Dedicated

To

My Wife

SIREESHA

RURAL DEVELOPMENT

Dr. I. Satya Sundaram
Economist and Writer
12/354-1, Rustumbada,
MACHILIPATNAM - 521 001.

Himalaya Publishing House
MUMBAI • NEW DELHI • NAGPUR • BENGALURU • HYDERABAD • CHENNAI • PUNE
LUCKNOW • AHMEDABAD • ERNAKULAM • BHUBANESWAR • INDORE • KOLKATA • GUWAHATI

First Edition : 1997
Reprint Edition : 1999
Second Revised Edition : 2002
Third Revised Edition : 2007
Fourth Revised Edition : 2011
Reprint Edition : 2013
Reprint Edition : 2015

Published by : Mrs. Meena Pandey
for **HIMALAYA PUBLISHING HOUSE PVT. LTD.,**
"Ramdoot", Dr. Bhalerao Marg, Girgaon, Mumbai - 400 004.
Phones: 23860170, 23863863, Fax: 022-23877178.
Email: himpub@vsnl.com • Website: www.himpub.com

Branch Offices:

New Delhi : "Pooja Apartments", 4-B, Murari Lal Street, Ansari Road, Darya Ganj, New Delhi-110 002. Phones: 23270392, 23278631, Fax: 011-23256286

Nagpur : Kundanlal Chandak Industrial Estate, Ghat Road, Nagpur - 440 018. Phones: 2738731, 3296733 Telefax: 0712-2721216.

Bengaluru : No. 16/1 (Old 12/1), 1st Floor, Next to Hotel Highlands, Madhava Nagar, Race Course Road, Bengaluru - 560 001. Phones: 22281541, 22385461, Telefax: 080-22286611.

Hyderabad : No. 3-4-184, Lingampally, Besides Raghavendra Swamy Matham,Kachiguda, Hyderabad - 500 027. Phones: 040-27560041, 27550139.

Chennai : No. 8/2, Madley 2nd Street Ground Floor, T. Nagar, Chennai - 600 017 (Tamilnadu). Phones: 044-32463737, 42124860.

Pune : First Floor, "Laksha" Apartment, No. 527, Mehunpura, Shaniwarpeth, (Near Prabhat Theatre), Pune - 411 030. Phones: 020-24496323, 24496333.

Lucknow : House No. 731, Shekhupura Colony, Near B.D. Convent School, Vikas Nagar, Aliganj, Lucknow - 226022. Mob: 09307501549.

Ahmedabad : 114, "SHAIL",1st Floor, Opp. Madhu Sudan House, C.G.Road, Navrang Pura, Ahmedabad - 380 009. Phone: 079-26560126.

Ernakulam : 39/176 (New No: 60/251) 1ST Floor,Karikkamuri Road,Ernakulam, Kochi - 682011, Kerala. Tel : (91) (0484) 2378012, 2378016.

Bhubaneswar : 5 Station Square, Bhubaneswar (Orissa) - 751 001. Phone: 0674-2532129,9338746007.

Kolkata : 108/4, Beliaghata Main Road, Near ID Hospital, Opp. SBI Bank, Kolkata - 700 010. Phone: 033-32449649.

Guwahati : House No. 15, Behind Pragjyotish College Near Sharma Printing Press, P.O. Bharalumukh, Guwahati-781 009 (Assam). Mobile: 09883055590/36.

Printed at : Geetanjali Press Pvt.Ltd., Nagpur on behalf of H.P.H.

PREFACE TO THE FOURTH REVISED EDITION

The growing popularity of this book is understandable. It is the most comprehensive text book on the subject available in the market.

Two new chapters have been included in this edition. These are: (i) Rural Development in the Eleventh Plan, 2007-12, and (ii) Food Security in India. The data have been updated. Suggestions for further improvement of the book are welcome.

— DR. I. SATYA SUNDARAM

PREFACE TO THE FIRST EDITION

Rural Development has been receiving increasing attention of the governments across the world. In the Indian context, rural development assumes special significance for two important reasons. First, about two-thirds of the population still lives in villages and there cannot be any progress so long as rural areas remain backward. Second, the backwardness of the rural sector would be a major impediment to the overall progress of the economy. The industrial sector cannot think of sufficient demand for its products so long as the rural incomes are low.

Rural development does not imply setting up of major industries in rural areas. Rural development on a sustainable basis is possible only when the rural resources are put to optimum use, enhancing a steady growth in rural output and generating surplus income. This strategy would ensure self-reliance in the rural population. According to Dr. Y. Nayudamma, self-reliance implies self-competence, resourcefulness, problem-solving capability, the ability to discern and wisdom to use knowledge.

Rural development remains an uphill task due to the complexity of problems existing in the rural sector. The rural sector requires a multi-dimensional approach to reach cost-effective solutions to these problems.

The rural areas suffer from poor infrastructural facilities. The villages are yet to emerge as the main centres of production activity. The proclivity is to produce goods in urban areas, even to meet the basic needs of rural consumers. This apart, the rural population requires not one but a few inputs and services. These have to be provided at the right time and in the right sequence. This demands the right kind of co-ordination amongst agencies extending help to the rural sector.

It has been rightly pointed out that a purely agricultural country remains backward even in respect of agriculture. Much of the labour force in India depends on agriculture, not because it is remunerative but because there are no alternative employment opportunities. This is a major cause for the backwardness reportedly seen in the Indian agricultural sector. We must opt for a type of rural industrialisation which extends full support to the agricultural sector. A part of the labour force now engaged in agriculture needs to be shifted to non-agricultural occupations.

The new agricultural technology is responsible for the present comfortable foodgrain position. But the Green Revolution too has created some problems. Moreover, the first phase of the Revolution is said to have reached the saturation point. Agricultural scientists are laying stress on its second phase which alone can give the real boost needed for India's agricultural sector. Irrigation has emerged as a crucial input contributing to the success of the Revolution. The farmers no doubt require price incentives, but their problems can be solved only when there is a steady increase in agricultural productivity. Technology should be cost-effective and give good financial returns to the farming community.

Given the unfavourable power structure in rural India, the benefits of the Revolution or even the anti-poverty programmes do not reach to benefit the rural population. The workers and small producers in India cannot put in their best in an inequitous atmosphere. Therefore, production suffers. Also, the rural sector cannot take advantage of opportunities available so long as the institutions are dominated by the rich.

For various reasons, particularly for lack of political will, land reforms have been neglected. The rural population requires support in terms of assets like land to improve their income levels and social status. Diversification of agriculture is needed to improve the plight of the agricultural labourers. The rural artisans and other sections would benefit only when the rural economy is diversified with stress on non-farming activities. Of course, organisation of the rural sector is needed to put an end to all kinds of exploitation continuing in the sector for a long time.

The Government has been implementing special schemes for the benefit of the rural sector since the early 1970s — worth mentioning are those for wage employment generation; others for asset distribution, leading to generation of self-employment. However, studies show that these schemes have been implemented in a perfunctory manner. The income generating capacity has failed to register an increase and thus remains limited. The situation worsened subsequently because of the absence of cost-effective groundwork to implement these schemes.

However, if these resources don't exist, strategies should be worked out to generate the same to meet the needs and demands of the rural sector. Studies relating to special schemes show irregularities in the identification of beneficiaries and programmes. The schemes should be based on available resources and needs. The industries being set up in rural areas must have forward and backward linkages which alone can ensure their steady progress. Above all, the special schemes must form an integral part of micro level planning. The stress should be on economically viable schemes which alone can strengthen rural economy. The implementation, monitoring and evaluation stages are crucial for the success of and financial sustainability of the rural sector.

The rural sector also requires institutional credit to take up economically viable projects. But it needs to be noted that credit alone cannot deliver the goods. There is what is called the credit absorption capacity of the region. This depends on the implementation of economically viable schemes. Hence, the formulation of economic plans should precede the preparation of credit plans. There are certain agencies like the co-operatives, regional rural banks and farmer's service societies which are most appropriate to serve the rural population, but their performance needs to be toned up. Of course, cheap credit needs to be discouraged.

The rural sector can derive due benefits from development schemes only with the help of the administration which needs to be strengthened. The panchayat raj institutions should assume their new responsibilities in the development sphere. Of course, they should enjoy both functional and financial autonomy.

The rural people should take active part in all stages of the planning process. At present, they look up to the government for each and everything. This dependency syndrome needs to be dispelled. People's participation in the development sphere is crucial. The people must be made fully aware of the opportunities available and how to take advantage of them.

In a vast sphere like rural development, voluntary agencies play an important role in providing infrastructure, in educating the public on development issues and opportunities available and in curbing leakages. They see to it that the government machinery becomes more responsive to the growing needs of the rural sector. They can tone up the rural delivery system by improving the performance of public agencies like the public distribution system. In short, the voluntary agencies are expected to provide the missing links in the long chain of rural reconstruction.

Concerted efforts are needed to bridge the widening gap between rhetoric and reality in the rural sphere. Untrammelled flow of credit into the rural sector is not the answer to unemployment and poverty problems. External assistance may be necessary to cross the Rubicon, but ultimately, success on the rural front depends on the optimum utilisation of the available local resources. Economic development ought to be based on individual and group initiatives.

The present book covers all the aspects of rural development in the Indian context. Suggestions from the readers for further improvement of the book are welcome.

— DR. I. SATYA SUNDARAM

CONTENTS

PART ONE

Rural Development: An Overview

Chapter

1 Rural Development: Nature and Scope

Rural development involves raising the socio-economic status of the rural population on a sustainable basis through optimum utilisation of local resources, both natural and human. While external help is necessary and appreciated, rural development can be achieved only when the rural people actively participate in the development process.

The essence of development is not in *'providing'* but in *'promoting'* the rural sector. The rural population should know how to sustain itself financially and gain economic independence. Therefore, the stress of rural development should be on self-reliance. Also, rural development should result in greater access to the rural population to goods and services.[1]

Importance of Rural Development

The emphasis on Rural Development (RD) in most developing countries is understandable. The majority of the population lives in the rural areas. As such, their backwardness would be retarding growth in other sectors and in the economy as a whole. The growth of towns and cities (urbanisation) will be possible, it is backed by prosperity in rural areas. Rural backwardness is the major cause for the falling demand (recession) for most products.

The stress on rural development is also due to many constraints facing the rural areas, which generally suffer from inadequate infrastructural facilities and technological advancements. The rural areas are not well placed in terms of even minimum needs like safe drinking water, primary health and road transport. This apart, the rural population suffers from indigence, ignorance and illiteracy. Their traditional outlook towards development has been preventing them from taking full advantage of the incentives offered by the Government. But with substantial exposure to media, both electronic and print media, the rural sector is moving towards self-reliance and economic independence. Also, the ownership of land and other assets has been heavily concentrated in the hands of a few. It is precisely for this reason that the benefits of rural development programmes failed to reach the rural population targeted for these benefits to the extent expected.

It is true that the process of economic development involves a shift from agricultural and allied activities to non-agricultural activities. It is, however, erroneous to believe that the increase in non-agricultural activity should be confined to towns and cities. After all, villages with growing non-agricultural activity will without doubt, become towns in course of time. What needs to be done is that non-agricultural activities in the rural areas need to be focussed upon and strengthened on priority basis.

The rural areas remain impoverished with remunerative economic activities initiated to be carried out only in towns and cities. Thus, even an essential commodity like soap is being produced in urban areas. The argument generally advanced for this is that rural areas lack the basic infrastructural facilities for setting up industrial units. But, it is conveniently forgotten that such facilities would be available in rural areas only when these areas become centres of growing economic activity. It is not for nothing that Gandhiji laid stress on village development.

So long as rural areas are deprived of minimum facilities, there will be *rural exodus.* Migration of rural people to urban areas has serious implications proving to be of burden on the available resources and facilities in urban areas. It is estimated that urban population is growing at 4% per year and 2% of the increase in urban population per year is reportedly caused by migration from rural areas.

The administration in the urban areas has been finding it difficult to provide employment to the rural labour force migrating to towns and cities. According to Michael Todaro, *"Migration in excess of job opportunities is both a symptom and a contributing factor to third world under-development."* The social consequences of rural exodus like growing slums are too serious to be ignored by the urban administration authorities.

Another disturbing trend in the rural sector is that the surpluses generated in the rural areas are being invested in urban areas for various reasons. While the Government has stepped up its investment in rural areas, the rural surpluses are diverted to urban areas. When rural services are heavily subsidised by the Government, the rural rich have an obligation to step up their investment in rural areas.

NATURE AND SCOPE OF RURAL DEVELOPMENT

Over the years, rural development has emerged as *"a strategy designed to improve the economic and social life of a specific group of people — the rural poor. It involves extending the benefits of development to the rural population who seek a livelihood in the rural areas."*[2]

Rural development is three dimensional in nature. As a method, it seeks people's involvement in all programmes. As a process, it seeks to modernise, through the application of science and technology, the traditionally-oriented rural cultures. Its major objective is to bring about improvement in the quality of life of the rural people.

'Rural development' denotes overall development of rural areas with a view to improving the quality of life of the rural people. The concept is comprehensive and multi-dimensional in nature. It encompasses development of agricultural and allied activities, cottage and small-scale industries, traditional crafts, socio-economic infrastructure, rural manpower and improvement in community services and facilities.

Rural development covers, besides agricultural development, a comprehensive set of activities, pertaining to all aspects of rural economy. It confers benefits on a number of classes like cultivators, landless labour and rural artisans.

Agriculture, in its broad sense, itself is very vast. It covers activities like horticulture, irrigation, land development, soil and water conservation, animal husbandry, dairying, poultry, pig-farming, fishery, handloom and other village industries, social forestry and setting up of agro-based industries and forest-based industries.

But rural development which is much more than agricultural development, ought to take into account the existing local and area-wise resources and complementary links among them. There are various classes in rural India and sometimes the relations among them may be conflicting. These conflicts have to be resolved.

Rural development requires a vast infrastructure. Provision of this is no easy task, because it has to be undertaken by the Government. Private investment in this area has been meagre and continues to be so. But the trend of meagre investments in the rural sector is gradually changing in terms of economic sustenance. However, evolving an appropriate technology for rural development is no easy task. Such a technology has to simultaneously achieve the twin objectives of raising growth rates and stepping up opportunities of employment. The setting up of appropriate institutions and co-ordinating their activities are crucial to any rural development strategy. The potential of self-reliance in rural areas needs to be exploited in a planned manner.

A single approach to rural development would not be effective. In fact, rural development is the product of interaction between various physical, technological, economic, socio-cultural, institutional and environmental factors. Indeed, the rural sector should experience the required changes so that it can join the mainstream of national development and contribute its share for economic development. It has been rightly said, *"In the end, however, rural development should not be seen as a package of specific needs but as a transformation of rural life and conditions."*[3]

OBJECTIVES OF RURAL DEVELOPMENT

Rural development programmes, in the Indian context, have aimed at achieving a number of objectives. These include:[4]

(i) Changing the attitude of the rural people towards development/transformation of the village community;

(ii) Promotion of democratic leadership at the grassroots level by setting up local self-governments;

(iii) Provision of basic needs such as drinking water, health care, better sanitation, housing and employment;

(iv) Development of both farming and non-farming activities so as to generate gainful employment without adversely affecting the environment;

(v) Improving infrastructural facilities in villages, particularly transport and communication facilities and

(vi) Ensuring a tension-free life for the rural population by promoting communal harmony and unity, levels of literacy, education and cultural activities.

Rural development should have the following major objectives: *(i)* full employment of labour and physical resources, *(ii)* setting up of agro-industrial complexes, *(iii)* laying down minimum standards of productivity or efficiency for those owning or using precious resources, *(iv)* minimum standards of performance by public agencies by making them accountable to the local people and *(v)* creating a scientific temper which implies a changing of the mind and old habits of thought and action.

According to ESCAP (The Economic and Social Commission for Asia and Pacific), the criterion for rural development involves: *(i)* drawing the entire rural labour force into the mainstream of economic activity; *(ii)* realising the creative energies of the rural people, *(iii)* checking the drift of the rural population to cities, *(iv)* enhancing participation of women and youth in the rural development process, *(v)* improving the quality of life through integration between development and environment and *(vi)* the all-round development of the rural population by tapping the abundant manpower.[5]

Rural development involves generating employment opportunities for the rural people so that they are able to meet their basic needs and ultimately become major agents of economic progress and social change. A climate has to be created which enables the rural poor to realise their full potentialities to attain a higher quality of life with economic security to sustain themselves. This alone can prevent rural exodus.

FUTURE TASK

Rural development is a complex process. It can, therefore, be achieved only through concerted efforts on various fronts. It is rightly said, *"It seems that of major weak links in rural development planning are absence of total approach at the strategy level, lack of co-ordinated planning at the programme level and weak planning component of individual programmes."*[6]

Rural development programmes cannot be successful without adequate regional planning, strong central co-ordination, effective local level organisation and people's active participation at the planning and implementation stages.

Even well-conceived rural development schemes have run into rough weather because of inefficiency and corruption at various levels which are again attributed to *"the absence of proper accountability and deterring punishment for failures."*[7]

The rural population is said to be coping with a dependency syndrome, forcing them to look up to the Government for financial help. While external help is necessary and desirable, the initiative for developing areas should come from the rural people themselves. It may be necessary to form self-help groups. These have to be linked with formal financial institutions before chalking out location-specific development schemes in the rural sector.[8]

Rural exodus could be arrested through a wider dispersal of industries which would generate financial returns for the development of the rural sector. This indicates that the feasibility of setting up of economically viable industries is important before investing in the rural sector. There is, however, a strong case for intensifying non-agricultural activities in rural areas in the service sector as much as in manufacturing. The tendency towards *'rurbanisation'* (urbanisation of rural areas) is quite welcome. The latest NSS data indicates that non-agricultural activity in the rural areas is on the rise. If this trend is strengthened, it would be easy to convert villages into small towns.

Rural development can be possible if only there is proper balance between service-oriented programmes and development-oriented and self-reliant centred programmes. The importance attached to service-oriented schemes, besides retarding rural development, has also resulted in the wastage of precious resources.

REFERENCES

1. Vasant Desai (1988): *Rural Development,* Himalaya Publishing House, Mumbai, Vol. 11, p. 18.
2. World Bank (1975): *The Assault on World Poverty,* Baltimore. Johns Hopkins University Press, p. 3.
3. Hernan Santa Cruz: 'The Three Tiers of Basic Needs for Rural Development', *Finance and Development,* June 1979, p. 30.
4. *Kurukshetra*, April 1, 1976.
5. S. K. Sharma and S. L. Malhotra (1977): *Integrated Rural Development: Approach, Strategy and Perspectives,* Abhinav Publications, New Delhi - 16, p. 68.
6. K. Dhanasekaan: 'Micro Level Planning as an Approach to Integrated Rural Development', *Khadigramodyog,* September 1990, p. 488.
7. K. Deb (1986): *Rural Development in India Since Independence,* Sterling Publishers Pvt. Ltd., New Delhi, p. 6.
8. R. N. Sinha: 'Self-Help Groups and Rural Development', *Financial Express,* June 2nd 1990.

Chapter

2 Approaches to Rural Development

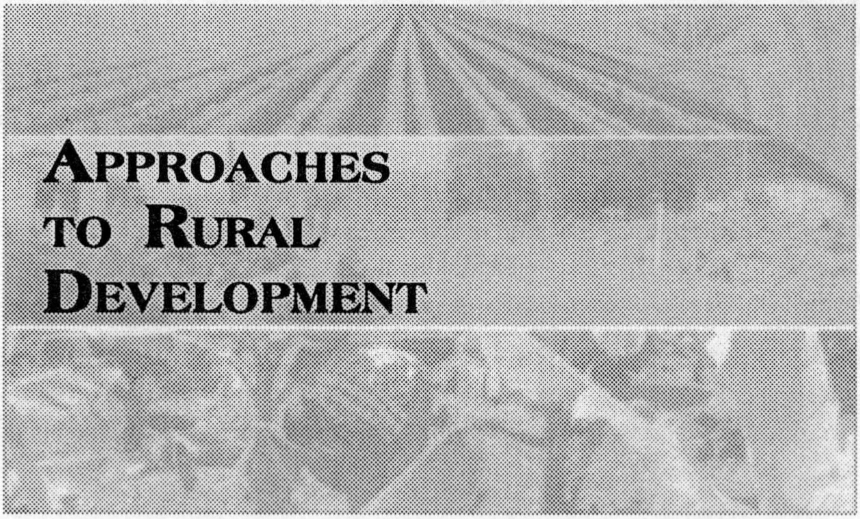

India has gained vast experience in the implementation of rural development programmes. The approaches to rural development and area planning have also changed over a period of time. In the light of the experience gained by following a particular approach, a new approach has been evolved. The shift in emphasis is intended not only to accelerate the pace of growth in the rural sector but to ensure social justice by minimising wastage and leakages.

The choice of interventions in planning rural development programmes has shifted from the target sector to the target area and to the target group approaches and their combinations as shown in Table 1.

Any pragmatic approach to rural development in the Indian context should concentrate on: (i) removal of disabilities (lack of necessary skills, absence of access to crucial inputs etc.) from which the rural population generally suffers and (ii) programmes meant to enhance gainful employment opportunities and raise the productivity levels of the rural sector.

Community Development Programme

India launched the First Five Year Plan in 1951. It was rightly thought that planning would not be effective without substantial participation of the people, thus suggesting that planning ought to be a 'people's movement.' Surely development effort cannot be the sole responsibility of the Government. The Government may create a climate conducive to development, but the pace of development depends on the initiative and dynamism exhibited by people who must be equipped with necessary skills and resources to take advantage of and benefit from the government-sponsored programmes.

The National Community Development Programme (NCDP) was launched in 1952 — its aim being to bring about the overall development of the rural community with people's participation in the development process. The Government, on its part, decided to provide technical and other services in a co-ordinated fashion. An institutional structure was provided in the form of panchayati raj, co-operative and village schools. The approach to rural development is a holistic one.

Table 1: Rural Development Strategies: Evolution

Approach	Emphasis
(i) Rural reconstruction	Village centred movement based on principles of voluntary effort.
(ii) Community development	Rural development based on ideas of motivation, self-help and self-reliance.
(iii) Target sector	Intensive development of a selected sector or sectors of activity with emphasis on concentrating in areas of comparative advantage.
(iv) Target groups	Growth with social justice for the weaker sections of the population.
(v) Growth centres	Spatial planning and development.
(vi) Backward area development	Reduction of regional imbalances in development.
(vii) Minimum needs	Equalisation of social consumption.
(viii) Area planning with full employment	Rural development in an area frame with the removal of unemployment and poverty as an important aim.

An important objective of the NCDP was to develop local leadership and self-governing institutions. Of course, the emphasis was on raising food and agricultural production by strengthening programmes of resource development, improving the effectiveness of farm inputs, supply systems and by providing and extending agricultural services to farmers.[1]

Initially, the NCDP was launched only in some parts of the country, but sooner or later, the entire country had to be brought under the programme. Therefore, a new programme of National Extension Service (NES) was launched in 1953. The intention was to provide the essential staff and funds so as to speed up development in the rural sector.

The tasks entrusted to NCDP and NES were enormous involving an all-round development of rural areas. They had to cover a vast area for agricultural and related programmes, communication, education, health, training, social welfare, supplementary employment and housing.

These tasks cannot be successfully undertaken without organisational support at the national, state, district and block levels. At the national level, a central committee was formed. At the State level, a State Development Committee or similar body was constituted. At the district level, a District Development Officer was made responsible for the implementation of Community Development (CD) programmes. Of course, all the districts do not have the same organisational structure.

The block level is specially important so far as CD programmes are concerned. The Block Development Officer (BDO) is made responsible for the implementation of the programme within the block. He is assisted by eight or nine extension officers specialising in fields like agriculture, animal husbandry, rural engineering, public health, co-operation, social education, women's and children's programmes and rural industries.

The responsibility for successfully implementing CD programmes in a cluster of villages was entrusted to ten Village Level Workers (VLWs) or Gram Sevaks and two Gram Sevikas. They work under the advice and control of the BDO.

The CDP met with limited success since the environment required for its success was absent. The agricultural sector remained weak. The block team neither exhibited the required unity and co-ordinated effort, nor did it secure the help of non-official leadership. The local level organisations like co-operatives and panchayats remained weak. The quality of services provided at the block level lacked essence. The social structure of the village society did not undergo much change. Too much stress on welfare at the expense of development is not feasible.[2]

The financial, material and administrative resources of the CDP were spread too thinly. Therefore, the programme could not produce a lasting impact on any sector, particularly the agricultural sector. There are other problems too: while the success of CDP largely depends on people's co-operation, people remained passive and the extension workers lacked the necessary training. As such, the programme was carried out in a perfunctory manner. In the absence of functional responsibility, inter-departmental jealousies assumed ominous dimensions.

The CDP also suffered because of paucity of trained and managerial staff. There has been shortage of professional managers for local enterprises and agencies. As such, even well conceived programmes could not be successfully implemented.

An appropriate combination of populistic and paternalistic approaches to development will, without doubt, ensure rural development on a sustainable basis.

Though CDP met with limited success, the experience gained is worth recalling and implementing its future programmes. It has drawn attention to the crucial role of agriculture in economic development and also the need for extending incentives to farmers. It also made it clear that resources are to be diverted to most responsible areas to ensure and realise maximum gains in the shortest possible time.

A mere bureaucratic approach to rural development is not enough. Local people and organisations (voluntary agencies, co-operatives etc.) are to play a positive and productive role in rural reconstruction. The Government has been working on strategies to implement and co-ordinate their community development programmes.

INTENSIVE AGRICULTURAL DISTRICT PROGRAMME

As the agricultural yields were very low, the Government thought it wise to evolve a new strategy to boost foodgrain output. Whereas CDP is based on equity principle, the Intensive Agricultural District Programme (IADP), launched in 1960, aimed at concentrating resources in better agriculturally placed areas.

The essence of IADP strategy has been to attain foodgrain self-sufficiency in the shortest period possible, calling investment for substantial in favourable areas with maximum irrigation facilities and minimum natural hazards, providing simultaneously all the requisite essential inputs and services which was needed. Thus, a package approach to step up agricultural production was evolved.

Seven districts were selected initially for IADP. These were: Thanjavur (Tamil Nadu), West Godavari (Andhra Pradesh), Shahabad (Bihar), Raipur (Madhya Pradesh), Aligarh (Uttar Pradesh), Ludhiana (Punjab) and Pali (Rajasthan). The Government of India declared these seven as IADP districts in June 1960, and suggested that one district in each state may be selected for IADP.

For the successful implementation of the IADP, appropriate infrastructure was made available at the national, state and district levels. At the block level, the staff responsible for implementing the CDP was strengthened with additional staff. The subject-matter specialists provided technical assistance and training to the block level staff.

Credit must be given to the efficiency of IADP that it has achieved its major objectives. It has created a new dynamism in the farming community, popularised the High Yielding Variety (HYV) programme. greatly enhanced the technical inputs at the district level and also contributed to the growth of marketing and storage facilities as well as supporting services.

However, the IADP strategy faced many problems. The administration at the district level failed to generate benefits for the rural sector because of inadequate staff and inadequate training. Crucial inputs like fertilisers, co-operative credit and supporting services were not given to the rural population for becoming self-reliant. A unified responsibility at the district level with full control over all inter-related disciplines was absent.

GROWTH CENTRE STRATEGY

It is argued that if investment activities are intensified in select areas of a region, they will produce sufficient 'spread effect' leading to the all-round development of the region. A leading industry exerts its influence on the economy through inter-industrial linkages, itself playing a leading and innovative role through backward and forward linkages. When once inter-industry linkages are well established, the process of development becomes smooth.

The concept of 'growth pole' was first introduced by Perroux in 1955, is based on one simple truth: human activities must cluster together to generate internal and external economies. This may, however involve some social costs which can be minimised in due course through policy interventions.

The village is neither a homogeneous unit nor is it necessarily a viable unit. In order to avoid wastage of resources, Prof. V. K. R. V. Rao has suggested formation of clusters of villages implying that, it is necessary to determine the minimum size of rural settlements. Regrouping of a small cluster of census villages with a central village or a small town as its focus point and with functional inter-linkages should be the ideal unit/area for planning.

After the formation of clusters of villages, it is necessary to identify the dynamic clusters among them and locate the growth foci within them. These growth foci have to be interlinked with one another in such a way that hierarchy is established with service centres at the local level, growth points at the sub-regional level, growth centres at the regional level and growth pole at the national level. Obviously, the focus should be on those clusters which have the largest development potential.

In India, in the Fourth Five Year Plan (1969-74), a pilot research project for growth centres was launched, establishing 20 centres in various states. Each growth centre consisted of about 20 blocks (two million population). An attempt was made to intensify location-specific activities.

The Draft-Five Year Plan (1978-83) suggested setting up of rural growth centres. The selection of such centres is to be based on the availability of infrastructure including co-operative institutions, presence of progressive farmers and effective local participation.

Walter Stohar has observed that *"growth centres have essentially led to a shift of disparities from the inter-regional to the intra-regional level, but rarely seem to have led to an overall reduction of spatial disparities in living levels."*[3]

The policy of growth centres in India is concerned more with the development of areas rather than with their rates of growth. However, the growth pole theory is inapplicable to all developmental situations and is too rigidly linked to industrialisation[4]

In the Indian context, two approaches have emerged towards integration of spatial units, namely, villages. These are: *(i)* the growth centre approach as developed by Gadgil and Sen, and *(ii)* the village cluster approach as developed by V. K. R. V. Rao and V. M. Rao. The former suggests a vertical integration between the hierarchy of human settlements, i.e., villages and towns. It is assumed that such a link up will transmit to the lower point in the hierarchy growth impulses from the top growth centres. The latter, on the other hand, advocates a horizontal link-up among the villages themselves so that they support each other functionally so as to make the cluster of villages an economically viable unit. Of course, both approaches stress on linkages, backward and forward.[5]

CONCEPT OF 'INTEGRATION'

It has been realised that development should be an integrated one. This is possible when sectoral development programmes, human resource development programmes, social welfare schemes and infrastructural development programmes *"are brought within the framework of a prospective plant for implementation, where each programme reinforces the other through their linkages."*[6]

The *'integration,* in the decentralised framework has three dimensions : *(i)* spatial balance, which is to be achieved through location, accessibility, efficiency and viability, *(ii)* sectoral balance, to be achieved through national and state priorities, local relevance, economic efficiency and internal consistency and *(iii)* the operational balance which can be achieved through organisation, delegation of functions, management procedures and personal systems.[7]

The most important single reason for laxity in the performance of various rural development programmes has been the negligence of inter-sectoral linkages and lack of co-ordination among various functionaries. For instance, when programmes for agricultural development are planned, an assessment of the backward linkages which include supply of seed, fertilisers and pesticides, agricultural implements, water, draught animals, power, storage and credit facilities gain priority. The forward linkages include supply of raw materials, fodder and provision of storage, transport, marketing and agricultural processing facilities.

Spatial integration refers to *'spatial planning'* which in turn, implies appropriate location of social and economic activities over a physical space for the development of a region. Proper spatial planning is necessary to provide adequate inputs and infrastructural facilities to various rural sectoral programmes. As inputs and infrastructure are scarce, they have to be put to the optimum use. A uniform spatial planning may not be appropriate to all regions, in a country like India, because of their diverse nature. However, appropriate methodologies for spatial planning have been evolved through identification of central places (growth centres, service centres and central villages).

It has been rightly observed by John P. Lewis : *"A serviceable rural development programme in India must deal with the several aspects of the rural economy in an integrated fashion. An isolated agricultural development effort unrelated to, and unsupported by other kinds of rural policies would be doomed to failure almost surely."*[8]

There is need for integrating objectives, namely, more production, more employment and more equitable distribution of income. A particular growth model may be successful in stepping up growth rates, but very often it fails to solve the more important problem of poverty elimination and unemployment. While a high rate of growth is no doubt welcome in the Indian context, how it has been achieved is also important. In other words, the economic and social costs of development cannot be ignored, particularly in a country suffering from inequalities in income and wealth and regional disparities in development. Hence, the increasing stress on rural development and local level planning.

The concept of integration is also viewed as integration of low income segments with the rest of the rural community by ensuring them a better participation in the production process and a more equitable share in the benefits of development.[9]

MICRO LEVEL PLANNING

In a vast country like India, problems of poverty and unemployment cannot be solved unless attention is paid to local level planning. Developmental programmes ought to be related to local resources and needs. This alone can make both quantitative and qualitative difference to the planning process. The quantum of output can be increased by better utilisation of resources, both natural and human. It can also lead to a socially relevant production pattern.

One of the lessons learnt during the period of experimentation is that, rural development must focus on manageable areas in which development activity can be responsive to the specificity of natural endowment and social order.[10] But, planning at the micro level faces a number of problems. It cannot be effective unless attention is paid to production programmes for the target groups, manpower planning and skill development, provision of basic minimum needs and a programme for institutional support.[11]

The tasks before block level planning are many. It has to compile an integrated resource inventory, prepare draft action plans and undertake a malady remedy analysis and select appropriate programmes with the involvement of the local community. [12] The stress should be obviously on the generation of gainful employment.

Briefly, the methodology for block level planning may be envisaged in seven phases which are not necessarily sequential: *(i)* the acquaintance phase, *(ii)* the resource inventory phase, *(iii)* project formulation phase, *(iv)* employment planning phase, *(v)* spatial planning phase, *(vi)* credit planning phase and *(vii)* the co-ordination and implementation phase.[13] The most important formation which the planning team should collect involves listing of the number of families living below the poverty line.[14]

Of course, there must be consistency between macro and micro planning. Macro-planning naturally gives importance to growth, while micro-planning lays stress on redistributive aspects of development. But funds cannot be wasted on projects of doubtful utility at the micro-level in the name of social justice. Both macro planning and micro planning should strive to step up growth rates. This is possible only when there is consistency between both the levels of planning.

Thus, it is clear that the approaches to rural development in India have changed over a period of time. Each approach, while achieving its basic objective, has also created certain problems. However, because of the rich experience gained by India in the rural field, planning process at the micro level has become pragmatic. The country has been able to eliminate a number of constraints on rural development.

References

1. Katar Singh (1986): *Rural Development: Principles, Policies and Management,* Sage Publications, New Delhi, p. 165.
2. R.P. Misra, K.V. Sundaram and V.L.S. Prakasa Rao (1976): *Regional Development Planning in India,* Vikas Publishing House, New Delhi, pp. 143-144.
3. Walter Stohar and Franz Stodtlins: 'An Evaluation of Regional Policies — Experiences in Market and Mixed Economies', in V.M. Hansen (Ed.), *Human Settlement Processes,* Ballingar Publishing Co., Cambridge.
4. S.K. Sharma and S.L. Malhotra (1977): *Integrated Rural Development: Approach, Strategy and Perspectives,* Abhinav Publications, New Delhi-16, p. 78.
5. For further details, see Abdul Aziz: 'Approaches to Micro Area Development Planning', in Sundaram, I.S. (1989): *Rural Poverty and Area Planning,* B.R. Publishing Corporation, New Delhi.
6. S.K Mitra: 'Rural Development: Need for Holistic Approach', *The Economic Times,* November 21, 1992.
7. Das Kumar: 'Spatial Framework for Rural Development in India', *Khadigramodyog,* February 1988, p. 215.
8. John P. Lewis (1970): *Quiet Crisis in India : Economic Development and American Policy.* Asia Publishing House, Mumbai, p. 142.
9. F.A.O. (Rome): Joint Report on the Expert Consultations, Policies, and Institutions for Integrated Rural Development, Colombo and Nairobi Sessions, Rome, 1977.

10. K.V. Sundaram: 'Some Recent Trends in Rural Area Development Planning in India' in R.P. Misra and K.V. Sundaram (Ed. 1979): *Rural Area Development: Perspectives and Approaches,* Sterling Publishers Pvt. Ltd., New Delhi, p. 25.

11. Planning Commission (1978): Report of the Working Group on Block Level Planning, pp. 3-4.

12. M.S. Swaminathan: 'Self-Replacating Process for Employment Generation', *Yojana,* March 1,1979, p. 20.

13. R.P. Misra, and K.V. Sundaram (1980): *Multi-level Planning and Integrated Rural Development in India,* Heritage Publishers, New Delhi, p. 42.

14. Report of the Working Group on Block Level Planning, *op. cit.,* p. 16.

Chapter

3 Gandhian Approach to Rural Development

Mahatma Gandhi (1869-1948) was not only a freedom fighter but also a greater thinker of the 20th century.

Gandhiji's views on rural reconstruction are an integral part of his philosophy of life which is characterised by truth and non-violence, respect for human nature, dislike for all kinds of injustice and exploitation.

Gandhiji did express his views on a number of economic and social issues. Majority of the population of India lives in villages. As such, it is but natural that Gandhiji paid attention to the problems of our villages. Gandhiji did anticipate the problems of unplanned growth. True Economics, according to Gandhiji, must be life-oriented and a servant of humanity at large. Gandhiji was not a pessimist. He declared: "Earth provides enough to satisfy every man's need but not for every man's greed."

On the economic plane, Gandhiji strongly believed in certain principles. These include:

(i) The aim of economic planning is self-sufficiency, full employment and decentralisation of power;

(ii) The promotion of the village industries is basic to the economic development of the country and

(iii) The principles of 'trusteeship' and 'cooperation' are capable of achieving both growth and social justice.

LABOUR AND MECHANISATION

According to Gandhiji, human resources are precious. For him, keeping human resources idle is a sin. All countries, rich and poor, should therefore know how to utilise the abundantly available manpower. There is no point in stepping up output by degrading, fragmenting and alienating labour.

The ILO feels that fuller employment is the means for producing more goods and simultaneously for acquiring the purchasing power to gain access to them. Better employment opportunities is an essential step towards fuller participation in society. What Gandhiji wanted was production by masses, not mass production.

Gandhiji's views on mechanisation have not been properly understood: Gandhiji was against machines if they keep people idle, if they create an employment problem for them. Otherwise, mechanisation is welcome. Gandhiji made his stand clear when he declared in *the Harijan:* "Mechanisation is good when hands are too few for the work intended to be accomplished. It is an evil when there are more hands than required for the work as is the case in India. The problem with us is not how to find leisure for the teeming millions inhabiting our villages. The problem is how to utilise their idle hours which are equal to the working days of six months in a year."

According to Gandhiji, machines should help man improve his productivity, but they should not throw men out of employment. Man should handle machine at will without being its slave. Gandhiji wrote:[1]

We should not substitute lifeless machines for the living machines scattered over the seven lakh villages in India. The machine is well used if it aids men's labour and simplifies it. Today it is used to pour wealth in the pockets of the chosen few. Little attention is paid to crores of people from whom the machine snatches away their bread.

Thus, Gandhiji thought that machines should not be allowed to dominate men. What he really objected to was not machinery as such but the craze for machinery. Indiscriminate use of machines is not desirable. Gandhiji observed, "What I object to is the craze for machinery, not machinery as such — the craze is for what they call labour saving machinery." He also said, "I am aiming, not at eradication of all machinery, but its limitation."

Gandhiji was clear on the actual place of machinery. He declared that in a labour surplus economy like ours, too much dependence on machines will create problems for the labour, and this would adversely affect the performance of the economy sooner or later.

VILLAGE ECONOMY

The Gandhian strategy of 'rural reconstruction' is based on his programme of 'village swaraj' and the 'swadeshi' movement. Under these two programmes, he introduced many apparently very simple activities like Charkha (spinning wheel and khadi — handmade cloth), revival of household/cottage industries and village handicrafts, village sanitation and hygiene, basic education for harmonious development of the whole personality etc.

Gandhi advocated a self-sufficient village economy and 'self-reliant village community' and emphasised the full utilisation of local resources for development purposes.

Most of the decision making powers will vest in the village panchayat rather than in the regional or national government.

The villages would be self-sufficient as far as their basic needs like food, clothing, shelter, education, health etc. are concerned. In certain matters, inter-dependence would also be necessary. No village can be totally self-sufficient, but it would strive to attain that goal.

Describing the conditions of the villages of his time, Gandhiji said, "Go to the village and you will find misery and despair written in the faces of the inhabitants. Both they and their cattle are underfed; mortality is on the increase, they have no resisting power against diseases like malaria which carries away thousands of villagers year by year."[2]

According to Gandhiji, as far as possible, every activity should be conducted on cooperative basis.[3] Gandhiji favoured cooperative cattle farming because individuals cannot raise cattle in a proper and scientific manner. Cooperative activities, said Gandhiji, would develop fellow feelings and would abolish poverty and idleness from the villages.[4] Gandhiji thought of village republics, completely free to manage their own affairs and united by mutual help.[5]

According to Gandhiji, the village is the ideal social order. He saw an inherent contradiction in the city and the village. He declared: "the village civilisation and the city civilisation are totally different things. One depends on machinery and industrialisation and the other on handicrafts."[6]

RURAL INDUSTRIALISATION

According to Gandhiji, revival and encouragement of village industries would create opportunities for self-employment. This would make man independent and free so that his creativity and expression are stimulated.[7]

Gandhiji believed that rural prosperity can be ensured by setting up a large number of small industrial units in villages. Gandhiji observed: "When our villages are fully developed, there will be no dearth in them of men with a high degree of skill and artistic talent."[8] Gandhian economic units have a degree of specialisation, according to the natural skill talent, aptitude and capabilities of its inhabitants.

Production by masses is production to meet local needs.

Gandhiji pleaded for revival of khadi and village industries. He gave 'charkha' the highest place of honour. Promotion of village industries will not create heavy demands on capital. A policy of decentralisation and modernisation of rural industries would provide immediate solution to the problem of open unemployment.

Of course, there must be a spirit of 'Swadeshi'. People should attempt to produce all the necessities they require in the villages themselves. 'Swadeshi' according to Gandhiji, is the key to the economic salvation of India. It is also the responsibility of the Government to extend protection to small units until they became economically viable. Small units also do not adversely affect the environment.

If industrialisation is spread to the villages, it has many advantages. It facilitates integration of villages and towns. It curbs economic disparities — inequalities in income and wealth. It also reduces regional disparities in development. In India, these disparities are wide. For instance, Punjab's per capita income is more than double the per capita income of Bihar. This situation changes when all villages are industrially developed. Above all, when industrialisation spreads to villages, rural infrastructure facilities develop. The economic dualism (vast income and regional disparities) disappears.

DECENTRALISATION

Gandhiji chose the village to be the basic operational unit in India to be developed along the lines of decentralisation and self-sufficiency. He wrote:[10] "independence must begin at the bottom, thus every village will be a republic or panchayat having full powers."

According to Gandhiji "every village of India will almost be a self-supporting and self-contained unit exchanging only such necessary commodities with other villages where they are not locally producible."[11]

Capital should flow into the rural areas rather than that labour should flow into urban areas.[12]

Gandhiji strongly believed in the principle of decentralisation not only to step up growth but to ensure distributive justice. It ends concentration of economic power. It also promotes local initiative.

Gandhiji disliked the practice of producing commodities in towns and cities while the majority of the population lives in the villages. Even a small, essential item like soap is now produced in towns and cities.

According to Gandhiji, work places have to be created in the areas where the people are living now. This would create demand for labour and generate employment opportunities. Production should be mainly from local materials and mainly for local use.

Rural India can prosper only through the revival of Gram Panchayats and creation of self-sufficient and self-governing village republics.

When Gandhiji talked of self-sufficient village units, what he had in mind was that a village community should not depend on the higher government for those needs which it could satisfy with local resources and local efforts. He visualised decentralised planning with local participation.[13] This would put pressure on local representatives to respond to local needs.

According to Gandhiji, distribution can be equalised only when production is localised. He pointed out:[14] "When production and consumption both become localised, the temptation to speed up production, indefinitely and at any price, disappears. All the endless difficulties and problems that our present day economic system presents, too, would then come to an end.... There would be no unnatural accumulation or hoards in the pockets of the few, and want in the midst of plenty in regard to the rest, as is happening today."

Decentralisation curbs all kinds of exploitation, restores human freedom and dignity and promotes human values like fellow feelings and cooperation. According to Gandhiji, the essence of non-violence is decentralisation.

CONCLUSION

Gandhian economic ideas are becoming increasingly relevant to the world today, particularly the Third World countries. Economic development ought not to be the job of the government alone. People should know how to utilise precious resources. Economic growth alone is not important. Equally important are fair distribution of income and wealth, and also protection of the environment.

REFERENCES

1. *Harijan,* September 15th 1935.
2. J.S. Mathur and M.S. Mathur (ed. 1962): *Economic Thought of Mahatma Gandhi,* Chaitanya Publications, Allahabad, p. 284.
3. *Harijan,* July 26,1942, p. 238.
4. P.M. Bora: 'Relevance of Gandhi's Vision of Rural Development in the 21st Century', *Khadigramodyog,* November-December 1997 & January 1998, p. 135.
5. Yogesh Upadhyay and Shiv Kumar Singh: 'Rural Development'.
6. *Hindustan Standard,* December 6th 1944.
7. I. Satya Sundaram: 'Relevance of Gandhian Economics', *Khadigramodyog,* March 1996, p. 268.
8. *Harijan,* November 10th 1946.
9. Shashi Prabha Sharma: (1992): *Gandhian Holistic Economics,* Concept Publishing Company, New Delhi, p. 122.
10. *Harijan,* July 28th 1946.
11. M.K. Gandhi (1967): *The Gospel of Swadeshi,* Bharatiya Vidya Bhavan, Mumbai.
12. A.K. Das Gupta: 'Plan Priorities: Some Basic Issues', *Yojana,* January 26th 1978.
13. Ramesh Chandra: 'Decentralised Planning: Problems and Prospects', *The Economic Times,* November 13th 1989.
14. *Harijan,* November 2nd 1934.

Chapter 4

The Political Economy of Rural Poverty

The implementation of various poverty alleviation programmes has resulted in reduction in the level of poverty rates in rural areas. It is assumed that the rural people were ignorant about the benefits of either growth or welfare which remains a priority area. Planners and administrators thus hold the responsibility to frame rural development programmes. Any rural development strategy, under these assumptions, is bound to experience limited success.

Poverty in India has become very complex with many of the variables influencing it. But the relationship among these variables is not clear. For instance, states which show high levels of calorie intake also report high infant mortality, thus blurring the relationships between malnutrition and mortality. Likewise, states which enjoy higher income may also suffer from low cereal consumption. On the other hand, Kerala, with a low per capita state income and also low calorie intake, has registered low mortality rates and the longest expectation of life.[1]

According to the estimates of Dr. Minhas et al., the rural poor numbered 284 million in 1990 while the number of urban poor was around 77 million. According to the National Sample Survey (NSS) 1983-84, the population below the poverty line had shrunk to 37 per cent and according to the NSS (1987-88), the same had shrunk to around 30 per cent. However, based on the recent methodological corrections, those below the poverty line were placed at 37 per cent of the total population.

In the developed countries, much of the poverty could be related to the interruption, reduction or loss of earnings from contingencies such as temporary unemployment, sickness, disability, old age, death of main earners in the family and large household sizes. This type of poverty persists even in India. Poverty in India is however, largely structural in nature.

It needs to be noted that the level of intensity of poverty in urban and rural areas are not independent of each other. Poverty in urban areas has worsened because of the exodus of the rural population to urban areas. The greater the intensity of poverty in rural areas, the larger would be this exodus. It is also equally true that rural poverty worsens when the urban based industrial and services sectors are not able to absorb and tap the potential of the growing labour force in the rural areas which suffer from poor land-man ratio.

The level of poverty is not therefore influenced by investments in a single area. It is influenced by the entire set of economic activities, in urban and rural areas, including agriculture and industry. Poverty alleviation schemes may be necessary to provide relief to the rural poor, but they cannot eradicate poverty even in rural areas unless other policies too aim at this laudable objective.

There is no doubt about the growing levels of poverty in rural areas. Studies show that between 1963-64 and 1977-78, the proportion of agricultural labour households below the poverty line for rural India as a whole increased from 52 per cent to 56 per cent.

The Rural Labour Enquiry Reports pertaining to the period, 1964-65 to 1974-75, observed that the average daily earnings in agricultural operations by men in agricultural labour households, deflated by the consumer price index for agricultural labourers, declined by 12 per cent during the ten-year period.

In the Indian context, relative poverty is less important than absolute poverty. Prof. Amartya Sen said that relative deprivation cannot be the only basis for the emergence of poverty. He observed, *"there is an irreducible core of absolute deprivation in our idea of poverty which translates reports of starvation, malnutrition and visible hardship into a diagnosis of poverty without having to ascertain first the relative picture."*

Distribution of land and other assets continue to be skewed. The rural poor standing at 30 per cent had access to 2 per cent of the assets as compared to the ownership of 81.9 per cent of the assets by the top 30 per cent. Hence, rural poverty has emerged due to the absence of access to productive assets to the rural population.

POVERTY LINE

In India, poverty is measured by the yardstick of minimum needs. The Planning Commission's Task Force, in 1977, defined the 'poor' in terms of daily consumption. A person is said to be poor if his daily consumption is less than 2,400 calories in the rural areas and 2,100 calories in the urban areas.[2]

In monetary terms, the poverty line has been fixed at ₹ 49 (in rural areas) and ₹ 56.55 (in urban areas) per person per year based on the 1973-74 prices. For the family (consisting of five members), the poverty line in the rural areas is placed at ₹ 2,946 and for the urban area at ₹ 3,402 per year. The figures were refixed at ₹ 6,400 and ₹ 7,300 (corresponding to per capita monthly consumer expenditure of ₹ 107 and ₹ 122 respectively for rural and urban areas) for the Seventh Five Year Plan period with the 1984-85 prices.

According to the Planning Commission study, the poverty line figures should have been ₹ 7,980 and ₹ 9,120 for 1987-88, taking into account the rise in prices. The Commission has assessed that 37.4 per cent of India's population was below the poverty line in 1983-84. The study has also taken note of the decline in the birth rate over the years, and reckoned that the family size has changed from 4.81 in 1951 to 5.55 in 1981 as a result of reduced morbidity and mortality rates primarily on account of better health delivery systems.

For the base year of the eighth plan (1992-93), poverty line is estimated as the average monthly per capita expenditure of ₹ 181.50 in rural areas and ₹ 209.50 in urban areas in 1991-92 prices. On an annual basis, the rural and urban poverty line is equivalent to the annual household expenditure of ₹ 11,060 and ₹ 11,850 respectively.

Prof. Nilakantha Rath observed that though poverty line is defined in terms of a particular level of income, a person may cross the poverty line even with less than this income level, by a 'judicious' choice of the items of food and their quantities or by spending more on food and less on non-food than the general run of the poor. Likewise, some non-poor households may remain below the poverty line by not consuming food that ensures the specified calories.

It is therefore essential to distinguish between poverty line and under-nutrition. Poverty line helps us identify the households who are unable to get the level of per capita income (or total expenditure) that would enable their members to get food with adequate calories. The concept of poverty line is not meant to identify households suffering from undernutrition.

It may be noted that countries like Sri Lanka, China and Costa Rico reportedly enjoy a high standard of living even with a reasonable rate of growth whereas countries like Brazil, Mexico, South Africa and Oman suffer from poor quality of life though they enjoy a high rate of growth. Even within India, Kerala, with a low per capita income, is well placed in terms of literacy and life expectancy. In this context, Prof. Amartya Sen wrote, *"Poverty alleviation has to be seen not only in terms of the growth of GNP or even in terms of raising the level of personal incomes of the poor population, but primarily as the enhancement of people's capability to lead minimally acceptable lives."*

Income may not be a satisfactory indication of poverty. When comparing living standards of countries, one must take into account the public provision of medical care, education etc. at subsidised rates or free of cost. Current income may not indicate current consumption because of inadequate saving or borrowing. The joint family system also provides higher level of standard of living. Likewise, elderly people benefit when they live with children. However, income still remains a *proxy* for good living standards.

The poverty line, based on headcount ratio, has been criticised by many who argued that the headcount index simply measures the ratio of the rural populations below the poverty line, but it does not throw light on the intensity levels of poverty or income shortfall of the poor. Also, if crossing the poverty line is the sole aim of anti-poverty programmes, the administration may concentrate on those who are very near to the poverty line. This will not significantly alter the growing levels of poverty.

The calorie-based criterion has been criticised on many grounds.

First, it may exaggerate poverty level as good consumption does not increase at the rate at which income increases. Hence, it fails to take into account the improvements seen in the realm of poverty barring food intake.

Second, calorie-based poverty fails to take into account other forms of poverty pertaining to literacy, health etc. The poor rural have felt better with access to these priority services for meaningful existences.

Last, the conventional poverty line takes into account only the personal expenditure and not other services which the poor obtain freely or at subsidised rates. These include education, health and subsidised items supplied through the public distribution system.

Thus, if we take into account the subsidised services of education, health etc., we obtain a better picture of the poverty levels in the rural sector. However, such a conclusion may not be entirely acceptable because in terms of quality of services rendered, our progress on education and health leaves much to be desired. Prof. Khusro has observed that, *"with the reduction of poverty, in quantitative terms, the decline in quality seems to have taken over and is washing away the percentage improvements."*[3]

The poverty line, based on consumer expenditure data from NSS, has some serious limitations. They are susceptible to under-estimation of the consumption. They do not impute for the consumption of free goods or forest products like fuel wood. Also, the wage goods received in kind and consumed at home may not be fully taken into account in the data collection. Moreover, such data covers only private expenditure. The social consumption portion (subsidised services relating to health, education, transport etc.) does not receive the attention it deserves.

An expert group (constituted by the Planning Commission in September, 1989) under the chairmanship of late Prof. D. T. Lakdawala, on estimation of proportion and the number of poor, has suggested a new methodology to estimate poverty. The Committee submitted its report to the Planning Commission on July 25th 1993. The members of this committee included Prof. V. M. Dandekar, Prof. P. V. Sukhatme, Dr. R. Radhakrishna, Dr. A. Vaidyanathan, Mr. S. N. Ray and Prof. S. R. Hashim.

The states' administration have shown dissatisfaction with the current assessment of poverty situation. The main points of criticism are: *(i)* the procedure of adjustment of consumption expenditure data produced by the national sample survey, *(ii)* choice of deflators to represent price changes in the poverty line, *(iii)* the assumption of absence of price differentials across the states, *(iv)* the assumption of fixed consumption basket over time, and *(v)* the assumption of a uniform consumption basket for all the states.

The Committee had suggested an indepth study linking poverty to living standards and employment as well as free social services provided by the Government and the state administration.

The Seventh Plan (1985-90) assumed that poverty could be abolished and near full employment situation could be created by 2000 A.D. But this seems an uphill task, given the current trends in the growth rates. A study by Operations Research Group (ORG) has stated that only 45 per cent of the rural poor would be crossing the poverty line by the turn of the century. The study also noted that poverty eradication in rural areas may take another 50 years unless the rate of growth in GDP is substantially stepped up and anti-poverty programmes effectively implemented.

It needs to be noted that while the percentage of population below the poverty line will come down, the actual number of the poor may increase. We must therefore aim at progressive reduction in the absolute number of the poor rather than the percentage reduction of the poor.[4] We must also pay attention to another dimension to the poverty problem: those who crossed the poverty line may fall below it at any time.

INCIDENCE OF RURAL POVERTY

Using the poverty line of ₹ 200 per capita per annum at base year (1960-61) prices, the proportion of the rural poor below the poverty line was found to be 52.4 per cent in 1956-57; 46.0 per cent in 1960-61. According to one study, the rural poverty ratio increased from 38 per cent in 1960-61 to 54 per cent in 1968-69.

According to the Planning Commission estimates, the poverty ratio had fallen from 51.5 per cent to 29.2 per cent and the number of poor from 291.5 million to 232.4 million during 1972-73 to 1987-88. However, this assessment has been strongly criticised by many economists. Minhas *et al.* argued that the number of poor actually increased from 308 million to 361.2 million during this period.

According to one estimate, the proportion of people below the poverty line in rural areas for 1972-73 was 54.1 per cent for 1977-78, it was 51.2 per cent and for 1984-85, it was placed at 39.9 per cent.

On the eve of the Sixth Plan, in 1977-78, the percentage of below the poverty line was placed at 48.3 for all India, 51.2 for rural India and 38.2 for urban India.

The poverty estimation in the Seventh Plan document is based on the consumption expenditure survey carried out by the NSS organisation during 1983-84. The preliminary tabulation of these data showed that 37.4 per cent of the total population was below the poverty line in that year — 40.4 per cent for rural India and 28.1 per cent for urban India.

The sharp decline in poverty ratio during a period of six years was attributed to a significant increase in agricultural production and the continuation of direct attack on poverty by implementing anti-poverty programmes. The Planning Commission has observed that the poverty ratio in India has declined from 37.40 per cent in 1983 to 29.2 per cent in 1987-88.

The Seventh Plan (1985-90) aimed at bringing down the population below the poverty line from 273 million in March 1985 to 211 million by the end of 1989-90 (with the poverty ratio declining from 37 per cent to 26 per cent). The plan was to extricate about 62 million people from the grip of poverty of whom about 54 million would be the rural poor. The incidence of rural poverty was recorded her on the high side at 48.7 per cent in 1987-88, according to Minhas et al.

There is also the regional dimension to the eradication of rural poverty which is concentrated mainly in backward, drought-prone and flood-prone areas.5

RURAL POVERTY DURING REFORMS

The reform process started in mid-1991. The reforms make impact on prices and income. For instance, the stress on commercial crops may bring down output of foodgrains and raise their prices.

A recent Expert Group Report (also known as the Tendulkar Report), commissioned by the Planning Commission estimates India's aggregate poverty to be 37.2 per cent According to the Report, 41.8 per cent of the rural population and 25.7 per cent of the urban population were poor.

But, according to NSSO data of 2004-05 (61st Round), only 27.5 per cent of the population was below the poverty line. The difference arose because of the changed definition of what constitutes poverty.

The Planning Commission has estimated, based on uniform recall period (URP), that 28.3 per cent of rural population and 25.7 per cent of the urban population was below the poverty line. For the country as a whole, 27.5 per cent of the total population was below the poverty line in 2004-05. It came to the conclusion that the average decline in percentage of population below the poverty line over the period 1993 to 2004 is 0.74 percentage points per year. The estimated number of poor was about 300 million in 2004-05.

It may be recalled that the official estimate for poverty in 1999 to 2000 was 26.1 per cent for the country as a whole and 260 million were below the poverty line.

Of course, the incidence of poverty differs from state to state. In 2004-05, five states namely, Uttar-Pradesh , Maharashtra, Bihar, West Bengal and Orissa accounted for 166 million poor (about 55. per cent of the total poor estimated at 302 million).

Table: 1

Poverty Estimates (%)

	1993-94	*2004-05*
Rural	37.3	28 3
Urban	32.4	26.7
Total	36.0	27.5

*based on Uniform recall period (URP)

Table: 2

Absolute Number of poor and Very poor in India on the URP basis

	1983	*1993-94*	*2004-05*
Rural	252.0	247.2	232.2
Poor	140.6	102.0	76.7
Very poor	(55.8)	(41.3)	(33.1)
Urban	72.3	77 4	83.3
Poor	38.4	38.0	38 4
Very poor	(53.1)	(49.1)	(46.1)
All India	320.4	324.6	315.5
Poor	179.0	140.0	115.1
Very Poor	(55.2)	(43.2)	(36.5)

Note: Figures in brackets refer to percentage share of very poor to the to total poor

Table: 3
Mean and quintile monthly consumer Expenditure for rural India

	1997-78	*1983*	*1987-88*	*1999-00*	*2004-05*
Per capita average Consumption expenditure (at 1997-78 prices, in ₹)	66.89	71.17	78.27	84.55	90.35
Quintile consumption Expenditure (at 1977-78 prices, in ₹)	29.14	31.43	35.91	42.79	44.91

Source: Economic survey 2009-10. p.23.

Table: 4
Percentage Distribution of Rural Poor

Social Groups	*1993-94*	*1999-2000*
Scheduled Castes	28.19	27.10
Scheduled Tribes	15.46	17.41
Others	56.35	55.45
Total	100.00	100.00

Source: Sundaram and Tendulkar, *Economic and Political Weekly*, December 13, 2003, pp.5264-65.

SALIENT FEATURES OF RURAL POVERTY

Rural poverty in India has some distinct characteristics. The majority of the rural poor are landless agricultural workers and small farmers with large families. Poverty is more widespread among females than males. They have limited access to land, irrigation and credit facilities. They were reported to be rather slow in adopting modern agricultural techniques. More than 70 per cent of the heads of poor households are reported to be illiterate.

The socially disadvantaged groups of scheduled castes and tribes in India account for more than 30 per cent of the rural poor and less than 12 per cent of the rural population. The above mentioned arises is the result of inadequate infrastructural facilities and environmental deterioration. Besides, poverty is correlated directly with family size and inversely with the number of income earners in a family.[6]

The size of the plan and the growth rate appear to be exercising less influence on the incidence of poverty could also achieve a growth rate of 5.4 per cent against the target of 5 per cent. Yet, no significant effort was made to eliminate poverty, unemployment, illiteracy and ill-health from the rural scene. What appears to be crucial is the way inter-sectoral priorities are fixed.

The available NSS data shows that agricultural and other labour households account for 37 per cent of the total rural households, the self-employed in agriculture account for 41 per cent and the self-employed in non-agriculture for 12 per cent. The incidence of poverty is the highest among agricultural labour households (46 per cent), followed by other labour households (28 per cent), self-employed in non-agriculture (27 per cent) and self-employed in agriculture (24 per cent).

More and more rural poor are made to depend on the market. This is evident from the fact that the proportion of the landless increased from 9.6 per cent in 1971 to 11.3 per cent in 1982. There has been a decline in the ratio of the self-employed and a simultaneous increase in the ratio of casual labour. Thus, the structure of the workforce indicates increasing landlessness.

Studies also show that the prices of coarse cereals like jowar, bajra, ragi, maize, barley, gram and small millet rose faster than those of superior cereals like wheat and rice. The cereal consumption pattern of the rural population changed in favour of superior cereals.

A rise in the unemployment rate among rural males which is likely to result from the process of substitution of women for male labour, and a reduction in the wage earnings due to the employment of cheap (women) labour are all indicative of increasing incidence of rural poverty. Studies have revealed that migration of labourers from their native villages to other villages to take up jobs has by and large improved the poverty scene in the country. The migrated labourers save some amount to fall back upon during the lean periods. Remittances are an important source of income for several families, whose members are living and working away from their usual place of residence. These tend to help the family to cross the poverty line while it would have been at the subsistence level in the absence of such remittances.

Profile of Rural Poor

According to NCAER studies, rural poverty in India is spread across all the occupation groups. The self-employed in agriculture and allied activities have 38.50 per cent of the rural poor followed by agricultural labourers (23.22 per cent), non-agricultural labourers (15.80 per cent), self-employed in non-agriculture (15.01 per cent), salaried earners (5.66 per cent) and others (1.71 per cent). This data are based on NCAER, 1996.

However, there are large inter-state variations in distribution of rural poor across occupation groups. In Andhra Pradesh, Gujarat, Kerala, Maharashtra and Tamil Nadu, agricultural labourers have major share of poor as compared to self-employed in agriculture. Punjab and Kerala have maximum proportion of poor from non-agricultural labourers.

Relative incidence of poverty across occupation groups indicates that poverty is more severe among agricultural labourers followed by non-agricultural labourers; self-employed in non-agriculture, self-employed in agriculture and allied activities, others and salaried.

Strategic Measures Needed

Statistics support the view that the levels of living of the rural poor move up the graph in the good agricultural years and move down in the years of bad harvests. For instance, when foodgrains output was lower in 1972-73 at 97 million tonnes as against 105 million tonnes in 1971-72, the poverty line jumped up to 51.5 per cent. In 1977-78, when the foodgrains production had gone up to 126.4 from 121 million tonnes in the previous year, the poverty level came down to 48.3 per cent. This underscores the need for stepping up foodgrain output to bring down the rural poverty level.

The World Development Report 1990 observed that countries had been most successful in reducing poverty by following a two-pronged approach: *(i)* policies that promote efficient growth, making use of the most abundant asset in the rural sector labour, and *(ii)* public expenditures and institutions that provide equitable access to education, health care and other social services. It also underscored the need for a social safety net for the most vulnerable groups in society.

Rural poverty is a multi-dimensional phenomenon. The approach to rural poverty alleviation should be a realistic one. In the Indian context, rural poverty alleviation calls for — *(i)* according high priority to basic needs and agricultural growth, *(ii)* strengthening the asset base of the poor rural households, *(iii)* effective implementation of anti-poverty programmes, both employment generation programmes and asset distribution programmes and above all, *(iv)* changing the rural power structure in favour of the poor by closely associating the weaker sections with the functioning of organisations at the grassroots level.

Rural poverty alleviation needs concerted efforts at various levels. Implementation of anti-poverty programmes in a perfunctory manner would only increase the incidence of leakages instead of reducing the incidence of poverty.

REFERENCES

1. T.N. Krishnan: *'Food Strategy: Inadequate Attention to Distributional Implications', Financial Express*, June 16th 1993.
2. For a discussion of the various dimension of the concept of poverty line, see *Economic and Political Weekly,* August 21st 1993, pp. 1748 to 1768.
3. A.M. Khusro: 'Gauging Poverty', *Indian Express,* July 30, 1993.
4. K. John Mammen: 'The Enigmatic Poverty Line', *The Hindu,* September 20th 1989.
5. *Kamta Prasad:* 'Rural Development in the Eighth Plan', *Yojana,* August 15th 1992, p. 75.
6. M. Lakshminarasaiah: 'Characteristics of Rural Poverty in India', *The Hindu,* January 19th 1993.

Chapter

5 Rural Unemployment in India

Employment is the bedrock of both development and social upliftment, particularly in the rural sector. As such, each country must concentrate on evolving an effective employment policy. The International Labour Organisation (ILO) has therefore argued that employment should become the target and overall growth, the by-product of rural development rather than the other way round.

If a country cannot fully utilise its own human resources, it can achieve nothing on the economic front.[1] If a large percentage of the work force remains unemployed, it will not be able to meet even the basic needs for want of necessary purchasing power.

True, most developing countries suffer from shortage of capital. But that cannot be a justification for growing unemployment and underemployment. The shortage of capital may explain low productivity. But work opportunities can be created if other resources are available. In fact, human resources can also be used to enhance capital formation. We must, therefore, aim at proper development of skills, tap the knowledge and talents of the labour force, and then chalk out a plan for fully utilising them. The fact remains that tapping the potential of the labour force would go towards meeting the basic needs and substantial employment generation in the rural sector.

Countries like China have successfully exploited human resources for creating productive assets. What is most important is the planning of human resources and its maximum utilisation. Mere generation of employment is not going to deliver the goods. The Eighth Five Year Plan has rightly observed, "Employment, to be gainful and sustainable, has, therefore, to be productive in character; it should be able to yield a reasonable level of income to the worker and also generate surplus for further growth and employment generation."[2]

Unemployment is a major problem facing both the developed and developing countries. While in advanced nations, the problem is a product of cyclical and technological factors, in developing countries, poverty and unemployment are products of deficiencies at the structural level. A high percentage of population in these countries depend on primary occupation with a very low resource base, low incomes and savings potential, traditional skills and attitudinal patterns.

The growth in output has not been matched by a corresponding growth in employment. The employment elasticity has been declining. Even when the economy experienced a growth rate exceeding five per cent per annum, employment generation has failed to keep pace with the growth in labour force which is estimated at around two and a half per cent per annum.

CHARACTERISTICS OF RURAL EMPLOYMENT

Though rural India is having abundance of labour force, most of it remains categorised unskilled. The other important features of the rural labour force are:

(i) According to the 1981 census, the total workforce was 240.57 million of which 33.66 million was child labour below the age of 5 years, constituting 12.5 per cent of the total workforce. Female workers in the total workforce were 98.05 million constituting 30.2 per cent;

(ii) Unemployment and underemployment were recorded to be high among rural women than men and their limited mobility focuses on the need to provide them employment in their own villages. As the family income level rises, female workers show a tendency to withdraw from labour force;

(iii) It is difficult to quantify unemployment at any particular point of time. The persons who are unemployed in any given reference period may get some employment later on; and

(iv) The rural labour force suffer from limited mobility. According to the National Sample Survey (NSS), mobility is inversely related to the size of their land-holdings. This means that marginal farmers are more mobile than small farmers and landless labourers are more mobile than marginal farmers.

One important structural change in the rural labour force is that while the daily status of unemployed labour in person days has declined from 8.25 per cent in 1983 to 6.09 per cent in 1987-88, the percentage of unemployed workers increased from 2.77 per cent to 3.77 per cent during this period. This means that the focus has been shifted from predominant underemployment to increased open unemployment. Also, there has been a sharp and steady increase in the casualisation of labour at the cost of the self-employed and the wage-employed.

The rural unemployment scene has certain characteristics. These are:

(i) The availability of employment in the country has not kept pace with the increase in the labour force;

(ii) The proportion of labour depending on wage paid employment is increasing;

(iii) There is a growing casualisation of wage paid labour and

(iv) The labour absorption capacity of the agricultural sector is declining.

In India, rural unemployment including underemployment, is large in its absolute incidence; persistent rather than cyclical. Also, the high incidence of poverty among the rural poor has resulted due to unemployment, including the low earnings or wages in self or wage employment.

The bulk of unemployment is in the rural areas where agriculture and agriculture-based activities are the mainstay of life. As these operations are seasonal, rural India also suffers from seasonal unemployment. Also, with high incidence of underemployment, marginal productivity of surplus labour has to a great extent remained low.

During the 1970s and 1980s, employment had grown at about 2.2 per cent a year, but owing to a faster growth of the labour force (2.5 per cent), the backlog of unemployment has increased. The declining trend in employment elasticity has further aggravated the crisis of unemployment. The challenging task was to create jobs for about 40 million in rural India.

An indepth analysis of unemployment as a crisis and poverty in India would reveal:

(i) A high incidence of disguised unemployment in the agricultural sector. Of course, there are wide variations in development across the regions;

(ii) Highly skewed distribution pattern in resource base in the form of landholdings, productive assets and levels of technology adopted;

(iii) Wide differences in the pattern of incomes, savings potential, investment capabilities, risk taking and entrepreneurial potentialities;

(iv) Marked differences in educational levels and also access to knowledge about modern technologies in the agricultural and industrial sectors and

(v) Presence of social structural constraints like caste system which restrict the ability to develop among the rural population.

It is generally believed that generation of employment opportunities is the best method to eliminate poverty and bring about social welfare. However, Dr. D.T. Lakdawala has argued that low levels of unemployment have failed to eliminate poverty. He observed, "In many parts of the country like Northern and Eastern Madhya Pradesh, Southern Orissa, Western and Southern Rajasthan and almost the whole of Uttar Pradesh, low standards of living of landless labourers are associated with fairly low unemployment rates. These are also parts of the country in which agricultural productivity is substantially low compared to the national average.[3]

The argument of Dr. Lakdawala underscores one point: the need for stepping up labour productivity and levels of agricultural wages, if employment has to reduce the incidence of poverty. He drew the following four significant conclusions in his analysis of the rural population:[4]

(i) Growth, even agricultural growth, is no solution by itself to the problem of poverty in India though it exists as a necessary pre-requisite for tackling poverty;

(ii) The extent of rural unemployment does not vary inversely with the level of consumption in rural areas;

(iii) Though unemployment and underemployment are grave problems, poverty is a more severe problem and mere achievement of full employment at the current wage rate may not contribute in the reduction or elimination of poverty and

(iv) The real problem of the Indian economy is of deployment of resources at a higher level and more efficiently to upgrade the production capabilities of those left out of the process of economic development.

In the rural areas, the proportion of persons employed in agriculture (including mining and quarrying) declined steadily from 86 per cent in 1972-73 to 79 per cent in 1987-88.

Rural areas still account for 78 per cent of employment. However, due to urbanisation, the share of urban employment went up from 16.1 per cent in 1977-78 to 21.6 per cent in 1987-88, with a corresponding decline in the share of rural employment. In fact, in the rural areas, the annual compound growth rate of employment declined steadily from 2.3 per cent between 1972-73 and 1977-78 to 0.8 per cent in the period 1983 to 1987-88.

In the rural areas, among males, 59 per cent were self-employed in 1987-88, while casual labour accounted for 31 per cent and the share of regular employees was only 10 per cent. Between 1972-73and 1987-88, while the share of the regular employees and the self-employed had declined, that of casual labourers had gone up from 22 per cent to 31 per cent. Among the rural families also, the share of casual labour had gone up from 31 per cent in 1972-73 to 36 per cent in 1987-88. The share of the self-employed has dropped in rural areas while it has gone up in urban areas.

As per the 1991 population census, the workforce participation, defined as the proportion of all (main plus marginal) workers to total population had declined among males in rural India (excluding Jammu & Kashmir) from 53.77 per cent in 1981 to 52.50 per cent in 1991. However, in the urban areas, it has remained more or less stable around 49 per cent.

On the other hand, the corresponding ratio among rural women has shown an upward trend from 23.06 per cent in 1981 to 27.20 per cent in 1991. Even in the urban areas, the women workforce participation rate showed an improvement, although quite modest from 8.31 per cent to 9.74 per cent over the same period.

The fall in workforce participation rate among rural males has been due to a fall in the ratio of main workers to the male population rather than that of marginal workers. The proportion of rural male population working as main workers declined from 52.61 per cent to 51.42 per cent between 1981 and 1991 whereas the corresponding ratio for male marginal workers registered a marginal decline of 1.16 per cent in 1981 to 1.08 per cent in 1991.

Along with a decline in the work participation rate for males, the percentage of rural male workforce (main workers) engaged in agriculture also fell from 79.22 per cent to 78.09 per cent between 1981 and 1991 probably because of increasing flows of labour from rural to urban areas.

INCIDENCE OF RURAL UNEMPLOYMENT

The employment elasticity for the economy as a whole has been recorded as low. In fact, it declined from 0.54 during the period 1977-78 to 1983 to 0.30 during 1983 to 1987-88.

The number of days for which employment was available in a year to rural workers had declined by 10 per cent for men, 7.5 per cent for women and 5 per cent for children between 1964-65 and 1974-75 as revealed by the Rural Labour Enquiry Report.

The NSS date based on usual activity status, has highlighted chronic unemployment/open unemployment. The Government treats this chronically unemployed as the backlog. However, the Dantwala Committee (1970) Report had pointed out that "in an economy like ours, there is very little open or outright unemployment but considerable seasonable unemployment and/or underemployment."

The Hiteswar Saikia Committee Report has stated that the total employment at the beginning of the Eighth Plan was 301.7 million. Open unemployment was of the order of 17 million. Those severely underemployed comes to 23 million. The net addition to the labour force was placed at 35 million for the Eighth Plan and 36 million for the Ninth Plan.

It was therefore estimated that employment had to grow at an average annual rate of 3 per cent to reach near full employment level by 2000 AD. The share of the educated unemployed in the total unemployment was placed at 40 per cent in 1987-88.

The usually unemployed in rural areas were estimated at about 7 million during 1987-88 as against the estimated 4 million during 1983. Of the 7 million unemployed during 1987-88, a little less than 2 million had some 'employment' in a subsidiary capacity.

In 1990, it was estimated that there existed a backlog of nine million unemployed agricultural labourers. This is based on two assumptions : *(i)* three-fourth of the 16 million unemployed are in the rural areas, and *(ii)* two-thirds among the rural unemployed are the agricultural labourers.

The Seventh Plan (1985-90) assumed that the backlog of unemployment would be reduced to 8.2 million compared with 9.2 million at the end of the Sixth Plan. The Seventh Plan hoped to create additional jobs to the tune of 40 million Standard Person Years.

The seriousness of the situation can be understood from the fact that between 1961 and 1988, total employment in the organised sector increased from 12 million to 26 million while additions to the labour force have been of the order of 175-200 million. Here again it is the services sector which contributed the most.

In 1985, it was estimated that 37 per cent of the population was below the poverty line. This meant that 273 million people (55 million households) were poor. However, even in 1990, it was estimated that about 50 million households were below the poverty line. Now, even if one member of two-thirds of such households is chronically unemployed or underemployed, the total unemployed would be about 34 million, and most of them would be agricultural labourers.[5]

As part of the annual series in the 60th Round of the NSSO, an all India survey on the situation of employment and unemployment was conducted in January to June, 2004 with a moderately large sample of households. The survey points out the large rural-urban and male-female divide in not only literacy, but also in employment and wages.

According to the survey, in the rural areas, about 66 per cent of usually employed males and 84 per cent of usually employed females were engaged in agricultural sector.

In rural India, on an average, per day, a male casual labourer earned ₹ 56.53, ₹ 20.38 more than a female casual labourer who earned ₹ 36.15.

On the basis of current daily status, during the reference period (1993-94 to 2004), unemployment rate for males increased from 5.6 per cent to 9.0 per cent in rural areas. Similarly, unemployment rate for females increased from 5.6 per cent to 9.3 per cent.

Table: 1 Unemployment Rates* in Rural India in 2004

Status	*Male*	*Female*	*Total*
Usual principal status	24	22	23
Current weekly status	47	45	46
Current daily status	90	93	91

*Unemployment rates (number of persons or person days) unemployed per 1000 persons (or person days).

Source: NSSO, 60th Round survey on employment and unemployment conducted in January-June, 2004.

The Eleventh Plan (2007 -12) rightly stated, "Generation of productive and gainful employment, with decent working conditions, on a sufficient scale to absorb our growing labour force forms a critical element in the strategy for achieving inclusive growth.

The NSSO 55th round had shown a deceleration in the growth of employment from 2 per cent per annum in the period 1983 to 1993-94 to less than one per cent per annum in the period 1993-94 to 1999-2000.

However, according to the NSSO 61at Round, employment growth increased from an annual rate of 0.98 per cent in the period 1993-94 to 1999-2000 to 2.89 per cent in the period, 1999-2000 to 2004-05.

There is another development - a decline in the share of agricultural employment in total employment. It declined from 61 per cent in 1993-94 to 52.1 per cent in 2004. In terms of absolute figures, however, the sector absorbed almost half (30 million) of the incremental workforce.

The share of the manufacturing in employment has marginally declined from 12.1 per cent to 11.7 per cent though in absolute terms the workforce in the sector increased by 5.5 million. The service sector improved it share from 22.7 per cent to 23.4 per cent adding 16.8 million workers in the five-year period.

The survey shows that cutting across the rural-urban divide, the share of self employed workers has increased sharply with an off-setting decline in the share of casual labourers.

During 1999-2000 to 2004-05, about 47 million work opportunities were created compared to only 24 million in the period between 1993-94 and 1999-2000. Employment growth accelerated from 1.25 per cent per annum to 2.62 per cent per annum. However, as the labour force grew at a faster rate of 2.84 per cent than the workforce, unemployment rate also rose. The incidence of unemployment on CDS (current daily status) basis increased from 7.31 per cent in 1999-2000 to 8.28 per cent in 2004-05.

The projected increase in the labour force during the Eleventh Plan is now estimated at 45 million. The backlog of employment in 2006-07 was estimated at 36.7 million. Thus, the total requirements of employment opportunities work out to about 82 million. With the generation, additional employment opportunities of the order of 58 million in the Eleven th Plan, the backlog of the unemployed at the end of the Eleventh plan (2012) will be of the order of 23 to 24 million. At a resu1t, the rate of unemployment will decline from 8.36 per cent in 2006-07 to 4.83 per cant in 2011-12.

Table: 2 Employment Scenario during 1993-94 to 2004-05
(current daily status)

All India	*1993-94*	*1999-2000 (million persons)*	*2004-05*
Population	893.4	1005.0	1092.8
Labour	334.2	364.9	419.2
Workforce	313.9	338.2	384.9
No. of employed	20.3	26.7	34.7
Unemployment rate (%)	6.1	7.3	8.3

Source: Planning Commission (2007), Eleventh Five Year Plan. Vol I.p.71.

Table: 3 Population, Labour force and Employment Projection
(in million)

	2004-05	*2006-07*	*2011-12*	*2016- 17*
Population	1092.8	1128.1	1208.0	1283.2
Labour Force	419.6	438.9	483.6	524.0
Employment opportunities	384.9	402.2	460.3	518.2
Unemployed	34.7	36.7	23.3	5.80
Unemployment rate (%)	8.28	8.36	4.83	1.12

MEASURES NEEDED

Different types of unemployment and underemployment require different strategies. Prof. Raj Krishna said, *"Poverty of the employed, unemployed, the self-employed and the unemployable receive different treatment. The unemployable need simple income transfers, the self-employed need additional input, credit and knowledge; the self-employed need more effective unionism and the unemployed need work and a means of production."*[6]

Employment generation is no doubt a function of growth rates. But even a high rate of growth is not generating enough employment in the context of declining employment elasticity of growth. We have to therefore concentrate on the structure of growth. Emphasis should be on sectors and sub-sectors having high employment elasticity, without lowering efficiency and productivity levels.

There is considerable scope for generating employment in regions which have so far lagged behind in agricultural development and poverty is also relatively high in these areas. If agricultural output is boosted in these areas through availability of assured irrigation, followed by provision of modern inputs and appropriate price policies, considerable employment would be generated. These would facilitate changes in cropping pattern in favour of high value crops, most of which also happen to be more labour using.

Some studies have shown that shift from inferior to superior cereals and from the cereal production to commercial crops would enhance employment opportunities. It is agreed that paddy and wheat show higher labour intensities than inferior cereals and pulses. Of course, enhancing irrigation potential is bound to lead to better employment opportunities in the agricultural sector. Also, employment per hectare of land is higher in the high yielding varieties as compared to the local varieties.

Of course, there is need for strengthening activities allied to agriculture. These include animal husbandry, fisheries, horticulture, aquaculture, forestry and wasteland development. There is a strong case for diversification of agriculture and the rural sector itself.

Land reforms are not likely to adversely affect rural employment opportunities. Farm management studies in the fifties have shown that labour intensity per hectare of land is much higher in small farms as compared to large farms.

Thus, rural unemployment has remained as grave as before. But, there are vast opportunities to generate gainful employment in the agricultural sector as this sector in particular and the rural sector in general remained backward.

REFERENCES

1. Frederick H. Harbison (1973): *Human Resources as the Wealth of Nations,* Oxford University Press, London, p. 3.
2. Planning Commission (1992), Government of India, *Eighth Five Year Plan* 1992-97. Vol. I, p. 116.
3. Presidential Address at the All-India Labour Economics Conference, Tirupati, December 1977.
4. *Ibid.*
5. J. S. Sodhi: 'The Field Theory of Labour', The *Economic Times,* May 10th 1990.
6. Raj Krishna (1973): *Unemployment in India.* Presidential Address, Indian Society of Agricultural Economics.

Chapter

6 Rural Migration

Most developing countries are experiencing the phenomenon of migration of the rural population to urban areas. This is attributed to industrialisation and urbanisation. However, in developing countries, such a migration is creating not a few problems.

Nature of Rural Migration

The Harris-Todaro model of rural migration is basically a two-sector model. The two sectors are urban and rural sectors. The urban sector specialises in the production of manufactured goods, while the rural sector specialises in agriculture. The basic concept behind the model is that rural urban migration will continue so long as the expected urban real income is more than real wage rate in the agricultural sector. The model further assumes that there is no uncertainty in the rural labour market.[1]

Even the developed countries, in their initial stages of development, had to experience rural migration. For instance, in England, migration took place in a wave-like fashion from villages to small towns and from small towns to cities. The situation was no different in other industrialised countries of Europe. The migrant work force from the villages and semi-towns was the main source of industrial labour for the emerging industrial centres and towns.

According to Todaro, "Migration today must be seen as a major contributing factor to the ubiquitous phenomenon of urban surplus labour and a force which continues to exacerbate already serious urban unemployment problems caused by a growing economic and structural imbalance between urban and rural areas.[2]

A unique feature of the Indian scenario is that rural-rural migration continues to be predominant. In the case of unskilled and semi-skilled jobs, it is generally true that any shift from the primary to the secondary and tertiary sectors represents migration. Initially, this kind of migration is usually within the rural areas — from agricultural to non-agricultural and subsequently from rural to urban areas.

The migration of landless labourers from Bihar to Punjab and Haryana, the two agriculturally prosperous states, is a good example of rural-rural migration.

More literate and higher educated are migrating to the metropolitan cities than the illiterates. The push factors may be important in the case of illiterates, but the positive push and pull factors are important in the case of the educated.[3]

There are two aspects of the problem of migration. One relates to the lack of opportunities in rural areas and small towns which compels the people to leave their homes and hearth, the other relates to the miserable conditions of living in the large cities. The earnings of majority of the migrants do not support a life with desirable standards. The rural poverty and urban misery, therefore, appear as two faces of the same coin.[4]

The inter-sectoral migration of labour is a multi-dimensional issue. Generally, as development picks up in an economy, there will be migration of labour from the primary to the secondary and tertiary sectors.

Inter-sectoral migration of labour is influenced by factors like social customs, unequal distribution of resources, technological advances, rural urban linkages, structural factors, psychological disposition, income differentials and so on.[5]

Of course, the migrants are not a homogeneous group. There are different streams of migrants with different causes and motivations underlying their movement.

A majority of the agricultural population depends on rainfed cultivation. A failure of monsoons will have tremendous destabilising effects on the agricultural economy, and subsequently on those who depend on agriculture. However, the impact would not be uniform but would vary across classes.[6]

Because of constraints on urban growth, there is nothing like a steady growth in rural-urban migration. In fact, the net rural urban-migration (decadal), registered a considerable decline even in absolute terms. Around 19.73 million people were estimated as net migrants over the decade 1971-81. This figure decelerated to 12.73 million during 1981-91, reducing its relative share in total increase in the urban population, from 39.40 per cent to 22.62 per cent. The decline in the growth rate of urban population during the last decade can, therefore, be attributed mainly to the decline in the net rural-urban migration.[7]

Some say that migration is rational, and households respond to economic incentives in selecting employment location. Earning differentials, according to them, is an important determinants of migration in the Third World countries.

However, according to Todaro, a proponent of the rationalist approach to migration, migrants respond rather to expected earning differentials than to current earning differentials.

It is not proper to lay stress only on wage differentials. We should give importance to differentials in the cost of living, availability of amentities etc.

Migrataion itself is not bad. But, it should be smooth, producing minimum adverse consequences. In fact, labour migration (with rural-rural and rural-urban) is natural and also essential from the overall development of the economy.

ADVERSE EFFECTS

Large influx of the rural population to urban areas has resulted in housing shortage and over congestion in urban centres. The formation of slums and squatter settlements further worsen the situation. Cities have to face pollution hazards and sky-rocketing land prices.

Migration also led to social tensions. The situation worsened because of over-population and unequal distribution of assets.

Most of the labourers who migrate to towns suffer from poor health facilities. A large number of labourers who migrated from Bhiar have been suffering from diseases like leprosy. They also do not take the prescribed medicines regularly.[8]

Thus, mass migration from the rural to urban sector tends to destroy both the spirit, growth and physical quality of life. This subsequently accentuates the rural urban divide, leading to social rift and tension accompanied by urban overload.[9]

The school drop-outs who migrate to urban areas lead pathetic life as casual labourers in construction, as domestic servants, chowkidars, footpath tea-makers and washermen.

MEASURES NEEDED

Economists like Lewis, Ranis and Fei have developed the dualistic theories of development. According to them, the ultimate limit to urban growth is agriculture either through the disappearance of the surplus rural labour and/or through the rise in the relative price of agricultural products.

Arresting rural migration is no easy task. The problem can be satisfactorily solved if villages become the focal point of development. We have to develop rural areas by creating infrastructure facilities and job opportunities there. Also, we have to improve urban governance and urban management to improve the quality of life in cities.

Agriculture by itself cannot solve the problem of rural poverty and unemployment. The solution lies in rapid rural industrialisation. Village life can be made attractive provided non-agricultural job opportunities are greatly stepped up.[10]

The rural economy should be diversified with special stress on agro-based industries, animal husbandry, poultry farming, bee-keeping etc. Provision of better irrigation facilities will not only increase farm productivity but also provide employment througl.out the year by encouraging multiple cropping.

Also, measures should be initiated to develop institutional capability in rural areas. There exists institutional potential even in the traditional rural sector. When this is properly utilised, it ensures effective implementation of the policies and plane directed at low income groups.

Some measures may be necessary to make labour migration painful and to arrest rural exodus.[11]

These should include:

(i) Effective implementation of land reforms;

(ii) Expansion of non-farm employment opportunities;

(iii) Enforcement of minimum wages;

(iv) Improving rural infrastructure like roads and communications;

(v) Special attention to development of industries in rural areas; and

(vi) Strengthening the self-employment sector.

We shall have to stop further urbanisation by arresting migration of rural people by developing rural areas and creating infrastructural facilities and job opportunities. We have to improve urban governance and urban management to improve the quality of life in cities.

REFERENCES

1. Amit Kundu: 'To Migrate or Not to Migrate', *The Indian Economic Journal,* October-December 1998-99. p. 121.
2. Macheal P. Todaro (1977): *Economics of Developing World,* Longmans Group, London.
3. D.L. Narayana: 'Migration to Cities: Its Implications for Rural Development', in R.C. Choudhury and S. Rajakutty (Ed. 1998): *Fifty Years of Rural Development in India: Retrospect and Prospect,* National Institute of Rural Development, Hyderabad. Vol. 1, p. 416.
4. U.C. Mallick: Planning for Small Towns for Balanced Regional Development (Commerce Pamphlet, Mumbai), pp. 18-19.
5. A. Amarender Reddy and A. Ravishankar : 'Inter Sectoral Labour Migration: Dimensions and Emerging Perspectives', *Kurukshetra,* October-November 1997, p. 81.
6. Rukmani Ramani: 'Migration: An Offshoot of Agrarian Stress', *The Hindu,* September 6, 1998.
7. Arup Mitra: 'Rural-Urban Migration', *The Economic Times,* October 8th 1996.
8. Shankar Lal Tulsyan: 'Labour Migration from Bihar', *Kurukshetra,* May 1999, pp. 5-6.
9. M.L. Khurana: 'Time to Dam the Row', *The Economic Times,* July 2nd 2000.
10. I. Satya Sundaram: 'Arresting Rural Exodus', *Kurukshetra,* February 16th 1978, p. 18.
11. A. Amarender Reddy and A. Ravishankar: *op. cit.,* p. 83.

Chapter

7

Rural Development and the Eighth Plan

India has acquired substantial experience in the implementation of various rural development (RD) programmes with schemes being designed and redesigned to make these programmes contribute effectively to eliminate rural poverty and unemployment. Like the Seventh Plan (1985-90), the Eighth Plan (1992-97) has aimed at economic growth in conjunction to social justice. The plan has recognised that opportunities of productive employment on a sustainable basis alone can eliminate rural poverty and unemployment. The plan also recommends the implementation of special schemes for the rural sector as the process of growth bypasses some sections of the population.

Plan Outlay on RD

The central plan has made substantial increase in the outlay for rural development from ₹ 4,900 crore approved in the Seventh Plan (against which actual expenditure was about ₹ 10,800 crore) to ₹ 30,000 crore in the Eighth Plan. Also, these programmes are being restructured in order to make them more cost effective and generate productivity. The emphasis has shifted from creation of relief type of employment to building up of durable productive assets in the rural areas.[1]

Table 1: The Eighth Plan Outlay for Rural Development

Centre	₹ 24,320 crore
States	₹ 11,677 crore
TOTAL	₹ 35,997 crore

The Finance Ministry has been working on strategies to down the fiscal deficit. Since there is very little scope for reducing expenditure on general administration, interest payments, law and order, security etc., the axe has fallen on development expenditure, especially on rural development and poverty alleviation programmes.

Economists are of the opinion that the provisions made for rural development in various budgets are inadequate. The budgetary outlay for 1992-93 stood at ₹ 3,113.24 crore as against budgetary provisions of ₹ 3,521.24 crore for 1991-92 which was later revised down to ₹ 3,021.24 crore. Given the price rise, the Outlay on rural development in real terms would be lower in 1992-93 than in 1991-92.

The worst hit were the rural water supply and sanitation programmes as the provision for accelerated rural water supply programme suffered a steep decline from ₹ 758.67 crore in 1991-92 to ₹ 460.58 crore in 1992-93. The budgetary allocation for sanitation, almost halved, as only ₹ 20 crore has been allocated in 1992-93 against ₹ 37.61 crore for 1991-92. In the revised budget for 1991-92, the provision had been brought down drastically to a mere ₹ 4 crore.[2]

Table 2: Plan Outlay on Rural Development

(₹ crore)

Item	*1992-93 budget*	*1993-94 budget*
Water supply and sanitation	480.000	770.000
Special programmes for RD	499.46	819.00
Rural employment	2,046.00	3,306.00
Land Reforms	25.02	35.50
Other RD programmes	32.50	53.50
Food storage and warehousing	—	—
Other agricultural programmes	7.01	11.00
Housing	10.00	15.00
	3,100.00	5,010.00

EMPLOYMENT GENERATION

According to the Eighth Plan, strategies for rural development should aim at ensuring not only economic benefits, but also social transformation in the post angle. Improvements in health, education, clean drinking water, energy supply, sanitation, housing and also attitudinal changes need to be prioritised without delay.

The Eighth Plan drew attention to the fact that poverty is more alarming than unemployment. Though the unemployment rate in rural India appears to be very small, the poverty ratio is high. A large proportion of the rural population is 'working', but they cannot make both ends meet. The plan document rightly observes, "More employment needs to be generated at higher levels of productivity in order to generate higher output. Employment at miserably low levels of productivity and income is already a problem of far greater magnitude than unemployment as such."[3]

Issues related to ongoing anti-poverty programmes (to be discussed these schemes in subsequent chapters) like Integrated Rural Development Programme (IRDP), Training Rural Youth for Self-

Employment (TRYSEM), Development of Women and Children in Rural Areas (DWCRA), Jawahar Rozgar Yojana (JRY) and Drought Prone Area Programme (DPAP). More were incorporated in the Eighth Plan for implementation on priority basis.

The employment generation programmes, the plan observed, must be integrated with other sectoral development programmes as this alone would generate larger and more sustainable employment. The plan gives priority to rural transportation and minor irrigation works.

In the Indian context, the success of a plan has to be judged in terms of its capacity to generate productive employment. This has been realised in the Eighth Plan. A geographically and crop wise diversified agriculture, wasteland development for crop cultivation and forestry, rural non-farming sector, small-scale manufacturing, urban informal sector, rural infrastructure, housing and services have been identified as sectors and areas on constituting the basic elements of an employment-oriented growth strategy.[4]

Land Reforms

In the Indian context, institutional reforms are as important as technological changes. Hence, land reforms have engaged the attention of the Government even in the 1950s. Of course, the performance of the Government on this front is not satisfactory for various reasons. However, it is also realised that mere provision of land alone cannot raise a family above the poverty line. The Eighth Plan therefore observes that the allottees of surplus ceiling land require assured access to inputs. It has also been realised that revenue administration needs to be strengthened in order to update land records. Towards this goal, by the end of the Seventh Plan, ₹ 25.57 crore have been allocated to 29 states and Union Territories for purchase of equipment and strengthening of training infrastructure.[5]

Development Administration

The poor can hope to get due benefits from RD programmes only when they get support from the development administration. At the district level, there is District Rural Development Agency (DRDA) to co-ordinate RD programmes. But the administrative machinery at the block level has to be strengthened. The Block Development Officer (BDO) has lost control over the extension officers who are functioning under their own departmental hierarchies.

The Panchayati Raj (PR) institutions work out strategies for the implementation of rural development programmes. This would ensure participation of local representatives in the planning process. These representatives can give due weight to the needs and aspirations of the local people. Of course, they must be made accountable to the people they represent.

The Eighth Plan clearly recognises the need for an integrated area plan, at the block level, based on the availability of local skills and resources. The plan document also observed that planning and implementation of sectoral activities should be decentralised and integrated into a unified activity, with horizontal co-ordination at the district level. With a view to activating the village panchayats, Jawahar Rozgaar Yojana (JRY) funds were placed at their disposal.

VOLUNTARY SECTOR

The Eighth Plan, like the Seventh Plan, gave priority to voluntary action and people's participation in the sphere of RD. The voluntary agencies have been working in close proximity to the rural population by chalking out and implementing new approaches towards integrated rural development. They have developed as appropriate institutions to assess the impact of anti-poverty programmes on rural people. The Plan also recognised the need for a cadre of trained animators and social organisers. Also, a massive programme for training the identified persons was prepared with the help of established voluntary agencies. It is felt that voluntary agencies are best suited to take up activities like organisation of the beneficiaries.

The Eighth Plan admits that funds alone cannot deliver the goods. In fact, the implementation of rural development programmes must lead to greater participation by rural people in programmes initiated through public relation institutions, co-operatives and other self-managed institutions. The rural population should take the help of development administration.

RURAL ENERGY

Modernisation of the rural sector depends on the availability of energy. The Eighth Plan gives importance to Integrated Rural Energy Programme (IREP). The share of the rural areas in the total commercial energy produced in the country is around one-fifth, though the rural areas account for nearly three-fourth of the total population. There is widespread scarcity of commercial energy in rural areas.

The IREP, which was taken up in the Seventh Plan, aimed at improving the share of rural areas in total commercial energy consumption. The IREP in the Eighth Plan will focus on two major areas :[6]

(i) Provision of energy for meeting the basic needs of cooking, heating and lighting, especially for the weaker section, by utilising locally available energy resources to the extent possible and

(ii) Provision of energy as the critical input in economic development of the rural areas which would result in the creation of employment, increasing productivity and income and accelerating the process of decentralised development. In this category will be included energy for sustainable agricultural production as well as promoting sustainable rural development activities.

The Eighth Plan document has summed up the task of rural development front thus: "Increased participation of people in the rural development process, decentralisation of planning, better enforcement of land reforms and greater access to credit and inputs go a long way in providing the rural people with better prospects for economic development."[7]

CRITICAL APPRAISAL

The real problem with rural development programmes in India relates to shortfalls in the achievement of physical targets. The returns from these programmes have not been impressive, mainly because of flaws in the identification of appropriate programmes, deficiencies at the implementation stage and poor evaluation and monitoring of the schemes. The document should have concentrated on implementation of programmes taking into consideration these issues. Allocation of larger funds for these programmes is no doubt welcome, but unless the incidence of leakages is minimised, the target rural group may not benefit much from schemes meant for them.

The document is also silent over the multiplication of the schemes for the rural poor. This tendency should be curbed. When there are too many schemes, all of them may not become economically viable or cannot be effectively implemented. Also, there would be duplication of work, leading to wastage of time and funds. Though this is well-known, multiplication of schemes continue more for political than for economic reasons.

Rural development programmes can be effective if only the decentralised planning set-up is strengthened. A few committees have submitted reports on decentralised planning. We have institutions at the district and block levels to implement and supervise these programmes. Yet, planning at the micro level remains perfunctory. The document has also not paid sufficient attention to these issues.[8]

Rural development should not remain a rhetoric and the development administration for these programmes should face the hard realities. It should implement productive programmes, ensure forward and backward linkages, minimise the leakages by proper identification of beneficiaries, create a climate conducive to people's active participation in the planning process and ensure periodical evaluation and monitoring of these programmes.

References

1. Pranab Mukherjee: 'Approath to the Eighth Five Year Plan', *Yojana,* August 15, 1992, p. 9.
2. *Kurukshetra,* April 1992, p. 16.
3. Planning Commission, Government of India (1992): *The Eighth Five Year Plan* 1992-97, Vol. II, p. 27.
4. Nitish Sengupta: 'Philosophy of the Eighth Plan', *Yojana,* August 15th 1992, p. 33.
5. *The Eighth Five Year Plan. op. cit.,* Vol. II, p. 34.
6. *Ibid.,* p. 46.
7. *Ibid.,* p. 27.
8. Dilip Shah: 'Eighth Plan Belies Rural Development Hopes', *Financial Express,* October 1, 1993.

Chapter

8 Rural Development in the Ninth Plan (1997-2002)

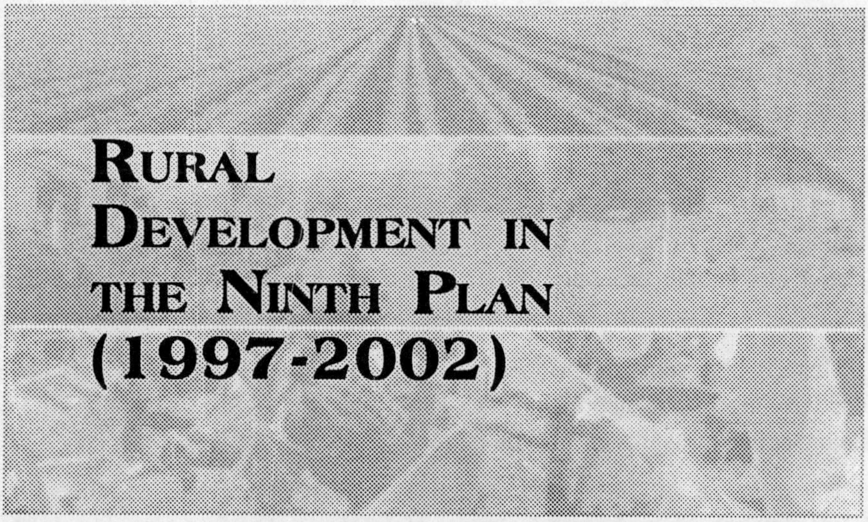

India's Ninth Five Year Plan (1997-2002) has given importance to agriculture and allied activities in view of the need for reducing the incidences of rural poverty and unemployment. It recognises that high growth of incomes is by itself not enough to improve the quality of life of the poor. The focus of the Plan is on human development.

According to the Plan's document, direct poverty alleviation programmes are important, and will continue on an expanded scale. But, these programmes would be oriented towards strengthening the productive potential of the economy and providing more opportunities for involving the poor in the economic process. Also, poverty can effectively be eradicated only when the poor start contributing to growth by their active involvement.[1]

Indian Agriculture

The Plan admitted that Indian agriculture continues to remain vulnerable to weather related shocks. Hence, the need for accelerating investment in agriculture. Credit availability needs to be stepped up as it has remained almost stagnant. Public investment, particularly in irrigation, has in fact dropped sharply. Also, the Plan realised that in view of the constant, and even the declining area available for cultivation, agricultural growth can come about only through rapid increase in productivity and changes in the cropping pattern.[2]

Agricultural development is marked by regional disparities. Therefore, the strategy of agricultural development has to be tailored to the requirements of different regions. There is large untapped potential in the eastern region and this region accounts for a major proportion of the poor people in India.

Agriculture economy of the eastern region is dominated by small and marginal farmers. The region has abundant surface and ground water, though it is flood-prone. The entire region is characterised by weak agricultural institutions.

In the eastern region, input subsidy is likely to play a major role in stimulating greater input use, and hence higher production and productivity. Given the high incidence of share-cropping, large reforms assume great importance.[3]

In the Ninth Plan, a target of 4.5 per cent annual growth rate in gross value of agricultural output, excluding forestry has been fixed. The investment for agriculture and allied activities in this plan is projected, at ₹ 220206 crore at 1996-97 prices, which is nearly 40 per cent higher than in the Eighth Plan. Of course, private investment accounts for a major share of investment in agriculture.

There is little scope for further expansion of the net sown area. Hence, cropping intensity and productivity need to be stepped up. The Ninth Plan proposed a regionally differentiated strategy for achieving agricultural growth and equity.[4]

The strategies for agricultural development will focus on the social objectives of employment generation, food and nutrition security, gender equity, poverty alleviation and environmental sustainability.[5]

The Plan gives importance to a positive agricultural price policy which included subsidies on inputs and a minimum support price for output. The minimum support price is meant to provide an incentive to the farmers to adopt high-risk new technology and to cover possible hazards of high input costs.[6]

Rural Poverty

Rural poverty is largely concentrated in the landless and marginal farmers. Access to land therefore assumes importance in any anti-poverty strategy in rural areas. The programme of action for land reforms in the Ninth Plan would include:[7]

(i) Detection as well as redistribution of ceiling surplus land;

(ii) Upgradation of land records on a regular basis;

(iii) Tenancy reforms providing for recording the rights of tenants and share croppers;

(iv) Consolidation of holdings;

(v) Preventing alienation of tribal lands;

(vi) Providing access on a group basis to the poor on wastelands and common property resources;

(vii) Leasing-in and leasing-out land will be permitted within the ceiling limits and

(viii) Preference to women in the distribution of ceiling surplus land and legal provisions for protecting their rights on land.

The Ninth Plan observes that updating of land records would have to be expedited as this is a necessary prerequisite of any effective land reform policy. Also, a massive programme of organising the rural poor for participation in the implementation of land reforms and poverty alleviation programmes would be undertaken with the help of voluntary groups with good track records, social activists and other community leaders.[8]

It is estimated that 20 per cent of the rural households are *de facto* female-headed. Yet, very few women have titles to land and even fewer control it. Hence, ensuring women's effective command over land will be one of the new priorities of the Ninth Plan.[9]

RURAL DEVELOPMENT PROGRAMMES

True, rural India is having abundance of manpower. But most of it is unskilled. Hence, imparting skills to the labour-force should receive priority. Of course, there is a class of rural artisans which is not receiving the required institutional support.

The rural artisans, in spite of their rich heritage and skills are poor. It is therefore necessary to support them with appropriate product design and training, improved technology on the one hand and professional management and marketing support on the other. The rural artisans will be serviced through a package approach wherein the distribution of improved tool-kits is supplemented with the supply of credit and raw material, marketing support and upgradation of existing technology.[10]

Regarding wage employment programmes, the stress should be on assuring at least 100 days of employment per person per year by coordinating all the wage employment schemes including the state schemes.

Both the Employment Assurance Scheme (EAS) and the JRY are operating in all the districts/ blocks in the country. At present, the JRY is being implemented through the panchayats and the EAS through the administrative apparatus. In future, however, the EAS would also be implemented through the panchayati raj institutions. Under JRY, the allocations are made on the basis of a specified criteria. On the other hand, the EAS is a demand-driven scheme, i.e., only initial/notional allocations are made, and depending on the demand for supplementary employment and actual utilisation, requests for additional allocations are made by states/districts. It is therefore argued that there is a strong case for merging these two schemes.

However, the Ninth Plan feels that funds released to states should be made on the basis of the incidence of poverty in order to prevent the better-off states from cornering a larger share of the funds.[11]

The Ninth Plan observes that a major constraint on effective implementation of IRDP is sub-critical investments, making projects unviable. It seeks to enhance credit flows and average level of investment per family in the range of ₹ 24,000 to 50,000 depending on the estimate of poverty line and the poverty gap.[12]

Also, the IRDP will seek to develop close linkages with the credit mechanism in such a manner as would promote repeated/multiple doses of credit rather than a one-line loan for the beneficiary. The emphasis is on establishing a continuous line of credit for the beneficiary. The intention is to make the project economically viable.[13]

In the case of IRDP, the Centre and the States's shares are 50:50 and in the case of wage employment programmes, the ratio is 80:20. Hence, the states are not showing sufficient interest in self-employment schemes. In the Ninth Plan, it is proposed to alter the funding pattern under IRDP and bring it at par with the rural wage-employment programmes. In fact, the cost sharing formula both for IRDP and the wage employment programmes would be revised to a uniform ratio of 75:25 between the centre and the states.[14]

The IRDP will also aim at diversifying the investments into high-value-addition sectors and non-traditional activities which have a market potential. Also, the IRDP would service the beneficiaries through a package approach wherein the beneficiary would have access to credit, training as per requirements, upgradation of technology, delivery of essential inputs and marketing tie-ups in an integrated manner.[15]

In order to strengthen the self-employment sector, the Ninth Plan envisaged a shift in strategy under IRDP, from an individual beneficiary approach to a group and/or cluster approach. This would facilitate higher investment levels to ensure viability of projects. This requires development of skills of the poor through an inbuilt training component, upgradation of technology, establishment of forward and backward linkages, availability of appropriate infrastructure and market tie-ups.[16]

A greater integration of DWCRA with IRDP and TRYSEM will be attempted to provide women's groups with greater access to financial resources and training.[17]

The Ninth Plan underscores the need for integration among the various poverty alleviation programmes, area development programmes and sectoral schemes within a district plan based on the physical and human endowments of the area the felt needs of the people and the total financial resources available.[18]

In the implementation of anti-poverty programmes, the Government policy is to reduce the role of government departments and entrust the responsibility to elected bodies. Hence, efforts have been initiated to strengthen the panchayati raj institutions through constitutional amendments.

REFERENCES

1. Planning Commission, Government of India, *Ninth Five Year Plan (1997-2002),* Vol. II, p. 9.
2. Planning Commission, Government of India, *Approach Paper to the Ninth Five Year Plan,* p. 6.
3. *Ninth Five Year Plan*, Vol. I, p. 111.
4. *Ibid.*, Vol. II, p. 416.
5. *Ibid.*, p. 418.
6. *Ibid.*, Vol. I, p. 107.
7. *Approach Paper to the Ninth Five Year Plan: op. cit.*, pp. 60-61.
8. *Ninth Five Year Plan*, Vol. II, p. 25.

9. *Ibid.*, p. 41.

10. *Ibid.*, p. 28.

11. *Ibid.*, p. 35.

14. *Ibid.*, p. 37.

15. *Ibid.*, p. 24.

16. *Approach Paper to the Ninth Five Year Plan, op. cit.*, p. 59.

17. *Ibid.*, p. 59.

18. *Ninth Five Year Plan*, Vol. II, p. 25.

Chapter

9 Rural Development in the Tenth Plan

India's Tenth Five Year Plan (2002-07) has some ambitious targets to achieve. The public sector outlay at 2001-02 prices is proposed to be ₹ 15,92,300 crore out of which the central plan would have an outlay of ₹ 9,21,291 crore, and the outlay for the states and union territories would be ₹ 6,71,009 crore. The central budgetary support to the plan is targeted at ₹ 7,06,000 crore. The disinvestment proceeds are expected to bring ₹ 78,000 crore. Foreign Direct Investment (FDI) annual inflow in the 10th plan period is placed at $7.5 billion, but the present level is only $4 billion.

The Tenth Plan aims at an annual growth rate of 8 per cent. However, the annual growth rate of real GDP for the entire Ninth Plan (1997-2002) was just 5.36 per cent much below the targeted 6.5 per cent (original target was 7 per cent). The annual rate of growth achieved in the Eighth Plan (1992-97) was 6.7 per cent.

Agriculture and Irrigation

In the agriculture and allied activities sector, the 10th plan aims at an annual growth rate of 3.7 per cent, and the incremental capital output ratio is placed at 1.99.

The foodgrain production fell from 212.9 million tonnes in 2001-02 to 174.8 million tonnes in 2002-03. It was high at 213.5 million tonnes in 2003-04. This fell to 204.6 million tonnes in 2004-05. The estimate for the year 2005-06 is 209.3 million tonnes.

The total public sector outlay for agriculture and allied activities in the Tenth Plan is ₹ 58,933 crore which forms 3.9 per cent of the total outlay. Rural development gets ₹ 1,21,928 crore which forms 8 per cent of the total outlay. An amount of ₹ 30,879 crore (1.3 per cent of the total) has been allotted to special area programmes. Irrigation and flood control get ₹ 1,03,315 crore which forms 6.8 per cent of the total outlay. All the four heads are thus allotted an amount of ₹ 3,05,055 crore, forming 20 per cent of the total outlay.

The Tenth Plan seeks to lay special stress on employment generation mainly in agriculture, irrigation, agro-forestry, small and medium enterprises and other services. The objective is to provide employment to 50 million people in the Tenth Plan.

The rate of growth of employment, on current daily status basis, declined from 2.7 per cent per annum in 1983 to 1.07 per cent in 1994 to 2000. The decline was attributed largely to near stagnation of employment in agriculture.

The share of agriculture in total employment dropped from 60 per cent to 57 per cent during this period. Clearly there is need for stepping up investment, both public and private, in rural areas. The aim should be asset creation initially and sustainable job creation subsequently.[1]

Table 1: Allocation for Ministry of Rural Development (₹ Crore)

Department	*Annual Plan 2005-06 (BE)*	*Annual Plan 2005-06 (RE)*	*Annual Plan 2006-07 (BE)*	*Outlay earmarked for North East 2006-07 (BE)*
Dept. of Rural Development	18,334.00	21,334.00	24,025.62	2,252.56
Dept. of Land Resources	1,396.00	1,396.00	1,418.00	134.00
Dept. of Drinking Water Supply	4,750.00	4,760.00	6,000.00	600.00
Total	24,480.00	27,490.00	31,443.62	2,986.56

Source: Budget 2006-07.

THE NEW SCHEMES

A few new schemes have been introduced during the 10th Plan for rural development. Only important schemes are discussed here.

NATIONAL RURAL HEALTH MISSION (NRHM)

This scheme was launched on April 12th 2005 with the objective of providing greater access of the rural population, especially the rural poor, to the public healthcare facilities. Major components of the scheme include training of health volunteers, providing more medicines and strengthening the primary and community health centres. NRHM has an initial outlay of ₹ 6731 crore in 2005-06 (BE).

JLNNURM

Jawaharlal Nehru National Urban Renewal Mission (JLNNURM) has been launched on December 3, 2005 in selected cities which include an urban infrastructure development scheme for small and medium towns to provide reform linked assistance to the State governments for infrastructure projects including water supply and sewerage projects for all towns and cities.

NATIONAL FOOD FOR WORK PROGRAMME

The National Food for Work Programme (NFWP) was launched on November 14th 2004. The scheme has been merged with the National Rural Employment Guarantee Programme (NREGP) which has been discussed elsewhere in this book.

The NFWP was 100 per cent centrally funded scheme, and it was implemented in 150 most backward districts of the country. The programme promises to provide 100 days of work per person for below poverty rural family. The annual requirement is estimated at ₹ 5400 crore and 37 lakh tonnes of foodgrains. Allocation for NFWP has been enhanced from ₹ 4020 crore in 2004-05 to ₹ 11,000 crore in 2005-06.

According to the guidelines, a minimum of 25 per cent of wages is to be paid in cash and the rest in foodgrains. It is further stated that a maximum of 5 kg of foodgrains is to be given to the workers.

A case study relating to adivasi dominated Beitul district of Madhya Pradesh revealed that labourers worked for nine hours against the stipulated eight. Even a tractor was hired to clear the mud from the tank instead of employing women to do so.[2]

Another study relating to three backward districts of Maharashtra (Yeotomal, Hingoli and Nanded) revealed a horrific picture of inhuman conditions at the worksite — extremely low piece rate wages for hard manual labour and what is worse, women had to work for nine hours in a day at public worksites without payment.[3]

The NFWP had no reservation provision for women. It is a highly centralised and the District Collector is the nodal agency to prepare the plan with the help of any professional agency.

Moreover, barring Rajasthan, the programme has virtually failed to achieve the target. Also, it was run by contractors instead of panchayats. And there were no fixed minimum wages.[4]

UNION BUDGET 2005-06

During the year, 2005-06, the scheme of Bharat Nirman was launched to improve infrastructure facilities. The aims of the scheme are:

- to bring an additional one crore hectares under assured irrigation.
- to connect all villages that have a population of 1000 (or 500 in hilly and tribal areas) with roads.
- to construct 60 lakh additional houses for the poor.
- to provide drinking water to the remaining 74,000 habitations that are uncovered.
- to reach electricity to the remaining 1,25,000 villages and offer electricity connection to 2.3 crore households.
- to give telephone connectivity to the remaining 66,822 villages.

Assured irrigation facilities to an additional one crore hectares of land over a period of five years will generate employment for an additional one crore people at the rate of one person per hectare.

For job generation on a sustainable basis, the budget 2005-06 lays stress on agro-processing, textiles, information technology and the like. The budget pointed out that the rate at which the food processing industry is growing, it can generate around 2.5 lakh jobs every year. The textile sector alone has the potential to create about 1.2 crore jobs over the next five years. And the information technology industry can be expected to offer about 70 lakh jobs by 2009.

The total central plan outlay for the rural employment sector has been pegged at ₹ 1000 crore. Of this, ₹ 4000 crore is allocated for the Sampoorna Grameen Rozgar Yojana (SGRY) and ₹ 6000 crore for the National Food for Work Programme, besides setting apart ₹ 1000 crore exclusively for the North-east region and Sikkim. In addition, the Swarnajayanti Gram Swarozgar Yojana (SGSY) has been allocated ₹ 862.24 crore from the total central plan outlay for 2005-06.

The 2005-06 budget has earmarked ₹ 196.65 crore for the PMRY and ₹ 369.95 crore for REGP.

The Central government's expenditure on agricultural research and education, plan plus non-plan, in 2005-06 (revised) was ₹ 1900 crore which was ₹ 42 crore less than the budgeted amount.

The budget 2005-06 announced a corpus of ₹ 8000 crore in 2005-06 for Rural Infrastructure Development Fund.

UNION BUDGET 2006-07

According to the Common Minimum Programme of the UPA Government, irrigation should receive top priority. Under the Accelerated Irrigation Benefit Programme (AIBP), the Centre has been assisting the State governments. Projects approved under the AIBP would require balance investment of ₹ 50,000 crore provided upto March 2006, for bringing in eight million hectares under irrigation.

Allocation for the AIBP in 2005-06 was ₹ 4500 crore. The budget 2006-07 increased the amount to ₹ 7181 crore. It may be difficult to achieve the Bharat Nirman target of bringing an additional one crore hectares under irrigation during the period 2005 to 2009.

Union budget 2006-07 also announced a programme for repair, renovation and restoration of 20,000 water Bodies with a command area of 1.47 million hectares at a cost of ₹ 4481 crore with the participation of states and with possible funding from multilateral agencies.

The budgetary allocation for agricultural research and education for 2006-07 is ₹ 2160 crore — a rise of mere 10 per cent. An amount of ₹ 245 crore has been allocated by the budget for agricultural extension. This is also inadequate. However, an amount of ₹ 1000 crore has been allocated for the food processing sector by the budget.

The budget 2006-07 has stepped up allocation for SGSY to ₹ 1200 crore, up from ₹ 1000 crore in 2005-06. It is expected that the government would be able to provide revolving fund and subsidy to the groups which have already been formed and have been grounded and eligible for financial support.

The budget proposed to credit link additional 3.85 lakh SHGs in 2006-07 under the microfinance scheme. Upto 2005-06, 8.01 lakh SHGs could get credit to the tune of ₹ 4863 crore under this scheme.

The allocation for Bharat Nirman has been stepped up to ₹ 18,696 crore in 2006-07 up from ₹ 12,160 crore in 2005-06.

The financial allocations made for rural development sector including agriculture are impressive, but the achievements fell short of the targets. Even the new schemes suffered from the deficiencies from which the earlier programmes suffered.

REFERENCES

1. Surinder Sud, "Budget and Employment", *Kurukshetra*, April 2005.
2. *The Hindu*, June 4th, 2005.
3. Brinda Karat, "Issues in the Food for Work Programme", *The Hindu*, June 3rd, 2005.
4. *The Hindu*, July 3rd, 2005.

Chapter

10 Rural Development in the Eleventh Plan, 2007-12

The growth rate achieved in the Ninth Plan (1997-2002) was only 5.5 per cent. However, the Tenth plan (2002-07) could achieve a growth rate of 7.8 per cent. The Indian Economy on the eve of the 11th plan was in a much stronger position than it was a few years earlier.

The Tenth Plan achievements were close to the targets set. While the growth rate anticipated was 8 per cent per annum, the plan could achieve a growth rate of 7.8 per cent. It is the highest growth rate achieved ever in any plan period.

However, the performance of the agricultural sector during the 10th plan was not up to the mark. The growth rate achieved was 3.42 per cent per annum against the target of 4 per cent. This vital sector could achieve a growth rate of 3.5 per cent in 2002-03, 3.7 per cent in 2003-04, 4 per cent in 2004-05, 4.2 per cent in 2005-06, and 1.7 per cent in 2006-07.

The total eleventh plan outlay for centre, states, and Union Territories is projected (at 2006-07 prices) at ₹ 36, 44,718 crore Agriculture ansd allied sector have been allocated ₹ 1,36,381 crore. Rural development has been allocated ₹ 3,01,069 crore. amount of ₹ 26,329 crore has been allocated to special area programmes. The amount allocated to irrigation and flood control is ₹ 2,10,326 crore. All these four subject claimed 18.5 per cent of the total outlay (Economic Survey, 2009-10. p.A-46).

Agriculture and Rural Development in the 11th Plan

Agriculture GDP grew at around 3.6 per cent between 1980 and 1996 after which it collapsed to less than 2 per cent. **The Paper, Approach to the 11th Plan**, observed, "one of the major challenges of the 11th plan must be to reverse the deceleration in agricultural growth from 3.2 per cent observed between 1980 and 1996-97 to a trend average of only 1.5 per cent subsequently." It said that the stress should be not only on small and marginal farmers, but even middle and large farmers who also suffer from production stagnation arising from a variety of constraints.

The Steering Committee Report on agriculture for the 11th Plan has identified the possible reasons for deceleration in agriculture since the mid-1990s. It said the major sources of agricultural growth are public and private investment in agriculture and rural infrastructure including irrigation, technological change, diversification of agriculture and fertilisers. The progress on all these sources slowed down in the 1990s particularly since mid-1990s.

Public investment in agriculture and allied sectors (at 2004-05 prices) was ₹ 23, 039 crore. This has gone up to ₹ 24,452 crore in 2008-09. During this period, private investment increased from ₹ 86,967 crore to ₹ 1,14,145 crore.(Economic Survey 2009-10, p.180).

During the period 2005-06 to 2008-09, food grain production recorded an average annual increase of over 8 million tonnes. Total food grain in 2008-09 was estimated at 233.88 million tonnes as against 230.78 million tonnes in 2007-08.

Distribution of certified/quality seeds stood at 179.05 lakh quintals in 2007-08. It may be around 190 lakh quintals in 2008-09.

Total fertiliser consumption in nutrient terms (NPK) was 203.4 lskh tonnes in 2005-06. It increased to 225.70 lakh tonnes in 2007-08, and to 249.09 lakh tonnes in 2008-09.

Growth in GDP in agriculture and allied sectors was 4.7 per cent in 2007-08, but it fell to 1.6 per cent in 2008-09. The share of agriculture and allied sector in GDP was 16.4: per cent in 2007-08, but it fell to15.7 per cent in 2008-09. The share of agriculture and allied sectors in total gross capital formation was 7.01 per cent in 2007-08, but increased to 9.05 per cent in 2008-09 (all figures at constant prices, 2004-05). In 2004-05, the agricultural sector accounted for 52. 1 per cent of the total employment.

THE UNION BUDGET 2010-11

The Budget laid stress on the following: (i) agricultural production, (ii) reduction in wastage of produce; (iii) credit support to farmers; and (iv) a thrust to the food processing sector.

The Budget strongly feels that the green revolution need to be extended to the north-eastern region consisting of Bihar, Chattisgarh, Zharkhand, Eastern UP, West Bengal and Orissa. To achieve this, the Budget made a provision of ₹ 400 crore.

It is proposed to organise 60,000 pulses and oil seed for villages in rain-fed area during 2010-11, and provide an integrated intervention for water harvesting, watershed management and soil health to enhance the productivity of the dry land farming area. The Budget made a provision of ₹ 300 crore for this.

The Government has advanced a Nutrient Based Subsidy Policy for the fertiliser sector. It became effective from April 1,2010. The policy is expected to promote balanced fertilisation through new fortified product and focus on extension services by the fertiliser industry. The new system will move towards direct transfer of subsidies to the farmers.

There is wastage of grain procured from buffer stocks and public distribution system due to acute shortage of storage capacity in the Food Corporation of India (FCI). Of course, the scheme of private partnership is there. The FCI has been hiring godowns from private parties for a guaranteed period of 5 years. This period is now being extended to 7 years.

Regarding institutional credit to agriculture, for the year 2010-11, the target has been raised to ₹ 3,75,000 crore from ₹ 3,25,000 crore in 2009-10.

The Budget also gave priority to food processing sector which is getting state of the art infrastructure. In addition to the ten maga food park projects already being set up, the Government has decided to set up five more such parks.

The Budget made a provision of ₹ 66,100 crore for rural development for the year 2010-11. The Mahatma Gandhi National Rural Employment Guarantee Scheme covers more than 4.5 crore households. The allocation for this scheme has been stepped up to ₹ 40,110 crore in 2010-11.

Bharat Nirman has made a major contribution to the development rural infrastructure through its various programmes. The allocation for this scheme during 2010-11 is ₹ 48,000 crore. Rural housing scheme Indira Awas Yojana gets ₹ 10,000 crore.

Thus, during the 11th plan period, the Government is keen an taking up some concrete measures to boost agricultural production and productivity, and also protect the interests of vulnerable sections like agricultural labourers. The well conceived programmes need to be implemented effectively.

PART TWO

Agriculture and Allied Programmes

Chapter

11 Rural Development Nature and Scope

Agricultural progress has emerged as a potential strategy to economic progress in most developing countries including India. Failures on the agricultural front would create formidable problems for the future development of any country. China gave priority to agriculture in order to absorb the surplus rural population and use its growing productivity for local diversification. Even the classical writers realised the importance of the agricultural sector, particularly in the context of the growing rural population.

Agriculture and Economic Development

Simon Kuznet argued that agricultural development should receive top priority because cost effective production can be raised more easily in this sector than in any other sector. A country cannot think of a large-scale transfer of the farming population to the non-farming sectors without sufficient food surpluses or considerable reduction in food deficits. A rise in agricultural productivity precedes or accompanies economic development.

Extensive use of modern inputs gradually lead to greater commercialisation and increased levels of agricultural produce. This would help farmers not only to produce more output per unit area, but also to generate surplus crops which would contribute to economic development, raise the income levels of farmers and meet the food requirements of the ever-increasing population.

An increased market surplus resulting from the commercialisation of agriculture would help in releasing the labour force from the agricultural sector to the non-agricultural sector without causing a decline in agricultural output. The boost in agricultural exports would enable the country to import the much needed capital goods and other raw materials required for rapid industrialisation.

Kulp has distinguished four main stages in the agricultural development process in the rural sectors: *(i)* traditional subsistence agriculture; *(ii)* institution-building development; *(iii)* institution-based development; and *(iv)* capital intensive development.

Although the share of agriculture in national income declines over the long run, this trend should occur naturally; neglecting agriculture and *forcing* its share to go down faster which depresses economic growth.[1]

The reasons for the growing importance of the agricultural sector in most developing countries are not far to seek. It is the agricultural sector which *supplies basic goods* like foodgrains. The demand for food products is bound to go up with the population levels and the per capita incomes in these countries going up. If foodgrain output is not satisfactory, food prices go up affecting the rural population to a great extent the poor, besides raising the prices of industrial goods. In other words, the general price level largely depends on the availability of agricultural goods. Also, food shortage would force a country to resort to food imports on which a poor country cannot afford to spend its precious foreign exchange.

Agricultural prosperity certainly exercises a *positive impact on poverty* situation. Several studies have shown that the incidence of poverty is lower in regions which have experienced a satisfactory rate of growth in agricultural production. Given the limited progress achieved by the non-farming sector, the agricultural sector had opened up adequate employment opportunities for the rural sector. Agricultural backwardness would be a major factor leading to low levels of employment in rural areas and increasing rural poverty subsequently. If stagnation and sharp fall in agricultural production are also accompanied by sharp price rise, the proportion of people below the poverty line is bound to increase.[2]

The *interdependence of agriculture and industry* is well known. The agricultural sector supplies raw materials and labour force to the industrial sectors which could be met only through the utilisation of surplus labour in the agricultural sector. Agricultural prosperity provides considerable demand for industrial goods. Industrialists get worried in a drought year not only because of fall in the supply of raw materials but equally because of fall in demand for their products from the farming community. Also, the foreign exchange earned through agricultural exports enable a country to import machinery and equipment required for industrialisation.

Agricultural prosperity contributes significantly to *capital formation.* It is possible to raise agricultural productivity with relatively low investment because of the low capital output ratio in the agricultural sector. If the existing terms of trade move in favour of agriculture, agricultural incomes go up faster than non-agricultural incomes. Also, the consumption pattern in the agricultural sector is such that consumption does not increase at the rate at which the farming incomes rise. All these factors are conducive to a rise in capital formation in the agricultural sector.

When agriculture is well developed through commercialisation, the incomes of farming communities will go up as a result of enhanced market and surplus. This provides stimulus to demand for industrial goods and raises the profits of capitalists, savings and capital formation. Also, adequate availability of food enhances the quality of the labour force.

However, in India, the agricultural sector suffers from reduced capital formation, which is only 10.2 per cent for its contribution of 33 per cent to the Gross Domestic Product (GDP).

In the case of industry, capital formation is said to be around 41 per cent for its 20 per cent contribution to GDP.

AGRICULTURE AND INDIAN ECONOMY

The agricultural sector occupies a predominant place in the Indian economy for various reasons. The prosperity of this sector is important not only to the local population but even to the Government. For instance, in a drought year, the Government has no alternative but to arrange for substantial relief funds towards drought relief. A good year would avoid such non-development expenditure besides boosting the government revenues.

Out of the country's geographical area of 329 million hectares, the cultivated area then was estimated at 186 million hectares, the gross cropped area at 175 million hectares and the net area used for agriculture at 143 million hectares.

Till the starting of economic planning in India in 1951, growth of foodgrain output recorded was low at 0.3 per cent per year. Canal irrigation was the major input in agriculture. During the period (1950-51 to 1964-65), more area was brought under irrigation including wastelands which were also reclaimed. The foodgrain output consequently increased during this period by 2.9 per cent per year. Besides, there have been significant improvements in productivity also mainly because of improved cropping practices, new crop varieties and increased use of chemical fertilisers.

During 1965 to 1980, foodgrain output rose only by 2.4 per cent a year because of lower contribution from increase in cropping area, while rise in productivity through better seeds played an important role. In the eighties, increase in foodgrain output was mainly due to better management of inputs and a strong infrastructure in the agricultural sector.

During the three decades (1950-1980), agricultural output increased on an average by 2.5 per cent per annum, which was only marginally above the population growth rate of 2.2 per cent per annum. Till 1967, agricultural growth was brought about mainly by bringing more land under cultivation. However, since 1967, agricultural growth was sustained by new agricultural technology which required more investments. The share of agriculture and allied activities in the total outlay has fluctuated between 5.7 per cent in the Second Plan and 12.9 per cent in the Fourth Plan.

In the Seventh Plan, food production increased by 20.2 million tonnes; it was 150.4 million tonnes in 1985-86 and 170.6 million tonnes in 1989-90. There was thus an average annual increase by about 4.0 million tonnes and strategies were implemented to raise it to 7.0 million tonnes in the Eighth Plan which envisaged a target of 210 million tonnes.

The country has yet to achieve a breakthrough on the food front. The present food availability per capita per annum is low at 200 kg. in India whereas it is 330 kg. in China. The country had to produce 270 million tonnes to feed a population of 910 millions by 1994-95 in order to catch the level of consumption achieved by China. The area under cultivation has not been increasing significantly. The required production levels of foodgrains by the year 1997 and 2007 has been estimated to be 210 million tonnes and 285 million tonnes respectively.

In the Indian economy, the agricultural sector still holds a pre-eminent position for various reasons. First, agricultural sector's *share in national income* is significant. The share of agriculture and allied sectors in national income was 58.9 per cent in 1950-51; it declined to 41.6 per cent by 1978-79. The percentage also came down to 33 per cent in 1990-91 and was only 25 per cent in 2000-01.

It has fallen to 20.8 per cent in 2005-06, to 19.9 per cent in 2006-07, to 18 per cent in 2007-08 and to 17.1 per cent in 2008-09.

Table: 1
Recent Trends in Foodgrain Production in India (million tonnes)

Crop/Year	*2001-02*	*2005-06*	*2006-07*	*2007-08*	*2008-09*
Rice	93.3	91.8	93.4	96.7	99.2
Wheat	72.8	69.4	75.8	78.6	80.6
Coarse Cereals	33.5	34.0	33.9	40.7	39.4
Pulses	13.3	13.4	14.2	14.8	14.7
Foodgrains	**212.9**	**208.6**	**217.3**	**230.8**	**233.9**

*Estimates.
Source: Economic Survey 2009-10.

The average annual growth rate of value added in the agricultural and allied sectors declined from 4.7 per cent in the Eighth Plan (1992-97) to 2.1 per cent in the Ninth Plan (1997-2002). It was -6.9 per cent in 2002-03. It was around 10 per cent in 2003-04, 0.7 per cent in 2004-05 and 2.3 per cent in 2005-06 (the figures for the last three years are provisional).

Table: 2
Public Sector Outlay for Agriculture : All India

(₹ in crores)

Five-Year Plans	*I 1951-56*	*II 56-61*	*III 61-66*	*IV 69-74*	*V 74-79*	*VI 80-85*	*VII 85-90*	*VIII 92-97*
Agriculture Including Co-operation	238	275	591	2,059	3,356	6,440	10,524	12,467
All Sectors	2377	4,800	8,099	15,902	39,322	97,500	1,80,000	4,34,100

Source: Eighth Five-Year Plan (1992-97) Vol. II, p. 1. and Ninth Five Year Plan.

Table 3
Ninth Plan and Tenth Plan Outlays on Agriculture and Rural Development (₹ Crore)

Item	*Ninth Plan (1997-2002)*	*% to the total*	*Tenth Plan (2002-07)*	*% to the total*
Agriculture and Allied Activities	42,462.0	4.9	58,933.0	3.9
Rural Development	74,686.0	8.7	1,21,928.0	8.0
Special Areas Programmes	3,649.0	0.4	20,879.0	1.4
Irrigation and Flood Control	55,420.0	6.5	1,03,315.0	6.8
Total Plan Outlay	8,59,200.0	100.0	15,25,639.0	100.0

Source: Economic Survey 2005-06, pp. S.43, S.44.

Table: 4

Eleventh Plan (2007-12) outlay by the centre, states and Union Territories (₹ crore)

Head	Outlay
Agriculture & Allied Activities	1,36,381
Rural Development	3,01,069
Special Area Programmes.	26,329
Irrigation & Food Control	2,10,326

The total outlay, including outlay on all other heads, is placed around ₹ 36,44,718 Crore.
Source: Economic Survey.2009-10. p.A-46.

As the economy makes progress, the share of agriculture in national income declines. Though the same has happened in India also, the rate of change has been rather slow. One important reason for this is that the industrial sector's share in national income has not shown significant improvement.

Second, agriculture provides employment to the largest percentage of the labour force in the rural sector. The country's labour force was 419.6 million in 2004-05, and 438.9 million in 2006-07. It may be around 483.6 million in 2011-12. The percentage of workforce depending on agriculture was 61 in 1993-94, 56.6 in 1999-00, and 52.1 in 2004-05.

However, all major sectors except agriculture, experienced over 3.0 per cent growth of employment per annum during the period 1978 to 1988. Agriculture registered an annual growth of only 0.92 per cent.[3] The farming sector has been suffering from unemployment, all kinds of underemployment and low productivity levels.

Third, *agricultural exports* play an important role in the country's exports. The agricultural and allied products exported from India include marine products, oilcake, spices, cashew kernels, rice and sugar. The traditional export items included tea, coffee and raw cotton. Exports of agro-based commodities have been steadily increasing, touching a ₹ 5,585.39 crore mark in 1992-93 as against ₹ 2,819.38 crore in 1990-91. Agricultural exports increased from ₹ 28,582 crore in 2000-01 to ₹ 65,230 crore in 2007-08. While agricultural exports generate significant foreign exchange, modernisation of agriculture does not imply a drain on foreign exchange as this sector's dependence on imports is relatively low.

PROBLEMS FACING INDIAN AGRICULTURE

The share of agriculture in GDP declined from about 60 per cent in the early fifties to about 33 per cent by the end of the eighties, with a very moderate change in occupation structure. Thus, while production structure changed significantly, the occupation structure remained almost stable. The share of agriculture in the total occupation force is still over at 70 per cent. These trends not only widened the disparity between the average standard of living and income in the rural and urban areas but also restricted the impact of agricultural development on rural poverty.[4]

Indian agriculture experienced two distinctive changes in the eighties. First, real investment in agriculture declined, both absolutely and as a ratio to total investment. This is true in the case of both public and private sectors. Probably because of better utilisation of growth potentialities created in the past, incremental capital output ratio turned favourable. However, this also implied serious limitations to raise agricultural output in future.

Second, there has been a fall in employment elastically of output in agriculture from about 0.5 in the seventies to less than 0.4 in the eighties.The average annual growth rate of employment in agriculture has fallen from about 1.3 per cent during the period 1977-83 to 1.1 per cent during 1983-88.

There is a general impression that agriculture is not receiving the attention it deserves has been confirmed with a steady decline in the plan allocatiion or agriculture, rural development and irrigation from 37 per cent during the First Plan (1951-56) to 21.7 per cent of the total outlay in the Seventh Plan (1985-90). One reason for this is that more than 75 per cent of the farmers belonged to the small and marginal category. As such, they are unorganised, often become victims of financially strong lobbies existing in the rural sector lobbies. No wonder, the disparity ratio between the per capita farming and non-farming incomes which was nearly 1:2.2 in 1970-71 has gone up to 1:4.2 in 1988-89.

The agricultural sector has yet to be strengthened at least for two important reasons: *(i)* stagnation in the real per income of the agricultural population and *(ii)* decline in their incomes relative to that of the non-agricultural population. According to a study done by Quizon and Buiswanger for the World Bank (1985), the real per capita income of the rural population increased only by about two per cent in twenty years between 1960-61 to 1980-81.[5]

The greatest challenge facing the agricultural sector has been mounting *pressure on land available for cultivation* because of the growing number of people depending on agriculture. The pressure is there not because agriculture is remunerative but because non-farming employment opportunities are very limited. This obviously leads to underdevelopment and low consumption levels of the farming population. As a result of excess labour force, there is the phenomenon of disguised unemployment. Even if a part of the labour force is withdrawn from agriculture, it is argued that there will not be any fall in agricultural production. It is said that at least 20 per cent of the labour force in the agricultural sector at present is in excess of what is actually required.

The agricultural sector is not in a position to generate enough surpluses as it is forced to support unproductive workers. Dobb wrote, "if there is any factor to be singled out as the fundamental limiting factor upon the face of development, then it is this marketable surplus of agriculture; this rather than the total product, or the productivity of agriculture in general."

A major problem facing the agricultural sector is *instability in production;* which is largely attributed to the fact that only about 30 per cent of the cultivable land has irrigation facilities. Dry farming technologies have yet to become popular. It is also better to evolve drought resistant varieties rather than high-yielding varieties.

Foodgrain output was 131.9 million tonnes in 1978-79. It fell to 109.7 million tonnes the next year, that is 1979-80. It rose to 133.3 million tonnes in 1981-82, but fell to 129.5 million tonnes in the following fiscal 1982-83. The output also rose sharply to 152.4 million tonnes in 1983-84. It again fell to 140.4 million tonnes in 1987-88. It was placed at 169.9 million tonnes in 1988-89, 171.0 million tonnes in 1989-90 and 176.4 million tonnes in 1990-91. As against the target of 182.5 million tonnes, it was only

167.1 million tonnes in 1991-92. The foodgrain production reached a record level of 208.87 million tonnes in 1999-2000.

In view of severe drought in 1987, the Government formulated a Special Foodgrain Production Programme (SFPP) which was implemented in the districts having potential for substantial foodgrain production with the available strong and cost-effective infrastructure and a large resource base. The focus of SFPP was on five crops, viz., rice, wheat, maize, gram and arhar which can respond well under suitable conditions. A higher output was sought to be achieved through increased use of fertilisers, control of pests, diseases and weeds, harnessing of water resources and proper supply of improved seeds and credit to the farming community.

Indian agriculture still suffers from *low productivity.* Productivity trends of individual crops have been discussed elsewhere. Foodgrain productivity, though low, has made significant progress over a period of time. It was 566 kgs. per hectare in 1050-51, which rose to 710 kgs. in 1960-61, 872 kgs. in 1970-71, 1,023 kgs. in 1980-81, 1,041 kgs. in 1983-84 and 1,182 kgs. in 1985-86 respectively.

However, land productivity has shown marked regional variations being low in states like Rajastan and high in states like Kerala. These variations are due to variations in natural factors, availability of inputs and institutional support. Only a few (48) districts covering less than 13 per cent of the area experienced high growth (more than 4.5 per cent per annum); a large number of districts (102) had medium growth (1.5 to 4.5 per cent); 62 districts experienced low growth (0 to 1.5 per cent) and as many as 70 districts had no growth or negative growth.[6]

Many factors have contributed to low agricultural productivity. The pressure of population on land led to sub-division and fragmentation of land and made holdings economically unviable. While new technology could raise yields considerably in certain areas, plans are on anvil to strengthen dryland farming at the earliest. The small farmers are yet to benefit from the green revolution on a war footing. The agrarian relations are hardly favourable for the actual cultivators. Semi-feudal production relations still exist. The infrastucture support to agricultural sector still remains inadequate.

Indian agriculture suffers from imbalances in the cropping pattern. The share of wheat and rice in total food grain output has been showing an upward trend, but that of coarse grains and pulses shows a declining trend.

There are *regional imbalance in* agricultural growth. The spread of new agricultural technology is not uniform throughout the country. According to Bhalla and Tyagi, the authors of *Patterns in Indian Agricultural Development: A District Level Study,* "in the incremental output, between the early sixties and early eighties, the contribution of the north-western region was as much as 53.1 per cent, while that of the eastern region was only 7.7 per cent. Thus, the increase in output added to the already existing inter-regional inequalities in production."

Naturally, the rich regions account for a lion's share in input use. To quote Bhalla and Tyagi, "During the overall period 1962-65 to 1980-83, about half of the incremental output was contributed by the north-western states whereas the eastern-region contributed only about 8 per cent. The contribution of the central region to aggregate incremental output was 24 per cent and that of the southern region 15 per cent... there is more stability in output levels of those districts which have assured of profitable levels of irrigation compared with those districts mainly dependent on rainfall."

The small holdings have the potential to register of a higher output per hectare than the large holdings through the intensive use of agricultural labour. However, as pointed out by C.H. Hanumantha Rao in his work, *Technological Change and Distribution of Gains in Indian Agriculture,* this phenomenon is not valid in the case of new agricultural technology which is characterised by widening income disparities between the large and small farmers.

During the seventies, a fairly high rate of growth has been recorded by Andhra Pradesh. Among the central states, Gujarat and Maharashtra improved their performance during the seventies, but Rajasthan and Madhya Pradesh did not show any improvement. In the south, Andhra Pradesh recorded a growth rate of 4.32 per cent, but other states have done poorly on the agricultural front. The performance of Tamil Nadu and Kerala has been disappointing.

But, it is the eastern states which are causing anxiety. Except Assam, all the other eastern states, namely, Orissa, Bihar and West Bengal have remained low on the rung of potential contributors in the agricultural sector. This is attributed to poor infrastructure and water management and also institutional constraints.

The agricultural growth pattern across the states has registered a serious imbalance in development. For instance, the average per capita income from agriculture (1986-87 to 1988-89) was ₹ 4,208 in Punjab and only ₹ 456 in Bihar against the national average of ₹ 1,564. Also, the per capita foodgrain production in 1989-90 was high in Punjab at 913 kg. and 551 kg. in Haryana. But, it was very low at 36 kg. in Kerala. Efforts were therefore directed towards stepping up investment in agriculture in states which experienced low agricultural growth rates.

Concerted efforts were emphasised upon to remove the existing imbalance in the spread of the green revolution, both in terms of crops and areas affected. As things stood at that time, three states (Punjab, Haryana and Uttar Pradesh) accounted for nearly 70 per cent of the total marketable surplus of wheat and only four states accounted for 80 per cent of the marketable surplus in rice.

The public investment in agriculture in real terms has witnessed steady decline from the Sixth Five Year Plan to the Tenth Plan. Trends in public investment in agriculture and allied sectors reveal that it has consistently declined in real terms (at 1999-2000 prices) from the Sixth Plan to the Ninth plan. It was ₹ 64,012 crore in the Sixth Plan, ₹ 52,108 Crore in the Seventh Plan, ₹ 45,565 Crore in the Eighth Plan and ₹ 42,226 Crore in the Ninth Plan. However, in the Tenth Plan (2002-07), public investment in agriculture registered an increase of ₹ 25,034 Crore and stood at ₹ 67, 260 crore .

The gross capital formation in agriculture and allied sectors as a proportion of total GDP stood at 2.66 per cent in 2004-05 and improved to 3.34 per cent in 2008-09. Similiarly, the gross capital formation in agriculture and allied sectors relative to GDP in this sector has also shown an improvement from 14.07 per cent in 2004-05 to 21.31per cent in 2008-09.

Table:5
public and Private Investment in Agriculture and Allied Sector
(at 2004-05 prices)

₹ Crore

Year	*Public*	*Private*	*Total*
2004-05	16,183	62,665	78, 848
2005-06	19,909	73,211	93,121
2006-07	22,978	71,422	94,400
2007-08	23,039	86,967	1,10,000
2008-09	24,452 (17.6)	1, 14 145 (82.4)	1,38,597 (100.0)

Notes: figures in brackets. are percentages to the total.
Source: Economic Survey 2009-10 p.180.

STRENGTHENING AGRICULTURAL SECTOR

The performance of the Indian agricultural sector has shown resilience in recent years. Even during the drought year, i.e., 1987-88, the decline in agricultural production was only 0.8 per cent when compared with 1986-87, although foodgrain output declined by 2.1 per cent.

For strengthening the agricultural sector, three areas which deserve top priority include rise in the growth rate of productivity by raising inputs; modernisation of the irrigation system and improved water management to reduce the gap between irrigation potential and utilisation and acceleration and resilience of growth in rainfed dryland agriculture and in crops like paddy, oilseeds and pulses.

There is nothing wrong with agricultural subsidies. But a lion's share of these subsidies is claimed by wealthier and agriculturally advanced regions and also the large farmers. For instance, Punjab received ₹ 1,027 per hectare on an average in 1980-87 compared to the All India average of ₹ 511 per hectare. Thus, these subsidies failed to serve as effective instruments for poverty alleviation.

The thrust of the agricultural programme in the Eighth Plan is on diversification of agriculture and development of horticulture, livestock, fisheries etc., accelerated growth in the North-Eastern region through improvement in the productivity levels, development of rainfed areas, increasing production of oilseeds and pulses, revitalisation of co-operatives, agricultural credit structure and improving marketing of agricultural produce and development of post-harvest technology.

The Draft Agricultural Policy Resolution (DAPR) was placed in Parliament in December, 1992 with emphasis on dove-tailing agricultural development and research programmes to boost the Indian agriculture sector. DAPR representatives believe that problems of underemployment, unemployment and malnutrition can be solved only through diversification of the agriculture sector and promotion of the agro-based industry. Augmenting facilities for processing, marketing and storage, development of rainfed and irrigated horticulture, segmentation of biomass production and increased utilisation of irrigation potential and promotion of water conservation are some of the major objectives of DAPR. Stress has also placed on strengthening the co-operatives and local communities and enhancing the involvement of voluntary agencies in agricultural development.

Top priority should be given to diversification of the cropping pattern through shifting of marginal and degraded land from low productivity crops to horticulture. Strategies should be developed to explore foreign market as well.

REFERENCES

1. Anandarup Ray: 'Trade and Pricing Policies in World Agriculture', *Finance and Development,* September 1986, p. 3.
2. J.P. Memorial Lecture delivered by B.S. Minhas in New Delhi on November 21,1985.
3. Eighth Five Year Plan 1992-97, *op. cit.,* Vol. I, p. 117.
4. B.B. Bhattacharya: "Its Participatory Development Approach is Welcome", *Kurukshetra,* June 1992, p. 18.
5. H.S. Shergill: 'Growing Imbalance in Agricultural Sector', MAINSTREAM, March 5,1988, p. 15.
6. C.H. Shah and C.N. Vakil (Ed. 1979): *Agricultural Development of India: Policy and Problems,* Orient Longman Ltd., Mumbai, pp. xxiv-xxv.
7. Malcolm S. Adiseshaiah: 'Agriculture and National Economy', *Yojana,* August 15,1993, p. 31.

Chapter

12 Food and Non-Food Crops and Trends in Yields

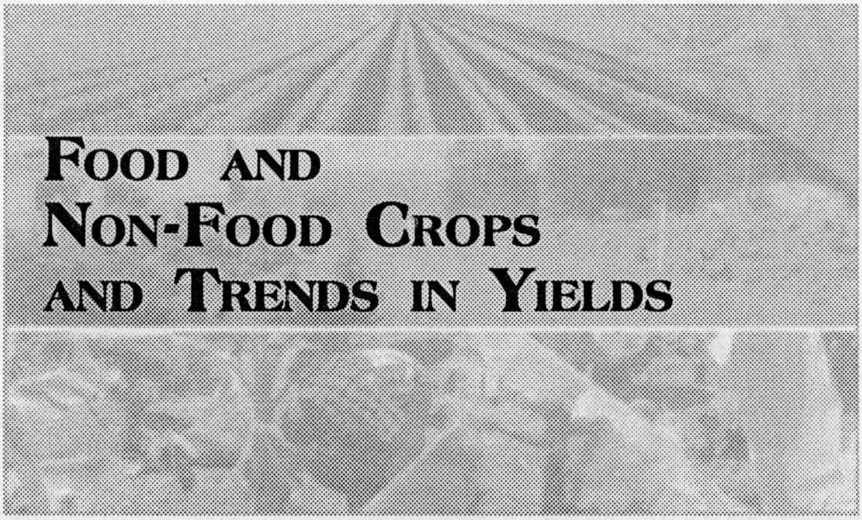

Indian agriculture still suffers from crop imbalances. Considering this it is necessary to study trends in production and productivity of food and non-food crops. The Green Revolution has not been able to offer an optimum cropping pattern. On the other hand, it appears to have brought about some distortions in the cropping pattern.

Rice: Rice is the most important food crop in India, contributing about 40 per cent to the total foodgrain output. Rice production has increased from about 20 million tonnes during 1950-51 to 74 million tonnes by 1991-92, with an annual compound growth rate of 2.86 per cent. Rice production was 89.5 million tonnes in 1999-2000. However, the additional area brought under rice cultivation is not impressive. Thus, additional output is largely due to improvement in yields.

There has been dramatic improvement in rice production with the introduction of semi-dwarf high yield potential varieties like Jaya, IRB, IR 20 etc. including a package of modern production technologies coupled with incentive output prices since the midsixties.

Rice productivity has reportedly stagnated at 1750 kg/ha for the four years since 1989-90. For the year 1999-2000, it is estimated at 1990 kg/ha. There are regional differences in productivity: it is high at 3500 kg/ha in Punjab, and 2000-2300 kg/ha in Tamil Nadu, Haryana, Andhra Pradesh, Jammu & Kashmir and Pondicherry in the irrigated belts.

In 2008-09, the gross area under rice was 45.4 million ha. production was 99.2 million tonnes, and yield per ha. was 2816 kgs.

Wheat: Wheat production was 56.86 million tonnes in 1992-93, five times more compared to figures in the period 1960-61. It was 75.6 million tonnes in 1999-2000. Wheat yields have shown steady improvement since 1950-51 to 851 kg/ha in 1960-61, to 1307 kg/ha in 1988-89. It, however, fell to 2121 kg/ha in 1989-90. It was placed at 2397 kg/ha for the year 1991-92. It was 2590 kg/ha in 1998-99.

Of course, there are regional variations. The average yields of wheat were as follows: Punjab 3.77 tonnes/ha; Haryana 3.58 t/ha as compared to the national average of 2.35 t/ha. In order to break the yields barriers of existing varieties, hybrid wheats can be exploited for good financial returns and development of the Indian agricultural sector.

In 2008-09, the gross area under wheat was 27.9 million ha. production was 80.6 million tonnes, and yield per ha. was 2891 kgs.

COARSE CEREALS

Annually about 40 million hectares, approximately a third of the area under foodgrains are planted with coarse cereals which include jowar, bajra, maize, ragi, a number of small mallets and barley. They are cultivated predominantly under rained conditions (90 per cent) mostly by resource-poor farmers. Their production has not shown encouraging trends because of their low value status and consumption by the poorer sections of society. However, jowar and ragi experienced a growth rate higher than that of the population.

Table: 1
Area, Output and Yields of Coarse Cereals

Period	*Area (m. ha)*	*Production (m. tonnes)*	*Yield (Kg/ha)*
1949-50 to 1958-59	4.02	19.75	467.9
1959-60 to 1968-69	44.91	22.30	534.8
1969-70 to 1978-79	43.86	28.03	639.8
1979-80 to 1988-89	40.18	29.12	724.9
2008-09	NA	39.4	NA

During the eighties, there was a perceptible fall in area under cultivation. However, the production and productivity steadily increased. For instance, during 1989-90, the production of coarse grains touched a new high of 34.3 million tonnes, the major contributions coming from jowar, maize and ragi. The coarse cereals on the whole, fared a shade better than pulses and oilseeds with the exception of repassed and mustard. Coarse grain output was 30.5 million tonnes in 1998-2000.

Coarse grains continue to be contributing to low input and low profit crops with a diminishing demand. An impression was created that hybrid cultivation may not be amenable to inter-cropping which has been rejected by the agricultural community. In fact, hybrid based inter-cropping systems have emerged productive, profitable, more stable and less risk-prone as compared to the traditional agricultural systems.

There is the need to raise productivity by 100 per cent. As support prices for jowar, bajra, ragi and maize are announced by the government, area under production of coarse cereals has marginally risen from 344.37 lakh hectares between 1950-51 and 1990-91. There is need for augmenting productivity and use of these agricultural yields. An integrated approach to crop production can, to some extent, alleviate economic constraints and contribute to the sustainability of the agricultural production system.

Coarse cereals production was 31.1 million tonnes in 2000-01, 33.4 million tonnes in 2001-02. It fell to 26.1 million tonnes in 2002-03, and rose to 38.1 million tonnes in 2003-04. It was estimated at 39.4 million tonnes for 2008-09.

Bajra: The yield in respect of bajra had risen from 290kg/ha in 1950-51 to 610 kg/ha in 1989-90, and then to 769 kg/ha in 1992-93. It was 748 kg/ha in 1998-99. In bajra, the initial advances in production with the introduction of hybrids had a setback due to widespread occurrences of the disease called downy mildew.

Yet, hybrids like BK 560 and MH 179 continue to be popular. Downy mildew resistant composites have been developed. These include WCC 75 and MP 171. The situation assured improving the development of ICMH 451 and 23. The extra-early hybrids such as MHB 67 and RHRBH 8609 and composites such as ICTP 8203, maturing in about 75 days, are expected to do well under acute drought conditions.

In 2008-09, the gross area under bajra was 8.7 million ha. production was 8.8 million tonnes, and yield per ha. was 1011 kgs.

Jowar: The yield in respect of jowar had gone up from 353 kg/ha in 1950-51 to 533 kg/ha in 1960-61. But, it fell to 466 kg/ha in 1970-71. It however, rose to 660 kg/ha in 1980-81, but fell to 576 kg/ha in 1986-87. The yield level fluctuated in the 1980s. It was high at 869 kg/ha in 1989-90, but fell to 664 kg/ha in 1991-92. It was 859 kg/ha in 1998-99.

In 2008-09, the gross area under jowar was 7.7 million ha. production was 7.3 million tonnes, and yield per ha. was 952 kgs.

Maize: Maize has always been a poorman's crop. India ranks fifth among the 29 maize producing countries in terms of area, and eighth in terms of output. During 1980-81 to 1989-90, maize recorded the following compound growth rates : Area 0.29 per cent; production 3.41 per cent and yield 3.69 per cent. India has around 6 million hectares under maize cultivation. But the yield per hectare is only 1.5 tonnes per hectare which is lower than the world average of 3.8 tonnes. The yield had risen from 550 kg/ha in 1950-51 to 1632 kg/ha in 1989-90 and then to 1684 kg/ha in 1992-93. It was 1797 kg/ha in 1998-99.

Hybrids like Deccan 1, High Starch, Ganga Safed 2 and Ganga 5 are doing well and they cater to both traditional and industrial needs. India has the right climatic conditions and soil textures to produce high variety maize. The Indian Maize Development Association (IMDA) has been involved in indepth research in maize. Their experiment in the Yamunanagar district in Haryana has showed positive result with a farmer having the capacity to produce 30 quintals per acre.

In western countries like the US, the corn and corn-based industry is very rich. Maize starch is used right from making chewing gum to Ale Beer to breakfast food. Extracts from maize like estrous, glucose syrup, maltodextrins, alcohols and oil are used in a whole lot of industries like chemicals, beverages, canned food, animal feed, building material, confectionery, dairy products and packaging material.

In 2008-09, the gross area under maize was 8.2 million ha. production was 19.3 million tonnes, and yield per ha. was 2355 kgs.

Pulses: Pulses constitute an important source of protein. They account for about 18 per cent of the foodgrains' area but their share in output is around 10 per cent only. Pulses are relegated to less fertile lands that get less irrigation. While the rate of growth of population has been around 2.2 per cent, that of production of pulses was only 0.78 per cent per annum during the period 1967-68 to 1989-90.

The annual production of pulses has fluctuated in the narrow range of 11 to 13 million tonnes. Of course, it was 14.06 million tonnes in 1990-91. The shares of pulses in the overall foodgrains basket has declined from 10.9 per cent in 1970-71 to 8 per cent. According to the National Commission on Agriculture, the country has to produce 35 million tonnes of pulses by 2000 AD. The output was only around 15 million tonnes in 1998-99.

There has been significant decline in the growth rate of pulses production. During the pre-green revolution period (1949-50 to 1964-65), the rate of growth was 1.39 per cent per annum, which declined to 0.78 per cent per annum in the post-green revolution period (1967-68 to 1989-90).

The higher growth rate in the earlier period was due to expansion of the area under pulses which took place at the rate of 1.9 per cent as compared to 0.3 per cent per annum in the latter period. In contrast, growth in productivity played a larger role in the latter period, when it increased by 0.6 per cent per annum as compared to a declining rate of 0.2 per cent in the pre-green revolution period.

In 2008-09, the gross area under pulses was 22.4 million ha. production was 14.7 million tonnes, and yield per ha. was 655 kgs.

Table: 2
Growth of Area, Production and Yield of Pulses

Year	*Area (m.ha)*	*Production (m.tonnes)*	*Yield (kg/ha)*
1950-51	19.09	8.41	441
1960-61	23.56	12.70	539
1970-71	22.54	11.82	524
1980-81	22.46	10.63	473
1989-90	23.22	12.61	549
1998-99	23.50	14.90	634
2004-05	22.50	13.40	595
2008-09	22.40	14.70	655

Table: 3
Productivity of Foodgrains Kg/ha

Product	*1960-61*	*1970-71*	*1980-81*	*1990-91*	*1998-99*	*2008-09*
Foodgrains	710	872	1,023	1,380	1,571	1,898
Cereals	753	949	1,142	1,571	1,778	2,175
Pulses	539	524	473	578	634	655
Rice	1,013	1,123	1,336	1,740	1,747	2,186
Wheat	851	1,307	1,630	2,281	2,590	2,891
Jowar	533	466	660	814	859	952
Maize	926	1,279	1,159	1,518	1,797	2,355
Bajra	286	622	458	658	748	1,011

Oilseeds: The oilseeds sector accounts for about 10 per cent of the nation's gross cropped area and 5 per cent of its gross product. Oilseeds account for about 10 per cent of the total agricultural production in terms of value, engaging about 30 million cultivators in the production process and another 50 lakh in the processing industries.

India has an environment well suited for cultivation of a wide variety of oilseeds crops like groundnut, rapeseed-mustard, sesame, niger, safflower, sunflower, coconut, castor and linseed. India is the world's largest producer of groundnut, sesame and niger, the second largest producer of castor and safflower and the third largest producer of rapeseed-mustard, linseed and coconut.

The oil seeds production was 24.7 million tonnes in 1998-99. The Green Revolution has not touched the oilseed sector. The growth rate of oilseeds production was only 2.04 per cent per annum against 5.3 per cent for wheat and 2.54 per cent for paddy during the period 1949-50 to 1988-89. The low yield is the major problem. For instance, the per hectare yield of groundnut in India averaged to 826 kg during 1988-89. It increased to 1214 kg/ha in 1998-99. The average yield of rapeseed-mustard is around 904 kg/ha in 1990-91, and 1017 kg/ha in 1996-97, but fell to 870 kg/ha in 1998-99.

In 2008-09, the gross area under oilseeds was 27.5 million ha. production was 28.2 million tonnes, and yield per ha.1016 kgs.

Cotton: The yield per hectare of cotton crop increased from 88 kg/ha in 1950-51 to 125 kg/ha in 1960-61. But it fell to 106 kg/ha in 1970-71. It, however, increased from 152 kg/ha in 1980-81 to 225 kg/ha in 1990-91. It was 224 kg/ha in 1998-99.

Cotton still depends on the vagaries of the South-West monsoon. The yield per hectare was 505 kg in Pakistan, 783 kg in the USA, 659 kg in China and 988 kg in Egypt during 1992-93.

In 2008-09, the gross area under cotton was 9.4 million ha. production was 23.2 million bales (of 170 kgs each) and yield per ha. was 419 kgs.

Sugarcane: Sugarcane production was 110 million tonnes in 1960-61. This increased to 288.7 million tonnes in 1998-99.

Productivity of sugarcane showed steady progress from 33,422 kg/ha in 1950-51 to 45,549 kg/ha in 1960-61 to 48322 kg/ha in 1970-71, to 57,844 kg/ha in 1980-81 and to 65,395 kg/ha in 1990-91. This was 71000 kg/ha in 1998-99.

During the period 1987-88 and 1991-92, productivity declined by 0.7 a year. Although productivity declined in all the tropical states, it increased in Andhra Pradesh.

In 2008-09, the gross area under sugarcane was 4.4 million ha. production was 273.9 million tonnes, and yield per ha. was 62 tonnes.

Tea: As there is limited scope for extensive tea cultivation, the output levels of this commodity has to be raised only through tide in productivity. Successful efforts in the spheres of R & D and extension services are responsible for higher yields. The average yield has nearly doubled from 900 kg/ha in 1950-52 to 1717 kg/ha in 1990-92. It was 1875 kg/ha in 1996-97. These are national averages. South India tops in tea productivity with 2278 kg/ha in 1990-92.

In 2008-09, the gross area under tea was 0.6 million ha. production was 0.9 million tonnes, and yield per ha. was 1500 kgs.

Coffee: Coffee is a traditional export crop with an average annual output of 1.8 lakh tonnes. Currently, about two-third of the crop is exported.

At present, 3.4 lakh hectares are under coffee cultivation of which 65 per cent is in Karnataka and the rest in Kerala and Tamil Nadu.

Productivity of the crop showed an encouraging trend touching 930 kg/ha in 1985-86 compared to 235 kg/ha in 1944-45. It was 877 kg/ha in 1998-99. Of the 1.17 lakh coffee growers in 1990, as many as 1.10 lakh operate on less than four hectares each.

In 2008-09, the gross area under coffee was 0.3 million ha. production was 0.3 million tonnes, and yield per ha. was 1000 kgs.

Rubber: India is the fourth largest natural rubber producing country after Thailand, Indonesia and Malaysia. In India, 93 per cent of the rubber is used for manufacturing rubber products for domestic consumption. About 65 per cent of the rubber goes for making tyres and tyre products.

The average yield has steadily increased from 284 kg/ha in 1950-51 to 653 kg/ha in 1970-71, to 1076 kg/ha in 1990-91 and to 1154 kg/ha in 1992-93. It was 1563 kg/ha in 1998-99.

In 2008-09, the gross area under rubber was 0.5 million ha. production was 0.9 million tonnes, and yield per ha. was 1800 kgs.

Jute: The yield per hectare of jute and mesta rose from 1043 kg/ha in 1950-51 to 1,183 kg in 1960-61, to 1186 kg/ha in 1970-71 and to 1245 kg/ha in 1980-81. It stood at 1710 kg/ha in 1985-86. It, however, fell from 1649 kg/ha in 1986-87 to 1496 kg/ha in 1987-88. It rose to the level of 1842 kg/ha in 1991-92. It was 1722 kg/ha in 1998-99.

In 2008-09, the gross area under jute was 0.8 million ha. production was 9.6 million bales (each of 180 kgs) and yield per ha. was 2194 kgs.

CONCLUSION

Yield levels in India continue to be low in respect of both commercial and non-commercial crops. There is vast scope for improving yield levels. The gap between potential yields and actual yields need to be bridged through concerted efforts on the research front and a well thought-out system of incentives to the farmers. As scope for extensive cultivation is limited and higher levels of output are to be achieved by boosting yields.

Chapter

13 The Green Revolution

The need to keep the rate of growth of agricultural production, particularly foodgrain production, on par with that of population is an issue of priority, considering the advancements being made in the agriculture sector on the whole. Otherwise, the problem of poverty would worsen. Among the economic priorities, food self-sufficiency has a special place which calls for concerted efforts to boost agricultural production and productivity mainly through the improved agricultural technology which is often referred to as *'Green Revolution.'* In the case of India too, improved methods of production are largely responsible for comfortable foodgrain situation which would meet the needs of the Indian population.

The new agricultural technology was initially confined to wheat in a few north-western states. But it gradually spread to other crops and regions. The success of new strategies is attributed to large scale investments in irrigation and scientific research. The positive price policy also has served as an incentive to boost agricultural production in the country.

As against a growth rate of 3.1 per cent during 1949-50 to 1964-65, agricultural output registered a rate of growth of 2.6 per cent per annum during 1966-67 to 1984-85. During this period, the contribution of productivity increased to total output growth rate to about 75 per cent compared with only 43 per cent during the earlier period while that of area under cultivation declined from 58 per cent to 25 per cent.[1]

After the mid-sixties, the High Yielding Variety technology in terms of seeds was introduced in wheat and rice. Also, public investment in the agricultural sector was stepped up significantly. The new technology succeeded in raising profitability of investment for the farmers. The gross irrigated area also increased, besides a rise in the annual gross capital formation in agriculture. Of course, the growth of the net sown area slowed down considerably.

Though the agricultural sector has suffered a fall in capital formation in recent years, growth in foodgrain output registered an upward trend. This was made possible with the better utilisation of advanced technological infrastructure. The Green Revolution has been extended to crops and regions hitherto lagging behind. Unlike in the seventies, in the eighties, fertiliser consumption in the kharif season increased at a much faster rate than in rabi season, particularly in the eastern region. This means that the new technology spread to the rain-fed and unfavourable areas.

There has been some improvement in the productivity of land, labour and capital, thanks to better utilisation of the available infrastructure. Economists say that between one-fifth to one-fourth of the increase in the output of foodgrains in the post-green revolution period can be attributed to an increase in the productivity of inputs. Use of high yielding varieties of seeds and fertilisers in rain-fed areas in the kharif season has become an important source of agricultural growth during the eighties.

Table 1
Production of Commercial Crops: Recent Trends

(million tonnes)

Item	*1996-97*	*1997-98*	*1998-99*	*2003-04*	*2008-09*
Oilseeds (million tonnes)	24.4	21.3	24.7	25.3	28.2
Sugarcane (million tonnes)	277.6	279.5	288.7	237.3	273.9
Cotton (million bales)	14.2	10.9	12.3	13.9	23.2
Jute and Mesta (million bales)	11.2	11.0	9.8	11.2	10.4

* bales of 170 kg. each.

** bales of 180 kg. each.

ASPECTS OF GREEN REVOLUTION

Agriculture certainly occupies an important place in the Indian economy. Employment generation in future has to come mainly from the agricultural sector, including agro and rural industries. It needs to be noted that there is vast scope for raising agricultural output through better use of available resources and inputs.

Agricultural development in India has produced effects, both desirable and undesirable. The growing income disparities between different regions and classes of farmers, witnessed in the first decade of the Green Revolution have been mitigated to some extent. The real wages in agriculture have risen during the 1980s in the less developed regions. There has been some improvement in technology for rice and oilseeds. Farmers have now better access to extension services and institutional credit. In recent years, there has been a decline in the relative prices of foodgrains mainly due to rise in the productivity of inputs.

However, there has been a steep decline in employment generated per unit of output throughout the green revolution period. The green revolution has not helped much to step up the purchasing power of the rural poor. Also, there has been degradation of the rural environment mainly due to deforestation and excessive use of chemical inputs in agriculture.[2]

Farm inputs like irrigation, fertilisers, insecticides and machinery cannot be effective unless farmers have access to HYV seeds. It was during the mid-sixties that the HYV in respect of wheat was evolved. Subsequently, paddy and other cereals also came under the HYV technology.

However, the HYV seeds remained confined to food crops like paddy, wheat, maize, jowar and bajra. The non-food crops have yet to take advantage of this technology. Even among the food crops, the initial success was confined to wheat whereas 90 per cent of the total cropped area under wheat makes use of HYV seeds, and the percentage is around 69 in respect of paddy.

The HYV technology is said to contribute to sustained agricultural growth and poverty alleviation not only through its contribution to improved agricultural performance but also through strong linkages between the agricultural sector and the non-agricultural sector.[3]

Productivity of rainfed crops which continues to be low, has increased slowly but steadily over the years. For example, coarse cereal yield had risen from 665 kg a hectare during 1970-71 to 911 kg a hectare by 1989-90.

Table: 2
Production of breeder and foundation seeds and distribution of certified seed

Year	*Production of breeder seeds(quintals)*	*Production of foundation seeds (lakh quintals)*	*Distribution of certified/quality seeds (lakh quintals)*
2004-05	66,460	6.9	113. 10
2005-06	68,654	7.4	126.74
2006-07	73,829	7.96	155.01
2007-08	91,960	8.22	179.05
2008-09*	1,00,000	9.69	190.00

*Anticipated.
Source: Economic Survey 2009-10.p. 185.

The strength of the new agricultural technology in the Indian context lies in evolving dryland fanning technology as 70 per cent of the land under cultivation is rainfed. This technology is also the answer to the problem of agricultural instability. There are two approaches: *(i)* the watershed management approach under dryland and rainfed situation and *(ii)* comprehensive land use management approach.

During the year 1983-84, dryland farming practices yielded 42 per cent of the total foodgrain production and about *75* per cent of oilseeds production in the country. About two-thirds of the rice crop, one-third of the wheat crop and nine-tenths of sorghum, pear, millet and groundnut crops in the country are still grown without conventional methods of irrigation. The dryland sector also supports a significant population of livestock, besides producing fodder and firewood. It is forecast that there is going to be no significant improvement in irrigation availability in the near future and the importance of the share of dryland farming in the national agricultural output will have to increase at the earliest.

There are a number of schemes to optimise the use of water resources in dryland agriculture for which a national watershed development programme is being implemented, in addition to special programmes for major crops like rice, pulses, coarse grains and oilseeds, there exists the need to initiate subsequently and enhance their research system by being totally responsive to resource poor farmers' needs and working out strategies for generating good agricultural output capabilities.

Scientific dryland farming implies appropriate treatment of land for conservation of moisture. The technology of this fanning involves crop rotation and adoption of varieties and practices adjusted to the moisture regimes of an agro-climatically homogeneous area. The aim is to make the best of a limited water supply by storing in the soil as much rain water as possible and growing suitable crops. Dryland agriculture emphasises water conservation, sustaining crop yields with limited inputs of fertilisers and protecting the soil from the ravages of both wind and water erosion.

Table: 3
Fertiliser consumation in nutriment termes

Product	*2005-06*	*2006-07*	*2007-08*	*2008-09*
Nitrogenous (N)	127.23	137.73	144.19	150.90
Phosphatic (p)	52.04	55.43	55.15	65.06
Potassic (K)	24.13	23.35	26.36	33.13
Total N+P+K	203.40	216.51	225.70	249.09
Per ha. consumption (kg)	105.5	111.80	116.80	128.60

Source: Economic Survey 2009 -10. p.186.

The new agricultural technology also has stepped up fertiliser consumption considerably. In fact, fertiliser availability is critical for accelerated food production.

There has been steady increase in the production of fertilisers. The consumption of fertilisers was only 0.13 million tonnes in 1995-56 which has more than doubled since 1981-82 from 60.68 lakh tonnes to 130 lakh tonnes in 1991-92. It was 180.70 lakh tonnes in 1999-2000. The share of imports in total availability came down from 57.1 per cent in 1951-52 and 71.6 per cent in 1960-61 to 12.1 per cent in 1987-88, though it increased to 23.35 per cent in 1990-91.

Of course, there are some problems relating to fertiliser consumption. There are vast differences in the levels of fertiliser consumption across the regions and crops. Rainfed areas, constituting about 70 per cent of the total area, consume only 20 per cent of the total fertilisers. The per hectare use of fertilisers has been very low in states like Nagaland, Mizoram, Arunachal Pradesh, Assam and Orissa and is very high in states like Punjab, Tamil Nadu and Andhra Pradesh.

Among crops too, wheat, rice and sugarcane account for the largest share in fertiliser consumption. On the other hand, pulses, coarse grains and oilseeds suffer from inadequate fertiliser application.

There are certain constraints on the use of fertilisers. In spite of subsidy element, fertilisers are not yet accessible to small and marginal farmers. The farmers have been to a great extent reluctant to invest in fertilisers because of risk caused by crop failures. In the case of inferior cereals, returns from fertiliser use have been low and unremunerative for various reasons. Because of the failure of the delivery system, the problem of scarcity of fertilisers has been seen in certain areas.

Fertiliser consumption can be boosted by increasing the use of high-yielding, disease resistant, fertiliser responsive, water economising varieties of seeds, regulation of fertiliser strategies and their application, expansion of irrigation facilities, improved soil and moisture conservation techniques.

Irrigation is a crucial input contributing to the successful implementation of new agricultural technology. Yet we have failed to step up considerably the irrigation potential. What is worse, there exists a gap between irrigation potential and its utilisation for various reasons. These problems associated with irrigation management have been discussed in Chapter 9.

As a result of employment of the new technology of HYV seeds and chemical fertilisers, the need to shift from human and bovine power to machine power was inevitable. But this mechanisation of agriculture in the Indian context has become a subject of controversy. However, mechanisation is essential to realise optimum returns from other inputs like water resources and fertilisers.

Mechanisation is helpful in increasing farm productivity, with the cost effective adoption of multi-cropping practices and in realising the full potential of lands under cultivation. Of course, there is controversy with regard to the effects of mechanisation on farming and rural employment. Studies have shown that labour use in agriculture subsequently declines with mechanisation.

However, some studies have opined that the overall employment situation may not be adverse because of the mechanisation of the farming sector. When mechanisation steps up farm production and productivity, the existing level of unemployment may decline. Moreover, there is acute labour scarcity during the peak sowing and harvesting seasons. The mechanisation process in the farming sector is capable of generating off-farm employment in the areas of manufacture of farm machinery, distribution of spare parts, fuels and lubricants, repair of equipment etc.

It must be admitted that farm mechanisation is inevitable in the context of new agricultural practices like crop rotation, double cropping, multiple cropping and mixed cropping. Also, the timing of mechanisation is important. For instance, China began to mechanise agriculture after achieving a significant diversification of the rural economy in which a sizeable proportion of the rural population had already been absorbed in non-agricultural activities and many communes were facing labour shortages in peak seasons.[4]

Green Revolution: Some Problems

The positive effects of the Green Revolution are slowly disappearing. According to a study by Dr. Minhas *et al.*, while between 1970-71 and 1982-83, the initial years of the green revolution, the number of the poor in Punjab fell at the annual rate of 2 per cent, which in subsequent years, between 1982-83 and 1987-88, increased by 4 per cent per annum. Similarly in Haryana, the number of the poor decreased by 2.1 per cent in the first twelve years period, then increased by 0.9 per cent in the subsequent four years.

The new agricultural technology is *capital intensive.* True, as a result of spread of irrigation and resort to multiple-cropping, it is possible to increase the labour absorptive capacity of the agricultural sector. All aspects of the Green Revolution are not labour saving. Studies show that adoption of HYV technology has increased human labour employment. The installation of pumping sets has decreased labour use. Tractorisation has reduced labour employment. However, tractorisation has enabled farmers to increase the intensity of cropping which again has a positive effect on labour employment.[5] It needs to be noted that agricultural technical change may affect employment not only in agriculture but in all industries linked with agriculture.

NEGATIVE ASPECTS OF MECHANISATION

As a result of farm mechanisation in Punjab, Haryana and parts of Uttar Pradesh, between 5,000 to 10,000 people die every year from agriculture-related injuries. Around 15,000 people lose some parts of the body and another 1.5 lakh people suffer serious injuries. Those working in the sugarcane fields are known to have suffered eye injuries.

The high incidence of deaths and injuries is largely due to poor handling of farm machines and defective farm equipment. For instance, threshers are still being sold with feeding chutes which do not conform to safety specifications. Manual fodder cutters, powered fodder cutters and threshers are primarily responsible for hand amputations. More accidents occur with fodder cutters than with threshers. Spades and sickles cause minor injuries. There are a few deaths due to electrocution from tubewell pump sets.[6]

Pesticides are powerful biocides which possess the ability to kill insects which destroy the crops. They interfere with basic bio-chemical and physiological processes common to life, leading to wide-ranging health hazards.

There have been pesticides related miscarriages, genetic birth defects, premature births, psychological problems, memory loss, immuno-deficiencies, kidney and liver damage and skin allergies topped with various forms of cancer. Pesticides have been found responsible for nerve and eye damage, dizziness, nausea, fatigue and even impotence in farm workers. Pesticide use is also said to be responsible for epilepsy and dwarfism.

The use of chemical fertilisers and pesticides has become harmful both to the soil and the health of consumers. Experts feel that both fertilisers and pesticides are perpetrators of a vicious circle of dependence on chemicals. The crisis has reached alarming proportions because most farmers lack adequate training or information on handling pesticides.

Pesticide use is said to be responsible for the contamination of ground and surface water and damage to soil organisms like earthworms. However, the farming system is also adversely affected with the elimination of pollinating insects, specially honeybees. All these have ultimately affected plant bio-diversity besides heavy monetary loss world-wide.

Even conservative estimates level put the annual global pesticide deaths at 20,000 in addition to some two million poisoning cases of severe dimensions. Three-fourths of these deaths usually occur in the Third World which uses one-fifth of the world's pesticides.

The International Labour Organisation [ILO] has been expressing concern about the increasing number of deaths from pesticide poisoning in developing countries, which use 20 per cent of the chemicals, with 99 per cent of the deaths from toxic poisoning, from handling of pesticides being reported. Upto five million people are poisoned each year by pesticides, 40,000 of them fatally. The incidences are very high in the third world countries, though the industrialised countries use 80 per cent of the agro-chemicals.

The progress on the irrigation front is disappointing. Irrigated area increased at the rate of over half-a-million hectares per annum during the seventies which declined to the 0.3 million hectares per annum and the average annual addition, after the mid-eighties, fell below 0.05 million hectares.

The gap existing between yield potentials and actual yields is glaring in the case of important crops like rice, wheat, jowar, groundnut, cotton and tobacco. This gap needs to be filled up through an efficient extension work.

Boosting agricultural yield is the only way to sustain a high level of farm output. This calls for strengthening agricultural research. As rightly observed by the National Commission on Agriculture, *"It is now recognised that agricultural research in one enterprise which has got a high pay-off. Our impression is that where extension has failed, the impact of scientific research has been minimised."*

The challenges on the agricultural front have been well summed up by the Eighth Plan document thus:[7]

- The strategy for agricultural development in the Eighth Plan must aim at not only achieving self-sufficiency in food but also generating surpluses of specific agricultural commodities for export. Though the progress of agriculture in the recent period has been satisfactory, there are striking regional and crop imbalances. Productivity varies considerably from one region to another.
- The benefits of the Green Revolution which remain confined at present to the north and north-west must spread to other regions, more particularly to the eastern and north-eastern region, which have adequate rainfall, fertile soils and unlimited scope for stepping up agricultural production. Since two-third of the cultivated area is still unirrigated, a more balanced regional development would call for a greater emphasis on dry land farming.

STRENGTHENING NEW AGRICULTURAL TECHNOLOGY

New strategies have to be evolved to strengthen the agricultural sector. The basis of research needs to be widened so as to cover a large number of new crops grown in diverse agro-climatic situations. The gap between the potential and the actual yields has to be bridged through adaptive research. The reverse communication from land to agricultural research laboratories should be encouraged.

We have been laying stress on adequate availability of modern inputs for individual crops. But future efforts should be directed towards maximising the combined income from all the crops in an agricultural year. This calls for research in inter-cropping and cropping systems including the rotation of crops for the entire year suited to different agro-climatic conditions.

We have to intensify research to conserve and save on inputs. Research in water management including water harvesting techniques, biological fixation of nitrogen, minimising wastages in the use of chemical fertilisers and evolution of high-yielding seeds incorporating multiple resistance to pests and diseases and adverse environmental conditions.

The new priorities being emphasised upon for agricultural research in India are:

(i) To reduce yield variability in rainfed areas by evolving high stability varieties rather than introducing merely high yielding varieties. This requires varieties with multiple resistance to pests and droughts as also conservation of soil moisture;

(ii) To minimise costs incurred by farmers through various input-saving practices including biological fixation of nitrogen and

(iii) To evolve cropping and farming systems to raise the incomes of farmers by making the optimum use of their resources throughout the year.[8]

Major inter-crop growth imbalances witnessed in the early years of the Green Revolution are being gradually corrected. Also, the existing GR disparities in growth between the irrigated and rainfed areas may not be as sharp as in the early years of the Green Revolution. The eastern region has shown some improvement in rice yields in the eighties including registering some higher growth than the national average.

The gap between potential yield and actual yield can be bridged only by strengthening extension service. The Training & Visit (T & V) system, aided by the World Bank, underwent modifications. The system of selecting a contact farmer and following it up with disseminating the information through more farmers has not been effective. The current stress is on diversification of agriculture, giving due importance to horticulture, poultry, fishery and animal husbandry. Experts feel that the computer-aided information system will be of immense help.

Training infrastructure in the central and state sector has been developed substantially. The National Institute of Agricultural Extension Management, 4 Extension Education Institutes and 15 Advanced Training Institutes have been established within the country for training of extension personnel at various levels.[9]

There are four major pre-requisites for technological change in agriculture: *(i)* an incentive system that encourages acceptance of innovations, *(ii)* a set of improved production processes created for local conditions, *(iii)* an educational system to teach farmers how to choose and adopt technology to gain substantially from specific conditions, and *(iv)* efficient supply to farmers of the added inputs in which technological change is embodied.[10]

It would be necessary to evolve HYV which has a built-in protection against pests. Use of bio-technologies in agriculture has the potential to eliminate the negative effects on the environment. The use of hazardous chemical pesticides too has to be gradually replaced by the use of herbal pesticides, e.g., the pesticides based on neem which are now commercially available.[11]

Every effort should be made to maximise the yields from agricultural inputs in respect of both irrigated and rain-fed lands. At the same time, the harmful dimensions of the Green Revolution if any, need to be reviewed.

REFERENCES

1. G.S. Bhalla: 'Agrarian Transformation: Interaction Between Tradition and Modernity', *Yojana,* August 15,1993, p. 41.
2. C.H. Hanumantha Rao: 'Recent Performance and Prospects', *Seminar,* June 1994 (Special Issue on Agriculture), p. 16.
3. G. Parthasarathy: 'HYV Technology: The Polarisation and Immiserisation Controversy', *Economic and Political Weekly,* June 29, 1991, p.A-74.
4. Sartaj Aziz (1978): *Rural Development: Learning from China,* The Macmillan Press Ltd. London, p. 41.
5. Raj Kumar Singh; 'Impact of New Agriculture Technology on Employment', *Southern Economist,* February 15,1987, p. 11.
6. Usha Rai: 'Green Revolution's Blood Stained Harvest', *Indian Express,* February 27,1992.
7. Eighth Five Year Plan 1992-97, Vol. I, p. 13.
8. Presidential Address by Ch. Hanumantha Rao at the Golden Jubilee Conference of the Indian Society of Agricultural Economics, Mumbai (December 4-7,1989).
9. Ministry of Finance, Government of India, *Economic Survey,* 1993-94.
10. Indian Institute of Public Administration, New Delhi (1979): *Management of Agriculture* (Collection of Papers), p. 30.
11. Avadhoot Nadkarni: 'The Green Revolution: Twenty Five Years After', *Social Action,* July-September, 1993, p. 290.

Chapter

14 Food Security in India

India is no doubt an agricultural country. Yet, its food security is weak. We do have foodgrain stocks but, food security is *different from* foodgrain security. There is a change in consumption pattern. Non-food grain items such as edible oils, sugar, milk, meat, eggs, vegetable and fruits have assumed importance. They now account for over 60 per cent of the Consumer expenditure on food[1]. Besides food availability, the poor ought to have enough purchasing power. Otherwise, there will be no food security.

Food security, as internationally understood, involves physical, economic and social access to a balanced diet, safe drinking water, environmental hygiene and primary health-care. The Government has prepared the National Food Security Bill. The draft of the Bill seeks to give the poor a right to get 25 kg of rice or wheat every month at ₹ 3 a kg. Of course this places huge burden on public exchequer.

FAO (1983) HAS ENLARGED ITS CONCEPT OF FOOD SECURITY.

It observed that

(1) the ultimate objective of world *foo*d security should be to ensure that all people at all times have both physical and economic access to the basic food they need, and (2) food security should have three specific aims: namely ensuring production of adequate food supplies; maximizing stability in the flow of supplies; securing access to available supplies on the part those who need them.

(I) STATE OF FOOD SECURITY IN INDIA

There are various estimates of poverty. The number of below poverty line (BPL) families calculated (taking four persons as the average size of the family) varies from 9.25 crore (Suresh Tendulkar Committee) to 20 crore (Justice D.P. Wadhwa). While the Planning Commission estimates that there are just over 62 million BPL families, the state government claim the existence of nearly double that number. The Arjun Sengupta Commission on the unorganised sector came to the conclusion that 77 per cent of India's adult population spent less than ₹ 20 a day. It is not possible to meet food requirements with this amount.

The National Family Health Survey (2006) showed that the child under-nutrition rate in India is 46 per cent. In Global Hunger Index (2008), India ranks 66th among the 88 countries surveyed by the International Food Policy Research Institute (IFPRI). The recent rise in food prices might have further worsened the situation. In India, the number of under-nourished persons has increased from about 210 million in 1990-92 to 252 million in 2004-06. India has about half the world's under-nourished children. Also, there has been a general decline in per capita calorie consumption in recent decades. The percentage of children below five years of age who are under-weight is now 42.5 per cent. The percentage of children below three years who are under nourished is 40 per cent.

It is true that the food grain production increased significantly during the 1970s and 1980s. But, food- grain production continues to fluctuate. It was 82 million tonnes in 1960-61, 108.4 million tonnes in 1970-71, 129.6 million tonnes in 1980-81, and 176.4 million tonnes in 1990-91.

However, food grain production which was 209.8 million tonnes in 1999-2000 fell to 196.8 million tonnes in 2000-01. I t again fell from 212.6 million tonnes in 2005-06. It may be around 234 million tonnes in 2008-09.

The estimates made of the requirement of cereals in 2020 range from 224 million tonnes to 296 million tonnes. Some put it at 260 million tonnes.

There is no progress in the output of pulses. It was 12.7 million tonnes in 1960-61, but fell to 10.6 million tonnes in 1980-81. It was high at 14.3 million tonnes in 1990-91, but fell to 11 million tonnes in 2000-01. It was high at 14.8 million tonnes in 2007-08. However, the growth in output is not commensurate with growth in population.

Milk production was only 17 million tonnes in 1950-51. It increased to 20 million tonnes in 1960-61, to 60.6 million tonnes in 1992-93, to 80.6 million tonnes in 2000-01 and to 108.5 million tonnes in 2008-09.

Production of eggs was only 1832 million in 1950-51. It increased to 21101 million in 1990-91 and to 36632 million in 2000-01. It was around 55638 million in 2008-09.

Fish production was 752 thousand tonnes in1950-51. It increased to 5656 thousand tonnes by 2000-01. It was around 7608 thousand tonnes in 2008-09.

The per capita net availability of cereals (per day/grams) was 334.2 in 1951. It increased to 404.1 by 1968, and to 468.5 in 1991. There are year to year fluctuations. In 2008, it was placed around 374 only.

Regarding pulses, it was 60.7 in 1951, increased to 74.9 in 1959 but fell to as low as 30.9 by 1980" There are year to year fluctuations. It was around 42 in 2008.

The per capita availability of edible oils was 2.5 kg in 1955-56. It of course increased to 5.8 kg in 1987-88, and to 7 kg in 1995-96, and to 12 kg. in 2008-09.

An important factor adversely affecting food security is inflation, especially food inflation. It seems the perishables will keep food inflation high. For instance, in 2009, price rise in respect of food articles was 12.43 per cent. But it was high at 14.57 per cent in respect of meat, eggs and fish. Of course, in the case of fruits and vegetables, it was high at 11.96 per cent.

The overall food inflation touched a decade high of 19.8 per cent in the second week of December, 2009. In 2009-10, while food inflation soared, non-food sector was free from inflation. The FCI and other government organisations have to initiate action as soon as the inflationary situation in food crosses a threshold.

Even subsidised grain is not going to ensure food security. For instance, at the prevailing price of pulses, the poor families will not have access to protein rich foods[2].

India has carry over stock of rice of 15 million tonnes as of October 1, 2009 with FCI and other state agencies. On top of this, there is accumulated wheat stock of 30 million tonnes as of 0ctober 1, 2009 against a buffer stock norm of only 11 million tonnes of wheat. Thus, total grain stocks were of the order 45 million tonnes. Of course, total covered capacity to store in the country is less than 27 million tonnes. Moreover, though the buffer stocks are rising, the off-take of grains for PDS and other schemes is not increasing.

NSS 61st Round reveals that more than half of rural manual labourers, the section most in need of subsidised food, do not have BPL cards. In Bihar and Uttar Pradesh, such exclusion was 71 percent and 73 per cent respectively.

(II) Measures to Strengthen Food Security

The country will need about 260 million tonnes of food grains, about 140 million tonnes of vegetables, about 90 million tonnes of fruits, about 12 million tonnes of meat, 35 billion eggs, about 13 million tonnes of fish, and 12 million tonnes of edible oils to provide adequate nutrition to 1.35 billion people by 2020 AD.

Measures required to strengthen food security in the Indian context should include:[3]

- Setting up of local level community food banks for easy availability of grains in periods of scarcity;
- Promoting the cultivation and consumption of fruits, vegetables and dairy farming;
- PDS should be enlarged to accommodate more items;
- Mid-day meal, scheme need to be implemented effectively;
- fodder and feed banks should be set up;
- agro-based industries and food processing units should be encouraged;
- contract farming with private participation should be encouraged;
- farmer' cooperative should be strengthened;

- the increasing area under bio fuels should be reversed; and
- quality input delivery system should be ensured.

(III) The Public Distribution System

A major problem facing PDS is the existence of bogus cards. This leads to diversion of PDS items to open market. It also enhances financial burden on the government by increasing food subsidy. The PDS also suffers from high levels of theft, wastage, spoilage and administrative costs. The Planning Commission had estimated, that there are around 6.52 crore poor families, but states have issued over 10.58 crore ration cards.

The Government is contemplating to introduce food coupons for providing the poor with food security. The system of food coupons would end dual pricing of foodgrain. The new system may lead to more efficient private grain handling as beneficiaries would be allowed to directly buy grain of their choice from retail shops against food coupon[4]. Of course, food coupons could' leak' to the undeserving, given the corrupt administrative machinery we have.

Some have suggested, in the place of PDS, cash transfers. But experts feel that food is far more likely to actually reach the mouths of children and women in a household than cash in the hands of the male adult family head.

A well functioning universal PDS can be the means to ensure adequate physical access to food at affordable prices at he household level.

The PDS has to be supplemented with specific food and nutrition interventions to meet the specific consumption needs of various classes — infants, children, teenage girls, manual worker, pregnant and lactating women and the elderly,[5]

A National Programme of mid-day meals in schools has been in existence But, it suffers from leakages. Recently, the government has revised the food norms for upper primary children by increasing the quantity of pulses from 25 to 30 grams, vegetables from 65 to 75 grams of course, transportation assistance is also provide to special category states.[6]

Thus, ensuring food security to the poor is a challenging task. Concerted efforts need to be made on various fronts.

References:

1. C.H. Hanumantha Rao: ' Food Security', The Hindu March 23, 2002.
2. M.S. Swaminathan: ' Pathway to Food Security for all', The Hindu, March 29, 2010.
3. Harender Raj Gautam: 'Food Security... Need to Strengthen the Agricultural Sector', Kurukshetra. June 2008 p.p. 9-10
4. The Economic Times (editorial'), February 19,2010.
5. Madhura Swaminathan: Eleventh Plan Ignored food and Nutrition Insecurity', The Hindu, September 1, 2006.
6. Ministry of Finance, Government of India: Economic Survey 2009-10. p. 281.

Chapter

15 Irrigation and Indian Agriculture

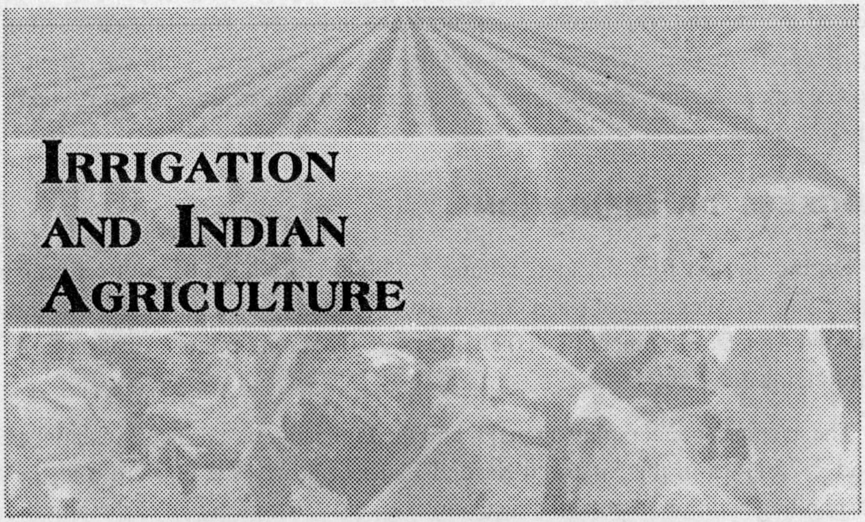

The new agricultural technology would be effective only when the farming community has access to crucial inputs like irrigation. Irrigation plays a vital role in agricultural development as it leads to desirable cropping pattern, registers an increase in yield rates and better labour utilisation. Also, the success and efficiency of other farm inputs largely depend on quantity, quality and timing of water supply, the methods of its use and adequacy of control over it.[1]

Importance of Irrigation

As a consequence of increased yields and more intensive agriculture, irrigation has left a significant impact on the quality of life of the rural population, viz., the agricultural labourers.[2] Irrigation is capable of increasing, besides agricultural wages, the number of working days available for the agricultural workers. Investment in irrigation leads to multiple benefits, both at the micro and macro levels.[3]

According to a World Bank Study, even one per cent increase in irrigation will definitely enhance crop production by 1.6 per cent. Authoritative data reveal that production on irrigated lands is three to five times the output on unirrigated lands. Irrigation is the *sine qua non* for increased agricultural productivity.

Some economists give top priority to irrigation among all the agricultural inputs. It is said, "none of these is as important as the availability of irrigation which alone is the key pre-requisite for determining, the domain of the new technology or of its applicability."[4] The irrigation factor alone accounts for half the inter-state variation in crop intensity.[5]

Case studies have revealed certain beneficial effects of implementation of irrigation projects. These include: *(i)* diversification in the cropping pattern, *(ii)* increased employment due to irrigation, *(iii)* increased income and *(iv)* increased consumption and asset formation as a result of increased income. Irrigation performs best in the matter of stability of cultivated area, yield and output.[6] Irrigation indirectly provides a base for the establishment of agro-based industries, servicing, repair centres and other business centres.

PROGRESS OF IRRIGATION

During the last four decades, around ₹ 45,000 crore have been directly invested by the public sector in various categories of water control works. Of this, major and medium irrigation works including Command Area Development (CAD) claimed ₹ 28,000 crore; minor irrigation ₹ 14,000 crore and flood control claimed ₹ 2,500 crore.

The average annual outlay on major and medium irrigation projects including CAD has risen from around ₹ 75 crore in the First and Second Plans to nearly ₹ 2,500 crore in the Seventh Plan. The corresponding addition to potential has, however, been, between two to three million hectares per Five Year Plan with the exception of Second Plan (1.05 m. ha) and Fifth Plan (4.02 m. ha).[7]

The Eighth Plan outlay for irrigation, CAD and flood control sector as a whole stood at ₹ 32,525.25 crore.

Yet, out of the total 266 million hectares of land, only 46 million hectares held access to irrigation. About 70 per cent of Indian agriculture is rainfed. Only 20.6 million hectares of land was irrigated till 1951. It increased to 73.1 million hectares in 1991-92 averaging about 1.3 million hectares per annum. The average annual increase during fifties was only 0.5 million hectares which went up to 1.6 million hectares during the eighties. It is targeted to grow by about 2.7 million hectares per annum during the Eighth Plan period.

At present, only about 30 per cent of the net sown area is provided with irrigation. The country's cultivated area stands at 186 million hectares, the gross cropped area at 175 million hectares and the net sown area at 143 million hectares.

The ultimate irrigation potential of the country, as estimated by the National Commission on Agriculture (1976) is 113.5 million hectares. This figure has since been revised to 178 million hectares as per the national perspectives of available water resources.

As per the 1986-87 Minor Irrigation Census, to ensure availability of water resources, 95 lakh wells, 0.64 lakh deep tubewells and 4.75 lakh shallow tubewells have been dug; 4.22 lakh surface works completed and the number of pump sets energised rose from 0.2 million in 1950-51 to 11.2 million by 1989-90.[8]

By the end of 1991-92, the cumulative irrigation potential created was 81.2 million hectares comprising 30.9 m. ha under major and medium and 50.3 m. ha under minor irrigation projects. The target for the year 1992-93 was set at an additional 2.7 m. ha (0.7 m. ha under major and medium projects and 2.0 m. ha under minor irrigation projects). Thus, the total potential likely to be created by the end of the year 1992-93 has estimated to be 83.9 m. ha.[9]

A centrally sponsored Command Area Development (CAD) Scheme was initiated in 1974-75 with the sole objective to bridge the existing gap between potential created and potential utilised and increasing agricultural production from the irrigated commands. The programme also made provision for execution of on-farm development works like construction of field channels, land levelling and shaping, implementation of warabandi (network of distributors and minors over the command area) for rotational supply of water and construction of field drains. The programme also gives importance to adaptive trials, demonstration and training of farmers and introduction of suitable cropping patterns. Upto March 1992, ₹ 3,214 crore were spent on the programme.

The share of the irrigation sector (states only) in the total public sector investment came down from 14.7 per cent in 1980-81 to only 5.6 per cent in 1990-91. The total public sector investment (at 1980-81 prices) increased at a rate of 6.3 per cent per annum from ₹ 11,767 crore in 1980-81 to ₹ 21,613 crore in 1990-91.

Investments made in the irrigation sector declined at 3.5 per cent per annum from ₹ 1,735 crore in 1980-81 to ₹ 1,215 crore in 1990-91. This decrease was more pronounced at the rate of 6.1 per cent per annum during the Seventh Plan as compared to 2.2 per cent per annum during the Sixth Plan.[10]

Table: 1
Development of Irrigation potential (cumulative)
Though Plan periods
(In million ha.)

Plan Period	*Potential created*	*Potential utilised*
First Plan	26.26	25.04
Second Plan	29.08	27.80
Third Plan	33.57	32.17
Annual Plan	37.10	35.75
Fourth plan	44.20	42.19
Fifth Plan	52.02	48.46
Sixth plan	65.22	58.82
Seventh Plan	76.53	68.59
Annual Plan	81.02	72.86
Eighth Plan	86.26	77.24
Ninth Plan*	93.95	80.06
Target for Tenth plan ' 2002-07)*	109.11	90.42

*Provisional
Source : India 2006. Government of India.

The Bharat Nirman Programme envisages creation of 10 million hectares additional assured irrigation during the 4 year period (2005-09). To achieve this, the pace of potential creation will have to increase from 1.42 million hectares per year in recent years to 2.5 million hectares per year. Of the new potential envisaged under Bharat Nirman, about half is planned for 2007-08 and 2008-09 that first 2 years of the 11th plan. Assuming the same rate continues thereafter a total of about 11 million hectares of new potential can be expected in the 11th Plan consisting of 5.5 million hectares in major and medium irrigation,

3.5 million hectares through minor irrigation and about 2 million hectares through ground water development. In addition, another 3 to 4 million hectares of land is to be restored through modernisation of major, medium and minor projects and restoration of tanks (Draft Approach paper of 11th Plan)

Various Systems of Irrigation

The inadequacies of canal and tank irrigation have increased dependence on tubewells. This has resulted in lowering of the water table. The problem is becoming serious even in a state like Punjab. However, groundwater possesses the following virtues:

(i) Groundwater resource is much more bountiful than surface water;

(ii) In comparison to big dams, groundwater irrigation is a low cost option for our economy;

(iii) Groundwater based farming has much higher land productivity;

(iv) Environmental degradation, forest submergence, population dislocation and rehabilitation problems of dam oustees are absent in groundwater irrigation;

(v) Unlike substantial under-utilisation of irrigation capacity observed in the case of big dams, there is almost full utilisation in the case of wells and tubewells and

(vi) Time lag between investment and returns is low in groundwater case, whereas construction of big projects lingers on for decades.[11]

Tank irrigation is the oldest system. It is simple, efficient and environment friendly. Water from the catchment areas flowed into the tanks during the rains. Once a tank is filled up, it overflows, not wastefully into the surrounding areas, but into canals that led to other, bigger tanks in a series. Thus, every drop of water is conserved in the tanks. This method also recharges groundwater, as otherwise the rains would simply go into rivers and thence into the sea.

Of course, tanks need maintenance. They are to be periodically desilted, the fertile silt going into the fields, the tanks and canals are reinforced and repaired and trees are planted in the catchment areas. The new technology removed the need for silt to fertilise the fields.

The canal system has created problems like waterlogging, salinity and weaker sections and tail-end farmers not getting water. In the case of groundwater, over pumping also caused serious problem of drinking water and salinity ingress in coastal areas. It also affected vegetation growth.

A watershed is generally referred to the area of overland drainage which contributes water with the flow of a particular stream at a chosen point. It embraces all the land and water areas which contribute run-off to a common point. It is the drainage area that contributes to the flow of a tertiary river having an area of 4,000 to 40,000 hectares.

Water shed management implies a project type operation developed and applied to all the land and water available in a specific watershed, taking into account physical conditions, needs and problems of the watershed, its relationship to the larger catchment areas and facilities available to accomplish the project. A watershed is used as a unit for planning and management of land, water and other resources in a systematic manner.

The scope of integrated watershed development include levelling and terracing: improving soil quality and productivity, watershed reclamation, *in situ* water harvesting and conservation, percolation ponds, open wells, tanks and small reservoirs, improving water quality and conjunctive use of water from different sources.

The watershed-based technology gives importance to post-harvest cultivation following the post-rainy season crop before the soil hardens; land levelling and shaping, dry-seeding before the monsoon; use of improved seeds and optimum fertiliser doses and timely plant protection.

The watershed based technology has ensured some social benefits also, for instance, reducing the loss of top soil and deep infiltration of water to recharge ground water. Also, farm labour employment is substantially high (and more stable) under the watershed based technology than under traditional technology.

Drip irrigation is the regulation of irrigated water for a longer period through orifices at frequent intervals near the root zone. This system has the potential to convert vast areas of wasteland into productive farmers generating substantial revenues.

The main advantages of drip irrigation are: low application rate, uniformity of water application, controlled root zone environment, improved disease control, water conservation, water and energy conservation, improved tolerance to salinity and crop control, reduced labour costs and suitability to various crops. Though the government is extending 50 per cent subsidy, yet drip irrigation covers just 75,000 acres only.

The drip irrigation system ensures ideal soil moisture condition in the root zone and reduces water loss due to evaporation since the area wetted is limited. Also, it does not require any special knowledge and can be used even by farmers not well acquainted with this system.[12]

In sprinkler irrigation, water is sprayed evenly on the crops through revolving nozzle-fitted emitters. Water is applied once in four to seven days. This reduces its moisture stress of the crop area to some extent. However, the water application being controlled only the needed water can be regulated in this system. This has an efficiency of upto 7 per cent. In the conventional method of flooding the fields, losses from evaporation and percolation down to below root zones are high.

IRRIGATION MANAGEMENT

Irrigation related agriculture, unless carefully managed, can lead to many problems like soil salinity, waterlogging and low yields. Basically, there are three elements of irrigation water management: (i) when to irrigate, (ii) how much irrigation water to be used and (iii) how to irrigate.

With area based water charges presently in use, those who manage to divert disproportionately large quantities of water deprive others their due share, besides non-payment for the excess water drawn.

Lining of water courses has been recognised as an effective measure to minimise water losses in the transit and to avoid subsequent damage to the crops. Unlined watercourses lead to deep seepage and reduced water supply to crops. Salinisation and alkalisation adversely affect land productivity. Moreover, the watch and ward requirements of unlined watercourses is certainly more due to its very structure.[13]

Regarding groundwater management, field studies have drawn the conclusion that the existing cropping patterns have to be adjusted to the available source of water in order to get the maximum output from the tubewell command areas. Also, private tubewell owners are close to the optimum crop plan than the farmers getting water from state tubewells.[14] It is also noticed that many of the crops are planted at the dates that do not give highest yield potentials.

The irrigation potential created is not properly utilised. This can be attributed to a number of factors. Most farmers are not familiar with appropriate agro-economic practices. The supporting facilities such as land levelling, land shaping, land consolidation, efficient field channels etc. for optimal use of irrigation facilities are absent in many parts of the country. There is no proper maintenance of major and medium irrigation works. Open wells remain neglected. It has been estimated that about 10 million hectares get affected by waterlogging.

There has been a lag in the utilisation of created potential, particularly in major and medium irrigation projects. At the end of 1991-92, utilisation was 73.1 m. ha against a created potential of 81.2 m. ha. This leaves a gap of 8.1 m. ha (4.3 m. ha. in major and medium and 3.8 m. ha in minor irrigation).

However, the underutilisation of irrigation potential has been over-estimated for two important reasons: (i) deliberate over-assessment of the irrigation capability of an irrigation work being promoted for clearance from the Centre and (ii) the incompletion of distribution network because of resource paucity.

A decentralised irrigation management system under the control of effective panchayats could be highly useful, if panchayats are effective and accountability is assured through regular local body elections.

Of course, the management of any irrigation system becomes effective only when consumers are prepared to pay a much higher price for the benefits of irrigation than is currently the case.

We must solve the problem of low water efficiency. The efficiency of lined canals is almost 90 per cent. The unlined canals' efficiency needs to be improved. The use of plastic to line canals is yet to take-off.

The optimum utilisation of irrigation facility requires infrastructural support such as better transport, marketing, communication, banking, veterinary services, education etc.

FINANCING IRRIGATION

In view of the resource crunch, financing irrigation projects has become a big problem. In the First Plan, ₹ 300 crore was spent on major and medium irrigation projects and ₹ 66 crore on minor irrigation projects. These figures rose to ₹ 11,556 crore and ₹ 6,305 crore respectively in the Seventh Plan.

The development of irrigation has become highly expensive. The per hectare cost of irrigation potential under major and medium projects, which was ₹ 1,530 in the First Plan, rose to ₹ 38,000 during the Seventh Plan and may go up to ₹ 60,000 during the Eighth Plan.

The resources available to the state governments for the maintenance of irrigation projects have been squeezed by their failure to collect meaningful user charges and by the growth of staff costs.

By the 1980s, irrigation subsidies accounted for about 70 per cent of total agricultural subsidies. The financial performance of the irrigation sector is poor because of poor maintenance, ownership issues and absence of cost effective technologies. There has been a large spill over of incomplete irrigation projects from plan to plan. Today, 142 major and 216 medium projects are incomplete.

The Vaidyanathan Committee has observed, "It is difficult to accept the case of subsidising such a user-oriented and capital intensive infrastructure as irrigation. The Government is not in a position to sustain the subsidies on irrigation, or for that matter or any infrastructure on the present scale."

Under the present arrangement, the disadvantaged farmer who can use water only once, pays the same charge as the advantageously placed farmer who generally opts for multiple cropping. The system has thus failed to ensure equity. By introducing changes at the field level operations, it is possible to link water charges to number of waterings given by a farmer to the crops.[15]

Increased revenues from irrigation need not necessarily come from higher rates. There is scope for increasing the revenues from industry, urban areas and non-agricultural users who should be charged at full cost for the services being used. It is said that strict enforcement and collection of dues at the existing rates should increase collections by at least 35 to 40 per cent on an average. There is also the need for rationalising the rate structure in such a way that the cost per unit of water consumed by different crops is equalised.[16]

Low water rates have not only deprived the government funds for improving irrigation potential, but resulted in the inefficient use of water. The low returns also mean that there is little incentive to monitor the use of irrigation water.

STRENGTHENING IRRIGATION SCHEMES

In 1992, the Report of the Committee on Pricing of Irrigation Water (Chairman: Dr. A. Vaidyanathan) emphasised the importance of farmers' involvement in water pricing and utilisation. It also recommended incentives for the formation of user groups and farmer groups, including discouragement of individual service. There should be a mutually beneficial obligation : the farmers pay full charges and the government ensure timely and contractual water supply. Switch over to volumetric supply of water and volume-based charges rather than area-based ones would emerge as incentives to farmers to use the water saved during the flush season later in the lean season.

Two things appear to be important in irrigation management: (i) maximum agricultural production per unit area where water potential is in excess of land potential and (ii) maximum production per unit of water where land potential is in excess of the utilisable water potential.

All efforts should be made to avoid both cost over runs and time over runs in implementing irrigation projects and to avoid the time lag between the creation of irrigation potential and its full utilisation.[17]

The new irrigation policy, drafted by the Government, seeks to raise water rates and also make improvements in the monitoring of both surface and ground water irrigation. There is the need for directly linking the recovery of dues with the operation and maintenance of irrigation facilities in each area. The relationship between land and water varies from region to region.

The new policy recognises that the approach to water efficiency must be based on the existing agricultural conditions. It emphasises that the yield per unit of land in areas where usable water potential is greater than land potential and the yield per unit of water where the reverse is true. It also recognises the need for state level irrigation policies that are consistent with the national policy on agriculture.

References

1. B.L. Patil: 'Irrigation Constraints and Efficiency Measures', *Yojana*, February 16-28.
2. Bharat Singh: 'Water Resources Development and Environment', *The Hindu*, July 21,1992, p. 17.
3. V. Subramanyam Chetty: 'Role of Irrigation in Agricultural Development', in Subramanya, S. and I. Satya Sundaram (Ed. 1987), *Growth of Agriculture and Rural Development in India*, Deep and Deep Publications, New Delhi - 27, p. 158.
4. Bandhudas Sen (1974): *The Green Revolution, in India: A Perspective*, Wiley Eastern Pvt. Ltd., New Delhi, pp. 26-27.
5. Khattar, Parveen: 'Impact of Irrigation on Crop Intensity', *Eastern Economist*, November 26,1976, p. 1044.
6. B.D. Dhawan: 'Indian Irrigation: An Assessment', *Economic and Political Weekly*, May 7,1988, p. 966.
7. *Eighth Five Year Plan* 1992-97, Vol. II, p. 57.
8. *Ibid*., p. 61.
9. *Economic Survey*, 1992-93.
10. Jayant Patil: 'Agriculture and the Eighth Plan', *Yojana*, August 15, 1993, p. 18.
11. B.D. Dhawan: 'Canal Versus Well Irrigation: Myths and Realities', *Facts For You*, August 1992, p. 43.
12. Himmat Patel: 'Drip Irrigation: Gujarat Farmers Experience', *The Economic Times*, August 12, 1988.
13. K.M. George: 'Is Lining of Watercourses an Answer for Better Water Management: A Case Study', *Southern Economist*, October 1, 1987, p. 11.
14. V.K. Sarma (1985): *Water Resource Planning and Management*, Himalaya Publishing House, Mumbai - 400 004.
15. M. Venkata Reddy: 'Irrigation Water Rates Need Increase', *The Economic Times*, July 7, 1988.
16. A. Vaidyanathan: 'Proper Pricing of Irrigation Water', *The Hindu*, March 21, 1993, p. 12.
17. A.P. Srinivasa Murthy: 'Irrigation Planning in India: A Critical Appraisal' in Gandhi, P. Jegadish (1989): *Indian Economic Issues*, Vol. I, Pointer Publishers; Jaipur, p. 145.

Chapter

16 Trends in Agricultural Exports

In a predominantly agricultural country like India, agricultural exports play an important role in boosting the total volume of exports of the country and thereby earning the much needed foreign exchange.

Agricultural exports do enjoy an advantage over non-agricultural exports. These include low import requirements, cheap labour costs and favourable climate conditions. Some people therefore argue for an agro-export led growth which can augment foreign exchange reserves and ease the pressure on the balance of payments.

While total exports increased from ₹ 6,611 crore in 1981 to ₹ 20,295 crore in 1989, agricultural exports during this period increased marginally from ₹ 2,057 crore to ₹ 3,283 crore. However, exports of agro-based commodities have been steadily on the rise, touching ₹ 5,585.39 crore in 1992-93. Such exports are likely to be around four to five billion dollars at the end of the Eighth Plan against the projected total exports of around 35 billion dollars.

Agricultural exports (other than raw cotton, including wastes) have registered remarkable growth from ₹ 7,430 crore in 1992-93 to ₹ 10,062 crore during 1993-94. The total exports of agricultural products (including tea, coffee and raw cotton but excluding marine products) during 1995-96 was ₹ 15,659.31 crore. Exports of agricultural and allied products were ₹ 24,576 crore in 1999-2000. India's share in the world trade in agricultural commodities is just about one per cent.

The share of agricultural exports in the country's total exports gradually declined from 44.2 per cent in 1960-61 to 31.8 per cent in 1970-71, to 30.7 per cent in 1980-81 and further to 19.4 per cent in 1990-91. By 1993, the percentage further fell to 16.5 per cent.

The proportion of agri exports to total exports came down from 11.9 per cent in 2003-04 to 10.2 per cent in 2004-05.

There are some problems on the agricultural export front. The primary commodity prices in the world market are unstable and to an extent unremunerative. A strong emphasis on agricultural exports has to be followed by steps to insulate the farmers against price fluctuations. Agriculture, in general, has been facing adverse terms of trade as compared to industry. Moreover, a huge domestic market inhibits the volume of exports.[1]

The country's poor performance in the sphere of agricultural exports can be attributed to a number of factors; poor research efforts on crops other than cereals, low yields and outdated technology, stagnant output, rising domestic demand and growing competition from other countries in the international market. The disintegration of USSR has also adversely affected Indian agricultural exports particularly the export of tea, coffee and tobacco. The recession in the US too has aggravated the situation.

A sharp decline in the share of farm exports in the total exports can be largely traced to infrastructural bottlenecks, a poor linkage of storage requirements and movement of transports, dearth of quality seeds, lack of gradation, inept handling, absence of quality controls, poor packaging facilities and for sometimes, growing home consumption etc.[2]

However, two major developments in the sphere of agricultural exports are discernible: (i) there has been a marked rise in the unit value realisation in respect of important agricultural export items, and (ii) diversification in favour of non-traditional items. For instance, during 1970-71, tea, spices, tobacco, oilcakes and cashew kernel were the principal items. By 1980-81, the relative share of these five commodities stumped while that of coffee, rice, meat, fish, fruits and vegetables increased. During the 1980s, there has been an upsurge in the share of fish, fruits and vegetables and oilcakes.

Rice: India is the world's second largest producer of rice with an area of 41 million hectares and a production of 73 million tonnes. The country became an exporter of rice only in the 1980s. There has been growing demand for basmati rice in the international market. India's rice exports reached a level of over four lakh tonnes by 1989-90. In 1991-92, rice exports reached a record level of 7.5 lakh tonnes valued at ₹ 750 crore. But, the level declined to 5.6 lakh tonnes in 1992-93, though value increased to ₹ 900 crore. Rice exports were valued at ₹ 3,105 crore in 1999-2000. Indian rice exports are a mere 0.5 per cent of the national output.

Rice exports were valued at $907.1 million in 2003-04 and $1478.2 million in 2004-05.

Export market for Indian rice is sluggish. The Persian Gulf countries, the biggest importer of Indian rice, are said to be carrying a large inventory, particularly of basmati rice. Moreover, Pakistan offers rice at a much cheaper price to the Gulf markets. The rise in domestic rice price has also an adverse effect on rice exports. India should diversify its direction of export.

Table 1
Exports of Agricultural Commodities
(in ₹ Crore)

Year	*Agricultural Exports*	*Ag. Exports as % of total exports*
1991-92	7,894.75	17.80
1995-96.	20,344.00	19.18
2000-01	28,567.37	14.23
2001-02	29,728.61	14.22
2002-03	34,653.94	13.58
2003-04	37,266.52	12.70
2004-05	41,602.65	11.20
2005-06	49,802.92	10.95
2007-08	65,210.00	9.90
2008-09	77,783.00	9.10

Wheat: In 1977, India made a beginning by exporting 1.36 lakh tonnes of wheat. This rose to one million tonnes in 1978. Wheat exports continued afterwards, though they experienced wide fluctuations. The wheat exports remain confined to a few countries because Indian varieties of wheat are appropriate for making chapatis. The US is heavily subsidising its wheat exports subsequently to Indian wheat which had to face heavy competition.

More than 72 per cent of extraction from whole wheat is exportable as flour, maida or bran. India exported wheat bran worth ₹ 7.3 million in 1976-77. Thereafter, the exports decreased but again rose to ₹ 19.5 and ₹ 14.0 million during 1985 and 1987.

Wheat exports were valued at $520.4 million in 2003-04, and $322.3 million in 2004-05.

It would be difficult to sell Indian wheat at more than $100 per tonne. Durum wheats fetch higher price in the export market. Instead of exporting a low-valued bread wheat, India should export durum wheat which is mainly used by pasta manufacturers in Europe and other Western countries.

COARSE CEREALS

Export of coarse cereals was only 18,000 tonnes during 1992-93 fetching ₹ 10 crore foreign exchange. During 1993-94, exports sharply increased to 1.1 lakh tonnes fetching ₹ 36 crore of foreign exchange. Though exports in volume had gone up by over 4.5 times, foreign exchange earnings rose by only 2.6 times. Of the 1.1 lakh tonnes exported, maize alone accounted for 0.75 lakh tonnes, fetching ₹ 25 crore worth foreign exchange.

Cotton: India's share in the world trade of cotton of 25 million bales estimated for 1992-93 was five per cent, while that of the US stood at 21 per cent. For 1992-93, the total export quota issued has been the highest on record at 17.85 lakh bales, of which 16.60 lakh bales are staple cotton. One lakh bales of short staple Bengal Deshi and 25,000 bales of yellow pickings have been exported. Rawedton exports were placed at ₹ 81 crore in 1999-2000.

Factors that helped to bring about good export sale are: (i) early announcement of export quota in November 1992, (ii) demand due to the fall in output in Pakistan, the US, China and Brazil, (iii) domestic prices ruled lower than international prices, (iv) favourable dollar exchange rate and (v) realistic minimum export prices. It would be better to follow a liberalised policy in cotton exports.[3]

Jute: Exports of jute goods were placed at 4.399 lakh tonnes, valued at ₹ 327.42 crore in 1980-81. These, however, fell to 2.996 lakh tonnes, valued at ₹ 341.26 crore in 1984-85. There was further decline to 2.400 lakh tonnes valued at ₹ 225.94 crore by 1987-88. In 1991-92, volume of exports was placed at 2.371 lakh tonnes valued at ₹ 387.24 crores. These were worth ₹ 514 crore in 1999-2000.

Owing to restriction on export of jute seeds, there was no free flow of seeds to other countries. This crisis called for modifying the restrictions on export for exchange of varieties. India has the capacity to produce seeds of elite varieties of jute and kenaf on a large scale for countries which have a less favourable climate.

Oilseeds: The Union Ministry of Commerce fixed an export target of ₹ 1,362 crore (equivalent to $ 480 million) for oilseeds sector for 1992-93. However, the export earnings of this sector for 1992-93 were at a new peak of ₹ 1,616 crore ($ 560 million) against ₹ 1,031 crore in 1991-92. Export earnings, thus, exceeded the target both in rupee and dollar terms. Oil cakes exports were worth ₹ 1,603 crore in 1999-2000.

The factors responsible for the record exports are: (i) peak production of 21 million tonnes in the nine major oil seeds during 1992-93, (ii) fall in world output of some oil meals like those of cotton, rapeseed and sunflower and (iii) China, a major supplier of soya and other meals to Asian countries, restricting exports due to increased domestic demand.[4]

Fruits and Vegetables: India, with a wide variety of soils and agro-climating conditions, annually produces 26 million tonnes of fruits and about 54 million tonnes of vegetables including potato. The annual growth rate of these commodities has been to the order of 1.66 and 3.96 respectively during the Seventh Plan. The Eighth Plan hopes to step up this rate to 7 per cent.

India ranks third in the production of fruits after Brazil and the US. It is the second largest producer of vegetables after China. India's share in the world production is about 8 per cent in fruits and 12 per cent in vegetables.

All horticultural crops put together cover 12 million hectares (mh) which is approximately 7 per cent of cropped area of the country. The estimated production from this area is about 100 million tonnes (mt) annually, contributing over 18 per cent to the gross agricultural output of the country.

The major horticultural products having potential for exports include mango, grapes, banana, lychee among fruits and mushrooms, tomato, onion and garlic among vegetables. Indian exports of vegetables stood at 18,000 tonnes valued at ₹ 16 crore in 1993. Exports of fresh fruits in 1991-92 were placed at 45,000 tonnes valued at ₹ 59 crore.

Exports of fruits and vegetables were placed at $378.2 million in 2003-04, and $361.7 million in 2004-05.

However, due to large internal demand, the quantities available for processing and exports are limited. There is another problem; the quality of products, post-harvest management, standardisation, handling and transport have failed to satisfy India, with natural advantages of cheap labour, abundant sunlight and a skilled farming community should be in a position to export fruits and vegetables valued at ₹ 1000-1200 crore by 2000 AD[5]. This is possible through extending the infrastructure needed by the farming community and professional training.

Flowers: Floriculture certainly enjoys many advantages with high export potential. The internal demand for flowers is also growing. Flowers also command high value in the market and hence a profitable business venture for farmers. Flowers have different kinds of chemicals in them from which perfumes are manufactured. Besides, flowers have adaptability that many other crops do not have.

At present, there are some 35,000 hectares under flower cultivation and the annual production of flowers is placed at ₹ 150 crore and at the retail level, floriculture trade turnover may be of the order of ₹ 200 crore per annum. Exports of floricultural products fetched ₹ 420 lakh in 1988-89 and ₹ 865 lakh in 1990-91. The exports are handicapped by undue delay in quarantine inspection of imported seeds and planting materials. High tech cleaning and packing standards are required by foreign companies who pay substantially to the Indian farmers.

LATEST DEVELOPMENTS

India's agricultural sector exports were up by 4.14 per cent during 2008-09. The exports in the plantation segment rose 10.72 per cent and agri and allied products registered an increase of 5.56 per cent but marine products dipped 10.77 percent. (The Economic Time, September 28, 2009)

In 2009-10, agri exports may go up by 35 percent in rupee terms. Agri exports in 2008-09 were placed at ₹ 77,783 Crore or $16,914 million. This formed 9.1 percent of the total earnings. In 2007-08, these were ₹ 65,230 crore $ or 16.202 million (9.9 per cent of the total export earnings)

The current stress is on higher value added products. Processed foods now account for ₹ 10,000 crore of export earnings. A new item is banana. Its exports brought ₹ 100 crore in 2008-09. There is rising demand abroad for Indian products like pomegranates which earned ₹ 70 crore in 2008-09

MEASURES NEEDED

On the agricultural export front, consistent and persistent efforts to enhance agricultural productivity, processing and preservation facilities for agri-producers are needed. These will result in added agri-exportable surplus, reduced post-harvest loss and enhanced value added exports.[6]

Value added products should be exploited for export rather than raw materials. Essential support in research and development for value addition should receive high priority.[7]

Intensive research on post-harvesting grading, packaging and quality improvement of material being exported is required. This includes extending necessary assistance on matters such as communication, packaging, warehousing, transportation and speedy customs clearance. It is also equally important to ensure co-ordination with various organisations both within the country and abroad.[8]

Some of the measures initiated by the government to boost farm exports include cash assistance, import replenishment, duty drawback, abolition of excise duties and imposition of export duties where necessary. Also, importance has been given to strict quality control and pre-shipment inspection systems.

A number of policy changes have been introduced to make agricultural exports viable. Market determined exchange rate policy has favoured agricultural product exports. Lowering of import duties on capital goods, particularly for greenhouse equipment and plant and machinery necessary for food processing industries as well as easier availability of credit for exports have also helped. Some of the restrictions on exports have been removed. The items on the restricted list have been pruned down and only a few items now remain subject to either licensing or quantitative ceiling.

A number of new agricultural products have been introduced in our export basket. These include floriculture products, fresh fruits such as bananas, lychees, grapes, pomegranates and fresh vegetables such as broccolli and asparagus *(Economic Survey 1996-97).*

Export growth of the agricultural sector has got special attention in the new Export-Import Policy of 1992-97. Various incentives have been accorded to set-up Export Oriented Units (EOUs) in this sector. Units engaged in the agricultural and allied sectors can now avail of the benefits of duty-free imports even if they export only 50 per cent of their production. They can sell the remaining 50 per cent in the domestic market as against the limit of 25 per cent for the non-agricultural sector. This would go towards building up a strong domestic base and thereby open the international market for these products and enable them to face global competition. The definition of 'capital goods' under the EXIM policy has been expanded to include capital goods used in agriculture and allied activities, so that units engaged in this sector can avail of the Export Promotion Capital Goods (EPCG) Scheme for importing their production at a concessional rate of duty. Certain inputs and materials required by the agricultural sector such as edible wax for waxing fresh fruits and vegetables, grape guard paper, dipping oil for treatment of grapes etc. have been removed from the negative list of imports so that they can now be freely imported without a licence.[9]

It is necessary to identify a few items depending on the demand for them in the competitive international market. For instance, there is a growing demand for good quality seeds. It is possible to boost up exports of seeds by ten times in a short period. Likewise, marine food (especially fish) holds tremendous potential for export.

Any strategy to boost agricultural exports should give priority to: (i) raising productivity, particularly that of foodgrains, (ii) planned marketing strategy which can generate surpluses for exports, (iii) rationalisation of financial and fiscal incentives, (iv) price competitiveness through vital backward linkages, and (v) spread of risks by diversifying the commodities exported as well as the rules and regulations of exports.

The Economic and Scientific Research Foundation has estimated that the value of agricultural exports is expected to touch the level of $ 36 billion by the year 2000 AD. Concerted efforts should be made to boost output of meat and other animal husbandry products as the demand for these items is increasing in developed countries. Also, special attention should be paid to items having high unit value. Otherwise, export earnings may show a declining trend in spite of increase in the volume of exports. In order to boost farm exports, agriculture should be treated on par with industry by the government in respect of tax incentives.

REFERENCES

1. Deepa Kamat: 'Domestic Demand: An Inhibiting Factor', *The Economic Times*, May 6, 1993.
2. *Ibid*.
3. E.K. Vasudevan: 'Cotton: Pragmatic Policy Vital', *The Hindu Survey of Indian Agriculture 1994*, p. 59.
4. E.K. Vasudevan:'Oilseeds Sector's Remarkable Show on Exports', *The Hindu*, July 29, 1993, p. 18.
5. Jayant Patil: 'Agro Exports: Future in Fruits', *The Economic Times*, July 7, 1992.
6. M. Selvam: 'Scope to Boost Farm Exports', *Financial Express*, January 21, 1994, p. 7.
7. R.S. Paroda and O.P. Makhija: 'Strategy for Boosting Agricultural Exports', *Yojana*, September 30, 1992, p. 13.
8. S.S. Khanna: 'Agricultural Export: Present Status and Future Strategies', *Yojana*, August 15, 1990, p. 65.
9. *Yojana*, Cover Page 2. November 15, 1993.

Chapter

17 Agricultural Price Policy of India

The agricultural price policy has become the most controversial issue in the sphere of agricultural economics. The price policy indeed faces a dilemma : the policy considers issues as to how to keep food prices high enough to encourage agricultural production and low enough to protect buyers' interests.

In both developing and developed countries, price policy has been an effective tool in controlling price levels, mopping up surpluses, encouraging farm production and supporting the weaker sections of the rural population. The agricultural price policy pertains to reshaping allocation of resources and income distribution not only within the agricultural sector but between agricultural and non-agricultural sectors. During the first two plan periods (1951-61), price policy remained largely consumer-oriented, with restrictions on product prices. The real beginning of the price support policy started with the launching of the Third Five Year Plan (1961-66).

Importance of Agricultural Price Policy

An appropriate agricultural price policy has to provide incentives to producers to step up production and at the same time protect the interests and cater to the demands of the consumers. The Agricultural Prices Commission (APC) was set up in January 1965. It was since renamed as the Commission for Agricultural Costs and Prices (CACP). The commission is expected to keep in view at least three points:

(i) The need to provide incentives to the producer for adopting and using improved technology for maximising production;

(ii) The need to ensure rational utilisation of land and other productive resources and

(iii) The likely effect of price policy on the rest of the economy, particularly on the cost of living, level of wages, industrial cost structure etc. In spite of food surpluses, there is need for 'developing a production pattern broadly in the light of national requirements.' It was sometime later in 1980, when adverse terms of trade of agriculture became a hot issue, that the CACP was asked to look into:

(iv) The terms of trade between the agricultural sector and the non-agricultural sector.

Besides the cost of production of the commodity for which it recommends the procurement price, the CACP has been entrusted with the responsibility to assess the trend in the wholesale price of the commodity, the need to achieve a balanced growth of different crops and the terms of trade between agricultural and non-agricultural commodities.

Along with wheat, CACP has recommended procurement price for gram, rapeseed, mustard and barley. However, coarse grains including barley, hardly figure in the public distribution stocks, reflecting the inadequate growth of marketable surplus of these grains. Thus, CACP's pricing policy has not been quite successful in achieving a balanced growth of different crops. Of course, the cropping pattern does not entirely depend on price incentives.

In the Indian context, a positive price policy has to correct market imperfections which are the result of unequal competition due to various rigidities and information gaps. It has also to provide proper market signals to achieve desired national objectives in terms of overall production, cropping patterns, remunerative incomes to farmers and assured supply of essential goods at reasonable prices to the consumer.

In the short run, the price policy has to provide stability in crop prices to avoid uncertainty. The medium-term goal is to achieve stability in terms of trade for agriculture to encourage investment. It is observed that agricultural prices have greater flexibility than the industrial prices both in the up and down swing.[1] The greater flexibilities of agricultural prices are suggestive of the low price elasticities of demand and supply of agricultural products. The long-term policy aims at gradual adjustment of all prices towards their equilibrium level. A rational price policy should be one which is designed to take advantage of the price responsiveness of producers to ensure adequate supply of agricultural products and at the same time safeguard the interests of the weaker sections of the consumers.[2]

The principal objectives of the price policy are:

(i) To step up agricultural production by assuring the producer that the prices of his produce will not fall below a certain minimum level;

(ii) To prevent excessive rise in prices and thereby protect the consumer interest; and

(iii) To stabilise prices to curb speculative activities.

The main constituents of the price policy are:

(a) Announcement of minimum support prices for major farm products well in advance of the sowing season;

(b) Fixation of procurement prices of major foodgrains for purchasing a part of the marketable surplus at below market prices;

(c) Running a public distribution system for safeguarding the interests of low income consumer and

(d) Building up buffer stocks to meet emergency situations and to mitigate seasonal and annual price fluctuations.[3]

TRENDS IN AGRICULTURAL PRICE AND SOME ISSUES

The CACP was set up on a permanent basis 'with a view to evolving a balanced and integrated price structure in perspective of the overall needs of the economy and with regard to the interests of producer and consumer.' The CACP announced minimum support prices to the producers so that 'any temporary glut in the market caused by either the supply or demand factor will not be permitted to depress their incomes to unduly low levels.'[4] These minimum support prices will ensure price stabilisation, improvements of agriculture's terms of trade and insurance to the producers.

In the place of minimum support prices, the Government has declared procurement prices. Normally, the procurement prices are kept below the level of market prices and above that of minimum prices. The trend of open market prices of inputs, the need to narrow down inter-state price disparities and the endeavour to promote a fair return to the grower without being harsh to the consumer, generally influence the fixation of procurement prices. One of the important ingredients of price policy is to ensure a floor price so that in a period of glut, prices do not fall below a given level. The price support policy aims at maintaining the present level of output and the tempo of growth at a high level. The support price acts as an incentive to the farmers to make long-term investments in agriculture without worrying about the possibility of a sudden and precipitous fall in prices of their products.[5]

The functions of CACP have been thus summed up by the Economic Survey 1991-92 : 'The CACP formulates its recommendations after making a comprehensive review. Of the entire structure of prices, they are : costs of production, paid out cost and the imputed value of owned assets including land and family labour, changes in input prices, input/output price parity, demand and supply situation, inter-crop price parity, effects on the industrial cost structure, on the general price level and on the cost of living, international market prices, parity between prices paid and prices received by farmers (terms of trade) etc.

Of course, fixation of procurement prices should take into account the trends in productivity, but this rule is hardly observed in practice. For instance, in the case of rice, procurement price is on the increase in spite of rise in both production and productivity. A reduction in procurement price may be helpful in moderating regional imbalances and income and wealth inequalities. Higher procurement prices for wheat and rice confer benefits mainly on a few states like Haryana, Punjab and U.P.

The cereal prices are rising by 8 per cent to 10 per cent per year which is happening in spite of the fact that the foodgrain stocks with the Government are at a record high. Most consumers are said to be buying cereals in the open market. This may be because the price of cereals issued through the public distribution system is considered excessive in relation to their quality and open market prices. Open market supplies at higher prices are perhaps preferred on quality grounds. Perhaps there is the need for augmenting open market supplies by adequate release from official stocks.[6]

It may be noted that there is no realistic price support for goods like cotton, sugarcane and potato. Hence, we find periodic gluts, causing price crashes and distress to farmers at one time or the other. Moreover, price policy will be successful only when it is backed up by an efficient procurement machinery. For an item like potato, support price is announced but there is no procurement machinery.

The commission has been recommending prices for wheat, rice and other commodities separately. It takes into account the cost of production and the general rise in the prices in the economy as a whole. Procurement prices are fixed in such a way that the farmers recover the cost of production and also enjoy a reasonable margin of profit. An attempt is made to ensure parity between the prices of various crops. Of course, since the consumers' interests are to be protected, the procurement prices should not worsen the inflationary situation. It is generally felt that the procurement prices fixed on the recommendation of the CACP are fair to the farmers.

The economy as a whole is experiencing an inflationary situation. Hence, the rise in the prices of agricultural commodities has been certainly less than the rise in the prices of commodities in general. But, it is not desirable to keep strict parity between agricultural and non-agricultural commodities. If higher and higher procurement prices are fixed, it may push up the general price level. However, some relationship in prices between what the farmer sells and what he buys will have to be established, since farm input prices have also risen abnormally:

Of late, the CACP is said to be favouring higher procurement prices on the plea that the unit costs are increasing. But economists argue that such a move is not desirable. First, the supply response to price increase is not encouraging. Second, a higher procurement price is conferring benefits neither on the consumers nor on the producers but only on middlemen and traders. For instance, the consumer price is almost double the producer price. Large number of small farmers do not get the price fixed by the Government : they sell their produce immediately after the harvest at throwaway prices and traders take advantage of this.

It is argued that the procurement price adequately compensates the farmer for the rise in the fertiliser cost which is the single largest item of cost of production. The fixation of procurement price should be studied from the point of view of income distribution among different classes. A higher procurement price is not likely to benefit much the small and marginal farmers as they have little marketable surplus. The fertiliser cost is observed to be very high on small and marginal farmers. Thus, the fertiliser price hike would adversely affect them. And, with little marketable surplus, they cannot take advantage of a higher procurement price. Further, higher procurement prices lead to higher open market prices, adversely affecting vulnerable sections like the agricultural labourers.[7]

In view of the general inflationary situation, the prices of all farm inputs have increased in varying degrees. Hence, the average cost of production of almost all farm products has gone up considerably in the recent past. This trend could not be arrested in spite of major technological breakthroughs already achieved particularly in respect of wheat production. We have yet to evolve an appropriate technology leading to increased farm output, keep costs stable in the immediate future and bring them down gradually. This can be done through better resource use and much better management of farm organisations.

One of the important objectives of price policy is to eliminate the mischief played by the middlemen. The farmer has to be brought close to the purchasing agency mainly through the setting up of regulated markets and the strengthening of co-operatives. Price support policy becomes ineffective in the absence of an effective market structure. The cultivators are exploited not by the mechanism of lower prices fixed by the Government but by the machinations of the large traders. Therefore, efforts of the Government should be directed towards eliminating the grip of private traders.

The timing of announcement of support prices makes the objective of higher prices self-defeating. Coming as the decision to raise support prices does almost on the eve of the marketing season, it leaves no scope for farmers to interchange the cropping pattern. The Government should take an immediate decision on procurement prices for different agricultural commodities well before the commencement of a sowing season. In fact, the support prices were announced at the time of the sowing seasons in some years. It has subsequently become essential for the Government to follow a well-defined procedure regarding an important matter like the fixation of procurement prices. It is true that the producers of rice would still benefit from enhanced prices but the delayed announcement of the decision robs it of its broader significance for agricultural growth.[8]

There is a plea for linking the prices of agricultural produce with the prices of inputs. Though this is justifiable, one major difficulty is that in agriculture, a variety of inputs are used and indexation of input prices is difficult. Increase in input prices may not have any direct and immediate impact on farm produce. Price incentives alone cannot step up output of certain items like pulses which are in short supply. Technological breakthrough and institutional improvements are necessary. Moreover, the farmers buy so many commodities for household consumption. Trends in their prices are also important.[9] A higher procurement price is not desirable as it leads to concentration on cereals and neglect of pulses. Moreover, as the marketable surplus mainly comes from big farmers, a higher procurement price would further worsen income disparities in the fanning sector.[10] Further, fixation of procurement prices based on comprehensive costs and not on paid-out costs, would only benefit affluent farmers.

The CACP is generally against higher procurement prices because crucial inputs like fertilisers are subsidised. The stress should be on reducing unit cost of production through improved technological practices. Evolving an appropriate price policy would be of limited use unless all important crops are served by adequate inputs and other services. There should be crop discipline to avoid fluctuations in areas under different crops.[11]

The procurement prices ought to be related to the actual cost of production which is not easy to arrive at. Therefore, an expert committee was set up in January 1990 under the chairmanship of Prof. C.H. Hanumantha Rao to review, *inter alia*, the methodology for the estimation of cost of production of crops and adjustment of procurement/support prices before the arrival of the crop to the market with a view to improving remuneration for crop production and safeguarding the interests of the farmers.

The expert committee submitted its Interim Report on March 15, 1990 and the Final Report on March 31, 1990. After studying the recommendations of the Standing Advisory Committee, the Government revised the methodology for the estimation of cost of production of crops as follows:

(i) Valuation of labour at statutory minimum wage or actual wage rate whichever is higher;

(ii) Evaluation of managerial input as an element of cost at 10 per cent of the total cost and

(iii) Adjustment of procurement/minimum support price announced before the sowing season in case the increase in output turns out to be higher than the anticipated rise.

There has been steep rise in procurement prices in respect of certain cereals. For instance, the increase in minimum support price/procurement price inclusive of bonus in respect of wheat after 1989-90 has been rather steep. These increased from ₹ 183 in 1989-90 to ₹ 330 per quintal in 1993-94, an increase of ₹ 147 per quintal or 80 per cent over a period of four years, i.e., an average of 20 per cent per annum.

There were substantial increases in the procurement price of wheat in 1991-92 (22.2 per cent) and 1992-93 (20.0 per cent). For 1993-94, wheat crop was to be marketed in April 1994, Minimum Support Price (MSP) was raised by a modest 6.3 per cent to ₹ 350 per quintal as against ₹ 330 per quintal in 1992-93. For rice too, the MSP/procurement price hikes have been substantial in 1991-92 (12.2 per cent), 1992-93 (17.4 per cent) and 1993-94 (14.8 per cent). As a rule, revisions in MSP should be guided primarily by the recommendations of the CACP and revision of procurement prices should normally follow general inflationary trends *(Economic Survey 1993-94)*.

The Government is aware of the limited success of MSP regime. Hence, the price policy for rabi and kharif crops announced modest price increase in recent years as shown in Table 1.

Table: 1
Minimum Support prices for 2009-10 Crop Year
(₹ Per Quintal)

Commodity Kharif corps		Commodity Rabi crops	
Paddy (common)	950+ ₹ 50 per Quintal bonus	Wheat	1,100
Paddy (Gr. A)	980+ ₹ 50 per quintal bonus	Gram	1,760
Jowar (Malindi)	860	Masur(lentil)	1,870
Arhar(Tur)	2,300	Rapeseed/mustard,	1,830
Moong	2,760	Barley	750
Cotton (F-414/H-777/J34)	2,500	other crops	
Groundnut in shell	2,100	Sugarcane	129.84

Source: Economic Survey 2009-10. p. 189.

The Government has fixed the MSPs of 2009-10 Kharif and rabi crops. The MSPs for paddy (common) and paddy (Grade A) have been raised by ₹ 100 per quintal and fixed at ₹ 950 per quintal and ₹ 980 per quintal respectively. An incentive bonus of ₹ 50 per quintal is also payable over and above the MSP of paddy. The MSP of arhar (tur) had been raised over the 2008-09 level by ₹ 300 per quintal and fixed at ₹ 2,300 per quintal while that of moong has been raised by ₹ 240 per quintal and fixed at ₹ 2,760 per quintal.

The MSP of sesamun has been fixed at ₹ 2,850 per quintal, raising it by ₹ 100 per quintal. The MSPs of other kharif crops have been retained at their 2008-09 levels. The MSP of wheat had been raised to ₹ 1,100 per quintal from ₹ 1,080 per quintal and of barley to ₹ 750 per quintal from ₹ 680 per quintal. The MSPs of gram and safflower have been raised by ₹ 30 per quintal each. The MSPs of mesoor and rapeseed/mustard have been retained at their previous year's levels of ₹ 1,870 per quintal and ₹ 1,830 per quintal respectively (Economic Survey 2009-10.Pp. 188-189).

For the crop year 2005-06, the minimum support price/procurement price has been fixed at ₹ 570 per quintal for paddy (common) and ₹ 600 for Grade A. For wheat, it was ₹ 640. For coarse cereals (jowar, bajra and ragi), it was ₹ 525. For maize it was ₹ 540, for Arhar it was ₹ 1,400, and for moong it was ₹ 1520. For sesamum it was ₹ 1550, and for niger seed, it was ₹ 1200.

PUBLIC DISTRIBUTION SYSTEM

State trading in foodgrains is justified to protect the interests of the consumers by curbing hoarding and speculative activities of traders. It is also necessary to ensure reasonable price for the farmers. The state has, therefore, taken up the task of ensuring availability of the minimum requirements of food to the vulnerable sections at reasonable prices in times of scarcity, genuine or artificial. State intervention and operation for the purpose of solving the food problem has two aspects:

(i) The production aspect which refers to agricultural policy and administration; and

(ii) The distribution aspect which refers to food policy and administration.[13]

Since a policy 'decontrol' has only led to undesirable consequences, public procurement and public distribution along with several other control measures have become necessary. The Foodgrains Policy Committee (FPC) appointed in 1966 observed that national management of foodgrains was urgently called for. National management of food implies a national plan of supply and distribution of food. The means of implementing the plan are four fold:

(i) Procurement to ensure necessary supplies;

(ii) Control over inter-state movement to facilitate procurement and keep prices at reasonable level;

(iii) A system of public distribution to ensure equitable sharing and

(iv) The building up of buffer stock to provide against difficult years.[14]

Sharp fluctuations in agricultural production necessitate measures to gather buffer stocks "to even out year-to-year fluctuations in supplies and the consequent erratic movement." The FPC (1966) felt that in order to achieve the objective of inter-seasonability in supplies, the Government should have adequate buffer stock, at least four million tonnes, which could be released to increase availability during a really bad season. The Government decided to build up buffer stocks from 1967-68 onwards. Since then buffer stock operations have become an integral part of the national food policy.

The Government set up, in January 1965 the Food Corporation of India (FCI) for implementing the 'buffer stock' policy. The primary function of buffer stocks is to take up the responsibility of protecting producers' interests in a year of bumper crops. However, the problem is basically one of instability and uncertainty in prices rather than simply one of ensuring a minimum reasonable price.[15]

The number of fair price shops functioning in the country was about 1,60,000 at the end of 1971 and it increased to about 2,43,000 at the end of 1977. By the end of the Sixth Plan (1985), their number was around 3.5 lakh. As on March 31,1993, there were more than 4 lakh FPSs in the country: 3.13 lakh in rural areas and 96,000 in the urban areas. The country is now said to having a buffer stock of 23 million tonnes of foodgrains. A systematic and comprehensive procurement programme aimed at acquiring a substantial part (about half) of the marketed surplus at administered price was deemed.[16]

Under the Public Distribution System (PDS), selected essential commodities are distributed through fair price shops and co-operatives which operate under governmental control and direction. Of course, the free market mechanism is retained and allowed to operate. The Government maintains a buffer stock and replenishes the same through the system of procurement. Prices charged are no doubt lower than the market prices, but the PDS is to a great extent said to be urban-oriented.[17]

The revamped PDS came into being in 1992, subsequent to which the Government identified 1,700 blocks in desert areas, hill regions, drought prone areas and tribal belts for special focus thus expected to benefit about 16 crore people living in these identified areas. A decision has been taken to open 11,000 more fair price shops in these areas to cater to the needs of the people.

Delivery of commodities to the FPSs on an individual basis would be taken up by the state governments in the identified areas wherever feasible. Vigilance committees would be set up at the fair price shop level to reported cases, of FPSs using and issuing these cards.

Table 2

Central Foodgrains Stocks and Minimum Buffer Norms: Wheat and Rice (in lakh tonnes)

Beginning of the month	*Minimum buffer norms*	*Actual stock*
January 2004	168	244.14
January 2005	168	216.94
January 2006	200	188.29
January 2007	200	174.00
January 2008	200	191.87
January 2009	200	357.88
January 2010	200	474.45

Source: Economic Survey 2009-10. p.202.

Of course, the PDS suffers from certain deficiencies — the inadequate procurement and storage facilities, finance, administrative capability etc. The cost of operating the system is also very high. The subsidy to the PCI was only ₹ 650 crore in 1980-81, it rose to ₹ 3,000 crore in 1994-95 though during this period, foodgrains actually distributed went up only from 15 million tonnes to less than 17 million tonnes.

The FPSs and co-operatives suffer from certain weaknesses. The malpractices include issuing ratio against bogus cards, charging higher prices for controlled commodities, delay in lifting the stocks etc.

The procurement-cum-PDS policy has been criticised on some grounds. The major beneficiaries of the scheme are: (i) farmers accounting for bulk of marketable surplus, namely, large and medium farmers, (ii) urban areas particularly larger cities receiving the major part of distributed grains and (iii) the expanding bureaucracy in the procurement-cum-distribution operations.

The PDS has not been very effective which is clear from the fact that a large section of the poor are outside the purview of the system. Even those who come under the PDS have failed to get the benefits of issue prices. The PDS burden on the government is said to be rising.

The PDS needs to be targeted and to a great degree group-oriented. The non-poor should be completely excluded. It would be better if the PDS gets closely linked to the ongoing employment generation programmes. Also, better results would emerge if the fair price shops are operated and managed by the actual beneficiaries and supervised by specially recruited and trained officials.

The Eighth Plan is trying to reorient and reform the PDS by excluding the non-poor and making the procurement and distribution system more efficient and cost effective.

THE TERMS OF TRADE

Under its revised terms of reference, the CACP is required to keep in view changes in terms of trade between the agricultural and non-agricultural sectors so that neither industry nor agriculture suffers from a substantial fall in incomes. It is pointed out that prices of industrial products (1970-71 = 100) have risen much faster than the prices of agricultural products. Prices of industrial products went up from 100 to 231.9 and of agricultural products from 100 to only 193.5 in 1981.

A study conducted by economists of the Indian Agricultural Research Institute has revealed that the terms of trade in agriculture are not favourable and have been worsening in recent years. According to the study, the terms of trade remained favourable up to 1974-75, but from 1975-76, the rise in prices of inputs became faster than the rise in prices of agricultural products. During 1980-81 and 1981-82, the terms of trade worsened further. The report has suggested immediate steps to reverse the trend since agriculture accounts for 50 per cent of the gross domestic product.[18]

There are people who feel that there is wide disparity between the prices received and paid by farmers which in turn results in lesser savings and investments in agriculture. Factors contributing to depressed farm prices are:

(i) Distribution of foodgrains procured within the country, or purchased from abroad, at prices which are much lower than their economic cost, at considerable loss to the public exchequer;

(ii) Placing restrictions on the movement of foodgrains;

(iii) Reducing the stocking limit of private traders;

(iv) Denying credit at reasonable rates against stored foodgrains and

(v) Imposing levy on traders/millers.[19]

It appears that the prices of agricultural products have not risen in the case of manufactured products. The parity ratio between agricultural and manufactured products has been more favourable in the case of manufactured products in 10 out of 12 years since 1971-72. This means that farmers have had to pay higher prices for manufactured products than what they had received for their produce.

Among agricultural commodities also, the increase in prices has not been uniform. In order to study the increase in relative prices of rice, coarse grains and pulses, parity ratios have been worked out between individual products and the general agricultural price level. It has been pointed out that the parity ratio for rice remained above 100 till 1975-76, but declined thereafter, indicating thereby that the rise in the price of rice was lower than the increase in the general agricultural price level after 1975-76.

The parity ratio in the case of jowar remained over 100 in 7 out of 12 years and in the case of bajra, it was 4 out of 12 years. This means that the increase in prices of coarse grains has lagged behind the increase in the general agricultural price level. Their prices have also shown considerable fluctuations during 1971-72.

In the case of pulses, except in 1976-77, the parity ratio has remained above 100 throughout the period since 1971-72. It is interesting to note that despite relatively higher prices, pulse production has remained stagnant. This is largely due to the lack of availability of short duration high yielding varieties of seed. Dependence on traditional pulse varieties lowers yield and therefore gives a lower return compared to other competing crops. Therefore, there is no incentive for farmers to cultivate pulses.[20]

Had land been owned in an equitable manner, a revision in agricultural prices would have benefitted the peasantry in a uniform manner. But where not only the urban population, but the rural poor have had to buy foodgrains; any rise in agricultural prices, particularly those of foodgrains will prove economically non-feasible then. More than half of the rural population (55 per cent) having holdings of one hectare or less have to buy foodgrains and another 20 per cent in the size category of 1 to 2 hectares cannot be said to have any surplus as such. Thus, three-fourths of the rural population has very little to gain by rise in the agricultural prices.[21]

In view of the rise in the procurement price of wheat, incentives have been offered to produce more wheat. But, consumption of wheat is lagging behind production and there is little possibility to export, as wheat is outpriced in international markets. It is therefore, desirable to encourage a partial shift away from wheat to other crops which are in short supply. A strong case can thus be advanced for altering the structure of relative prices in agriculture.

An increased foodgrains output is likely to bring down prices, as the elasticity of demand for foodgrains is low (given the level of per capita income). The ratio of index of industrial price to agricultural prices is on the increase. However, it is undesirable to raise procurement prices on the plea that industrial prices are high. A right step suggested is to stabilise industrial prices through various measures.

The Terms of Trade are important as they affect the flow of resources to various sectors of the economy. More generally in a developing agrarian economy, the terms tend to be unfavourable for the agricultural sector. It is suggested that these terms favouring the industrial sector is the right way in the initial stages of development when huge capital investment is required for the development of the agricultural sector.

It is said that the administered prices have caused unfavourable terms of trade for agriculture by keeping prices artificially low. This in turn reduces the incentive to invest. The terms of trade for agriculture stood at 82.9 in 1981-82, 82.4 in 1985-86, 88.2 in 1990-91 and 89.0 in 1991-92. Although they have shown some improvement recently, they remain to a great extent unfavourable.

The Tenth Report of the Lok Sabha's Committee on Agriculture (1993-94) has observed, *"An extraordinary alarming situation is being faced currently by Indian agriculture as there has been a steep fall in the prices of almost all commodities produced by the agricultural sector on one hand and a simultaneous sharp shooting up in prices of non-agricultural goods purchased by the farm sector on the other."* This means that the terms of trade have failed to benefit the agricultural sector.

The Chokka Rao Report reviewing India's agricultural sector observed that the index prices paid out by the farm sector shot up from 100.5% in 1970-71 to 567.3% in 1991-92. During this period, the price index for the agricultural commodities sold increased from 100.5 to 516.3%. There is need to redress this imbalance.

The Report also observed that though the farming sector is crippled due to depressed prices, the consumers have not gained. In fact, they had to pay exhorbitant prices mainly because the retail prices have behaved disproprotionately.

The Chokka Rao report, in view of the recent deterioration in the inter-sectoral terms of trade for agriculture, pleaded for removal of movement restrictions on foodgrains. Some criticised the suggestion saying that the report has been voicing the interests of the surplus farmers, often called the *farm lobby*.

Economists say that terms of trade moved against agriculture between the mid-1970s and the mid-1980s, with a record low registered in 1985-86. There was a modest improvement in the late 1980s, but the terms continue to be unfavourable for agriculture. In particular, the prices of farm inputs rose sharply and attached the agricultural surplus substantially.

The index of prices paid out by the farm sector shot up from 100.5% in 1970-71 to 567.3 in 1991-92. The price index for agricultural commodities sold increased from 100.5% in 1970-71 to 516.3% in 1991-92.

This cannot be an argument for rise in procurement prices, argued Prof. G.S. Bhalla. Any improvement in productivity is bound to entail a decline in prices. What is important is the link between productivity and the income terms of trade. The farmer is more concerned about the return on his investment, he having ploughed in the fields and which led to income generation from his marketable surplus.[22]

Of course, the government policy has been partly responsible for raising the level of farm prices in relation to the prices of the industrial goods.

If the terms of trade turn unfavourable for the farming sector, the expected long-term consequences are: (i) the rich farmers may diversify their cultivation from traditional foodgrain cultivation to more remunerative areas like cash crops and exports and (ii) farmers with smaller holdings will continue to be at the mercy of depressed end-product prices and soaring input costs.[23]

The relative movement of the price index of agricultural and manufactured products shows a mixed trend. The ratio of the index of manufactured products when expressed as per cent of index of agricultural products, fluctuated between 85.5% (August, 1992) and 91.2% (March 1993). It remained unchanged till April 1993 and rose marginally to 91.3% in May 1993. Since then, it has fallen to reach 88.5% in December 1993 (provisional).[24]

A study made by Thamarajakshi has mentioned that there have been three phases in the long-term trend in the net barter terms of trade. These remained relatively stable during 1951-52 to 1960-61 along with the highest growth rates both in the agricultural and industrial sectors; subsequently during 1960-61 to 1973-74, the terms of trade showed an impressive improvement in favour of agriculture after which these considerably deteriorated between 1973-74 and 1983-84.

The terms of trade moving against agriculture for long may not be desirable, and favourable terms of trade for agriculture are needed as the majority of the workforce depends on agriculture. There is also need for stepping up real income with agriculturists year after year in comparison to those in the industrial sector. After all, higher income with the farming population would mean larger demand for industrial goods also. There is also the need for stepping up investments in the farming sector.

At the suggestion of the C.H. Hanumantha Rao Committee, the Government set up a 13-member task force under the chairmanship of A.S. Kahlon, to study the entire gamut of terms of trade between agriculture and other sectors. The panel had to examine the composition of inputs structure and output mix in the farm sector with a view to assigning appropriate weight to each of the items/commodities purchased and sold by the farmers.

The Kahlon Panel had to subsequently prepare appropriate index numbers of terms of trade reflecting parity between prices received and prices paid by the farmers for both domestic and farm expenses, identify items purchased by the farmers and the output-mix sold by them and assign appropriate weights to each item.

SOME POLICY ISSUES

The foodgrain sector is the most important one, both in terms of total output and employment generated. Inflationary pressures normally emanate from this sector. A significant percentage of the family budget in respect of the poor is devoted to the consumption of foodgrain. Higher foodgrain prices often lead to higher industrial wages which in turn lead to higher production costs in the industrial sector. Thus, a hike in foodgrain prices raises the cost of the living index.

In recent years, foodgrain prices have recorded an increase which is much more than that recorded by the procurement prices. This increase has been attributed to the fact that traders engaged in the foodgrain business may be finding an excuse in higher procurement prices for fixing prices at which they sell their products, particularly in the open market. Consequently, the price of foodgrains rises more than what is warranted by the rise in procurement prices.[25]

There must be some parity between prices received and the prices paid by the farmers, but the agricultural price policy is having only a limited role in this regard. Experience has shown that the interests of farmers, consistent with social goals, are served more by improved technology resulting in higher yields than by increased prices.[26] A.S. Kahlon therefore observed that a solution *"has to be largely found outside the purview of the price policy via such measures as greater public investment in rural development, discrimination in the supply of inputs, credit, essential consumer goods and social services in favour of rural areas and all farmers, rural work projects and provision of strong market infrastructure*." Dantwala has rightly suggested that increase in productivity is more rewarding than the increase in farm price in augmenting farmer's income.[27] Of course, price support policy and technological development should go together.

What is often missed is that farmers need to be compensated not only for higher prices of inputs, but also for higher cost of living.[28]

Economists are not in favour of the steep rise in procurement prices for various reasons. First, the buffer stocks at present are estimated to be 23 million tonnes. Besides, carrying costs are proving a prohibitive drain on budgetary provisions for food subsidy. Second, the domestic foodgrain prices are too high to promote export competitiveness in these commodities. Lastly, the country is not able to contain inflationary trends. Any increase in food prices is bound to push up the general price index. Since 1990, the procurement price of wheat has been increased by over 50 per cent. The state governments too should therefore appreciate the moderation in hiking procurement prices.

The agricultural price policy suffers from certain shortcomings. The official procurement covers only a small percentage of the farmers. Thus, even if the price policy intends to confer benefits on the farming community, it may not succeed. Yet, the Government is made to bear the cost of a huge food subsidy. Also, when prices do not move in tune with costs, farmers are discouraged from producing maximum level of agricultural output.

A continual increase in procurement prices may not be in the long-term interests of the agricultural sector itself. Price increases which over-compensate cost increases may discourage investment in the farming sector and undermine the objective of raising farm productivity. The rich farmers may not be interested in improvement in productivity when the softer option to step up profits (through higher procurement prices) is available. Obviously, the price factor as a policy instrument needs to be employed judiciously.

The heavy subsidisation of food and fertiliser appears to be unsound. The Economic Survey 1992-93 has pertinently pointed out : *"Depressing administered prices artificially by subsidisation from the exchequer only alters the source of price rise; it does not remedy the malady of price rise. Subsidies reduce the incentives to producers to compete and reduce costs. In fact, when accompanied by retention pricing, subsidies reward the least efficient producers at the expense of the efficient ones."*

The IIM study by Prof. S. Raghunath and Prof. D. Ashok found that the farmer's share of the produce price *vis-a-vis* the end consumer price was dented badly by a battalion of middlemen. High cumulative wastage across the supply chain (24 per cent for potato to 40 per cent for tomato) played a key role in determining the farmer's price for his produce. Add to that, the poor infrastructure and poor strategies to check post harvest loss and the woes increase. The study points out that merely focusing on more credit access to farmers cannot change the picture greatly (*The Economic Times*, March 28, 2006).

It is suggested that the price policy has to protect only the efficient producers so that a climate is created for raising productivity in the agricultural sector. Non-viable farmers have to be helped by measures other than price policy. Also, protection has to be given only to prevent losses being made by the efficient producers, and not to unnecessarily boost their profits.

REFERENCES

1. G.S Kainath: 'Recent Trends in Sectoral Terms of Trade', *Productivity*, October-December 1981, p. 8.
2. T.P. Dhirawat: 'Agricultural Price Policy', *Yojana*, October 31, 1971. p. 19.
3. G.S. Gupta: 'Agricultural Price Policy and Farm Incomes', *Economic and Political Weekly*, September 27, 1980, p. A-123.
4. *Report of the Agricultural Price Commission on Price Policy Cereals for 1965-66, Season*, p. 1.
5. Kamta Prasad: 'Support Prices for Farmers', *Kurukshetra*, April 16, 1977.
6. *The Economic Times* (Editorial), October 8, 1985.
7. Tara Nair : 'Procurement Price Hike Likely to Widen Farm Income Disparities', *Financial Express*, September 12, 1980.
8. *Commerce* (editorial), October 19, 1985.
9. A.S. Kahlon and M.V. George: 'Farm Produce Input Prices Link Up', *Financial Express*, April 24, 1981.
10. G.S. Gupta: 'Price Policy and the Small Farmer', *Commerce*, March 14, 1981.
11. N.P. Nawani: 'Price Policy for What, Current Scenario', *Yojana*, June 30, 1994, p. 7.
12. V.M. Rao: 'The Wheat Story: Recent Changes in Price Policy', *Economic and Political Weekly*, October 30, 1993, p. 2386.
13. P.M. Bora: 'Food Distribution: Rationale of State Intervention', *Mainstream*, March 22, 1980, p. 24.
14. *Report of the Foodgrains Policy Committee 1966*, Government of India, Ministry of Food and Agriculture, New Delhi, p. 3.
15. M.V. Nadkarni: 'Farm Prices: A Rational Approach', *Mainstream*, May 8, 1982, p. 18.
16. Rajbans Kaur: *Agricultural Price Policy in Economic Development*, Kalyani Publishers, New Delhi, p. 103.
17. Jos E. Mooij: 'Public Distribution System: Safety Net: Who is Saved?', *Economic and Political Weekly*, January 15, 1994.
18. *The Hindu*, February 7, 1984.
19. Bhanu Pratap Singh: Farm Economy Mismanaged', *The Hindu*, February 25, 1986.
20. *State Bank of India Monthly Review*, September 1985.
21. Kripa Shankar: 'Should Agricultural Prices be Raised', *Mainstream*, March 3, 1984, p. 27.
22. Sabyasachi Mitra: 'Agricultural Prices: Fluctuating Fortunes', *The Economic Times*, April 19, 1993.
23. Sunil Batra: 'Agricultural Price Policy: Need for Rethinking', *Social Action*, April-June 1994, p. 80.
24. *Economic Survey* 1993-94.

25. Keya Sengupta: 'Procurement Prices and Inflation', *Yojana*, October 15, 1991, p. 11.

26. Kamta Prasad: 'Foodgrains Policy 1966-76 in Cham D. Wadhva (Ed. 1978): *Some Problems of India's Economic Policy*, Tata McGraw Hill Publishing Co. Ltd., New Delhi, p. 487.

27. M.L. Dantwala: 'Incentives and Disincentives in Indian Agriculture', *Indian Journal of Agricultural Economics*, April-June 1967.

28. Bhanu Pratap Singh: 'Support Prices: Myth and Reality', *The Hindu*, October 10, 1991.

Chapter

18 Forest Resources of India

Economic growth is no doubt important, but equally important is retaining ecological balance. What is required is a satisfactory rate of growth without causing serious damage to the immediate ecology. The proper management of forest resources thus assumes special significance as forests, besides ensuring ecological balance, confer innumerable benefits on the community, particularly the poor.

Importance of Forestry

Forests play an important role in maintaining ecological balance, in the conservation of natural resources and in providing livelihood to vulnerable sections like tribals. Forests cushion the rain and storm, discipline the rivers and control the floods. They are rightly described as the natural defenders of dust storms. They prevent soil erosion and contribute substantially to environmental conservation.

Forests are one of the most important renewable natural resources of the country. They have multifarious uses and as such are considered to be of immense help to human beings. They moderate the climate, maintain the soil mantle and regulate water supplies. By their photosynthetic activity, the plants take in carbon-dioxide from the atmosphere and release oxygen, thus purifying the air and also have the potential to convert solar energy, into various forms of energy such as fuel, food, oil and oil products which can be directly used by human beings. Forests offer protection to soil against erosion by wind and water.

Forests meet the recreational needs of human beings. They are capable of absorbing noise, and thus help in noise abatement. They certainly provide relief from the unpleasantness caused by unplanned urbanisation. Forests also act as homes for rich and varied wildlife and promote the aesthetic beauty of the nation. The conservation of wildlife and their habitat largely depend on the growth of forestry. Forests are useful even from the defence point of view.

Forests provide raw materials for a number of industries such as paper and pulp, fibre board, chip board, silk worm rearing, lac, toy making, saw mills, match, plywood, stationery, agricultural implements, playing equipments and so on. They also provide major and minor forest products such as timber, round-wood, pulp-wood, charcoal, bamboos, canes, drugs, spices, edible fruits and vegetables, non-edible oils, fibres and flosses, gums, resins, sandalwood, bidi leaves, fodder and grazing grass. Also, the rural poor depend on forests for their firewood and building their huts.

In the tropics, protection of the forestry serves five closely related purposes: (i) soil stabilisation, (ii) prevention of erosion, (iii) watershed management, (iv) provision of shelter and shade and (v) reclamation of sites and arresting desertification.

The crowns of trees, which together form the forest canopy, act as a barrier between falling rain and the soil surface. This confers three benefits. First, the force of rain is spent on the tree tops which absorb most of the kinetic energy of the rain drop. Second, the water from rain falling on the crown takes longer to reach the ground as it trickles down the branches and the trunk and drips off the leaves. Third, the total quantity of water reaching the ground is reduced because some moisture evaporates from leaf surfaces. These effects greatly moderate rainfall intensity at the ground surface and virtually eliminates raindrop erosion.[1]

It needs to be noted that forestry is a highly labour intensive primary activity. Not only will forestry provide employment, but by raising fuel and fodder supply, it will enhance the productivity of land and livestock.[2]

When forward and backward linkages are fully taken into account, the contribution of the forestry sector to India's GNP is around 10 per cent. For every person directly employed in forestry, four people are employed externally as a result of forward linkages.[3]

DECLINE OF FORESTS

The 1952 National Forest Policy Resolution of the Government had recommended that the country should have one-third of the total land area under forests. But only about 23 per cent of the total land area is under forests and not more than 40 to 50 per cent of this has good forest cover. In 1900, forests covered 40 per cent of the land area. Today, the cover is less than 13 per cent. It has been estimated by the Ministry of Environment that since independence, nearly 4.3 million hectares of forest land have been lost due to developmental activities like river valley projects, setting up of industries, construction of roads etc. According to the satellite survey, the per capita forest area is only 0.1 hectare in India against the world average of 1.1 hectare.

There has been indiscriminate felling of trees because of demographic and commercial pressures. Of the 75 million hectares classed as forest land, as much as about 20 million hectares are affected by soil erosion. The 'permanent pastures' also suffer from over grazing encroachments.

No less than 3.4 million hectares of forest land were deforested during 1951-52 to 1972-73. Fifty per cent of the 3.4 million hectares involved was deforested in 17 years, 1951-52 to 1968-69 and the rest in just four years, 1968-69 to 1972-73.

This means deforestation is taking place at an accelerated rate. By 1975-76, it was estimated that 4.14 million hectares of forest areas were deforested. It may also be noted that if the forest cover is thinned by 40 to 50 per cent, its power to protect soil and water may well be lost. Another disturbing trend is that while the plantation of commercially profitable trees is on the increase, natural forests are neglected though they are responsible for the maintenance of ecological balance.

As a result of low productivity of forests in India, the contribution of forestry to GNP is said to be as low as 1 per cent in spite of its inherently larger potential. India is likely to face a grave situation, if the conservatively estimated toll of deforestation of 1.5 million hectares a year is not checked. Out of about 75 million hectares of land, over 40 million hectares have been deprived of natural forest cover.

In 1954, the Government of India had set up a target that the land under forest should at least be 25 per cent of the total land area. In 1983, this percentage was only 10, and the forest trees are being cut down at the rate of 1 per cent every year. If this rate of deforestation continues, in other 10 years, we have destroyed all our jungle wealth and a serious situation may arise when we may have food but not the firewood to cook the same. Deforestation in the country has been carried out to such an extent during the three decades (1955-85) we have destroyed forest wealth worth ₹ 600,000 crore.[4]

The demand for fuelwood has grown faster than its supply through forests. The Report of the Fuelwood Study Committee (Planning Commission) 1982, has estimated that in order to meet the demand for fuelwood, it would be necessary to raise fuelwood plantations at the rate of 1.5 million hectares manually and to distribute 800 million seedlings per year to the public. The Centrally Sponsored Scheme of Social Forestry, including Rural Fuelwood plantations, is at present in operation in all fuelwood deficit areas.

The per capita availability of forest area is 0.14 hectares as against the world average of 1.6 hectares. Even though the forest area is 50 per cent of that under agriculture, the contribution of forestry to gross national product is neglible, being a mere 1.6 per cent in 1969-70 as against that of the farming sector which was 47 per cent.[5] Though 75 million hectares are under forests, only about 45.6 million hectares are serving as sources of fuel supply and another 14.8 million hectares are considered as potentially productive.[6]

The fuelwood production should be integrated with the cultivation of food crops, cooking one kg. of food requires 1.2 kg. of fuelwood. Thus, self-sufficiency in fuelwood can come, if its production exceeds that of food in the country. Secondly, attention should be paid to 14.68 per cent of land area which is neither suitable for forestry practices nor for cultivation. The total availability of fuelwood at present can be assumed to be 49 million tonnes, against the requirement of 133 million tonnes (this excludes the use of cow dung and vegetable wastes). Possibly a new cropping pattern, combining the twin objectives of producing foodgrains and fuelwood can be evolved.[7]

A colossal investment of nearly ₹ 5,000 million annually will be required with a proper institutional and organisational support if the task of adequate fuelwood production is to be achieved successfully. Some states view forests as revenue yielding only and this results in over-exploitation of forest resources.

In parts of Northern and Western India like Pubjab, Haryana, Rajasthan and Gujarat, the forest cover forms less than 10 per cent of the land area. However, in Andaman & Nicobar Islands, Sikkim, Manipur, Arunachal Pradesh and Tripura, this percentage is about 50. Also, one million hectares are available along railway tracks which can be used for growing trees.

The forest region, intersperesed all over the country consists of evergreen forests, deciduous forests, dry forests, alpine forests and riperian forests and tidal forests. Measures so far undertaken to rehabilitate the degraded forest areas have met with limited success. Past experience shows that the Forest Policy sought to protect forest wealth from forest dwellers, not from the unscrupulous contractors.[8]

The rate of soil erosion has gone upto 12,000 million tonnes a year. During the period 1971 to 1980, the flood-prone area doubled to 40 million hectares and the drought-prone area to 59 million hectares.[9]

In 1982, the Planning Commission estimated that the fuelwood demand would be 133 million tonnes against the availability of 39 million tonnes, leaving a shortage of 94 million tonnes. As a result of the growth of population, by 2000 AD, the fuelwood demand may go up to 230 million tonnes.

Even when estimates of the loss caused by the damage done to ecology is made, the loss caused to forest dwellers is not taken into account. Also, in the afforestation programme, top priority is given to quick-growing species which can be used as raw-material for forest based industries.[10] Even in respect of afforestation programmes, the interests of industry and revenue seem to predominate.[11]

An independent evaluation of Rural Fuelwood Plantation (REP) scheme was carried out by the National Council for Applied Economic Research (NCAER) at the behest of National Wastelands Development Board (NWDB). The study has revealed certain deficiencies in the scheme, namely, low survival of plantation (between 40 to 50 per cent) and poor health of the surviving plants; inadequate consolidation of effort and discontinuity; poor maintenance and after care of plantations, predominance of non-fuel species in most states, ambitious targets and bad advance planning, leading to poor choice of planting material and lack of people's involvement.[12]

It is said that in the implementation of the forest policy, the national interest remained confined to augmenting revenue earnings from the forests.[13]

Social Forestry

Social forestry includes farm forestry, extension forestry and recreational forestry. Forestry practices for the benefit of the society is social forestry. Farm forestry is a practice of forestry on the farmer's land in conjunction with other farming operations. The areas for social forestry are the village wastelands, canal banks, road's avenues, foreshores of tanks etc. and under farm forests, we can tap the field bunds and also the dry land extent. It is well to remember that the financial return from forestry are also attractive. It is estimated that fuel wood alone could yield an income of ₹ 7,000 per year (₹ 10,000 to ₹ 12,000) per hectare.[14]

Social forestry is a new concept of forest creation, management and judicious utilisation of goods and services generated therefrom. It aims at combining idle land, labour and water resources to optimise production of farm manure, firewood, fodder, food, small constructional timber and to stabilise soil. In a way, social forestry is the product of integration of agriculture, forestry and animal husbandry aiming at self-sufficiency, economic growth and community development.

Unlike other developmental programmes, the social forestry programme is unique in character since it simultaneously cuts diverse aspects of rural communities: their ecology, environment, climate, agriculture, livestock rearing, power structure, political participation, status of women and so on.[15]

We should not argue against commercialisation of forests. In fact, commercialisation of forests and rational, environmentally sound and economic management of forests can be made consistent with each other. Commercialisation, properly handled, can be a progressive force, increasing the productivity of resources and income of all people concerned.[16]

The afforestation programme, particularly the social forestry programme, made rapid progress from 1982-83 onwards when afforestation was included in the new 20-point Programme. The survival rate of seedling has been quite encouraging. There is, however, scope for improvement in the qualitative content of the programme, especially in terms of choice of suitable species, involvement of local people and meaningful sharing of forest wealth.

Evaluation studies have revealed serious lapses in the implementation of the social forestry programme. Only big farmers are able to pick up the saplings. Eucalyptus is not being used as fuelwood, but it is used for commercial purposes. By and large, the programme has ignored the needs of the local people.

FOREST POLICY AND DRAFT FOREST BILL, 1994

A Forest Policy for India was announced in 1894, which recognised, among other things, that *"forests situated on hill slopes should be maintained as protection forests to preserve the climatic and physical condition of the country and to protect the cultivated plains below them from the devastating action of hill torrents."* Soon after independence, the Government enunciated a new Forest Policy which was issued as a Resolution in 1952.

Table: 1
Progress of Afforestation Through Successive Plan Periods

Five Year Plan Period	Area Afforested in Plan Period (lakh ha)	Cumulative (lakh ha)
First	0.52	0.52
Second	3.11	3.63
Third	5.83	9.46
1966-69	4.53	13.99
Fourth	7.14	21.13
Fifth	12.21	33.34
1979-80	2.22	35.56
Sixth	46.50	82.06
Seventh	88.70	170.76
1990-91	7.01	177.77

Source: Developing Wastelands, Ministry of Environment and Forests.

The essential features of the new policy emphasised:

(i) That a system of balanced and complementary land use is evolved under which each type of land is used according to its land use capability so that it could produce more and deteriorate less of the forest wealth.

(ii) That it satisfied the need for checking:

(a) Denudation on mountainous regions on which depends the perennial water supply of the river systems whose basins constitute the fertile core of the country;

(b) The erosion progressing space along the treeless banks of the great rivers (leading to ravine formations and vast stretches of undulating waste land depriving the adjoining fields of their fertility) and

(c) The invasion of sea sands on coastal tracts, and the shifting of sand dunes (more particularly in the Rajasthan desert);

(iii) That the tree lands should be established wherever possible for improving the general well-being of the people;

(iv) That progressively increasing supplies of fodder (for grazing), timber (for agricultural implements) and firewood (for releasing the cowdung for use as manure) should be ensured to the cultivator;

(v) That the forests should be maintained on the principle of progressively increasing and eventually the highest sustained yield to meet the requirements of defence, communication and industry;

(vi) That the maximum annual revenue should be realised (in perpetuity) to fulfil the above- mentioned needs.

The Forest policy laid stress on:

(i) Weaning the primitive people, by persuasion of the baneful practice of shifting cultivation;

(ii) Increasing the efficiency of forest administration having adequate forest laws;

(iii) Providing adequate facilities for the management of forest and for conducting research in forestry and forest product utilisation;

(iv) Controlling grazing in the forests and

(v) The needs for promoting the welfare of the people.

The National Forest Policy was presented in 1988. The salient feature of the policy are: (i) environmental stability, (ii) conservation, (iii) meeting the basic needs of the people and (iv) maintaining the intrinsic relationships between the forest and the tribals and the rural people.

The policy has stated that priority would be given to the protection of the existing forest cover and improving its productivity. Also, the need for expanding the forest cover was emphasised. The biological diversity will have to be preserved at the earliest. People need to be involved in all these tasks.

The policy declares that "forest conservation and ecological balance have to be ensured while at the same time meeting the essential requirements of the people. The policy, however, acknowledges (sub-section 4.6) that one of the major causes of degradation of our forest wealth is illegal felling of trees by contractors."

The Union Ministry of Environment and Forests has been drafting a new law on the forests to replace the Indian Forest Act, 1927. The Bill will lay stress on conservation and ensure people's participation substantially. The Draft Bill, however, has decided not to mention the Joint Forest Management (JFM) Scheme being implemented by West Bengal. The Bill gives priority to reserved forests in which the people do not have rights over any produce. The powers of the forest officials have been enhanced in the Bill. Penalties for offences have been increased substantially. These provisions are likely to be misused.[17]

The Government has urged NGOs to prepare a comprehensive Bill, forwarding the concept of forests as community assets. The alternative forest bill, submitted by the NGOs on October 24, 1994, called for the local communities having full control over all public lands and waters and managing them in conjunction with the private lands and waters of the localities.

The basic management unit should be a single compact village rather than larger cluster of villages with 10,000 or more people as the case with Panchayat Raj institutions. The key institution in the alternative forest bill is the Village Natural Resources Management Committee (VNRMC) which is accountable to the Gramsabha. The VNRMCs would come together to constitute higher level natural resource management committees at the panchayat, taluk, district, state and national levels. It is proposed that the membership at higher levels must derive from membership at the lower levels so that people close to earth will have a say in environmental issues which concern them.[18]

JOINT FOREST MANAGEMENT

In 1990, the Government of India adopted a resolution on Joint Forest Management (JFM) with a view to enabling the people and the forest department to work together for protection as well as regeneration of forest resources. The JFM provides for community protection of forests by assigning to the villagers a forest guard and a regular watchman in addition to the special watch being kept by each member by rotation to protect the regenerating areas from theft, illicit cutting, fire and encroachment.[19] However, JFM can succeed only when local people's effective participation is ensured through education, awareness building, motivation and persuasion. A positive attitude on the part of forest officials is also important.

The West Bengal government has developed a model for the success of the social forestry programme. The village protection committees held the responsibility for the protection of reserved forests. The forest department shares the forest produce with the villagers and permits them to collect fuelwood and fodder at a nominal fee. The programme yielded good results thanks to the extensive motivation campaign taken up jointly by the officials and local panchayat raj institutions. Women were involved in a big way in the programme.

As joint forest management represents a new style of interaction between communities and forest departments, it is important that both the parties receive some orientation to the objectives and operation of the forestry programme.[20]

There is also a need to increase the powers of JFMs and to empower people by introducing changes in other spheres — land tenure laws, resource control policies etc., on the one hand, and clearly define their relationship to the existing panchayats and other formal organisations in one area or the other.[21]

By January 1,2000, in all the 25 states, 44,943 JFM committees have been formed. The area under the committees was 11,629,539 hectares.

The JFM requires, an effective monitoring and evaluation mechanism to study: (i) the relationship between forest department and people; (ii) people's participation in the programme; (iii) village committee's ability to get rid of encroachment on forest land; (iv) control of smuggling of forest products; (v) improvement in regeneration and development of forest lands; and (vi) extent of additional employment generation.

MEASURES NEEDED

Some states have established Forest Development Corporations in order to expand and spee ' up afforestation programmes by utilising institutional finance. The area under plantations of quick growing forest trees has increased substantially to cover about 14.8 lakh hectares by 1979-80. As a result of amendment to the Constitution in 1976, forests and the protection of wild animals and birds are brought under the Concurrent List of the Constitution. A need for a national forest resources survey for providing continuous and reliable information on the existing and potential forest resources was emphasised. An Institute of Forests Management has come into being, which worked for about 1½ years in collaboration with the Institute of Management, Ahmedabad.

It is possible to step up productivity of man-made forests by a closer spacing of plants and through irrigation and fertilisation. The returns in this case have been quite attractive. The central subsidy during 1977-78 has been raised considerably to enable the states to implement the programmes of plantation activity on a much larger scale than before. However, the outlays provided by states for the forestry programme declined to ₹ 5.61 crores during 1979-80 from ₹ 11.99 crores in 1978-79 when it was transferred to them.

For the scientific management of forests, the National Commission on Agriculture and the Central Board of Forestry have recommended the abolition of contractors and favoured departmental working. In some states, the entire work of forests is done by forest labourers' co-operatives. There is also need for some institutional changes in education, training and motivation of the rural masses, research and administration.

The National Commission on Agriculture has suggested that:

(i) Forests must have an adequate share of land and deforestation should not be permitted without the approval of the state government;

(ii) All forests, under the management of other departments of the Government, should be transferred forthwith to the Forest Department;

(iii) Private forests should also be regulated and controlled;

(iv) Bearing in mind the future demand on the forests, all forest lands should be functionally classified into protection forests; production forests and social forests. Protective influence of the forests, specially on hill slopes, watershed of rivers, sea forests and other localities, vulnerable to erosion and degradation should be developed by suitably managing existing forests and providing for their rehabilitation and improvement. Production forests must be managed to meet the needs of the existing and projected industries and for well established uses. Growing of plantation crops in suitable localities on forest lands should be undertaken. The social function of forests should meet these needs of the community of agricultural timber and fuelwood; grazing and grass and recreation;

(v) Steps should be taken to provide employment to local people, specially the socially backward and unemployed and underemployed agricultural labour.

(vi) The National Forest Policy should be revised to take into account the above-mentioned and also other related needs, like controlled grazing, regulation of shifting cultivation, welfare of tribals, protection of wild life and plants, forest research and education, extension and publicity, legislation on forestry and strengthening of forest administration at all levels.[22]

All-India co-ordinated research projects in bamboo, neem and leguminous trees and shrubs have been carefully envisaged in the Sixth Plan to cover:

(i) Survey and exploration of major areas where neem and leguminous trees occur;

(ii) Selection of suitable eco-types and assembling the variation in germ plasm bank;

(iii) Studies on vegetative propagation techniques;

(iv) Breeding and improvement work, provenance and progeny trials and

(v) Cytological and chemical studies. The agricultural Universities too, are taking interest in certain aspects of forestry research. It is necessary to involve people of every block in the development of forests through proper publicity. The school children should be actively involved in 'Tree for Every Child Programme.'

A pre-investment survey of Forest Resources was created in 1965. The Forest Survey of India was created on June 1, 1981 on the recommendations of the National Commission on Agriculture. The Forest Survey of India has been working on such activities as forest inventory and reinventory, photo interpretation and mapping, data processing and training, consultancy and some special studies. An area of 28.8 million hectares had been surveyed by this survey of forest resources between 1965 and 1981, while 13.15 million hectares were surveyed after the establishment of the Forest Survey of India between 1981 and 1985.[23]

During the Sixth Plan (1980-85) period, the Forest (Conservation) Act, 1980 was enacted with the main objective of checking the diversion of forest land for non-forestry purposes. The rate of diversion has been brought down to about 4,600 hectares per year, as against 0.15 million hectares during the period 1951-52 to 1979-80.

The Forest Bill of 1980 has been criticised on the ground that it gave importance to the bureaucrats and the police and not to the forest dwelling communities. This is likely to increase the already large-scale corruption and malpractices associated with forest management, much to the disadvantage of the rural people. It may be noted that it is the ultimate requirement of forest based industries, rather than the limited needs of villagers, that are responsible for the substantial and rapid loss of forests.[24]

The National Commission on Agriculture was convinced that if forest programmes are based on *"the needs and interests of the people and with the active involvement of the people at the planning and operational levels, the people would accept the programmes irrespective of their illiteracy or other difficulties."* There is need for an association that brings together all those interested or involved in forests or forest-related activity; tribals and other forest dwellers, foresters, administrators and planners, ecologists; academics, wildlife lovers, persons associated with forest based industries, activities and voluntary agencies working in forest areas or among forest people.[25]

Forestry has acquired a multi-disciplinary dimension. Therefore, the Indian Institute of Forest Management was established in March 1981 at Bhopal. This Institute was concerned with a wide range of activities covering research, development of teaching materials, executive development programmes and consultancy/management needs in terms of community social forestry and farm forestry programmes.

With a view to harvesting the forest produce on better scientific management patterns, it was recommended in the Sixth Plan that the contractor agency should be eliminated in all the states. Action has accordingly been taken by 13 states.

To support the massive social forestry programme, adequate research input was needed in respect of fuelwood, biomass, fodder-trees, agro-forestry and genetic engineering.

A programme like social forestry cannot be successful without people's participation. There is need for evolving a viable, effective and operational model for this. People should be actively involved in formulating and implementing the schemes based on local needs, potential and availability of inputs. This would also result in the reduction of unit cost of afforestation. The Seventh Plan observed: "The association of people in the implementation of afforestation programmes would further result in the creation of awareness, exchange of views, especially on the impact of forestry programmes and better appreciation of the realities in the field."[26]

The local population residing near forest areas will continue to depend on the forest for many of their basic requirements. The pressure on forests would be regulated by making them partners in forest management. This would also ensure their full co-operation in the rational management of forests.[27]

Over one million hectares have been brought under afforestation during 1991-92. About 140 crore seedlings were distributed for this purpose. An outlay of ₹ 26 crore was earmarked to the reconstituted NWDB during 1992-93. The NWDB is now placed under the newly created Department of Wasteland Development in the Ministry of Rural Development in July 1992.

Unfortunately, there has been little evidence of political commitment to strengthening community forestry. Without such a commitment, even schemes which are good on paper will fail to deliver the goods.[28] Forestry schemes should be viewed as people's programmes as such schemes confer benefits on the entire community.

Also, forest management requires a new decentralised, people-oriented and environment-friendly set up.

REFERENCES

1. K.N. Gopikrishnan: 'Protective Role of Social Afforestation', *The Hindu*, May 14, 1985.
2. Kripa Shankar: 'Employment Policy for Rural Areas', *Mainstream*, February 21, 1981, p. 20.
3. Michael Burgess: 'Dangers of Environmental Extremism: Analysis of Debate over India's Social Forestry Programme', *Economic and Political Weekly*, October 3, 1992, p. 2198.
4. S.A.N. Peerzade: 'The Vanishing Forests: The Impact on Indian Economy', *The Economic Times*, August 6, 1983.
5. 'New Concepts of Forestry', *THE HINDU*, May 18, 1977.
6. N.D. Bachkheti: 'Fuel Wood Crisis in India: A Solution', *Yojana*, January 26, 1982, p. 87.
7. L.C. Sharma: 'Fuel Crisis in Rural India', *Commerce*, November 1, 1980, p. 834.
8. Gopa Joshi: 'Forest Policy and Tribal Development: Problems of Implementation, Ecology and Exploitation', *Social Action*, October-December 1981, p. 461.
9. Vikash N. Pandey: 'National Forest Policy 1988', *Mainstream*, August 22,1992, p. 29.
10. Planning Commission, Government of India, New Delhi: *Draft Five Year Plan 1978-83*, p. 149.
11. Walter Fernandes: 'Afforestation Programmes, Voluntary Action and Community Organisation', *Social Action*, July-September 1987, p. 293.
12. Planning Commission, Government of India, New Delhi, *Eighth Five Year Plan 1992-97*, Vol. II, p. 98.
13. Gopa Joshi: *op. cit.*, p. 448.
14. G.S. Kamat: 'Role of Social Forestry', *Khadigramodyog*, March 1982, p. 293.
15. M.P. Boraiyan: 'Social Forestry: A Way of Life', *Kurukshetra*, October 16-31, 1985, p. 6.
16. M.V. Nadkarni: 'Deforestation in India', *The Economic Times*, January 23, 1985.
17. Walter Fernandes: 'Draft Forest Bill Ignores the People's Rights', *The Economic Times*, September 25,1994.
18. Madhav Gadgil and Seshagiri Rao: 'The People's Ecological Bill', *Indian Express*, November 20, 1994.
19. Sushma Arya: 'Forest Management Scheme to Help Poor Tribals', *Indian Express*, March 5, 1994.
20. S.B. Roy: 'Forest Protection Committees in West Bengal', *Economic and Political Weekly*, July 18, 1992, p. 1530.
21. Dolly Arora: 'From State Regulation to People's Participation: Case for Forest Management in India', *Economic and Political Weekly*, March 19, 1994, p. 695.
22. Ministry of Agriculture and Irrigation (1977): Government of India, New Delhi, *Report of the National Commission on Agriculture*, Abridged Report p. 428.
23. Planning Commission, Government of India (1985): *Seventh Five Year Plan 1985-90*, p. 38.

24. Vandana Shiva and J. Bandyopadhyay: "The Forest Bill: Old Wine in New Bottles', *Indian Express*, June 19, 1982.
25. *Voluntary Action* (editorial), March 1982, p. 317.
26. *Seventh Five Year Plan, op. cit.*, p. 41.
27. S. Madhav Gadgil, Narendra Prasad and Rauf Ali: 'Forest Management and Forest Policy in India: A Critical Review', *Social Action*, April-June 1983, p. 150.
28. N.C. Saxena: 'Social Forestry and Panchayat', *Seminar*, June 1993, p. 32.

Chapter

19 RURAL INDUSTRIALISATION IN INDIA

Indian economy suffers from high incidence of rural poverty, unemployment and underemployment. The agricultural sector by itself cannot provide productive employment to the growing labour force — whose potential needs to be tapped structurally to overcome the economic crisis. The employment potential of the agricultural sector is also limited thanks to low employment elasticity. There is therefore the need the for intensifying non-farming activities in rural India. If this is not done, more and more workers will consider migrating to towns and cities, swelling the informal sector both in the rural and urban areas.

Diversification of agriculture through animal husbandry, dairying, forestry, fishery, sericulture etc., would benefit both the landless and the landholders and this should form an important ingredient of any strategy for integrated rural development.[1]

Too much dependence on the agricultural sector is not desirable. The occupation structure should change in favour of the industry.

Only rapid rural industrialisation can help developing countries substantially increase opportunities for employment in the non-agricultural sector, expand the production of inputs needed to increase agricultural output and multiply the number of plants available for processing farm commodities.[2] It can successfully revitalise the rural masses and assist the urban sector too.[3] There is a close relationship between employment generated in rural non-farming activities and the spread of prosperity resulting from agricultural growth.[4]

The value productivity per worker in the secondary and tertiary sectors is much higher than in the primary sector. The shift in occupational structure therefore would be associated with rise in per capita income.[5]

Even to reduce pressure of population on land and strengthen the agricultural sector, rapid rural industrialisation is indispensable. Industrialisation has to perform the role of the leading sector in the process of structural transformation.

The general pattern of structural transformation in a country should be from agriculture to industry and then to services. But, in India, there has been a faster transition from agriculture to services, with the industry lingering behind. In 1970-71, agriculture's share in GDP was placed at 45.7 per cent, but this came down to 34.5 per cent in 1985-86. The secondary sector's share during this period increased marginally from 20.7 per cent to 21.9 per cent, and that of tertiary sector increased significantly from 31 per cent to 41 per cent. There is therefore the need for intensifying non-farming activities as our objective is to improve the standard of living of the masses by stepping up output of wage goods.

Progress and Problems

It is necessary to study the progress and problems of small scale and ancillary units. India has 2.2 million units belonging to the small scale Industry SSI category — the largest number in the world. The small scale sector produces as many as 5,000 products in a bigger or smaller way.

An industrial undertaking is regarded as small scale if its investment in plant and machinery does not exceed ₹ 1 crore (from December 1999). The investment level was ₹ 3 crore from December 1997 to 1999. Prior to that, from April 1991 to December 1997, it was ₹ 60 lakh.

During 1996-97, the small scale sector contributed over 40 per cent to the gross turnover in the manufacturing sector, 45 per cent of manufacturing exports and 34 per cent of total exports.

The All-India census of SSIs conducted in 1973 and 1988 has revealed the following: the number of SSI units increased from 2,57,797 as on November 30,1973 to 9,86,861 as on March 31,1988. But, the number of working units over the two periods was 1,59,321 and 5,93,769 respectively. A majority of the SSI units are located in the backward areas. In 1988, the backward areas accounted for 3,62,174 units or 62 per cent of the total SSIs.

During the Seventh Plan (1985-90), the SSIs output rose annually by 12.7 per cent against the targeted 9.7 per cent (from ₹ 50,520 crore to ₹ 92,080 crore). The employment increased from 90 lakh to 119.6 lakh. The Eighth Plan (1992-97) envisages a 5.6 per cent growth in the manufacture with SSI exports at 10 per cent.

Between 2000-01 to 2004-05, the small enterprises sector registered continuous growth in the number of units, production, employment and exports (see Table 1). During this period, the average annual growth in the number of units was around 4.1 per cent and in employment 4.3 per cent annually. Further, the annual average growth in production, at current and constant prices was 12.4 per cent and 8.1 per cent respectively (*Economic Survey 2005-06*, p.151).

The number of small unite increased from 97.15 lakhs in 1999-00 to 123.43 lakhs in 2005-06, and to 133.68 lakhs in 2007-08.

Employment rose from 229.10 lakhs persons in1999-00 to 299.85 lakh,persons in 2005-06 and to 322.28 lakh persons in 2007-08.

Output value increased from ₹ 2,33,760 crore in 1999-2000 to ₹ 4,97,886 crore in 2005-06 , and to ₹ 6,95,126 crore in 2007-08 .

Exports increased from ₹ 54,200 crore in 1999-2000 to ₹ 1,77, 600 crore in 2005-06.

The contribution of small and medium enterprises (SMEs) to GDP is projected to go upto 22 per cent by 2012. Over 60 per cent of SMEs are aggressively upgrading themselves technologically to reduce their input costs.

The small scale sector now produces a wide variety of products. Starting from the production of simple consumer goods, this sector has branched out to some of the highly precision-oriented products. It produces goods like leather and leather goods; plastics and rubber products, readymade garments, iron and steel goods, soaps and detergents, safety matches, toothpaste and powder, wooden and steel furniture, paints and varnishes, electrical irons, TV cabinets, electrical capacitors, electro-medical equipments, air conditioning equipments, bulbs, optical lenses, drugs and pharmaceuticals, machine tools, electric motors, automobile spare parts, confectionary items and razor blades.

Financial, technological and infrastructural sickness is very alarming in the small scale sector. The number of sick small scale industrial units in December 1980 was 23,147 which increased to 1,45,776 in December 1986, showing a 6.3 fold increase in the six year period; the number of sick units in large units during the same period increased from 409 to 714, showing a 1.75 fold increase.

Table 1
Performance of Smallscale Enterprices

Year	*No. Of units (in lakhs)*	*Employment (Lakh persons)*	*Output (₹ Crore at current prices)*	*Exports (₹ Crore)*
1999-00	97.15	229.10	2,33,760	54, 200
2000-01	101.10	238.73	2,61,297	69,797
2001-02	105.21	249.33	2,82,270	71, 244
2002-03	109.49	260.21	3,14,850	86,013
2003-04	113.95	271.42	3,64,547	97,644
2004-05	118.59	282.57	4,29,796	124,417
2005-06	123.42	299.85	4,97,886	177,600
2006-07	129.44	312.52	5,65,112	NA
2007-08	133.68	322.28	6,95,126	NA

By the end of December 1987,200,259 small scale units were declared sick showing an increase of 40 per cent over the previous year. At the end of 1986, the outstanding bank credit against sick small scale units was estimated at ₹ 4,874 crore. It can be observed that sickness has been spreading faster in the small scale sector than in the large and medium scale sectors.

As on 31st March 1999, there were 309,013 sick/weak units consisting of 3,06,221 units in the SSI sector and 2,792 units in the non-SSI sector.

As on 31st March 1999, the total bank credit blocked in the sick units was ₹ 19,464 crore. The small scale sector has ₹ 4,313 crore (22.2 per cent), blocked in its units.

The technology base of small units is weak. There is also no clear idea yet of the technology absorptive capacity of small units. The process of technology development in the small scale sector passes through four distinct phases at the micro level, namely, evaluation of current technology level, preparation of the improvement model, acquisition of inputs and implementation.[6] All these require involvement of multiple agencies. Besides, the traditional skills and capabilities available in the tiny sector need to be upgraded. The inability of rural enterprises to adapt to the changing market conditions has quite often proved detrimental to rural industrialisation.[7]

Industries having backward and forward linkage with agriculture, irrespective of their size and having a direct bearing on agriculture and rural economic life may be placed in the category of agro-based industries. These industries provide the essential inputs and also function as potential outlets for the agricultural output.[8]

Agro industries do play an important role in modernising the agricultural sector, in raising the incomes of the farmers and in stepping up agricultural productivity. These industries contribute greatly towards diversification of the rural economy which is the real answer to the twin problems of rural poverty and unemployment. However, over optimisation with respect to raw material supply and markets has led to widespread underutilisation of capacity in agro industrial investments.[9]

The ancillaries are also facing a number of problems. Capacity utilisation is low, ranging from 40 per cent to 50 per cent. While parent units give priority to diversification, ancillaries are not able to change their modes of production. The ancillaries should make some efforts to upgrade their technologies instead of entirely depending on parent units. Parent ancillary relationship is also impaired because of a lack of sufficient communication linkages between them which is vital in the development of any bilateral relations.[10]

The parent units should assist ancillaries in the transfer of technology and arrange for supply of quality raw materials so that the end-product comes upto the requisite specifications.[11] Generally, an ancillary depends on only one parent unit; it may be good for both the parent and the ancillary unit to have alternatives available.[12] The ancillaries should be protected from unscrupulous and unfair competition from the small scale sector — which enjoys subsidies and other incentives.[13]

A Rational Approach

India has realised the importance of rural industrialisation. But, various approaches adopted towards rural industrialisation have not been quite successful. High priority was given to capital goods industries even during the Second Five Year Plan. The country should have opted for a labour intensive pattern of industrialisation, starting from simpler consumer goods and moving gradually thereafter to intermediate and capital goods.

The rural industrialisation programme should be area-specific. The setting up of big units in backward areas is not going to help local people. The Rourkela Steel Plant was set up in a tribal region in Orissa. But, the plant did not help tribal people to improve their financial conditions and day-to-day living. On the other hand, it created problems for them by destroying their culture and way of life.

For instance, in a tribal region, emphasis should be on education and social infrastructure, gradual application of modern farm technology, market facilities, simultaneous development of agriculture and forestry, agro- and forest-based small industries with effective co-ordination between block administration and government departments and other institutions.

The linkage between small and big units should be strengthened for mutual benefit. The complementary nature between small and big units is also due to the fact that the different stages of the production process of a good manufacturing unit can be carried out in different scales. It should be therefore possible to undertake the capital and technology intensive parts of the process in the large scale, leaving the labour intensive part to the decentralised small scale, but again the marketing of the products being done by large scale industries. An example would be that of textiles: preparation of cotton and spinning is best done by large scale. Weaving can be decentralised. But again, the finishing, quality control and marketing can be done advantageously by large scale industries.[14]

The Chinese pattern of industrialisation is said to have been based on forward and backward linkages. The Chinese rural projects are based on diversity in rural resources and needs, whereas those in India appear to be almost of a straight-jacket and uniform model. Since rural industrialisation in China is an outcome of the total area planning in its comprehensive terms, it does not suffer from a deficiency in one sector for the benefit of another sector.[15] The Chinese pattern of rural industrialisation has also underscored the need for — *(i)* effective linkage between local and extension services, and *(ii)* local initiative, innovation and self-reliance.[16]

If the aims of rural industrialisation are to provide full employment through balanced occupational structure, to prevent rural exodus and to improve the structure of income and asset distribution within rural areas, rural industrialisation should cover household based industries, agro-based industries and industries aimed to producing consumer goods in demand in rural areas, besides secondary goods and services required for primary business activities. The viability of demand for the products of rural industries should be studied in-depth. Underlying the viability of demand is the question of generation of income and its disposition. Unless we know how much is likely to be generated and the associated pattern of expenditure, demand for rural industries cannot be ascertained. Sustained progress on the rural industrialisation front requires policies to strengthen the linkages.[17]

INSTITUTIONAL SUPPORT

The governmental support to small and rural industries has taken many forms. The reservation of items for production exclusively in the small sector and exclusive purchase from this sector by the government organisations and the price preference for such purchases is one of them. However, most of the benefits emerging from this preferential treatment are appropriated by large units within the small scale sector and the near urban units.[18]

The number of items reserved for exclusive manufacture in the small scale industry has increased to 873 as of December 1985 from 313 in 1973-74 and 126 in 1967-68. The entry of bigger units is barred except when they undertake to export 75 per cent of the total production.

The industrial estates programme has been in operation since 1955. Though there are about 800 industrial estates in the country, not all of them are functioning. Nearly ₹ 10 crore has been spent till now on the construction of government sponsored industrial estates. However, the functioning of those set up in the interior regions is disappointing, with poor use of capacity created. On the other hand, those set up near industrial conglomerates and cities have succeeded beyond exceptation.[19] It has been observed that the construction of industrial estates is more suited to accelerating the development of rural industries than to initiating them.[20]

The Rural Industries Projects (RIP) programme was introduced in 1962-63, initially started in 49 districts, each covering three to five blocks. The programme aimed at the development of entrepreneurs in rural areas, identification of industrial ventures and promotion of extension services. The Central Government provided 100 per cent grants to meet the establishment cost. Entrepreneurs were given loans at *5.5* per cent rate of interest. The programme was finally extended to 111 districts, excluding towns having a population of 25,000 or more. The RIP programme was subsequently merged with the DIC programme.

An evaluation of the RIP programme has revealed serious deficiencies at the implementation stage. These include: *(i)* some part of the assistance being provided to relatively larger amongst small scale units, *(ii)* assistance diverted to towns which were excluded from the purview of the scheme and *(iii)* rural artisans did not receive adequate credit, training and marketing.[21]

The DICs have been set up to co-ordinate the industrial expansion and to serve as 'single window service' institutions. However, in actual practise, most DICs have failed to discharge this function effectively. The performance of DICs in respect of conducting techno-economic surveys, identifying market potential for various products, assisting perspective entrepreneurs, imparting training to them and initiating quality control measures is not upto the mark. The lead bank, the DRDA and the DIC have to function with perfect understanding. However, the linkage among them is very weak.

Also, the staffing pattern of the DIC remained to be streamlined. The unscheduled transfer of the DIC personnel, including the general manager, usually casts an adverse effect on the general functioning of the development programme. Generally, the DIC personnel should be transferred only after completing a five-year term.

The technical information available with DICs is almost negligible. It would be desirable if the DICs possess reliable information relating to projects, technology, machinery suppliers etc., in respect of industries relevant to the district concerned. The DICs should have a shelf of projects with all relevant information, which can be implemented without any difficulty.[24]

While the DICs were required to make provision in their action plans for the establishment of rural marketing centres, most DICs do not make any such provision, as pointed out by the Public Accounts Committee in its 219th Report submitted in August 1984.

An intensive review of the DIC programme was done by a high level team. Following this review, the Government decided in August 1981 to restructure the DIC programme with one general manager, four functional managers and upto three project managers in disciplines considered relevant to the needs of the particular districts. But, this restructuring has been very slow probably because there was a fear that this centrally sponsored programme would be wound up after the Sixth Plan. Again, while many of the DICs did prepare action plans, they were not based on any detailed survey or study.

The Small Industries Service Institutes (SISIs) are state level agencies rendering coordinated industrial extension services. There are also extension centres whose activities are limited to one or more specific industries and restricted to a smaller area. The extension centres like SISIs assist individual entrepreneurs to solve common technical problems, suggest improved designs and more up-to-date techniques of manufacture, train workers in improved techniques of production management, marketing etc. and serve as common service facilities centres.

The Small Industry Development Organisation (SIDO) with its network of nearly 100 small industries service institutes, branch institutes, extension centres and production centres provide a wide range of services to the small units. The SIDO maintains a close liaison with institutes and other organisations with a view to getting the rnaximum allocation of imported and indigenous raw materials for the small sector. The National Small Industries Corporation (NSIC) helps small units to get supplies of up-to-date plant and machinery on hire-purchase basis. Both indigenous and imported machinery is supplied on easy instalments.[26]

In 1986, the Small Industries Development Fund (SIDF) was set up in the Industrial Development Bank of India (IDBI) with an initial corpus of ₹ 2,500 crore. This measure has been taken *"in order to provide a focal point for co-ordinating financial assistance to the small scale sector at the apex level."* One financial problem facing the small sector which needs immediate attention is that the small units are often asked to repay the loans even before they could organise themselves and generate surpluses. What is therefore required is provision of a minimum initial moratorium, say for two years. There is also the need to widen the range of the equity type of institutional support.[27]

The Government announced the new Industrial Policy in June 1991. In August 1991, the Government came out with a new policy — exclusively for the development of SSIs and the tiny sector. The thrust of the policy was directed to the following areas:

(i) Financial support to SSIs;

(ii) Rendering better infrastructural facilities;

(iii) Increased support for better marketing of products of small scale industries at home and abroad;

(iv) Modernisation, technological and quality upgradation;

(v) Promotion of entrepreneurship in the small scale sector;

(vi) Promotion of the tiny sector;

(vii) Promotion of the handloom sector and other village industries and

(viii) Simplification of rules and procedures for industrial development.

Investment limits in small scale and ancillary industrial units have been raised respectively to ₹ 60 lakh and ₹ 75 lakh. In 1985, these limits were raised for ₹ 20 lakh to ₹ 30 lakh and in the case of ancillaries, from ₹ 25 lakh to ₹ 45 lakh. A separate category of export-oriented units has been introduced where the limit of investment is ₹ 75 lakh, with 30 per cent export obligation.

Limit of investment of tiny units has been raised from ₹ 2 lakh to ₹ 5 lakh. Locational restrictions have been removed.

Investment limits on plant and machinery for the small scale industries have been raised from ₹ 60 lakh/75 lakh to ₹ 3 crore and that for tiny units has been raised from ₹ 5 lakh to ₹ 25 lakh. Export obligation on non-SSI units manufacturing reserved items has been reduced from 75 per cent to 50 per cent *(Economic Survey 1996-97).*

A new category of industry-related service and business enterprises have been introduced. They will be treated at par with SSIs up to investment limit of ₹ 5 lakh in fixed assets excluding land and building.

The new policy observed that emphasis would henceforth shift from subsidised and cheap credit except for specified target groups and efforts would be made to ensure both adequate flow of credit on a normative basis and quality of delivery for viable operations of this sector.

A significant step in this direction is the decision to allow equity participation by other industrial undertakings in SSIs upto a limit of 24 per cent of the equity shareholding. This step is likely to help modernisation of, and technological upgradation in the small scale sector. It would also provide a powerful boost to ancillarisation and sub-contracting leading to expansion of employment opportunities.

It has been decided to widen the scope of the National Equity Fund Scheme to cover projects up to ₹ 10 lakh for equity support up to 15 per cent of the total equity shareholding. Single window loan scheme has also been enlarged to cover projects up to ₹ 20 lakh with a working capital margin upto ₹ 10 lakh.

The budget for 1994-95 has introduced some measures to revamp the small scale sector. These include: extension of excise to 26 new products and withdrawal of 389 exemptions. Some of the items from which exemptions have been withdrawn include products of steel, rubber, plastic, foundry, shoes and aluminium wires.

Excise concessions upto ₹ 75 lakh will now be available to both the registered and unregistered units. Unregistered units could have concession upto only ₹ 30 lakh earlier. Also, there is a shift in excise duty from specific to *ad valorem.*

Commercial banks have been asked to meet the credit requirements of the small scale industries in 45 districts all over the country. There is a large concentration of SSI units in these districts. This is being done in accordance with the Nayak Committee's recommendations. Banks have also been instructed that henceforth, for the credit requirements of village industries, tiny industries and other SSI units having aggregate fund-based working capital limit up to ₹ 1 crore from the banking system are to be provided working capital limits — computed on the basis of a minimum of 20 per cent of their projected annual turnover of new as well as existing units. The Nayak Committee, which was set up in September 1992 to examine the adequacy of institutional credit to the SSI sector and related aspects, has observed that the small scale sector, as a whole received a level of working capital of only 8.1 per cent of its output. The village industries and the small tiny industries between them could get working capital finance to the extent of only about 2.7 per cent of their output.

The RBI (vide circulars dated April 17,1993 and July 3,1993) announced a special package of measures to ensure adequate and timely credit to the SSI sector. The salient features of this package are:

(i) Banks should give preference to village industries, tiny industries and other small scale units in that order, while meeting the credit requirement of the small scale sector;

(ii) The banks should step up the credit flow to meet the legitimate requirements of the SSI sector in full during the eighth five year plan;

(iii) An effective grievance redressal machinery within each bank which can be approached by the SSI in case of difficulties would be set up; and

(iv) Banks should adopt the single window clearance scheme of SIDBI for meeting the credit requirements of small scale units.

Several new measures have been adopted for improving the efficiency and performance of the small scale units. These include provision of infrastructural support in an integrated manner through Integrated Infrastructure Development (IID) Scheme, enhanced technology support for modernisation and quality upgradation through opening of five new tool rooms with Danish and German assistance, enhancing entrepreneurship development programmes by involving voluntary agencies, strengthening special employment generation programmes through Prime Minister's Rozgar Yojana (PMRY) Scheme and enhancing the information and database of the small scale industries sector. *(Economic Survey 1996-97).*

FUTURE TASK

The relatively poor performance of the rural industrial sector can be attributed to the restrictive approach adopted to the problem. The preservation of traditional rural industries is often viewed as an objective in itself, without examining their likely role in the process of overall rural and national development. Thus, protection of small units has become more important than development and modernisation of such units.[28] The protective and promotional measures should aim at increasing the growth potential rather than merely consider the survival of rural industries.[29] It has been pointed out that there is a case for providing protection to the small sector through differential taxation rather than reservation.[30]

Besides, various fiscal incentives offered to the small units are often misused. Surely, the objective of such incentives is not to keep the unit 'small' but to help them grow into efficient sized units. If the small units are made clear that incentives like excise concessions will be gradually withdrawn, the units will work towards improving their efficiency and the urge for fragmentation and remaining small will no longer exist.[31]

Some have strongly criticised the reservation policy for the SSI sector, claiming that the policy initiated for developing the SSIs has become regressive. The country is now committed to liberalising imports, including imports of many of 836 reserved items. Under the liberalisation policy, the import of received items made by large scale companies abroad is being seriously contended for, and not allowing their large scale manufacture in India may prove detrimental to the Indian economy.

India's rural industrialisation programme should take into account two things: *(i)* the pace of non-farming activities in rural areas will be greatly influenced by the trends of agricultural incomes and productivity, and *(ii)* as the private sector is still predominant, the tendency towards geographical concentration of the industry is strong.[32]

The reservation policy followed in respect of the small sector has failed to enhance quality consciousness of manufacture and pre-empting the entry of potentially more efficient units into these product lines. As this policy has been operating for a long time, the small units must be exposed to competition so that they are compelled to produce quality products at reasonable prices. Responding to this crisis, experts are of the opinion that about 200 items maybe deserved. The Narasimhan Panel, while commending provision of infrastructure and support facilities to the small sector, felt that the policy of reservation may not achieve the desired objectives.

Without a political will or policy support, the rural entrepreneurs and their products may fail to enter the competitive market and avail of the benefits of economic liberalisation. Tax relief and exemption from octroi etc., should be liberally given to small producers. The fiscal policy and policies relating to purchase of raw materials, inputs and the subsequent marketing of the products should be so formulated as to favour small entrepreneurs.[33]

The rural industrial sector requires not a generalised thrust as has been the policy so far, but specific attention and a specially designed package of programmes conducive to its own characteristics. For any such package to be developed and implemented, there has to be a detailed survey, adequate database and indepth analysis of the market.[34]

In future, an attempt should be made to tap the 'potential' of the rural population from among the children of the traditional artisans and give them intense training and orientation to convert their establishments into real industrial-cum-business establishments. Further, the focus of training for self-employment in rural areas should be on motivating and training of the educated youth to become rural entrepreneurs for organising decentralised production and develop as leaders in their area of business. The emerging entrepreneurs need trained to take up those lines of production which could be best organised, using the available local raw materials, manpower, markets etc.[35] This makes it necessary to develop regular and appropriate training programmes for the rural entrepreneurs to upgrade their present skills and acquire new ones.[36]

The rural artisans who have the potential to contribute to the country's economy, fail to do so, having less access to credit and raw materials. Another problem relates to the size of the market which is small. There are of course clusters of artisans engaged in specific industries, but their operations are not viable. A strategy based on industry-cum-area development approach leading to vertical and horizontal integration of the programmes can alone sustain the industries in rural areas. This calls for integration of beneficiary-oriented schemes with the overall 'area' development plans to be drawn up after taking the resource endowments into account.[37]

Establishing production linkages of rural industries with the farm sector, as in the case of China, would contribute effectively in revitalising the rural economy.[38] In the case of agro-industries, it is necessary to evolve an appropriate organisational set-up for the growth of agro-industries. Perhaps a strong case can be advanced in favour of organising agro-industries on co-operative basis.[39]

Marketing continues to be a major problem facing small units. The rural industries sector has to depend on the local rural and semi-urban markets for marketing its products. It must of course constantly strive to capture the urban markets first and then tap foreign markets to the extent possible. Positive measures are necessary to help the small sector to emerge as potential contributors to the Indian economy. There is need for inter-sectoral harmonisation in both production and marketing.[40]

At present, there are different agencies engaged in the technology transfer to rural areas. There is need for co-ordinating their efforts by evolving a single forum at the national level. It is also felt that there should be an extension agent of DICs at the block or sub-block levels and a technology centre at the district level. Perhaps there is need for an institution at the district level to help rural artisans with financial inputs and strategic marketing.

NEW INITIATIVES

In 1967, only 47 items were reserved for small industry. This increased to 180 by June 1976 and to 504 by April 1978. However, the dereservation process started from April 1997 when 15 items were dereserved. In May 2002, 51 items were dereserved, and in May 2003, 75 items were dereserved. In November 2004, 85 items were struck off from SSI reserved list. In 2004-05,193 items were dereserved to bring down the total number of reserved items to 506.

In September 2005, the government approved an increase in the subsidy for small scale industries from 12 to 15 per cent to make the sector competitive. Along side, it raised the ceiling on loans under the Credit Linked Capital Subsidy Scheme for modernisation and technology upgradation from ₹ 40 lakh to ₹ 1 crore. The validity period of the scheme has been extended to March 31, 2007. Also, the capital subsidy is to be calculated with reference to the purchase price of plant and machinery instead of the term loan disbursed to the beneficiary.

The Government has proposed to take up 100 clusters of traditional industries in the small scale sector for their development over the next 5 years. Among these, 25 clusters will be for khadi, 25 for the coir sector and 50 will be for village industries. The scheme will greatly benefit artisans, weavers, potters and other workers engaged in traditional industry activities.

In pursuance of the announcement of the Finance Minister in the Budget 2005-06, a fund titled 'Scheme of Fund for Regeneration of Traditional Industries (SFURTI)' was approved for the holistic development of traditional clusters.

REFERENCES

1. Planning Commission, Government of India (1981): *Sixth Five Year Plan 1980-85,* p. 210.
2. Dannis A. Rondinelli: 'Small Industries in Rural Development: Assessment and Perspective', *Productivity* (Special Issue on Rural Development), January-March 1979, p. 458.
3. R.V. Rao (1987): *Rural Industrialisation in India,* Concept Publishing Company, New Delhi, p. 78.
4. FAO, Rome (no year): Review and Analysis of Agrarian Reform and Rural Development in the Developing Countries since the mid-1960s, p. 63.

5. Manmohan Singh: 'Indian Economic Planning and World Economy', Valedictory Address at the VIII World Economic Congress in New Delhi on December 5, 1986.
6. K.L. Nanjappa: 'Small Scale Sector: Need to Upgrade Technology', *The Economic Times,* July 10, 1986.
7. FAO (no year): *op. cit.*
8. Badar Alam Iqbal, Javed Alam Khan and Sibghat Ullah Farooqi: 'Role of Agro Industries in Agricultural Economic', *Khadigramodyog,* February 1979, pp. 281-282.
9. James G. Brown: 'Improving Agro Industries in Developing Countries', *Finance and Development,* June 1986, p. 43.
10. K.V. Rao: 'Wide Scope for Closer Parent Ancillary Ties', *The Hindu,* March 6, 1986.
11. Planning Commission, Government of India (1985): *The Seventh Five Year Plan 1985-90,* Vol. II, p. 101.
12. M.S.S. Vardhan: 'What Ails the Ancillaries', *The Hindu,* August 27, 1971.
13. I. Satya Sundaram: 'Ancillaries Face Rough Weather', *Industrial Times,* May 17-30, 1982, pp. 35-37.
14. T. Thomas: 'Relationship Between Small-scale and Large-scale Industry: A Different View', *Economic and Political Weekly,* March 3, 1979, p. M-36.
15. O.P.L. Jain: 'Rural Industrialisation : China's Experience', *Monthly Commentary on Indian Economic Conditions,* June 1978, p. 111.
16. *Ibid.,* p. 12.
17. D.B. Gupta: 'Rural Industry in India: Need Policies and Prospects', *Kurukshetra,* October 1984, p. 62.
18. B. Sudhakara Rao: 'A Pragmatic Approach to Rural Industry Needed', *Kurukshetra,* December 1984, p. 14.
19. *The Economic Times* (Supplement), June 12, 1986, p. 1.
20. FAO (no year): *op. cit.,* pp. 65-66.
21. Rajula Devi: 'Industrialisation Holds Key to Rural Development', *Kurukshetra,* December 1984, p. 34.
22. I. Satya Sundaram: 'DICs at the Crossroads', *The Economic Times,* December 9, 1983.
23. Ajit Kumar Gaur: 'Success and Failure of DIG. A Case Study: *Khadigramodyog,* April 1987, p. 325.
24. B. Sudhakara Rao: *op. cit.,* p. 17.
25. *Economic and Political Weekly,* November 1-8, 1986, p. 1915.
26. Vivek S. Deolankar: 'Assistance and Incentives to Small Scale Industries', *Southern Economist,* June 1, 1986.

27. K.R. Pillai: 'Small Industry: New Dimensions', *The Economic Times,* October 4, 1986.

28. Vivek Deolankar: 'Role of Rural Industries', *Khadigramodyog,* February 1987, p. 215.

29. *Ibid.,* p. 216.

30. *The Economic Times* (editorial), November 22, 1985.

31. Isher Judge Ahluwalia: 'Industrial Policy: Priorities in Reform', *The Economic Times,* January 16, 1985.

32. Manmohan Singh: *op. cit.*

33. R.N. Kapoor. 'Rural Industrialisation: Existing Trends and Future Strategies', *Khadigramodyog,* November 1986, p. 103.

34. S.P. Vishnoi: 'Required An Integrated Approach to Rural Industrialisation', *Kurukshetra,* October 1984, p. 103.

35. C.S. Rao: 'Need to Promote Rural Entrepreneurship', *Kurukshetra,* December 1984, p. 29.

36. S.P. Vishnoi: *op. cit.,* p. 56.

37. *Sixth Five Year Plan: op. cit.,* p. 191.

38. Swapna Mukhopadhyay: 'Rural Non-Farm Sector in Asia: A Characterisation', *Economic and Political Weekly,* June 1, 1985, p. 968.

39. Badar Alam Iqbal *et al., op. cit.,* p. 39.

40. I. Satya Sundaram (1984): *Anti-Poverty Rural Development in India,* D.K. Publications, Delhi, p. 220.

Chapter

20 Technology for Rural Development

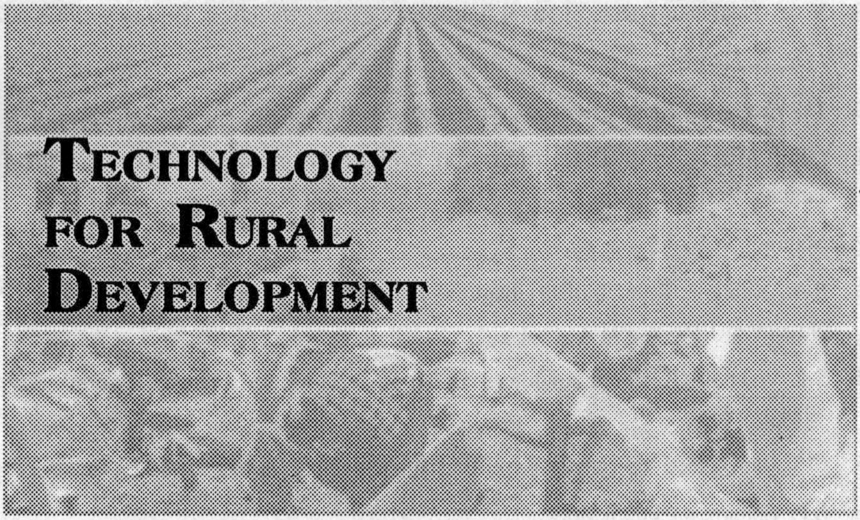

Rural India is endowed with vast and potential reserves of both natural and human resources. Subsequently, a need has arisen for obtaining optimum returns from these resources without causing any damage to the ecology which will, without doubt, prove detrimental. In rural India, there is need for enhancing the incomes of the currently employed persons, besides providing additional employment opportunities. These two tasks can be achieved only through strategic 'marketing' and the use of current 'technology'.[1]

For developing any technology plan for rural people, the stress should be on the rural society, its culture and traditions be taken as the basic objective to improve the standard of living of the rural population.[2]

Importance of Rural Technology

The technology selected for rural development should meet the local needs; be in conjunction with the raral culture and the social and economic aspirations of the rural people; be able to promote local talents and skills, enhance existing incomes and generate additional/new employment opportunities; generate entrepreneurial temper and create widest possible involvement of the rural poor and other disadvantaged groups.[3]

In the sphere of rural technology, an integrated approach will definitely be desirable — planning out cost — effective activities which would be interlinked with each other so that the output, by-product or waste material of one activity would be the raw material of the other. For instance, about the Centre for Rural Development (of the Indian Institute of Technology, Chennai) situated at Narayanapuram near Chennai, it is said:[4]

Soil was excavated and used for raising bunds and roads. Brick was also manufactured from it. The areas from where soil was removed were converted into fish ponds. A rice mill was set up and the paddy husk from the mill was used in the brick kilns and for cattle. A dairy was also set up which, besides providing milk, also provided dung which was used in producing bio-gas. The bio-gas in turn was used for firing bricks, as well as in the bakery and for running an engine to generate electricity. In addition to bio-gas, attempts are also being made to tap solar and wind energy.

The Centre started units for carpentry and building sections, a unit for recycling of waste paper, a printing press and a tailoring unit. The Centre also took electronics technology to the rural areas. It has evolved construction technology to suit the local conditions and worked towards contributing sufficiently to the rural economy.

The Murugappa Polytechnic in Sathyamurthi Nagar, Avadi, near Chennai has been doing a commendable job in the sphere of rural technology. It also produced a variety of equipment and tools suited for economic upgradation of the local people. These include domestic and community solar cookers, biogas plants, solar driers and water heaters, pedal operated paddy threshers and groundnut decorticators, sieves, tool sharpeners as also hydraulic presses and wind-mills for pumping water and for generating electrical power for the rural sector to avail of.

PLASTICS AND AGRICULTURE

Rural development, particularly agricultural development, cannot be insulated from technological growth. We have to depend heavily on new products and technology for the modernisation of the agricultural sector. For instance, plastics offer a new potential for further increasing agricultural yield. The use of plastics in irrigation has proved to be a boon in increasing water use efficiency, decreasing waterlogging and soil salinity and minimising wastage during water conveyance etc. Polythenes are useful in lining of water storage structures, particularly in laterite and sandy soils as also in canals, reducing water loss through seepage.

The wastage during the post harvest storage and preservation can be minimised by using plastics. By using black plastics on floor for sun drying of agricultural products, 15 per cent time can be saved.

Storage life and quality of fruits and vegetables can be increased by simply storing them in polythene packings. Polythene storages are also used for enhancing ripening of fruits like banana, mango, lemons etc. Post harvest losses of fruits and vegetables can be significantly reduced by using polythene lined packing material not only in wooden or hard board cases but also in country made bamboo basket packings.

Use of plastic green houses for increasing the yield and productivity of horticultural crops, vegetables, flowers and ornamental plants by controlling the environment is gaining global acceptance. Such green houses help in growing out-of-season crops and quality produce besides producing disease free and better quality planting material of horticultural crops. Low cost plastic houses for developing nursery plants is said to be becoming popular.[5]

BIOGAS TECHNOLOGY

The energy crisis has come to exist as a serious threat. We have to go in for new and cheap sources of energy. There has been increasing pressure on oil and coal reserves and also forest resources. Biogas has been identified as an alternative source of clean and cheap energy.

Biogas is produced from cattle dung in a biogas plant commonly known as 'gobar gas plant' — through a process called digestion. It is a gaseous mixture containing 60 per cent methane, a high value fuel, and 40 per cent of carbondioxide, an inert gas, plus traces of other gases such as nitrogen and hydrogen sulphide obtained from anaerobic fermentation of dung in the presence of micro-organisms. Thus, a biogas plant helps in obtaining both fuel and manure from a given quantity of cattle dung.

Out of the total estimated production of 132.4 million tonnes of animal dung (air-dry), about 73 million tonne have been estimated to be burnt for energy purpose, which is said to exceed the total fertiliser consumed in the agricultural production in India.

It is estimated that by 2000 AD, nearly 250 million additional people will not have fuel for cooking and heating and they will be forced to burn dried animal dung and agricultural/crop residues, which would otherwise increase the food crops yield substantially.

The Khadi and Village Industries Commission's Directorate of Gobar gas and the Structural Engineering Research Centre, Roorkee, are among institutions that have developed ferrocement gas holders which are cheaper, stronger, better insulated and easier to fabricate, maintain and repair than the steel units previously used.

The Planning Research and Action Division of the State Planning Board, Lucknow, has achieved success in developing a Janata biogas plant in which a lined pit drug underground, substitutes the conventional digester with its requirements of cement and steel. This pit has been patterned on the Chinese model. The Janata biogas plant is even cheaper than the ferro-cement variety, and will be a boon if it can be fully stabilised in the rural field conditions. However, the Janata unit has no automatic slurry-escape and the pit has to be broken open and emptied annually.

Another unit, the KVIC ferro cement digester-cum-gas holder bio-gas unit, is now available in sizes ranging from two cubic metres (60 cubic feet) to six cubic metres (200 cubic feet) — which is claimed to be 20 per cent cheaper than the conventional unit and takes only a day to construct as against 10 days required for the cement and steel variety. This hand-process, labour intensive ferro-cement technology requires only six bags of cement as against 20 bags for the conventional 100 cubic feet biogas unit.[6]

Most of the small units have been made with movable dome as developed by KVIC. The only other type, fixed dome or Chinese type digester has gained wide acceptance due to their low cost. The cost of $2m^3$ Janata Model Chinese type bio gas digester was found to be 25 per cent less than the same capacity KVIC digester.

One of the problems identified with the Chinese type relates to gas leakage from the displaced slurry. A $2m^3$ Janata model Chinese type biogas unit was designed to displace 0.66 m^3 of slurry in 8 hours to store the gas produced. The gas produced from the displaced slurry leaks and gets mingled in the atmosphere and cannot be recovered. This problem has been overcome by displacing water instead of slurry to store the gas produced.[7]

The National Project on Biogas Development (NPBD) set a target of installing 1.47 lakh biogas plants during the year 1991-92 with an investment of ₹ 64 crore. 1.64 lakh plants were installed in 1990-91, which is reported to have exceeded the set target of 1.37 lakh plants. The implementing agencies for the project included nodal departments of state governments, state corporate bodies, the KVIC and the National Dairy Development Board. Since the inception of the Project in 1981-82, a total of 14 lakh family size biogas plants have been installed by 1992 which is against an aggregate target of 12 lakh. The 13 Regional Biogas Development and Training Centres in the country decided to provide technical and training services and also bear the cost for repairs, maintenance and publicity support for effective implementation of the project.

Table: 1

Non-Conventional Sources of Energy Achievement at a Glance

Sl. No.	*Programme*	*Cumulative Achievement up to 31-3-1992 (Numbers)*
1.	Family size biogas plants (in lakh)	15.75
2.	Community /Institutional biogas plants	819.00
3.	Improved chulhas (in lakh)	125.00
4.	Domestic solar water heating systems	10,127.00
5.	Industrial solar water heating systems	4,829.00
6.	Solar stills	9,651.00
7.	Solar timber kilns	71.00
8.	Solar air heaters	61.00
9.	Solar cookers (in lakh)	2.27
10.	Villages provided with photovoltaic street lights	8,100.00
11.	Photovoltaic water pumps	1,171.00
12.	Photovoltaic power units (KWP)	750.00
13.	Photovoltaic community lights/TV and community facilities	968.00
14.	Photovoltaic domestic lighting units	9,050.00
15.	Photovoltaic lanterns	-
16.	Wind pumps	2,916.00
17.	Wind farms (MW)	2,916.00
18.	Mini-micro hydro (MW)	86.53
19.	Urjagram Energy Surveys	1,557.00
20.	Urjagram Projects	155.00
21.	Biomass Energy plantations (hectares)	17,110.00
22.	Biomass Gasifiers/Stirling engines	1,000.00

The sixteen lakh biogas plants in operation had the estimated capacity to generate fuel equivalent to saving about 50 lakh tonnes of firewood per year valued at ₹ 200 crore per year. Besides, these plants have been producing about 240 lakh tonnes of enriched manure-containing about 2.4 lakh tonnes of nitrojgn, phosphorous and potash, and which have been valued at ₹ 160 crore per year.

Taking the average life span of plants to be about 20 years, large economic benefits would thus be generated to enable the nation to emerge successful in the competitive global market.

In addition, the programme has brought about employment generation of about 70 to 75 lakh mandays per year for both skilled and unskilled workers in the rural areas.

In order to make community biogas plants viable, it was deemed necessary to identify various organic wastes as available cattle dung was considered to be insufficient. We can also use human excreta, water hyacinth and other agricultural wastes to develop such plants. The use of gas and manure have been diversified by providing motor power for supply of drinking water, running flour mills and the like.

The enriched manure so produced can be either used for growing vegetables or supplied to farmers for raising potential crops of economic importance.[8]

The bio-gas research and development programme aims at:

- 5 per cent to 8 per cent enhancement of biodigestibility of cattle dung and other organic wastes;
- Doubling of gas production rate and
- Enrichment of manurial value.[9]

A co-ordinated Project on Microbiology and Bio-process Engineering of Methane Production has been in operation in eight institutions, namely, Annamalai University, Haryana Agricultural University, Indian Institute of Sciences, Bangalore, Maharashtra Association for Cultivation of Sciences, Pune, National Dairy Research Institute, Karnal, Tamil Nadu Agricultural University, Coimbatore and Tata Energy Research Institute, New Delhi.

Of course, the amount of subsidy granted to a biogas plant depends on its size, location and the type of beneficiaries. The NPBD provides for —

- Turnkey job fee with two years free maintenance guarantee @ ₹ 400 per plant to corporate bodies, registered voluntary societies and approved self-employed workers.
- Promotional cash incentive @ ₹ 50 per plant to village functionaries.
- Service charges and staff support to state governments, nodal agencies and KVIC.
- Promotion of sanitary toilet linked biogas plants; ₹ 150 per such plant as additional subsidy or turnkey job fee.
- Repair charges; one time @ ₹ 750 per plant for repair of structural defects and higher charges on a case by case basis;
- Training Programmes.
- Demonstration on the utility of manure in farmers' fields @ ₹ 1,000/- per demonstration.

- Setting up new models for demonstration purposes.
- Incentives for saving of diesel-oil by using biogas; subsidy amounting to ₹ 5,000 for setting up a 8 or 10 cubic metres capacity plant and @ ₹ 2,800 per beneficiary for 2 or 3 balloons for transportation of gas.

Both commercial and co-operative banks have been providing loan facilities at concessional rates of interest. Some of the state governments like Himachal Pradesh, Orissa and Gujarat have emerged as supporting categories of beneficiaries. Different departments of some state governments have also provided funds for promoting biogas plants among scheduled castes and scheduled tribes and in and around forest reserves, sanctuaries and the like with a view to reducing dependence on the cutting of trees for firewood.

The Ministry of Non-Conventional Energy Sources is promoting setting up of large sized biogas plants of community and institutional uses. So far, 401 community plants, 359 institutional plants and 50 night soil based biogas plants totalling 819 plants, have been set up in the country. The gas is used for cooking purposes and also for running duel fuel engines for drinking water supply system and generating electricity for small scale industries according to the growing needs of villages and demands of emerging institutions in the rural sector. Night-soil based biogas plants exist as low cost sanitary disposal systems for converting human wastes for manurial purposes. The programme has become acceptable widely in Punjab, Gujarat, Tamil Nadu, Uttar Pradesh, Orissa and Maharashtra.

Gobar gas has its own problems: each gobar gas plant owner must have 3 to 5 cattle heads; the technical information should be available; besides dung, other biodegradable materials have to be used; water scarcity should not be there; fuel shortage problem has to be solved in the absence of dung cakes and it is important to see that the community gas plant does not confer benefits on a few rich people only. The administrative problems are: co-ordination of finance, production, distribution and political activities backed by competent staff.[10]

Biogas production slows down at low temperatures. People have higher fuel needs for making tea etc., during winter just when biogas output gets reduced. To overcome this difficulty, the Regional Research Laboratory at Jammu has been experimenting with various solutions: building underground plants, adding solar heated water and insulating the fermentation pit.[11]

Amongst the various new feedstocks that are being used in experimental plants are animal wastes like the excreta of cows, buffaloes, poultry, sheep and goats; human night soil; agricultural wastes like sugarcane trash, weeds, spoilt fodder and straw; and aquatic wastes like forest litter which mainly consists of twigs, barks and leaves.[12] Efforts should be made to use poultry, sheep and goat excreta, night soil, water hyacinth and other vegetable wastes.[13]

IMPROVED CHULHAS

Around 40 per cent of the total energy is consumed in rural areas. The domestic sector accounts for about 60 per cent of this. The rural poor heavily depend on non-conventional energy sources like firewood, agro-based residues and animal wastes.

Attempts are being made to replace traditional and inefficient chulhas by more fuel efficient improved cooking devices with a view to conserving fuelwood and forests and also to improve health by prioritising hygienic conditions, reduction of drudgery of women and children and improvement in the overall quality of life.

A national programme on Improved Chulha has been launched to ensure the above mentioned areas of priority which aims at fuel conservation from women and children.

The number of improved chulhas was only 0.8 million in March 1985. It increased to 8.4 million by March 1990; to 10.4 million by March 1991 and to 12.5 million by March 1992.

By the end of the Eighth Plan, 30 million rural householders are likely to benefit from the improved chulhas (25 per cent of the potential households). Financial assistance and incentives are being provided for various activities coming under the programme. Fixed models of chulhas are constructed in the kitchens of different households by using locally available material by self-employed workers. The portable chulhas are manufactured by small scale units and are distributed to the beneficiaries. The minimum thermal efficiency of over 25 per cent and 25 per cent has been set for fixed and portable chulhas respectively as against thermal efficiency of 5 per cent to 10 per cent of traditional chulhas.

Table: 2
The Economics of Improved Chulha

Item	*Traditional Chulha*	*Improved Chulha*	*Remarks/ Benefit Per Year*
Capital cost	Free (made from locally available materials)	Average cost (₹ 100/- including pottery/ceramic liners pipe or metallic parts)	
Running cost (average annual consumption of wood in kgs.)	2000-2500	1000-1500	1000 kgs. of wood*

Notes: * Considering various factors, actual savings may be assumed at 700 kgs/family per year of wood or equivalent.

Thus, an improved chulha pays back the investment within three months of its installation. This benefit is of recurring nature. Apart from monetary benefits, other benefits are also there.

A wide variety of chulhas in improved models are now available. These include: *(i)* mud-fixed chulhas with or without chimney, *(ii)* mud-clad pottery lined, fixed chulhas with or without chimney, *(iii)* portable metallic chulha, *(iv)* portable metal-clad-ceramic lined chulha, and *(v)* portable chulha with separated hood chimney system.

The fixed and portable chulhas are 1.38 and 1.48 times more efficient respectively than the traditional chulhas. There is need for increased emphasis on users training for optimum fuel use and maintenance.[14]

The National project on demonstration of improved chulha was designed and launched in 1983 by the Department of Non-Conventional Energy Sources with the following objectives:

- To conserve and optimise the use of the fuelwood specially in the rural and semi-urban areas;
- To help in preventing deforestation;
- To reduce women's drudgery and health hazards by eliminating smoke from the kitchen;
- To help in improvement of this domestic environment.

The project was subsequently converted into a national programme with effect from April 1985, in view of the overwhelming response from the beneficiaries. It now forms part of the Twenty Point and the Minimum Needs Programmes of the Government of India.

Nearly 12.5 million improved chulhas have been installed in domestic households from the inception of the programme till March 31, 1992. A target of an additional 18 million chulhas has been envisaged during the 8th Five Year Plan period, 1992-97, striving to achieve nearly 25 per cent coverage of the potential households.

The traditional wood chulha has very low efficiency ranging from 2 per cent to 10 per cent. The result is long hours spent on cooking in smoke filled kitchens and in collecting cooking fuel, especially for the rural poor who cannot afford to buy fuel. The slow deterioration in the health of most of the rural women caused due to respiratory diseases and deterioration in the eye sight are direct results of the hours they spend in poorly ventilated smoky kitchens.

The improved chulha incorporates an optimum size of combustion chamber, air inlet, grate, baffles and dampers. It is with or without a chimney. The improved models of chulha are of thermal efficiency ranging from 20 per cent onwards.

The new strategy for implementation envisages large scale extension of the programme from a level of nearly 10 per cent coverage as at present to about 25 per cent coverage of the potential households by the end of the 8th plan. It focusses on greater association of beneficiaries in selection of models, their financial participation, education and awareness through wide publicity over the electronic and print media.

The programme thrust during the 8th plan also attempts liberalised marketing and easy availability of various models of chulhas, including ISI marked portable chulhas for quality satisfaction.

The new strategies for the extension of the programme include:

- Association of beneficiaries in selection of models;
- Modification of the designs appropriate to users' local needs;
- Greater financial participations of users;
- More thrust on users' education;

- Introduction of incentive schemes for various levels of field functionaries, depending upon functionality percentage;
- Wider publicity through Radio, TV and other modes;
- Easy availability of various models of chulhas;
- Providing liberalised marketing through decentralized registration of models; and
- Introduction of ISI marked portable metallic chulhas for better quality, durability and longer life.

IMPROVED BULLOCK CART

Efforts have been made to improve the designs of the bullock carts, the primary source of transport in rural India. About 20 million people are involved in the bullock cart business. The employment potential of a bullock cart has been found to be more than four times that of a truck.

Whereas the net loading capacity of the traditional cart is as low as 750 kgs, the four wheel cart specially made of steel axles and body as a carrying capacity of three tonnes. The traditional wheel with an outer rim of hard rubber is best suited for rural roads as it causes least damage to roads. It is cheaper than pneumatic tyres and requires less maintenance.

Ball bearings, by minimissing friction, ensure extra speed with minimum effort. Instead of pulling reins, the breaking device should be installed. The adjustable fixed yoke to the height of bullocks should be replaced by providing better balance and causing minimum strain to the animals. The improved bullock cart can be made with local resources and expertise; hence, the need for training the local artisans. The advantages of the improved bullock carts over the traditional ones are manifold.

In 1980, S.R. Salvi had developed an elastic bullock cart with the following features:

The rapid and stiff framework of the conventional wooden bullock cart was replaced by all-steel elastic body designed to free the bullocks from jerks and jolts to enable them to carry double the load and prolong the life of bullocks. Each sturdy wheel with two-feet level arms has its own separate axle; the axle friction is minimised by using an assembly of pin-roller bearings; when the cart rolls downhill, automatic brakes come into operation; it can be attached to a tractor or jeep as a trailor; and it can be converted into a passenger carrier or a milk or kerosene 'tanker', a mobile stall or shop or even a mobile dispensary or library. It is capable of carrying three tonnes of cargo for over 10 to 12 miles at a stretch.[15]

TECHNOLOGY FOR RURAL WOMEN

Technology should be extended to rural women who take up a number of onerous tasks. In addition to participation in economic activities, they have to bear the additional burden of house and cattle management. The rural women's contribution to the national economy is significant. Moreover, the income earned by women goes directly for satisfying the basic survival needs of the family. Earlier, we have seen how an improved cooking stove can help rural woman in a big way. Reducing the drudgery of rural women should receive attention.

Most rural women take up the task of fetching firewood or preparing cowdungs, collecting water and looking after the children in the family. With drastic reduction in the forest cover, day- by-day, collection of firewood from the forest is becoming increasingly difficult. In fact, after performing various tasks, the rural women hardly find time to attend adult education classes.

As we have seen earlier, rural women and children would be greatly benefitted from the use of biogas plants. They would be saved from the hardship of collection and head-loading heavy bundles of firewood everyday, making arrangements for storage of firewood in the rainy season, exposure to smoke in the kitchen and resultant eye troubles and lung diseases, time-consuming and tedious cooking and cleaning of utensils.

The solar cookers, improved chulhas and family type biogas plants go a long way in reducing the drudgery of rural women. The rural women no longer should be allowed to perform cooking in an uncongenial environment which could prove to be detrimental to their health. Use of modern devices do influence the life-style of the rural women by decreasing their workload, increasing the leisure time and reducing the drudgery of work.[16]

Rural Technology: Some Problems

Transfer of technology to rural areas is no easy task. However, the technology should be extended to the rural people and cater to their needs: otherwise, they will not adopt it. Development does demand social change, particularly in the rural context.

There does exist a vast gap between the cultural patterns of scientists and those of the target groups. When a programme is directed towards a target group, there will be resentment on the part of other groups. Moreover, development of those technologies which have no linkages with the old technology do create problems in their diffusion. Another constraint in the transference and acceptance of technology is the lack of interaction between the R&D systems and socio-cultural institutions.[17]

Rural people's attitudes to new technologies should be changed. For instance, even biogas is resented for various reasons, though it is cheap. Rural people do resist collecting the human waste for any purpose, let alone cooking purpose. They have been accustomed to cook food on the traditional chulhas. They think that the food cooked by any other means cannot be better. But the trend of cooking has charged over the years.

Before introducing any technology into rural areas, the rural people should be properly educated to enable them to modify their ideas and attitudes. The rural society is having diversified cultural patterns. Innovations which are based on the socio-cultural environment will be easily absorbed by the targetted rural people.

It needs to be noted that any technology which helps rural people meet the basic needs is highly acceptable. The new technologies should not disturb the environmental balance of the area where the technologies developed.

Thrusting any programme on people leads to its rejection. The approach should be slow and smooth. Before introducing any technology, the level of awareness on the part of people should be raised through the mass media. This is necessary to ensure people's participation in the implementation of any programme.

The Government is fully aware of the need for evolving technology appropriate to rural areas. Even voluntary agencies are showing interest in the field. The Council for the Advancement of People's Action and Rural Technology (CAPART) is now serving as a national nodal point for promoting the design and development as also the demonstration and dissemination of technologies relevant for the rural areas.

Under its 'Advancement of Rural Technology Scheme' (ARTS), CAPART extends financial support to agencies undertaking projects for technology transfer through demonstration and training programmes. Voluntary agencies with a proven track record in adaptive R&D and technology transfer are supported with a one time grant by CAPART under its scheme for development of Regional Resource Centres of Rural Technology (RRCRT). These centres act as focal points of referral of technology gaps in the areas they serve besides undertaking research and training.

In order to provide R&D support to the community polytechnics, some polytechnics have been identified by the Government as Centres for Development of Rural Technologies (CDRTs). Of the 31 CDRTs in the country, eight are located in the southern region which are engaged in development, modification, fabrication, production and manufacture of various technologies appropriate and relevant to the demands of rural areas. The CDRTs also conduct various training programmes mostly orientation and refresher courses for the staff of the community polytechnics in order to equip the latter with the latest technology and equipment designed and invented by them.[18]

Thus, the challenges are many on the technological front. But these can be easily overcome because rural India is endowed with rich potential manpower and related resources. The only thing is that the rural poor should be properly educated and apprised of the new opportunities available on the technological front. The Government is extending all possible help in this regard.

REFERENCES

1. M.C. Gupta: 'Appropriate Rural Technology', *Kurukshetra*, November-December 1986, p. 32.
2. Dil Bagh Kaur: 'Human Problems in Technical Change', *Khadigramodyog,* February 1989, p. 251.
3. J.C. Srivastava: 'Integrated Rural Development: A New Concept and Approach', *Khadigramodyog,* April 1978, pp. 363-364.
4. S.R. Govindarajan: 'Technology for Rural Areas', *The Hindu,* October 9, 1984, p. 17.
5. L.S. Srivastava: 'Use of Plastics in Agriculture', *Yojana,* October 15, 1993, p. 28.
6. *Voluntary Action*, March 1979, p. 15.
7. J. Rajakumar and V. Subramanian: 'A Modified Digester to Increase Biogas Production', *Yojana,* June 30, 1992, p. 23.
8. *Usha Patel and Mahendra:* 'Biogas Models: Low Cost Sources of Energy for Farmers', *The Economic Times,* October 19, 1983.

9. K.C. Khandelwal: 'Biogas: A Useful Source of Energy', *Yojana,* January 26, 1993, p. 122.

10. Wallace Edward Tyner (1978): *'Energy Resources and Economic Development in India,* Boston, p. 122.

11. 'Is Biogas a Life Belt for the Rural Poor?', *Commerce,* August 8, 1981, p. 267.

12. *Ibid.,* p. 267.

13. *H.S. Srinivasan:* 'Revolutionary Promise of Gobar Gas', *Commerce* (Annual Number) 1977, p. 87.

14. D.K. Mittal: 'Improved Cookstove Programme', *Yojana,* June 15, 1993, pp. 24-28.

15. *Financial Express,* October 15, 1980.

16. Ashima Sharma: 'Modern Household Technologies — Boon for Rural Women', *Kurukshetra,* July 1990, p. 40.

17. Dil Bagh Kaur: *op. cit.,* p. 252.

18. V.K. Natrajan: 'Technology Transfer to Rural Areas: Role of Technical Institutions', *Kurukshetra,* September 1993, pp. 35-36.

PART THREE

Rural Power Structure

Chapter

21 Land Reforms in India

Agrarian relations do influence the levels of production and productivity and also the pattern of income and wealth distribution in the agricultural sector. The pre-requisites for a productive land tenure system are direct ownership of land, absence of intermediaries, reasonable land rent, consolidation of holdings and efficient land record system.[1]

Land reforms refer to measures initiated by the state in relation to ownership, tenancy and management of land. Thus, land reforms encompass the whole agrarian structure. We must have a land ownership pattern which is socially just and economically efficient. Concentration of ownership of land in a few is not desirable. Also, the actual tiller of the soil must have proper incentives so that he takes interest in strategic activities of agricultural development.

The term land reforms includes not merely redistribution of land but also tenancy and other land management aspects, measures to conserve land use, prevention of its degradation etc. Land reforms provide a real sense of participation in rural life for the rural poor.[2]

The pattern of land relations in rural India does influence both agricultural growth and distributive justice. During the British rule, new classes emerged in rural areas like money-lenders-cum-landlords, tenants and sub-tenants, sharecroppers and an agricultural proletariat.

The evolution of the comprehensive land reforms policy is mainly based upon the recommendations of the Congress Agrarian Reforms Committee set up in December, 1947 under the chairmanship of J.C. Kumarappa.

After independence, due to pressure from opposing groups, the Government had to think on the following lines: either to redistribute land in favour of the actual cultivators or to induce the landlords to cultivate the land themselves, through hired labour, instead of renting it out to tenants and sharecroppers. The course of action chosen was an intermediary one.

The Government had decided to abolish Zamindari and creating a class of owner-cultivators from among the landlords' class as well as the upper strata of the peasantry. There was no radical distribution of land in favour of the rural poor. To end Zamindari, most states enacted legislations which took four to five years to come through. This gave enough time for the landlords to manoeuvre the records in their own favour. However, it is said that about 20 million tenants benefitted from the Zamindari abolition.

True, Zamindari abolition made it illegal for landlords to secure rent from their tenants, thereby eliminating the intermediaries. But, this also led to widespread ejectment of tenants and the land belonging to the land owners was recorded in the name of each of their family members and also several fictitious names. Thus, there was no marked change in the ownership pattern of landholdings. In any case, this abolition did not concern itself with the condition of the poorest, namely, the marginal farmers, the sharecroppers and agricultural labourers.[3]

RURAL POWER STRUCTURE

In spite of land ceiling and tenancy reforms, a skewed distribution of assets has been reported, particularly land in rural areas. While there is no change in the concentration ratio of ownership holdings, inequality in the distribution of operational holdings has worsened, with the Gini Coefficient rising from 0.58 in 1961-62 to 0.63 in 1982. This suggests considerable leasing of land.

The rural power structure, as revealed by the all-India Debt and Investment Survey of 1971-72, is quite uneven and unfavourable for the poor: about 9 per cent cultivated households in the country with assets below ₹ 2,500 possessed less than two per cent of total assets of cultivators, while over five per cent of them having assets of ₹ 50,000 and above owned 32 per cent of the total assets.

Land is still the main asset held by the rich rural households. The importance of land has not changed over a period of time in many states.[4]

In 1995- 96, the bottom 61.6 per cent of operational holdings accounted for only 17.2 per cent of the total operated area as against 40.1 per cent accounted for by the top 7.3 per cent. The picture in respect of ownership holding is unlikely to show any dramatic change.

Table: 1
Percentage Share of Land in Total Assets of Rural Households

States	1971-72	1981-82
Andhra Pradesh	68.00	60.70
Assam	60.00	50.00
Bihar	74.00	65.60
Gujarat	57.00	53.00
Haryana	72.00	63.90
Jammu & Kashmir	55.00	58.30
Karnataka	65.00	54.60

Kerala	63.00	68.20
Madhya Pradesh	65.00	61.20
Maharashtra	71.00	65.40
Orissa	66.00	64.30
Punjab	72.00	71.80
Rajasthan	56.00	53.20
Tamil Nadu	65.00	50.10
Uttar Pradesh	66.00	65.00
West Bengal	60.00	59.00

Source: All India Debt and Investment Survey Report, 1971-72.
All India Debt and Investment Survey Report, 1981-82.

Agrarian structure in India has undergone significant changes during the last few decades. We can summarize major change in the pattern of land ownership as revealed in the Agricultural Census (1995-96) and NSS round as follows:

- Proportion of landless agricultural households in the rural area has stabilized around 12 per cent. Trends towards prolitarianisation has come to an end.
- Nearly 80 per cent of the cultivators own marginal (less than 1ha.) and small (between 1 and 2 ha.) holding. Their number as well as area has increased. They accounted for 36 per cent of the total cultivated area in 1995-96.
- Nearly 18 per cent of cultivating households own semi - medium (between 2 to 4 ha) and medium (between 4 to 10 ha) holdings, and accounted for 49 per cent of the cultivated area in 1995-96. There is no perceptible decline in their number or in the area owned by them in recent years.
- Number and area under large holdings (10 ha. And above) has continiously declined.

There is enough evidence to suggest that large holdings do not have any intrinsic advantages in crop production. However, the small and medium size holdings should go in for high value remunerative agriculture.

Table: 2
Distribution of operational Holdings

Size (ha)	Class of holdings	1985-86	1990-91	1995-96
Marginal (Less than 1)	Share of holdings (%)	57.8	59.4	61.1
	share of area operated (%)	13.4	15.0	17.2
Small (1 to 2)	Share of holdings(%)	18.4	18.8	18.7
	share of area operated	15.6	17.4	18.8
Semi-medium (2 to 4)	Share of holdings (%)	13.6	13.1	12.3
	share of area operated (%)	22.3	23.2	23.8
Medium (4 to10)	Share of holdings (%)	8.2	7.1	6.1
	share of area operated (%)	28.6	27.1	25.3
Large) (above 10)	Share of holdings (%)	2.0	1.6	1.2
	share of area operated (%)	20.1	17.3	14.8

The landlords have become politically powerful. They therefore worked towards restricting the governments to mobilise additional resources.

While the feudal order had been eliminated, the feudal elements emerged stronger and more powerful. The elite refused to surrender their power and status so easily. One cannot be therefore indifferent to the present power structure in our villages while implementing programmes for the poor. This power structure is heavily in favour of big land owners who hold numerous positions in public life. In fact, they have also created their vested interest through their own lobby in assemblies of states and the Parliament at the Centre.

The Government is not serious about mobilising rural surpluses. The importance of land revenue and agricultural taxes has been reduced over a period of time. For instance, in 1951-52, taxes on agriculture accounted for seven per cent of the total tax revenues of the Centre and the states. By 1987-88, although the absolute amount increased from ₹ 52 crore to ₹ 573 crore, the proportion of agricultural taxes declined to a mere one per cent. The land tax demand by the state is relatively light, particularly for large cultivators who pay little by way of direct taxes and yet receive maximum benefits from ever-increasing subsidies.[5]

IMPORTANCE OF LAND REFORMS

In the rural context in India, land is not only a means of livelihood, it is also a source of prestige and social identity.[6] In many countries, land ownership and tenure may actually define social status. Indeed, evaluation studies relating to poverty alleviation programmes have revealed how the very poor, without any asset support, are margin. Hence, a blind emphasis on growth without eliminating exploitative elements in the agrarian structure is neither economically nor socially desirable.[7]

Poverty is the end product of the process of monopolisation of means of production. The problem has to be tackled on two fronts: curbing the monopolisation process and improving the capacity of the poor to participate and share in the development.[8] Technological changes in the rural sector are no doubt desirable, but these have succeeded only in accentuating inequalities in the absence of institutional changes.

It was soon realised that the absentee landlordism had resulted in agricultural stagnation. The landlords were content with receiving rents. They did not show any interest in land improvement. The actual tillers of the soil had neither the means nor the incentive to invest as they did not own the land. Under these circumstances, the best way to increase agricultural production was the transfer of ownership of land to the actual cultivator. However, land reform is not only a reform of the way the land is held and maintained, but just as much reform of the man who tills the land.[9]

Land reforms aim at restructuring the agrarian relations to achieve egalitarian social structure. They seek to end all exploitative tendencies. Land to the tiller is an important objective of land reforms. Land reforms aim at improving the socio-economic status of the rural poor so that they participate actively in the functioning of local level institutions.

Land reforms do exercise a positive impact on agricultural development. After all, their primary aim is to remove disincentives in the agricultural sector. Those who acquire land as a result of land ceilings are bound to take advantage of new incentives and opportunities for more work and investment. Smaller units are expected to use the available inputs more intensively, leading to higher cropping intensity. Consolidation of holdings provide better opportunities to adopt new farm technology.

Thus, land reforms aim at achieving the twin objectives of growth through optimum utilisation of land and 'equity' by means of re-distribution of ownership holdings and security of tenure.

Redistribution of land in favour of the poor no doubt will enable the beneficiaries to make their lands emerge as sources for greater agricultural production. Land redistribution compels governments to take better care in the provision of services and make the state policy more development-oriented.[10] As a result of the implementation of land reforms, the leadership would be vigorous and tenacious rather than ephemeral and unreliable.[11]

Several case studies have revealed the positive impact of land reforms on the economic life of the rural people. According to a study relating to the Kangra district of Himachal Pradesh, land reforms could reduce the number of fragmented land holdings. The distance from fragment to fragment and from house to fragment was also reduced due to land reforms. The crop productivity of all the important crops increased after the land reforms were undertaken, but higher yields per hectare were noticed on tenant-cum-owner farms.

Also, the income from agriculture on tenant-cum-owner farms increased from 25 per cent to 40 per cent of the total household income. This income decreased on owner farms from 54 per cent to 50 per cent. The income from hired-out labour decreased substantially from 81 per cent to 33 per cent on land allottees' farms after the land reforms. The corresponding figures for tenant-cum-owner were 26 and 6.

Regarding the impact of land reforms on employment situation, the study indicated that the total days of employment increased from 49 to 57 per cent in the case of land allottees, 51 to 60 per cent for tenant-cum-owners and 52 to 69 per cent in respect of owner farms as a result of land reforms.[12]

I. CEILINGS ON LAND HOLDINGS

The agricultural sector has no doubt experienced technological changes. But, in the absence of institutional changes, these have only accentuated the economic disparities between those who own land and other productive resources on the one hand and those with little access to productive assets. The case for land ceilings arises from the absolute and permanent shortage of land; land ceiling is more urgent than other kinds of ceilings.[13]

The fixation of a ceiling on land holdings and the distribution of surplus land among the landless need to be supported on many grounds. There has been heavy pressure on land, particularly because of limited employment opportunities in the non-farming activities. Land ceilings would eventually step up agricultural output along with employment opportunities.

The case for land ceilings is strong particularly because of absolute and permanent shortage of land. When land ownership is concentrated in a few hands, there is bound to be tension in the rural areas, particularly between poor peasants and landless labourers on the one hand and big land owners on the other.

The fixation of ceilings on holdings at a viable level in terms of improved technology will facilitate distribution of a sizeable area of land among landless labourers and small landholders. This would ensure fuller utilisation of the work-force in agriculture and will also enhance the social status of the rural poor.

Distribution of Surplus Land

The Government has announced its commitment of land reforms in the first five year plan document itself. Prior to that, the Report of the Agrarian Reforms Committee of the Congress, published in 1949, had recommended the imposition of a maximum limit on agricultural holdings. The second five year plan supported the view that there should be an upper limit to the extent of land which a person should be permitted to hold. The panel on Land Reforms of the Planning Commission in 1956 and another Panel on Land Reforms of the Planning Commission in 1961 have studied the issues relating to land reforms.

The Third and Fourth plan documents reiterated the views on land reforms contained in the second plan document. It was made clear that a reduction in disparities in the size and distribution of holdings was a necessary concomitant for building up a progressive co-operative rural economy. The move is meant to provide a measure of opportunity to the landless section of the population. The tenants and share-croppers reportedly were to acquire ownership rights in due course.

However, the progress of land reforms programme has been tardy. After a review of the progress of land reforms, the standing committee of the National Development Council decided in 1957 that the states which had not yet enacted necessary legislation should do so by the end of March 1959 and the laws should be implemented within a period of about three years.

The Indian National Congress at its session held at Nagpur in January 1959, passed a resolution urging the states to enact the ceiling legislation expeditiously. In view of this policy direction, most states were compelled to enact ceiling laws by 1961. Two states, namely, Jammu & Kashmir and West Bengal had enacted the laws well before the Second Plan.

The question of implementation of land reforms was reviewed at a conference of Chief Ministers held in Delhi on September 26-27, 1970. The conference felt that sufficient attention should be given to the new social and political pressures which were getting built up in the rural areas. The need was felt to ensure minimum subsistence to the landless agricultural workers.

At the Chief Ministers' Conference on Ceiling on Agricultural Holdings held on 23rd July 1972, various aspects of the ceiling laws were discussed and certain conclusions were reached with regard to the level of ceiling, unit of application, exemptions, compensation, distribution of surplus land etc.

Studies reveal the following information regarding the record of land reforms:

- Less than 2 per cent of the total area operated has been redistributed.
- Other than in three states, the area redistributed is less than 1 per cent of the area operated in the state.
- Ownership rights over only 3.8 per cent of total area operated were conferred on the tenants.

Even at a ceiling level of 20 acres, it was estimated in the 1950s that 63 million acres would be available as surplus land. The surplus in 1970-71 was placed at 40 million acres.

By end-September 1991, 72.49 lakh acres had been declared surplus, 62.53 lakh acres had been taken possession of, and 48.12 lakh acres had been actually distributed to 45.98 lakh persons. As of March 31, 2002, 73.73 lakh acres had been declared surplus, 65 lakh acres had been taken over, and 53.94 lakh acres had been distributed to a total of 56.47 lakh persons.

The achievement in respect of distribution of government wastelands was considerably higher in absolute tems. As of September 30,1991, 124.61 lakh acres of such lands had been distributed, the bulk of it from Andhra Pradesh (30.4 lakh acres), Uttar Pradesh (22.28) Gujarat (13.73), Karnataka (13.22) and Maharashtra (10.23) By March 31, 2002, the total amount of government wastelands distributed had risen to 147.47 lakh acres, with Andhra Pradesh contributing the largest chunk of 42.02 lakh acres.

EFFECTS ON PRODUCTION

It is feared that land ceilings by reducing the size of the operational holding, would adversely affect agricultural production. The argument is that farm size becomes very uneconomical for cultivation. However, studies show that there is inefficiency among small as well as big farms. What the big or small farms require urgently is an efficient farm management extension which can eliminate distortion in the factor proportions responsible for high costs. The resource utilisation pattern of the most efficient small farms is no way different from that of most efficient large farms.[14] What the small farms urgently require is institutional support.

Some economists believe that small farms have an edge over large farms in respect of traditional labour intensive irrigated farming, though the new agricultural technology is favouring the big farms more than the small ones. But with the adoption of new farm practices and double cropping, a small farm may even produce a marketable surplus. Both the cropping pattern and cropping intensity may be favourable on small farms. The only pre-condition is that such farms have to secure access to crucial inputs.

Moreover, possession of resources is not the criterion to judge efficiency. Rather the right criterion is how best the resources like family labour, bullock power and the capital assets are utilised. Farm management studies reveal that the productivity per acre is greater on the small than on the large farms. Also, the employment per acre is a decreasing function of the size of the farm. Generally, the intensity of cropping decreases as the size of farm increases. The small farmers, however, could benefit only when there is no divorce of resource ownership and resource use.[15]

A small farm need not be inefficient if the experience of Japan, Taiwan and South Korea is any guide. In Japan, a one hectare farm uses three to four times more labour as well as capital and produces four to five times more than a farm of the same size in Orissa. Even a small farm can be productive if it has access to appropriate technology, reinforced by an occupancy right for the land with substantial input and credit support.

LAND CEILING PROGRAMMES: LIMITED SUCCESS

The ceiling laws have been by and large ineffective. Transfers have been permitted under the law as well as those indulged in a clandestine manner. Also, numerous exemptions were granted by various states. The ceiling limits are also open to question. They were fixed at a time when farm productivity and prices were low. The advent of new agricultural technology, the policy of support prices and the exemption of agricultural income from taxation have altered the situation and strengthened the case for lower land ceilings.

Most state governments fixed a very high land ceiling limit and the range is also very wide. Moreover, these ceiling limits were fixed on the basis of the individual holder as a unit instead of a family. This enabled a large family to retain as much as 1000 acres, defeating the very purpose of land ceilings.

The numerous exemptions granted by state governments have made the ceiling laws ineffective. Exemptions were available for plantations, sugarcane farms operated by sugarcane factories, cattle breeding farms, orchards and groves, grazing lands, efficient farms, mechanised farms, religious and charitable institutions and trusts and co-operative farms etc.

After deliberations with the state governments, it was decided to re-enact dealing legislation, fixing a limit on the size of ownership holdings. The essential features of this legislation are:

(i) 10 to 18 acres was the limit of perennially irrigated land capable of yielding two crops a year;

(ii) In the case of a single crop, the ceiling was 27 acres;

(iii) In a household of more than five persons, additional land was allowed for each extra member over 18 years of age.

The legislation is of little help to the rural poor. For paying compensation, the poor used to borrow from the money-lenders. When they failed to repay loans taken, the lands were appropriated by them. Thus, the move proved to be self-defeating.

Moreover, the concept of both sufficient irrigation as well as quality of land were subject to different interpretations. The individual may also assert that he cultivated only one crop. By using their power, the landlords could easily make illegal transfers. In the absence of birth registration, minors claimed that they were above 18 years so as to enable a family to acquire more land.

A case study has revealed that land is considered a basic input, substantially contributing to the socio-economic status of its holder.

However, giving plots of less than one acre to the landless do not help. With the increase in farm size, more and more family members were found to be engaged in their own farm work. The study also revealed that the new land owning class is showing interest in the working of village panchayats and political organisations.

However, the study also noticed many weaknesses in the system of land ceilings. The allottees had suffered because of the procedural delays, judicial decisions, lack of inputs, capital and technical know-how and the overall indifference towards the comparatively weaker sections.

The Lok Sabha was informed on July 28, 1993 that an area of 13.27 lakh acres of ceiling surplus land is involved in litigation in the states, with Andhra Pradesh heading the list with 2,05,324 acres followed by Bihar 1,83,188 acres and West Bengal 1,77,275 acres.

The ten-member Task Force on Agrarian Relations, headed by P. S. Appu, was appointed by the Planning Commission in 1972. It submitted its Report in March 1973. The Report aptly observed, "that in the context of the socio-economic conditions prevailing in the rural areas of the country, no tangible progress can be expected in the field of land reforms in the absence of the requisite political will. The sad truth is that this crucial factor has been wanting.

"The lack of political will is amply demonstrated by the large gaps between policy and legislation and between law and its implementation. In no sphere of public activity in our country since independence has the hiatus between precept and practice, between policy-pronouncements and actual execution been as great as in the domain of land reforms."

"With resolute and unambiguous political will, all the other shortcomings and difficulties could have been overcome; in the absence of such a will, even minor obstacles become formidable road-blocks in the path of the Indian land reforms. Considering the character of the political power structure existing in the country, it was only natural that the required political will was not forthcoming."

The beneficiaries of ceiling laws are passive, unorganised and inarticulate. They do not constitute a homogeneous social or economic group. They are not mutually exclusive. The Task Force of the Planning Commission observed,[16] "The mixed economic status of the different groups and their conflicting economic interests have rendered organised collective action very difficult."

In the absence of a suitable administrative organisation, ceiling laws cannot be effective particularly when the bureaucracy itself does not favour them. The situation worsened in the absence of correct and up-to-date record of rights.

The land reforms programme lacked an integrated approach: consolidation of holdings was conceived of and undertaken without providing for village roads, irrigation and drainage channels, land shaping, soil conservation etc. There is also no effective political organisation at the grassroot levels to minimise and eliminate the tensions that are bound to emerge with the implementation of land reforms.[17]

While the redistribution of land is essential, it is necessary to see that too uneconomic and small holdings do not emerge.[18]

II. TENANCY REFORMS

The term 'land tenure' refers to the system of land-ownership and management. Land tenure assumes importance because it has a direct bearing on agricultural productivity and production. For instance, under the Zamindari system, the landlord who provides land is made responsible for the payment of land revenue to the state. The landlord gets a pre-determined share of the produce. The tenant provides the labour and managerial inputs. Thus, the actual tiller does not come into contact with the state. The landlord, acts as an intermediary. Besides, the Zamindari system does not serve as an incentive to boost agricultural production.

The relationship between the farmers and the owner of the land has a direct bearing on agricultural production. A research study of the Intensive Agricultural District Programme on the tenancy pattern in Thanjavur district has pointed out that "if the relationship is cordial, production goes up, if not, production suffers."[19]

In fact, one of the main reasons for inadequate rice production in the eastern-region has been the prevalence of share croppers in Bihar and Orissa which, in turn, has led to inadequate flow of inputs and credit as well as inadequate development of land and inappropriate use of ground water.

There is no doubt about the primacy of tenants in rural India. At the all-India level, there were 17.4 million rural households reporting leasing-in. These formed 18.55 per cent of the total rural households which were estimated at 93.6 million as in 1982. The distribution of households reporting leasing-in by households category, showed heavy concentration in the landless, marginal and small owner category. These groups accounted for 91.55 per cent of the total tenants in rural India. Again, at the all-India level, those who leased out land were 5.2 million rural households, mostly small owners.[20]

Aspects of Tenancy Reforms

Tenancy reforms were enacted in all states except Nagaland, Meghalaya and Mizoram. They provide for conferment of ownership on the tenants by the state, execution of ownership by tenants on payment of reasonable compensation, security of tenure and fixation of rents.

Along with legislation for the abolition of intermediaries, tenancy laws were carried out in order to ensure a large measure of protection to tenants. However, this set into motion a contradictory social process, namely, the mass eviction of tenants and share croppers. The major elements of tenancy legislation carried out by various states are: *(i)* regulation of rents, *(ii)* security of tenure and *(iii)* the right of ownership.

On the eve of independence, the rents paid by tenants to the landlords were high at 50 to 70 per cent of the total produce. The tenants were also forced to render certain free services. The government, after reviewing the situation, came to the conclusion that the rent should be fixed between 20 to 25 per cent of the total produce. Of course, the actual rent fixed varies from one state to another. Rents also vary depending on the type of agricultural land, dry or wet. Rents have also been differentiated on the basis of differences in land revenue.

Security of tenure is important for the tenant. Legislation relating to the security of tenure has the following features: *(i)* ejectments do not take place except in accordance with the provisions of the law, *(ii)* land may be resumed by the land-owners for personal cultivation and *(iii)* in the event of resumption, the tenant is assured of the prescribed minimum area.

Of course, in some states, all tenants in cultivation and possession of land have been given full security of tenure without the land owners having any right to resume land for personal cultivation.

In some states, land owners are permitted to resume a limited area for personal cultivation, subject to the condition that a minimum area or a portion of the holding is left with the tenants.

In some states like West Bengal and Jammu & Kashmir, a limit has been placed on the extent of land which a land owner may resume but the tenant is not entitled to retain a minimum area or a portion of his holding in all cases.

Measures have been initiated in some states in the form of an order for staying ejectments to grant temporary protection to tenants.

As a result of measures taken by the government, about 110.42 lakh cultivators have been conferred ownership rights in respect of 144.29 lakh acres of land which constitutes approximately five per cent of the cultivable land.

LIMITATIONS OF TENANCY LEGISLATION

Tenancy legislation aims at making ejectment difficult for the landlords. Ejectment can take place only on certain grounds — *(i)* non-payment of rent, *(ii)* performance of an act which is destructive or permanently injurious to the land, *(iii)* sub-letting the land, *(iv)* using the land for purposes other than agriculture and *(v)* resumption of land for personal cultivation by the landlord.

The ultimate aim of land reforms is to confer rights of ownership on the tillers. Legislation has been passed to achieve this objective: *(i)* by declaring tenants as owners and requiring them to pay compensation to owners in suitable instalments, *(ii)* through the acquisition of right of ownership by the state on payment of compensation and transfer of ownership by the state on payment of compensation and transfer of ownership to tenants and *(iii)* through acquisition by the state on the basis of rights given to landlords and bringing tenants into direct relationship with the state, an option being given to tenants to continue as such on payment of fair rent to the government or to acquire full ownership on payment of the prescribed minimum. As a result of the tenancy legislation, about 90 per cent of the cultivated land is wholly owned and self-operated by the tenants.

However, the tenancy legislation does suffer from certain loopholes. Some of these are listed below:

In most cases, leasing takes place on the principle of share cropping. The exclusion of share croppers from the scope of security of tenure limits the utility of tenancy legislation.

Ejectment of tenants from their holdings still takes place on many grounds. Some elements of feudal system still exist and are implemented as they were done earlier.

Voluntary surrenders are hardly done by tenants. Very often the tenants are forced to surrender their lands and the law is ineffective because such lands are recorded as having voluntaries been surrendered.

The right of resumption contained in the tenancy reform legislation is very often misused. This leads to concealed tenancy. The actual tenant is shown as a farm servant.

Not much progress has been made in respect of regulation of rent. The fair rent remains undefined in most states. When the security of tenure is denied, it is difficult to ensure a fair rent.

The spirit of land to the tiller remains only on paper. The tenants are not in a position to pay high rates of compensation. It is also difficult for the tenants to provide proof of continuous possession of land for twelve consecutive years. The landlord is capable of manipulating the land records. The onus of proof rests on the tenants.

There is provision for pre-emption, that is, when the landlord is selling the land, he should give first preference to the tenant. But the trouble is that the landlord may offer his land at a time when it is not convenient to the tenant.

Without bringing the tenants and share croppers on records, the security of tenurial rights cannot be ensured and these persons cannot get even a crop loan from the credit institutions. Many tenants just could not afford to pay the purchase price while others were unwilling to purchase as landlords pressurised the tenants into submitting that they were no interested.

The Wadhwa Committee appointed by the Planning Commission to evaluate the situation concerning record of rights in land suggested establishment of an autonomous statutory corporation called 'Land Title Corporation.' The Committee also recommended a change over from the present system of presumptive titles to land to conclusive titles.

The sad part of the story is that there is absolutely no agency to effectively supervise the implementation of tenancy provisions. That is why the gap between state policy and the actual field situation is wide.

BETTER DEAL FOR THE TENANTS

The tenancy reforms have not been uniformly successful across the states. West Bengal, Karnataka and Kerala have achieved some success. By 1993, in West Bengal, 14 lakh share croppers have been recorded under 'Operation Barga.' In Karnataka, three lakh tenants were settled on 11 lakh acres of land by special 'land tribunals' set up for this purpose. In Kerala, through the tenants' association, applications of 24 lakh tenants for conferment of ownership were accepted.

The tenancy legislative provisions are also said to be ineffective. Tenancy can be ended legitimately on very frivolous grounds. There must be provision to restrict termination of tenancy only to misuse of land, denial of rent or denial of the landlord's right. It may be necessary to prescribe a fairly long-term as the minimum period of tenancy and automatic renewal of the tenancy agreement on the expiry of the first term of lease. Also, 'personal cultivation' should include not only personal supervision of the land but also personal labour.

Some tenants were removed on the ground of voluntary surrenders. It would be more useful, if all surrenders are made in favour of the state to enable it to dispose of surplus land according to rules framed for this purpose.

The FAO observed that the governments should[21] —

(i) Give precedence in the redistribution of land to established tenants, small landholders and landless agricultural labourers, with particular attention to the most deprived groups, and strength on such redistribution with programmes for improving productivity, including the formation of co-operatives and other forms of associations of peasants with comprehensive state assistance;

(ii) Implement redistribution with speed and determination backed by preventive legal sanctions to avert disinvestment and evasive transfers;

(iii) Create and support post-reform institutions, including farmers associations, co-operatives, collective and state farms and development activities with the widest feasible participation of the beneficiaries to prevent the emergence of new patterns of concentration of resources of other forms of exploitation.

It may also be noted that a complete ban on future tenancies will also adversely affect social mobility. The small land owners may be allowed to lease out land subject to the following conditions:

- A small landowner may be defined as one who owns less than five acres of land;
- The lease should be for a period of five years and there should be provision for six months' notice if the lease is to be terminated at the end of five years;
- All lease deeds should be reduced to writing and lodged with the Gram Panchayat;
- The rent payable should not exceed one-fourth of the gross produce and it may be fixed in cash for different categories of land in different areas. In a year of serious failure of crops, the tenant should have the option to pay the rent by showing the produce and
- If any landowner leases out his land in violation of these conditions, penal action should be taken against him and ownership rights should be conferred on the tenant.[22]

Land reforms would be incomplete without tenancy reforms. Incentives are important in all sectors, more so in the agricultural sector.

III. CONSOLIDATION OF HOLDINGS

As a result of increasing pressure of population on land, the holdings are not only sub-divided but also fragmented (the holdings of a cultivator are scattered over a number of places). The average size of a holding was about 3.1 hectares in 1953-54; it came down to 2.6 hectares by 1961-62 and further to 2.06 hectares as revealed by the agricultural census for 1970-71.

The sub-division and fragmentation of land holdings are becoming more and more serious for various reasons:

- Pressure of population on land;
- The laws of inheritance and succession;
- The break-up of the joint family system;
- The tardy progress of rural industrialisation programme;
- Growing indebtedness of small and marginal farmers; and
- The desire of each sharer to have a fractional share of each kind of land in every plot.

Sub-division and fragmentation of land holdings do produce very harmful effects. These make cultivation very uneconomic. The small farmers had to acquire fixed assets at a high cost. Precious land is wasted because of too many restrictions and fixed boundaries. When holdings are fragmented, the cultivators have to move from one place to another to carry on agricultural operations, resulting in wastage of time and money. Personal supervision of land and making available modern technological infrastructure on the firm become quite difficult. Also, sub-division and fragmentation often create disputes regarding boundaries, rights of tenancy which compel farmers to undertake expensive litigation.

Due to population growth and sub-division of holdings, 70 per cent of total holdings were below 2 ha. The per capita availability of arable land is 0.18 ha. This has made holdings quite uneconomical. To bring about economical feasibility, the remedy lies in *'consolidation'* of holdings. *Consolidation* means rearrangement of holdings in a unit amongst several tenure holders in such a way as to make their respective holdings more compact and economically viable for intensive cultivation.

Consolidation of holdings is bound to produce some economic gains. The increase in production can be attributed to additional land brought under cultivation as a result of removal of boundaries. Besides, productivity will definitely go up due to development of land, greater availability of private irrigation facilities, use of highest level of inputs and adoption of improved agricultural practices and latest technological infrastructure.

A study of agricultural holdings in India with special reference to Punjab and Uttar Pradesh has revealed that the process of consolidation of holdings has led to a significant reduction in cost of cultivation, increased cropping intensity and bringing about a remunerative cropping pattern.

The study also showed that as a result of consolidation of agricultural holdings, there was reduction of dependence on share croppers and greater investment in development of agricultural infrastructure such as mechanisation and minor irrigation.

The study, commissioned by the Food Production and Rural Development Division of the Food and Agricultural Organisation (FAO), was carried out by the Centre for Research and Training in Rural Administration, University of Lucknow.

The study has clearly brought out that consolidation of holdings has almost uniformly resulted in better-planned provision of common services and facilities like roads, irrigation channels, grazing lands and housing sites. It has also led to harmonious relations in the village community.[23]

Fifteen states have passed laws for consolidation of holdings. In selected areas of Andhra Pradesh, Tamil Nadu, Kerala, Pondicherry and North Eastern States, these laws have not been enacted. Consolidation of holdings has made very good progress in states like Punjab, Haryana and U.P. which has facilitated agricultural growth.

Consolidation of land holdings was carried out without taking effective steps to ensure security of tenure to tenants, particularly share-croppers. This led to large-scale ejectment of insecure tenants.

When land holdings are scattered, it is not possible for land owners to cultivate land personally. When consolidation of land holdings is effected, the land owners find it feasible and profitable to cultivate personally the entire area. The task of getting rid of the share-croppers becomes easy.

The Task Force of the Planning Commission observed, "Consolidation of holdings was conceived of and undertaken without providing for village roads, irrigation and drainage channels, land shaping, soil conservation etc. An integrated approach would have yielded much better results."

As a result of sub-division and fragmentation of holdings due to increasing pressure on land, top priority becomes necessary to bring about consolidation of holdings.

IV. CO-OPERATIVE FARMING

The sub-division and fragmentation of land holdings make the operational holdings quite uneconomical. Under these conditions, it tends to become difficult for small farmers to take advantage of the modern agricultural practices. These farmers cannot derive the economies of scale for undertaking meaningful cultivation.

Under co-operative farming, lands held by a number of uneconomic holders are brought under common management in order to create a landbase on which economic agricultural operation is possible.

The co-operative planning committee had in 1945 suggested the organisation of four types of co-operative farming societies, namely: *(i)* better farming, *(ii)* tenant farming, *(iii)* joint farming and *(iv)* collective farming societies. It was thought that the first two types are not suited to developing countries because under them, the members have to take decisions and bear the risks individually.

The Indian government has over the years concentrated mainly on joint farming, which implies pooling of land and joint cultivation. In the joint farming societies, members owned the lands but cultivated the pooled lands jointly. In the collective farming societies, the pooled lands were held by the society on either free hold or leasehold. [24]

Under the co-operative better farming society, independent land holding members 'agree to follow a plan of cultivation' laid down by the society. "In furtherance of its object, it may undertake . . . joint ploughing, joint harvesting or joint arrangements for watch and ward or joint use of machinery. However, joint cultivation is not obligatory."

The co-operative tenant farming society leases out (freehold or leasehold) plots to members for individual cultivation. The rental becomes the income of the society, and this is meant to provide support and guidance to members for improvement of cultivation.

Under co-operative joint farming society, the landowners pool their lands under the society for joint cultivation. The ownership of each member in this holding continues and is recognised by the payment of a dividend in proportion to the value of his land.

The co-operative collective farming society holds land in lease-hold or free-hold and undertakes joint cultivation. It is supposed that the co-operative farming system has to ultimately take this shape and joint farming society is the first step forward to achieve this.

Under the banner of co-operative farming, the landlords have almost legally consolidated their position in the face of the land ceiling laws. A number of societies have been formed by bigger farmers for their own benefit. The dominant group in such societies takes no interest in farming operations. The actual work is entrusted to casual labourers engaged on a daily wage basis.

There are also societies formed by small farmers who have pooled their holdings in the co-operative. Such societies are generally homogeneous in character. The majority of members in such societies are invariably engaged in farm operations.

There is another category of societies formed on lands that have been assigned to them or required for them. There are usually government waste lands and the members of such societies are usually landless agricultural labourers.[25]

In India, the co-operative farming movement was launched in the early fifties and prospered during the late fifties and the early sixties. D.R. Gadgil considered co-operative farming an "obvious and logical solution to the basic problems of agriculture in the country."

Indian planning has given importance to co-operative farming. A beginning was made even in the First Five Year Plan (1951-56) when small and medium farmers were encouraged to group themselves voluntarily into co-operative farming societies. The number of joint farming societies increased from 1758 in 1959-60 to 5328 in 1966-67. But subsequently their number declined to 4844 in 1972-73. The Government did sincerely try to implement the recommendations of the Report of the Working Group on Co-operative Farming (1959) under the chairmanship of S. Nijalingappa.

Co-operative farming was considered most desirable particularly in the context of ceiling laws and distribution of surplus land among the landless. Those who receive small holdings under the ceiling laws may not be able to cultivate them most productively. On the other hand, if these holdings are brought under co-operative farming, it is possible to obtain optimum returns from them.

There were, at the end of June 1974, over 9700 co-operative farming societies, with a membership of 2.7 lakh, commanding a total area of 5.25 lakh hectares. But more than 60 per cent of these societies are admittedly not functioning properly.

However, co-operative farming has not received the attention it deserves in the absence of sustained interest on the part of the government machinery and positive interest on the part of farmers concerned. In many states, partial pooling of lands had been allowed. There is only inadequate appreciation of benefits of joint farming. The farmers feel that they would not be able to obtain loans from the money-lenders for urgent domestic needs under joint farming societies.

In some cases, the small cultivators are reluctant to accept the idea of collective farming, if big farmers do not join them. Also, in most states, finance has not been readily available to societies to undertake development programmes. The old debts of the members may also create problems. By the end of the third five year plan, the enthusiasm about co-operative farming disappeared.

The Gadgil committee, which submitted its report in 1965, regretted that co-operative farming had not taken firm roots in India. Even when societies are formed, their functioning has been far from satisfactory. It was pointed out that on the eve of the fifth plan, nearly 40 per cent of the societies were not functioning properly. Out of 9,400 societies with a membership of over two lakh and covering a total area of over five lakh hectares, only 4,580 were actually working and of them, 2,500 societies were running at a loss.[26]

Soon enough, it was discovered that the movement bristled with a number of deficiencies, inconsistencies and even surreptitiousness, experienced a gradual but inevitable decline.[27] The bigger plot holders have not shown any interest in this system, except in controlling and dominating the minor and medium plot holders.

Though there is arrangement for proportionate share in the total surplus, there are still discrepancies in remuneration. However, the payment system became unworkable because though there is upward revision with the rising level of market prices, any drop in dividends for genuine reasons like crop failure was resented. There are also difficulties in the measurement of work to determine the share of each owner. This leads to distrust.

In actual operation, the co-operative societies suffered from serious drawbacks. The spirit of co-operation was replaced by fissiparous tendencies. Distrust gradually increased. Also, there was no sound financial management. Many societies remained defunct. The co-operative movement slackened due to inefficient monitoring, guidance and supervision by the state.

Co-operative farming cannot be successful through bureaucratic initiatives. It is necessary to build up a base for people's initiative which can be generated by mass organisations of the rural work force. Experts feel that co-operative farming would be successful only if it is preceded by the consolidation of holdings.

The Centre has advised the state governments to encourage collective farming: compact blocks of land belonging to the government need to be converted into co-operative farming societies. The government has to take up reclamation of land and provide technical guidance to the societies. It was envisaged that the Centre would provide societies by way of contribution to the share capital, loans for development, loan-cum-subsidy for godowns and subsidies towards managerial expenses.

The Committee of Direction on Co-operative Farming, 1969 (Chairman: D.R. Gadgil) recommended that 10,000 new co-operative farming societies ought to be organised. However, the interest, encouragement and even indirect participation of the government had also disappeared to a large extent.

The merits of co-operative farming have not been well appreciated by the farming community. The farmers show positive interest in the programme if only they are properly educated.

V. LAND REFORM: THE TASK AHEAD

In the past, there have been discussion for a long period on the merits and demerits of land reforms. This gave landlords plenty of time to conceal large amounts of land, with the connivance of the local revenue administration and the collusion of the party in power.

The major hurdle in the distribution of surplus land is that a large extent of such land which is around 12.92 lakh acres is usually involved in litigation at various levels. In order to make this land available for distribution, state governments have been urged to constitute land tribunals under Article 323-B of the Constitution or create special benches in the High Courts in consultation with them to expedite the issue in the least possible time.

The states of Bihar, Kerala, Tamil Nadu and West Bengal have already enacted legislations for setting up Land Tribunals under Articles 323-B of the Constitution. Also, land reforms tribunals are functioning in Gujarat and Maharashtra while a special bench has been set up in the Bihar High Court as well as in Andhra Pradesh where two additional primary tribunals and six full time district level Appellate Tribunals have been set up.

There have been differences of opinion on the quantum of compensation to be paid. The Working Group rejected the view that compensation should be at the market value. It said, "It will be impossible for the state to undertake its social responsibilities if full compensation is given. The very purpose of breaking the concentration of economic power will be lost, if a rich land owner who is to lose his power on land is given financial resources to gain in other sectors. Moreover, equity participations demand that there should be different slabs of compensation, the scale of compensation going down along with higher holding to be compensated, as has been done at the time of abolition of intermediary interests."

The enforcement of land reforms is a state subject. As such, the states have the responsibility of creating conditions favourable for land reforms. Under the Gadgil formula, the states doing well on the land reform front get a higher allocation from the general pool of central assistance to the states.

The Task Force of the Planning Commission has pertinently pointed out, "No state has taken necessary steps to forge a suitable administrative organisation and keep it in proper term by systematic in-service training and periodic orientation courses. Nor has any conscious effort been made to post able and dedicated men with faith in land reforms to key positions in the administrative set up. As a matter of fact, there have been cases where administrators who tried to implement land reform laws honestly and efficiently were transferred elsewhere."

It is necessary to update land records, in order to know whether ceiling surplus land is distributed or the erstwhile landless tenants acquire rights or land is transferred through inheritance, sale or gift.

The centuries old land records system in the country is being computerised in line with technological changes taking place. As many as 21 pilot projects on computerisation of land records are being implemented in one district each of 21 states and Union Territories. The scheme has to be extended to all districts in the country.

The Centre had started a scheme in 1988 to help the states and Union Territories as part of its efforts to modernise land records and strengthen revenue administration. A sum of ₹ 5,972 lakh has been provided as central assistance to all States and Union Territories up to June 1993. The funds were released to the states on 50:50 basis except for Union Territories where central assistance was 100 per cent.

The Constitution (49th) Amendment Act, 1983, was passed by the Parliament in August 1984, which placed 14 more land reform laws in the Ninth Scheduled of the Constitution, providing immunity to these measures from being challenged in a court of law.

The Working Group on Land Reforms appointed by the National Commission on Agricultural Land observed that in the distribution of surplus land, first priority should be given to landless persons. If surplus land is available in larger blocks, the allotment of land to co-operative societies consisting of eligible beneficiaries should be encouraged.

Also, the surplus land should be allotted to the beneficiaries on the specific condition that they will not be permitted to sell or mortgage these lands. The Working Group observed, "If at any time the beneficiaries want to leave the profession of cultivation, the land will revert to the government. The beneficiaries will enjoy permanent heritable rights in the lands concerned."

Considering the poor quality of surplus ceiling land assigned to the beneficiaries, financial assistance at the rate of ₹ 2,500 per hectare was decided under the centrally-sponsored scheme of financial assistance to assignees of ceiling surplus land.

The benefits of this scheme have all been extended to Scheduled Castes/Scheduled Tribes, allottees of bhoodan land and the government wasteland and also to SCs/STs who have been given back their alienated lands.

Land reforms succeed only when there is enhanced awareness among the actual cultivators about their rights. The 73rd Constitutional Amendment Act enables people to take active participation in the functioning of panchayati raj institutions.

The organisation of the beneficiaries of land ceilings and tenancy reforms is absolutely essential. Otherwise, the benefits of radical reforms remain only on paper. The Task Force of the Planning Commission has observed, "In our view, a certain degree of politicisation of the poor peasantry is a pre-requisite for any successful legislative-administrative action for conferring rights and privileges on them. Of course, there must be massive economic support to the share-croppers through institutional sources."

REFERENCES

1. S.L. Ghosal: 'Land Reforms and Access to Technological Change', *The Hindu,* September 21, 1993, p. 17.
2. R.K. Sharma, Anil Kumar and S.K. Chauhan: 'Impact of Land Reforms on Farm Production', *Kurukshetra,* February 1993, p. 8.
3. Rohini Nayyar: 'Land Reforms: Still a Relevant Issue', *Kurukshetra,* August 15, 1993, p. 55.
4. *Southern Economist* (editorial), July 1, 1992, p. 4.
5. Ritu Dewan: *'Political Economy of Agrarian Reforms in India'*,Himalaya Publishing House, Mumbai.
6. Andre Beteille (1974): 'Studies in Agrarian Social Structure', Oxford & I.B.H. Publishing Co., New Delhi, p. 65.
7. N.C. Saxena: 'Land Reforms and Equity', *Seminar,* June 1994, p. 31.
8. R.P. Misra: 'Target Groups and Regional Development', in Brahmananda, P.R., D.M. Nanjundappa and B.K. Narayan (Ed.1979): *Indian Economic Development and Policy,* Vikas Publishing House, New Delhi, p. 258.
9. FAO (1953): 'Inter-relationship between Agrarian Reform andAgricultural Development', p. 63.
10. Keith B. Griffin, John L. Enos: 'Planning Development', Addison-Wesley Publishing Co. London, pp. 130-131.
11. Sachchidanand Sinha (1975): The Bitter Harvest: Agriculture and *the Economic Crisis',* Manas Publications, New Delhi, p. 108.
12. R.K. Sharma *et al., op. cit.,* p. 6.
13. A.M. Khusro (1973): 'The Economics of Land Reform and Farm Size in India', Macmillan, p. xiv.
14. Karam Singh: 'Economic Efficiency and Farm Size', *EasternEconomist,* November 11, 1977, p. 928.

15. G. Parthasarathy (1971): *'Agricultural Development and Small Farmers: A Study of Andhra Pradesh'*, Vikas Publishing House, New Delhi, p. 25.

16. M.P. Mathur: 'Distribution of Surplus Land: Impact on Beneficiaries', *Financial Express*, June 7, 1990.

17. G. Parthasarathy: 'Land Reform and the Changing Agrarian Structure', in C.H. Shah (Ed. 1979): *Agricultural Development of India: Policy and Problems,* Orient Longman, p. 365.

18. 'Organisation of Economic Co-operation and Development', Paris (1964); Low Incomes in Agriculture: Problems and Policies, p. 48.

19. *The Hindu,* January 27, 1978.

20. G. Parthasarathy: 'Lease Market, Poverty Alleviation and Policy Options', *Economic and Political Weekly,* March 30,1991, p. A-31.

21. FAO (1979): 'Report on World Conference Agrarian Reform and Rural Development', p. 6.

22. P. S. Appu: 'Tenancy Reform in India', *Economic and Political Weekly* (Special Number) August, 1975, p. 1360.

23. *The Economic Times*, April 11, 1983.

24. B.S. Padmanabhan: 'Co-operative Farming Still a Far Cry', *The Hindu,* December 10, 1975.

25. *Economic and Political Weekly,* December 25, 1975, pp. 1942-1943.

26. B.S. Padmanabhan, *op. cit.*

27. S.K. Ray: 'Co-operative Farming: A Review', *Facts For You,* April1986, p. 41.

Chapter

22 PLIGHT OF AGRICULTURAL LABOURERS

The landless agricultural labourers constitute one of the disadvantaged sections of rural India. Their conditions should receive special attention because they form about 25 per cent of the total labour force. Indeed, the composition of the workforce in agriculture has been changing for the worse. We find declining proportion of cultivators and increasing proportion of agricultural labourers. However, the occupational structure has remained more or less stagnant over the last three decades. The proportion of agricultural workforce was 69.51 per cent in 1961; 69.79 per cent 1971 and 66.69 per cent in 1981.

As a result of worsening rural poverty and alienation of the rural sector from land and growth of commercial agriculture, the number of landless agricultural labourers is rapidly increasing. Out of a total workforce of 184 million in India in 1971, 26 per cent (48 million) were agricultural labourers. The percentage was 16.71 in 1961. The number of agricultural labourers have increased from 13 million in 1961 to 64.4 million in 1981 and to 78 million in 1990.

During 1971 to 1981, the proportion of agricultural labourers increased at the rate of 3.3 per cent per annum. This is nearly 50 per cent higher than the growth rate of total population of the country. The position of the eighties is no different from the previous decade. There has been a sharp decline in the proportion of self-employed households in agriculture. As a result of sub-division of holdings among the small and marginal farmers, some of the self-employed labour force is becoming redundant. The only option left to them was to become wage labourers.

It is observed that 'attached labour households' which constituted 9.7 per cent of the total agricultural labour households in 1950-51 had increased to 26.63 per cent by the end of the sixties. Capitalism in Indian agriculture is fast expanding but the relationship between farmers and labourers continues to be semi-feudal in most parts of the country.

The number of agricultural labourers in the country including marginal workers was 64.4 million in 1981. Their number is said to be increasing at the rate of 2.5 per cent. The number of agricultural labourers, including marginal workers in 1987 was about 74.68 million. This figure does not include the self-employed agriculturists, whose number as per the 1981 census was 92.53 million.

The agricultural labourers can be identified by some peculiar characteristics. These labourers are unorganised and unskilled. Hence, they suffer from weak bargaining power. Very often, they migrate to the place of work. Also, there is direct contact between the agricultural labourers and their employer. Considering the nature of work they take up, agricultural labourers are hardly governed by any rules and regulations.

The Second Agricultural Labour Enquiry Committee defined an agricultural labourer *"as one whose principal means of livelihood in wage income arise out of the farm labour and other allied activities."* The agricultural labourer, according to the census of India, is one who works on another person's land for wages in money, kind or share.

I. PREDOMINANT WORKFORCE

About two-thirds of the total workers are engaged in agriculture and these proportions have decreased marginally since 1951. A little more than one-third of the agricultural workers are landless labourers and the rest are cultivators.

The special employment generation schemes of the eighties like RLEGP, NREP and JRY have only marginally helped the labourers in getting employment. A number of programmes have been taken up under employment generation schemes. These included road-building, reclamation and development of land, water conservation, minor irrigation, soil conservation and afforestation. Yet, agricultural labourers remain unemployed for most part of the year.

According to the 1981 census, the female agricultural labourers constituted 23.9 per cent of the rural workforce as against 15.9 per cent in 1971. This means that there is increased rate of participation of women in agriculture and its allied activities. This can again be attributed to sheer poverty and deteriorating economic conditions.

There has been a steady increase in the proportion of agricultural labour to the total workforce of the country. This proportion stood at 16.71 per cent in 1961, but rose to 26.15 per cent in 1991.

The proportion of agricultural labour households to total rural households also increased from 21.8 per cent to 25.3 per cent during the decade 1964-65 to 1974-75.

According to the NSS 55th Round Survey on Employment and Unemployment (1999-2000), the total workforce of the country was 393 million: 298 million in rural areas engaged in agriculture and allied activities. About 80 per cent of the total rural labour households (over 30 per cent of the total rural households) are agricultural labour households. Of them, SC/ST constitute nearly 50 per cent.

The agricultural labourers are greatly handicapped because their supply is far in excess of their demand. The slow growth of non-farming sectors is responsible for this.

Not a few factors have contributed to the rapid rise in the number of agricultural households. In some parts of rural India, the old, semi-feudal forms of bonded and attached labour still continues, giving impetus to capitalist production for profit. The ranks of the landless are swollen by evictions of poor peasants.

Table: I
Growth of Agricultural Labour in India

(in lakhs)

Years	*Number*
1881	75
1891	187
1911	216
1931	299
1951	280
1961	320
1971	480
1981	555
1991	747
2001	1074

Source: Population Census Reports.

The rapid growth of population is mainly responsible for a significant rise in the number of agricultural labourers. More and more people are forced to depend on land for their livelihood.

Of course, the proportion of agricultural workers to the total number of workers varies from state to state. This was 3.52 per cent in Himachal Pradesh; 37.21 per cent in Bihar, 40.76 per cent in Andhra Pradesh, 25.66 per cent in Kerala and 34.2 per cent in Tamil Nadu.

II. CONDITIONS OF AGRICULTURAL LABOURERS

The agricultural workers constitute the most backward, unorganised and downtrodden section of the rural community. Most of them are below the poverty line. Very often, they are deprived of the benefits of their own labour.

As the fortunes of the farm sector fluctuate from year to year, the worst affected are casual workers in agriculture. In a year of scarcity, the farm labour households do try to maintain their real incomes constant by: *(i)* encouraging women to enter the workforce and *(ii)* stepping up the non-wage and non-agricultural income.[1]

By 1990, it was estimated that there existed a backlog of nine million unemployed agricultural labourers. The assumptions in arriving at this magnitude are: *(i)* three-fourth of the 16 million unemployed being in rural areas and *(ii)* two-thirds among the rural unemployed being the agricultural labourers.[2]

Generally, female agricultural workers are paid less than the male workers. Women perform a number of social and domestic functions and go to the field, only to earn less than men. Women are preferred in certain categories of work like transplantation. The system of fixing lower wages for agricultural operations predominantly performed by women is undesirable and it should be stopped.[3]

Real wages of agricultural labourers increased on an average per annum by 4.89 per cent during the period 1983 to 1987-88. But, this came down to 2.94 per cent during the period 1993-94 to 1999-2000. Thus, the relative position of agricultural labourers has worsened during the 1990s.

According to NSSO, the real wages of male agricultural labourers increased by 4.7 per cent during 1980-89, by 1.5 per cent during 1990-99 and by 0.1 per cent 2000- 04. For females, the increased during these periods were 4.5 per cent, 1.42 per cent and 0.1 per cent.

Table: 2
Growth in Real Wages of Agricultural Labourers (Per cent)

Period	*Males*	*Femals*
1980-89	4.70	4.50
1990-99	1.50	1.41
2000-04	0.10	0.10

The male casual labourer in agriculture got a wage of ₹ 25.48 in 1999-2000. The corresponding figure for females was ₹ 17.99.

Most agricultural labour households do not own any land. As per the 32nd Round of the National Sample Survey (NSS), about 51.37 per cent of the agricultural labour households did not own any land. The average size of land cultivated per agricultural labour household was 1.33 acres only.

Agricultural labourers remain unemployed for more than four months in a year. This is the main reason for the growing indebtedness of agricultural workers. During the period 1964-65 to 1974-75, employment declined from 235 days to 218 days in a year in the case of male agricultural workers and from 194 days to 180 days in the case of female agricultural workers. Studies show that even in agriculturally prosperous districts, farm workers, could find employment only for 150 days in a year.

The Rural Labour Enquiry Report (1974-75) revealed that 75 per cent of agricultural labour households held less than 1.50 acres each. The proportion of agricultural labour households with land and without land was early equal, 49 per cent and 51 per cent respectively. The World Bank Staff Working Paper No. 320 (published in 1972) estimated the number of landless labour households in India at 24 million and their population at 114 million in 1977. The Sixth Plan (1980-85) estimated that 50 per cent of the agricultural labour households had no land.

The Report has shown the deteriorating economic conditions of farm labourers. The money wage no doubt increased from ₹ 1.43 in 1964-65 to ₹ 3.24 in 1974-75. But, during this period, the All-India Consumer Price Index Number for agricultural labourers (base July 1960-61) went up by 157% from 143 in 1964-64 to 368% in 1974-75. Therefore, the average daily earnings of ₹ 3.24 for men in agricultural operations in 1974-75 got reduced to ₹ 1.26 in real terms, compared to ₹ 1.43 in 1964-65, thus showing a decline of 12 per cent. According to rough estimates, the money income in 1974-75 per agricultural labour household was ₹ 1,404. The abnormal price rise brought down the real wage, based on the 1960-61 price level, the income worked out to only ₹ 381.52 per household in 1974-75. In 1964-65, the per capita income of agricultural labour was only 59 per cent of the average rural net national product and this declined to 42 per cent in 1974-75.[4]

The system of payment of wages in kind is being increasingly replaced by cash and monetisation of the agrarian economy. It is easier to administer, and is very convenient to the migrant labour not familiar with local customs. However, replacement of kind payment by cash has eroded the real income of labour class due to price rise.

According to a study (1988) carried out by the International Labour Organisation — Asian Regional Team for Employment Programmes (ILO-ARTEP), the real wages of farm workers during the period 1970 to 1985, fell even in the two agriculturally prosperous states, namely, Punjab and Haryana. The study pointed out that wages in Punjab, Haryana and Kerala were far higher than those prevailing in other states.

However, the study observed that the rising trend in wages in Punjab and Haryana was arrested because of — *(i)* large scale migration of labour from Bihar and Uttar Pradesh into these states and *(ii)* use of modern farming implements which reduced the farm sector's ability to absorb and finance labour.

The study pointed out that in Kerala, the rise in wages took place in spite of stagnation in output because of certain favourable factors. These include high literacy rate, increased political awareness and spread of trade unionism in the agricultural sector.

The conclusion of the study is that in states where the number of agriculture labourers is large, the wages have remained stagnant for a long time. Thus, Andhra Pradesh, Bihar, Maharashtra and Tamil Nadu which account for more than half of the agricultural labour population, had wages which are substantially lower than those prevailing in other states.

There has been sharp decline in rural employment. The average number of days worked by rural males dropped from 331 days per annum in 1993-94 to 327 days per annum in 1999-2000. However, the average number of days worked by rural females increased slightly from 241 to 246 during the same period. This may be due to the fact that incomes earned by males are inadequate.

A study by a sub-committee of the Union Labour Ministry observed that a farm hand finds work only for two days in a week in the best of time and just a day when conditions turn adverse. This is so in the case of areas having assured irrigation facilities. The plight of farm workers in non-irrigated areas is worse.

According to the All-India Debt and Investment Survey 1971-72 of the Reserve Bank of India, while the percentage of households with assets up to ₹ 1,000 was 19.7 for all rural households, it was 69.1 for agricultural labourers. As regards indebtedness, the Rural Labour Enquiry (1974-75) revealed that the percentage of agricultural labour households in debt to total agricultural labour increased from

61 in 1964-65 to 66 per cent in 1974-75. The average debt per indebted agricultural labour household was ₹ 584 in 1974-75 as against ₹ 244 in 1964-65, an increase of 135 per cent. Money-lenders accounted for about 48 per cent of the total debt raised by agricultural labour households in 1974-74 — higher by about 17 per cent than in 1964-65.

At the national level, as per the NSS estimates, about 52 per cent of agricultural labour households were said to be in debt.

The highest proportion (about 80 per cent) was in Kerala and the lowest proportion (11.75 per cent) was in Assam. The total outstanding debt per household at the all-India level was reported to be ₹ 680. It was highest at ₹ 1,808 in Rajasthan and lowest at ₹ 244 in West Bengal.

Only about 20 per cent of the loans is productively utilised. Also, money-lenders, friends and relatives provide about 75 per cent of the loans.

The new farm implements are also causing serious injuries to the farm workers. When agricultural labourers sustain injuries, the land owners do not take care of them. In case of death, the responsibility of extending compensatory benefit becomes an issue of great debate.

The trade union movement has practically no impact on the conditions of agricultural labourers. Therefore, the violation of minimum wage notification goes unnoticed. There were strikes in some states by the farm workers. But this resentment is of little consequence in the absence of a strong trade union movement.[5]

III. MEASURES TO IMPROVE STATUS OF AGRICUTURE LABOURES

Minimum Wage Legislation

All state governments passed laws, fixing minimum wages. Of course, these vary from state to state. However, there are many difficulties in enforcings the Minimum Wage Acts. Even when the minimum wages are paid, the labourers cannot get even 40 per cent of the per capita income of India. Strangely, wages prescribed under the minimum wage laws are usually fixed below the prevailing wage rates.

There are many practical difficulties in the implementation of the Minimum Wage Acts. Those include: *(i)* poverty and illiteracy of farm workers, *(ii)* the scattered nature of agricultural farms, *(iii)* casual nature of employment and *(iv)* the character of agricultural labour.[6] The administrative machinery to enforce minimum wages is ill-equipped and therefore ineffective.

From the field studies, we understand that the implementation of the Minimum Wages Act is far from satisfactory. First, different state governments have been fixing different rates of minimum wages and subsequently revising them. The variations in 1983 range from ₹ 6 to ₹ 10 which is very wide. Second, wages of agricultural labourers are determined by market forces and administrative measures to implement them have not succeeded. Third, even if the present prescribed rates of minimum wages are implemented, they will fail to enable the relevant population cross the poverty line. This is so because the agricultural labourers are not able to get continuous employment. Fourth, the highly unorganised agricultural labour force accepts the dictates of the landlord. Lastly, the anti-poverty programmes have not produced a decisive impact on poverty eradication by enlarging the volume of employment.[7]

Provision of employment and payment of minimum wages must be looked at simultaneously. The minimum wages fixed by the state government do not enable the labourers to cross the poverty line. Not only this, in most places, agricultural labourers do not get even minimum wages.

The existing administrative machinery for the enforcement of minimum wages is often blamed for the present state of affairs. The labour inspectors do not visit the remote villages and they may even align with the rural rich.

The labourers are ignorant about the laws and other matters related to the minimum wages. Generally, they are reluctant to complain due to the fear of repercussions.

The implementation of the Minimum Wages Act is difficult because of the size of agricultural labour and its location in remote and at times inaccessible villages.[8] The litigation process is also cumbersome, both time and money consuming. In such a situation, the possibility of legal enforcement of the Minimum Wages Act appears to be remote.

The Sub-committee of the Parliamentary Consultative Committee attached to the Ministry of Labour, which submitted its report in 1987, observed, "The lack of job opportunities, the preponderance of mono-crop areas in the national agricultural today, the tardy development of agro-industries and limited expansion of agro-irrigation together with inadequate growth of the industry contribute to the low level of the agricultural wage."

ABOLITION OF BONDED LABOUR SYSTEM

Some people say that the 'attached' form of labour is also a type of bonded labour. It is, however, true that a large number of agricultural labourers are forced to work with a particular employer to pay back the loans taken particularly during the lean period of the year. The labourers have no alternative but to accept wages below the minimum wages fixed by the respective state governments.

Though bonded labour has been abolished by law in India, it still persists in some parts of the country. The law envisages release of all the bonded labour and simultaneous liquidation of their debts. Of course, this task is primarily the responsibility of the state governments.

The Bonded Labour System (Abolition) Ordinance came into force on October 25, 1975, was replaced by an amendment in February 1976. Efforts are being made towards identification, release and rehabilitation of bonded labourers. Yet, the situation is really serious. According to the National Sample Survey Organisation, the number of bonded labourers in 1977-78 was 3.4 lakh at the all India level.

The Seventh Five Year Plan document has observed, "An extreme manifestation of the sorry plight of rural unorganised, labour is the bonded labour system. The conditions which have created it have to be rooted out in order to prevent relapse. Extreme poverty, total lack of skills or assets, inequitous social customs, the state of helplessness of a large number of these people and their dependence on the private money-lending system are the causes which have led to this situation."

The obnoxious practice of human bondage has its roots in abject poverty and extreme social oppression based on caste rigidities and ignorance on the part of rural masses.[9] The bonded labourers lead a life of servitude mainly because they are illiterate and ignorant. They are not in a position to remember for a long time the amount of loans or advances taken by them at the time of migration; the amount repaid by them and the amount outstanding. In fact, there may not be any written agreements at all. Also, as bonded labourers suffer from extreme poverty and helplessness, they fear intimidation by the masters if they disclose the actual conditions.

According to the information available with the Union Ministry of Labour, the total number of bonded labourers identified and freed by March 1991 was 2,55,608.

According to some voluntary organisations, notably the National Labour Institute and the Gandhi Peace Foundation, the estimated number of bonded labourers was around 26 lakh. Orissa accounts for 3.5 lakh, Tamil Nadu 2.5 lakh, Andhra Pradesh 3.25 lakh and Uttar Pradesh 5.5 lakh. The number of bonded labourers is insignificant in Kerala, West Bengal and Assam. It is difficult to estimate the number of bonded labourers. Bihar is said to have the largest number of 5 lakh bonded labourers while the figure for Southern states is reported to be around 50 lakh.

A study done by the Programme Evaluation Organisation (PEO) of the Planning Commission has revealed a long gap between release and rehabilitation. It found that only 41.2 per cent of the released bonded labourers were rehabilitated till the end of 1981. Nearly 60 per cent of the beneficiaries had to wait for periods well beyond two years. During this period, they either starved or resorted to other ways of earnings. The study also recommended a rise in assistance to a bonded labourer to ₹ 10,000 or ₹ 15,000.

The PEO Report suggested involvement of reputed voluntary organisations in the task of rehabilitating the bonded labourers freed. Social workers may be appointed to guide and help bonded labourers. The district administration has to provide enough subsistence allowance to the released labourers during the intervening period between release and rehabilitation. Also, after release from bondage, the bonded labourers should not be allowed to become victims of debt again.

Sometime back, the Union Labour Ministry formulated a scheme for involvement of voluntary agencies in the identification and rehabilitation of bonded labourers. As per the scheme, such agencies are paid managerial subsidy of ₹ 5,000 per annum and ₹ 100 for each release order in excess of 20 cases, with a maximum yearly amount of ₹ 10,000 for both. The selection of voluntary agencies is done either by the states or the Council for Advancement of People's Action and Technology (CAPART). The voluntary agencies are also permitted to lodge reports with the police in terms of the provisions of the Act.

With a view to supplementing the efforts of the state governments, a centrally sponsored scheme is also functioning under which the state governments are provided central assistance on a 50:50 basis, for rehabilitation of bonded labourers. To speed up the pace of rehabilitation, the state governments have been allowed to delegate powers for sanction of rehabilitation schemes to the district level authorities. The centre has also issued a set of guidelines for the purpose of preparing village level schemes for the rehabilitation of bonded labour.

The state governments have been urged to set up vigilance committees to provide for the economic and social rehabilitation of freed bonded labour. Almost all the state governments have already set up these committees at the district and sub-division level for the purpose.

It would be better if bonded labourers are assisted through self-employment schemes like IRDP. These schemes are to be integrated with area development plans, formulated by elected institutions to ensure democratic decentralisation. The schemes to be adopted for rehabilitation of bonded labour must suit the conditions in which they live and for which they have aptitude.[10]

Legislation has been tightened in favour of bonded labourers. Information to district magistrate/ sub-divisional magistrate or members of the vigilance committees can be given in the form of an affidavit. To avoid procedural delays, the civil courts are barred from entertaining any such cases. Every state government is expected to have vigilance committees at district and sub-divisional levels for release and rehabilitation of bonded labourers.[11]

The practice of bonded labour is deeply rooted in the socio-economic structure particularly in the rural sections of our society. Therefore, measures to wipe it out must be of long-term in nature.[12]

DIVERSIFICATION OF RURAL ECONOMY

Poverty in rural areas is largely due to too much dependence on land. As such, dependence on agriculture is not remunerative. The agricultural sector is not able to generate surpluses and employment opportunities to absorb the growing labour force. The agricultural productivity is low.

One factor which can change this situation for the better is ensuring the provision of irrigation facilities. This would enable farmers to adopt new agricultural technology and raise their agricultural productivity. This would also raise demand for agricultural labourers. When wages are low, top priority should be given to provision of employment to agricultural labourers throughout the year.

Diversification of the rural economy, with stress on rural industrialisation, is the best remedy to the problems of rural poverty and unemployment.[13] There is large scope for setting up of agro-based industries, cottage and small-scale industries, improvement of animal husbandry and dairy farming. New industrial units have to be set up to process farm produce. Of course, there is need for strengthening rural infrastructure. Training programmes for the rural labour should be intensified.

ORGANISING THE RURAL POOR

The agricultural labourers, because of their growing numbers, suffer from weak bargaining power. This is one of the important reasons for low agricultural wages. Generally speaking, higher wages prevail in areas, as in Kerala, where powerful agricultural labour unions exist. Of course, too high a wage may also lead to unemployment.

However, powerful agricultural unions emerged only in Kerala and Tanjavur (Tamil Nadu). In these places, labour unions were successful in eliminating feudalistic tendencies in rural areas. They were able to command higher wages through collective bargaining.

The Rural Labour Enquiry (1974-75) observed that trade unionism was highest in Kerala where 9.33 per cent of agricultural labour households were reported to be the members of trade unions followed by Tamil Nadu (3.81 per cent). For the rest of the states, unionism is less than one per cent and for the entire country, it is one per cent.

Any strategy to tone up the socio-economic status of farm workers should give priority to —

- Shifting the excess labour force from the agricultural sector to other sectors;
- Organising the rural labour force;
- Proper implementation of Minimum Wages Act by strengthening the enforcement machinery;
- Diversification of the agricultural sector to provide better employment for more days and
- Integrating anti-poverty programmes with block plans so that the employment generated becomes productive and durable.

We cannot think of rural development without raising the socio-economic status of the agricultural labourers. Modernisation of the agricultural sector is no doubt important, but this modernisation should help raise the economic and social conditions of the farm workers. The majority of the workforce in rural India will continue to depend on agriculture for some years to come.

The major provisions of the Agricultural Workers (Employment, Conditions of Service and Welfare Measures) Bill, 1997 include a definition of agricultural workers, fixation of hours of work, wages and harvesting wage, special provision for women workers, penalties for violation of dispute resolution at local levels by conciliation and compulsory arbitration.

REFERENCES

1. *Economic and Political Weekly,* June 25, 1988, p. A-67.
2. J.S. Joshi: 'The Field of Labour', *Financial Express,* May 10, 1990, p. 6.
3. D.R. Deoras: 'Agricultural Labourers: Swelling Ranks and Emptier Bellies', *Commerce,* December 27, 1980.
4. P.T. George: 'Status of Agricultural Labour in Rural Development in India: Some Facets', National Institute of Rural Development, Hyderabad.
5. P.K. Sharma: 'Farm Labourers', *The Economic Times,* April 21, 1983.
6. K.C. Alexander: 'Fixing Minimum Wage for Farm Labourers', *Kurukshetra,* August 1, 1980, p. 11.
7. Ruddar Dutt: 'Minimum Wages Act and Farm Labour: Lessons from Three Studies', *Mainstream,* March 24, 1984, p. 25.
8. U.V.N. Charyulu: 'Social Legislation for Agricultural Labour: Trends in Implementation', *Social Action,* July-September, 1980, p. 271,
9. I. Satya Sundaram: 'Of Human Bondage', *Social Welfare,* May-June 1993, p. 22.
10. *Kurukshetra,* August 16, 1980, p. 9.

11. Kashiram Thakare: 'Bonded Labourers: Release and Rehabilitation', *Yojana,* May 15, 1994, p. 19.

12. N. Lingamurty and K. Mohan Rao: 'Bonded Labour: Unkept Promises', *Mainstream,* December 20, 1980, p. 18.

13. I. Satya Sundaram: 'Farm Workers' Worsening Plight, *Financial Express,* July 4, 1992.

Chapter

23 Conditions of Rural Artisans

The rural artisans constitute an important segment of the rural economy. But in terms of economic and social status, they are no better than agricultural labourers. Rural artisans belong to the poorer sections of the rural population. Nearly 75 per cent of the artisans fall in the category of weaker sections of the rural families with their assets remaining below ₹ 2,500 in 1971.

Artisans constitute an important segment of the rural community. In 1971-72, out of the total 770 lakh households, 19 lakh (2.4 per cent of the total) were rural artisan households. There were about 6.5 million rural artisans engaged in various industries according to the 1981 census.

The rural artisan is a skilled worker in a traditional village craft, who works on his own account. The rural artisans mostly utilise locally available resources for manufacturing, processing and servicing of a product or an activity. They are engaged in procuring a wide variety of products like carpets, brassware, earthenware, textiles and artistic pieces for the local people. They also supply a wide variety of implements to agriculturists.

The rural artisans who lack new skills are made to abandon their traditional occupations. The artisans, could not be integrated with the process of modernisation of agriculture. As a result of intensification of the rural industrialisation programme and modernisation of the farming sector, the demand for artisans has been gradually increasing. But unless they upgrade their skills to a large extent in tune with new developments in the rural sector, they cannot hope to get gainful employment. The formal training to rural artisans is imparted through specific training institutions like District Industries centres, Industrial Training Institutes and Khadi and Village Industries Commission (KVIC).

In almost all development programmes, rural artisans were not given their due place. However, the artisan is an important person in the rural society because he contributes a lot to the development of techniques of making a bullock cart, a chaffcutter, plough, agricultural tools etc. The present technological development has broken the traditional linkages between the farmers and artisans. We find a fall in the number of artisan households.

PLIGHT OF RURAL ARTISANS

According to the All-India Debt and Investment Survey 1971-72, the rural artisan households formed just 2.4 per cent of the total number of rural households. They are among the poorest among the poor. Their holdings of assets were estimated at ₹ 445 crore, constituting a negligible proportion of 0.5 per cent of the total assets of rural households in 1971. The average holdings of the assets by the artisans was found to be ₹ 2,381 of which not more than eight per cent were in the form of implements and machinery, while the humble dwellings accounted for as much as 57 per cent of the assets.

The average debt per household was ₹ 287 out of which cash debt totalled to ₹ 283. Bulk of cash debt was due to non-institutional agencies (95 per cent) among whom the most important ones were agricultural money-lenders. The Government provided 2.7 per cent of the total, followed by co-operatives (1.7 per cent) and commercial banks (0.3 per cent). Of the total outstanding cash debts of the artisan households of ₹ 52.69 crore as on June 30, 1971, loans taken for production purposes was a marginal ₹ 12 crore.[1]

Commercial banks' advances to artisans stood at only ₹ 127.67 crore, having 6,27,120 borrowal accounts as at the end of June 1983.

A study conducted in 1981 by the Madras Institute of Development Studies (MIDS) on rural artisans revealed that the new earnings per artisan per year worked out to be ₹ 1,081 in village leather, ₹ 1,816 in village pottery, ₹ 2,750 in carpentry and blacksmithy and ₹ 2,858 in bamboo and cane activities.

No doubt, the importance of rural artisans has declined due to the emergence of industrial alternatives. But it needs to be noted that artisans still play an important role in the growing industrialised economies. Given the socio-economic conditions in rural India, the rural artisans need to be projected and encouraged to expand their operations to get maximum financial benefits.

With the modernisation of agriculture and small scale units, the demand for skilled manpower has substantially increased. Thus, the rural artisans can stay in their own villages and enhance their incomes if enough employment opportunities are available.[2]

PROBLEMS OF RURAL ARTISANS

Most of the problems facing the rural artisans emerge from the conditions in which the artisans are placed. The rural artisans —

- are poor, scattered, unorganised and illiterate,
- have poor productive asset base,

- use outmoded equipment which are not productive,
- are exploited by usurious middlemen, contractors and master-artisans and
- do not have the benefit of an organised market and depend on private marketing systems.

Taking cognisance of these problem issues, the Union Government has activated 'benefit schemes' to help the rural population.

There has been an increase in the number of schemes and institutions to help the artisans, but there are no adequate arrangements for co-ordination and monitoring of their activities. Further, most of the artisans and small entrepreneurs failed to get a package of services, especially scarce raw-materials.[3] Economic prosperity of farmers has changed their consumption requirements. Manufactured commodities of industry are cheap and refined as compared to goods produced by local artisans. Hence, the artisans had no option but gradually shift to other occupations.[4]

The rural artisans suffer from lack of financial resources at their disposal. They work mostly in their own houses, but these are very small. Most of the artisans are compelled to shift from their traditional occupations to other professions for their livelihood. It is essential to give due emphasis to the skill formation of rural artisans. Those who are able to upgrade their skills are also facing some problems:

(i) Non-availability of financial resources to purchase new tools;

(ii) Lack of awareness of entrepreneurial and management problems involved in setting up of an industry;

(iii) Lack of marketing ability and

(iv) Inability to derive much benefits from the facilities created for the development of artisans under various programmes.[5]

The artisans are facing special problems in procuring raw materials. There is substantial competition from the organised sector, which has to a great extent affected the regular and assured supply of raw materials. Middlemen who supply raw materials, usually tend to exploit artisans in a number of ways.

Marketing a product subsequently becomes a major problem for the rural artisans. The artisans lack staying power and are also ignorant of the true market potential and are unable to tap the same to establish a market for their products. Government assistance in the form of sales through state-owned corporations and emporia is leading artisans to a better life which was earlier not available to artisans in the rural sector.

Most artisan enterprises lack the requisite managerial and technical expertise. Most units suffer from poor planning and execution of programmes. Other problems include outloaded designs and models and the lack of market intelligence.

The incomes of rural artisan households are generally low. The borrowed amounts are not put to productive use by them. According to one case study, about 78.90 per cent of the sample artisans have used the borrowed amount for non-productive purposes, particularly towards individual consumption purposes.[6]

The rural artisans depend on both institutional and non-institutional sources for their working capital requirements. However, there is no exact estimate of the working capital lent to rural artisans which need to be done to ascertain the economic feasibility of the artisan's planned project. The information available from the RBI Banking Statistics showed that the total limit given to them at the end of June increased from ₹ 76.77 crore in 1980 to ₹ 4,684.48 crore in 1989, while the amount outstanding during the same period rose from ₹ 60.19 crore to ₹ 620.66 crore. The working capital employed by the rural artisans may range between ₹ 4,000 crore to ₹ 5,000 crore.

Besides, institution credit provided is inadequate. It is also not provided at the right time. An important factor contributing to the non-viability of artisan enterprises is lack of adequate working capital.

Case studies reveal that the requirement of working capital of a rural artisan ranged between ₹ 500 in cane and bamboo industry to about ₹ 5,000 in tanning — depending on seasons — for raw materials and marketing. In some cases like brick-making or wooden furniture/structurals, the working capital requirement was estimated to be ₹ 7,000 and ₹ 8,000.

Inadequate credit is the cause for low financial returns. Also, when the artisans get money after the season, they spend it for non-productive purposes and are labelled as *defaulters.* Lack of entrepreneurial skill which continues to be a major problem should be tackled through proper monitoring by agencies, guidance and training facilities.

Even where there is provision for sanctioning a second loan, it is not of much help to the artisans. Very often, the second loan is adjusted by the banker towards the repayment of the first loan as he is under pressure to show progress in respect of loan recovery.[7]

As the rural artisans face a number of problems, there must be appropriate institutional agencies to help them. In most states, though a few agencies have been created, they lack co-ordination and in many cases, the artisans have failed to utilise the facilities provided by such organisations.[8]

SUGGESTIONS TO IMPROVE ARTISANS' CONDITIONS

Most artisans face the problem of inadequate accommodation. The artisans must be provided with house sites through housing co-operative societies or government housing schemes. Training institutions should be involved in training the artisans with the main purpose of upgrading skills to enable them to handle jobs requiring better skills.[9]

Financial institutions should take a positive interest in helping the artisans and ensure links between the artisans and co-operatives, rural banks and commercial banks through the agency formed to help the artisans. Introduction and popularisation of new designs to cater to the increasing domestic demand and export demand will have to be attempted at various trades.[10]

The District Industries Centres have to help the artisans in a big way. Some immediate measures to help the artisans are:[11]

(i) Artisans from atleast 10 villages should form professional associations under the leadership of responsible persons having some background in social work, preferably from amongst themselves. The leadership should get them together, for a unified effort to claim and avail benefits from various development programmes sponsored by the government;

(ii) Facilities for technical education and training should be made available to the artisans' groups by considering them as weaker sections of the society;

(iii) Schemes for providing subsidies to artisans to enable them to upgrade production to the level of small-scale industries should be worked out and implemented. Under these schemes, tools, machinery, raw-materials etc., should be provided to them with some guidance in management etc.

(iv) Efforts to impart theoretical/academic knowledge through mass media may be identified to the artisans so that they are able to push up their productive potentialities.

Banks have rightly thought of financing village craft industries and services as they are having a large employment potential. Bank assistance to rural artisans should be on the following lines:[12]

(i) Commercial banks should equip themselves with technical and trained manpower to deal with rural artisans. Certain percentage of total bank credit should be earmarked specifically for financing rural artisans as a part of integrated development programmes.

(ii) Extensive surveys should be conducted to identify block-wise and trade-wise artisans and also the number of artisans assisted by commercial banks under different programmes;

(iii) Research studies evaluating the impact of bank credit on asset-base, income and employment generation are of great importance;

(iv) Artisans' co-operatives should also be financed in addition to financing individual artisans;

(v) Banks need not favour artisans having assets. In fact, the purpose of the financial assistance by banks aims at strengthening the productive asset-base of the rural poor;

(vi) Financial assistance should be given for establishing market-cum-service centres which act as multi-functional centres and serve as centres of guidance to the rural artisans and

(vii) Area-specific schemes should be drawn up and financed so that such crafts could be preserved and their employment possibilities be fully exploited.

The Composite Term Loan Scheme, which was framed in 1979 took into account the total financial needs of the rural artisans, village and cottage industries. Under this scheme, units set up in villages and towns with a population not exceeding 50,000 and which used local resources were eligible for loans not exceeding ₹ 25,000 at concessional rates of interest. To meet the consumption needs of the artisans, a consumption loan not exceeding ₹ 500 was also granted under the Scheme. The loans could be repaid over a long period of seven-to-ten years in small instalments, depending on the surplus generated, after an initial moratorium of 12 to 18 months.

The rural artisans whose annual family income does not exceed ₹ 6,400 (₹ 7,200 in urban and metropolitan areas) are extended financial assistance up to ₹ 6,500 under the Differential Interest Rate (DIR) Scheme at four per cent interest for working capital as well as for acquiring appropriate equipment.

In 1984, NABARD announced a new scheme providing term loans of ₹ 10,000 to rural artisans at 10 per cent interest. The repayment period varied from three-to-ten years depending on the customer's repayment capacity. NABARD's refinance scheme covers settlements with population upto 10,000. Refinance is available to primary lending institutions for infrastructural support proposed for the rural artisans' sector in centres with population upto 50,000.

NABARD, in the 1996-97 fiscal, was sanctioned ₹ 500 crore as advance additional share capital — ₹ 100 crore by the Government and ₹ 400 crore by the Reserve Bank of India (RBI). The above-mentioned share capital was considered to be augmented by similar amount of ₹ 500 crore as announced by the Union Finance Minister P. Chidambaram in the 1997-98 Union Budget. The amount was for the 1997-98 fiscal.

For increasing the viability of both enterprise and credit, provision of entrepreneurial training to borrowers and some special training to the bank employees for monitoring the rural industries including rural orientation programme is required.[13]

The whole training curriculum should be based on the philosophy that an attitudinal change is indispensable for the rural artisans to make the best use of the facilities provided to them.[14]

Artisans' training in the Khadi and Village Industries (KVT) sector is arranged mostly through institutions engaged in the development of the industry. It is the in-plant training with emphasis on learning by doing rather than on lectures.[15]

The rural artisans to a great extent depend on outdated technology, resulting in failure to avail of economic liberalisation. They require technology to tap the existing local resources and environmental conditions. There is a need to develop an effective linkage of modern science and technology with the rural community, focusing mainly on rural industries and village artisans.

The process of adaptation of modern technology to suit the conditions prevalent in rural India has begun on a modest scale which emphasizes the need to evolve a strategy for blending the traditional and modern technologies in the context of local requirements.

Artisans and craftsmen should be given opportunities to receive new technologies first and then transfer them to user groups in villages through systematised liaison with R&D agencies. The artisan, after acquiring training, tools, and raw-materials should be encouraged to use the acquired skills to benefit other user groups. Technology transfer becomes easier because the artisan is born and brought up in the village and his language and culture are those of the user groups. Also, if there is anything wrong with the technology, the user can approach the artisan immediately in the village itself and ask him to amend or modify the technology at short notice.[16]

The Rural Artisans Programme (RAP) was launched in 1971-72 as part of the Small Farmers' Development Agency (SFDA) and Marginal Farmers and Agricultural Labourers Development Agency (MFALDA). RAP was started in 87 selected areas all over India and it was handled by the Development Commissioner, Small-scale Industries. Later on, the programme was taken over by the District Industries Centres (DICs).

The RAP aimed at providing training in varying skills so as to induce in artisans the urge to open up opportunities to take up small enterprises, primarily to meet local needs, with improved tools. RAP gave priority to village trades like poultry, masonry, carpentry, blacksmithy, repair and maintenance of agricultural implements, machinery, tractors, pumpsets, diesel engines and electric fittings. RAP provides subsidy to artisans to help them stabilise in their chosen professions. The subsidies maybe of different kinds like tool kits, plant and equipment, managerial subsidy and subsidy for worksheds.

The Rural Artisan Complexes (RACs) emerged during 1981 with a view to providing better living and working conditions for those artisans who lacked accommodation in their villages. The RACs have been set up on the outskirts of villages and each one accommodates at least 20 artisans. The unifunctional complex accommodates artisans from the same trade while multi-functional ones accommodate artisans from diverse trades. Priority should be given to integrate programmes of RACs with rural housing schemes.

The artisan development programmes receive help not only from the DICs but also other agencies like District Rural Development Agency (DRDA), the Khadi and Village Industries Commission/ Boards and Handicrafts/Handloom Boards. But proper co-ordination is lacking in formulating and implementing programmes for the benefit of rural artisans.

The DICs conduct detailed surveys to identify artisans and also the type of training needed by them. The training programme is arranged on the spot for those who require training for a short period, say a fortnight. For others, requiring training for three months to one year, the same is arranged on priority basis in suitable institutions. Occasionally training is imparted in industrial units also.

There is need for improving the financial viability and sustainbility of various schemes. Measures should be initiated to improve extension services to promote artisan based activities to enable them to tap the domestic as well as foreign market for their products. There is also a need for developing service-type rural artisan trades.

The artisans can survive in a competitive world only when they possess the capacity to diversify and modernise their skills in tune with the present needs. The needs of the modern rural consumer are changing fast. Of course, area specific schemes should be drawn up and effectively implemented. The artisans may form into co-operatives to take advantage on several fronts, particularly marketing.

What the rural artisans urgently require is a package of services which include training, new designs, raw materials, credit, marketing and general guidance.

REFERENCES

1. *Reserve Bank of India Bulletin,* March 1978.
2. I. Satya Sundaram: 'Better Deal for Rural Artisans', *Financial Express,* March 19, 1991.
3. D.B. Mahatme: 'Helping the Artisan', *Commerce,* July 8, 1978, p. 92.
4. Such a Singh Gill: 'Development and Its Impact on Rural Artisans', *Mainstream,* January 12, 1980.
5. S.S. Solanki: 'Rural Artisans and Modern Technology', *Kurukshetra,* February 16,1982, p. 12.

6. Yashavantha Dongre and K.C. Praveen Kumar: 'Indebtedness Among Rural Artisans: A Case Study', *Khadigramodyog,* April 1991.

7. Abdul Aziz: 'Rural Artisans and Bank Credit: Some pointers from Karnataka Experience', in L.K. Naidu (Ed. 1988): *Bank Finance for Rural Artisans,* Ashish Publishing House, New Delhi, p. 79.

8. S.N. Nanje Gowda: 'Rural Artisans of Channapatna: A Socio-Economic Profile', in L.K. Naidu (Ed. 1988), *op. cit.,* p. 181.

9. P. Malyadri: 'Development of Rural Artisans: A Case Study', *Kurukshetra,* August 1984, p. 20.

10. D. Nagaiya: 'Development Strategy for Rural Artisans', *Kurukshetra,* September 1, 1980, p. 20.

11. S.S. Solanki: *op. cit.,* p. 20.

12. B. Nagaraja: 'Commercial Banks and Rural Artisan', *Kurukshetra,* September 1985, pp. 40-42.

13. *Khadigramodyog,* September 1992, p. 668.

14. K. Ravi, P. Harish and P.D. Deenadayalu: 'Banks and Rural Artisans — An Integrated Approach', in L.K. Naidu (Ed. 1988), *op.cit.,* p. 62.

15. M.V. Raghava Rao: 'Technology and Artisan Training in KVI Sector', *Khadigramodyog,* October 1987, p. 58.

16. S.S. Solanki: 'Modern Technology and the Indian Rural Artisan', *Khadigramodyog,* May 1994, p. 553.

Chapter

24 Organising the Rural Poor

Given the rural bargaining power structure, the benefits of targeted welfare programmes for the rural sector do not reach the target groups to the extent expected. Consequently, they suffer from weak bargaining power and tend to become passive. No wonder, the legislation relating to minimum wages etc. has remained only on paper.

Plight of the Unorganised Workforce

The unorganised workforce is vulnerable to all kinds of exploitation. They have not joined any major trade union. However, a large number of programmes are being implemented for the upliftment of the weaker sections of the rural labour. But there is no guarantee that the benefits of such programmes reach the target groups. There is therefore an urgent need for organising the unorganised rural poor.

The agricultural sector is having the largest workforce in the country. The unorganised rural labour constitutes a major chunk of the agricultural sector.

It is only in the process of organisation of the rural poor and through 'conscientisation' (a term used by Paulo Freire) that it is possible to educate the rural poor in India to avail of these benefits.

The rural poor, whatever may be their occupations, share some common characteristics like a high degree of vulnerability to the unexpected climatic changes, seasonal pattern of employment, low income participation, exclusion from many agrarian programmes, social exploitation through unwritten contracts which lead to economic deprivation and social degradation, limited access to public services and powerlessness in the labour market.[1]

The unorganised labour in the Indian context suffer from meagre wages, inadequate employment opportunities, lack of welfare facilities and discriminatory treatment — social and economic — meted out to them.

The unorganised labourers are not having unions of their own; have limited or no access to the Government and are said to be unprotected by the state legislation, regulating conditions of work. They are engaged in a set of survival activities on the margin of poverty. The rural labour enquiry has estimated that only about one per cent of the agricultural labour is covered by trade union activities. The general observation is that the minimum wages are much higher and more promptly paid in regions having powerful worker unions than in regions without such unions. However, their conditions of work and living patterns have been showing gradual improvement over the years.

The plight of the rural poor has been well summed up by Justice P.N. Bhagavati in his keynote address to the National Seminar on 'Organising Unorganised Labour.' He declared, "The poor are worsted in their encounters with the dominant sections, not only in the courts but also before public authorities. They suffer in the exercise of discretionary powers by public officers at the lower levels because quite a few of these officers, hardened by mechanical routine and bureaucratic rigidity, exercise their powers sometimes indifferently, irresponsibly and dishonestly — regardless of the interests of the rural poor."

NEED FOR UNIONISATION

The implementation of land reforms and other progressive programmes are bound to generate tensions in the rural sector. The rural poor can protect themselves from the opponents of change only when they are organised.

A number of special schemes are being implemented for the benefits of the rural poor. Studies have revealed of leakages in the implementation of these schemes and the exploitation of labour continues even when wages are paid partly in kind. One reason identified for this is that the beneficiaries do not actively contribute either at the planning stage or at the implementation stage of the welfare programmes. Indeed these schemes are generally implemented in such a way that the needs of the target groups are ignored.[2]

The rural power structure continues to be unfavourable for the rural poor. Even institutional credit mainly meant for the weaker sections is mostly appropriated by the better off sections as in the case of co-operative credit. Only the organised workforce commands attention and get their grievances redressed.

The organisation of the rural poor aims at promoting self-determination and assertion among the vulnerable sections. The aim of unionisation is to break social and psychological barriers which inhibit self-assertion. It also develops awareness in them about their own potential and power in protecting their legitimate interests. In short, it functions as countervailing power against the vested interests. Also, organisations of the rural poor can motivate field level functionaries to perform their duties better.[3]

In areas where powerful organisations emerged, the traditional relationship between the rural rich and the workers has changed. The unions were able to raise wage levels, arrest discrimination in payment, raise the consciousness of the rural peasants, retrieve the illegally alienated land and redistribute it among the peasants.[4]

The peasant organisations and labour unions are reported to have emerged in new centres of power in the countryside. Such organisations enable the rural poor to forward their needs and demands to the authorities concerned. The presence of these authorities is necessary not only for the better implementation of the minimum wage provisions but to ensure flow or benefits to the rural poor from the developmental and welfare programmes.[5] In view of their importance, the late Prof. Raj Krishna has suggested that governments may even extend subsidy to such organisations.

PROBLEMS IN ORGANISING THE UNORGANISED

The reasons for lack of unionisation among the rural poor are not far to seek. The rural poor are unaware of their rights guaranteed under the laws. They lack the much needed correct perception about forces which generate dependence and subordination. They are reluctant to articulate their feelings which can be attributed to fear, lack of confidence, isolation and apprehension of retaliation by the rural rich. These apprehensions of the rural poor are gradually disappearing.

The existing laws and traditions heavily favour the better-off sections of rural society. Naturally, the bureaucracy has reportedly developed a bias against any movement which aims at alternation of the existing social order which needs immediate redressal.

In the Indian context, the rural labour unions are bound to experience some initial difficulties, the reason being the heterogeneous nature of various segments of the rural poor and their conflicting economic interests. There is a danger of caste considerations becoming more dominant than economic and social considerations.[6] An FAO study has observed that unless governments are atleast willing to tolerate rural unions, it is difficult to establish them on a firm platform to contribute to the rural sector in a major way.

The Working Group Report, which emerged from the Round Table on the 'Adaptation of Administration to Rural Development' jointly organised by the Government of India and the UN Economic and Social Council for Asia and the Pacific (New Delhi, August 16-18, 1978) has observed:

- There are numerous factors which inhibit the organisation of the poor in rural India. Some of these are external to them such as the coercive power of the propertied class, the economic dependence of the poor, the inbuilt bias of the local law and order machinery to maintain the status quo, the lack of supportive legislation and non-implementation of existing laws enacted in their favour etc. Other inhibiting factors arise from the heterogeneity of poverty itself.
- The poor are differentiated and divided by such factors as conflicting economic interests, caste and community differences, sex discrimination and other divisive mechanisms which compel the poor to compete among themselves for limited opportunities and resources.

One problem with the existing organisations is that they are never concerned with such larger issues as the allocation of resources between agriculture and industry or rural development versus urban development.[7]

Given the rural power structure, the task of unionising the farm workforce is a delicate one. Perhaps voluntary agencies are best suited to take up this task. But most voluntary agencies, depending as they are on liberal donations and government funds, do not come forward to take up this task lest they should incur the wrath of the bureaucracy and the rural rich.

MEASURES NEEDED

It is essential to create conditions conducive to mobilisation and organisation of the rural poor. Otherwise, our attempts towards democratic participation and decentralised administration may remain only on paper. There must be institutional devices to strengthen the political and material base of the poor.

The International Labour Organisation (ILO) Convention No. 141 relating to the organisation of rural workers observed that all categories of the rural poor should be organised. The ILO convention added that such organisations should emerge on a voluntary basis so that they participate in socio-economic development and avail themselves of the benefits resulting therefrom.

The Council for Advancement of People's Action and Rural Technology (CAPART) has been administering the scheme of organising the rural poor. CAPART identified the leadership potential within the target groups. The leaders are provided with necessary skills and given other assistance leading to high quality action.

CAPART has also been encouraging voluntary organisations to undertake two types of training programmes. One type of programme is meant for the rural poor who belong to the village. After acquiring necessary skills and confidence, they have to work for mobilisation of their fellow-men for extending the needed assistance under various development and regulatory programmes. The catalyst in this stream is called an *animator* whose function is to inspire, facilitate and help people in getting their programmes. The second requisite benefits out of these training stream of training is for persons known as *rural organisers* whose goal is to help people to form organisations of their own to achieve specific objectives they have in view.[8]

The Working Group Report of the Round Table (1978) quoted earlier has also made certain suggestions to strengthen the movement towards the organisation of the rural poor. These include:

(i) Effective agrarian reforms;

(ii) Total redemption of debts of the rural poor;

(iii) Guaranteeing alternative employment;

(iv) Amendment of the Conduct Rule providing for disciplinary action for acts of omission or commission by officials in cases of atrocities on the rural poor;

(v) Posting of local functionaries generally away from their home districts;

(vi) Free legal aid and waiving of stamp duty for the rural poor and

(vii) Constituting special investigating agencies and special courts for atrocities committed on the rural poor.

A scheme for organising rural workers was introduced in 1981-82 in eight states by the Centre. The scheme aimed at motivating a large section of the rural workers to organise themselves on the basis of laws enacted for their welfare. Initially, 415 Honorary Rural Organisers (HROs) were appointed under the scheme by the state governments at the block level. The expenditure required is released to the states by the Central Government. By 1992, the scheme successfully covered 14 states with around 1500 HROs.

Another scheme for educating the workers was already functioning through the Central Board of Workers Education. The scheme aimed at creating awareness among the rural poor, developing their individual organisations and helping them to seek benefits of various welfare and legislation measures. The scheme also covered landless labourers, agricultural workers and marginal farmers. Its aim has been helping the emergence of the quality of leadership among the rural workers themselves.

Another scheme for organising the rural labour which was started in the Sixth Plan has been dovetailed into the anti-poverty programmes of rural development. It aimed at organising workers in the form of unions and educating rural workers about setting up co-operatives by the Centre and its various programmes.[9]

The National Commission on Rural Labour (NCRL), set up by the Government, submitted its Report in July 1991 in which it laid stress on achieving two major objectives — improvement in the living standards of the rural labour and ensuring their effective participation in the development process as incorporated in welfare programmes targeted for the rural sector.

The Commission felt that benefits of development can reach the 'target groups' only through agricultural growth, employment guarantee programmes, infrastructure development for rural industries, developing human resources and provision of rural credit to enable them to meet their needs. Today, agriculture has emerged as the 'life blood' of the Indian economy. As per the Common Minimum Programme of the Union government, increasing the flow of credit to the agricultural sector and its related agro-industries two-fold within five years has been assured in the Union Budget, 1997-98.

In 1996-97, credit flow was expected to increase from ₹ 22,000 crore to ₹ 28,600 crore — an increase by ₹ 6,600 crore.

The Commission, to meet their needs, also recommended prohibition of child labour in all occupations and processes. For the benefit of poor women, the Commission recommended a 'National Credit Fund for Women' with which they could get credit without any collateral security upto a specified financing limit. Other recommendations of the Commission included fixation of a national basic minimum wage of ₹ 20 per day at December 1990 prices and a provision for higher wages automatically every six months on the basis of rise in the Consumer Price Index (CPI) and easier accessibility of institutional credit to rural labour households through co-operative banks.

The rural labour camps, though few and far between, have produced good results. They have become effective instruments for 'conscientisation' of the rural poor. Of course, mere awareness of one's conditions and the factors leading to such a plight is not enough. It should encourage the rural poor to do something significant to improve their financial ar.d social status. In other words, the centre of emphasis has to be shifted from conscientisation to sensitisation of authority in charge of implementation of laws and programmes meant for the rural poor leading to its degradation in the eyes of the Centre.

The established power structures may thwart any attempt to organise the rural poor which may generate conflicts in the rural sector with the rural administration. This underscores the need for political commitment of the government, both central and state. A close interface between the agencies organising the rural poor and the local administration would not merely be needed but would have to be suitably institutionalised.

The Sixth Plan rightly felt that institutionalised action can be distinctly more effective in mobilising local resources, articulating needs and co-ordinating the developmental tasks for the benefit of the rural poor.[11]

Of course, unionisation by itself cannot solve the problems of the unorganised. The expansion of job opportunities alone would be a permanent palliative to the problems of this sector. There is therefore a need for diversifying the agricultural sector and stepping up investment in agro-based industries and other allied activities in order to bring down pressure on land under cultivation. Even payment of reasonable wages is not possible unless employment is productive enough to justify such payments.

REFERENCES

1. K.B. Saxena: 'Organising the Rural Poor', in B.N. Yugandhar (Ed.1991); *Studies in Village India,* Concept Publishing Company, NewDelhi, p. 43.
2. Mona Mehta: 'Organising the Beneficiaries', *Kurukshetra,* May 1986, p. 27.
3. K.B. Saxena, *op. cit.,* p. 49.
4. Pradhan H. Prasad: 'Agrarian Unrest and Economic Change in Rural Bihar: Three Case Studies', *Economic and Political Weekly,* June14, 1975.
5. *Sixth Five Year Plan 1980-85,* p. 407.
6. S.C. Mathur: 'Organising the Rural Poor: Some Basic Issues', *Kurukshetra,* November 16, 1978, p. 17.
7. K.C. Alexander: 'Emergence of Peasant Organisations in South India', *Economic and Political Weekly,* June 28, 1980, p. A-83.
8. K.B. Saxena: *op. cit.,* p. 57.
9. *Yojana,* June 30, 1992, pp. 17-18.
10. K.B. Saxena: *op. cit.,* p. 66.
11. *Sixth Five Year Plan 1980-85,* p. 182.

PART FOUR

Special Schemes

Chapter

25 Rationale of Special Schemes

The high incidence of poverty and unemployment in rural areas has compelled most developing countries to resort to special schemes. It is said that 95 per cent of the increase in the labour force in the next quarter of a century will take place in the countries. India has already started implementing special schemes since the early 1970s. There are about 260 centrally sponsored schemes initiated by the Centre.

Stress on Special Schemes

There is a plea for ensuring 50 per cent of the total plan outlay for rural development. However, the immediate task is to enhance returns from investments made in the rural sector which suffers from high incidence of leakages. During the 1980s, a huge amount of not less than ₹ 25,000 crore was spent on poverty alleviation programmes. Of this, ₹ 15,000 crore was the budgetary support from the Centre and the States and ₹ 10,000 crore as credit support through the banks.

Some have argued that because the implementation of special schemes suffer from high incidence of leakages, these schemes should be jettisoned. However, this is no answer to the problem of worsening poverty in rural areas. What needs to be done is that these programmes should be suitably restructured. Besides increasing financial assistance, priority should be given to the choice of schemes and strengthening of the rural infrastructure. Equally important is the need for injecting professional inputs into the government's delivery system so as to realise optimum financial returns from the investments made.

Table: 1
Rural Development Programmes Under Different Plans

Plan Period	*Programme*	*Year of Introduction*
First Five Year Plan	Community Development Programme	1952
	National Extension Service	1953
Second Five Year Plan	Khadi and Village Industries Programme	1957
	Village Housing Scheme	1957
	Multi-purpose Tribal Development Blocks Programme	1959
	Package Programme	1960
	Intensive Agricultural District Programme	1960
Third Five Year Plan	Applied Nutrition Programme	1962
	Rural Industries Projects	1962
	Intensive Agricultural Areas Programme	1964
	High Yielding Variety Programme	1966
Annual Plan 1966	Farmers Training and Education Programme	1966
	Well Construction Programme	1966
Annual Plan 1967	Rural Works Programme	1967
Annual Plan 1968	Tribal Development Block	1968
Annual Plan 1969	Rural Manpower Programme	1969
	Composite Programme for Women and Pre-School Children	1969
Fourth Five Year Plan	Drought-prone Area Programme	1970
	Crash Scheme for Rural Employment	1971
	Small Farmers Development Agency	1971
	Tribal Area Development Programme	1972
	Pilot Projects for Tribal Development	1972
	Pilot Intensive Rural Employment Programme	1972
	Minimum Needs Programme	1974
	Command Area Development Programme	1974
Fifth Five Year Plan	Hill Area Development Programme	1975
	Special Livestock Production Programme	1975
	Food for Work Programme	1977
	Desert Development Programme	1977
	Whole Village Development Programme	1979
	Training Rural Youth for Self-Employment (TRYSEM)	1979
	Integrated Rural Development Programme (IRDP)	1979
Sixth Five Year Plan	National Rural Employment Programme (NREP)	1980
	Prime Minister's Twenty Point Programme	1980
	Development of Women & Children in Rural Areas (DWACRA)	1983
	Rural Landless Employment Guarantee Programme (RLEGP)	1983
Seventh Five Year Plan	New Twenty Point Economic Programme	1986
	Indira Awas Yojana (IAY)	1986
	Jawahar Rojgar Yojana (JRY)	1989

Note: Only important programmes are included in this table.

In its Foreword to the Special Report (1990), the World Bank observed:

> .... The most effective way of achieving rapid and politically sustainable improvements in the quality of life for the poor has been through a two-part strategy. The first element of the strategy is the pursuit of a pattern of growth that assures productive use of the most abundant rural resource — labour.
>
> The second element is widespread provision to the poor of basic social services, especially primary education, proper health care and family planning. The first component provides the opportunities, the second increases the capacity of the poor to take advantage of these opportunities. The strategy must be complemented by the well-targeted transfers to help those not able to benefit from these policies and safety nets to protect those who are exposed to shocks.

The implementation of various programmes for the benefit of the rural poor is the product of the working with the theory and practice of economic development. The traditional growth theory lays emphasis on enhancing Gross National Product (GNP), generation of surpluses, investing and reinvesting such surpluses. While this approach may result in higher rate of growth, it has failed to ensure distributive justice as it neglected the distributive part of the GNP. It was soon realised that a rising growth rate by itself is no guarantee against worsening poverty. As such, a direct attack on mass poverty is attempted by most developing countries by the formulation of projects specially designed for the target groups.

It has been rightly observed that "the Indian experience with economic growth has also brought to light that poverty is the product of the system with interlocked political, economic and social components and the eradication of poverty involves a change in the value system or an attack on the prevailing socio-economic system."[1]

The implementation of various anti-poverty programmes has provided an opportunity to discover the dormant resources and skill in the rural areas and to *activise* them. This is possible only when constraints, structural, technological and institutional, are removed. The ultimate objective of these schemes is to shift the workforce from agriculture to non-agricultural sectors so as to reduce the incidence of underemployment in the agricultural sector, particularly disguised unemployment.

One study has made the following observations about the impact of rural development programmes on the quality of life of the rural poor:[2]

(i) During the period 1977 to 1983, reduction in the incidence of poverty was greater in magnitude than in the early period of high growth;

(ii) The beneficial impact of reduction in income inequality is more pronounced for the ultra poor than for the poor and

(iii) These results lend significant credibility to the consumption equalising intervention initiated since mid-1970s such as IRDP.

Rural development projects ought to aim at accelerating economic growth besides increasing the productivity of the rural poor. It is further said that such poverty-oriented rural development projects should reach large numbers of the rural poor at a cost per beneficiary low enough to allow replication, given the availability of additional resources.[3]

The implementation of too many programmes has come under fire. When the number of schemes is large, it becomes difficult to co-ordinate their activities. Also, when the resources are thinly spread out, optimal deployment of resources becomes difficult. Any such resource deployment is likely to dilute the impact of the programme and defeat the core objective of the anti-poverty philosophy itself.[4]

LIMITATIONS OF SPECIAL SCHEMES

In actual practice, the anti-poverty programmes suffer from many limitations. It has also been rightly observed that "Poverty in the country cannot be eradicated by investments in anti-poverty measures only, however large, while other investments in the economy are not oriented to this objective and therefore, offer no assistance to poverty eradication and may, on the contrary, add to its volume."[5]

Prof. C.T. Kurien has criticised: "the anti-poverty programmes on the ground that they are the programmes without a framework considering realities of the situation on the ground. As a result, what the government gives to the poor through anti-poverty programme is taken away not unstealthily by the social process dominated by the rich."[6]

It is also argued that the target-oriented programmes are prone to confer more benefits on the 'transiently poor' than on the 'chronically poor.' This is so because the former can exercise influence, are better educated and can incur the costs of search and bribery more easily. Moreover, the Government officials themselves often prefer to deal with the less poor among eligible households.[7]

One difficulty with the anti-poverty programmes is that financial allocations and physical targets are determined without taking into account the local conditions such as incidence of poverty, size of population and resource endowments.

Most rural areas/households suffer from limited credit absorption capacity. As such, the Seventh Plan suggested group-oriented activities through co-operatives, registered societies, informal groups etc. By adopting this approach, economies of scale inherent in some activities in the services sector could be fully realised and beneficiaries can also be protected from adverse operations of the market forces.

It is, however, admitted that the anti-poverty schemes suffer from high incidence of leakages. This is attributed to many factors. The rural sector (in particular the poor) is unorganised and as such, does not have correct information about developmental programmes.

There has been wrong identification of beneficiaries. Most studies say that not less than 20 per cent of benefits are pocketed by the non-poor. The land records are absent and even if they are there, they are manipulated through political and money power. As the rural poor are dependent on the rural rich, the latter take advantage of the former to get the benefits of subsidised food, inputs, credit and even subsidised rationed food and sugar which are made available to the rural poor.

The over-centralisation of development programmes has to a great extent institutionalised corrupt practices. Some of the beneficiaries receive milch cattle only on paper. The enhanced role of intermediaries and undue delay in the release of assistance are also responsible for high incidences of financial leakages.

There is also the tendency to overprice the assets. For instance, higher prices paid by IRDP participants in the livestock market are not compensated by higher quality of the animals purchased. This has naturally eroded development funds.

Of course, the beneficiaries themselves are responsible for these leakages. They may not properly utilise bank funds. The pressure of consumption needs and social obligations are always there.[8]

Most rural schemes are being implemented in a haphazard manner. About the rural housing schemes, a journalist has this to say.[9]

In parts of Rajasthan, houses constructed under the Indira Awaas Yojana for the Scheduled Castes and Scheduled Tribes were cornered by the affluent. All over the country, there are several thousands of these houses lying desolate. Built without consulting the people, they are away from the rest of the village and nobody wants to live in them. Doors, windows, roofs and even bricks of these ghost houses have been stolen. Lakhs of rupees have gone down the drain and the Government has yet to decide what to do with these abandoned houses.

The situation may not be different in other states where the leakage of benefit is said to be increasing substantially.

A major drawback of the special schemes is that the assets provided do not match with the requirements of the beneficiaries. The demand patterns of the poor stand completely ignored. As such, the goods and services provided by the programmes and official agencies fail to confer benefits on the target groups to the extent expected.[10]

The foodgrain supply under the anti-poverty programmes has reportedly declined in recent years. This is a disturbing development particularly because both the government and the World Bank are harping on the need for new social safety net to protect the poor from the adverse impact of economic reforms.

The distribution of foodgrains under the anti-poverty programmes declined from 22 lakh tonnes in 1986-87 to 1.26 lakh tonnes in 1990-91 and to a merely 17,000 tonnes in 1991-92. This decline is attributed to inadequate availability of foodgrains in the buffer and the Government's repeated emphasis on releasing the stocked grain to the public distribution system.

The productivity of these schemes seems a distant dream. There is heavy concentration on the construction of roads and buildings. Realising this, the Government declared that under the new schemes, at least 50 per cent of the funds would be spent on land development activities such as soil conservation and water harvesting while expenditure on buildings and road construction should not exceed 25 per cent.

In the implementation of special schemes, geographical targeting is usually forgotten. As a result of the implementation of special schemes for well over two decades, poverty ratio is said to have come down in some areas. Therefore, there is no point in allocating funds uniformally among all the blocks under a particular scheme.

Delivering the J.P. Memorial Lecture in New Delhi on November 21, 1985, Prof. B.S. Minnas observed, "Our approach to overcome poverty since the early 1970s has been extremely flawed. The anti-poverty programmes have been over-centralised. The best model of development for the removal of poverty, shorn down to its essentials, has been reduced to schemes for dispensing of political and bureaucratic patronage on an individualised basis. It is not only leading us into inefficiency and corruption, but we also run the danger of its being used for perpetuation of poverty on a patron-client basis."

The existing schemes were centrally planned, designed, managed and controlled by bureaucrats with no participation by the intended beneficiaries or by agencies truly representing them.

Also, these schemes failed to realise the need for a critical minimum level of resource inputs to break out of the poverty cycle. There is no systematic effort to mobilise resources on the scale needed to eradicate poverty.[11]

The main drawback in our planning for the weaker sections appears to be lack of clear understanding of the prevailing environment and the factors associated with them.[12]

There is ample evidence to show that strategies based on the trickle down theory will not be enough to tackle the problem of rural poverty. In most developing countries, not only is the growth rate inadequate, but even the pattern of growth is such that it helps widen the income inequalities.

While a strong case is advanced for the continuance of special schemes, efforts should be made to see that the poor do not depend on the government permanently. These schemes should help the target groups equip with income earning capacities so that they can cross the poverty line within a reasonable period of time.

Prof. Dantwala has observed that the success of the special employment schemes should be judged by the progressively reduced reliance on them.[13]

STRENGTHENING SPECIAL SCHEMES

The rural poor suffer from despondency constraint and tend to look forward to programmes to improve their socio-economic status. The implementation of anti-poverty programmes would revive confidence in them which would be boosted when the beneficiaries get properly organised.

Considering the high incidence of unemployment and poverty in rural India, the need for these special schemes increases. However, these schemes need to be strengthened by —

- integrating them with planning at the block level,
- providing appropriate training to the personnel responsible for implementing these schemes,
- minimising wrong identification of beneficiaries through ensuring people's participation and
- selecting projects having maximum forward and backward linkages.

Because of the high incidence of leakages, some economists have argued in favour of strict targeting of poverty alleviation programmes. This would reduce the cost of support programmes. However, Prof. Amartya Sen has argued that such strict targeting also involves some economic and social costs. These include administrative costs for executing the programmes for the deserving; the deterioration in quality of services as the beneficiaries (the poorest of the poor) may not be in a position to monitor the quality and ensure the soundness of the services offered. Also, helping the largely disadvantaged rural sector may amount to a demeaning process.

There are also some social costs when the target group is reduced in size, there will be attempts to distort the relevant information for the inclusion of the non-poor in the list of beneficiaries. According to Prof. Sen, there may even be 'incentive distortions.' The beneficiaries tend to adjust their work and other activities to qualify for support from the government, causing significant loss in social output and activity. The socially disadvantageous groups may not like policing and probing into their lives.[14]

While implementing special schemes, we should give priority to geographical targeting. For instance, the revamped Public Distribution System (PDS) does concentrate on 2,184 blocks in backward and remote areas. We should follow the same approach while implementing special schemes for rural development. Otherwise, achievements are likely to fall short of the targets.

It is necessary to bring all the programmes of human resource development — employment generation, assets endowment, minimum needs, training and skill formation etc., under a single umbrella with the objective of enhancing their mutual reinforcing potential.[15]

The functionaries at the block level should explain the benefits of different schemes so that beneficiaries can be motivated to adopt a suitable scheme. Also, the functionaries have to maintain links with beneficiaries even after the schemes have been sanctioned in order to be aware of the problems coming in the way of effective implementation of the programme.[16]

No doubt, saving and investment ratios have gone up significantly since the commencement of the planning era, but the growth rate has not gone up significantly. Therefore, what matters is not additional resource mobilisation, though this is also important but efficiency in resource utilisation.

REFERENCES

1. S.D. Chamola: 'Remove Weaknesses of R.D. Programmes', *Kurukshetra,* August 1990, p. 33.
2. N. Kakwani and K. Subba Rao: 'Rural Poverty and Its Alleviation in India', *Economic and Political Weekly,* March 31, 1990.
3. *Focus on Poverty* (1983): A World Bank Publication, pp. 10-11.
4. K.M. George: 'Integrated Rural Development Programme: Need for Recasting', *Kurukshetra,* September 1987, p. 18.
5. R.C. Dutt: 'It's Corruption that Intercepts Rural Progress', *Kurukshetra,* October 1991, p. 45.
6. C.T. Kurien: Asian Session on Rural Development: Dantwala and Others (edited 1986).
7. Peter Lanjouw and Nicholas Stern: 'Poverty in Palanpur', *The World Bank Economic Review,* January 1991, pp. 33-34.
8. D.R. Shah: 'Plugging Leakages of Resources', *Kurukshetra,* October 1991, pp. 96-97.
9. Usha Rai: 'The Promises that are Beyond Redemption', *Indian Express,* January 19, 1995.
10. Neela Mukherjee: 'Lessons of Poverty Alleviation Programmes', *Yojana,* August 15, 1990, p. 38.

11. P. K. Gopinathan and V.L. Srilatha: "The Kerala Experience', *The Hindu,* Apri l 2, 1995.

12. P. Hanumantha Rayappa and Deepak Grover (1980): *op. cit.,* p. 2.

13. Speech of Prof. M.L. Dantwala at the Labour Economic Conference in Ahmedabad, on 28th December 1978.

14. Convocation Address of Prof. Amartya Sen, Lamont Professor of Political Economy at Harvard University, Boston, USA, at the Management Development Institute, Gurgaon, in July 1992.

15. M.L. Dantwala: 'Making Administration Responsible', *Kurukshetra,* October 1991, p. 14.

16. Ajay Kumar Singh: 'Administrative Personnel in the Implementation of IRDP', *Kurukshetra,* August 1985, p. 22.

Chapter

26 Employment Generation Programmes

Employment generation, particularly in rural areas, appears to be the most challenging task for planners and policymakers in India. The unemployment situation has worsened over a period of time.

The main objective of the Eighth five-year plan is to create employment avenues for over six million rural people every year. The addition to the number of unemployed in rural areas is reportedly increasing at the rate of nearly one million a year. The problem can be solved in the near future if only rural employment increases from the present 2.2 per cent to 2.6 per cent per annum.

The rural labour force is adversely affected due to meagre wage rates and rising unemployment. The government sought to improve the plight of the rural labourers by implementing: *(i)* special programmes for supplementing work opportunities and *(ii)* programmes for increasing labour absorption in agriculture. While the former provides temporary relief, the latter is crucial for long-term employment growth. But programmes so far implemented to enhance the labour absorption capacity of the agricultural sector have failed to reach the point of success.

In this chapter, an attempt has been made to present the nature, progress and problems of major employment generation programmes.

The Rural Works programme was taken up towards the end of 1960-61 in 32 community development blocks on a pilot basis for utilising rural manpower to provide employment for 100 days to at least 2.5 million persons by the last year of the Third Five Year Plan, specially in areas exposed to pronounced seasonal unemployment and underemployment. However, due to resource constraints, a little over 20 per cent of the outlay of ₹ 150 crore, originally envisaged could be provided and the programme ended in 1968-69, resulting in generation of 137 million man-days of employment.

The centrally sponsored schemes for employment generation have suffered from serious irregularities in implementation besides providing opportunities to unscrupulous politicians and their allies in the bureaucracy for illegal gratification. The delivery system has also been defective and ineffective. No significant changes in the administrative structure have taken place since the days of Rajiv Gandhi as Prime Minister. The state governments have been working on strategies to collect central funds for various employment schemes and divert them for various other unintended purposes. The canon of accountability is skirted.[1]

There is very often no proper maintenance of assets created. As such, they cease to be a source of service to the poor sooner or later.

A uniform pattern of rural employment programmes may not be suitable to the entire country. For instance, a study of Andhra Pradesh has revealed that the agriculturally prosperous regions experienced higher wage rates but lower levels of employment, and of course lower levels of poverty. In backward regions, the employment schemes should ensure raising both employment and wage levels. In the developed regions, the stress should be on generating more employment opportunities in the rural sector.[2]

A study of some important employment generation programmes would offer us many useful lessons.

I. CRASH SCHEME FOR RURAL EMPLOYMENT

The Crash Scheme for Rural Employment (CSRE) was initiated in 1971-72 for generating employment opportunities in rural areas. It lasted for three years. During this period, it is supposed to have generated employment to the tune of 3.150 lakh man-days. Its achievements are related to minor irrigation works, land development including reclamation, soil and water conservation, groundwater recharging, drainage and water-logging and flood protection. It also contributed to the development of pisciculture and the extension of roads and culverts.

It is argued that a programme like CSRE cannot be successful as it was launched on an ad hoc basis and the works under this scheme did not form an integral part of rural development planning as such.

Table: 1

The year-wise allocation of funds, amounts actually released, expenditure incurred and employment generated under the Crash Scheme for Rural Employment

Year	*Allocation of Funds (₹ in lakh)*	*Amount Released (₹ in lakh)*	*Expenditure Incurred (₹ in lakh)*	*Employment Generated (lakh man-days)*
1971-72	5,000.000	3,373.430	3,116.580	789.660
1972-73	5,040.745	4,711.395	5,334.480	1,344.070
1973-74	4,233.550	4,178.000	4,265.880	1,023.660
Total	1,4274.295	12,262.825	12,716.940	3,157.390

Source: Annual Reports of Ministry of Agriculture and Irrigation.

The CSRE was designed to generate on an average 2.5 lakh man-days of employment in every district. According to the guidelines, the projects were to be labour-intensive and to promote the development of districts. The cost of material, equipment etc. was not to exceed 25 per cent of the total cost. The scheme was administered by the Department of Rural Development at the Centre and its counterparts at the state level.

Table: 2
Physical Achievements under the CSRE

Categories of Works	*Physical Achievements*
Minor Irrigation	1,84,132 (Ha)
Land Reclamation	10,549 (Ha)
Soil Conservation	33,496 (Ha)
Water Conservation and Groundwater Recharging	1,516 (Ha)
Afforestation	32,559.5 (Ha)
Flood Protection	1,35,028.0 (Ha)
Drainage and Anti-waterlogging	1,89,172.0 (Ha)
Community Orchards	599.0 (Ha)
Panchayat Land Development	847.0 (Ha)
Pisciculture Tanks	3,147.0 (Ha)
Roads	86,197.0 (Kms.)
Culverts	6,769.0 (Nos.)

Source: Annual Reports of Ministry of Agriculture and Irrigation.

The scheme was financed outside the plan during 1971-72 and as part of the central plan during 1972-73 and 1973-74. The entire cost of the scheme was borne by the Centre and released to the states/ union territories as 100 per cent grant.

During the three year period 1971-74, the central assistance released was of the order of ₹ 122.6 crore out of a total allocation of ₹ 142.7 crore and resulted in the creation of employment to the extent of 3160 lakh man-days.

Two objectives of CSRE are:

(i) the direct generation of employment in all the districts of the country through the execution of projects which are essentially labour-intensive and

(ii) the production of assets of a durable nature in consonance with local development plans so that the all round development of the districts is assisted.

The Programme Evaluation Organisation (PEO) of the Planning Commission carried out in 1975 an evaluation study of CSRE in 29 districts spread over 18 states. The study revealed that each state government evolved its own system for the allocation of funds to different agencies and to different areas. The relative share of the wage and material components in the expenditure under the scheme varied from state to state.

The PEO study further revealed that the CSRE concentrated on road construction, land development and minor irrigation without taking into account the needs of the districts. The study observed, "Had the focus of the programme been on land development and minor irrigation works rather than on roads, perhaps larger benefits would have accrued to agriculture through the creation of durable productive assets." Also, the CSRE employed contractors contrary to the norms laid down.

However, it was noticed that the weaker sections of the village community by and large benefitted more than others under the scheme. The maximum participation was noticeable in the case of scheduled tribes.

II. PILOT INTENSIVE RURAL EMPLOYMENT PROJECTS

The Pilot Intensive Rural Employment Projects (PIREP) was launched as action-cum-research studies in 1972 for a period of three years in 15 selected blocks in the country—one block was selected from each of the major states. In order to understand the nature of poverty and unemployment in rural India, the blocks were selected based on the diversity in their agro-climatic conditions.

The works selected under PIREP have been directly related to agricultural operations. The states were made responsible for the actual implementation of PIREP. The programme gave top priority to minor irrigation strategies and roads.

Table: 3
Pilot Intensive Rural Employment Projects: Allocation, Amounts Released, Expenditure Incurred and Employment Generated

Year	*Allocation Made (₹ in lakh)*	*Amounts Released (₹ in lakh)*	*Expenditure Incurred (₹ in lakh)*	*Employment Generated (lakh man-days)*
1972-73	150.00	150.00	118.31	33.70
1973-74	248.85	248.85	218.30	50.14
1974-75	594.14	594.14	621.63	97.76
Total	992.99	992.99	958.24	181.60

Source: Annual Reports of the Ministry of Agriculture and Irrigation.

However, PIREP has not produced results commensurate with the investments made. The programme faced the same problems experienced by earlier programmes, namely, RWP and CSRE.

Table: 4
Physical Achievements under PIREP 1972-75

Category	*Physical Achievements*
Minor Irrigation (Ha)	352
Soil Conservation and Afforestation (Ha)	-
Land Reclamation and Flood Protection (Ha)	1148
Pisciculture Tanks (Ha)	26
Fodder Development (Ha)	7

Soil Conservation (Ha)	20
Roads Constructed/Repairs (kms.)	931
Drinking Water Wells (Nos.)	8
School Rooms (Nos.)	54
Rural Godowns (Nos.)	4
Houses for Weaker Sections (Nos.)	20
Culverts (Nos.)	118

Source: Annual Reports of Ministry of Agriculture and Irrigation.

III. ANTYODAYA

Realising the limitations of the usual rural development programmes in conferring benefit on the poor, the Government of Rajasthan launched the 'Antyodaya' programme on October 2,1977— the first of its kind in the country. Subsequently, the programme was launched by the government of Uttar Pradesh, Bihar, Himachal Pradesh, Gujarat, Manipur, Orissa and Karnataka. Literally 'Antyodaya' means 'raising/lifting the last man.'

The special features of *Antyodaya* include:

(i) Involvement of the village representatives in identifying the antyodaya families inclusive of non-agricultural labourers and self-employed persons in various petty occupations and

(ii) Laying emphasis on economic criterion for the selection of families without any differentiation on grounds of caste, colour and religion.

The Planning Commission brought out the following features of Antyodaya:

First, under this approach, poverty does not remain a statistical abstraction. The poor family is identified as a concrete human reality. Second, emphasis is laid on the delivery of productive assets so that a poor family begins to get a regular income from self-employment. Third, the administration goes out and identifies potential areas to generate employment and assists the poor people, instead of waiting for people to come for assistance. Fourth, the criterion of identification is strictly economic — that is income below the poverty line.

The following criteria were laid down for selection of families under this programme:

(i) Families not having any economic assets or earning member in the age group of 15-59 years due to infirmity or old age;

(ii) Families without any economic assets but with one or more members capable of undertaking economic activity where the total income of such a family of five members is not exceeding ₹ 1,200 a year;

(iii) Landless labourers and artisan families whose annual income for a family of five members falls between ₹ 1,200 and ₹ 1,800 a year and

(iv) Other families with some land or other assets but are living below the per capita consumption level of ₹ 55 per month.

The identification of families is done in *gram sabhas* which are organised by the BDO (Block Development Officer). The *gram sabha* meetings would be supervised by an officer nominated by the collector. The Patwari/VLW would prepare a tentative list of 10 to 15 of the poorest families eligible for assistance under the programme. The decision of the *gram sabha* is final in the selection of beneficiaries. The *gram sabha* discusses the needs of the selected families. Each identified *antyodaya* family under the programme would be issued an identity card.

With a view to ensuring proper utilisation of the benefits provided, the state government had authorised the village panchayats to keep vigil on the beneficiary families.

At the district level, the district *antyodaya* committee chaired by the District Collector consisting of officials and non-officials is responsible for the implementation of the programme. At the block level, the BDO is incharge of the programme. He is assisted by co-operative officials, revenue officials and other departmental officials. The sarpanches have been given the responsibility to check on the proper utilisation and continuance of the benefit given to the selected families.

Some of the programmes included under *antyodaya* are: old age and disability pension, allotment of land, bank loans (there is also a provision to help the *antyodaya* families in digging wells on their lands), khadi board programmes, public works, government service and other schemes.

There are some ancillary benefits too. These include:

(i) No registration is required with employment exchanges for getting a job, the identity card issued to select families is sufficient;

(ii) Maximum age-limit for employment in class IV categories is raised to 45 in case of antyodaya family members;

(iii) School going children of antyodaya families need not pay school fees and contribution to student-fund upto the 11th class and obtain free school dress and books and

(iv) Priority is given to children of antyodaya families in getting admission into the hostels run by social welfare departments.

The PEO of the Planning Commission has evaluated the *antyodaya* programme in Rajasthan during September-October 1978. The evaluation study revealed: *(i)* greater awareness about the programme on the part of beneficiaries, *(ii)* identification of beneficiaries was by and large fair and *(iii)* old age pension scheme existed earlier, but its coverage was extended to cover *antyodaya* families with large financial allocations.

The evaluation study made certain recommendations to strengthen the programme. These include:

(i) Strengthening the supervisory field staff of commercial banks, specially to ensure proper utilisation of loans advanced;

(ii) Strengthening of package of services of technical know-how together with provision of raw materials and marketing facilities;

(iii) Provision of consumption credit particularly for those whose assets start giving benefits of income after sometime;

(iv) Land allotment to the beneficiaries should invariably be followed by the loan assistance for land improvement;

(v) Strengthening the machinery for implementation and follow up of the programme and

(vi) There should be a regular system of concurrent evaluation of the working of the programme to adopt timely corrective measures.

The choice of programme for economic upliftment of these families was to be guided by the preferences of the identified families, preset status of the village economy, availability of resources including institutional finances etc.[3]

IV. EMPLOYMENT GUARANTEE SCHEME

The Employment Guarantee Scheme (EGS) was launched by the Maharashtra Government in May 1972, but because of relief works till 1973-74, the implementation of the programme was not a high priority issue till 1974.

Legislated in December 1974, the EGS aimed at providing employment to all those who seek it with special emphasis on daily wages. The aim is to provide manual jobs particularly during the land dry season.

The scheme covered all the rural areas of Maharashtra plus 'C' class municipal areas. The EGS guarantees work to anyone who seeks it within a radius of 8 kms. from his or her village of residence. Two modifications were made in the scheme: the person seeking work must be 18 years of age and above and that work will be provided only in the rural parts of Maharashtra.

The EGS has been in operation in the rural areas as well as in the areas of 'C' class municipal councils since 1972-73. The salient features of the programme are:

(i) All adult persons are covered under the programme;

(ii) The guarantee is given at the district level, though operationally works are normally provided within the panchayat samiti area;

(iii) The person demanding the work has no choice regarding the nature of work;

(iv) The employment seeker has to get his name registered under the scheme;

(v) Failure to provide employment creates the liability on the state for payment of unemployment allowance at the rate of ₹ 2 per day;

(vi) Only productive works are permitted under the scheme; for instance, to minimise the recurrence of drought in the state, moisture conservation and water conservation given priority;

(vii) The wages are paid on the piece rate basis;

(viii) Ex-gratia payment up to ₹ 5,000 is admissible in the case of death or disablement of a worker on work and;

(ix) Welfare amenities are provided to workers such as potable water, creches, rest shade, first aid facilities etc.

It was stipulated that 48 per cent of EGS expenditure should be wage expenditure and the remaining 60 per cent for all other expenses, i.e., cost of materials, tools, project planning and supervision etc. Till March 1990, ₹ 2,400 crore has been spent on the scheme and the annual outlay continues to be around ₹ 250 crore. Of course, the average cost per man-day has gone up.

A three-tier administrative set up has been evolved to ensure close and effective liaison and continuous supervision over the programme. Committees for planning, direction, control and co-ordination have been set up at the state, district, and panchayat samiti level. The works are implemented through the government departments (and not through contractors) like irrigation, public works, agriculture, forest and zilla parishads.

The state government raises much needed resources from the urban areas for the implementation of EGS. The special taxes and levies are:

(i) tax on professions, trades, callings and employment,

(ii) additional tax on motor vehicles,

(iii) additional tax on sales tax,

(iv) special assessment on irrigated agricultural lands,

(v) surcharge on land revenue and

(vi) tax on non-residential urban lands and buildings under the Education Cess Act.

The State government makes a matching contribution equal to the net collection of taxes and levies every year. The net collection of taxes and levies and the matching contribution from the state government are credited to a separate fund called the Employment Guarantee Fund. The resources thus collected have to be used for the purpose of EGS only. If there is any balance in a particular year, the same is carried forward to the subsequent year.

The EGS has done a good job in the Maharashtra State during the drought period of 1970-73. The scheme was used as a relief programme. After the drought period, the government has continued the EGS and used it as an anti-poverty programme. From a modest beginning with only ₹ 1.88 crore in 1972-73, the scheme expanded to a total of ₹ 235 crore in 1990-91.

It is said that between 1977 and 1983, the percentage of population below the poverty line in rural Maharashtra declined from 54.7 per cent to 35.7 per cent. The EGS proved to be a boon for the rural poor, particularly in the context of poor performance of the agricultural sector in Maharashtra during this period.

The EGS has also succeeded in providing employment particularly to the rural women. Female employment has been highly helpful in raising the nutrition and health status of poor families. The scheme's provision of employment also increased from 0.45 crore person days in the first year to around 19 crore in 1985-86; but has reportedly declined to 8 to 9 crores since 1988-89.

Of course, the EGS has been facing some problems. The procedure of getting employed under the EGS is lengthy and is riddled with bureaucratic procedures. This needs to be corrected particularly because the labourers are illiterate. Also, very few people know about the procedures followed under the EGS.

Table: 5
Expenditure Incurred on EGS and Mandays Generated

Year	*Total Expenditure (₹ in crore)*	*Total Mandays (in crore)*	*Average Cost Per Manday (in ₹)*
1972-73	1.88	0.45	4.18
1973-74	1.89	0.51	3.71
1974-75	13.72	4.81	2.85
1975-76	34.62	10.95	3.16
1976-77	51.11	13.65	3.74
1977-78	51.54	11.73	4.39
1978-79	74.17	16.35	4.49
1979-80	109.23	20.54	5.32
1980-81	122.12	17.15	7.12
1981-82	126.17	15.60	8.09
1982-83	130.94	12.80	10.23
1983-84	184.98	16.45	11.24
1984-85	232.04	17.80	13.14
1985-86	271.37	18.95	14.37
1986-87	246.27	18.76	12.98
1987-88	288.32	13.32	19.06
1988-89	254.23	8.13	31.27
1989-90	239.28	7.80	30.28
1990-91	235.00	8.94	26.28

Source: Planning Department, Government of Maharashtra, Mumbai.

The officials have, however, failed to take up the EGS scheme seriously as an anti-poverty programme expecting labourers to take up better employment opportunities. They have to turn to EGS only if they fail to get better jobs. This attitude would also undermine the quality of EGS.

Also, the administration has forced difficulties in identifying and designing works in the vicinity of the villages and consequently the EGS is not able to provide continuous employment in relation to the needs of the rural sector.

Table: 6
Categorywise Percentage of Expenditure Incurred from 1974-75 Onwards

Category	*1974-75*	*1978-79*	*1982-83*	*1986-87*
Irrigation	77.8	42.3	40.7	24.5
Soil Conservation and Land Development	12.2	25.3	18.2	13.1
Afforestation	2.7	2.3	6.2	7.2
Roads	5.7	19.3	32.4	31.0
Other works	1.6	1.0	0.7	1.1
Staff expenditure including machinery expenses etc.	-	9.8	1.8	23.1
Total	100.0	100.0	100.0	100.0
	(13.72)	(74.17)	(130.93)	(246.27)

Figures in bracket show total expenditure ₹ in crore.

Source: Planning Department, Government of Maharashtra, Mumbai.

The employment guarantee is there only at the district level and many labourers are unwilling to migrate from one tahsil to another. Besides, the earnings and the extent of employment under the EGS have failed to attract labourers to migrate from their region.

The landless workers are interested in daily wages and not weekly or fortnightly wage payments. There is considerable uncertainty about the period of employment as the state is required to provide employment for a minimum of 30 days at a stretch. There have been reports of cases of inherent corruption and political interference.

Under the EGS, the unskilled workers could not get higher wages. There is a condition that the full requirements of labour on various farm operations and other allied activities in the rural areas are met. Thus, the unskilled worker has no option to choose between work under EGS or work with a private landholder.[4]

The PEO study has revealed that in majority of the cases, necessary complementary investment in the form of construction of wells, land levelling and land shaping, application of fertilisers and other essential inputs had not been made. This had resulted in the sub-optimal use of the potential created. No specific agency seemed to have been assigned the responsibility of the follow-up, including extension and credit supplies in order to realise optimum benefits. Funds were wasted on assets of doubtful utility. Also, nearly 30 per cent of the works remained incomplete till the end of 1989.

The EGS has in essence contributed to the stabilisation of incomes of the poor. It also prevented, to some extent, rural-urban migration. It has been noticed that the delivery system has fared much better in areas where voluntary organisations have been active.

It may be noted that the poor could derive continuing benefits if there is agricultural development due to EGS assets.[6] What is necessary is to stipulate that a socio-economic cost-benefit analysis of each proposed project be taken up — for a proper selection of the projects to meet the various objectives of the scheme.[7]

V. FOOD FOR WORK PROGRAMME

The Food For Work Programme (FFWP) was taken up in April 1977 as an integral part of the strategy to tackle the problem of rural unemployment and poverty. The works taken up under the scheme are aimed at creating durable community assets and strengthening the rural infrastructure. The central government issues detail guidelines to the state governments for planning, implementation and monitoring of the programme.

The major objectives of FFW programme are:

(i). To generate additional gainful employment to a large number of unemployed and underemployed persons, both men and women, in the rural areas, which will improve their incomes and consequently their nutritional levels,

(ii) To create durable community assets and strengthen the rural infrastructure, which will result in higher production and better living standards in the rural areas and

(iii) Utilisation of surplus foodgrains for the development of human resources.

According to the Sixth Plan, the FFW programme aims *"at creation of additional employment in rural areas on works on durable utility to the community with the use of surplus foodgrains available in the buffer stock for payment as wages."*

According to revised guidelines, the FFW lacks provision of contractor's system as the programme is based on foodgrain assistance by the central government.

It was felt necessary to fix responsibility for the maintenance of assets created under the programme in those states where there was no specific agency for such maintenance.

The foodgrains are to be utilised for the payment of part or whole of the wages of the labour engaged in the execution of specified works taken up under the scheme. Work projects under the scheme can be implemented throughout the year.

The state government /union territories are required to show additional expenditure over and above the amount provided in their budget for the respective items to the extent of value of the foodgrains utilised and calculated at the prescribed rate.

The panchayati raj institutions have been auhorised to execute work under the programmes. The state governments/union territories have been given the discretion to entrust the execution of works under the scheme to voluntary agencies of repute and standing.

The states are also given freedom in the implementation of FFW. Broadly the states have adopted the following three methods:

(i) in some states, the bureaucratic machinery has been used to implement the programme,

(ii) some states used the political machinery (the panchayats) to implement the programmes and

(iii) in many states, private contractors have been sold the rights to use the foodgrains and organise projects.

During 1977-78, 2.04 lakh tonnes of wheat was allocated to different states. The total utilisation was about 1.27 lakh tonnes.

In 1978-79, 12 lakh tonnes of foodgrains were utilised creating 372.8 million man-days of employment. During 1979-80, the utilisation was estimated at 23 lakh tonnes of foodgrains inclusive of the special allotment which was made to the states affected by drought that year, resulting in about 600 to 700 million man-days.

About 438 lakhs of man-days of employment were generated in 1977-78 through this programme. During 1978-79, about 2,864.18 lakh man-days were generated under the programme. During both these years, the highest man-days were generated in West Bengal.

The Programme Evaluation Organisation (PEO) has noticed, in its study, a number of irregularities in the implementation of the FFW programme. These include:

The actual days as shown in the muster roll were more but the workers were paid for lesser days or one man appeared two times in the same muster roll. Thus, things were not viewed seriously by the supervising officers.

In some blocks, even if some workers did not work up to the prescribed extent, they managed to get the certificate of satisfactory work.

It was also reported that the modified ration shop dealer supplied bad quality wheat. Probably the dealer sold out the actual foodgrains in the open market and distributed the worst quality of grains purchased at lower prices.

The state governments had also issued instructions that wages should be paid according to work, but it appeared that the agencies in charge of this programme were ignorant about these instructions. Therefore, they did not pay more even if some workers had put in extra work hours. In some blocks, some money by way of shares was demanded by the supervisory staff at the time of distribution of foodgrains.

In some districts, it was noted that the contractors paid the wages fully in cash and in turn sold bulk of the foodstocks in the open market for saving transportation costs. Due to delayed supply of foodgrains, the contractors had to pay the wages in cash and on receipt of the supply, the foodgrains were sold in the open market. Malpractice in weighing of foodgrains by ration shop owners was also reported.

In some cases, most of the assets created are not durable. It has also been observed that no agency has been made responsible for the maintenance of works.

Majority of the beneficiaries reported that the benefits of FFW programme were only of short-term nature and seasonal.[9]

A nation-wide evaluation of the programme revealed a number of deficiencies in its implementation. These included erratic disbursement of foodgrains, delay in measurement of earthwork, non-durability of assets created under the programme, inadequate technical support and lack of supervision leading to dilution of the technical specifications at the stage of implementation. Moreover, the programme was implemented on an ad hoc basis. No attempt was made by the states to prepare a shelf of project taking into account the local needs.

It is true that the primary aim of FFW programme at the time of its initiation was to raise the purchasing power with the rural people. If the beneficiaries spend on goods produced locally, the 'multiplier effect' would be effective. In the case of a public work programme like FFW programme, the beneficiaries have spent their income on goods produced in states or districts other than their own. Thus, the programme was affected resulting in a largely weak 'multiplier effect.'

It is again argued that the infrastructure provided by FFW programmes has not been of much help in raising agricultural production. As such, the ambitious anti-poverty programme has been reduced to a one-time relief programme.[10]

VI. NATIONAL RURAL EMPLOYMENT PROGRAMME

The National Rural Employment Programme (NREP) was launched in October 1980 in place of the erstwhile FFW programme. NREP was made an important part of the Sixth Plan in April 1981. It was implemented as a centrally sponsored programme on a 50:50 financial sharing basis between the central and state governments. The NREP had also the same objectives as the FFW programme. The basic objectives of the programme are:

(i) Provision of gainful employment opportunities for the unemployed and underemployed persons in the rural areas;

(ii) Strengthening the infrastructural facilities in rural areas, through construction of public utility assets.

It is further laid down that:

(iii) The NREP must create permanent assets;

(iv) The expenditure against labour and material component of the schemes included in the programme should have a ratio of 60:40 respectively;

(v) At least 10 per cent expenditure should be on the works specifically benefiting the weaker sections and

(vi) At least 10 per cent expenditures should be on afforestation etc.

The programme was implemented through the District Rural Development Agencies (DRDAs). The works were to be taken up for execution on the basis of a series of projects and annual action plans prepared by the DRDAs. Works were mainly executed through panchayati raj institutions. Workers were to be paid minimum wages fixed under Minimum Wages Acts. Part of the wages were paid in terms of subsidised foodgrains.

The outlay for NREP includes both the wage and the 'material' component of works. For no individual work should 'material' component exceed 40 per cent, though for the programme as a whole 33 per cent should normally be the proportion. With a view to ensuring the durability of assets created, the percentage of expenditure on materials has been raised to 50 with effect from 1983-84.

A major step was taken in 1983-84 when it was decided to subsidise the cost of foodgrains to be distributed under NREP. A subsidy to the extent of 37 paise to 40 paise per kg. was provided for wheat and rice to be distributed under the programme. According to the guidelines, foodgrains were to be provided at the rate of one kg. per man-day.

An outlay of ₹ 980 crore has been provided for the programme for the Sixth Plan period in the central sector. Of course, there was provision in state plans for this programme from 1981-82 onwards as it was implemented on 50:50 sharing basis.

The employment generated during the year 1986-87 under the NREP was 395.39 million man-days which substantially exceeded the plan target of 290 million man-days. In 1987-88, 208.52 million man-days of employment were generated under NREP up to December 1987 against the plan target of 290 million man-days for the whole of the year.

The outlays provided in the central and state plans were meant to generate 300 to 400 million man-days of employment on an average per year during the plan period.

Table: 7

Performance of NREP in the Sixth Five Year Plan

Year	*Resource Availability (₹ crore)*	*Expenditure (₹ crore)*	*Employment Generation (in million man-days)*	*Man-day Cost (₹)*	*Wage-Material Ratio*
1980-81	346.32	219.03	413.58	5.25	62.38
1981-82	460.37	317.63	354.52	9.04	69.31
1982-83	540.15	394.76	351.20	11.24	62.38
1983-84	535.59	393.22	302.76	13.08	62.38
1984-85	590.68	519.14	352.31	14.74	60.40

*For the first six months, the FFW programme was in operation.

Source: The Seventh Five Year Plan 1985-90, Vol. II, p. 58.

Table: 8

Performance of NREP in the Seventh Five Year Plan

Year	*Resource Availability (₹ crore)*	*Expenditure (₹ crore)*	*Employment Generation (in million man-days)*	*Man-day Cost (₹)*	*Wage-Material Ratio*
1985-86	593.08	531.95	316.41	16.81	60:40
1986-87	765.13	717.77	395.39	18.45	60:40
1987-88	888.21	788.31	370.77	21.26	59:41
1988-89	845.68	901.84	394.96	22.83	57:43

Source: Eighth Five Year Plan 1992-97, Vol. p. 29.

Major problems experienced by NREP include: absence of a specific survey for assessing the size of unemployment and underemployment, selection works is generally done at the state level without taking into account the felt-needs of the people; too many schemes are taken up for execution resulting in a very thin distribution of the funds; there is no provision for adequate administrative and technical staff at the district level and the involvement of contractors has also contributed to the limited success of NREP.[11]

It has become difficult to select schemes under NREP when the conditions laid down for the programme are observed. For instance, studies show that it is rather impossible to construct permanent capital assets by maintaining a ratio of 60:40 in labour and material.

Studies show that nearly 50 per cent of the funds meant for NREP are spent towards the close of the financial year, i.e., during January, February and March. As such, it seemed not possible to strictly follow the guidelines. This would dilute the quality of the schemes and encourage corruption among the officials.

Most of the NREP workers want more work on the programme and demand that work be made more regular and permanent. Indeed, in spite of NREP, an overwhelming proportion of households of NREP workers live below the poverty line.[12]

The NREP also experienced problems relating to incomplete works, recovery of unutilised funds, selection of labourers and payment of wages, lack of technical support, short life-span of assets created and absence of arrangements for the maintenance of assets created.

The NREP could provide only short-term employment, had limited coverage of programmes and allocation; could not undertake a systematic survey of nature and extent of employment, could not prevent leakage of funds, could not evolve an efficient monitoring machinery at the micro and macro levels and could not ensure people's participation in the planning and execution stages.

Moreover, inflated estimates of employment generation have been reported by various evaluation studies. This is attributed to a situation of actual wages being higher than the minimum wages; higher share of skilled labour, higher material component, outright misappropriation etc.

The Seventh Five Year Plan noticed some irregularities associated with works taken up under NREP. Undue importance was given to all kinds of building works under local pulls and pressures. Ten per cent of the outlays had been earmarked for works of direct benefit to members of SCs and STs. Many states were not able to spend the earmarked outlays.

Moreover, road construction too received high importance, but this lacked meaningful relationship with priorities arising from the minimum needs programme.

The NREP could achieve its employment targets. It also succeeded in stabilising wages in rural areas, containing prices of foodgrains and creating a wide variety of community assets which could be expected to help in raising the levels of living of the rural population.

The NREP would be effective only if the portfolio of projects indicating the precise man-days of labour needed for completing each specific task is prepared carefully. The project preparation and task implementing agencies should ensure that the economic output of the project is at least equal to the wages paid and total amount spent.[13]

The priorities should be determined taking into account the felt-needs of the area and potentials of employment. Only those works should be taken up which are labour intensive and which are preferred by the local people. Some of the works which can come under NREP included: village link roads, soil conservation, construction of tanks and bundhies, afforestation etc.

VII. RURAL LANDLESS EMPLOYMENT GUARANTEE PROGRAMME

The Rural Landless Employment Guarantee Programme (RLEGP) came into being on 15th August 1983. As in the case of NREP, wage and material cost ratio is 50:50. The wages are to be paid both in cash and kind.

The specific objectives of RLEGP are:

(i) improving and expanding employment opportunities for the rural landless with a view to providing guarantee of employment to atleast one member of every landless household up to 100 days in a year and

(ii) creating durable assets for strengthening the infrastructure in rural areas.

The objectives and stipulations under RLEGP are similar to those of NREP. But, RLEGP is limited only to the landless, with guaranteed employment of 100 days.

Funds have been earmarked specifically for certain activities — 25 per cent for social forestry, 10 per cent for works benefitting only the SCs and STs and 20 per cent for housing under Indira Awaas Yojana.

An outlay of ₹ 500 crore, fully financed by the central government, was provided under this programme in the Sixth Plan. However, during 1983-85, the central committee approved 320 projects with an estimated cost of ₹ 906.59 crore. The target for employment generation in 1983-84 and 1984-85 was fixed at 360 million man-days against which 260.18 million man-days of employment were actually generated.

An outlay of ₹ 1,743.78 crore for the country during the Seventh Plan has been provided to be borne entirely by the Centre. At an average wage of ₹ 8.61 per day as in 1984-85, total employment of 1013 million man-days is likely to be generated during this plan, at an average rate of around 200 million man-days per annum.

However, in the seventh plan, ₹ 2,412 crore were spent and 115 crore man-days generated with an average expenditure of ₹ 21 per man-day. Only 16 per cent had been spent on social forestry but 22 per cent had been spent on housing, with over 5 lakh houses created for SC/ST and freed bonded labourers. Rural roads accounted for 22 per cent while other construction, minor irrigation, soil conservation etc. each had a small share.

Studies have revealed a number of weaknesses of RLEGP. It is suggested that only those villages should be selected for this programme, which are predominantly inhabited by scheduled castes and landless labourers. But there is no systematic selection of villages for field operations of the programme.

The objective of the scheme is to guarantee employment to atleast one member of every landless agricultural household upto 100 days, but no record is being maintained to ensure that the beneficiary get employment of 100 days in a year.

While RLEGP has to provide employment during the slack agricultural season, the employment under the scheme came mainly during the busy season. This may be due to the tendency to utilise funds provided at the fag end of the financial year, i.e., in the month of March.

Other problems faced by the scheme include:

(i) the reluctance of the beneficiaries to accept a part of the wage in kind. Much time is wasted in getting grains from fair price shops,

(ii) the wages paid are generally lower than the prevailing wage rates,

(iii) though the class of contractors was abolished for this scheme, the practice of incorporating fictitious figures of man-days in the records continued,

(iv) the ratio between labour and material is fixed at 50:50. If this ratio is observed, certain works remain unfinished and

(v) there is absolutely no provision, whatsoever, for the maintenance of the projects constructed under this programme.[14]

The Seventh Plan observed that for the selection of assets under RLEGP, the basis was department plans and not local requirements. The objective of providing requisite quantum of employment to the landless labourers too remained neglected.

The report of the Controller and Auditor General of India (CAG) for the year ending March 31, 1989, pointed out that rice meant for distribution as part wages to workers under the RLEGP was diverted to the public distribution system, thus seriously affecting the implementation of the programme during 1983-89.

The Report further said that identification of rural landless households was not made. Identity cards were also not issued to the individuals concerned to serve as a record of employment guaranteed. Also, contrary to the instructions, works were entrusted on contract basis to nominees of gram panchayats and payments were made to them. There was also no verifiable record to show that the nominees distributed wheat as wages to workers.

VIII. JAWAHAR ROZGAR YOJANA

The Jawahar Rozgar Yojana (JRY) was launched on April 1, 1989 by merging NREP with RLEGP. JRY is financed by the Centre and the States in the ratio of 80:20. It has developed as the most important scheme for employment generation meant for those below the poverty line. Sixty per cent of the total allocation on a project under this scheme has been earmarked for payment of wages and the balance 40 per cent for purchase of materials. The scheme provides for creation of durable community assets such as roads and irrigation canals.

The primary objective of JRY is to generate additional gainful employment for the unemployed and underemployed persons, both men and women in the rural areas. Creation of productive community assets for strengthening rural infrastructure is another major objective of JRY. A secondary objective of JRY is to bring about improvement in the overall quality of life in the rural areas.

JRY is being implemented by the village panchayats all over the country. Over 440 lakh families which are below the poverty line are intended to benefit from this scheme. The programme is to provide employment to atleast one member of each poor family for 50 to 100 days in a year in the vicinity of places of their residence.

Of the total expenditure incurred, 15 per cent will be transferred to village panchayats to be used exclusively for the benefit of the Scheduled Castes and Scheduled Tribes. Diversion of funds meant for SCs/STs is not permitted. Thirty per cent of the JRY beneficiaries should be women.

Before the beginning of the financial year, every DRDA/Zilla Parishad is required to prepare the Annual Action plan equivalent to 12.5 per cent of its share of funds allocated in the preceding year. No work can be taken up unless it forms part of the Annual Action Plan. While preparing the Annual Action Plan, completion of incomplete works is to be given priority over new ones. No work is to be taken up by the DRDA/Zilla Parishad which cannot be completed within two financial years.

All plans for development are required to be discussed at the Gram Panchayat meeting. While preparing the work plan, care has to be taken to safeguard the interests of the weaker sections in a village. Top priority is given to the works benefitting SCs/STs, women and other weaker sections of the village society. The Gram Sabha (village assembly) has to be apprised of the progress of implementation of the programme at least twice a year.

JRY funds are kept in a nationalised or a co-operative bank or in a post-office in an exclusive and separate savings bank account by the Zilla Parishad/DRDAs/Village Panchayats. Withdrawal of funds from a JRY account can be made only for incurring expenditure under the Yojana. At the Gram Panchayat level, the cheques would have to be signed by the Head of the Panchayat along with another representative specially authorised by the village panchayats. The representative must be a member of the village panchayat or hold post of secretary of the panchayat. The village assembly should be informed about this payment.

Wages under JRY are to be paid at the rate notified for the prescribed schedule of employment under the Minimum Wages Act for the relevant works and may be paid partly in foodgrains and partly in cash. The village panchayats maintain a muster roll indicating the details of the labourers employed, their record of attendance and the wages paid to them.

JRY: Salient Features

Of the total funds allotted, five per cent should be on administrative expenses and 10 per cent on maintenance of assets. The remaining amount has to be distributed on the following lines: 35 per cent on the economically productive assets, 25 per cent on social forestry works, 15 per cent on million wells scheme and 25 per cent on other works including roads and buildings.

The wage component is kept at 50 per cent, the rest being on materials, administration and maintenance. Wages may be paid partly in cash and partly in kind, i.e., foodgrains (wheat and rice). The ratio of distribution of foodgrains shall not exceed 1.5 kg. per man-day. The foodgrain component of wages should as far as possible be given on the site itself.

Central assistance is provided to the states on the basis of proportion of the rural poor in a state/union territory to the total rural poor in the country. From the states to the districts, the allocations are made on an index of backwardness which is formulated on the following basis:

(i) 20 per cent weightage for the proportion of agricultural labourers in the total workers in the rural areas,

(ii) 60 per cent weightage to the proportion of rural SCs and STs population in relation to the total rural population and

(iii) 20 per cent weightage to the inverse of agricultural productivity.

However, these criteria have been changed. The main implications of the change in criteria for allocation of funds are:[15]

(i) districts with low agricultural productivity now get higher JRY allocations,

(ii) weightage for SC/ST population has been decreased from 60 per cent to 50 per cent and

(iii) no more weightage is given for percentages of agricultural labourers in a district.

The criteria for the distribution of resources to village panchayats from the districts are on the basis of the population of the village panchayat. If the population of a village panchayat is less than 1000, then it is assumed 1000 for the allocation of funds. Panchayats with a population of 3000 to 4000 would receive funds to the order of ₹ 80,000 to ₹ 1,00,000; others would get on a *pro rata* basis.

Not less than 80 per cent of the allocations under JRY are received by the district in respect of both the central assistance and state contribution. They are required to be given to the village panchayats. The gram panchayats are assigned a crucial role in the implementation of JRY not only to cover all the rural areas but to ensure people's active participation.

Under JRY, five per cent of the total funds, subject to a maximum of ₹ 75 crore, will be earmarked for taking up special and innovative projects such as those aimed at prevention of migration of labour, enhancing women employment, special programmes through voluntary organisations aimed at drought proofing as well as watersheds development resulting in sustained employment.

Twenty per cent of the funds, subject to a minimum of ₹ 700 crore were to be used to implement an intensified JRY in 120 backward districts in different states of the country where there was a concentration of unemployment and underemployment.

For better implementation of JRY, some modifications have been made in the Yojana from 1993-94. The aim is to provide 90 to 100 days of employment per person in backward districts which have higher number of unemployed and underemployed persons. JRY has been successfully implemented in three streams:

First, it has been implemented on the existing pattern with its two sub-schemes, Indira Awaas Yojana (IAY) and Million Wells Scheme (MWS).

Second, an intensified JRY has been launched in 120 backward districts with additional allocations. The type of works undertaken in the second stream include construction of all-weather roads, minor irrigation works, soil and water conservation works, water harvesting structures, wasteland development, farm forestry and drought proofing.

In the third stream, special and innovative projects are being taken up in rural areas to prevent migration of labour, enhance women's employment, drought proofing as well as watershed development resulting in sustained development.

Under JRY, strategies have been worked out to prevent diversion of resources from one district to another. Likewise, diversion of funds from a village panchayat to another village panchayat will also not be permissible. However, additional allocations can be considered for those districts which are reported to be performing better within the overall state allocations.

Two or more districts/gram panchayats may decide to pool the resources together to take up a work for the common benefit of the concerned district/panchayat. Central assistance is released in two instalments subject to certain conditions.

The state government is required to release its share to the DRDA/Zilla Parishads within a month after the release of the central assistance. The DRDAs/Zilla Parishad shall distribute the funds to the

Gram Panchayat within a month of the receipt of central grant. Likewise, the state share of funds will also be distributed to gram panchayats within a month of the receipt of the state share.

It is also stipulated that payment of every amount is to be authorised in the meeting of the village panchayat and the village assembly which is supposed to meet twice in a year.

Stress has been laid on simplification of the procedure of works. The block samiti or district level panchayati raj body will prepare and approve standard design and cost estimates. Village panchayats can execute works on the basis of approved cost norms and designs. Village panchayats are also allowed 10 per cent of annual allocation towards the maintenance of assets.[16]

In the selection of projects, state intervention is not there. The DRDAs/Zilla Parishad prepare annual action plans for JRY. A committee of the gram panchayat will oversee, supervise and monitor implementation of the projects undertaken, physical and financial audit of the works implemented by gram panchayats has been made compulsory. An important feature of JRY is that it has done away with the employment of contractors.

Another aspect of resources distribution is that foodgrains will be provided under JRY to the implementing agencies in those states and union territories which accept the same. The foodgrains will form a part of the overall resources to be shared in the ratio of 80:20 between the Centre and the states. The foodgrains to be released will generally be in two equal six monthly instalments — one in April and the other at the time of release of the second instalment of funds in money.

There is provision for 'social audit' at the village panchayat level. For this purpose, meetings, of village panchayats shall be held every month at a fixed state, time and place to consider issues regarding planning, execution, monitoring and supervision of JRY.

JRY: Targets and Achievements

A large part of plan resources meant for rural development was allotted for JRY. Between 1987-88 and 1992-93, as much as ₹ 11,800 crore, nearly 70 per cent of the plan allocations for rural development was spent on JRY and 405 crore man-days were generated.

JRY is expected to provide employment for 50 to 100 days during the year to one member of the 44 million rural families living below the poverty line.

Under JRY, works which result in creation of durable productive community assets can be taken up. During 1989-90, the scheme provided 8,643 lakh man-days of employment agaist the target of 8,757.25 lakh. A sum of ₹ 2,458 crore was spent during this year — against the total availability of ₹ 2,678.11 crore.

During 1990-91, 8,722 lakh man-days of employment was achieved against a target of 9,291.04 lakh man-days. During this year, a sum of ₹ 2,554.89 crore was spent as against the availability of ₹ 3,253.51 crore.

According to official statistics, 3,300 million man-days under JRY were generated in the country from 1989-90 to 1993-94.

Between 1983-93, a major chunk of 23.5 per cent of the allocation was for building of roads; 16 per cent for construction of wells; 12.5 per cent for housing; 11.4 per cent for minor irrigation; 7.9 per cent for schools and community buildings; 5 per cent for social forestry and 23.7 per cent for other rural projects.[17] For the year 1994-95, 1150 million man-days of employment were reported.

As part of the efforts to meet the housing needs of the rural poor, the Indira Awaas Yojana (IAY) was started in May 1985. This programme aimed at construction of dwelling units free of cost for the poorest of the poor. Scheduled Castes, Scheduled Tribes and the freed bonded labourers in the rural areas were given preference. This programme was implemented as a sub-scheme of Jawahar Rozgar Yojana. Ten per cent of the resources at the national level under JRY were earmarked for this programme.

The allotment of houses has been in the name of a female member of the beneficiary household. The beneficiaries would make their own arrangements for construction to suit their requirements. To the best possibility, houses were built in clusters so as to facilitate the provision of common facilities.

A total of 14.42 lakh houses have been constructed under the Indira Awaas Yojana (IAY) since the inception of the Scheme.

Out of this, about 7.68 lakh houses were constructed during 1990 to 1994.

The central allocation for this scheme for 1994-95 was estimated to be ₹ 300.90 crore as against an allocation of ₹ 254.00 crore in 1993-94.

Table: 9
Expenditure under Different Heads in JRY

Head	*1989-90 to 1993-94 (₹ crore)*	*Per Cent of Total*
Minor Irrigation (including wells)	2,786	25.2
Rural Roads	2,478	22.4
House sites and House construction	1,660	15.0
School and Community Buildings	868	7.8
Social Forestry	480	4.3
Other Items	2,800	25.2
Total	11,072	100.00

Table: 10
Physical Achievements Under JRY

Item	*Unit*	*Achievements*
Construction of wells under MWS	lakhs	4.47
Development of house sites	Nos.	49,478.00
Construction of houses	lakhs	14.80
School buildings	Nos.	1,68,993.00
Rural roads	000 kms.	674.00
Drinking water wells	thousands	489.00
Construction of village tanks	thousands	329.00
Area covered under social forestry	thousand Ha	655.00

Source: Ministry of Rural Development, Annual Report 1994-95.

JRY: MAJOR PROBLEMS

The utilisation of funds under JRY has been lower than the allocations in recent years due to inadequate attention paid by the state governments and the local administration.

Table: 11
Progress of Million Wells Scheme

Year	*No. of Wells Constructed (₹ crore)*	*Expenditure Incurred Per Well(₹)*	*Average Expenditure*
1988-89	50,345	123.0	26,416
1989-90	87,634	108.2	12,342
1990-91	56,433	279.7	49,570
1991-92	1,72,328	495.2	28,734
1992-93	1,80,995	534.0	29,506
1993-94	1,49,335	638.8	42,776
1994-95 (up to November 1994)	87,810	309.4	35,240
Total	7,84,880	2,498.3	31,831

Source: Ministry of Rural Development, Annual Report 1994-95.

Table: 12
Progress of Indira Awaas Yojana

Year	*No. of Houses Constructed*	*Expenditure (₹ crore)*	*Average Expenditure Per House (₹)*
RLEGP			
1985-86 to 1988-89	5,19,943	592.1	11,388
JRY			
1989-90	1,86,023	188.5	10,133
1990-91	1,81,800	213.1	11,710
1991-92	2,07,299	263.1	12,687
1992-93	1,92,585	238.8	12,402
1993-94	3,59,933	464.4	12,904
1994-95 (up to November 1994)	1,95,607	237.5	12,142
Sub-total	13,23,247	1,605.4	12,132
Total (1+2)	18,43,190	2,197.5	11,922

Source: Ministry of Rural Development, Annual Report 1994-95.

Table: 13
Expenditure on JRY during the Eighth Plan 1992-97

(₹ in crores)

Year	*I Stream*	*II Stream*	*Total*
1992-93	2709.59	—	2709.59
1993-94	3590.21	288.50	3878.71
1994-95	3359.88	098.45	4268.33
1995-96*	3966.08	493,41	4459.49
1996-97*	2156.93		2156.93
Total	15782.69	1690.36	17473.05

* provisional

Source: Ninth Five Year Plan Vol. II p. 51.

Table: 14
Employment Generated under JRY during the Eighth Plan (1992-97)

(lakh man-days)

Year	*I Stream*	*II Stream*	Total
1992-93	7821.02	—	7821.02
1993-94	9523.45	734.95	10258.40
1994-95	7453.59	2063.48	9517.07
1995-96*	7955.89	991.27	8947.16
1996-97*	3819.14	—	3819.14
Total	36573.09	3789.70	40362.79

* provisional

Source: Ninth Five Year Plan Vol. II, p. 51.

During the period 1989-90 to 1997-98, JRY could generate 69,690.83 lakh man-days.

In a comprehensive restructuring of the wage employment programmes on January 1,1996, JRY was further streamlined. The IAY and MWS which were till then sub-schemes of JRY were made independent schemes.

The second stream of JRY which was being implemented in 120 backward districts in the country was merged with the Employment Assurance Scheme (EAS) introduced in 1775 selected backward blocks in the country in 1993-94 in view of the similarity in these programmes. The Third Stream of JRY with its thrust on innovative projects was continued. Accordingly, the JRY is now being implemented in two parts, i.e.:

(i) The Jawahar Rozgar Yojana (Main Scheme) and

(ii) Special and Innovative Project.

The Centre has expressed regret over the passive performance of states which the latter refute, saying that low performance has been due to inadequate infrastructure, multiplicity of central agencies and insincerity at the top level of administration. Whatever may be the reason, large unutilised JRY funds are reportedly lying with the states.

The Programme Evaluation Organisation (PEO) of the Planning Commission took up a serious study of the JRY during 1991-92 in 10 major states: Andhra Pradesh, Bihar, Karnataka, Madhya Pradesh, Maharashtra, Orissa, Rajasthan, Tamil Nadu, Uttar Pradesh and West Bengal. The study covered 600 beneficiaries in 40 village panchayats of 20 districts. The main findings of the study were reported as follows:

(i) While the share of SCs/STs in employment generation was more than 50 per cent, the share of women in employment generation was only 22 to 25 per cent at the district level and 15 to 18 per cent at the village panchayat level;

(ii) The Yojana did not provide employment to the extent expected as the average number of days for which a person got employment was 11.44 days during 1989-90, 15.68 days during 1990-91 and 12.81 days during 1991-92 (upto September 1991);

(iii) Adequate attention was not given to the maintenance of assets;

(iv) Some of the Village Panchayats did not utilise the funds provided to them;

(v) 89 per cent of the selected beneficiaries described the assets created as useful and

(vi) Contractors were engaged by some of the Gram Panchayats for execution of some works.[18]

During 1992, the Government of India undertook concurrent evaluation of JRY through reputed research institutions covering all districts in the country. The main findings were reported as follows:

(i) Nearly 73 per cent of the available funds were spent by the village panchayats;

(ii) In almost all the states, the average wages paid per man-day to the unskilled workers were less or equal to the minimum wages prescribed under the Minimum Wages Act;

(iii) The wages and non-wages component of the expenditure of JRY works undertaken by the village panchayats at the All-India level was 53:47.

(iv) In about 84 per cent of the cases, the Muster Rolls were maintained;

(v) Of the total assets created, roughly 74 per cent was found to be good/satisfactory, 8 per cent of poor quality and the remaining 18 per cent were neither incomplete nor according to laid down norms;

(vi) At the All-India level, during the last 30 days preceding the date of the survey, a JRY worker got roughly four days of employment more than was received by the other members of the family;

(vii) In 17.5 per cent cases, assets created were not maintained by any agency.

The areas of concern as pointed out by the evaluation studies are:

(i) In majority of cases, panchayat heads were not given any training for undertaking JRY works;

(ii) In some states, the Annual Action Plan were not discussed at all in the Gram Sabha meetings;

(iii) In some states, viz., Andhra Pradesh, Kerala, Maharashtra, Tamil Nadu and Pondicherry, there were disparities in the average wages paid per day to male and female unskilled workers — the workers belonged to the category of 'ineligible' who also took advantage of the programme.

According to one case study, the major problems associated with JRY are:[19]

(i) Release of resources to Mandal Panchayat was delayed and as a result implementation of the scheme got delayed;

(ii) JRY wage rates have been reported low as compared to the locally prevailing wage rates;

(iii) Non-availability of workers and material during certain seasons caused delay in completing the works;

(iv) Foodgrains distribution to the workers as part of their wage is difficult due to irregular supply, lack of storage facility, low quality etc.;

(v) Lack of co-ordination between different agencies involved in implementing the scheme; and

(vi) Works are given on contract basis, though it is not permitted.

The occupational background of JRY workers was: 55 per cent were landless labourers, 39 per cent small and marginal farmers and 6 per cent rural artisans. Concurrent evaluation revealed that annual action plan in accordance with the JRY guidelines were discussed in Gram Sabha meetings only in 60.71 per cent cases at the national level.[20]

Much criticism has been levelled against the delivery mechanism. It is said that only about 57 per cent of the money is left to the panchayat to spend. The remainder is decided at the block/DRDA level. As a result of this, accountability disappears. This is so because government officials get frequently transferred and in some states, the duly elected panchayat system remains absent.

It was decided to restructure JRY during 1993-94. The ₹ 3,300 crore scheme was split into two major parts — about ₹ 2,000 crore would continue to fund the schemes as it exists today, the remainder of the money would go towards additional funding of 100 or so specially selected districts so as to augment employment opportunities in these more backward areas.

Also, the wage component and asset component ratio so far followed was 60:40. This resulted in the creation of poor quality assets. In order to solve this problem, efforts were made to dovetail JRY with other developmental activities in the gram panchayats area. While other schemes reportedly help to provide assets, the wage component was to be paid out of JRY funds.

JAWAHAR GRAM SAMRIDHI YOJANA (JGSY)

Three wage employment programmes have been integrated into JGSY in 1999 to be implemented at the village level by village panchayats to develop infrastructure. These are: (i) Jawahar Rozgar Yojana (JRY), (ii) Indira Awas Yojana (IAY), a sub-scheme of JRY, and (iii) Employment Assurance Scheme (EAS).

Salient Features of JGSY

- DRDA/Zilla Parishad will release funds including state's matching share directly to village panchayats. Emphasis is on creation of durable assets at the village level. Government will suitably relax the condition of maintenance of wage-material ratio of 60:40.
- As JGSY is implemented at the village panchayat level, 22.5 per cent of funds will continue to be earmarked for individual beneficiary schemes of SCs/STs at all the three levels of panchayati raj institutions.
- The village panchayats will have power to sanction works/schemes upto ₹ 20,000.
- Village panchayats are permitted to incur (i) administrative expenditure/contingency, and for taking technical consultancy upto ₹ 7,500 or 7.5 per cent of funds, whichever is less in a year, (ii) maintenance expenditure upto 15 per cent of funds in a year.
- Wages under JGSY will either be minimum wages as notified by the states or higher wages fixed by states through the procedure prescribed by the State governments.
- Allocation of funds under JGSY will be made on the basis of actual population of the village panchayat.
- There is no separate provision for innovative and special projects under JGSY, unlike JRY. They form part of JGSY.

The cost sharing ratio between the centre and states is 75:25. While the primary objective of the scheme is to create demand driven community village infrastructure including durable assets, the secondary objective is to generate supplementary employment for the unemployed poor in rural areas.

Sampoorna Grameen Rozgar Yojana (SGRY)

SGRY was launched on September 25, 2001 by merging the ongoing schemes of Employment Assurance Scheme (EAS) and the Jawahar Gram Samridhi Yojana (JGSY).

The objectives of the programme is to provide additional wage employment in the rural areas as also food security, along side the creation of durable community, social and economic infrastructure in the rural areas. Under SGRY, with an annual outlay of ₹ 10,000 crore, fifty lakh tonnes of foodgrains, amounting to ₹ 5,000 crore, has been kept to meet the cash component of wages and material cost. The special component of the SGRY replaces food for work programme with effect from April 1, 2002.

Under the SGRY, during 2002-03, an amount of ₹ 3,684.64 crore as cash component and about 45.26 lakh tonnes of foodgrains has been released to the States/UTs. Under the Special Component of the SGRY about 63.41 lakh tonnes of foodgrains has been released to the drought affected states/ districts during 2002-03.

During 2003-04, an amount of ₹ 2661.55 crore against the allocation of 45 lakh tonnes have been released under the programme. During 2003-04, 49.14 lakh tonnes of foodgrains has been released under the Special Component (*Kurukshetra*, April 2004, 3rd Cover Page).

In 2004-05, 82.23 crore person days were generated with the centre releasing ₹ 4496 crore as cash component and about 50 lakh tonnes of foodgrains to the States/UTs. Besides, under the special component of the SGRY, with the States/UTs meeting the cash components, centre released 26 lakh tonnes of foodgrains to the 13 calamity affected states.

In 2005-06 (upto November 2005), the number of person days generated under SGRY was 48.75 crore, while the centre's contributions in terms of the cash and foodgrains components upto January 2006 were ₹ 4651 crore and 35 lakh tonnes, respectively. Under the special component, about 11.65 lakh tonnes of foodgrains have been released to the 11 calamity hit states in the year 2005-06.

Funds are to be spent by the village panchayat for which they are meant. Diversion from one village panchayat to another is not allowed. The JGSY will also be a rural infrastructure rather than the wage employment scheme by changing the accounting procedure and relaxing the 60:40 funding ratio where 60 per cent has to be spent on labour.

The states are not happy because the centre has empowered panchayats to spend upto ₹ 50,000 on a scheme, without technical and administrative sanction. All the JRY funds are sent directly to panchayats on the basis of population.

The panchayat should become a planning and guiding machinery at the local level. Group activities would be encouraged to reduce the chances of misuse of funds.

REFERENCES

1. S. Swaminathan: 'Poverty Alleviation — The New Channel for Corruption', *The Hindu,* October 18, 1995, p. 19.
2. S. Galab: 'Rural Employment Programmes: Case for Involving Voluntary Organisations', *Economic and Political Weekly,* March 6, 1993, p. 409.
3. PEO, Planning Commission Government of India (1979): 'Evaluation Study of the Working of Antyodaya Programme in Rajasthan', p. 10.
4. *Economic and Political Weekly,* July 31,1982, p. 1228.
5. PEO, Planning Commission, Government of India and Director of Economics and Statistics, Government of Maharashtra, June 1980, *Joint Evaluation Report on Employment Guarantee Scheme of Maharashtra,* p. 41.
6. S. Mahendra Dev: 'Alleviating Poverty: Maharashtra Employment Guarantee Scheme', *Economic and Political Weekly,* October 14-21, 1995, p. 2672.
7. S. Bagchee: 'Employment Guarantee Scheme in Maharashtra, *Economic and Political Weekly,* September 15, 1984, p. 1637.
8. Kaushik Basu: 'Food For Work: Some Economic and Political Consequences', *Economic and Political Weekly,* March 27, 1982, P. A.-10.
9. PEO, November 1980: *Evaluation of Food For Work Programme* (August-October 1979) Final Report, Government of India, New Delhi.

10. K..K.Mohanty: 'From FFW to IRDP', *The Economic Times*, May 22, 1987.

11. Ethirajulu Naidu: 'Poverty Alleviation through NREP — A Study', *Yojana,* July 16-31, 1990, p. 32.

12. *Economic and Political Weekly,* May 14, 1988, p. 993.

13. Planning Commission (1981): *Sixth Five Year Plan 1980-85,* p. 175.

14. V.S. Singh and Banwari Lal: 'Anti-poverty Programmes: An Objectives Assessment', *Commerce,* June 27- July 3, 1987, pp. 26-27.

15. Parameswaran Iyer: 'Creating Rural Employment: JRY's New Thrust Areas', *Economic and Political Weekly,* August 6, 1994, p. 2065.

16. S.M. Shah: 'Are Panchayats prepared for JRY ?', *Kurukshetra,* January 1990, p. 15.

17. K.R. Sudhaman: 'Rozgar Yojana: Widening Horizon', *Yojana,* July 15, 1994, p. 21.

18. Annual Report of the Ministry of Rural Development, 1993-94.

19. K.P. Shripathi: 'Let Industrialisation Be Focus of JRY: A Case Study of Dakshina Kannada District', *Kurukshetra,* May 1994, pp. 13-14.

20. M. Neelakantan: 'Jawahar Rozgar Yojana', *Economic and Political Weekly,* December 3,1994, p. 3097.

Chapter

27 National Rural Employment Guarantee Programme

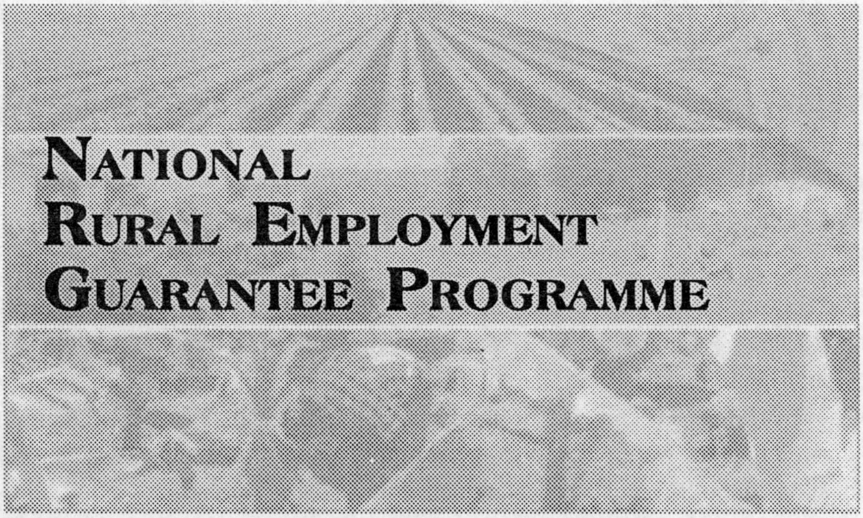

Rural India suffers from high incidence of poverty and unemployment. Hence, employment guarantee has special significance. The National Rural Employment Guarantee Bill, 2004, with necessary changes, was introduced in the Lok Sabha on August 18,2005. It was passed by the Lok Sabha on August 23, and by the Rajya Sabha on August 24,2005.

The National Rural Employment Guarantee Programme (NREGP) was formally launched on October 12,2005 in Bandlapalli of Anantapur district of Andhra Pradesh. To start with, the scheme would be implemented in 200 districts of the country. The NREGP covered all the districts of the country in 2008-09. At present, 619 districts are covered under the NREGP. During the year, 2008-09, more than 4.51 crore households were provided employment under the scheme. As against the budgeted outlay of ₹ 39,100 crore for the year, 2009-10, an amount of ₹ 24,758.50 crore has been released to the States UTS till December, 2009. During the year, 2009-10, 4.34 crore households have been provided employment under the scheme. Out of the 182.88 crore person days created under the scheme during this period, 29 per cent and 22 per cent were in favour of SC and ST population respectively and 50 per cent in favour of women. Union Budget 2010-11 provided ₹ 40,100 crore for NREGP.

Agriculture by itself cannot provide productive employment to the growing labour force. The rural non-farm employment has to be stepped up. What the rural poor require is not merely a guarantee of 1200 days of work in a year, but uninterrupted employment for most part of the year.[1]

As there are many irregularities in the implementation of wage employment programmes, meaningful employment guarantee scheme would be one that is not targeted, but is universal and demand driven.[2]

THE BACKGROUND

In July, 2004, a draft National Rural Employment Guarantee Act was prepared by concerned citizens and sent to the National Advisory Council (NAC).

Some important provisions of the draft Act have been watered down in the Bill. The NAC insisted on two principles — universality and self-selection. Under the Bill, there is no guarantee of time bound extension of the Act to the whole of rural India. The Guarantee of employment applies only "in such rural area in the state and for such period as may be notified by the Central Government." This means the guarantee can be withdrawn anywhere at any time.

The Bill stipulates that both the employment guarantee and the unemployment allowance are to be confined to "the poor households." There may be irregularities in identifying the households. The Bill defines poor households as those below the poverty line in the relevant financial year. But, the BPL (below poverty line) list is known to be highly unreliable. The Bill dispenses with minimum wages. In the NAC draft, labourers were entitled to the statutory minimum wage of agricultural labourers in the relevant state. In the Bill, this has been replaced by a central norm.

Also, the transparency provisions have been severely diluted. In the NAC draft, muster rolls and other records were to be made available for public scrutiny. But, the Bill states that these documents will be available on demand after paying such fee as may be specified in the scheme."

The Bill, in essence, leaves labourers to the mercy of the states. The state's discretionary powers under the Act can also be used at any time to phase out the whole projects.

On December 23, 2004, the National Rural Employment Guarantee Bill 2004 was referred to the standing committee on Rural Development whose final report has been placed before the Parliament.

The committee consisting of 31 MPs has suggested that

- A universal, self-targeting guarantee, ensured by the nature of the work, is to be provided;
- The guarantee should be not to a household, but to each workers; and
- There should be a time limit of four years for its extension to all rural areas of the country.

SALIENT FEATURES OF NREGP

The NREGP has some important characteristics. These should be kept in view while implementing the scheme.

THE APPROACH

A household is entitled for 100 days of work in a year. Within the household entitlement, all adult members of a rural household have the right to demand employment.

The household demanding work should submit name, age, sex and addresses of its adult members to the Gram Panchayat for registration.

Upon registration, a job card will be issued by the Gram Panchayat with photographs of adult members of the registered household. It will be valid for five years.

To get employment, the registered adult must submit an application on a plain paper in writing to Gram Panchayat or the Programme Officer (at the block level) and get a dated receipt of the application. The application should be submitted for at least 14 days of continuous work. One-third of persons who are given employment are women.

Within 15 days from submitting the application or from the date when employment is sought, employment should be provided by the Gram Panchayat. No contractor will be allowed to work under the scheme.

The Works

The main objective of NREGP is to create durable assets. As per schedule 1 of the Act, the focus of the programme should be on works like water conservation, drought proofing, minor irrigation works, land development, flood control, rural connectivity, and any other work that may be notified by the Central government in consultation with the State government. Work will be provided within 5 kms of applicant's residence. If it is provided beyond this distance, an additional 10 per cent wage is paid.

Implementing Agencies

At the village level, Gram Sabha and Gram Panchayat take up the responsibility. At the Block level, the responsibility is with intermediate panchayat, and programme officer. At the district level, the district panchayats and District Programme Coordinator are responsible. At the State level, the employment guarantee commissioners, and at the Central level, Central Employment Guarantee Council are responsible for the successful implementation of the programme. Local Vigilance and Monitoring Committees will be set up.

Wages

Every person working under the scheme shall be entitled to wages at the minimum wage rate fixed by the State government. Equal wages shall be paid to both men and women workers. It is recommended that wages should be paid on a weekly basis on a pre-specified day of the week in each Gram Panchayat. If workers are willing, a proportion of the wages may be earmarked and contributed to welfare schemes.

If a worker who has applied for work is not provided employment within 15 days from the date on which work is requested, an unemployment allowance shall be payable by the State Government at the rate prescribed in the Act. The payment of unemployment allowance shall be made no later than 15 days from the date on which it becomes due for payment.

Other Facilities

At work site, safe drinking water, shades for children, periods of rests and first aid box shall be provided. A person may be entrusted with childcare if there are more than five children brought along on the site. Such a person gets the usual wage. If a worker gets injured working on the site, free medical treatment will be given by the State government.

In case of death or permanent disability to the registered labourers due to accident at work site, an exgratia payment of ₹ 25,000 or such amount as may be notified by the Central government shall be paid to the legal heir of the diseased or to the disabled as the case may be.

Funding

The centre bears the entire cost of wages for unskilled manual workers, and also 75 per cent of the cost of material and wages for skilled and semi-skilled workers. It also bears administrative expenses.

The State government has to bear 25 per cent of the cost of material and wages for skilled and semi-skilled workers. It is also responsible for payment of unemployment allowance. The State meets the administrative expenses of the State Employment Guarantee Council.

During the year, 2005-06, states received 1,61,76,944 applications for registration, and 55,90,658 job cards have been issued. Funds released amounted to ₹ 1,46,498.71 lakhs.[3]

NREGP: Some Problems

One problem with the special schemes like NREGP is that works that are usually taken up for rural employment generation may be shown as NREGP works for funding by the centre. As a result of this, there will not be any substantial increase in employment level in the states.

From the employment data, we find that in nine of the 15 major states, the observed wage for earning members of rural labour households is less than the statutory minimum wage. If the workers under the NREGP are paid the statutory minimum wage, it might well attract participation from the non-poor as well.[4]

The provision for unemployment allowance if work is not provided within the time period specified is meaningless. There has been such provision in Maharashtra Employment Guarantee Scheme also but it remained only on paper.[5]

Some doubt the efficacy of the scheme. This is because of the gap between the predominantly central funding of the scheme and the predominantly state/local responsibility of its administration.[6]

The financial burden of the scheme needs to be examined. It is believed that the Draft Act has been diluted for financial reasons. According to Jayati Ghosh, around ₹ 40,000 crore would be needed to implement NREGP all over rural India which forms 1.5 per cent of the GDP. Of course, there is scope for raising the tax-GDP ratio.

The scheme suffers from three major drawbacks:

(I) confusion about the operational requirements of the Act;

(II) absence of any grievance redress system and

(III) lack of independent monitoring...

The CAG Report (2007) has pointed out a number of deficiencies at the implementation stage. These include lack of professional skill, lack pf proper project planning, bureaucratic resistance, lack of transparency and absence of social audit and inappropriate rates of payment.

Also, there remain considerable delay in the release of funds, leading to delays in initiating works, abandoning the work already started, and delay in payment of wages.

According to a study done by the National Council of Applied Economic Research (NCAER) in 2008, food secure households got more workdays compared to those who are food insecure. The survey covered 3,200 poorest households in villages in seven states.

NREGP: Measures Needed

Generation of productive employment in the Indian context requires diversification of agriculture, and also the entire rural sector. The priority areas are: raising farm productivity through improved management of micronutrients and water; expanding the total irrigated area, emphasising on more labour intensive crops (such as sugar, cotton, flowers and vegetables, sericulture, aquiculture etc.), reclamation of waste land and increasing income from animal husbandry and poultry.

All employment schemes suffer from high incidence of leakages. Very often employment figures are inflated. Hence, each worker is to be provided with a job card which is an official record of days of employment, work done, and wages paid. All records are to be subject to social audit in ward sabhas where utilisation certificates are to be issued after the works are completed.[7]

It is preferable to offer guarantee (with or without restrictions) to individuals rather than households.[8] Also, effective childcare facilities should be arranged so that women are free to take up employment without making their children suffer.[9]

It would be better if the NREGP is integrated with the on-going Bharat Nirman which aims at development of rural infrastructure like irrigation, roads, water supply, electrification, housing etc.[10]

Also, the list of permissible work should be expanded by an appropriate Central government notification. For instance, the types of work which would be required in the aftermath of a disaster should be added to the list.[11]

There should be incentive compatibility between the funding and the implementing agencies. A 90:10 centre-state funding ratio provides little incentive for the State government machinery to ensure that funds are spent efficiently.[12]

The NREGP has the potential to strengthen social security in rural India; strengthen community mobilisation, ensure better response from local administration to felt needs and priorities and also ensure better governance.[13]

We have to create institutional mechanisms to check rampant corruption, and strengthen social audit mechanisms.[14]

There is need to move away from large centralised bureaucracies that treat rural folk as clients to a more decentralised control over the programme anchored in the panchayati raj institutions.[15]

Some of the measures necessary to strengthen NREGP include: appointing full time professionals for implementing the scheme, specific efforts to reduce the gap between work done and payment received , evolving monitoring mechanisms to check leakages and misappropriation of funds.

The Government is making social audits compulsory. It has finalise procedures to ensure that Gram Sabha meeting be video graphed. The aim is to see that the NREGP fund is spent after adequate debate and preparation.

The panchayats should take up NREGP seriously, and create socially and economically useful infrastructure. There must be some arrangement whereby panchayats can access the expertise of line departments without pressure from these departments. Also, panchayats have to prepare and maintain a shelf of works as part of an overall village development plan.[16] The asset maintenance responsibility should be taken up by local people.

References

1. Srirang Jha (2004): 'Opportunities in Rural Non-Farm Sector', *The Hindu* (Magazine Section).
2. Prabhat Patnaik (2005): 'Need for a Universal EGS', *The Hindu*, January 5.
3. *Kurukshetra*, April 2006.
4. Bharat Ramaswami and Wilima Wadhwa (2005): 'Getting the Job Guarantee Plan Right', *The Economic Times*, March 21.
5. Anuradha Joshi (2005): 'For Effective Employment Guarantee', *The Hindu*, February 8.
6. Sankar Acharya (2004): 'Guaranteeing Action for Employment', *The Hindu*, August 15.
7. Aruna Roy and Nikhil Dey (2005): 'Guaranteeing Action for Employment', *The Hindu*, August 15.
8. Bharat Ramaswami and Wilima Wadhwa (2005): *op.cit.*
9. Kiran Bhatty (2006): 'Employment Guarantee and Child Rights', *Economic and Political Weekly*, May 20, p.1967.
10. C.H.Hanumantha Rao (2005): 'Rural Jobs Scheme and Tasks Ahead', *The Economic Times*, September 5.
11. J.Krishnamurty (2005): 'Employment Guarantee and Crisis Response', *Economic and Political Weekly*, March 4, p.790.
12. Arvind Virmani (2005): 'Should EGS be Universalised', *The Economic Times*, August 25.
13. Yamini Aiyer and Salimah Samji (2006): 'Improving the Effectiveness of National Rural Employment Guarantee Act', *Economic and Political Weekly*, January 28, p.325.
14. Mihir Shah (2005): 'Employment Guarantee — MPs Lead the Way', *The Hindu*, August 10.
15. Nitin Desai (2005): 'Work for Welfare', *Business Standard*, January 19.
16. A.Vaidyanathan (2005): 'Need for Involvement of States', *Economic and Political Weekly*, August 13.

Chapter

28 Integrated Rural Development Programme

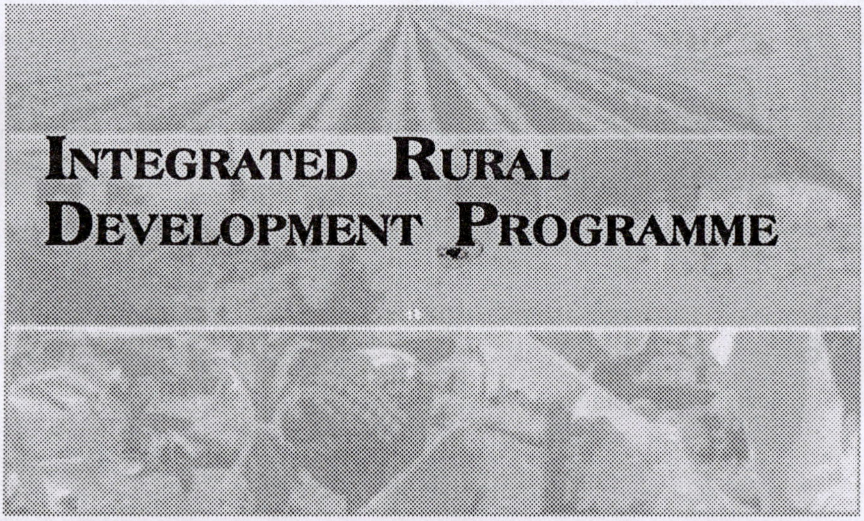

The rural poor have to be assisted to cross the poverty line either by providing wage employment or by providing assets to create self-employment. Generation of wage employment may not be feasible in all the regions. Hence, the Government has initiated certain programmes in the direction of self-employment.

I. SFDA/MFALDA PORGRAMMES

The central sector schemes of Small Farmers Development Agency (SFDA) and the Marginal Farmers and Agricultural Labourers Development Agency (MFALDA) were included in the Fourth Five Year Plan (1969-74) with the specific objective of ameliorating the economic conditions of small, marginal farmers and agricultural labourers and to bring them into the mainstream of national development. A sum of ₹ 103 crore was allocated for this purpose in the plan. The schemes were introduced gradually on a pilot basis in certain selected areas of the country from 1970-74 onwards.

The scope of activities of SFDAs was enlarged in November 1971 to cover not only small farmers but also those holding land smaller than the minimum limit fixed for small farmers.

The functions of each SFDA were to: *(i)* identify the eligible small farmers in its area, *(ii)* investigate and identify their problems, *(iii)* formulate programmes incorporating suitable measures to deal with the problems and *(iv)* devise ways and means for implementing the programmes.

The main objective of the scheme was to make potentially viable small farmers surplus producers.

The MFAL agencies are to promote interest, of marginal farmers and agricultural labourers. They were called upon to —

- identify eligible marginal farmers and agricultural labourers to be covered by the project,
- investigate their problems,
- formulate economic programmes for providing gainful employment to them,
- promote rural industries,
- evolve adequate institutional, financial and administrative arrangements for implementing various programmes,
- promote creation of common facilities for production, processing, storage and marketing of products and
- evaluate the programmes from time-to-time.

Generally, the SFDA and MFAL agencies were not expected to administer programmes directly. They are to be implemented through institutions sponsored by them. The agencies are expected to help —

- in strengthening the existing co-operatives,
- in organising and developing functional co-operatives (e.g., dairy and poultry assistance, labour co-operatives), and
- co-operatives and other agencies implementing the programmes to develop essential common facilities (e.g., poultry and cattle-feed mixing units, bulk coolers for milk).

However, these agencies did experience some difficulties. Inadequacy of the extension staff had been a major handicap in efficient implementation of the programme of the agencies. The block level staff have been over-burdened with numerous duties.[1]

The Co-ordination and Review Committees at the state level were expected to review the progress of work, assess and evaluate the programmes, discuss the difficulties/bottlenecks, if any, and suggest actions which may be taken. They also expected to bring about co-ordination between various development departments concerned at the state level. But these committees failed to perform their functions properly.[2]

The small/marginal farmers do not have access to institutional credit. The SFDAs do not provide credit directly to the beneficiaries. They help beneficiaries in securing credit from institutions, particularly co-operatives. Project agencies were also empowered to grant subsidy.

However, the PEO study has shown that project assistance has been least fruitful in areas where co-operative movement was weak.

The evaluation study carried out by the PEO has revealed many deficiencies in the implementation of SFDA/MFAL projects. The selection of areas in many cases was not in consonance with the guidelines issued by the Department of Rural Development, Ministry of Agriculture and Irrigation. Most of the project areas were poorly served by co-operatives.

The PEO study pointed out that the administrative set-up of agencies has generally not been effective. There have been delays in the appointment of executive staff. Their frequent transfers have also impaired efficiency. In most cases, measures were not taken to strengthen the extension staff. Supervision, co-ordination and direction have been neglected.

The progress of identification of the target groups was slow in most of the project areas. This is mainly due to the lack of understanding of the precise scope and extent of the identification work, absence of upto-date land records and inadequate instruction. The schemes taken up were not based on the actual needs of the area and often lacked co-ordination in their implementation. Naturally, income and employment generation was not upto the mark. Credit facilities were also inadequate because co-operative infrastructure was inadequate in most of the project areas.

The PEO study also pointed out that only physical and financial targets were monitored. The monitoring system needs to be restructured and oriented more towards the impact of various programmes. The study recommended the introduction of concurrent evaluation.

II. IRDP: SALIENT FEATURES

The provision of productive employment to the rural poor on a sustainable basis has become an issue of priority. It was realised that this can be achieved only when there is integration of major sectors of the economy. The linkages between these sectors need to be strengthened. The various programmes meant for the poor should be co-ordinated to minimise wastage. The concept of 'integration' thus assumes importance.

The IRDP was first introduced in March 1976 on a pilot basis in 20 selected districts, representing different socio-economic and ecological conditions. It was extended to 2300 blocks by 1979. All the 5011 blocks in the country were brought under the programme on October 2,1980. The IRDP is being implemented through the District Rural Development Agencies (DRDAs).

The major thrust of the programme has been to provide income generating assets to identified families below the poverty line through a mix of credit and subsidy and to enable them to improve their income levels so as to eventually cross the poverty line. It has been said that IRDP as a strategy of development[3]

Emphasises to begin with scientific management of resources and providing adequate work to the mass of workers in the region and in the process increases the internal potential rate of growth. It also emphasises the retaining of growth impulses in the region through providing backward and forward linkages in the non-agricultural sector and in the region.

The IRDP aims at providing assets to poor households so as to enable them cross the poverty line with the help of income generated from such assets. The scheme is in the nature of asset distribution through credit-subsidy with a view to providing self-employment.

The target group includes small and marginal farmers, agricultural and non-agricultural labourers, rural craftsmen and artisans, scheduled castes and scheduled tribes and virtually all families below the poverty line.

It was also envisaged that for the purpose of the grant of subsidy and sanction of loans for schemes under IRDP, atleast one-third of the beneficiaries should be the women heads of households.

For the selection of beneficiaries, the guidelines recommended a household survey covering all the clusters with the help of a prescribed proforma for collecting information and details regarding the size of the family, social status, literacy, occupation, land holding assets, income and indebtedness etc.

The families below the poverty line so identified were to be classified into various income ranges and the poorest amongst them were to be selected for providing the assistance. The final selection of the poorest families was required to be done in the scheduled meetings of the Gram Sabha.

The poverty line for a family was fixed at ₹ 11,000 in 1992-93. The IRDP is expected to first cover rural population with an annual family income below ₹ 4,800 (or ₹ 7,500 from 1992-93).

There are reservations for families belonging to the SCs and STs (50 per cent of the beneficiaries); women (40 per cent); physically handicapped persons (three per cent) and liberated bonded labourers (over-riding priority).

Financial assistance is provided through the District Rural Development Agencies (DRDAs) partly as a government subsidy and partly as bank loans. The expenditure on the subsidy as well as administration and infrastructure is borne equally by the central and state governments. The responsibility for implementing IRDP is that of the Ministry of Rural Development at the Centre, the departments dealing with rural development in the states and the DRDA at the district level.

The scheme for providing assistance towards the Risk Fund for Consumption Credit has been in operation since 1977-78. However, banks do not appear to encourage consumption credit unless the state governments make necessary provisions in their budgets.

In the selection of schemes, the basic approach is to select from a package of schemes sanctioned by the authorities one or more schemes in which the individual beneficiary had experience and motivation for deriving benefits from these schemes.

The typical schemes under the priority sector are minor irrigation works (individual and community); supply of milch animals; poultry units; sheep units; pig farming; goats; ducks; fisheries; sericulture etc.

Activities coming under secondary and tertiary sectors include setting up of cottage or artisan-based rural industries, shoe repairing units, tailorings, grocery and petty shops, rickshaw, bullock carts, camel carts etc.

The block level officials are expected to take care that only such schemes get selected which hold economic viability, are technically feasible and also acceptable, to the beneficiaries.

The choice of the schemes would ultimately depend on the availability of the requisite inputs, marketing facilities and other supporting infrastructure.[4] The schemes should be economically viable, keeping in view the resource potential and other conditions of the areas concerned.

In respect of schemes under the Industry, Services and Business (ISB) sector, it was visualised that arrangements for the supply of raw materials as well as the sale of the products be prioritised.

The capital cost of the assets under IRDP is subsidised to the extent of 25 per cent for small farmers, 33 1/3 per cent for marginal farmers, agricultural labourers, rural artisans and 50 per cent for tribal families. An individual family receives ₹ 3,000 by way of subsidy. For areas coining under Drought Prone Area Programme (DPAP), the limit is ₹ 4,000 and in tribal areas, the beneficiary is entitled to ₹ 5,000 as subsidy. Only tribals are entitled to 50% subsidy of the capital cost of the scheme.

A Pilot Project on Family Credit Plan (FCP) was launched in 40 districts during 1991-92 to ensure higher investment and consequently higher incremental income through provision of assistance to more than one member of an IRDP family. In each district, 200 families were to be provided multiple assets. By 1994, the FCP had been extended to 213 districts in the country. More than one lakh rural families were reported to benefit under the scheme during 1994-95.

The system of purchase committees in 50 per cent blocks has already been abolished. Under the new Cash Disbursement Scheme, the beneficiaries had the option to purchase assets of their own choice.

In order to discourage low investment which have poor returns and do not cause any viable impact on poverty, the Government decided to increase the level of investment per family to at least ₹ 12,000.

The allocation of funds to the districts, which until 1993-94 was on a state devised formula has been streamlined. Currently, district-wise allocation is made on the basis of poverty levels.

The compensation under life insurance for IRDP beneficiaries has been revised upwards from January 1, 1994. The nominee of IRDP beneficiary will henceforth receive ₹ 5,000 in case of natural death and ₹ 10,000 in case of accidental death.

III. IRDP: TARGETS AND ACHIEVEMENTS

IRDP is funded on 50:50 basis by the Centre and the States. It was estimated that each block was to be provided with an outlay of ₹ 5 lakh in the first year, ₹ 6 lakh in the second year and ₹ 8 lakh in each of the remaining three years of the Sixth Plan. Each block would thus have a total of ₹ 35 lakh for IRDP during the Sixth Plan period. The Centre and the States provide ₹ 1,500 crore for IRDP during this plan. Banks would provide ₹ 3,000 crore as credit. The total investment for IRDP during the Sixth Plan was fixed at ₹ 4,500 crore. The subsidy and loan components are expected, on an average, to be in the ratio of 1:2.

The IRDP, during the Sixth Plan period, aimed at assisting 15 million rural families to cross the poverty line (three million of the poorest of the poor families per year). It also envisaged to cover 600 families per year in each of the 5011 blocks. On an average, it was also proposed to assist 400 families in agriculture and allied activities including animal husbandry, poultry, piggery, fishery, forestry, sericulture etc. About 100 families were reportedly assisted in the secondary sector (rural industries) and another 100 families in the services and business sector. The segment of poor families were given financial cover under the ISB.

Against the financial allocation of ₹ 3,000.27 crore for IRDP during the Seventh Plan, the total utilisation of funds (taking into account the opening balances with the DRDAs and other miscellaneous receipts) totalled to ₹ 3,315.82 crore. The credit mobilisation amounted to ₹ 5372.53 crore. Thus, the total investment under IRDP during the Seventh Plan was ₹ 8,688.35 crore.

While the centre's allocation for IRDP in the Eighth Plan is ₹ 3,350 crore, states' share was fixed at ₹ 3,300 crore taking the total to ₹ 6,650 crore.

Against the target of 160.38 lakh families assisted during the Seventh Plan, it came to be 181.77 lakh which is 113 per cent of the target fixed on the basis of Annual Plans and 90 per cent of the target fixed as per the plan document. The coverage of SC/ST families ranges between 43 per cent and 46 per cent of the total families assisted. The coverage of women beneficiaries has been of the order of 18.89 per cent.

During the Eighth Plan, 1.26 crore families have been proposed to be assisted with central and state allocation of ₹ 6,650 crore.

By 1994, about 4 crore and 22 lakh families have been assisted at an investment of ₹ 18,728.3 crore under IRDP. Substantial portion of assistance (over 50 per cent) has gone to SC/ST families during 1993-94. Coverage of women under the programme has steadily increased from about 10 per cent to the total families assisted in 1985-86 to about 32 per cent during 1993-94.

The Eighth Plan provision for the centre as well as the states is ₹ 6,650 crore and the target is to assist over 1.25 crore families. Under the IRDP, the ceiling on subsidy has already been enhanced by ₹ 1,000 from April 1993.[5] During the Eighth Plan (1992-97), 108.36 lakh families were covered and ₹ 11.54 thousand crore were invested.

The approach of uniformity in allocation of funds target fixation has been changed to one of selectivity based on incidences of poverty in block/state. The coverage of women beneficiaries has also been increased to 30 per cent.

The budgetary outlay on IRDP has gone up from ₹ 356.46 crore in 1990-91 to ₹ 623.70 crore in 1994-95.

The budget allocation for IRDP during 1995-96 was ₹ 640 crore. The assistance should reach 19.5 lakh rural families below poverty line.

There has been a significant increase in per capita investment under IRDP from ₹ 3,746 during 1993-94 to about ₹ 11,000 in 1994-95. It was ₹ 16,917 in 1997-98.

The new scheme called 'family credit plan' has been under operation in 213 districts to give more than one asset simultaneously to all the adult members of the family. The scheme has seen a substantial level of success.

A new scheme of supply of modern tool kits to rural artisans has been in operation since 1992. The average cost of a tool-kit is ₹ 2,000 on which 90 per cent subsidy is given by the Centre. The scheme proposed to cover 5 lakh rural artisans during the Eighth Plan.

The beneficiaries now enjoy greater freedom in the purchase of assets. The purchase committees have been abolished in about 50 per cent of the blocks in each district. An experienced family credit plan scheme for higher incomes per family has been extended from 51 districts to 236. The scheme was devised to check out whether higher per family investment would lead to higher incomes.

Over the years, there has been diversification of activities under the scheme. Investments in the primary sector such as irrigation and animal husbandry have fallen from 94 per cent to about 51 per cent. The percentage in respect of secondary sector activities like weaving and food processing has risen from below three per cent to about 18 per cent. The tertiary sector (service and business) could improve its percentage from four to about 31.

Since the launching of the IRDP till the end of the financial year 1994-95, bank credit of ₹ 1,320 crore and government subsidy amounting to ₹ 3,202 crore, aggregating to ₹ 21,432 crore, had been provided to 447 lakh families below the poverty line.

Table: 1
Performance of IRDP in the Seventh Plan (1985-90)

Item	*Achievement*
Total Expenditure (₹ crore)	3,315.81
Total Term Credit Mobilised (₹ crore)	5,372.53
Total Investment (₹ crore)	8,688.34
Total No. of families covered	
Old (in lakhs)	51.80
New (in lakhs)	129.97
Total (in lakhs)	181.77
No. of SC/ST Beneficiaries (in lakhs)	81.97
Percentage of SC/ST to total	45.10
No. of women beneficiaries covered (in lakhs)	34.33
Percentage of women to total	18.92
Per Capita Subsidy (Gross) (₹)	1,824.00
Per Capita Credit (Gross (₹)	2,956.00
Per Capita Investment (Gross) (₹)	4,780.00
Subsidy Credit ratio	1:1.98
Sectorwise coverage (%) Primary sector	43.75
Secondary sector	18.64
Tertiary sector	37.61

* Net Subsidy Credit Ratio.

Sources: Eighth Five Year Plan 1992-97, Vol. II, p. 48.

Table: 2
Expenditure on IRDP during the Eighth Plan (1992-97)

(₹ in crore)

Year	*Expenditure*
1992-93	693.03
1993-94	956.65
1994-95	1008.32
1995-96*	1077.16
1996-97*	1139.49
Total	4874.65

* provisional
Source: Ninth Five Year Plan 1997-2002, Vol. II, p. 47.

Table: 3
Performance of IRDP in the Eighth Plan (1992-97)

(lakh families)

Year	*Target*	*Achievement*
1992-93	18.75	20.69
1993-94	25.70	25.39
1994-95	21.15	22.15
1995-96*	No Target	20.89
1996-97*	No Target	19.12
Total		108.24

* provisional
Source: Ninth Five Year Plan 1997-2002, Vol. II, p. 47.

IV. IRDP: MAJOR PROBLEMS

Studies have shown that the IRDP benefitted the rural population nearer to the poverty line and left out the poor at the bottom, either by keeping them out or by allowing them only petty small schemes. Also, in general, women have benefitted less from IRDP and female dominated households have had poorest access to it.[6]

In the Sixth Plan, nearly 30 per cent of the beneficiaries were actually ineligible due to incomplete survey of households, non-issue of *Vikas Patrikas,* non-holding of *Gram Sabhas* and general apathy.

A major problem facing IRDP is wrong identification of beneficiaries which is placed between 15 to 20 per cent in the Seventh Five Year Plan. This has been attributed to poor database, non-involvement of people's institutions in the survey and selection process, collision between the government functionaries and vested interests.

The IRDP has also suffered from certain deficiencies: no proper identification of beneficiaries, lack of infrastructural facilities, absence of technical guidance to beneficiaries, lack of co-ordination amongst the bank and block officials and under-financing of projects which subsequently resulted in poor returns. Also, insurance claims of animals failed to be settled expeditiously.

At present, considerable time is consumed between the processing cases of eligible beneficiaries and the actual distribution of assets. The beneficiary has to go through four stages :

(i) household surveys for identification of eligible families by block officials and approval of the lists of eligible families by gram sabhas,

(ii) selection of beneficiaries for assistance by the DRDAs and BDOs, filling up of application forms of DRDAs and forwarding these to the banks,

(iii) sanction of bank loans and completion of documentation and

(iv) procurement and distribution of assets to the beneficiaries, follow up by the bank and government officials by way of assisting the beneficiaries in grounding the scheme and repayment of bank loans.

Delays occur at several points due to lack of co-ordination between the various agencies. The time taken is approximately one year from the time the DRDA application form is filled up till the grounding of the scheme.

Those coming under the lowest income slabs are not able to cross the poverty line. Thus, according to one case study, only about 8 per cent of the sample beneficiaries belonging to this category are able to cross the poverty line.[7]

The IRDP guidelines are remaining only on paper. According to one case study, the 'gram sabha' was never convened; each IRDP beneficiary has to bribe the gram sevak and the household surveys were reportedly not conducted and the URDP list is nothing but a list drawn up *after* loans have been sanctioned.[8]

The concurrent evaluation of IRDP carried out by the department of rural development for the period October 1985 to September 1986 has revealed that though 78 per cent of the beneficiaries belong to the very very poor categories, in respect of income generation, the picture is not encouraging.

The survey also pointed out that 29 per cent of all the assets were simply not intact. Of the assets surveyed, about 24 per cent failed to generate any incremental income. This meant that over 45 per cent of the assets created under IRDP had failed to produce income flows.

However, the performance of the remaining 55 per cent of the assets has failed to reach a satisfactory level. The survey pointed out that in only 26 per cent of these cases, income generated by the assets exceeded ₹ 2,000. This meant that less than 20 per cent of the total number of beneficiaries could earn an annual income of over ₹ 2,000. In the Sixth Plan, the poverty line stands at ₹ 6,400, and the survey came to the conclusion that only 12 per cent of the old beneficiaries had managed to cross the revised poverty line.

The concurrent evaluation of IRDP for the year 1989 conducted by the Government of India revealed that only in 28 per cent of the cases, old beneficiaries had been able to cross the then poverty line of ₹ 6,400 per annum.

The PEO study of the IRDP in 1989-90 showed that 9 per cent of the selected families were ineligible; the working capital was needed in 59 per cent of the cases, but in fact was provided only to the 24 per cent; for 15 per cent of the cases, the repayment period was less than 3 years, and there were lapses in insurance in 26 per cent of the cases, in training in 32 per cent cases and in after-care support by government agencies is 54 per cent of the cases.[9]

A NABARD study has shown that 8 per cent of the IRDP funds went to ineligible families, 25 per cent of participants were not provided with the needed working capital, 22 per cent had no incremental income generated as a result of participating in the programme. The poor performance has been attributed to the lack of effective technical support to the local body and the lack of appropriate infrastructural development to supplement planning for the target groups. Also, most programmes failed to emerge as area specific[10] and benefit the rural population in the target areas.

The important findings of the concurrent evaluation, carried out by 29 research institutions on behalf of the Ministry of Rural Development are:

(i) The poorest of the poor had predominant coverage under IRDP. About 60 per cent of the assisted families belong to the destitute group;

(ii) About 40 per cent of the beneficiaries were selected in the meetings of the Gram Sabhas and the rest of the officials;

(iii) The assets had generated incremental income of more than ₹ 2,000 in about 26 per cent cases. It ranged between ₹ 1,001 and ₹ 2,000 in 22 per cent cases and between ₹ 501 and ₹ 1,000 in 12 per cent cases. It was upto ₹ 500 in about 12 per cent cases;

(iv) In about 20 per cent cases, the assets of the beneficiaries had not been insured;

(v) No incremental income was generated in about 20 per cent cases;

(vi) About one-fifth of the beneficiaries required training which was provided and

(vii) In about 45 per cent cases, after care and support by government agencies was not made available.

The quantum of investment available per beneficiary family under both JRY and IRDP has been very meagre. The per beneficiary family investment (subsidy plus credit) was ₹ 1,642 in 1980-81, ₹ 3,339 in 1984-85, ₹ 4,470 in 1987-88 and ₹ 5,507 in 1989-90.

The low investment would not enable the household to cross the poverty line. The option would be to reduce the number of families to be assisted or to double the assistance per household. Both these may not be acceptable for the Government, the first for political reasons and the second for financial reasons.

In some cases, the subsidy amount was not adjusted immediately after providing assets to the beneficiaries with the result that the beneficiary had to pay interest even on the subsidy portion of the cost of assets involved.

The greatest drawback of IRDP is that while assistance has been provided on the family basis, complementary linkages have not been adequately established to translate the IRDP assets into steady and adequate income. In other words, IRDP continued to fall outside the framework of area planning. Also, the beneficiaries would require a number of inputs and services (such as credit, fodder, veterinary services, marketing and technology). But in the absence of functional linkages, it becomes difficult to properly protect, maintain and utilise the assets provided.

It is said that in some cases, the IRDP may produce even negative results. This happens when the beneficiaries fail to meet the full costs, direct and contingent, of acquiring the assets. The costs of assets are going up in the local market because of the IRDP induced demand. The beneficiaries may have to supplement the IRDP aid with high cost informal borrowings. This, coupled with low returns, may result in a debt trap and/or loan default.[11]

The quality of the programme is poor. It lacks proper planning and identification of thrust areas, viable projects within the meaning capacities of rural families, tying up backward-forward linkages, mobilising adequate credit, ensuring higher family investment and marketing support. There has been no attempt to match the production capacities being created to local resources or demands.[12]

The evaluation studies have highlighted the insufficient backward and forward linkages, inadequate field staff, lack of adherence by the implementing agencies to prescribed procedures and guidelines, short training periods and irregularities in the supply and maintenance of assets.

According to the guidelines, the asset has to be purchased by a committee consisting of the representatives of the block, bank and the beneficiary. However, in majority of the cases, the involvement of the beneficiaries is minimal. This often leads to a higher price of the IRDP asset.[13]

Evaluation studies have revealed that when assets depreciate, the income flow would stop as the beneficiary is not in a position to replenish his stock of assets. It is thus clear that IRDP is not in a position to provide self-sustaining income growth.

There is too much emphasis on milch cattle. But the milch cattle available to the beneficiaries were reported to be of a relatively poor quality and did not give adequate milk yield. The necessary veterinary support was also said to be lacking in many areas, raising the morality rate of animals. Those who received the milch animals for the first time were not provided any instruction and training regarding better breeds and varieties, feed and fodder.[14]

Studies also showed that diversification of benefit schemes in secondary and tertiary sector activities was not noticeable to the extent envisaged.[15]

The direct consequence of the weak organisational support has taken the form of poor linkages of the programme and inadequate maintenance and support services.[16] The credit absorption capacity also varied from area to area. This is not generally taken into account.

The central government has shown concern in the decline in bank credit to the IRDP. In 1988-89, it was ₹ 1,231.62 crore and it went down to ₹ 1,038.80 crore in 1992-93. Banks have been unable to service small clients with regard to their working capital needs to the desired extent. Under financing and difficult repayment terms, they leave little or no surplus with the beneficiary after repayment.

The decline between target and credit mobilised increased from ₹ 22.70 crore in 1992-93 to ₹ 122.36 crore in 1993-94 and to ₹ 330.93 crore in 1994-95.

Several studies on IRDP have shown that beneficiaries had to resort to private borrowings in several cases for meeting their immediate household consumption needs.

The concurrent evaluation shows that working capital was required by 60 per cent cases but was not provided in 32 per cent cases to the beneficiaries. Insurance of the assets was required in 71 per cent cases, but could not be done in 23 per cent cases. Training was not imparted to beneficiaries in 21 per cent cases out of the 25 per cent requiring training. The assets were not intact in 29 per cent cases.[17]

The recovery performance in respect of IRDP loans granted by the public sector banks as a percentage to demand has declined to 30.8 per cent as at the end of June 1993 from 41.34 per cent as at the end of June 1991.

Not a few factors have contributed to the poor recovery of loans granted. According to one study, the obligation to meet the daily family expenses has been a major reason for poor recovery. About 35 per cent of the sample beneficiaries admitted this. Also, about 60 per cent of the incremental family income was spent on consumption. Other factors included diversion of incremental income towards settlement of old private debts, desire for broadening the asset-base, both business and non-business and the unhelpful attitude of the bureaucracy extending support to the bank.[18]

According to one study, 36 per cent of the households surveyed/reported that the returns from the benefit schemes were not adequate to make regular repayments of the loan instalments.[19] However, 88.2 per cent of the households reported that their income had increased while 10.6 per cent felt that there was no material change.[20]

Inadequate income has been taken to be the main reason for delays in repayment. Some beneficiaries felt that repayment schedules have been very tight and taxing. Natural calamities such as floods and drought are other reasons for their inability to paying on time: It is also observed that intermediaries, in many cases, mislead beneficiaries by saying that the loan is non-repayable.

It has also been observed that the tight repayment schedules fixed by banks, notwithstanding liberal guidelines framed by the Centre, is a major reason for the non-viability of schemes under the IRDP.

The Union Ministry of Rural Development had fixed ₹ 8,500 per family as IRDP assistance even though the Planning Commission had stipulated ₹ 11,000 as the basis of the poverty line.

Also, case studies revealed that capital output ratio used for calculating the incomes generated from IRDP grossly over-estimated the benefits flowing from the loans.

A matter of concern is the inadequate provision for assessment of skills, risk bearing capacity, working capital, local demand, inputs supply, price fluctuations and depreciation etc. under IRDP.[21]

Field studies have shown that funds allotted for creation of the infrastructure to the extent of 10 per cent of the total allocations were not adequate. This limit needs to be enhanced.

In sanctioning schemes, the beneficiaries' choices are very often ignored. This created formidable problems for the beneficiaries. For instance, a large number of spinning machines are lying idle because the beneficiaries do not find relevance of such machines in their livelihood.

Thus, for some products produced under IRDP, markets were not available locally and marketing centres were at a considerable distance. Even when goods are available, lack of purchasing power on the part of the local people may create a situation of surplus. The problem has been aggravated because generally these schemes which can be easily handled by the poor households are preferred. The IRDP schemes were promoted in excess of what the area could absorb.

The link between IRDP and TRYSEM is weak. The two schemes are being run almost independently. This would adversely affect the success of both.[22]

An evaluation of IRDP by the Comptroller and Auditor General (CAG) of India for the period 1985-93 has revealed the following defects:

About 11,000 families which were not eligible for the benefits under the scheme were aided to the extent of more than ₹ 3 crore; money misutilised in about 1.5 lakh cases added up to ₹ 14.5 crore; irregular diversion of IRDP funds to other projects amounted to ₹ 20 crore; expenditure incurred on administrative infrastructure exceeded the prescribed norms by ₹ 8 crore. The total amount spent on IRDP during the eight year period came to ₹ 14,000 crore (with a subsidy of ₹ 5,500 crore and bank loans amounting ₹ 8,500 crore).

The Report observed that the popular milch cattle scheme has not, been properly implemented. Under the scheme, two animals are to be supplied to the same beneficiary so as to ensure continuity of income from this source and prevent any sidebacks into the original state of poverty. The Report revealed that in about 1.7 lakh cases, the second animal was not provided.

The Report observed that household surveys of poor families for properly identifying the beneficiaries were not undertaken in most states. The DRDAs and banks did not conduct physical verification of assets in several states. Loan applications sponsored by the DRDAs were arbitrarily rejected by the banks in many cases. The recovery of loans given to the beneficiaries was reported far from satisfactory.

The Public Accounts Committee (PAC) of the Lok Sabha (Chairman: Bhagwan Singh Rawat) has identified major areas of concern in the implementation of IRDP. These include: low per capita investment, non-preparation of five-year perspectives and annual plans, failure to conduct household surveys for identification of beneficiaries; coverage of ineligible families; non-provision of assistance for the second milch animal, failure to verify misutilisation of assets and assistance and diversion of funds meant for IRDP to other programmes.

The Report also observed that only 14.81 per cent of the beneficiaries of IRDP has been able to cross the current poverty line of ₹ 11,000 per annum per family.

Further, the flow of credit and institutional financial assistance under IRDP were beset with shortcomings such as rejection of loan applications, low per capita disbursement, inordinate delay in sanctioning and disbursal of loans and poor recovery rate.

A major deficiency of the IRDP is that it was not based on decentralised micro level planning. It is more or less a desk exercise with no micro level investigations. Very often, production capacities being created are not linked to local resource endowments.

The rural development planning suffers from lack of co-ordinated planning at the programme level and weak planning component of individual programmes. There is also ignorance of inter-sectoral linkages and lack of co-ordination among various functionaries.[23]

Attempts towards integrated rural development should be followed by shifts in power to the target groups. Otherwise, IRDP may fail to achieve its broader objectives. It has been rightly pointed out that:[24]

> The route from the overthrow of GNP to target groups and from target groups to integrated rural development is quite logical. But, what is missing even here is the inadequate recognition of the need for shift of power to the groups who could be beneficiaries of new policies.

Rural development administration has yet to be strengthened. The Central Government has offered financial help to the states for creating and manning some of the additional posts required. However, the state level organisations lacked the required degree of support of the sectoral and subject-matter specialists in the formulation of projects and schemes and providing adequate technical guidance to the field staff.[25]

V. STRENGTHENING IRDP

In the Indian context, it is not possible to eradicate rural poverty only by providing productive assets. All the beneficiaries may not be in a position to use the assets productively. Entrepreneurial skills may be lacking in many cases. Some of the beneficiaries may be able to work on wage employment only rather than managing their own activities.[26]

However, in a country where nearly 62 per cent of the workforce is in the self-employment sector, the IRDP approach cannot be undermined. What is however required is a total approach that integrates the various strategies systematically, as observed by Indira Hirway.[27]

It would prove beneficial to opt for a mix of employment and asset development programmes for the poor, the mix depending upon the need of each location.[28]

Studies show that in general, the IRDP performance has been better in not only relatively more developed regions but also in other areas where follow-up measures had been undertaken and the people involved through their representatives.[29]

It has been rightly observed:[30]

> There is also need for a comprehensive review of the viability of the ongoing schemes including their integration with the local level plan schemes so as to make them more suitable for catering to the needs and conditions of different areas. This is necessary not only for ensuring that schemes devised, are area-specific but also for enhancing the productivity and returns from the investments made for this purpose.

There is need for a comprehensive review of the viability of on-going schemes specific to the areas including their integration with the local plans at the block and district levels.

The failure of infrastructural development is wide-spread and what is needed is a more systematic effort at its development and distribution than has been attempted so far.[31]

Almost all beneficiaries seek the second dose of financial assistance to consolidate the gains achieved through the schemes.[32]

The PAC of the Lok Sabha (Chairman: Bhagawan Singh Rawat) has also recommended, enhancing the minimum repayment period from the existing three years. For better recovery of loans, it has been suggested that a strategy of action against wilful defaulters and incentives for prompt repayment be worked out.

In some districts, there is the practise of holding back the subsidy and charging interest on the whole amount including subsidy element. This would be improper and unjust. It would be better if the practice of subsidy adjustment as a part of unit cost is replaced by the provision of depositing the subsidy as of Fixed Deposit Receipt which would be pledged to the bank. The withdrawal of this amount should be allowed only after three years after the certification of assets. Also, it would be better if the subsidy is provided in kind instead of in cash.

The Government has initiated a multi-level arrangement for credit co-ordination starting with setting up of committees at block, district, state and natural levels. These committees would monitor disposal of applications and will be in charge of planning and implementation at higher levels.

A group insurance scheme for the beneficiaries of IRDP was introduced throughout the country with effect from April 1, 1988. The scheme is being implemented through the DRDAs (Zilla Parishads in Karnataka).

The Government of India would pay a sum of ₹ 15 crore to the Life Insurance Corporation (LIC) during 1988-89 and ₹ 20 crore during 1989-90 as a lump sum premium to cover up to four million beneficiaries every year. Fifty per cent of the amount would be the central share and the balance fifty per cent would be contribution of states to be adjusted against the central release to the DRDAs.

IRDP beneficiaries aged not less than 18 years and not more than 60 years will be covered. The insurance cover for each beneficiary will be operative till the date on which he completes 60 years or the period of three years from the date of the commencement of cover, whichever is earlier.

Upon the death of the insured beneficiary, a sum of ₹ 3,000 shall become payable by the LIC to the nominee of the deceased. In the event of death due to accident, an additional sum of ₹ 3,000 would be payable to the beneficiary by LIC.

The Reserve Bank of India (RBI) appointed a committee under the chairmanship of Shri D.R. Mehta, to examine the present system of lending under IRDP. In its interim report, submitted in 1994, the committee made the following suggestions:[33]

(i) The subsidy payment system should be changed from the present front-end system to one of back-end system so as to avoid misuse of funds.

(ii) For the extremely poor, the Committee favours wage employment schemes. The committee observed that self-employment even for the very poor can be considered if they organise themselves into self-help groups or acquire skills after training.

(iii) For identifying beneficiaries, surveys should be systematically undertaken and the selection process be made completely transparent. The involvement of panchayat and the village population should also be enhanced. Bank should also have greater freedom in selecting beneficiaries. Voluntary organisations and self-help groups, should also be involved in the process.

(iv) The Committee also favours linking of recovery performance to subsidy allocation to some extent. Special recovery officers may be appointed in banks, both at the district and at lower levels.

(v) The amount of loan and subsidy provided under IRDP should be increased to ensure the viability of activities undertaken.

(vi) For the first time, the Committee recommended the provision of working capital for IRDP loans.

(vii) The Committee also recommended changes in the structure of DRDA so as to make it a compact and professional agency. For this, the committee wants officers from National Bank for Agriculture and Rural Development (NABARD), RRBs and state financial accounts services to be included in DRDA. Even private consultants can be associated with DRDA to improve the functioning of this agency.

(viii) It was further suggested that the DRDAs should prepare a detailed infrastructure plan in consultation with district consultative Committees and block level bankers committees. The limit of expenditure for improving and setting up infrastructure facilities can be raised from 10 per cent to 20 per cent of the DRDA's budget.

NABARD has asked all the state co-operative banks, rural and agriculture development banks to stretch the minimum repayment period in case of all loans under IRDP to five years from the present time limit of three years. NABARD has stipulated that the banks should fix realistic repayment schedules after taking into account the level of income generation and the economic life of these assets. This suggestion emerged from the recommendations of the expert committee headed by Dr. R. Mehta.

NABARD has also recommended that the banks should endeavour to provide group loans for various activities under IRDP including assistance towards infrastructure development. It has also called for the reorganisation of the DRDAs in compact teams of professionals and technical experts. The credit officers should be drawn from banks, RRBs or from within NABARD. NABARD has also suggested that the banks may be given the freedom to select the IRDP beneficiaries out of the below poverty line lists instead of the block authorities sponsoring applications on a pilot basis.

In order to improve the recovery performance, NABARD has indicated that recovery officers may be appointed by respective state governments to exclusively recover bank dues. There may be one recovery officer in every district together with the required complement staff whose costs will be borne by DRDAs and lead banks.

NABARD has asked banks to provide loans under IRDP for acquisition of land together with short-term credit for meeting current farm expenditure. For land valuation, NABARD has indicated that the existing system of land valuation being followed by the State Land Development Banks may be adopted. NABARD has also prescribed ₹ 25,000 as the limit for not obtaining mortgage in case of loans under IRDP.[34]

NABARD has further stated that district level technical groups consisting of lead district officer of the RBI, district development manager of NABARD, lead bank manager, technical officers of the state governments and non-government consultants will be set up for the identification of investment opportunities and preparation of such project profiles will have to be borne by the DRDAs.

NABARD has also advised banks not to ask from women any collateral security or third party guarantee for loans under IRDP upto the limit of ₹ 10,000 for agriculture and allied activities and ₹ 25,000 for other activities. NABARD has also stated that bank assistance under IRDP should not be denied to women only because ownership of land and other properties has not been entered in their names.

Following the recommendations of the Mehta Committee, banks have been asked to ensure that the loan components be enhanced suitably to cover project cost minus available subsidy so that the projects undertaken would be of adequate size to generate sufficient income to enable the beneficiaries to cross the poverty line at one go.

For all activities under IRDP upto ₹ 25,000, obtaining mortgage may be dispensed with. However, for loans above ₹ 25,000 but upto ₹ 50,000, normal banking norms including mortgage/margin etc. may be followed without asking for any collateral security. The minimum repayment period for IRDP loans needs to be fixed at five years as against the present three years.

The distribution of funds and implementation of plans should be entrusted not to the usual bureaucratic channels, but to a set of persons whose honesty and integrity are beyond doubts.[35]

Recently, the Government has decided to enhance the investment to be made available per family to ₹ 15,000 from ₹ 10,000 so as to improve the quality of lending. It has also decided to do away with the set targets.

While financial allocation has been raised by about 65 per cent during 1993-94, the physical targets have been raised by only about 37 per cent by the Centre to achieve higher percentage per family investment, following the recommendations of the Public Accounts Committee.

The subsidy element of the programme is very often misused. Making subsidy back-ended would reduce leakages at various levels to some extent. Under the revamped IRDP, if a beneficiary is regular in repayment, he or she need not pay-back the last few installments.

However, when repayment is not regular, as happens in two-thirds of the cases, the subsidy plus loan burden will simply be passed on to banks from the Central Government.

The revamped IRDP is expected to give a higher subsidy of 50 per cent, subject to a maximum of ₹ 7,500 to the educated rural poor.

In the Seventh Plan, emphasis was laid on: (i) provision of second dose of assistance to the beneficiaries, (ii) increasing the total assistance per beneficiary to ₹ 6,000 and (iii) diversifying the activities under the programme by increasing the number of beneficiaries under the secondary and services sector.

Other innovative strategies adopted to bring about qualitative improvement in IRDP included establishment of resource-based production and processing units, coverage of non-traditional areas like vegetable growing and prawn farming, and organisation of production groups for supply of goods for institutional requirements.

The beneficiaries should be properly educated about the proper maintenance of assets provided. Also, the concept of IRD would be meaningless without provision of forward and backward linkages.

The IRDP should not be left to the bureaucracy, professional politicians and the middlemen. It requires much more intellectual inputs and clarity of thought for conceptualisation and planning at all levels than what is provided at present.[36] Integrated rural development is an action-packed strategy which requires an action-oriented administration.[37]

The success of IRDP depends on the availability of efficient block level administrative machinery and its smooth co-ordination with the real linkage delivery systems on the one hand and the financial institutions on the other at each beneficiary household level.[38]

The success of IRDP depends on the availability of supporting services and facilities extended by the government departments. It maybe necessary to constitute at the block level a block co-ordinating committee to co-ordinate the activities of government departments, co-operative banks and commercial banks.

There must be an appropriate mechanism to give proper representation to the poor on the implementing agencies at the district/block levels.

IRDFs performance is better in West Bengal and Rajasthan where village panchayats are directly linked with the programme.

To be effective, the IRDP has to be conceived within the framework of the socio-economic structure and the opportunities provided by the overall rural development activities.[39]

For the success of IRDP, there is need for stepping up investment in agriculture and infrastructure. Also, the development administration at the district level needs to be strengthened.

REFERENCES

1. Programme Evaluation Organisation (PEO), Planning Commission, Government of India, 1979: Report on Evaluation Study of Small Farmers, Marginal Farmers and Agricultural Labourers Projects (1974-75), p. 12.
2. *Ibid.*, p. 13.
3. Sulabha Brahme, Kumud Pore and S.H. Pore (1975): 'Regional Planning: A Case Study of Marathwada Region', *Artha Vijnan*, pp.171-72.
4. PEO, Planning Commission May 1985: 'Evaluation Report on Integrated Rural Development Programme', p. 34.
5. *Yojana*, June 30, 1994.
6. Indira Hirway: 'Selective Development and Widening Disparities in Gujarat', *Economic and Political Weekly*, October 14-21, 1995, p. 2610.

7. Programme Evaluation Organisation, May 1985, *op. cit.*, p. 135.

8. Jean Dreze: 'Poverty in India and the IRDP Delusion', *Economic and Political Weekly*, September 29, 1990, p. A-98.

9. Annual Report: Department of Rural Development 1987-88, Government of India, New Delhi, 1988.

10. Annual Report: Department of Rural Development 1988-89, Government of India, New Delhi, 1989.

11. S. Guhan: 'On Reforming the IRDP', *The Economic Times* (supplement), January 26, 1989.

12. Sanjay Sinha: Poverty, Alleviation: Anything Goes', *Economic and Political Weekly*, May 10, 1986, p. 823.

13. N.J. Kurian: 'IRDP: How Relevant Is It?', *Economic and Political Weekly*, December 26, 1987, p. 165.

14. Programme Evaluation Organisation, May 1985, *op. cit.*

15. *Ibid.*, p. 84.

16. Dilip Shah: 'Carry Out Approach Directives Honestly', *Kurukshetra*, August 1990, p. 51.

17. *The Economic Times*, April 1, 1987.

18. *SB1 Monthly Review*, August 1987, pp. 385-386.

19. Programme Evaluation Organisation, May 1985, p. 93..

20. *Ibid.*, p. 116.

21. M. Seetharam: 'Integrated Rural Development: Trends and Challenges', *Kurukshètra*, November 1989, p. 33.

22. Alakh N., Sharma: 'Political Economy of Poverty in Bihar', *Economic and Political Weekly*, October 14-21,1995, p. 2599.

23. K. Dhansekaran: 'Micro Level Planning as an Approach to Integrated Rural Development', *Khadigramodyog*, September 1990, p. 488-489.

24. G. Parthasarthy: 'Integrated Rural Development: Concept, Theoretical Base and Contradictions', in T. Mathew (Ed. 1981), *Rural Development in India*, Agricole Publishing Academy, New Delhi-17, p. 30.

25. Programme Evaluation Organisation, May 1985, *op. cit.*, p. 136.

26. S.C. Bandyopadhyay: 'How to Reduce Poverty — The Experiences of IRDP', *SBI Monthly Review*, February 1986, p. 77.

27. *Economic and Political Weekly*, March 30, 1985, p. 564.

28. G. Parthasarathy: 'Reorientation of Rural Development Programmes: A Note on Some Basic Issues', *Economic and Political Weekly*, November 30,1985, p. 2128.

29. Sandeep Bagchee: 'Poverty Alleviation Programmes in Seventh Plan: An Appraisal', *Economic and Political Weekly*, January 24, 1987, p. 141.

30. Programme Evaluation Organisation, May 1985, *op. cit.*, p. 134.

31. Nilakantha Rath: 'Garibi Hatao: Can IRDP Do It ?' *Economic and Political Weekly*, February 9,1985, p. 246.

32. C.P. Vithal: 'ISB Component — Key to Success of IRDP (A Study)', *Kurukshetra*, April 1984, p. 30.

33. *Indian Banks Association Bulletin*, December 1994, p. 4.

34. K.K. Ammannaya: 'A New Strategy for IRDP Implementation', *Southern Economist*, January 1, 1996, p. 14.

35. Ashok Kumar Mishra: 'Integrated Rural Development Programme in Siwan', *Khadigramodyog*, June 1994, p. 598.

36. H. Ramachandran and J.P. De Campos Guimaraes (Ed. 1991): 'Integrated Rural Development in Asia', Concept Publishing Company, New Delhi, p. 68.

37. S.K. Sharma and S.L. Malhotra: 'Integrated Rural Development: Approach Strategy and Perspective', Abhinav Publications, New Delhi, 1977, p. 93.

38. K. Sundaram and Suresh D. Tendulkar: 'Integrated Rural Development Programme In India', *Social Action*, January-March1985, p. 24.

39. P. C. Bansil: 'Rural Poverty: An Appraisal', *Facts for You*, August 1994, p. 32.

Chapter

29 Swarnjayanti Gram Swarozgar Yojana (SGSY)

The S.R.Hashim Committee reviewed the rural development and poverty alleviation programmes in 1997. It recommended a single self-employment programme. It also suggested that the individual approach should be replaced by group approach and cluster approach for financial assistance.

The implementation of a number of programmes resulted in lack of proper social intermediation, absence of desired linkages among these programmes, undue importance given to target achievement instead of sustainable income generation.[1]

The SGSY, launched on 1st April, 1999, after restructuring the IRDP and allied schemes, is the only self-employment programme for the rural poor.

Six rural development programmes have been integrated into SGSY. These are: IRDP, TRYSEM, DWCRA, SITRA (Supply of Improved Toolkits to Rural Artisans), GKY (Ganga Kalyan Yojana) and MWS (Million Wells Scheme).

The SGSY aims at bringing the self-employed above the poverty line within a period of three years by providing them income generating assets through bank credit and government subsidy. The District Rural Development Agencies (DRDAs) implement the scheme.

The assisted families known as Swarozgaris can be either individuals or groups, and would be selected from BPL families by a three-member team consisting of Block Development Officer, Banks and Sarpanch.

The SGSY has some good features which make it an improvement over IRDP. These are:

- the cluster approach for selection of activities;
- credit channeled mainly through self-help groups;
- training and infrastructure component; and
- involvement of NGOs.

Salient Features of SGSY

According to the Ministry of Rural Development, the following are the salient features of SGSY:[2]

- Each district will draw up a comprehensive plan of the resources and the strategies for poverty eradication. Identifying 4 to 5 activity clusters in each block based on the resources and also on the occupational skills of the people.
- SGSY will focus on Group approach organising the poor and their capacity building. Self-help groups (SHGs) will be formed and steps will be taken to help them function effectively as well as to choose their economic activity.
- The Gram Sabha will authenticate the list of families below the poverty line identified in the BPL census.
- SGSY will seek to lay emphasis on skill development through well-designed courses.
- SGSY will seek to develop close linkages with the credit mechanism in such a manner as would promote multiple credit rather than a one-time credit 'injection.'
- The subsidy admissible to the general individual beneficiaries under the integrated programme will be uniform at 30 per cent (50 per cent for SC/ST) of the project cost subject to a ceiling of ₹ 7500 (₹ 10,000 for SC/ST). For group beneficiaries, the existing pattern of subsidy at 50 per cent of the cost of the scheme, subject to a ceiling of ₹ 1.25 lakh, will continue.
- SGSY will seek to ensure that the infrastructure needs for the identified activities are met in full so as to enable the rural poor to derive the maximum advantage from their investments. Critical gaps in investments will be made up under SGSY subject to a ceiling of 20 per cent (25 per cent in the case of North Eastern States) of the total programme allocation for each district. This amount will be maintained by the DRDAs as "SGSY-Infrastructure Fund."

  SGSY will ensure upgradation of technology in the identified activity clusters.

  SGSY will provide for promotion of marketing of the goods produced by the SGSY beneficiaries.

  In respect of land based activities, SGSY will focus on creation and extension of minor irrigation facilities to enable the small and marginal farmers to take up activities such as horticulture, floriculture etc.
- Credit is a critical component in SGSY, subsidy being only a minor and enabling component. It is proposed to involve banks and other financial institutions closely in the planning and

preparation of projects, identification of activity clusters, infrastructure planning as well as capacity building and choice of activity of the SHGs.

- Women and weaker sections will be the focus of poverty eradication effort under SGSY. Fifty per cent of the benefits under the programme will accrue to the SC/STs, 40 per cent to women and 3 per cent to handicapped persons.
- SGSY will seek to cover the rural artisans in a significant manner, enabling them to utilise the inherent skill to overcome poverty.

Funds under the SGSY are shared by Central and State governments in the ratio of 75:25. Emphasis is laid on multiple dose of assistance. This would mean assisting a swarozgari over a period of time with second and subsequent doses of credit enabling him/her to cross the poverty line.

All loans granted under the scheme are to be treated as advances under priority sector. Loan applications should be disposed of within 15 days and at any rate not later than one month.

For individual loans upto ₹ 50,000 and group loans upto ₹ 3 lakhs, the assets created out of bank loan would be hypothecated to the banks as primary security. In case where movable assets are not created as in land based activities such as dug well, minor irrigation etc. mortgage of land may be obtained.

Insurance cover is available for assets/livestock bought out of the loan. Swarozgaris are covered under the Group Insurance Scheme.

Banks are eligible for refinance from NABARD for the loans disbursed under SGSY as per their guidelines. The eligibility for refinance is related to the recovery position of the banks.

PROGRESS OF SGSY

During 1999-2000, as against an allocation of ₹ 1472.33 crore (₹ 1,105 crore central allocation and ₹ 376.34 crore state allocation), ₹ 1,131.02 crore were released under the programme. Against the total credit target of ₹ 3205 crore, credit mobilised was ₹ 1056.46 crore which was 32.96 per cent of the stipulated target. The credit subsidy ratio comes to 1.95:1 against the target of 3:1. Per capita investment was ₹ 17,113 against the target of ₹ 25,000.

In the year 2004-05, as against the budgetary allocation of ₹ 1000 crore, a sum of ₹ 523.49 crore has been released. During this year, 400 million mandays of employment were generated under SGSY.

Upto November 2005, the centre and states, sharing the costs on 75:25 basis had allocated ₹ 8,067 crore, of which ₹ 6,980 crore had been utilised to assisting 62.75 lakh self-employed.[3]

Up to December 2009, 36.78 lakh self help groups (SHGs) had been formed and 132.81 lash swarozgaris have been assisted with a total investment of ₹ 30,896.80 crore. (Economic Survey 2009-10. P. 277).

The National Institute of Rural Development (NIRD) conducted a study in 10 states of India in 2007-08. The study covered 1116 SHGs and 1111 members of SHGs in the 10 states and so one can imagine the magnitude of the study. According to the study, income of Swarojgaris has substantially gone up in almost all cases, as shown in the Table.

Table: 1
SGSY and Income Generation

State	*Before Project/Swarojgari/ Month (₹)*	*Afer Project/Swarojgari/ Month (₹)*
Andhra Pradesh	480	1705
Assam	982	1525
Bihar	661	1283
Chattisgarh	490	1057
Jharkhand	547	800
Rajasthan	433	1392
Orissa	423	641
Madhya Pradesh	304	398
Tripura	1418	2038
Uttar Pradesh	314	640

Source : Micro Credit for Self Employment, NIRD Study, 2007-08.

A Critical Appraisal of SGSY

The choice of activity under SGSY must be governed by the resources and skills available in the area, and also the market.

The process of technology identification should be closely inter-linked with the identification of key activity itself.

The technology identified for each activity should be such that it can be managed comfortably by the Swarozgaries, and at the same time leads to quality products.[4]

The DRDA could not effectively implement IRDP. As such, it will not be successful in monitoring and grading the assisted SHGs.[5] Also, the SGSY continues to be implemented and monitored in a deterministic manner.[6]

The Working Group for the Tenth Plan identified the following factors as responsible for slow progress of SGSY.

- delayed start of the programme during 1999-2000 and initial preparatory works;
- time involved in sensitisation of different stake holders;
- DRDA continued to assist individual swarozgaries more than the SHGs with the resource available with them under the scheme;
- Flow of bank credit was also not as desired during the period;
- inadequate delegation of powers to bank branches to sanction loan beyond a certain limit.
- demand by bank to collateral security for loan beyond ₹ 50,000.

Also, inadequate availability of credit has adversely affected average per family investment and credit subsidy ratio during the first two years of the programme.

The National Conference of the State Ministers of Rural Development, NGOs, Field Level Functionaries, Banks, SHG members held at the National Institute of Rural Development, Hyderabad, during 23-24 June, 2001 made some suggestions to strengthen SGSY. These include:[7]

- relaxation in the number of key activities per block/district;
- relaxation in the size of self help group;
- relaxation in minimum time involved for gradation of groups, first for Revolving Funds and then for assistance to take up economic activities;
- increasing the loan limit for collateral security both for individual and groups;
- increasing the amount of Revolving Fund;
- bankers accountability in implementation of the scheme;
- active involvement of voluntary sector in social mobilisation of the poor;
- continuous sensitization of all concerned; and
- gradual shift from individual finance to group finance and ultimately making group finance 100 per cent under the scheme.

The SHG movement should not be assessed by the number of groups formed, and the amount of credit disbursed. What is important is income generation on a sustainable basis. SGSY has now become target-driven. There is perceptible pressure put on village, block and district level administration to achieve group target within a limited time-frame. The groups formed should also be stable.[8]

It is necessary to see that the SGSY does not suffer from the irregularities associated with earlier schemes like IRDP. The self-employment created should be productive and durable.

REFERENCES

1. Mahi Pal: 'Swarnajayanti Gramswarozgar Yojana', Evolution, Assessment and Future Prospects, *Kurukshetra*, June 2002, p.29.
2. *Kurukshetra*, June 1999, pp.13-14.
3. Ministry of Finance, Government of India, *Economic Survey 2005-06*, p.206.
4. Sukhvir Singh: 'Swarnajayanti Gramswarozgar Yojana (SGSY), *Khdigramodyog*, October 2000, p.61.
5. Ananth P. Panth: 'Swarozgar Yojana:Old Wine, New Cocktail', *Economic and Political Weekly*, September 8, 2001, p.3430.
6. Nikita Sud: 'Experiences of SGSY in Gujarat:From Process-oriented Theory to Deterministic Practice', *Economic and Political Weekly*, September 27, 2003, p. 4087.
7. *Kurukshetra*, June 2002, p.33.
8. Amal Mandal: 'Swarnajayanti Gramswarozgar Yojana and Self-Help Group:An Assessment, *Kuruikshetra*, January 2005, p.7.

Chapter

30 Training Rural Youth for Self-Employment (TRYSEM)

Though rural India has been endowed with abundant labour force, most of it is reported unskilled. The majority of the rural poor are unable to take up productive programmes, even if institutional credit is available because of lack of the requisite skills.

Training occupies an important place in the efficient management of any development programme. Besides providing skills, training programmes bring about desired changes in the outlook and attitudes of trainees in tune with the ever-changing needs of the environment, the society and technology. Training, like education, is an investment in human resources management. The time, money and energy spent over this is bound to pay rich dividends like human tools for achieving social change and economic growth.[1]

Training also bridges the gap between rural and urban people in terms of attitude, language, value systems, social and religious customs.[2] Of course, there is also the need for periodically evaluating the training programmes. Training meant for the rural poor should discard its elitist character. The trainee must be in a position to clarify his doubt as he practices the vocation and attains a level of competence.

Rightly has it been said that the game of economic growth is neither interesting nor rewarding if we neglect improvements in skills and knowledge of people and confidence that go to make people more capable.[3]

The centrally sponsored scheme, Training Rural Youth for Self-Employment (TRYSEM) was launched by the Government of India in the Department of Rural Development on 15th August, 1979. The objective of the scheme is to provide technical and entrepreneurial skills to rural youth from families below the poverty line, to enable to take up self-employment in the broad fields of agriculture and allied activities, industries, the service sector and business activities. The main stress is on equipping the rural youth with necessary skills and technology to enable them to take up self-employment.

TRYSEM: NATURE AND SCOPE

The important features of TRYSEM are as follows:

(i) Providing basic technical and managerial skills to rural youth from families below the poverty line to enable them to take up self-employment and also wage employment in agriculture and allied sectors like industries, services and business activities;

(ii) Technical skills are imparted to rural youth in the age group of 18-35 years;

(iii) The minimum age is relaxable to 16 years for inmates of orphanages and the upper age limit is relaxable to 45 years for widows, freed bonded labourers, freed convicts, persons displaced by large development projects and cured leprosy patients;

(iv) A minimum of 50 per cent of selected youths should belong to the SCs/STs and a minimum of 40 per cent should be women;

(v) Training is imparted both through formal training institutions and non-institutional modes like master craftsmen;

(vi) Financial assistance is given for recurring expenses on training and for strengthening the infrastructure of training institutes;

(vii) During training, trainees are paid stipends ranging from ₹ 200 to ₹ 500 per month and a tool-kit costing not more than ₹ 800;

(viii) The master craftsmen are paid an honorarium of ₹ 100 each and the training institutes are paid ₹ 200-300 per trainee per month.

The centralised training system had many advantages: good infrastructure could be provided at one place; the training package could be standardised; the cost factor could be controlled; the trainees could interact among themselves; external supervision could be easy and quality of the programme should be ensured.[4]

There is need for diversification of the rural economy through the expansion of non-farm activities. TRYSEM should therefore place emphasis on non-traditional trades. An illustrative list of the traders identified under TRYSEM include: production of mushrooms, honey processing, cultivation of medicinal herbs and plants, poultry farming, fruit-plants-nursery, processing of fruits and vegetables, veterinary services on custom basis, collection, storage and marketing of livestock products, sericulture, farm equipment repairing, installation and maintenance of biogas plants, water pumps, rural transport services, masonry, tailoring, small business and retail trade.

Training is imparted in nearly 130 jobs including auto repair, production of soaps and detergents, bakery, battery recharging, diamond cutting, fishery, furniture making, food processing, fruit preservation, house-wiring, hand pump repairs, learner work, mat weaving, hosiery, plumbing, sericulture, tyre repair, welding, watch repair services and wood carving.

The period of training has been fixed at six months. This period can be increased with the approval of the state level co-ordination committee. Training is imparted through local servicing and industrial units, master craftsmen, artisans and skilled workers. Thus, emphasis is on learning by doing.

Generally, training is imparted through institutions and master trainers. In the non-institutional mode, the training is imparted through master craftsmen, skilled artisans, industrial and servicing units, commercial and business establishments etc.

On the successful completion of training, the youth should receive a combination of subsidy and institutional credit under the IRDP, acquisition of income-generating assets, if they so desire for activities which have relevance to the training imparted under the scheme.

The identification of beneficiaries is done by the Block Development Officer (BDO) after a scrutiny of applications from youth belonging to the target group in his area. Such an assessment can also be done at the time of the household survey prescribed under the IRDP so that a wide base of potential beneficiaries is available.

The BDOs are supposed to ensure that normally no more than three trainees are deputed to a master trainer as the latter, being a professional in his own field, is also expected to continue his normal vocation.[5]

The financial provisions for training under the scheme have been delinked from that of IRDP since 1991-92. The funds for training under the scheme are allocated to the states on the same criteria as the IRDP funds. The actual distribution of funds among the districts is left to the states. The funds available for training are released from a separate Budget Head from within the overall IRDP budget.

Subsidy provision is on the IRDP pattern. The entire expenditure on the scheme is shared on 50:50 partnership by the Centre and the state governments.

The trainees are also given a stipend of upto ₹ 200 per month (₹ 250 if no accommodation is provided) for the training period and course materials for trainees are provided free by the training institutes. If training is imparted in the village where the trainee resides, the rate of stipend is upto ₹ 100.

Those who have completed training are eligible to get assistance from the nationalised banks at a concessional rate of interest of four per cent. If the duration of the training is less than a month, a daily stipend of ₹ 9 is paid in case no free accommodation is provided (₹ 8 if free accommodation is provided). In both cases, the maximum limit is ₹ 125.

A toolkit costing up to ₹ 500 may be given free to the trainees preferably during the course of training itself.

The master craftsmen are paid a honorarium of ₹ 50 per trainee per month within the limit of 10 trainees at a time. The training institution would receive ₹ 75 per trainee per month.

There is provision for an amount of ₹ 40 per trainee per month for purchase of raw materials. This provision is subject to the ceiling of ₹ 350 per trainee per course.

Fifty per cent of the sale proceeds of the articles produced by the trainee during the training period is to be given to the trainee, and the remaining 50 per cent may be given to the trainer/training institution.

The individual master craftsmen may be given an additional amount of ₹ 50 per trainee as a reward in case of successful completion of the training.

The stipend amount has been enhanced from ₹ 300 to ₹ 500 per month per trainee in case they receive training in specific technical institutions. The honorarium for training institutions has also been increased from ₹ 100 to ₹ 300 per trainee per month. The states have also been advised to tie up with reputed technical institutions to improve the quality of training and make it more focussed towards achieving self-employment.

Entrepreneurship training should be developed depending upon the type of the entrepreneurship, viz., rural entrepreneur, woman entrepreneur, service entrepreneur, science and technology entrepreneur etc.[6] Some studies have shown that women have shown interest in developing their own business and also about the objective of the entrepreneurial programme.[7]

Training should also enable potential entrepreneurs to acquire necessary motivation to undertake a self-employment career; to face the ambiguity and risks associated with most projects; to properly choose the right type of enterprises and acquire the skills of managing an enterprise by organising the production and services, ensuring quality and capability of marketing the products and services via the entrepreneurial programme.

TRYSEM: Targets and Achievements

TRYSEM aims at providing training to 40 youths per block per annum. Thus, at least two lakh rural youths are to get training every year in the country and also avail of facilities made available to generate opportunities for self-employment.

During the Sixth Plan (1980-85) period, the achievements exceeded the target marginally. Against the target of 1,009,440, the actual achievement was 1,014,695.

During the Seventh Plan (1985-90), no target was fixed, but in absolute terms, the number of youth trained was marginally below than that during the Sixth Plan period. It was placed at 997,960. For the year 1990-91, target was 425,314, but the actual achievement was only 150,776.

During the Sixth Plan, about one-third of the trained youth belonged to the SCs/STs categories. The same is true of women. The proportion of SC/ST categories has moved to 42 per cent and that of women to 46 per cent during the Seventh Plan period.

A little less than half (47 per cent) of the youth trained during both the plans could engage themselves in self-employment.

The wage employment has come under the scheme during 1982-83. Between 1982-83 to 1984-85, the proportion of trained youth given wage employment was 30.8 per cent which was much higher than that during the entire Seventh Plan period (13 per cent).

During the Eighth Plan (1992-97), a total of 7.52 lakh youths were trained.

Table: 1
Progress of TRYSEM during the Eighth Plan (1992-97)
(No. in lakh)

Year	*No. of youths to be trained*	*No. of trend youths self-employed*	*No. of trend youths on wages employed***	*Total*
1992-93	2.76	0.99	0.42	1.41
1993-94	3.04	1.08	0.43	1.51
1994-95	2.82	0.86	0.45	1.31
1995-96*	3.02	0.98	0.48	1.46
1996-97*	3.64	1.31	0.52	1.83
Total	15.28	5.22	2.30	7.52

* provisional

** wage employment was included under the scheme with effect from 1982-83. *Source*: Ninth Five Year Plan, Vol. II, p. 48.

Table: 2
Coverage of SCs/STs and Women Among Trained Youth

Period	*SCs/STs*	*Women*
Sixth Plan	3,33,928	3,42,744
Seventh Plan	4,22,145	4,59,505
Annual Plan 1990-91	1,05,441	1,16,623
Annual Plan 1991-92	1,38,697	1,59,849
Eighth Plan 1992-93	1,16,464	1,34,929
1993-94 (up to Dec. 1993)	40,543	44,080
Total	11,57,218	12,57,730

By 1994, a total of 31,33,400 youths, including 12,60,300 from SCs/STs and 13,65,317 women were trained. Out of this, 17,99,829 youths were given employment.

TRYSEM: Basic Problems

All those who obtained training may not be in a position to start their own industrial units. Some of the beneficiaries should be prepared to take up wage employment in small and village industries and also work artisans.

The scheme would become popular and successful in a region only when that region experiences a high rate of growth, particularly in respect of industrial growth. The scheme has failed to produce positive results in regions which suffered from high poverty ratios. This can be taken as an indication that the absorption ratio was impressive in better-off regions.[8] The poor infrastructure has failed to help trainees in the rural sector to follow the pursuits in which they had attained skills under the programme.

Various evaluation studies have highlighted certain problems like lack of finance and lack of confidence among the trainees in the implementation of the TRYSEM.[9]

There are some special problems faced by beneficiaries. Travelling long distances involves waste of time and high expenses. The training period is stated to be too short to master the skill in trades like handloom weaving; silk weaving and TV and radio mechanisms.

Most trainees are of the opinion that the amount of loans sanctioned is inadequate to carry on their business. This often leads to diversion of loan amounts from productive to unproductive purposes. Also, there is considerable delay, in some cases even two years, in the disbursement of loans.

There has been too much stress on certain trades and skills. This led to shortage of skills in respect of certain trades and surpluses in respect of others. For instance, most women get stitching machines under TRYSEM. But tailoring may not be remunerative always and in all regions.

Concurrent Evaluation shows that in 78 per cent cases, TRYSEM beneficiaries were provided IRDP assistance for activities other than those for which they were trained. There is thus no correlation between the skills imparted and the job opportunities available.

In many cases, the training programme organised under TRYSEM and the activities chosen for assistance under the IRDP are totally unrelated.[10]

In certain cases, the duration of training has been very short. For instance, with three month's training, the electrician may not be in a position to undertake any remunerative enterprise.

It is also pointed out that the training imparted had less emphasis on practicals. Training should not be for less than one year. There is also the need for raising the subsidy.

The trainees need to be encouraged in terms of incentives and also helped in the preparation of projects. But in actual practice, there is hardly any effort towards this end. There is very little co-ordination among block level administration, banks, DIC and the DRDA to arrange these incentives.

Banks are no doubt taking interest in identifying the potential beneficiaries. But they have to take up a more active role. They must be associated with the scheme right from the stage of selection of trainees to identifying suitable trades and preparation of project reports and schemes introduced by the bank management.

STRENGTHENING TRYSEM

The selection of beneficiaries and trades should be rational which would recognize and tap the potential of youths to achieve qualitative results. The youths are selected from a particular target and age group. There is also the need for full involvement of the beneficiaries.

The consumer needs are fast changing even in rural India. There is therefore an urgent need to identify specific trades for training specific caste groups or occupational groups.[11] Units set up on traditional lines would not be of much help. There should be a thorough assessment of resources and markets to identify viable units.[12]

Suitable linkages should be established between TRYSEM and the ongoing programmes and projects in a particular area.[13] Training should be backed up by extension service and adequate supply of inputs and follow-ups. To be effective, the training programme should start from the actual field demonstration and at later stages, it should be centre-based.[14] The training imparted should be able to provide a permanent source of income to the beneficiaries.

A resource inventory survey should be done at the block level. There is no point in selecting trades in a routine manner. The selection should be based on the potentialities of the block and the employment prospects of the trainees.

The Committee on training for full employment had identified the following eight multi-skill trades under ISB (Industry, Service and Business): tractor mechanic, rural electrician, auto-mechanic, bakery, tailoring, knitting and embroidery, leather goods manufacturing, carpentry and furniture making, blacksmithy and sheet metal welding.

The training and extension service agencies play an important role in taking care of the trainees in the post-training period. These agencies have to adopt a liberal approach, taking into account genuine physical and financial needs of those who have successfully completed the training course. There is also need for a greater degree of co-ordination among various agencies.[15]

The training should also concentrate on developing the skills of the trainees not only in managing the enterprise but also in earning a profit and sustain the activity undertaken in the training schedule.[16]

The rural youths should become successful entrepreneurs after getting training under TRYSEM. It is therefore necessary to impart managerial techniques in addition to skills in the trade.[17]

The training becomes a priority issue to examine the feasibility of establishing a training-cum-demonstration-cum-production centre in each cluster of villages with the assistance of institutional support. The institutions should provide not only equipment, raw materials etc. but also on the job training to youth until they develop sufficient confidence to launch their own ventures.[18]

All the beneficiaries must be provided assistance for only those identified activities along with marketing support. If possible, these beneficiaries may be organised in the form of a co-operative society.

Also, it is not desirable for a person to depend only on one skill. The rural skill requirements are diverse and complex. A mechanic can become viable only if he is trained to do various jobs at the required level of sophistication. Therefore, rural training programmes should aim at multiple skill development and also be area-oriented.

REFERENCES

1. R. Rajendran: 'Training in KVIs: A Futuristic Approach', *Khadigramodyog*, February 1992, p. 298.
2. V.G. Rajadhyaksha: Convocation Address at the Indian Institute of Management, Ahmedabad, *Yojana*, June 1,1979.
3. Theodore W. Schultz: 'US Endeavours to Assist Low-income, countries improve economic capabilities of their People', *Journal of Farm Economics*, December 1961.
4. K. Pradeep Chandra: 'Linking TRYSEM and Integrated Rural Development Programme', *The Hindu*, January 10,1995, p. 25.

5. Programme Evaluation Organisation, Planning Commission (May1985), *Evauation Report on IRDP*, p. 40.
6. Editorial, *Khadigramodyog*, February 1993.
7. D.K. Ghosh: 'TRYSEM and Voluntary Action', *Kurukshetra*, September 1993, p. 32.
8. K. Subba Rao: 'Regional Variations in Impact of Anti-Poverty Programme: A Review of Evidence', *Economic and Political Weekly*, October 26, 1985, p. 1833.
9. Planning Commission (August 1983): *Sixth Five Year Plan: Mid-term Appraisal*, p. 52.
10. K. Pradeep', Chandra: *op. cit.*
11. R.S. Malik, R.K. Punia and Deep Punia: 'Achievements, Accelerators and Barriers in TRYSEM', *Khadigramodyog*, July 1986, p. 486.
12. B. Sudhakara Rao: 'TRYSEM and ISB Components of IRDP', *Kurukshetra*, May 1986, p. 19.
13. Malyadri: TRYSEM and Self-Employment in Rural Areas', *Khadigramodyog*, March 1986, p. 299.
14. S.S. Chakravarty: 'Integrated Rural Development: Some Critical Issues', *Decision*, October 1979, p. 429.
15. M.R. Das: 'Training Rural Youths for Self-Employment (TRYSEM): The Indian Experience', *State Bank of India Monthly Review*, December 1992, p. 636.
16. M. Loganathan: 'Rural Entrepreneurship: Behavioural Approach', *Khadigramodyog*, January 1988, p. 185.
17. P. Ramaiah and A. Muralidhar Rao: 'Impact of Special Employment Generation Programmes in Rural Areas: A Case Study', *Southern Economist*, July 1, 1991, p. 16.
18. Evaluation Report on IRDP, *op. cit.*, p. 42.

Chapter

31 TRIBAL DEVELOPMENT PROGRAMMES

The tribal population suffers from economic and social backwardness. According to the 1991 census, tribal population (87.8 million) formed 8.08 per cent of the total population of India. In spite of constitutional provisions, integrating the tribals into the mainstream remains a tough task. About 55 per cent of the Scheduled Tribes population is concentrated in the East and the Central tribal belt including West Bengal, Bihar, Madhya Pradesh, Orissa and part of Andhra Pradesh. The tribal areas, rich in forest and mineral resources, constitute 20 per cent of the country's total geographical area.

The tribal regions are rich in mineral and forest resources. True, most tribals have more than one occupation. But they live in poverty mainly because they are exploited, in several ways, by the middlemen, moneylenders, traders, landlords, labour contractors and officials. Moreover, in 1981, the percentage of literacy for the tribal population was only 16.35.

According to the Agricultural Census 1985-86, out of the total operational landholders (97.2 million) in India, tribal landholders amounted to 7.6 million (7.9 per cent). Of India's operated area (164.6 million hectares), 17.2 million hectares (10.5 per cent) of land belongs to tribals (net area cultivated was only 14.9 million hectares).

About 3.2 million tribal landholders (41.3 per cent) belong to marginal cultivators (less than one hectare) and about 93 per cent of the operational holdings is owned and cultivated by tribals themselves. Only 22.2 per cent of the area is wholly or partly irrigated. An average tribal holding in India is about 2.25 hectares.

ECONOMICALLY AND SOCIALLY BACKWARD

Though the tribals are backward economically and socially, the tribal groups differ from one another in physical features, language, culture, lifestyle and the nature and intensity of contact with non-tribals. Broadly, the tribal population can be classified into the following four groups:

(i) Tribal communities who confine themselves to original habitats in remote forests and still retain their distinctive pattern;

(ii) Semi-tribal communities who have more or less settled down and have taken to relatively improved type of cultivation and other allied occupations;

(iii) A cultured tribal communities who are more or less in the plains and are engaged in different industrial complexes, coal mines and other allied industries; and

(iv) Totally assimilated tribals who have migrated to cities and urban areas and have become part of the non-tribal society.[1]

Following the recommendations of the Balwantrai Mehta Committee in 1957, special multi-purpose blocks were started in 43 selected scheduled areas in different parts of the country. The Third Five Year Plan adopted the concept of tribal development blocks as one of the major approaches to eliminate problems of tribal development. At the beginning of the Fourth Plan, a new approach was adopted for tribal development where all areas with more than 50 per cent tribal concentration were clearly identified for preparing special plans.

The tribal sub-plans aim at the total development of tribal areas. They comprise four elements: (i) outlays from state plans; (ii) investment by central ministries; (iii) institutional finance and (iv) special central assistance.

MAJOR PROBLEMS

The emancipation of tribal communities is no easy task, and it has socio-political and economic implications. The powerful feudal and vested economic interests had to be fought against and new modes of role relations had to be established to ensure tribal claims.[2] Programmes implemented without institutional changes had helped to strengthen the already entrenched social interests marginally.[3]

The Eighth Plan observed, "The Scheduled Tribes problems arise from geographical isolation characterised by low level of techno-economic development and wide variation in the levels of living between different areas and different tribal groups but all the same assiduously retaining their distinct socio-cultural identity in a large measure."[4]

The beneficiary-oriented schemes are neglected with lower share of outlay. The schemes of sectoral fragmentation under the sub-plan do not reflect the felt needs of the tribals and these do not create the desired impact. In many cases, the project officer has been reduced to the status of a co-ordinator.[5]

The tribals are hardworking people. But they are not in a position to enjoy the fruits of their labour. They are victims of the tricks played by traders who provide loans to tribals on the condition that they have to deliver agriculture and forest produce to them only at prices much lower than the market prices. Lands assigned to the tribals very often are passed onto the rural moneylenders sooner or later, though laws exist to prohibit such transfers.

Attempts are being made to bring about development of tribal regions through industrialisation. However, such industrialisation has created new problems for the tribals. Any integrated approach to tribal development must take this into account.[6]

The main issues in tribal development are the right to land-based resources for survival and to cultural determination as these are fundamental human rights. Welfare-oriented programmes alone will create further disparities rather than reducing them.[7]

The real task is to involve tribals in the processes of articulation, assertion and action. Their struggles are to be brought to the Centre of political process.[8]

MEASURES NEEDED

Agricultural development alone cannot raise the socio-economic status of the tribal people. Development of agriculture and its allied activities alone can provide employment to tribals throughout the year. The Dhebar Commission (1961) had observed, "the problem of destitution and the sub-normal standard of living in the tribal areas owing to the low potential of agriculture can be mitigated, mainly through the development of village and cottage industries." Forest-based industries deserve special attention.

Of course, the tribals can obtain due benefits only through co-operatives. The tribals' bargaining power is low and therefore they need to be organised into co-operatives. The Large Sized Agricultural Multi-Purpose Societies are most appropriate for tribal areas. These societies can look into the credit needs (including consumption credit) of the tribal people, provide technical guidance for the modernisation of agriculture and arrange marketing facilities.

The outlay on tribal development programmes was only 1.0 per cent of the total outlay in the First Plan. This has steadily increased and reached 5.7 per cent in the Sixth Plan. While the outlay for tribal development was ₹ 5,535 crore in the Sixth Plan, it was placed at ₹ 13,000 crore in the Seventh Plan. This ensured developing infrastructure in the tribal areas. Their plight tends to worsen when they borrow for social functions.

The Integrated Rural Development Programme (IRDP) pays special attention to SC/ST families. The target of coverage of Scheduled Caste/Tribe beneficiaries in the Seventh Plan was 30 per cent of the total number of beneficiaries. However, the actual coverage was 32.05 per cent in the case of Scheduled Castes and 13.04 per cent in the case of Scheduled Tribe beneficiaries. A target of 50 per cent has been fixed for Scheduled Caste and Scheduled Tribe beneficiaries with effect from April 1990.

Since 1990-91, Scheduled Caste Beneficiaries are being treated on par with Scheduled Tribe beneficiaries for subsidy purposes, both getting 50 per cent subsidy subject upto a ceiling of ₹ 5,000.

In the wage employment programme of the Jawahar Rozgar Yojana, preference has been given to Scheduled Castes/Scheduled Tribes and freed bonded labourers. It has also been provided that at the village panchayat level, 15 per cent of the annual allocation must be spent on items of work which directly benefit the Scheduled Castes and the Scheduled Tribes. Diversion of funds meant for Scheduled Castes and Scheduled Tribes is not permitted.[9]

The comprehensive sub-plan approach to tribal development, introduced in the Fifth Five Year Plan, has the individual family as its focus. The sub-plan is reported to have covered over 75 per cent of the tribal population. In 1986, the number of integrated tribal development projects was 180.

The tribal sub-plan strategy (TSP) comprised of:

(i) Identification in a state of development blocks where tribal population held a majority and their constitution into integrated tribal development projects with a view to adopting therein an integrated and project-based approach for development;

(ii) Earmarking of funds for the central and state plan sectoral outlays from financial institutions and

(iii) Creation of appropriate administrative structures in tribal areas and adoption of appropriate personnel policies.

The focus of TSP has been on the socio-economic development of tribal areas and raising the status of tribal families. Currently, the TPS is laying special stress on infrastructure development, environment upgradation and development of vulnerable groups and areas.

At the end of the Seventh Plan, the Tribal Sub-plan strategy was being implemented through 191 Integrated Tribal Development Projects, 268 pockets of tribal concentration (Modified Area Development Approach — MADA), 74 clusters and 74 primitive tribal group projects.

However, there was limited involvement of Scheduled Castes/ Scheduled Tribes in the formulation and execution of programmes resulting in non-adaptability of schemes/policies to cater to their specific needs.[10]

The recommendations of the Working Group during the Eighth Plan for welfare and development of Scheduled Tribes indicated that:

(i) Outlays under crop husbandry, horticulture, social forestry and other related sectors should be channelised through integrated tribal development programmes;

(ii) Tribal sub-plan areas should be identified as sub-zones in each agro-climatic zones;

(iii) TSP areas should receive priority for agricultural research, education and extension services and

(iv) An integrated scheme of agro-forestry or agriculture with horticulture, sericulture and pisciculture should be designed and implemented in TSP areas.

Tribal agriculture needs to be strengthened through co-operative farming, mixed farming involving various high yielding varieties of crops, land shaping and provision of minor irrigation facilities through construction of small check dams across the perennial streams or facilities for lift irrigation from these streams.[11]

The Eighth Plan seeks to formulate co-operatives for different occupational groups amongst the Scheduled Tribes. In order to encourage self-employment avenues, programmes to enhance productive and managerial skills need to be planned to benefit tribals. Measures also need to be initiated to ensure greater participation of tribal people in conservation and development of forests and preservation of ecology.

The Government has made attempts to strengthen the vocational training centres in tribal areas and the State Tribal Development Co-operatives operating in minor produce. An amount of ₹ 5.40 crore has been provided for this purpose during the year 1993-94.

Under the central scheme launched recently to encourage literacy among tribal women, essential educational complexes were reportedly set up in 48 districts where the rate of literacy among tribal women has been less than two per cent. The scheme was developed to impart education and vocational training. A provision of free uniforms, periodical health check-up and incentives of ₹ 30 per month to parents for sending their children to residential schools has been given priority. The proposed scheme also provides for adult education in the evening. The scheme has been implemented by the Government through voluntary organisations.[12]

Administrative preparation is an important though a missing link in the tribal development programme. Implementation of major and medium irrigation projects often result in displacement of tribal people. This makes it the obligation of the concerned administration to see that they are properly rehabilitated.

It would be better if there is a single line administration in the tribal sub-plan areas. The village assistants should be from the tribal population and priority should be given to ensure land provision to landless tribals.[13]

The age-old links between forests and the tribal people needs to be clearly recognised. The various Acts passed to protect forests should take into account the level of dependence the tribals have on forests. After all, the tribals make a living by selling their produce; and they usually do not exploit forest wealth for profit.

The National Forest Policy has rightly observed that the life of tribals and other poor, living within and near forests, revolves around forests. The rights and concessions enjoyed by them should also be fully protected. Their domestic requirements of fuelwood, fodder, minor forest produce and construction timber should be the first charge on forest produce.

The success of tribal development schemes should not be judged in terms of funds allotted for such schemes. It should be assessed by the positive achievements attained in the direction of social transformation.[14] As such, voluntary agencies, with assistance from governmental departments, could play a useful role in raising the socio-economic status of the tribal population.

Tribal development should also maintain congruity with tribal culture and psychology or else the proposed scheme would remain only far-fetched.[15] Of course, tribal development strategies succeed only when there is inter-departmental co-ordination. More funds would be required for making tribal development schemes cost effective and meaningful. At present, a lion's share of the allocated finance for such schemes goes to infrastructure development. Also, intensive training to workers associated with tribal development programmes is also required. The selection of schemes should also take into account the needs and demands of the tribals and also the absorptive capacity of tribal regions.

THE SCHEDULED TRIBES BILL, 2005

The proposed Scheduled Tribes (Recognition of Land Rights) Bill 2005 has generated a lot of controversy. The Bill is aimed at looking into the extent of dependence on the forests and traditional conservation mechanism of the tribal people. It recognised the inalienable rights of the forest dwelling scheduled tribes (FDST) over the forests where they have inhabited from time immemorial.

The Bill has been criticised on many grounds. It lays stress on regularising 'encroached' lands in the forests. The allocation of 2.5 hectares of land to every FDST is also opposed to the recognition of corporate (community) and usufructuary rights. The soil quality in the forest zones is usually very poor and continuous cultivation without a break is counterproductive. Hence, the FDST would prefer usufructuary rights to permanent land tenure.

There is also opposition to conversion of forest villages into revenue villages. There is no reduction in state control. The Bill states "rights of forests can be exercised only to bonafide livelihood purposes and not for exclusive commercial purposes." There is thus less scope for self-management and self-determination. The Bill has not recognised the role of panchayati raj institutions.

FORESTS RIGHTS BILL, 2006

The Parliament has passed the Scheduled Tribes and other Traditional Forest Dwellers (Recognition of Forest Rights) Bill, 2006 in the winter of 2006 of the Parliament.

The Salient features of the Act are:

- The Act recognizes and vests the forest rights and occupation in forest land in forest dwelling Scheduled Tribes and other traditional forest dwellers.
- The Act provides for recognition of forest rights of other traditional forest dwellers provided they have for at least three generations prior to 13-12-2005.
- The Act provides for the ceiling of occupation of forest land for purposes of recognition of forest rights to the area under actual, occupation and in no case exceeding an area of four hectares.
- The Act provides for conferring rights in the National Parks and Sanctuaries also, renamed as 'critical wildlife habitat' on regular basis.
- The Act provides for the right to hold and live in the forest land under the individual or common occupation for habitation or for self- cultivation for livelihood by a member or members of a forest dwelling Scheduled Tribe or other traditional forest dwellers.
- The Act recognizes the right of ownership access to collect, use, and dispose of minor forest produce which has been traditionally collected within or outside village boundaries.

- The Act provides for the forest right relating to Government providing for diversion of forest land for the purpose of Schools, hospitals, anganwadis, drinking water supply and water pipeline roads, electric and telecommunication lines etc.
- The rights conferred under the Act shall be heritable but not alienable or transferable, and
- The Act provides that no member of forest dwelling Scheduled Tribe or other traditional forest dwellers shall be evicted or remove from forest land under his occupation till the recognition and verification procedure is completed.

REFERENCES

1. B. Janardhan Rao, P. Hussain Khan and P. Narendra Babu: India's Tribal Development: A Critique in N.L. Murthy and K.V. Narayana (Eds. 1989): *Rural Economy of India.* Mittal Publications, Delhi - 35, p. 390.
2. Alexander V. Verghese: Tribals and Sub-Plans', *Seminar*, February1983, p. 34.
3. *Ibid*., p. 35.
4. *Eighth Five Year Plan 1992-97*, p. 422.
5. Subhrendu Bhattacharya and T. Lakshmaiah: 'Development Perspectives for Tribals', *Yojana*, February 29, 1992, p. 21.
6. P. Ramaiah and K. Mohan Reddy: 'Planning for Tribal Development', in Sundaram, I. Satya (1989), *op. cit*., p. 209.
7. Suguna Pathy: 'Political Economy of the Ethnic Peoples in India: Some Reflections', *Social Action*, January-March 1993, p. 43.
8. Pradip Prabhu: 'Working with Tribals', SEMINAR (Social Issue on Tribals), December 1993, p. 30.
9. *Eighth Five Year Plan 1992-97*, p. 418.
10. *Ibid*., pp. 417-418.
11. D. Venkatesan: 'Strategies for Agricultural Development in Tribal Sub-plan Areas', *Yojana*, November 15,1993, p. 14.
12. *Yojana*, September 30,1993, Cover page III
13. Satya Sundaram: Travails of Tribal Development*, *Social Welfare*, November 1993, p. 33.
14. S.A.R.Sastry: 'Tribal Segment and Social Integration', *Yojana*, May 14, 1972, p. 385.
15. Nita Mathur: 'Evolving Strategies for Tribal Development', *Mainstream*, March 7, 1992, p. 22.

Chapter

32 Development of Women and Children in Rural Areas (DWCRA)

In rural areas, women take up a wide variety of agricultural and non-agricultural operations. However, the conditions under which these women work have not changed much. It has rightly been indicated that special efforts/schemes would be needed to improve not only income levels but also the working conditions of the rural women.

The sub-scheme for women's development under IRDP, previously called Basic Services in Rural development (BSRD) has been renamed as Development of Women and Children in Rural Areas (DWCRA). A mid-term appraisal of the implementation of IRDP revealed that flow of assistance to women members of target households or even women-headed households has been largely marginal.

DWCRA, a special strategy of IRDP, was first introduced in 1978 as a pilot project in 50 selected districts extended to all states in 1982-83, and one district in each Union Territory during 1985. Initially the districts were chosen on the criteria of low female literacy and high infant mortality rates. Promoted by the Centre, the scheme has also been supported by UNICEF. The expenditure is shared equally by the central government, the state government and UNICEF.

The focus of the scheme has been the upheaval of the rural households with women as heads of the families, and women members of rural families living below the poverty line. The programme also aimed at improving the status of poor women in rural areas. Whereas IRDP's focus has been on the family, the DWCRA has focussed its attention on groups of poor women.

DWCRA has emerged basically as an economic programme for providing opportunities for supplemental income to women. For helping the women's groups, DWCRA has included provision of multi-purpose community centres. Each Centre has been designed to provide space for training and demonstration, conducting of income generating activities, a balwadi for children and residential accommodation for gram sevikas. The centres have been bolstered with supplies and equipment of upto ₹ 50,000 provided by UNICEF.

Earlier state sponsored programmes have bypassed rural women. Only rural men have been mostly involved in rural development programmes while the rural women have usually associated with and contributed to social welfare schemes. Even these are half-hearted attempts towards adult education and family planning. Though rural women undergo tremendous physical labour, they usually have less control over their cash earnings. Also, rural women have emerged as a cheap labour category.

Another characteristic of rural women's work is that most of it is non-monetised type. The rural women are involved in time and energy consuming work which usually goes unpaid. Thus, their income earning capacity is greatly reduced. However, developmental activities, when related to rural women, needs to be kept within the traditional framework of their lives.[1] The problem of integrating women into processes of development remains to be solved. Probably a basic approach is needed to solve this problem and help the women financially with self-supporting schemes.

There was no effort to utilise the skills of women who, being experienced home-makers, are adept at managing frugal resources. They are more conscious of and concerned about the needs of the family and children.[2]

Studies show that female workers have been discriminated against in terms of availability of work, number of hours of work and wages.

There is no doubt that womenfolk in poor rural households are far more constrained than their male counterparts by the limited (and declining) resources and means at their disposal. Also, the poor peasant and tribal women largely depend on what are called Common Property Resources (CPR). But the growing tendency to privatise CPR is also a factor adversely affecting interests of rural women.[3]

In rural areas, earnings of women go a long way in improving the educational, nutritional and economic status of the families which they lead.

DWCRA: Nature and Scope

DWCRA's primary thrust has been on the formation of groups of 10-15 women from poor households at the village level, for delivery of services like credit and skill training, cash and infrastructural support for self-employment. The overall aim of the scheme has been to raise income levels of women of poor households by making them participate in organised socio-economic activities. As a result of group formations, women's access to basic services of health, education, childcare, nutrition, water and sanitation is bound to improve.[4]

Some of the activities coming under DWCRA are bee-keeping, honey processing, soap making, candle making, handprinting, pickle making, poultry, animal farming, carpet weaving, goat rearing, paper making, ram lamp rearing, palm mat-weaving, bamboo basket making, lime burning, vegetable vending, leaf plate making, silk weaving and rearing, palm basket making, dairy, quarry, beedi making, rope making, thunga mat-weaving, etha basket and mat-weaving, brick making, kambal weaving, tailoring, pottery and readymade garments.

The main objectives of the scheme are:

(i) Promotion of self-employment among the rural women below the poverty line by providing training in vocations;

(ii) Organising beneficiaries in group activities and promote economic and social self-reliance;

(iii) Generation of income for the rural poor by creating avenues for production of goods and services;

(iv) Organising production-enhancing programmes in rural areas and

(v) Promoting care for the children of working women by providing an improved environment, care and food and by establishing creches/balwadis.

The scheme also identifies women in the age group of 18 to 35 years who are below the poverty line in rural areas. The identified women are given training for six months and paid ₹ 200 as stipend per month. Also, a group of organisers is selected for each group. The organisers would have to undergo a separate training during which they are paid a stipend of ₹ 250 per month. After the completion of training, each beneficiary is given a loan ranging from ₹ 4,000 to ₹ 6,000 depending upon the nature of activity to start one's own business as a self-employed venture.

The DWCRA group consists of 15 to 20 women. The women select one of the members as a group organiser, who helps it to select an economic activity in accordance with its skill, aptitude and availability of facilities for procuring raw materials and marketing finished products. Fifty such groups can be formed in every block.

A one time grant of ₹ 15,000 is given to each group as revolving fund for the purchase of raw materials, marketing, child care facilities etc. and suitable training imparted to the rural women. They are also provided access to employment, skilled training, credit and other support services. In selecting the districts, priority is given to those with low female literacy and high rate of infant mortality.

For better inter-communication amongst women, a group approach was adopted. From April 1, 1991 onwards, each group consisted of 10 to 15 women. Training skills to members of the group are imparted under TRYSEM.

The group members, apart from deriving benefits under DWCRA, would also be entitled to loan facilities — beneficial and subsidy under IRDP.

To extend the benefits of the scheme to more women in rural areas, voluntary organisations are geared up to provide assistance in the implementation of projects for providing income-generation opportunities to these women.

Supportive services like mother and child care, immunisation, provision for working conveniences, adult education etc. are provided to rural women to improve their efficiency and reduce subsequent drudgery.

Apart from direct assistance from DRDA, financial assistance up to ₹ 5 lakh has been targeted to benefit eligible voluntary agencies through the Council for Advancement of Rural Technology (CAPART). The amount would be available for projects aimed at providing income-generating activities to the rural population, in particular women.

Those activities which involve training are brought under the scheme of TRYSEM. The National Institute of Rural Development (NIRD) is to act as the nodal institution for all the training activity undertaken by DWCRA.

The scheme is managed and supervised by an Assistant Project Officer (APO) preferably a woman, whose duty is to educate the target group of women.

In each block, there is one Mukhya Sevika, two Gram Sevikas and an additional Gram Sevika to supervise the functioning of groups. The number of groups in one block may be either 30 or 50.

For the effective implementation and monitoring of the DWCRA programme, a three-tier staff pattern at the state, district and village level has been evolved. At the state level, there is a separate cell to oversee the implementation. At the district level, the scheme would operate under the supervision of Assistant Project Officer (Women's Development) who works under the guidance of the project director of the DRDA. At the village level, Grant Sevika is the key functionary who works under the guidance of the BDO.

DWCRA: TARGETS AND ACHIEVEMENTS

Till December 1987, 3,085 groups with membership of more than 52,000 were formed. During the Seventh Plan period, over 28,000 groups with a membership of 4.68 lakh were formed. During 1990-91, 4,500 groups with a membership of 74,000 were added.

By the end of the Seventh Plan (1990), DWCRA was already operating in 240 districts and plans have been to add fifty districts each year. By December 1993, DWCRA has been extended to 355 districts. During the Eighth Plan, the scheme would cover all the remaining districts. In the selection of districts, priority has been given to low female literacy rates and high infant mortality. All the districts will be covered under DWCRA. Targets set under DWCRA failed to materialise in the Sixth and Seventh Plan periods.

The total amount sanctioned also increased from ₹ 26 lakh in 1983-84 to ₹ 738 lakh in 1988-89. On an average, an amount of ₹ 48.3 lakh was spent per year during the five year period. The Seventh Plan outlay for DWCRA was ₹ 48.05 crore.

Table: 1
Performance of DWCRA during the Eighth Plan (1992-97)

Year	*Groups formed*	*No. of Women benefitted*	*Utilisation of funds (₹ crore)*
1992-93	9092	128744	15.48
1993-94	15483	268525	23.65
1994-95*	37964	592026	31.00

1995-96*	37565	697088	63.65
1996-97*	41345	580434	56.94
Total	141386	2266817	190.72

* provisional

Source: Ninth Five Year Plan (1997-2002), Vol. II, p. 50.

The Council for Advancement of People's Action and Rural Technology (CAPART) would extend financial assistance to the economically deprived rural women through voluntary agencies. CAPART has also worked out strategies to provide grants to voluntary agencies to implement income generating projects for women.

DWCRA: BASIC PROBLEMS

The identification of trades is generally done without baseline surveys. Though only a few trades achieve good financial returns, they may not be relevant to the local situation or remunerative to DWCRA beneficiaries.

Case studies reveal that non-traditional units have failed to achieve popularity among the rural women. The reason attributed to this crisis is lack of technical skills among rural women. Moreover, the non-traditional items like wig-making, dress-making and cosmetics do not have sufficient marketing. The initial investment for setting up non-traditional units is substantially high.[5]

The women under DWCRA have not been trained in basic skills for appreciating and availing of the benefits of these viable income generating schemes. As a result of poor marketing infrastructure, they have been forced to switch over from product to product.

It has also been pointed out that the DWCRA products lack economic feasibility. Most products are left with no buyers in the absence of aggressive marketing. Some of the assets like machines obtained under DWCRA have failed to enter the market. The trouble would arise when schemes get implemented without conducting surveys to assess the reaction and acceptance levels of the target group or preparing feasibility reports.[6]

According to one study, the tailoring trade has faced the problem of developing an appropriate strategy for readymade garments. The major problem of dairy trade is uneven price realisation and that of mat weaving is scarcity of basic raw-materials.[7]

The scheme also suffers from the wrong selection of group activities by the groups, the reason being lack of skill, aptitude and local conditions at the initial stage. Lack of co-operative zeal among the members of the group was also observed. They generally lacked management skill.

The scheme suffered from inadequate availability and high cost of raw-materials. The products failed to secure local demand. The products suffered from poor quality and also competition from big companies. Product diversification was an uphill task for women members whereas the market situation required it.

Inadequate provision of backward and forward linkages needed for the smooth functioning of the scheme has emerged as another major shortcoming. It has also been observed that the amount sanctioned for revolving funds remains inadequate.[8]

The training period is too short to master the skill. The trainees had to wait for four to five years for starting the trades. During this period, the trainees tend to lose their grip over the skills they acquired.

It is argued that the field functionaries for women's programmes by and large have orientation in welfare rather than in development. Conceptual clarity is lacking in many cases. Selection of viable projects and ensuring forward and backward linkages are generally absent. In many states, training institutes are yet to be identified and set up.

Lack of skill training, staffing as per norms, low motivational levels of various functionaries, low literacy, lack of convergence with existing services, delay in release of funds from the states to DRDAs and resource constraints are some of the major problems in implementing DWCRA.[9]

The scheme also suffers from many organisational difficulties. It is said that women beneficiaries do not have any say in the kind of activity they could undertake. The choice of activities was further hampered by the stereotypical approach of the authorities towards what women can and cannot do.

Again, artificial groupings, lacking in cohesion, may fail to deliver the goods. Furthermore, they are unable to agree upon and select the most suitable activity that has some chance of succeeding. Also, frequent staff transfers and too many vacancies have put a question mark on the economic feasibility of the scheme.

In certain cases, the assistance has proved to be a liability rather than an asset. This happens when the asset fails to generate income, and the women groups have to repay loans with high interest rates.

An evaluation of DWCRA has revealed that:

(a) A low priority has been given to DWCRA by the DRDAs;

(b) Little convergence of other social services and programmes like nutrition, family welfare, immunisation, adult literacy; and

(c) Inadequate marketing outlets and infrastructure facilities.[10]

There is undue delay in the delivery of development assistance. This is mainly due to lack of functional co-ordination among the various agencies, viz., banks, DRDA and the beneficiaries. The Implementing agencies generally do not take proper interest in providing any supporting facility, viz., community centres, child care, adult education, immunisation etc.

Strengthening DWCRA

There is need for identifying suitable and viable trades, depending on the local resources, skills and markets.

The self-employed women need to be brought close to the administrative and welfare machinery. There must be a confidence-building attitude on the part of the officials.[11] Also, frequent change in the group organiser, as is now the practice, should be completely stopped.[12]

The ceilings for construction of multi-purpose community centres for use by DWCRA beneficiaries have also been raised to ₹ 1.90 lakh and ₹ 2.30 lakh for centres located in plain and hilly areas respectively. By 1988, about 270 such centres have been approved.

The DWCRA has been laying stress on easier processing of documents to help the women meet their credit needs. Simplified and field tested set of documents have been evolved. Thrift and credit is an important group activity of the DWCRA scheme. The women groups can enhance their savings by a matching share of upto ₹ 15,000 through the IRDP funds.

Another pilot project of Management Information Systems for DWCRA has been introduced in 19 districts: In 14 districts out of 19, planned intervention has been sought at all levels of DWCRA for better awareness, education and information through mass media, mainly All India Radio.[13] Today's technological boom demands extended use of the media in encouraging entrepreneurial ventures in the rural sector.

Marketing continues to be a major problem. Therefore, supply and marketing societies should be formed at different levels to help the groups in marketing their products. It is desirable to open sale points at the block and district headquarters to promote the sale of products. A suggestion was made that state government should make provisions for purchase of products made by women's groups.

REFERENCES

1. Ranjitha Padmanabha: 'The Rural Women and Development', *Hindu*, September 13,1978.
2. P.K. Gopinathan and V.L. Srilatha: 'The Kerala Experience', *The Hindu*, April 2, 1995.
3. Samir Dasgupta: 'Women: Bearing the Brunt', *Financial Express*, June 16, 1993.
4. Archna Sood: 'Development of Rural Women — Perception and Outcome', *Kurukshetra*, September 1994, p. 16.
5. A.R. Reddy, Y. Suresh Reddy and P. Mohan Reddy: 'Women and Rural Drvetopment — A Study of DWCRA in Cuddtapah District', *Kurukshetra*, September l994, p. 21.
6. Sunita Kaul: 'Employment Generation Schemes: Not Cutting a Wide Swathe', *Indian Express*, October 3,1993.
7. N. Prem Kumar and A. Rahul Kumar: 'DWCRA: A Case Study', *Yojana*, March 31, 1992, p. 28.
8. D.S. Dhillon and B.S. Hansra: 'On Making DWCRA Effective', *Kurukshetra*, September 1991, pp.25-26.
9. C.S. Singhal: 'DWCRA: Problems and Prospects', *Social Welfare*, July-August 1992.
10. Mahi Pal: 'Planning for Women's Progress Under Panchayat Raj',*Yojana*, February 28, 1994, p. 24.
11. Suman Singh and Manisha Goel: 'Bottlenecks in the Implementation of the DWCRA Programme', *Kurukshetra*, September, 1994, p. 24.
12. Neelam Mahajan: Women's Contribution in Economic Growth', *Kurukshetra*, March l992, p. 24.
13. Archna Sood: *op. cit.*, p. 17.

Chapter

33 Implementation, Monitoring and Evaluation of Rural Development Programmes

Many development programmes involving substantial investments have run into rough weather because of flaws reported in the implementation, monitoring and evaluation of such programmes. Monitoring and evaluation thus assume importance because development is a continuous process and the direction of development too needs to be well targeted and watched. Also, most socio-economic problems are multi-dimensional which need to be scrutinized by an indepth study. Higher allocations for rural development would not be of much help unless the implementation, monitoring and evaluation stages of these programmes are given priority. Of course, these three stages are closely related, in other words, a chain reaction. For instance, inputs are necessary to generate outputs. These inputs may take many forms — physical facility such as an effective irrigation system or a health clinic.

The inputs may be in the form of advice which the beneficiaries are to be encouraged to adopt. Likewise, the outputs may also be in the form of skill acquisition, larger school attendance and greater use of health facilities. These outputs will, in turn, generate effects amongst the target population such as changes in income and expenditure patterns and improvement in social conditions, e.g., health and economic upliftment etc. These effects will have an impact on the social and economic life of the community. As a result of improved incomes, better services may come up in the area providing wider income and employment opportunities. Likewise, better education, and health would mean a general improvement in the quality of life.

There is one clear distinction between monitoring and evaluation. Evaluations are meant to be a detailed assessment of all aspects of the implementations of schemes. They are therefore time-consuming. Monitoring, on the other hand, is needed by planners and administrators as a different process to deliver a substantial information at very short intervals, not exceeding three months in any case. It is said that:[1]

Its purpose is to help administrators keep track, every quarter or every month of the progress of the construction or operation of a project in relation to targets and the flow of expenditures and employment and to identify major slacks and bottlenecks which call for immediate remedial action.

Monitoring is an integral part of the project management structure, but evaluation need not be such an integral component. Evaluation is a kind of achievement audit and mostly takes place after the programme/project ran for some specific period.

Of course, implementation, monitoring and evaluation should go together to derive optimum results. It is rightly said:[2]

Thus, when one talks of failures of implementation, one should look upon planning, implementation and evaluation as an integral process, each deriving strength from the other land transmitting its weaknesses all the way through the process.

It must be admitted that the monitoring and evaluation techniques employed in the industry are more advanced than those employed in respect of elimination of poverty and restructuring of social services sectors.

The Eighth Plan document has identified the following defects in the implementation of rural development schemes:[3]

(i) Wrong selection of beneficiaries/type of assistance, without considering their needs, capabilities and skills.

(ii) Lack of flexibility. Straight-jacket guidelines, issued centrally, often ignore local needs/situations and variations.

(iii) Inadequate delivery mechanisms, pilferages, malpractices etc.

(iv) Lack of co-ordinated approach with many sectoral organisations working independently for different levels of the programmes and

(v) Lack of commitment of the part of agencies/agents responsible for the delivery of the programmes.

I. IMPLEMENTATION

The implementation of any project/programme involves two aspects: (i) proper utilisation funds and (ii) achievement of desired objectives and results.

The implementation stage at present suffers from many deficiencies:[4]

First, the involvement of the implementing agency in terms of efficiency and responsiveness in the programmes lacks commitment.

Second, the implementing agency is not fully aware of the implications of the guidelines received from the above. These guidelines often ignore the local conditions.

Third, the schemes, which are omnibus in character, are not based on realities, particularly regional variations. The details of the village economy do also not receive due attention.

Fourth, the, district administration has by and large remained a regulatory agency. When it is called upon to discharge the developmental functions, it may face many difficulties. The regulatory and developmental functions are not always complementary.

Last the implementing machinery is not concerned with as to how the resources for development would be raised and it has no responsibility towards raising of resources either.

The implementing agencies have to take seven steps. These are:[5]

(i) Planning which includes orientation-training for the functionaries. The field staff should be aware of the task ahead. The area has to be surveyed and the data has to be properly analysed.

(ii) Formulation of schemes and projects should be done taking into account the views of the intended beneficaries. Awareness building amongst beneficiaries is important. There should be interaction 'between functionaries and beneficiaries. The selection of schemes and projects and ensuring proper integration by following a cluster approach are important. The intention is to pool up mutually supportive programmes.

(iii) Planning and formulation of infrastructure development schemes are crucial to the success of schemes. Besides providing infrastructural faculties, the planners should see that backward and forward linkages are ensured. Implementation of schemes without provision of infrastructure amounts to putting the cart before the horse.

(iv) The execution of schemes/projects should be carried out in an orderly manner. The constraints like inadequate skills and inefficiency should be overcome and co-ordination amongst various departments should be ensured.

(v) Effective implementation of the project should be ensured by organising the beneficiaries and training the group leaders.

(vi) Monitoring of programmes is important to take mid-course correctives. Reports have to be obtained to analyse them for a follow-up action.

(vii) Evaluation is needed to judge the quality of implementation. This would help both to improve the plans and ensure effective implementation of programmes in future.

It has been rightly observed:[6]

The psychological needs of promoters of the target programme in terms of autonomy and motivation should be recognised. Decentralisation of decision-making gives, implementers (promoters) a personal stake in the performance of their jobs. Internal stimuli rather than only material incentives increase commitment .... Governments create a new bureaucracy whenever a social problem appears; the need is to carry it to its logical conclusion of sharing decision-making with field implementers and clients.

It has also been rightly pointed out[7] that:

There is further indication from experience that deficiencies in implementation may also be due to inadequate planning of projects at the initial stage, causing slippages in schedules, cost over-runs and poor performance generally.

II. MONITORING

Monitoring is the provision of information for the management to assess progress of implementation and the timely decisions to ensure that progress is maintained according to schedule.

Monitoring seeks to know whether project inputs are being delivered and being used as intended and are having the initial effects as planned.

The fruits of development are not percolating down to the poorest of the poor, mainly because of the ineffective monitoring system coupled with lack of will power.

According to the terminology of the World Bank, "monitoring is the provision of information and the use of that information to enable management to assess progress of implementation and take timely decisions to ensure that progress is maintained according to schedule. Monitoring thus examines whether —

(i) The inputs of the programme are properly delivered;

(ii) The use of inputs are according to programme intentions and the set goals and

(iii) The inputs are able to achieve initial impacts as desired. It has been rightly observed:[8]

> The essence of a good monitoring system is the speed of communication of dependable information on key result areas, the competence of the monitor to interpret the signals and the ability to lead to intervention in a constructive manner.

Monitoring process consists of three components:

(i) Information generating and gathering system;

(ii) Information processing and communication system and

(iii) Decision-making and follow-up action.

The imperative purpose of monitoring is to see whether the targetted activities are completed within a given time-frame and what are the factors influencing the progress.[9]

Monitoring systems are to determine whether —

(i) The project is being implemented according to the agreed plan and procedures and

(ii) The initial response by the intended beneficiaries is in accordance with expectations.

The monitoring system therefore concentrates on issues of physical and financial progress of a project. It has to ensure that inputs reach the intended beneficiaries and such inputs are utilised to the maximum.

A monitoring system must have the capacity to identify not only the deviations from targets but also the causes of these deviations. This would help the management to take decisions for remedial actions. Of course, the targets set must be realistic. Otherwise, deficiencies would reflect not only implementation deficiencies but inappropriate projections.

When some information is not already available, the monitoring unit has together required information either from project records or from sources external to the project. The project staff have to maintain appropriate records and resort to regular reporting.

There is a tendency to collect too much data. As a result, the reports become too long and they are submitted too late to allow timely action and subsequent implementation of the planned project. After all, the chief task of a monitoring system is the provision of information that contributes to effective decision-making.

III. EVALUATION

Evaluation assesses the overall effects — both intentional and unintentional, and their impact. It involves comparisons requiring information from outside the project. Evaluation is to be recognised not only as a management tool for those in charge of planning, but also as a medium through which the public are informed about how the programmes proceed.[10] The scale of evaluation depends on the type of project.

The objective of an evaluation system is to determine whether the project objectives set in terms of expected outputs, effects and impact are being, or will be, met. It is said that "evaluation assesses the overall project effects, both intentional and unintentional and their impact." The extent of coverage for purposes of evaluation will be determined by the constraints of time and availability of resources, both human and financial.

Evaluation assumes special significance in a planned economy. Without such a system, it would be difficult to know whether the planned schemes are moving in the right direction or whether the schemes are cost-effective. Any improvement in the future policy must be based on evaluation. As evaluation is time-consuming, it is confined to a few projects.

The evaluation exercise is essentially directed towards — (i) Identification of areas of success and failures; (ii) appraisal of efficacy of methods adopted and (iii) possible fresh approaches for restructuring of the programmes to attain the desired objectives.[11]

In the context of rural development administration, evaluation performs certain important functions: (i) It provides a sort of mechanism for measuring success; (ii) By measuring the outcome of programme, it shows the area of success and failures thereby helping in minimising failures; (iii) It acts as a guide for further programming by recommending improvements and (iv) It facilitates repeating the success stories of a particular programme.[12]

The essence of evaluation is reproved to be missing in the whole of IRDP system. The present evaluation is mostly target-oriented and does not give emphasis to socio-economic evaluation. Clientele dimension is missing in the current evaluation set-up. Without the clientele dimension, evaluation is meaningless especially in rural development.[13]

In June 1978, the Government of India set up a committee for Training in Evaluation. It has come to two major conclusions:

(i) Training facilities for evaluation personnel are lacking in almost all the States/Union Territories. Whatever little training is there, it is by deputing their staff for training to Central Programme Evaluation Organisation and other research institutes. There is a need to organise systematic training for the evaluation personnel and to tailor the train-ing programmes to suit the requirement of evaluation work and

(ii) There is scope for improving the quality, timeliness, and follow-up action of the reports completed by the various state evaluation organisations. Training would go a long way in improving the quality of these evaluation reports.

Conducting concurrent evaluation of major rural development programmes through independent research institutions has been given importance in recent years. This has thrown useful light on the working of the programmes and also the administration.

IV. MEASURES NEEDED

Monitoring has yet to be perfected. Evaluation is primarily carried out in terms of the targets. As such, it is very difficult to assess the quality of work submitted by the administration.

It needs to be noted that evaluation is more than a progress analysis and review or inspection. Also, it has been the general experience that evaluation by an independent organisation could eliminate possible bias in findings. In the ultimate analysis, the utility of an evaluation system rests on the quality and analysis of information gathered by the evaluator.[14]

The study group set-up by the PEO of the Planning Commission has made some useful suggestions:

(i) The system of qualitative monitoring should be introduced to take care of the quality aspect of the functioning;

(ii) Periodical evaluation of programmes/schemes in the context of the goals should be organised;

(iii) Studies should also be conducted periodically to examine the adequacy of the basic approach as well as the conceptualisation and designing of various programmes and schemes. This would enable the policy makers to assess the relevance of the programmes and schemes in the changing environment and

(iv) Upward communication in the system should be encouraged as this will throw light on the field level problems and prospects of the various programmes/schemes etc. Participative consultation should therefore be encouraged at all levels.

It would be better if monitoring and evaluation are undertaken by some independent external agency rather than by the implementing authorities themselves. Enough scope should be left for mid-term correction and imparting flexibility to the system. The three stages of evaluation should be adopted, i.e., ex-ante evaluation, mid-term evaluation and ex-post evaluation.[15]

The issue of decentralisation should be taken up seriously. Rural programmes ought to become responsive to local problems, needs and potentials. Distrist and block level implementing agencies will have to be given more flexibility.[16] The block level administration will have to be so structured and strengthened so that it would ensure the desired degree of horizontal co-ordination.

Rural development programmes can be successful only when people's active participation is ensured at various stages, particularly at the implementation stage. It has been observed:[17]

> The selection of the specific tasks, however, is governed by local conditions and in assigning priorities, it might be necessary to involve both the local administration as well as the representatives of people particularly of the beneficiary groups.

The Seventh Five Year Plan document has observed:[18]

> A measure of local flexibility in working out the details of each scheme is necessary. The geographically diffuse nature of development programmes makes it difficult to control implementation from a central level. Hence, leakages and misappropriation tend to take place. Greater local involvement can play an important role in reducing these abuses.

For the success of anti-poverty programmes, two things appear to be absolutely essential:[19]

(i) Involvement of beneficiaries in the implementation of the programmes through organisation of beneficiaries and/or panchayats and

(ii) Introducing flexibility in the programmes by giving more autonomy to the local bodies and panchayats to plan according to the needs and resources available at the local area level.

Thus, rural development schemes can deliver the goods only when the three stages, namely, implementation, monitoring and evaluation are strengthened.

REFERENCES

1. Raj Krishna: 'Improvement of Evaluation System', *Yojana*, March16, 1978, p. 14.
2. *Sixth Five Year Plan 1980-85*, p. 89.
3. *Eighth Five Year Plan 1992-97*, Vol. II, pp. 472-73.
4. Neela Mukherjee and Amitav A. Mukherjee: 'Let the Poor Be Arbiter of Their Own Future', *Kurukshetra*, October 1991, p.71.
5. R.K. Derhgawen: 'Seven Steps for Success of R.D. Programmes', *Kurukshetra*, October 1991, pp. 82-84.
6. Mukul Sanwal: 'Garibi Hatao: Improving Implementation', *Economic and Political Weekly*, December 7,1985, p. 2177.
7. *Sixth Five Year Plan 1980-85*, p. 89.
8. *Seventh Five Year Plan 1985-90*, Vol. II, p. 415.
9. D.K. Ghosh: 'Monitoring of Rural Development Programmes — Some Issues', *Kurukshetra*, March 1991, p. 8.

10. D.T. Lakdawala: 'Evaluation: New Dimensions', *Yojana*, March 16, 1978, p. 14.

11. C.H. Hanumantha Rao: 'Can Evaluation be more Proposeful?', *Yojana*, November 1-15, 1982.

12. B.S. Bhargava, Vijayakumar and N. Torgal: 'Need for an Effective Evaluation in Rural Development', *Kurukshetra*, July 1984, p. 26.

13. *Ibid.*, p. 27.

14. K.S.V. Sanjeeva Rao: 'Rural Development: Project Evaluation', *Social Welfare*, November 1995, p. 15.

15. S.D. Chamola: 'Revitalise P. R. Institutions to Plug Loopholes', *Kurukshetra*, October 1991, p. 62.

16. *Sixth Five Year Plan 1980-85*, p. 92.

17. *Ibid.*, p. 17.

18. *Seventh Five Year Plan 1985-90*, Vol. II, p. 413.

19. *Eighth Five Year Plan 1992-97*, Vol. II, p. 473.

PART FIVE

Rural Banking in India

Chapter 34

Rural Indebtedness and Rural Credit

Credit is a crucial input helping the rural poor in raising their incomes. As most farmers are small, they tend to borrow substantial finance from different sources to improve their agricultural output. The problem of indebtedness worsens when the loans are not put to productive uses. Providing adequate credit to the rural poor has become a problem because of the complex nature of the rural society. Moreover, it is not the borrowing that affects productivity but indebtedness which lowers productivity by eliminating the will to change and by creating a despondent outlook.[1]

Some of the major problems facing the rural credit system are:[2]

(i) It has not produced desired results in terms of the direction, quantum and quality of the flow of credit;

(ii) It is afflicted by alarmingly high overdues, bad debts, loan defaults, unviability, low profitability, over-burdening of staff, declining control and deteriorating customer services;

(iii) Information imperfections have contributed to inefficiencies like high transaction costs and low recycling of credit;

(iv) Motivation to perform has not been given due importance;

(v) Directed credit programmes and subsidised lending have badly affected viable functioning of credit disbursing units.

MAGNITUDE OF RURAL CREDIT

The All-India Rural Credit Survey (1951-52) collected data on the socio-economic conditions of farmers so that it would be of help to the Reserve Bank of India, the Government of India and the state governments in the formulation of an integrated scheme of rural credit. Another survey, the All-India Rural Debt and Investment Survey (1961-62) was conducted to arrive at statistically valid and reliable estimates of debt, investment and other related features of rural households both at the national and state levels. After the nationalisation of 14 major commercial banks in 1969, commercial banks started increasing their level of interest in the financing of priority sectors. Therefore, it was thought that a fresh look at the financial conditions of farmers was needed. During 1971-72, the All-India Debt and Investment Survey was conducted, covering the rural and urban household sectors of the economy. The results of the survey relating to the rural households were released in April, 1975.

The 1971-72 survey has thrown useful light on the extent of concentration of economic power and rural indebtedness.[3] Out of the total assets of ₹ 88,409 crore, cultivator households, which constituted 72.3 per cent of the rural households, claimed 93.6 per cent, with an average of ₹ 14,694 per household. The proportion of agricultural labourer households to the total rural households may be taken as an index of the inequality and poverty in the rural areas.[4] The proportion was 14.6 per cent on an all-India basis. The non-cultivated class had an average of ₹ 2,000. per household. Among the non-cultivators, 53 per cent were agricultural labourers with an average value of assets of ₹ 1,139 per household and 8.7 per cent were artisans with an average value of assets of ₹ 2,367 per household.

The survey revealed that land was the most important item of all the assets owned by the rural households, constituting about two-thirds of their total assets. For non-cultivator households, buildings constituted the most important item of all the assets, accounting for nearly two-fifths of the total assets. The concentration of land in the hands of a few is quite clear from the fact that cultivator households in the assets range of ₹ 2,500 to ₹ 20,000 accounted for slightly over 35 per cent of the total assets of all cultivator households. The corresponding share of cultivator households with total assets of ₹ 20,000 or more, each accounted for about 63 per cent of the total assets of all cultivator households.

Of course, inter-state variations are quite striking: the average value of total assets per rural household varied from ₹ 6,018 in Meghalaya to ₹ 31,833 in Punjab. The average value varied over a wider range from ₹ 6,504 in Meghalaya to ₹ 62,789 in Punjab in the case of cultivator households. For non-cultivator households, the variation was from ₹ 1,428 in Orissa to ₹ 8,556 in Punjab.

The liabilities totalling ₹ 3,921 crore were accounted for almost wholly by cash loans, the share of loans in kind being hardly 2.5 per cent. The Survey revealed that 46 per cent of cultivator households and 34 per cent of non-cultivator households suffered from liabilities. The outstanding liabilities per household averaged ₹ 612 among cultivators and ₹ 219 among non-cultivators. Among non-cultivators, the average outstanding liabilities per household were ₹ 162 for agricultural labourers and ₹ 261 for artisans. In all these groups, the outstanding liabilities were small in relation to the value of the total assets, the debt-assets ratio being 4.2 per cent for cultivator households, 14.2 per cent for agricultural labour households and 11 per cent for artisan households. The ratio for non-cultivator households was 8.4 per cent.

Regarding liabilities also, inter-state variations have been reported to be striking. The proportion of rural households reporting liabilities varied from 7 per cent in Meghalaya to 57 per cent in Rajasthan. The average outstanding liabilities per rural household ranged from ₹ 15 in Meghalaya to ₹ 1,084 in Punjab. The outstanding liabilities as a proportion of total assets were small in all the states. The ratio ranged from less than one per cent in Meghalaya to slightly over 10 per cent in Tamil Nadu.

During the decade 1951-52 to 1961-62, the percentage of indebted households to total households did not show any significant variation: it remained between 67 and 69 for cultivators and at 52 for non-cultivators. The average debt for an indebted household, however, recorded an increase and was ₹ 647 in 1961-62. The outstanding total debt increased from ₹ 750 crore in 1950-51 to ₹ 2,380 crore in 1960-61 and further to ₹ 3,921 crore in 1971-72.

Average debt per farm household is ₹ 1.39 lakh, 72 per cent of farm households are more heavily involved in debt; 17 per cent cannot pay back even the interest, 60 per cent of the debts trapped are small or marginal farmers.

Table: 1
Debt Owed to Different Agencies by Rural Households (All-India)

(Percentages)

Credit Agency	*Cultivators*				*Non-Cultivators*			
	1951	*1961*	*1971*	*1981*	*1951*	*1961*	*1971*	*1981*
Government	3.3	2.6	7.1	3.9	1.5	0.6	3.4	4.5
Co-operatives	3.1	15.5	22.0	29.8	1.5	5.3	6.0	13.9
Commercial Banks	0.9	0.6	2.4	28.8	2.0	1.4	0.8	17.3
Landlords	1.5	0.6	8.1	3.7	4.9	1.2	12.6	8.4
Agricultural Moneylenders	24.9	36.0	23.0	8.3	24.8	23.0	23.8	11.4
Professional Moneylenders	44.8	13.2	13.1	7.8	38.0	10.6	18.7	13.4
Traders	5.5	8.8	8.4	3.1	9.9	16.4	10.9	5.8
Relatives/Friends	14.2	8.8	13.1	8.7	15.5	8.6	19.0	14.4
Others	1.8	13.9	2.8	5.9	1.9	32.8	4.8	10.9
Total	100.0	100.0	100.0	100.0	100.0	100.0	100.0	100.0

Sources: (i) Report of the All-India Rural Credit Review Committee, RBI, Mumbai, 1969.
(ii) All-India Debt and Investment Survey 1981-82.
(iii) RBI Bulletin, June 1986, p. 447.

THE SITUATION ASSESSMENT SURVEY (SAS), 2003

The NSSO survey data relating to cash dues of rural and cultivator households for the year 1991 reveals that the share of institutional agencies was 64 per cent (61.2 per cent in 1981). Considering only the cultivator households, the share of institutional debt was 66 per cent (NSSO Report No. 420).

In 2003, the NSSO had undertaken SAS (Situation Assessment Survey) as part of the 59th Round. It was confined to farmer households. It covered 51,770 households spread over 6638 villages. This is a fairly large survey. It showed a decline in the share of institutional debt of cultivator households from 66 per cent in 1991 to 57.7 per cent in 2003.

According to SAS, about 49 per cent of farmer households were reported to be indebted in 2003 as against 23 per cent of the cultivator households indebted in 1991. Both agricultural and professional moneylenders accounted for 25.7 per cent of cash dues. The share of all institutions stood at 57.7 per cent (commercial banks 35.6 per cent).

According to the Report, the average debt of the lowest category of households was ₹ 6,121 and it increased with the size of holding. This indicates that the larger landholders were able to obtain higher loans probably because of their better asset position.

The Report revealed that money lenders constitute the second important source of finance accounting for 25.7 per cent of the loans advanced. The shares of cooperative societies has fallen to 19.6 per cent.

In spite of all the efforts made for their development, institutional finance accounts for 57.7 per cent of total loans and non-institutional sources like moneylenders, traders etc. still account for 42.3 per cent of the total credit.

An analysis of incidence of indebtedness among farmer households given by SAS brought out that a majority of them were indebted and that a very large proportion of their debt was from non-institutional sources, and that borrowing of productive purposes constituted 58.4 per cent of outstanding loans and the rest were for consumption purposes or for marriage and other ceremonies.

Also, the incidence of poverty among farmer households was much higher than among the other rural households and had increased in most of the states as compared with 1999-2000 situation.

INSTITUTIONAL CREDIT GAP

The active functioning of several special programmes require that 75 per cent of the credit should come through institutionalised sources. The availability of institutional credit to agriculture and allied activities has been projected to expand from the base level of ₹ 2,550 crore in 1979-80 to ₹ 5,415 crore in the terminal year (1984-85) of the Sixth Plan. The National Commission on Agriculture has, however, put the figure at ₹ 9,400 crore. An almost four-fold increase is projected in the commercial banks' short-term loans. The share of the priority sector in the total advances by commercial banks is to be increased to 40 per cent, of which the share of agriculture and allied activities will again be at least 40 per cent, i.e., 16 per cent of the total advances.

It is somewhat difficult to estimate the credit requirements of the agricultural sector. The farmers need credit for diverse purposes which include both production and consumption. However, reliable estimates place the credit requirements of the agricultural sector at ₹ 57,316 crore in 1994-95 and ₹ 1,10,873 crore in 1999-2000 AD. It is estimated that the gap between demand and supply in respect of agricultural credit was estimated to be of the order of ₹ 21,000 crore by the end of 2000 AD.

The important objectives of the new agricultural credit policy include:

First, provision of a total and cost effective system for building up and expanding all activities facilitating the modernisation of agriculture, including organisation of services and marketing, thus improving its productive capacity.

Second, it must have a comprehensive connotation of 'agriculture' to make it almost compatible with rural development, covering all production needs of targeted rural households.

Third, it must facilitate and provide for linkages between finance and services for current inputs as well as for investments in land development, wells and pumpsets and farm equipment. The new credit policy has thus, broadned the diversion of the credit needs and has placed emphasis on an integration of the different agencies supplying credit.[5]

Table: 2
Advances to Agriculture by Public Sector Banks (in ₹ crore)

(₹ crore)

In the month of	*Amount outstanding*
June 1969	162
March 2006	1,55,219
March 2007	2,02,614
March 2008	2,49,397
March 2009*	2,98,211

* provisional

Source: Economic Survey 2009-10. p.A-59

Table: 3
Relative Share of Borrowing of Cultivator Households from Different Sources
(per cent)

Sources of Credit	*1951*	*1961*	*1971*	*1981*	*1991*	*2002*
Non- Institutional of which	92.7	81.3	68.3	36.8	30.6	38.9
Moneylenders	69.7	49.2	36.1	16.1	17.5	26.8
Institutional of which co-operative	7.3	18.7	31.7	63.2	66.3	61.1
Societies/ Banks	3.3	2.6	22.0	29.8	23.6	30.2
Commercial Banks	0.9	0.6	2.4	28.4	35.2	26.3
Unspecified	-	-	-	-	3.1	-
TOTAL	100	100	100	100	100	100

Source: All India Debt and Investment Survey and NSSO

Regarding borrowings of cultivator households, the share of non-institutional sources was high at 92.7 per cent in 1951. But, by 2002, this fell to 38.9 per cent. Of this, money-lenders share stood at 26.8 per cent. Institutional share was 61.1 per cent. Of this, co-operative societies/bank share was 30.2 per cent and commercial banks share was 26.3 per cent as shown in the Table 3.

Advances to the agriculture sector can be in the form of direct finance or indirect finance. Indirect finance is limited to a maximum of 25 per cent of the specified 18 per cent (that is, a total of 4.5 per cent of loans and advances). Any shortfall from this 18 per cent requirement needs to be deposited in the Rural In frastructure Development Fund (RIDF) of National Bank for Agriculture and Rural Development (NABARD).

Table: 4
Indirect Agriculture Advance
(₹ crore)

Year	*Public Sector BanksAdvance*	*Private Sector Banks Advance*
2001	15,682.14	3,125.13
2002	18,173.68	5,489.12
2003	21,707.86	6,671.86
2004	24,229.65	8,934.00
2005	29,862.02	9,315.51
2006	43,263.88	13,867.37
2007	58,149.63	24,081.98

Banks have been consistently meeting the targets set for agriculture credit flow in the past few years For the year 2010-11, the target fixed is ₹ 3,75,000 crore. It was ₹ 3,25,000 crore for the year, 2009-10. Also, the Debt Waiver and Debt Relief Scheme for Farmers was to expire by December 31, 2009. However, in view of drought conditions, it has been extended by six months, up to June 30, 2010.

CAUSES OF RURAL INDEBTEDNESS

Rural indebtedness is influenced by a number of factors. While the farmers are responsible for indebtedness to some extent, the conditions in rural India too contributed to perennial indebtedness of the rural poor. The following factors stand responsible for the phenomenon of indebtedness.

First, the indebtedness is passed on from one generation to another. Thus, we find people making efforts to repay the loans taken by their fathers and forefathers. However, they are quite ignorant that if no property is inherited, there is no liability to pay the debt. In their anxiety to repay the loans taken from one moneylender, they borrow from another moneylender. Thus, the burden goes on increasing and is subsequently passed from one family (generation in a larger context) to another family. It is not for nothing that the Royal Commission on Agriculture remarked: "The Indian peasant is born in debt, lives in debt and bequeaths debt."

Second, the presence of uneconomic holdings is also responsible for rural indebtedness. When the holdings are small and fragmented, cultivation becomes unremunerative and the farmers' capacity to repay gets reduced. The situation worsens if the farmers face national calamities like floods, which result in partial or total failure of crops. As such, the farmers find it difficult to pay the interest charges, not to speak of the principal amount. The farmers are hardly in a position to set aside a part of their income for agricultural improvement.

Third, the illiteracy and ignorance of the farmers stand in the way of improving the economic conditions. The farmers are not serious about keeping their families reasonably small. When the families are large, the farmers are compelled to borrow finance for maintaining their families. The illiterate and ignorant farmers often become victims of malpractices indulged in by money-lenders.

Fourth, the farmers are hardly in a position to come out of the vicious system of money-lending. They borrow from the moneylender for paying rent (in times of crop failure) or performing the marriage ceremony etc. The rates of interest are very high. Sometimes, the farmers have to sell their produce to the moneylenders on terms not favourable to them. Thus, not only have they to pay higher rates of interest, but they have to sell their produce at lower prices. No wonder, the farmers are always dominated by moneylenders.

Fifth, though the farmers lead a simple life, they are often tempted to carry on their expenditure to extravagant limits. They spend a lot on unproductive activities like social ceremonies and ornaments. Another undesirable trait of Indian farmers is their passion for litigation, which adds to their poverty and unproductive debt. Thus, even when the harvests are good, the farmers are not able to repay loans or bring about much needed agricultural improvements. The cultivators hardly observe the principles of self-help and thrift. Hence, their dependence on moneylenders becomes total and permanent.

Last, even if the cultivator is hardworking, he is not able to improve his economic status because of inadequate infrastructural facilities and institutional arrangements. For instance, due to inadequate marketing facilities, the farmers are compelled to sell away the produce immediately after harvest at unfavourable prices in the villages. The heavy indebtedness of the farmers also makes it difficult for them to store the produce for sale on favourable terms at a later date.

CONSEQUENCES OF RURAL INDEBTEDNESS

The consequences of mounting indebtedness on farmers are very serious indeed. It is this indebtedness that is responsible for low standard of living and worsening poverty amongst the cultivating classes. As stated earlier, due to heavy debts, the farmers are unable to properly market their produce. No wonder, the moneylender is both the creditor and the village trader. The farmers are unable to properly market their produce. The farmers are compelled to sell their produce in an isolated market for the advantage of the trader. As a result of debts, the income of the farmers is mostly spent for repayment and agricultural improvements tend to get neglected. There is thus, little scope for the farmers to improve their economic status. They cannot live with integrity and confidence because as borrowers, they have to render certain services to the leaders without proper returns.

In countries like Japan, even the small farms are managed most efficiently by adopting the latest farm practices. The small farms need not be inefficient and they need not suffer from low productivity. In India, small farms also became unviable as they do not have access to crucial inputs like credit and irrigation.

If the small and marginal farmers are in debt, they will not be in a position to adopt modern farming practices. This would cripple their capacity to increase their income levels. This would also mean that they cannot repay the loans taken.

IDEAL CREDIT SYSTEM

There is need for evolving an ideal credit system which takes into account the peculiar socio-economic conditions of rural India. The credit system should be capable of meeting the short, medium and long-term credit requirements of the farmers. Credit should be accessible even to small and marginal farmers and other weaker sections. It should encourage productive investment in the desirable directions, not only to enhance the economic status of the farmers but to ensure prompt repayment of loans by them. Besides credit, the farmers require other services. It would be better if credit agencies take interest in providing these services. It is for this reason that farmers' service societies are recommended. To avoid the problem of overdues, it is necessary to streamline the recovery machinery. To ensure the full recovery of loans, credit may be linked to marketing of the produce. Above all, the interest rates must be reasonable and within the reach of the rural poor.

Under the ideal agricultural credit system:

(i) The quantum of credit should be related to the requirements of a good farm plan;

(ii) The kind of security should be such that the farmers should be able to offer it;

(iii) The period of repayment should be in tune with the repaying capacity of the farmer;

(iv) There should be an optimum measure of supervision and assistance in the utilisation of credit by the farmer and

(v) There must be flexibility to face unforeseen contingencies like floods or droughts.

An ideal credit agency should be owned by its patrons; controlled by member patrons themselves on a democratic basis; guided by service motive and not profit motive; have an elastic source of resources; able to adopt a supervised credit system; proximate to the borrowers; oriented to the needs and circumstances and welfare of the rural people in business and democracy as well.[6]

The 59th round of NSSO survey says that 51.4 per cent of the farmer households are financially excluded from both formal and informal sources. This is about 45.9 million farmer households out of 89.3 million farmer households in the country. Of the total farmer households, only 27 per cent has access to formal sources of credit; of which one- third also borrow from non-formal sources. Farm households not accessing credit from formal sources as a proportion to total farm households is especially high at 95.91 per cent, 81.26 per cent and 77.59 per cent in the north-eastern, eastern and central regions, respectively.

The bulk of the institutional credit is going to those farmers whom have a high assets base, rather than to the small and marginal farmers who actually need it the most. This is so because of the lending institutions' bid to keep transaction costs low, as otherwise they would have to deal with a very large number of small borrowers spread over large area.

Another sad feature is, the inclination of the banking sector to continue to prefer lending for crop production rather than non-crop based agricultural activitities, such as dairy, fisheries, bee-keeping and the like , most of which are relatively more lucrative and involve far less risks.

Debt Relief and Regulation of Money-Lending Acts

In view of the many evils associated with money-lending by private people, legislation for the regulation of money-lending has been enacted and enforced in most of the states. Under the earlier Acts, legal rates of interest were fixed. It was further provided that the amount of interest paid should not exceed double the principal amount. These Acts aimed at removing the need for borrowing by reducing the burden of land revenue, increasing irrigation facilities and improving means of communication, transportation and marketing legislation was also enacted to protect the assets of the agriculturist from passing to the hands of the non-agricultural moneylenders. The Acts allowed not only reasonable rates of interest but also restricted credit on the mortgage of land.

Attempts have been made to attack directly, the power of the moneylender and regulated his activities. Courts were allowed to study the contract of debt and remove irregularities, if any. In order to protect the debtor from manipulated accounts, states have prescribed form of accounts, and insisted on the debtor being supplied with these regularly. Further, money-lending without licence and registration was made an offence. Voluntary reduction of debts was undertaken, but when this proved to be unsuccessful, more effective and useful acts were passed. They aimed at exempting ancestral property from attachment as also standing crops, restoration of mortgaged lands on payment of nominal compensation etc.

However, the restrictions placed on moneylenders were not effective. There are several methods by which the money-lenders can violate the Acts. These methods include:

(i) Obtaining a pro-note for a large amount of principal than that actually lent;

(ii) Interest computed at illegal rate and deducted in advance from the amount lent; and

(iii) Forward purchase, together with false evaluation of the debtor's produce etc. Thus, because of the inadequacy of the supervising machinery, absence of an alternative source of credit and the compelling nature of the borrower's requirements, the money-lenders are able, without much difficulty, to evade almost all important provisions of these enactments.

The 20-point economic programme, initiated in July, 1975, aimed at moratorium on rural debt. It declared that measures should be undertaken for redemption of debts in case of the very poor and liquidation of rural indebtedness by stages in the case of others, amongst the weaker sections. The programme recommended total relief from indebtedness in one state for landless labourers and rural artisans whose annual household income does not exceed ₹ 2,400 and also for marginal farmers, owning up to one hectare of unirrigated land.

The programme also observed that in the case of small farmers owning unirrigated land more than one but up to two hectares, the debts should be scaled down in accordance with certain norms. Since the small farmers have to meet their consumption needs and also undertake agricultural improvements, it is stated that repayment of the scaled down debt should not exceed 20 per cent of the gross value of the produce. The debts will, therefore, be scaled down to fit in with the above formula. The interest rates under the law should be applied.

To avoid cumbersome procedures and eliminate all possible delays, it is suggested that jurisdiction of civil courts in respect of any settlement regarding scaling down of debts may be barred. To cut down delays, summary procedures maybe adopted by the officers for this purpose. To reduce the role of the moneylenders, the Sivraman Committee (1976) has suggested:

(i) Grant of consumption loans for purposes like marriages, ceremonies, education and medical expenses;

(ii) Grant of loans for similar purposes to marginal farmers by co-operatives and commercial banks; and

(iii) Implementation of employment schemes by states financially tight for the borrowers so as to ensure prompt repayment of loans.

It may be said that legislative measures alone cannot wipe out the evil of indebtedness completely as the disease is wide-spread. A real solution to the growing rural indebtedness lies in the provision of more productive and remunerative jobs to the rural poor and strengthening the institutional framework, particularly the co-operative movement. There is an urgent need for instituting vigilance committees to see that the villagers reap the full benefit of the many well conceived measures of the government.[7]

The National Bank for Agriculture and Rural Development (NABARD), which is the apex organisation in the field of rural credit has taken several initiatives for facilitating flow of credit to the agricultural sector. These include introduction of Kisan Credit Card Scheme in 1998-99 which is regarded as an innovative scheme to facilitate rural lending.

In order to ensure flow of enough credit to agriculture, the Reserve Bank of India (RBI) has advised the banks to prepare an annual action plan for disbursement of credit to agriculture under different heads. Accordingly, each bank is preparing a Special Agricultural Credit Plan (SACP) segregated into quarterly targets which is being monitored by the RBI. Every year banks should plan for at least 25 per cent growth in disbursements over the previous year.

LOAN WAIVER SCHEME

The loan waiver scheme announced in the budget 2008- 09 is one of the bold steps taken by the Union Government. The salient features of the scheme are explained here to highlight exactly the benefits gained by the farmers through this debt relief measure.

- All agricultural loans disbursed by Scheduled commercial banks, Regional Rural Banks and co-operative Credit Institutions up to March 31st 2007 and overdues as on 31st December 2007 are waived.
- For marginal farmers (holding up to one hectare of land) and small farmers (holding to 2 hectares), all loan overdues as 31st December, 2007 and remaining unpaid till 29th February 2008 are waived.
- For other large farmers, there is one time settlement scheme (OTS) for all loans that were overdue on 31st December 2007 and remaining unpaid till 29th February 2008; a rebate of 25 per cent is given against payment of the remaining 75 per cent.

- The re-scheduled loans, other loans rescheduled, as per the RBI guidelines are also eligible for a waiver or an OTS on the same pattern.
- THE implementation of Debt Waiver and Debt Relief scheme will be completed by June 30, 2008. Upon being granted debt waiver and signing an agreement for debt relief under the OTS, the farmers will be entitled to fresh agricultural loan in accordance with normal rules.

It is estimated that about three crore of small and marginal farmers and one crore of other farmers would be benefited from this scheme. The total value of overdues being waived is estimated at ₹ 50,000 crore and the OTS relief on the overdue loans is estimated at ₹ 10,000 crore to totalling a whopping ₹ 60,000 crore of relief package.

MULTI-AGENCY APPROACH TO RURAL CREDIT

The adoption of the multi-agency approach to agricultural financing has generally been accepted. To study the problems involved in this approach, the Reserve Bank of India constituted a Working Group in August, 1976 under the chairmanship of C.E. Kamath. The Group submitted its report in April 1978. Due to a large credit gap, multi-agency approach for credit to agriculture has been accepted as inevitable. The failure of co-operatives in meeting agricultural credit needs adequately, the slow march of commercial banks into the agricultural sector, the need for expanding facilities in rural areas and the need for introducing a broad-based agricultural credit system — all these have made the multi-agency approach a necessity.[8]

One serious drawback of the multi-agency approach to agricultural financing is that when a number of agencies function in a particular area, credit will not be supplied in a co-ordinated manner, resulting in multiple financing, over-financing, under-financing, financial indiscipline and diversion of scarce resources to unproductive purposes. There is thus much wastage and misuse of scarce resources. Moreover, the rich farmers and other influential people started appropriating a lion's share of institutional credit.[9] The Reserve Bank could not properly co-ordinate the operational mechanism of the multi-agency system. This task would be most effective in the hands of the National Bank for Agriculture and Rural Development (NABARD).

The credit agencies have been unable to formulate and develop meaningful agricultural credit programmes on an area approach basis.

In areas where co-operative and commercial bank sectors are well developed, generally there is multiple-financing, encouraging unproductive investment. There has also been needless competition amongst the commercial banks themselves and also between commercial banks and co-operatives. The starting of too many agencies in a particular area is expected to result in higher cost and declining profitability of bank branches.

A serious drawback of the multi-agency approach is that more than one credit agency may have claim on the same income/security. The borrower tries to play one agency against another and hence recovery becomes a problem. Thus, the multi-agency approach often leads to uneven flow of credit as between regions and also classes in the same region. The problem of overdues worsens, if a farmer is allowed to borrow beyond his repaying capacity.

The systems, procedures and policies followed by co-operatives are different from those followed by the commercial banks. The co-operatives follow the principle of co-operation and they have limited operation. They are backed up by the state patronage and local management. On the other hand, commercial banks observe commercial norms and are backed up by large resources, professional management and organisation. We find vast differences between these two institutions in respect of timeliness of the credit assistance, security norms, services and supervision charges, recovery performance and procedures.

Since the multi-agent approach has come to stay, there is need for improving it through the following measures:

First, as a result of the diverse character of financial institutions serving the rural sector, there are wide differences in cost of funds with them, purpose, duration and size of loans, difference in risks involved in respect of different category of loans, degree and extent of competition and considerations of social justice. The Working Group on Multi-Agency Approach has observed, "the glaring irregularities in the interest rates charged have not only created confusion but also given rise to feeling of discrimination among borrowers in the same area catered to by different agencies." Hence, there is need for the adoption of a uniform pattern of interest rates by commercial banks as well as the co-operative credit societies.

Second, unsupervised loans are often used for purposes other than those for which they are requested.[10] There is need for close supervision over utilisation of funds to ensure that the benefit from the loans accrues to the borrower, thus facilitating recovery of loans. The village headman has to act as co-ordinator or liaison officer between the bankman and the villagers. The problem of supervision can partly be met by assigning manageable areas to individual institutions and societies.[11]

Third, the Working Group felt that geographical demarcation was more appropriate and practical than functional demarcation. The style of 'scattered' lending is not convenient as it creates operational difficulties, supervision, follow-up and recovery. It would be better, therefore, if banks identify compact and contiguous areas comprising of cluster of villages for the purpose of agricultural lending. This approach also ensures intensive coverage of all viable and potentially viable farmers in a given area.[12]

Last, to see that the borrower does not borrow beyond his means, and so the credit card system has been recommended. The credit card contains relevant information such as extent and quality of land possessed, the crops raised and the total eligible credit limit. Some of those who had promptly repaid their previous loans are preferred in issuing the card. The problem of over financing will thus be eliminated and the problem of overdues disappears.

The Narasimham Committee Report on the financial system (1991) observed that the structure of rural credit will have to combine the local character of the RRBs and the resources, skills and organisational/management abilities of the commercial banks. The Committee therefore recommended that each public sector bank should set up one or more rural banking subsidiaries, depending on the size and administrative convenience of each sponsor bank, to take over all its rural branches and, where appropriate, swap its branches, with those of other banks.

The rural poor should be made more bankable. The loans to the poor should be adequate. If necessary, two or three loans to two or three members of a family may be provided. The block level planning should be strengthened to identify viable schemes. Loan procedures too should be simplified to a great extent for economic benefits.

NABARD should ensure convergence between credit availability and credit absorptive capacity of farmers, linking credit to technology suitable to farmers in rain fed/irrigated and even to specific crops in varied farming situation.

REFERENCES

1. International Co-operative Alliance (1966): 'The Role of Co-operation in Social and Economic Development.' (Collection of Papers), p. 27.
2. R.V. Bhavani: 'Restructuring Credit System for Rural Development', *State Bank of India Monthly Review,* April 1996, pp. 161-162.
3. R.P. Pathak, K.R. Ganapathy and Y.U.K. Sarma: 'Shifts in Pattern of Asset Holdings of Rural Households, 1961-62 to 1971-72', *Economic and Political* Weekly, March 19, 1977.
4. Subhash Chandra Sarkar: 'The Face of Rural Poverty and Inequality', *Khadigramodyog,* April 1977, p. 313.
5. Report of the National Commission on Agriculture, Part XII.
6. O.R. Krishnaswamy: 'A Critical Review of the Agricultural Finance System in India', *Agricultural Situation in India,* August 1979, pp. 295-296.
7. A.K. Dharamraj: 'Tackling Rural Indebtedness', *Financial Express,* November 25, 1980.
8. B.D. Sharma: 'Multi-Agency Approach to Farm Credit', *Financial Express,* July 7, 1979.
9. S.P. Sinha: 'Agricultural Credit: Development and Prospects', *Commerce,* Annual Number 1979, p. 105.
10. Food and Agricultural Organisation (1955): 'Manual of Supervised Agricultural Credit in Latin America', p. 4.
11. S.K. Rau: 'Strategy of Rural Development', in *Rural Development in India; Some Facets, op. cit.*
12. C.L. Khemani: 'Area Approach in Agricultural Lending', *State Bank of India Monthly Review,* January 1981, p. 33.
13. *Rural Reconstruction,* October 1971 and January 1972, pp. 15-16.

Chapter

35 THE CO-OPERATIVES

The rural co-operatives are doing a good job both in credit and non-credit spheres. They are fully familiar with local conditions and problems and as such are ideal institutions to serve the rural poor. The rural co-operative structure mainly consists of credit co-operatives, land development banks and farmers' service societies.

I. THE CO-OPERATIVE BANKS

The co-operative movement is more than 100 years old. The movement has a rural as well as an urban structure, a credit as well as a non-credit component and within its credit segment, has a short-term and long-term structure.

Historically, co-operatives in India have developed as an adjunct of the state activity. They have largely depended on state support even for their structural reorganisation and managerial upgradation and also financial viability.

The credit co-operatives have been able to develop a unique delivery system at the doorsteps of the farmers through a single window institutional structure providing not only credit but other farm inputs as well. They are rendering significant support for increasing agricultural production and productivity.

The International Labour Organisation (ILO) considered "co-operatives to be established and developed as a means of increasing national income, export revenues and employment by a fuller utilisation of resources ... aimed at bringing fresh areas into productive use and in the development of modern industrial, preferably scattered, processing local raw-materials." (Recommendation No. 127, 1996).

The state government assistance to the co-operative credit structure includes provision of managerial staff on deputation, financial assistance by way of equity participation, guaranteeing of their borrowings etc. As at the end of 1991-92, the state government contribution to the share capital of the co-operative credit institutions in both Short-Term (ST) and Long-Term (LT) sectors amounted to ₹ 592.76 crore accounting for 13.6 per cent of the total.

The agricultural co-operative credit structure has two parts: one engaged in short and medium-term credit consisting of three-tier system, state co-operative banks, central co-operative banks and primary credit societies. The other part is engaged in long-term credit, consisting of a two tier system, central land development banks and primary land development banks. The primary agricultural credit societies form the kernel of the co-operative movement in India and constitute the largest number of co-operative institutions.

> *"The agricultural primary credit society is the foundation stone on which the whole co-operative edifice is built."*

The primary credit societies provide short and medium-term credit supply, agricultural and other production requirements and undertake marketing of agricultural produce. They also help in formulating and implementing a plan for agricultural productions for the village and take such educative, advisory and welfare functions as the members might be willing to take up. They are expected to inculcate the habit of thrift and saving among their members.

The membership is open for agriculturists, artisans and small traders in villages. Universal membership has now been accepted as the policy so that the weaker sections would become members of the co-operatives and enjoy the services offered by them. Regarding management, the ultimate authority in the affairs of the society is the general body which could meet at least once a year. The General Body elects a small managing committee to look after the day-to-day working. The office bearers usually render honorary services, an honorarium out of the profits maybe paid to the President or Secretary in certain cases. A society with heavy transaction appoints a clerk on monthly salary basis.

The co-operatives operate through a multi-tiered federal structure, with the base or grassroot level institutions engaged in financing the ultimate user of credit with the funds provided by the higher tiers, which are mainly responsible for mobilising resources for the purpose by way of deposits and borrowings.

The ST credit structure comprises of the Primary Agricultural Credit Societies (PACS) at the grassroot level affiliated to Central Co-operative Banks (CCBs) at the district level, which in turn are federated at the apex level to the State Co-operative Banks (SCBs).

However, in some of the smaller states and union territories, the intermediate level structures, i.e., CCBs are dispensed with and the PACS are directly affiliated to the SCB. Thus, in this structure, while the individuals are members of the PACS, the membership of the higher tiers, i.e., CCBs and SCBs are generally restricted to societies. These institutions are engaged in the provision of short and medium duration credit mainly to meet the working capital requirements of the members and to a limited extent their investment credit needs involve relatively low outlays.

The co-operatives originated as an institutional agency for delivering crop loans in a minor way. There are now 3.53 lakh co-operative societies bringing within their fold a membership of ₹ 17.51 crore and employing a working capital of over ₹ 76,000 crore, enveloping almost every conceivable economic activity.

Table: 1
Distribution of Capital Base of Rural Cooperative Banks (as on 31.03.05)

	Short Term			Long Term	
	State Co-op. Banks	DCCBs	PACS	SCARDBs	PCARDBs
Number of Coop. Banks	31 (₹ Crores (%)	367 (₹ Crores (%)	2,08,779 (₹ Crores (%	20 (₹ Crores (%)	727 (₹ Crores (%)
(i) Owned Funds (Share capital + Reserves)	9495 (13.9)	20495 (16.4)	9197 (13.4)	5022 (22.1)	3494 (20.8)
(ii) Deposits	44316 (64.8)	82098 (65.5)	18976 (27.7)	566 (02.4)	0385 (2.2)
(iii) Borrowings	14608 (21.3)	22568 (18.1)	40250 (58.9)	17180 (75.5)	12873 (77.0)
Total capital base	68419 (100.0)	125161 (100.0)	68423 (100.0)	22768 (100.0)	16732 (100.0)

PACS

In 2007, there were 1,08,779 Primary Agricultural Credit Societies (PACS) at the village level. The PACS are struggling all over the country. Several of them are dormant. In 2005, only about 50 per cent of them were viable, 30 per cent potentially viable and the remaining unviable.

Out of more than 1 lakh units, only 62 per cent were found viable as on March 31, 2003. During 2004-05, PACS as a group incurred net losses of ₹ 1261 crore.

In 2006, as many as 40 per cent of country PACS are located in Maharashtra and West Bengal.

Table: 2
Number of PACS in India in 2006

State	*Number*
Maharashtra	20,866
West Bengal	18,788
Uttar Pradesh	8,929
Gujarat	8,482
Bihar	5,936
Rajasthan	5,236
All India	1,05,735

DCCBs

In 2005, of the 365 District Central Cooperative Banks (DCCBs) 104 incurred losses to the tune of ₹ 800 crore. The accumulated losses of DCCBs exceeded ₹ 5,500 crore. As on June 30,2006, 134 out of 367 DCCBs did not comply with the provisions of minimum requirement of paid-up capital and reserves under Banking Regulation Act, 1949.

The aggregated NPAs (non-performing assets) as on 31 March 2005 were estimated at ₹ 14,520 crore for DCCBs. In 2007, there were 367 DCCBs. The DCCBs are federated in to 31 apex or state cooperative banks (SCBs) at the state level, which is closely linked to NABARD.

SCBs.

During 2005, 27 out of 31 State cooperative Banks (SCBs) eamed profits and four incurred losses. As on June 30, 2006, 7 out of 31 SCBs did no comply with the provision of minimum requirement of paid up capital and reserves under the Banking Regulation Act, 1949. The aggregate NPAs as on 31st March 2005 were estimated at ₹ 6,072 crore for SCBs.

SCARDBs AND PSARDBs

In 2007, in the long term cooperative credit structure, There were 20 State Copperative Agriculture Rural Development Banks (SCARDBs) at State level and 727 Primary Cooperative Agriculture Rural Development Banks (PCARDBs) at district level.

In the case of SCARDBs and PCARDBs more than 60 per cent suffer form poor recovery, reduced recycling of funds and high overdue besides losses. The SCARDBs depend heavily on borrowings for raising their resources. As on 31st March, 2004, their borrowings accounted for 83.5 per cent of their total resources, and a major portion of these borrowings are from NABARD.

During 2004-05, SCARDBs and PCARDBs accumulated NPAs to the tune of ₹ 5,437 crore and ₹ 4,056 crore respectively.

Table: 3
Flow of Cooperative Credit to Agaiculture
(In ₹ Crore)

Year	*Cooperative Credit*
1999-2000	18,260.00
2000-01	20,718.00
2001-02	23,524.00
2002-03	23,716.00
2003-04	26,958.79
2004-05	31,424.23
2005-06	39,403.77
2006-07*	42,479.80
2007-08*	33,070.17

* provisional.

Table: 4
Number of Kisan Credit Cards and Amount Sanctioned by Cooperative Banks

Year	*Credit Cards Issued (in lakhs)*	*Amount Sanctioned (in ₹ crore)*
2001-02	54.36	15,952
2002-03	45.79	15,841
2003-04	48.78	9,855
2006-07	22.97	13,141
2007-08	20.91	19,991
2008-09	13.44	8,428

Advantages of Co-operative Institutions

What distinguishes a co-operative enterprise from other forms of business organisations is that in a co-operative, there is no 'sleeping partnership' concept. Members belonging to a co-operative must actively participate in that organisation. The participation is the essence of co-operative democracy. Of course, actually this participation is poor.

Co-operatives are said to be the ideal institutions as they enjoy several advantages. First, they are in close touch with the members and therefore aware of their repaying capacity or lack of it. Second, they can provide strong incentives for thrift and saving and promote a feeling of responsibility for repayment. Third, they follow financial operations which are simple and not complicated since identification and similar problems do not exist. Fourth, co-operative financing is not restricted to a class, it is the only means by which even the poorest of the poor can hope to get loans.

It is also observed that credit co-operatives are relatively better in areas where:

(i) The crop loan system is in vogue;

(ii) The number of large size societies is more and

(iii) Sizeable attempts have been made in introducing the integrated rural credit scheme.

The success of co-operatives largely depends on:

(i) The progressive role played by the Central Bank;

(ii) The satisfactory functioning of the institution of field workers conference and

(iii) Co-ordination between the departmental agencies and the central financing agency.

Problems of the Co-operative Structure

The co-operative structure suffers from a number of drawbacks. It has been observed that "the co-operative sector is being totally neglected, in fact, throttled by too much intervention. It is a case of killing with kindness, through over regulation, official diktat and curbing of freedom to perform."[1] The bureaucratisation of the co-operatives is complete. The movement is denied of the educative process and its experience in the democratic self-government has not been acknowledged.

The distribution of co-operative credit per borrower was found to be highly concentrated in the relatively developed states of Gujarat, Haryana, Kerala, Karnataka, Maharashtra, Punjab and Tamil Nadu, while the relatively backward states like Bihar, Orissa, Jammu & Kashmir, Rajasthan, Himachal Pradesh, Uttar Pradesh and West Bengal had comparatively low amount of co-operative credit per borrower.

Per hectare availability of co-operative credit in 1984-85 ranged from ₹ 24 in Bihar to ₹ 1,490 in Kerala. Bihar, Jammu & Kashmir, Madhya Pradesh, Orissa, Rajasthan, West Bengal, Uttar Pradesh and Karnataka had a relatively lower share of co-operative credit available per hectare than the national average of 165 per hectare. The amount of loan was the highest (₹ 2,551) in Gujarat and the lowest (₹ 231) in Bihar.

When measured in aggregate terms, the eight states of Andhra Pradesh, Tamil Nadu, Kerala, Karnataka, Punjab, Haryana, Gujarat and Maharashtra accounted for about 65 per cent of the total co-operative credit advanced during 1984-85. Thus, there are marked regional disparities in the flow of co-operative credit.[2]

The credit co-operatives have become unviable and uncompetitive mainly because of state government interference in their day-to-day operations and an antiquated management structure.

Though there is a substantial increase in the total membership of PACS, the percentage of borrowing members to the total membership has shown a steady decline from 54.8 per cent in 1960-61 to 24.0 per cent in 1987-88. This reveals the organisational weakness of PACS.[3]

The cooperative banks meet about 46 per cent of the credit needs of small farmers, marginal farmers, and sub-marginal farmers in the country. Yet, they are not healthy. It is estimated that the total accumulated losses of rural cooperative credit institutions amounted to ₹ 8,746 crore as on March 31, 2004.

Cooperative credit institutions have suffered from low resource base, high transaction cost (Because of standardized business model, overstaffing), high risk cost (because of low recovery level) with excessive dependency on the government.

Also, market share of credit cooperatives in rural credit is steadily declining. From a meager credit share of 2.7 per cent during early 1950s, the share in rural credit increased phenomenally to 62 per cent in 1990s. However, the market share declined sharply from 43 per cent in 1998-99 to 31 per cent in 2003-04, and to 27 per cent by 28 February, 2005.

Nearly half of PACS (50 per cent) made overall losses. Out of 31 State Cooperative Banks, 26 earned profits, 4 made losses and 1 reported neither profit nor loss as on 31st March, 2005.

Recovery position is a matter of serious concern. As at end March 2005 the recovery per cent was 83 per cent for SCB, 71.2 per cent for DCCB and 66.4 per cent for PACs. The above figures show the weak foundation of the cooperative credit structure.

State government's interference, dormant membership lack of professionalism, low skilled staff, weak MIS, poor house keeping and internal checks and control, lack of transparency and accountability for laxity in granting and monitoring loans have led to poor quality of loan portfolio.

STRENGTHENING CO-OPERATIVE STRUCTURE

For strengthening the co-operative movement, the Rural Credit Survey Committee has recommended:

(i) State participation in the share capital of co-operatives;

(ii) Strengthening of the co-operative credit structure at all levels;

(iii) Linking up of credit with marketing;

(iv) Development of processing on co-operative lines;

(v) Promotion of storage and warehousing and

(vi) Improvement of training facilities and the strengthening of administrative machinery.

Apart from effective state participation in capital management, co-operatives require close co-ordination between the revenue department, the panchayat, the agricultural department and the co-operative department.

The Committee on Co-operative Credit 1963 recommended that:

(i) As a general rule, co-operatives should be organised on the basis of the village community as the primary unit. There is need for ensuring viability with the inclusion of the smallest number of villages;

(ii) The state may participate in the share capital of primary agricultural credit societies under certain conditions;

(iii) Co-operative societies should admit to their membership all classes of cultivators including marginal and sub-marginal cultivators etc., and provide them adequate credit on the basic production requirements and repaying capacity and

(iv) All short and medium-term loans upto ₹ 500 should be given without mortgage of landed property.

The main recommendation of the Committee to Review Arrangements for the Institutional Credit for Agriculture and Rural Development (CRAFICARD), 1981 to strengthen the co-operative movements are:

(i) Even where reorganisation has been completed, the quality of operations has not improved to the desired extent. Therefore, there should be a drive for improving the efficiency and content of services as well as for increasing the business and membership of the societies, particularly from among the weaker sections;

(ii) In planning the future of reorganised societies, the aim should be to transform them into a single contact point in the village for all types of credit;

(iii) The PACS should correct the aberration in their working as mere lending agencies and take steps to spread banking habit and mobilise deposits in rural areas;

(iv) The district level central co-operative banks and the state level apex co-operative banks should provide a positive leadership in developing the strength and soundness of the co-operative credit system and

(v) In view of the need to cover vulnerable groups who are to take up non-land based activities, functional co-operative societies may finance their members wherever necessary.

For building a strong organised co-operative sector, the following points should be urgently considered:[4]

(i) Multi-agency approach to agro-financing should function as a supplement to co-operatives;
(ii) Absolute institutionalisation of agro-credit should be continued and the co-operatives should cater to the needs of the rural population;
(iii) Co-operatives should be allowed to advance more of consumption credit and for this, they must get refinances from NABARD;
(iv) All agro-credit agencies should administer uniform rates of interest;
(v) Definition of different categories of farmers should be uniform;
(vi) Co-operatives should build warehouses to store the agro-products at times of glut to give remunerative prices to the farmers;
(vii) Co-operative credit societies should have links with consumer co-operatives to sell the agro-products;
(viii) Area survey must be done before the Reserve Bank of India (RBI) gives licences to open new branches. Banks should not be allowed to open branches at a place where the co-operatives are already successfully meeting the credit needs.
(ix) Immediate steps to set up National Co-operative Development Banks should be taken up by the government.

At present, co-operative banking is governed by the Co-operative Societies Act of the respective state as also the Banking Regulation Act as applicable to co-operative societies — BRA (AACS) 1966. While the Co-operative Societies Act is the basic law related to the formation and operation of the co-operative society, the BRA (AACS) is the legislation for banking business.

In 1985, a committee headed by K.N. Ardhanareeswaran, then Additional Secretary in the Department of Agriculture and Co-operation, was constituted. The committee, in its report submitted in 1987, made some radical recommendations, particularly relating to the role of the state governments. However, the recommendations were not given serious attention by the government.

The major findings of the Ardhanareeswaran Committee are:

(i) The existing Co-operative Societies Act contains provisions which militate against the democratic character and the autonomy of co-operatives. Over the years, the Registrar of co-operative societies has acquired undue powers in respect of management decisions of the co-operatives, which should be curtailed;
(ii) The role of the Registrar should be made more positive and he should be looked upon as a development agent;
(iii) The Federal Co-operative Societies should play a more active part in the developmental functions relating to promotion, organisation, proper functioning and growth of affiliated co-operative societies and

(iv) The changing complexities of member management, human resources management and financial management have necessitated the availability of professional assistance to co-operatives through adequately trained and professional staff working under the guidance of a democratically elected body.

The Agriculture Credit Review Committee (ACRC), headed by Prof. A.M. Khusro, and appointed by the RBI, submitted its Report in 1989. It recommended that the supersession of the co-operative structure should stop; that laws should be made to prevent such supersession; that the government should withdraw from the co-operative movement and let the co-operatives perform their business independently.

The Committee also laid stress on effective mobilisation of deposits. The secretaries of co-operatives, numbering around 9000, should be persons of considerable calibre. They should be responsible to their societies, and not to the cadre system. Of course, they deserve incentive payments for their better performance.

The ACRC has recommended the setting up of National Co-operative Bank of India (NCBI). At present, the surplus deposits in a state cannot be utilised in a deficit state. The funds thus go out of the co-operative bank. The NCBI can be a balancing organisation, linking one co-operative state apex with another; transferring funds, enabling financially large ventures, providing leadership to the co-operative movement, undertaking training and other exercises to improve the efficiency of the co-operative sector.[5]

In March, 1990, the Planning Commission itself set up a committee under the chairmanship of Choudhary Brahma Prakash, a veteran co-operative leader. The Committee drafted a model Co-operative Societies Bill, which was submitted to the Government in November, 1990.

The aim of the draft law was to minimise government control and interference and develop self-reliance and self-confidence within these bodies. While co-operatives by and large welcomed liberalisation, the state governments showed resent in tapping the benefits associated with liberalisation.

The model law has recommended new norms of membership, suggesting that entry into a co-operative society should be voluntary and available to all without any artificial restriction. The draft law prescribes that membership should be granted to anybody who will make use of the services of the society and accept the responsibilities outlined in the byelaws. Of course, the West Bengal government feared that this may lead to domination by upper classes.

The simplified registration procedures in the model bill grant registration to any society within 60 days of application. This no doubt neutralises the role of the Registrar, who is a State Representative. Under the model bill, a formal declaration on the part of an applicant society expressing its willingness to abide by the co-operative's objective will suffice. Here again, the West Bengal government feared that any society can be formed with vague objectives by traders, middlemen and other powerful interest groups without any restrictions whatsoever.

The model bill also reported that any federal co-operative may be formed with signatures of authorised representatives of at least two primary co-operatives. It is again feared that this provision would endanger the basic structure of the co-operative movement as this would lead to the mushrooming of federations rendering both primary societies as well as federations weak.

There is a provision in the model bill that a co-operative society can acquire a holding company status. This would also enable co-operatives to float subsidiary organisations if they want. The move is meant to enlarge the avenues for business. But, the West Bengal government expressed fear that this may widen the scope for siphoning off funds.

The model bill contains an upper ceiling on borrowings by a co-operative — borrowings should at no time exceed ten times the sum of the member funds and organisation reserves less accumulated deficit. The West Bengal government argued that such a restriction would affect the viability of these co-operatives whose activities are capital intensive.[6]

The model co-operatives bill prohibits co-operatives from accepting funds from the government by way of equity. The committee's fear was that the state will virtually take over co-operatives by augmenting their share.[7]

The decision-making in a co-operative must ultimately lie with the general body which shall also elect an executive or governing body. The one-man one-vote principle may have to be amended in the interest of co-operative management. A more appropriate basis of voting should be the patronage (i.e., the extent of user-participation) by the members.[8]

The co-operatives need to be accorded more autonomous status with regard to membership emolument, management of business and other aspects of their operations. This is necessary to promote business-like structures to ensure greater efficiency and viability at every level as well as of the federal structure as a whole. The stress should be on the orientation of the upper-tier co-operative structure to strengthen the primary constituent units to fulfil their needs in totality.[9]

All co-operative societies which are in the banking business should be brought under an umbrella central legislation by suitably strengthening and amending the BRA Act (AACS) 1966. The Co-operative Societies Act in various states may be restricted to only non-credit co-operatives.

While some portion of the share capital held by state governments may be retained, the remaining portion may be returned to the state governments and the consequent shortfall may be made good by share capital contribution from the Union Government/NABARD.

With this, the tendency to prop up weak and unviable societies with government share capital will come to an end and those which are commercially unviable will have a natural eclipse.[10]

While it may not be possible to completely restructure the system, the apex institutions will have to take steps to revitalise, for which a beginning has already been made, and weed out those institutions which are not likely to become viable in the next five years and have them amalgamated with the neighbouring strong units.[11]

As per the recommendations of the ACRC, the government had introduced the concept of Business Development Plans (BDP) for PACS. An essential component of BDP would be adequate deposit mobilisation by the PACS which would be able to attract an equivalent amount of institutional finance for the purpose of implementing BDP evolved after intensive consultation between members and staff of PACS and the DCCB personnel to generate a business plan four times in size of the deposits mobilised.

It is expected that the 70,000 non-viable PACS of the total 87,305 will be covered by the revitalisation programme, each of the PACS reaching a minimum business of ₹ 10 lakh per year at 15 per cent annual growth rate. Of course, the BDP also aims at promoting backward and forward linkages.[12]

In order to improve ground level credit, NABARD's refinance support for production credit and investment credit was enhanced to ₹ 3,700 crore and ₹ 2,650 crore respectively during 1994-95.

It is suggested that the PACS should be transformed into a single contact point in the village for all types of credit and not merely for agriculture in the narrow sense. They should provide a package of integrated services to the members. They can also undertake services either directly or through forging links with other agencies such as marketing societies. The PACS can be economically viable if it taps the available potential for farm credit business.

The co-operative sector has turned down the report of the Vaidyanathan task force on the revitalisation of the co-operative credit structure. The task force was appointed by the Finance Ministry on August 5, 2004 to formulate a plan to rejuvenate the rural co-operative credit structure. The task force submitted its draft final report on December 30 for public debate and suggestions.

The Task Force has suggested a ₹ 14,839 crore rehabilitation package for the co-operative credit infrastructure but the sector leaders find the conditions attached to this assistance too harsh. Most of the credit societies will be rendered ineligible for the revival support.

According to experts, phased implementation of the revival package, as suggested by the Task Force, would be time consuming. They also disagreed with the panel recommendation that only those states that had passed the parallel co-operative laws should be eligible for the revival package.

The National Policy on Cooperaties (April 2002) aimed at

- Upholding the values and principles of cooperation
- The preservation of the distinct identity of cooperatives, its values and principles by providing an appropriate environment and taking the required administrative and taking the required administrative and legislative measures;
- Recognising cooperatives as a distinct economic sector and an imtegral component of the socio economic system of the country and an effective and potential instrument of socio-economic development.
- Accepting the regulatory role of Government, mainly limited to the conduct of timely elections, audit of the cooperative societies, and measures to safeguard the interest of the members and other stake holders in the cooperatives. There shall, however, be no interference in the management and working of the cooperatives. The Government recognizes the apolitical nature of cooperatives; and
- Protecting the interests of the SC/St women and other weaker sections of the society and their development through the cooperatives.

In Janurary 2006, the Government announced a package for revival of short-term rural cooperative credit involving financial assistance of ₹ 13,596 crore. The NABARD has been designated as the implementing agency for the purpose. States are required to sign memorandums of understanding with the Government of India and NABARD, committing to implementing the legal, institutional and other reforms as envisaged in the revival package. So far twenty- five states have executed MOUs with the Government of India and NABARD. This covers 96 per cent of the primary agricultural credit societies, and 96 per cent of the central cooperative banks in the country. As on November 2009, ₹ 7,051.75 crore has been released by NABARD as the Government of India share for recapitalization of ₹ 37,303 PACS. (Economic Survey 2009-10. p. 196).

In July 2007, World Bank has approved a financial package of $600 million (₹ 2,400 crore) loan towards revitalizing rural credit cooperative banks, with the aim to transform them into efficient and commercially viable institutions responsive to the financial service needs of India's poor farmers including small and marginal farmers. This is likely to reduce the accumulated losses of rural cooperative banks and will help them in restoring the value of members capital and for achieving a minimum capital to risk weighted assets ratio of 7 per cent.

The cooperative banks should go in for more diversification in lending and other activities, insurance, housing finance, handloom finance and extension of credit to processing industries, and production-oriented small units will greatly help is earning more. Products and services must be upgraded to compete with commercial banks. Collection of dues and overdues should receive top priority from all personnel of the cooperative credit movement. The huge scope for investment credit to agriculture should be exploited properly.

II. THE LAND DEVELOPMENT BANKS

The Land Development Banks (LDBs) have a two-tier structure with Central Land Development Banks at the state level and Primary Land Development Banks at the tehsil, sub-divisional/district level. They supply long-term credit to the cultivators. The Primary Co-operative Credit Societies cannot advance long-term loans as they themselves draw their funds from the Central Co-operative Bank for short and medium-terms. The co-operatives also lack necessary expertise to evaluate property in order to advance long-term loans. Commercialisation of agriculture requires long-term finance. Hence, the need for land development banks.

Under the federal type, the Central Land Development Banks work at the top level and the Primary LDBs at the base level. Under the unitary type, the Central LDBs advance loans directly to individuals operating through branches as well as Primary LDBs which serve the whole of the district or a group of talukas. The central LDBs open their branch offices at the regional or district level.

MANAGEMENT OF LDBs

The management of the LDBs vests in the Board of Directors consisting of 7 to 9 members. In some states, 2 to 3 Directors are nominated by the Government. In the case of Primary LDBs, one Director is nominated by the Central LDB. The members of the Board work for three years.

Regarding finances, the Primary LDBs depend on:

(i) Share capital;

(ii) Loans from Central LDBs;

(iii) Admission and other fees;

(iv) Grants and subsidies from the government and

(v) Borrowings from other agencies.

The central LDBs get funds from:

(i) Share capital;

(ii) Floating of debentures on the security of its assets and mortgage bonds transferred by primary LDBs to it;

(iii) Loans from State Bank of India on the guarantee of state government;

(iv) Admission and other fees;

(v) Grants and subsidies;

(vi) Deposits and

(vii) Other funds.

PROGRESS OF LDBs

Central Land Development Banks maintained a steady progress in terms of issue of loans and advances. They issued loans totalling ₹ 363 crore during the year 1980-81 as against ₹ 309 crore in 1979-80. The total loans outstanding as on 30th June, 1981 were at ₹ 1,697 crore as against ₹ 1,535 crore as on 30th June, 1980. Their borrowings by way of debentures, which formed the main source of their funds, stood at ₹ 1,984 crore as on June 30,1981 as against ₹ 1,873 crore as on 30th June, 1980. Overdues (principal) stood at ₹ 243 crore, forming 52 per cent of demand as on 30th June, 1981 as against 57 per cent at the end of the previous year.

The number of Primary LDBs was 858 at the end of June, 1981. The membership of these banks stood at 6.6 million compared with 6.2 million in 1979-80 while working capital increased from ₹ 1,130 crore to ₹ 1,259 crore in 1980-81. Loans outstanding stood at ₹ 986 crore as at the end of June, 1981 as against ₹ 891 crore at the end of the previous year. Overdues (principal) increased from ₹ 122 crore to ₹ 130 crore at the end of 1980-81; the percentage of overdues to demand decreased from 52 to 45.[13]

The co-operative LDBs are engaged in providing long-term credit to the rural population. There are about 2,100 offices of the co-operative LDBs in the country, claiming a membership of about 90 lakh. Outstanding loans provided by these banks total over ₹ 4,000 crore. During 1982-83 alone, these banks disbursed loans totalling ₹ 422 crore. The Sixth Plan target of loan disbursement by these banks was ₹ 2,150 crore; the banks may not be able to hit the target by the end of March, 1985, when they are expected to have disbursed loans of about ₹ 2,118 crore (about 98 per cent of the target). The target for the Seventh Five Year Plan is to provide fresh loans of ₹ 3,574 crore.[14]

PROBLEMS OF LDBs

The LDBs are facing a number of problems:

(i) High overdues;

(ii) Uneven development;

(iii) No uniform management structure;

(iv) Inadequacy of funds;

(v) Delay in granting loans;

(vi) Defective loan lending operations;

(vii) High cost of credit;

(viii) Lack of supervision and inspection;

(ix) Presence of a number of non-viable units and

(x) Poor economic coverage of small farmers and other weaker sections.

MEASURES TO STRENGTHEN LDBs

The LDBs have to chalk out a number of measures to improve their performance. These include:

(i) Uniform structural pattern;

(ii) Availability of adequate field staff;

(iii) Proper supervision over the primary units;

(iv) Loaning policies should be production-oriented;

(v) Timely assistance from the state government in respect of provisions of staff to evaluate strategic schemes of land development;

(vi) Mobilisation of rural savings;

(vii) Removal of delay in the granting of loans;

(viii) Timely recovery of loans and

(ix) Proper co-ordination between short and medium-term credit and long-term credit.

The Committee on Co-operative Land Development Banks, constituted by the RBI in March, 1973, headed by K. Madhavan Das, has urged that the banks should be enabled to grant loans on the basis of a charge on the land and other assets of the borrower instead of on mortgage of land. On the structure of land development banking, the Committee felt that suitable measures should be taken to strengthen or improve the efficiency of both federal and unitary structures such as the setting up o regional or divisional offices of Central LDBs with adequate staff, introduction of suitable training programmes for the staff of primary LDBs or branches of central LDBs and satisfactory arrangements for co-ordination between primary LDBs or branches of central LDBs on the one hand, and other institutions and departments of state governments.

III. Farmers Service Societies

The National Commission on Agriculture has recommended the organisation of Farmers Service Societies (FSS), one for each block or any other viable unit of convenient size. The strength of FSS lies in the fact that they take into account a comprehensive view of the problems of the small farmers. As is well-known, the small and marginal farmers require not only credit but timely availability of inputs and ancillary services, along with technical advice and services such as storage, transportation, processing and marketing, preferably through a single contact point. These societies have been organised since 1973-74 to meet the above-mentioned requirements of poor farmers. The National Commission on Agriculture has recommended a programme of establishing 2,500 such societies over a period of six years, commencing from 1974 with a capacity to form new societies at the rate of 1,000 per year. However, by the end of June, 1979, there were only 1,200 FSSs in the country.

Objectives of FSS

The main objective of the FSS has been to help farmers, particularly small/marginal farmers, agricultural labourers and rural artisans by providing them integrated credit, i.e., credit linked with input supply and marketing. Societies provide short, medium and long-term credit for agriculture and allied activities mainly for productive purposes.

The FSS supply agricultural inputs to farmers and required raw materials, machinery, appliances etc. to cottage and small-scale industrial activities, and they provide marketing, godown and agricultural extension services to members. Besides credit facilities, these societies were expected to provide the full package of services needed by the farmers such as supply of agricultural inputs, technical guidance, storage facilities, marketing/processing of the agricultural produce and distribution of consumer goods etc.[15]

Though FSS serves all farmers, the control over the society would rest with a Board of which two-thirds of the elected members would represent weaker sections. Each FSS has to cover a block so that it can maintain an expert as also trained managerial and technical staff for undertaking the diverse activities.[16] Thus, the FSS is an instrument to change the rural power structure in favour of the poor.

The assumptions underlying the recommendations of the National Commission on Agriculture relating to the FSS were broadly as follows:

(i) That small and marginal farmers in particular required a specialised agency which could simultaneously provide all the services required by them along with proper guidance for using the services effectively;

(ii) Any effort to reform the existing primary societies was not going to solve the problems of small and marginal farmers and weaker sections;

(iii) The FSS with its co-operative form would help in mobilising local initiative and local control, keeping in view the priorities for the use of credit and other services and

(iv) The FSS would not be modified credit society, borrowing loans from commercial or co-operative banks but would develop into a powerful local nucleus, integrating its credit function with inputs supply and other services under the guidance of competent professional management.

The Lead Bank of the district would assume leadership in organising the FSS, provide them technical and financial support, evolve norms and standards, rules and procedures, in respect of financing, also overall guidance and supervision fulfilling the requirements of an integrated service. The promoting bank is expected to provide managerial services and guidance atleast in the initial stages till the beneficiaries acquired requisite knowledge and competence to run the society on their own.[17]

These societies are organised and financed by commercial banks, central co-operative banks and regional rural banks. The uniqueness of the FSS lies in the stress on integrating the credit function with the function of organising the availability of inputs and services. Further, FSS being co-operative institutions, are vested with effective summary powers which can be utilised, if necessary, for recovering dues from recalcitrant borrowers.[18]

In actual operation, the FSS have not shown proper interest in discharging their non-credit functions. Their tardy progress may be attributed to slow receptivity on the part of the state governments, non-availability of experienced staff, delay in achieving the break-even stage for individual societies, paucity of share capital, inadequate discretionary powers of managers of financing institutions, reluctance on the part of farmers to make use of the facilities and political interference.[19]

The FSS should consider immediately the need for improving efforts with regard to recovery of loans, and bringing down the level of overdues. Greater initiative and enterprise are required for the marketing of members' agricultural produce, rice, wheat, onion, vegetables etc. This would add to the income of the society and would make its financial base broad and balanced.[20]

Most FSSs predominantly concentrate only on credit disbursement and very little attention has been paid to non-credit services. Again, within credit disbursement, short-term loans occupied a predominant position, followed by medium-term loans. Long-term loans have been reportedly neglected. Moreover, the coverage of rural artisans and agricultural labourers seem to be very unsatisfactory. The non-credit services of these societies reveal that custom services and consumer goods supply were insignificant in the integrated services activities. Marketing of agricultural produce was completely neglected by most of the societies, as observed by field studies.[21]

There is need for developing FSS into a powerful local nucleus, integrating its credit function with inputs supply and other services under the guidance of the competent professional management. Most rural institutions are under-managed. If the FSS acquires professional management, it can serve the poor in a better way than any other financial institution. Strengthening FSS is the need of the hour as that would ensure implementation of relevant programmes for the rural sector and also ensure flow of benefits to the really deserving.[22]

REFERENCES

1. A.M. Khusro: 'The Co-operative Sector: Neglecting A Vital Component of Economy', *Indian Express,* May 14, 1992.

2. Balishter: 'Need for Revamping the Rural Co-operatives', *Yojana,* January 15, 1994.

3. M.B. Patil: 'Who Can Save Primary Agricultural Co-operative Societies?', *Southern Economist*, November 1, 1992, p. 21.

4. Satyabadi Misra: 'Agro Financing by Co-operatives: Retrospects and Prospects', *Khadigramodyog*, May 1984, pp. 323-324.

5. A.M. Khusro: *op. cit.*

6. Ratna Ganguli: 'Co-operatives: Stating the Case', *The Economic Times*, May 20, 1991.

7. Nripendra Misra: 'Co-operatives: Paradigm Shift Needed', *The Economic Times*, July 25, 1995.

8. Nilakantha Rath: 'Restructuring the Co-operatives', *The Economic Times*, September 13, 1994.

9. M.V. Srinivasa Gowda: 'Co-operatives in the New Economic Scenario — Agenda for Liberalisation', *Southern Economist*, September 15, 1994.

10. P. Satish: 'Commercialising Co-operatives', *The Economic Times*, June 24, 1995.

11. P.V. Prabhu: 'Rural Development', *IBA Bulletin*, January 1994, p. 113.

12. U.M. Shah: 'Co-operative Development — Progress and Trends', *Kurukshetra*, November 1995, p. 7.

13. *National Bank News Review*, September 1985, pp. 25-26.

14. Subhash Chandra Sarker: 'Long Term Rural Credit', *Commerce*, February 25, 1984, p. 323.

15. P. Ramaiah, N. Lingamurthy and G. Sudarshan: 'Andhra Farmers' Service Societies: Promise and Performance', *Yojana*, February 16-28, 1983.

16. For a discussion of FSS, see D.M. Nanjundappa (1976): 'Development with Social Justice', Oxford and IBH, New Delhi.

17. G.S. Kamat: 'FSS: The Promise and the Prospect', *Kurukshetra*, November 16, 1982.

18. V.R. Gundannavar: 'Farmers' Service Societies: Position and Prospects', *The State Bank of India Monthly Review*, May 1979, p. 140.

19. *Ibid.*, pp. 142-143.

20. G. S. Kamat L., *op. cit.*, p. 11.

21. P. Ramaiah, N. Lingamurthy and G. Sudarshan: *op. cit.*, p. 26.

22. I. Satya Sundaram: 'Strengthening Farmers' Service Societies', *Khadigramodyog*, March 1986, p. 309.

Chapter 36

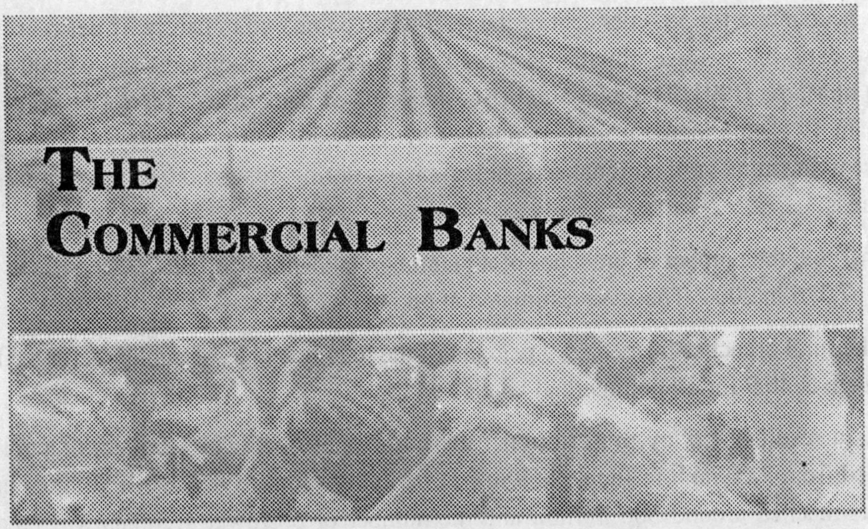

The Commercial Banks

The banking sector in India has undergone a sea-change during the past quarter century. It has emerged as one of the important agents of rural development. Gone are the days when commercial banks were only 'purveyors of credit', now they are *catalytic* agents in the nation's economic progress. It is for this reason that 14 major commercial banks were nationalised in July, 1969 and six more were nationalised in April, 1980. Efforts are also being made to see that at least 50 per cent of the institutional credit goes to the weaker sections. Separate sub-targets have been prepared for the weaker sections and further within this group for the landless labourers, artisans etc.

The social objectives would be achieved through — *(i)* rapid expansion of banking services through vigorous branch expansion programme specially in the unbanked and neglected areas and *(ii)* the provision of adequate liberal finances to the 'priority sector' which includes most neglected areas such as agriculture, small scale industries, professional and self-employed persons, education, transport operators etc.

Progress of Commercial Banks

The number of public sector banks increased from 22 in 1969 to 28 in 1980 and their share in deposits increased from 83.3 per cent to 90.9 per cent; in credit, from 83.8 per cent to 90.5 per cent; in offices, from 79.8 per cent to 87.9 per cent during the same period.

In 1992, there were about 100 major commercial banks with over 60,000 branches in the country. Together, they had more than 20 crore deposit accounts and over two crores of borrowal accounts. By the end of March, 1992, the total deposits of the banking sector were of the order of more than ₹ 1,30.000 crore while credit worth ₹ 96,000 crore had been advanced by India's commercial banks.

Between June 1969 and March 1991, the total number of commercial bank offices rose from 8,262 to as much as 60,190. The number of rural branches went from 1,833 to 35,187 during the same period, accounting for 58.4 per cent of the total when compared to hardly 22 per cent in 1969. In terms of these data, the average population served per bank office declined from 65,000 in 1969 to about 11,000 in March, 1991. The total number of nationalised bank offices increased from 7,015 in 1969 to 57,561 in 1994, the increase in their number being 50,561 during the 25 years' period. Of the total increase in the number of nationalised bank branches during this period, as much as 62 per cent were in rural areas.

In 1969, the number of branches of all commercial banks was 8,262. This rose to 65,907 in 2001, and to 67,376 in 2004. These are estimated at 68,500 in 2005.

The rural branches formed 49.9 per cent of the total branches of public sector banks in 2005. This percentage is 46.9 for all commercial banks.

As a result of policy prescriptions, the number of borrowal accounts of public sector banks increased from 2.60 lakh in June, 1969 to 331.01 lakh in June, 1989. By 1996, the number of deposit accounts reached around 500 million and the number of borrowal accounts was recorded to be 100 million.

Bank deposits which in 1969 constituted just 13 per cent of the GDP have increased to over 40 per cent of the GDP in 1993.

Total liabilities of all scheduled commercial banks rose from ₹ 6,168 crore at the end of December, 1969 to ₹ 95,483 crore at the end of December, 1983. Their deposits rose from ₹ 5,295 crore to ₹ 81,761 crore on December 20, 1985, that is, at the average compound annual growth rate of 18.7 per cent. On the other hand, total credit rose at an average annual growth rate of 18 per cent from ₹ 3,729 crore in December, 1969 to ₹ 52,423 crore on December 20, 1985. The number of bank offices which was only 8,262 on the eve of nationalisation of the 14 major banks in July, 1969 rose very rapidly to nearly 48,932 in February 1985. Of the increase of around 40,670 offices, 32,491 or four-fifth were in rural and semi-urban centres. All these are no small achievements.

The total bank credit of public sector banks increased from ₹ 3,017 crore to ₹ 3,16,427 crore in March 2001, to ₹ 3,41,291 crore in March 2002, to ₹ 3,94,064 crore in March 2003, and to ₹ 5,60,819 crore in March 2004.

Recent Trends

Indian bank's loan growth has slowed down from around 27 per cent in November 2008 to 15.8 percent in June 2009, recovering partially to 19.7 per cent in July 2009.

Total earnings of commercial banks have steadily increased from ₹ 1,72,116 crore in 2002-03, to ₹ 3,68, 884 crore in 2007-08, and total expenses increased from ₹ 1,39,454 crore kin 2002-03 to ₹ 2,85,212 crore in 2007-08. Profits increased from ₹ 11,175 crore in 2002-03 to ₹ 42,733 crore in 2007-08.

As against an increase of 22.3 percent in 2007-08 bank credit increased by 17.5 percent 2008-09. Non food credit during the same periods was 23 percent and 17.8 percent respectively. During 2009-10, on financial year basis, growth in bank credit extended by scheduled commercial banks (SCBs) stood at 8.4 percent (end March 2009 to January 15,2010) as compared to 11.9 percent during the corresponding period in 2008-09 (Economic Survey 2009-10. p.91).

Table: 1
Branch Expansion of Public Sector Banks and other commercial banks

Bank Group	*1969*	*2004*	*2009*	*Rural branches as on 30-06-09*
SBI and Associates	2462	13621	16294	5619
Nationalised Banks	4553	33359	39703	13425
Regional Rural Banks	-	14486	15100	11644
TOTAL OF PUBLIC SECTOR BANKS (A+B +C)	7015	61446	71196	30688
Other scheduled commercial banks	900	5807	8979	1126
Foreign Banks	130	218	295	4
ALL SCHEDULED BANKS	8045	67491	80470	31818
Non-Scheduled commercial Banks	217	32	44	11
All Commercial Banks	8262	68523	80514	31829

Source: Economic Survey 2009-10. P.A-58.

Table 2
Total Credits and Deposits of Scheduled Commercial Banks

Item	*June 1969*	*June 1979*	*June 1989*	*March 1999*	*March 2009*
Total deposits	4,646	28,671	1,47,854	7,22,203	38,34,140
(a) demand deposits	2,104	-	-	1,17,423	5,23,085
(b) time deposits	2,542	-	-	6,04,780	33,11,025
Total credit Credit/Deposit	3,599	19,116	89080	3,68,837	-
Ratio	77.5	65.87	60.32	51.1	72.39
Deposit per capita (in ₹)	-	417	1788	7264	33,225

Table: 3
Rural Credit by Scheduled Commercial Banks
(in ₹ crore)

Items	June 1969	June 1979	June 1989	March 1999	March 2006	March 2008
Rural Credit	55	1661	14553	53909	199423	323133
% share of rural credit	1.5	8.4	16.2	14.1	13.17	13.37
Total Credit	3609	19822	89361	382425	1513842	2417006

Table: 4
The Composition of NPAs of Scheduled Commercial Bank

Item	1998	2008	2009
Gross NPA (₹ core)	48,306	55,842	67,497
Gross NPA (percent)	14.78	2.39	2.42
Net NPA (₹ crore)	23,013	24,891	30,924

RECENT TRENDS

Advances to agriculture and other priority sectors by public sector banks increased from ₹ 441 crore in June 1969 to ₹ 7,20,083 crore in March 2009 (provisional). Advances to agriculture during this period increased from ₹ 162 crore to ₹ 2,98,211 crore (provisional).

Priority sector advances as percentages of total advances was 14.6 in June 1969. It increased to 44.8 by March 2008, but fell to 42.5 in March 2009 (provisional) (Economic Survey 2009-10. P.A- 59).

Table: 5
Advances to Agriculture and other priority Sectors by Public Sector Banks
(in ₹ Crore)

		June 1969	March 2009(P)
1.	Agriculture	162	2,98,211
	direct finance [a]	40	2,15,642
	indirect finance [a]	122	82,569
2.	Small scale Industries [b]	257	NA
3.	Micro and small enterprises	-	1,91,307
4.	Setting up of industrial estate	-	-
5.	Small road and water transport operators	5	-
6.	Retail Trade	19[d]	43,061
7.	Small business	-	-
8.	Professional and self employed persons	-	-
9.	Micro credit	-	3,943
10.	Education	1	26,913
11.	Consumption	-	-

12.	State sponsored organisation for ST/ST for purchase and supply of inputs and marketing of outputs	-	58
13.	State sponsored corporations/organisations for on-lending to other priority sector	-	-
14.	Housing loans	-	1,56,590
15.	Funds provided to RRBs	-	
16.	Advances to self-help groups	-	
17.	Advances to software industries	-	
18.	Advances to food & agro processing sector	-	
19.	Investment in venture capital	-	
20	Total priority sector advances[(e)]	441	7,20,083

P – Provisional

(a) excludes advances to plantations other than development finance.

(b) no. of units

(e) Total priority sector advances is the total of items 1 to 12 and 14 to 17 and half of item 13

Return on assets is an indication of the efficiency with which banks deploy their assets. During 2007-08, the net profits to assets ratio of scheduled commercial banks improved moderately to 1.0 per cent from 0.9 percent to 2006-07. Though net profits as percentage of total assets improved across all bank groups, the improvement was more pronounced in the case of old private sector banks. Foreign banks continued to show the highest returns on assets.

The flow of commercial banks credit to agriculture increased form ₹ 33,587 crore in 2001-02 to ₹ 81,481 crore in 2004-05, to ₹ 1,25,859 crore in 2005-06.

The total amount of priority sector advances to SSI increased from ₹ 31,542 crore in 1997 to ₹ 49,743 crore in 2002, to ₹ 67,800 crore in 2005 and to ₹ 104,703 crore in 2007. Total advances to micro and small enterprises by public sector banks stood at ₹ 1,51,137 crore and by private sector banks at ₹ 46,912 crore in March 2008.

PRIORITY SECTOR LENDING

The need for the rural orientation of commercial banks, with stress on neglected sectors and sections, was first highlighted by a Report of the National Credit Council.[1] The report pointed out that commercial banks met large proportion of the credit requirements of the large scale industry, wholesale trade and commerce whereas important activities like agriculture were left in the lurch. For instance, in 1967, over four-fifths of the advances of commercial banks went to the industry and commerce with only about two per cent of bank credit for agriculture (mostly to large plantations) and less than two per cent of the advances for retail trade.

In June 1969, total priority sector advances accounts of public sector banks numbered 260. These increased to 30,080 by March 2004.

The amount outstanding under priority sector for public sector banks was ₹ 441 crore in June 1969. This increased to ₹ 127478 crore in March 2001, and to ₹ 244456 crore in March 2004.

In 1969, priority sector advances formed just 14.6 per cent of total advances of public sector banks. This rose to 40.3 per cent in March 2001 and to 43.6 per cent in March 2004.

Banks were required to ensure that minimum of 33 1/3 per cent of total advances was lent to priority sectors by the end of March 1980 and this target was raised to touch 40 per cent at the end of March 1985. Within this overall target of 40 per cent, banks were advised to achieve a target of 15 per cent of the total bank credit in respect of direct finance to agriculture and 10 per cent in respect of advances to weaker sections by the end of March, 1985. Public sector banks exceeded the overall target and attained a ratio of 41.3 per cent and made good progress in achieving the sub-targets by achieving 14.2 per cent and 9.4 per cent as against 15 per cent and 10 per cent prescribed for direct finance to agriculture and advances to the weaker sections respectively.

In 1981, the Ghosh Working Group re-examined the components of the priority sector. It felt that the scope of 'weaker sections' needs to be enhanced to include: *(i)* Small and marginal farmers, landless labourers, tenant farmers and share croppers; *(ii)* Artisans, village and cottage industry; *(iii)* IRDP beneficiaries; *(iv)* Scheduled castes and scheduled tribes and Differential Interest Rate scheme (DIR) beneficiaries.

Earlier, the weaker sections included only small and marginal farmers, landless labourers, persons in allied activities with borrowal limits up to ₹ 10,000 and SSI units with borrowal limits upto ₹ 25,000.

The Group fixed a composite target for weaker sections, instead of separate targets for various sub-sectors. Within retail trade, the ceiling on the turnover was removed and all retail traders in fertilisers, mineral oils and fair price shops were included. A ceiling of ₹ 1 lakh was placed on credit to professional and self-employed persons. The following targets have been stipulated as per the recommendations of the Ghosh Committee:

(i) 40 per cent of the total advances should be for priority sectors;

(ii) 16 per cent in the total advances should be for direct agricultural advances;

(iii) One per cent of the previous year's advances should be under the Differential Interest Rate (DIR) scheme;

(iv) 40 per cent of the DIR advances should be lent to scheduled castes and scheduled tribes; and

(v) Two-thirds of the DIR advances or 25 per cent of the priority sector advances should be lent to the weaker sections

In order to ensure flow of adequate credit to the priority sectors, the Government has stipulated that 40 per cent of advances of commercial banks should be earmarked for the priority sector. From November 1978, the private sector banks were also expected to achieve the various targets and sub-targets for priority sector advances in the same way as public sector banks.

Within the priority sectors, the following sub-targets have been in force:

(i) Direct finance to agriculture — to reach 18 per cent by March 1990. This has been raised from 16 per cent in March 1987 and 17 per cent in March 1989 and

(ii) Advances to weaker sections to form 25 per cent of the priority sector advances or 10 per cent of total bank credit. The 'weaker sections' have been defined to conform to the Ghosh Committee recommendations.

The amount of the priority sector advances increased significantly from ₹ 441 crore to ₹ 34,874 crore during the period 1969 to 1989. Its share in total advances also spurted from 14.6 per cent to 44.6 per cent, thus exceeding the target of 40 per cent.

However, total priority sector advances stood at ₹ 46,652.77 crore — 36.64 per cent of the total credit of the banks. Public sector banks achieved a priority sector lending level of 36.54 per cent during 1994-95. Within the priority sector, direct agricultural advances of public sector banks formed 16.5 per cent of total bank credit at the end of June 1989, advances to small scale industries constituted 16.9 per cent. Advances to weaker sections within the priority sector at ₹ 8,641 crore at the end of June 1989 formed 11.1 per cent of the total outstandings as against the prescribed target of 10 per cent.

Total public sector bank credit to agriculture — direct and indirect — increased from ₹ 165 crore in June 1969 to ₹ 14,369 crore in June 1989. Commercial bank credit emerged as the major source of institutional credit for agriculture and at the end of June 1987, accounted for 58.2 per cent of the outstanding agricultural credit. The share of bank credit in the outstanding borrowings of rural households rose from 1.1 per cent in 1951-52 to 28.0 per cent in 1981-82.

In 1989, agriculture and allied activities constituted the largest portion of priority sector advances (41.2 per cent) followed by small scale industries (37.9 per cent). Taken together, they formed 79.1 per cent of priority sector advances or 35.3 per cent of net bank credit. Thus, within the priority sector, the other categories accounted for only 20.9 per cent of priority sector advances.

The priority advances as a percentage of total advances are reportedly on the decline. For instance, in 1991-92, the priority sector target fell by one per cent and in 1992-93 by more than 3 per cent.

The priority sector advances are in difficulty because of poor absorptive capacity. The viable schemes are difficult to come by Banks are not in a position to achieve artificial targets.

According to the RBI Report on Currency and Finance, 1993-94, priority sector lending as a percentage of gross bank credit has tended to lag behind the 40 per cent target. From 36.1 per cent in 1991-92, it came down to 33.8 per cent in 1992-93 which in 1993-94 improved to 34.4 per cent. The erosion seems to have occurred mainly in agricultural lending which came down from 14.4 per cent in 1991-92 to 13.5 per cent in 1992-93.

In March 2000, the total priority sector advances by public sector banks (PBS) accounted for 43.6 per cent of their net bank credit.

Within the priority sector, the flow of credit to agriculture from PBS accounted for 15.8 per cent in 2000.

Advances from PSBs to SSI accounted for 15.6 per cent of net bank credit in March 2000.

A system of mandatory allocation of credit to the relatively backward sectors of the economy was adopted. This envisaged the stipulation of targets and sub-targets for financing specific sectors — which were accorded a 'priority' status.

Targets have also been laid down for attaining credit-deposit ratio at rural and semi-urban branches, financing under the DIR scheme, IRDP, Self-Employment to Educated Unemployed Youth (SEEUY), Self-Employment Programme for Urban Poor (SEPUP), 20-point programme etc. Financing of women and minority communities is also being monitored.

In order to promote growth in the backward rural areas, only advances to professional and self-employed persons in notified backward regions and rural and semi-urban areas should be treated as priority sector advances and given concessional credit.[2]

The RBI is mulling over introducing tradable certificates to help banks to meet the mandatory priority sector lending target. It is proposed to constitute a working group to examine the issues involved in the introduction of priority sector lending certificates (PSLCs) and make suitable recommendations. These certificates could be traded in the open market, and banks having shortfall in meeting the priority sector lending targets could buy such certifications and thus meet the priority sector lending norms

Commercial Banks: Some Problems

As the commercial banks are actively involved in social banking, some operational problems do eventually arise. These include:

(i) Problems of reporting and control due to vast expansion of branches;

(ii) Adverse effect in yield on advances due to the high service cost of small accounts;

(iii) Increasing establishment and operational costs; and

(iv) Problems of recycling of funds.

These factors have placed pressure on the profitability of banks.

The viability of rural banking had been under great strain for several reasons. Priority sector lending carries low interest rates. A sizeable part of the lending is with concessional rates of interest. Several schemes have been sponsored by the state for the benefit of the weaker sections. Banks have been closely associated with these schemes. Rural lending by and large has become a losing proposition, with the negative margins for the credit institutions.

Among the internal causes are the absence of proper credit delivery mechanism, unwillingness of personnel to work in the rural branches, inadequate field work, deficiencies in lending schemes, non-viability of some of the schemes, faulty repayment schedules and inadequate appraisal and follow-up of loans.

Important among the external factors are target-oriented lending, undue political and bureaucratic pressure to reach targets, frequent disturbances in the recovery climate on account of announcement about loan waivers by political parties and wilful default by village influentials.[3]

The changing role of the commercial banks has created a number of problems. It has been rightly observed[4] that —

> With the multiple institutional agencies operating in the field of rural credit — co-operatives, RRBs and commercial banks — a number of problems arose, such as uncoordinated credit disbursal, diversion to unproductive purposes, inability of the credit agencies to formulate agricultural programmes on the basis of an area approach, overlapping and duplication of banking facilities, lagging recovery and numerous problems arising out of different systems, procedures, security norms, service charges, interest rates etc.

One has to admit that commercial banks are facing a number of difficulties in financing the agricultural sector for various reasons. First, the credit requirements of the agricultural sector have been rapidly increasing but commercial banks do not have refinancing facilities to meet these requirements. Second, credit absorption capacity is low due to the presence of a large number of uneconomic holdings. Third is the poor performance in respect of repayment of loans. The recovery performance of commercial banks has been unsatisfactory and was only 50.2 per cent in the case of public sector banks in June end, 1978. Fourth, commercial banks lack close contact with the borrowers. Fifth, absence of guarantee facilities has been reported in the case of rural advances to small scale industrialists. Lastly, the absence of proper securities for the farmers and the heavy risk involved in farming has been reported.

With regard to direct agricultural finance, there is uneven distribution of credit among farmers with different sizes of land holdings, and the disparity is more marked in the case of term loans. Over two-thirds of the term loans amount outstanding is accounted for by farmers with holdings over five acres.

While the banks' performance and progress of commercial banks are commendable, one also finds a few regional imbalances in their progress. It has been noticed that the credit of commercial banks has tended to flow largely to the very areas where co-operative credit structure was strong enough, while the areas of low credit availability continue to suffer from paucity of funds.

The Credit Deposit (CD) ratio of metro-centres is 77 per cent, urban centres with 51.6 per cent, rural 49.1 per cent and semi-urban centre has a low CD ratio or 38.6 per cent. In the process, public sector banks draw resources from small centres and deploy in large centres.

It has been pointed out that in 97 out of the 409 districts, the rural credit deposit ratio was 40 per cent or less. These districts, with total deposits of ₹ 2,582 crore, accounted for a third of all rural deposits. These 97 districts yielded surplus funds to the rest of the country. In the next higher ratio category are 43 districts with deposits of ₹ 981 crore. These had a CD ratio of 10 to 50 per cent. These districts too were generators of surplus funds. In the remaining 269 districts, the CD ratio in June 1983 exceeded 50 per cent, especially in 218 districts where the ratio was 60 per cent and above. The low average credit deposit ratio in the semi-urban centres suggests an outflow of funds from these centres to the cities and the metropolitan centres. Perhaps, there is a shortage of bankable projects in the semi-urban centres.[5]

The bias of commercial banks lending credit in favour of large farmers is particularly noticeable in Gujarat, Maharashtra, Punjab and Madhya Pradesh. Though commercial banks' agricultural credit has been additive, has failed to fill the geographical gap in the availability of credit not covered by co-operatives. The lack of interest on the part of commercial banks in the identification of right customers has led to the fulfilment of specified targets but failed in the attainment of genuine developmental goals.[6]

According to one study, the 46 Indian scheduled commercial banks together incurred a net loss of ₹ 3,316 crore in 1992-93, as against a profit of ₹ 875 crore in the previous year.

The huge loss incurred by 20 nationalised banks amounting to ₹ 36.48 crore in 1992-93 and ₹ 6,889 crore in 1993-94 could not be wiped out by the meagre profits of the State Banks of India and its associated banks, thus amounting to ₹ 280 crore and ₹ 357 crore respectively in these two years.

Priority sector lending is also facing many problems. For example, the recovery under IRDP has been below 30 per cent. According to evaluation studies, the main reasons for low recovery performance of banks are incorrect identification of beneficiaries and activities, inadequate availability of proper infrastructure and the lack of adequate marketing facilities.

Over ₹ 37,000 crore of assets of the banking system are non-performing. This means that 24 per cent of the assets do not yield income and repayment of the principal is suspect to varying degrees. Also, more than 73 per cent of these non-performing assets comprise loans in excess of ₹ 10 lakh, indicating that defaulters are mainly medium and large industries.[7]

Rapid expansion of the branches of banks had led to numerous problems like deterioration in customer service, strain on bank managements, dilution of control and lowering of motivation through reduced contact of the higher management with branches, delays in communication, decision-making and disposal of business, decline in profitability and inefficiency.[8] It is not necessary that banks should endeavour to maximise their net profits, and not that the net profits should grow from year to year. A steady profit trend may be an adequate and positive reflection on the health of the system.[9]

The old habit of monitoring performance merely by reference to quantitative targets of lending must yield place to the performance criteria which takes into account quality of lending as well. Within each bank or branch, the staff performance needs to be judged on comparable criteria, i.e., the innovative ability not merely in deposit mobilisation but also in improving the quality of loans, the latter requires an in-depth contact with the clientele and sustained work specially in backward regions to understand their needs and problems. The system of rewards and punishments does not always encourage such work.[10]

CO-ORDINATION BETWEEN CO-OPERATIVES AND COMMERCIAL BANKS

In order to serve the rural farmers better, there must be co-ordination between the co-operatives and commercial banks.[11] Some members of co-operatives may be eligible for loans, but they are denied co-operative credits because the resources of the co-operatives are meagre or the members may need medium or long-term loans which the co-operatives are not in a position to provide. Such members can be assisted by commercial banks. Second, the co-operatives also suffer from poor management. The commercial banks therefore should offer them technical advice on short-term financing. Third, since the co-operatives are in touch with local conditions, they can help commercial banks in identifying eligible borrowers or in recovering loans.

There has been no perceptible progress in the scheme for functional co-ordination between the PACS and the LDBs. The need for effective co-ordination between the short-term and long-term co-operative credit structure had been emphasised by various expert committees and the RBI, the latest of which was the committee to Review Arrangements for the Institutional Credit for Agriculture and Rural Development (CRAFICARD), 1981.

The Hazari Committee had even recommended the integration of these structures so that the credit needs of the farmer could be met at a single point. But CRAFICARD had recommended that a greater degree of functional co-ordination between PACS and LDBs at the grassroots level could ensure the same benefits as integration.

Following CRAFICARD's recommendations, the agricultural credit board of the RBI had proposed in 1977 that PACS might act as agents of the LDBs in the disbursement of long-term credit so that farmers could get credit and requirements of inputs at one contact point. In 1980, the PACS were probably entrusted with the responsibility to act as agents of LDBs in the disbursement of long-term credit. It was also suggested that the applications for term credit prescribed by the LDBs should also provide an indication of the sources from which the borrower would raise resources to meet the credit requirements for production expenses. The LDBs also were expected to send a list of their requirements for loans to beat the production expenses. The LDBs also were expected to send a list of their loanees to PACS so that the latter could be enrolled as members, if they were not already members.

Such functional co-ordination, it was felt, would not only give the convenience of a single contact point for borrowers but could also be mutual advantage to both credit agencies in ensuring better supervision and close monitoring of credit.[12]

Joint financing of individual projects by co-operatives and commercial banks should be innovated. The commercial banks should support the co-operatives:

(i) By subscribing to the debentures of co-operatives and

(ii) By rediscounting the bills of LDBs.[13]

In extending this linkage, banks should give preference to areas where:

(i) They have already done Some agricultural financing (i.e., direct) and gained experience in the field and

(ii) Environment and market conditions encourage the adoption of new (i.e., better) technology.

Thus, we have to study the option and potential of combining the resource mobilisation aspect of the commercial banks with the credit expansion function of the co-operatives.

MEASURES TO STRENGTHEN COMMERCIAL BANKS

The Government and the RBI have taken a number of steps time and again for strengthening the earnings of the banking system. Some of the steps taken are:

(i) Increase in rate of interest on food credit;

(ii) Increase in the coupon rates on central government securities;

(iii) Increase in the rate of interest on eligible Cash Reserve Ratio (CRR);

(iv) Rationalisation of service charges;

(v) Consolidation of banking operations;

(vi) Effective and timely monitoring of the banking operations and

(vii) Introduction of Action Plans and their effective monitoring by the RBI.

The overdues problem has also assumed ominous dimensions. It has to be tackled at the earliest. It is suggested that for re-establishing the ethics of repayment, some sort of group guarantee may also be adopted in suitable areas.[14]

There is need for redefining the economic feasibility of the priority sector. It is realised that not all priority sector advances go to the disadvantaged groups. This aspect has already specifically been examined by two committees in the past.

For instance, the Krishnaswamy Working Group suggested that all SSI units with limits upto and inclusive of ₹ 25,000 should be included under the weaker sections and advances to them should constitute 12.5 per cent of the total advances to the small scale industries.

The committees also suggested that direct advances to the weaker sections should reach a level of at least 50 per cent of the total direct lending to agriculture, including allied activities by 1983.

The Narasimham Committee Report on the Financial System (1991) observed that the priority sector should be redefined to comprise the small and marginal farmers, the tiny sector of the industry, small business and transport operators, village and cottage industries, rural artisans and other weaker sections in the rural sector.

The credit target for this redefined priority sector should henceforth be fixed at 10 per cent of the aggregate credit which would be broadly in line with the credit flows to these sectors at present. The Committee felt that a review may be undertaken at the end of three years to see if directed credit programmes need to be continued.

The concessional credit should only go to the weaker sections within the priority sector; others should be charged commercial rates of interest. The Chakravarty Committee[15] had observed that —

In the interest of promoting effective use of credit on the one hand, as also operational efficiency of lending agencies on the other, it would appear that in the present structure of interest rates, there is considerable scope for eliminating concessional interest rates or reducing the extent of concessionality apart from reducing the number of categories for which different concessional rates are specified.

The Khusro Committee[16] has also pointed out that —

While in the context of the present day socio-economic milieu, a degree of concessionality needs to be retained in favour of the very weak sections of the community, there is hardly any justification for continuing such concessionality in the case of other borrowers.

Given the complex nature of the rural credit system, it would be better if voluntary agencies, which are in touch with ground realities, are also involved in the rural credit system with a view to reducing the transaction costs and ensuring prompt repayment.[17]

Thus, the commercial banks have the only options to make concerted efforts to meet the new challenges. It is reasonable to assume that they can carry out the task successfully if they are allowed reasonable functional autonomy.

REFERENCES

1. National Credit Council: 'Organisational Framework for the Implementation of Social Objective', Mumbai, October, 1969.
2. Brinda Jagirdar: 'Need for Redefining Priority Sector', *SBI Monthly Review,* May 1991, p. 254.
3. B.L. Chadha: 'Toning Up the Rural Credit System to Improve Viability', *Financial Express,* April 23, 1995.
4. Satyabadi Misra: 'Agro Financing by Co-operatives: Retrospects and Prospects', *Khadigramodyog,* May 1984, pp. 323-324.
5. *The Economic Times* (editorial), January 15, 1985.
6. Arya Kumar: "The Role of Credit Planning in the Attainment of Development Planning in India', *Indian Economic Association, Annual Conference,* Pune, December, 1982.
7. P.V. Maiya: 'Changing Profile of Banking', *The Hindu Survey of Indian Industry 1995,* p. 431.
8. K. Ramanujam: 'Functioning of Public Sector Banks: Mis-carriage of an Enquiry', *Economic and Political Weekly,* November 24, 1979, p. M-99.
9. L.G. Kulkarni: 'Developmental Responsibility and Profitability of Banks': *Economic and Political Weekly,* August 25, 1979, p. M-99.
10. *The Economic Times* (editorial), December 12, 1985.
11. K. Madhava Das: 'Primary Co-operative Credit Societies', *The Economic Times,* February 14, 1981.
12. *The Economic Times,* June 7, 1983.
13. Agricultural Finance Corporation, Mumbai, *Co-ordination Between the Commercial Banks and Co-operative Banking Sectors,* pp. 15-17.
14. N.P. Kurup: 'Profitable and Socially Responsible Banking', *Economic and Political Weekly,* August 20, 1994, p. 2197.
15. Reserve Bank of India, Mumbai, 1985, Report of the Committee to Review the Working of the Monetary System.
16. Reserve Bank of India, 1989-90. Agricultural Credit Review Committee. A Review of the Agricultural Credit System in India.
17. N.A. Majumdar: 'Refocusing on Rural Credit: The Macro Dimensions', *Economic and Political Weekly,* October 15, p. 2733.

Chapter

37 The Differential Interest Rate Scheme

The Differential Interest Rate (DIR) Scheme was introduced in December, 1972, following the recommendations of a committee set up in September, 1970 under the chairmanship of Dr. R.K. Hazari. The scheme was meant to ensure and provide access to institutional credit for certain sections of the poor. The eligible obtain loans at a uniform concessional interest rate of four per cent.

The DIR scheme covers people with tiny holdings, self-employed institutions for handicapped persons, orphanages, women's homes etc. People engaged in tailoring, garment making, running wayside tea stalls, mending shoes (cobblers), basket making, purchase of milch animals, poultry farming etc., are eligible for assistance under the DIR scheme. No margin money is insisted upon under the scheme.

The DIR beneficiary would also be eligible for ₹ 1,500 as working capital and ₹ 5,000 as term loan. For the small scale industry and artisans in the decentralised sector, a loan of upto ₹ 6,500 is given under the scheme as composite loan, without making any distinction between working capital and the term loan. Of course, the poverty line for a family was currently placed at ₹ 11,000 per annum. Repayment period was for five years (including two years for the repayment of the principal amount) in the case of term loans for acquiring fixed assets.

Since 1981, the private sector banks have also been associated with the Scheme.

At the time of starting of the scheme in 1972, it was stipulated that the DIR advances should form 0.5 per cent of the total advances as at the end of the previous year. The percentage was raised to 1.0 in November, 1978.

Banks were also required to grant atleast 40 per cent of the DIR advances to borrowers belonging to SC/ST categories. The norms governing DIR loans have been revised from time to time. According to the latest norms, the beneficiaries under the DIR scheme are:

(i) Those borrowers whose family incomes do not exceed ₹ 6,400 in rural areas or ₹ 7,200 in urban and metropolitan areas.

(ii) The size of their land holdings should not exceed 0.5 hectares in the case of irrigated land and 1.25 hectares in the case of unirrigated land (borrowers belonging to SC/ST categories are exempted from this condition).

(iii) The borrower should not employ any paid worker on a regular basis. However, he can use his family labour. He should not resort to double sources of finance at a time.

(iv) In respect of housing loans upto ₹ 5,000 to SC/ST borrowers, the bank should bear the premium and, in the case of others, it can be passed on to the borrowers, subject to the maximum ceiling of 18 per cent including interest.

Banks have also been asked at that time to set aside about ₹ 400 million for lending at four per cent interest rate to Harijans for setting up of small industrial units and for engaging themselves in other gainful vocations. The DIR scheme now covers the entire country.

Besides the lower rate of interest, there are other relaxations associated with the DIR scheme. These include: *(i)* Waiving of margin requirements; *(ii)* No insistence on surety or security; *(iii)* Meeting of the cost of insurance (if any) by the banks; *(iv)* Extension of repayment period up to five years; *(v)* No insistence on production of documentary evidence etc.

The DIR scheme made rapid progress ever since its inception. The number of borrowed accounts increased from 0.26 lakh in December, 1972 to 48.14 lakh in December, 1987. The outstanding loan amount also increased from ₹ 87 crore to ₹ 597.60 crore during this period. The increase in the average amount has been reported to be from ₹ 334 to ₹ 1,436.

The DIR advances as percentage of total advances of the previous year have increased from 0.02 in 1972 to 1.10 in 1987, but fell to 1.0 per cent in 1988, and there was a further fall to 0.9 per cent by March, 1989. Also regarding lending to SC/ST categories, it has always exceeded the prescribed target of 40 per cent.

RECENT TRENDS

In the union budget 2007- 08 , the maximum amount that could be lent for housing is raised from ₹ 5000 to ₹ 15,000. For other purposes, the eligible amount was raised from ₹ 6,500 to ₹ 15,000.

The advances outstanding stood at ₹ 607.24 crore in 1990. These are fluctuating. They stood at ₹ 683.03 crore in 1995, at ₹ 422 crore in 2000, and at ₹ 634.46 crore in 2007.

After the introduction of financial reforms, the number of accounts came down sharply from 34.49 lakhs in 1991 to 19.46 lakhs in 1995, to 9.05 lakhs in 1998 to 3.70 lakhs in 2003, and to 2.60 lakhs in 2007.

Table:1
Progress of DIR Scheme

Year	*No of accounts (in lakhs)*	*Advances outstanding (₹ crore)*	*Share in total (%)*
1990	37.35	607.24	0.74
1991	34.49	618.82	0.67
1992	.31.94	716.25	0.67
1993	29.05	705.33	0.62
1994	24.25	694.18	0.51
1995	19.46	683.03	0.49
1996	15.52	677.66	0.41
1997	14.29	654.76	0.34
1998	9.05	543.65	0.28
1999	7.29	485.00	0.21
2000	5.89	422.00	0.13
2001	5.14	358.00	0.10
2002	NA	NA	NA
2003	3.70	300.00	0.08
2004	3.68	315.00	0.07
2005	3.33	385.27	0.07
2006	3.88	490.22	0.07
2007	2.60	634.46	0.06

DIR Scheme: Some Problems

The success of massive development programmes, which are implemented at the grassroots level throughout the country depends on: *(i)* How effectively these are administered by the implementing agencies at various levels and *(ii)* The extent of which the modus operandi of the schemes is understood and accepted by the target groups.

One serious problem facing the DIR scheme is the mounting overdues. The low rate of interest on loans makes the clients irresponsible in the use of credit and in its repayment. The majority of the DIR advances lacked follow-up on account of two main reasons:

(i) Large numbers getting out of reach for the limited staff; and

(ii) The lethargic attitude of the staff.

The worsening overdues position is due to the fact that banks not been able to undertake post disbursement supervision and study the problems of borrowers in taking up productive employments and getting the required inputs and services in time. In many cases, the beneficiaries are identified even from defaulters' families based on fictitious record of separation and the project recommended does not find favour with the beneficiaries.[1]

Banks have not paid sufficient attention to disbursement of adequate amount of credit required by the borrower and prescribing the repayment period as warranted by the activity and on the basis of repaying capacity of the borrowers. Consequently, the scheme suffered in respect of economic upliftment of the borrower and the subsequent recovery of loans. According to some case studies, differences in repayment rates between two groups of borrowers showed that economic circumstances could be very important. However, there may not be a clear pattern of overdues decreasing as loan size increased. Most bank branches lacked trained and professional personnel to successfully implement the scheme.[2]

There are institutional obstacles too. The procedure followed by banks for advancing loans is wrong and the attitude of doctors, banks and insurance companies is unhealthy in most cases. The borrowers do not get loans directly from banks; payments are made to persons from whom the animals are purchased. The beneficiaries could not exercise their choice in the selection of animals. All these are responsible for wiping out the benefits of subsidy and interest rate concessions.[3]

The DIR scheme could not make much progress with barely 20 per cent recovery performance. It has not increased the production capacity of the target population. One reason for the irregular payment and default is that the location of the branch office and its working hours proved inconvenient to the loanee. Going to the bank office involved travel expenses, besides loss of the day's earnings.[4]

In most of the banks which had disbursed loans under the DIR scheme, the recovery had hardly touched the 40 per cent mark. This was despite the subsidy component of 33.33 per cent given by the government in the loans. In certain banks, the percentage had not even crossed the 30 per cent mark, indicating that either the government had not paid the subsidy on time or had raised queries to the loans.[5]

The bank officials attribute various reasons to the poor recovery position. They state that an impression had been created amongst the beneficiaries that the loans were grants and so there was no need to repay them. In some other cases, wilful defaults and diversions of funds for consumption needs had contributed to poor recovery.

The factors responsible for poor recovery are: *(i)* inadequate income from/or the failure of the activities financed and *(ii)* unproductive use of loans granted. The inadequate staff and paucity of vehicles also restricted the recovery efforts at the branch level. The external factors included drought and rumour hinting at a waiver of the loans.

There has been considerable delay in the release of loans as well as subsidy. The delay has also been due to the mischief played by the middlemen. Other factors contributing to the delay are: *(i)* non-availability of the borrowers in time for the pre-sanction survey, *(ii)* incomplete application forms, and *(iii)* inadequacy of staff at the branch level to cope with the inflow of applications for small loans.

There are other problems too. Most beneficiaries are ignorant of the loan amount and other details of the scheme. There have been irregularities in the identification of beneficiaries. The rural branches lacked requisite technical expertise to guide the DIR borrowers. The co-operative banks also mere outside the purview of the DIR scheme.

The SBI study on the DIR scheme has announced that "there is no systematic planning by branches for lending under the scheme by properly identifying the potential and evolving appropriate strategies for exploiting it in a phased and optimal manner."[6] The state governments should organise specialised agencies to help the banks in the identification of eligible borrowers so that undesirable cases are weeded out and only the genuine ones considered to assist eligible borrowers.[7]

The interest rate under the scheme is only four per cent, which is far below the bank rate. The criteria evolved to identify beneficiaries under the scheme were so designed that almost all people below the poverty line be made eligible for assistance under the scheme. This has created innumerable problems at the branch level particularly in the light of the limited funds available (one per cent of the previous year's outstanding credit).

The working of the DIR scheme has been hampered by some personal and institutional factors. Most of the borrowers do not know the rate of interest being charged from them and the amount of subsidies they are getting. They fail to make use of banking, medical and insurance facilities available to them. Very few take loans to the maximum authorised limit. The loanees generally do not make special efforts in search of better and potential markets for their products like wool, milk and small animals.[8]

There have been institutional obstacles too. The procedure followed by banks for advancing loans is wrong and the attitude of doctors, banks and insurance companies is reported to be unhealthy in most cases. The borrowers failed to benefit from loans given directly by banks. Payments were made to persons from whom the animals were purchased. The beneficiaries also were restricted to exercise their choice in the selection of animals. All these turned out to be responsible for wiping out the benefits of subsidy and interest rate concessions.

Even well conceived schemes have been reported as running into rough weather in view of the deficiencies at their implementation stage. It is often pointed out that the credit planning in the country seemed to evade the issue of mass poverty.

MEASURES TO STRENGTHEN DIR SCHEME

There has recently been a number of suggestions to modify the DIR scheme to make it meaningful. Some of the suggestions call for amendments in the DIR scheme by dividing it into two schemes: DIR Scheme I and DIR Scheme II. Under DIR Scheme I, the credit limit was proposed to reduce from ₹ 3,000 to ₹ 2,000 and the rate of interest be kept unchanged at four per cent per annum. Under DIR Scheme II, the credit limit be kept at higher level at about ₹ 6,000 and the rate of interest be pegged according to the bank rate and may be kept at 8 per cent per annum. The existing criteria for loan eligibility under the DIR Scheme may also be retained as such for the DIR scheme I, whereas the criteria, viz., the income limit, land holding etc. be revised appropriately in the case of DIR scheme II. The present target of total DIR scheme advances should also be divided equally for both the schemes. A ceiling should be imposed on the total number of advances that an individual can take under both the DIR schemes.[9]

There is need for strengthening the District Rural Development Agencies (DRDAs) and the Block Development Offices by providing suitably trained and qualified personnel so that problems relating to identifying the beneficiaries and making them financially strong could be successfully achieved. At the grassroots level, preferably for a group of 20 to 30 villages, there existed the need for creating non-exploitative institutional infrastructure which could provide credit and convert credit into supplies and services.[10]

The DIR beneficiaries should also be educated about the loan content and its utilisation. In respect of the rural artisans, the bank staff should undertake market survey and help artisans overcome the marketing problem.

The loan amount should be increased keeping in view the prices of inputs. As the operating expenses for the beneficiaries are considerable, these should be taken into account while fixing the loan amount.

The approach to lending should be on consortium basis, i.e., banks, government and other bodies should be actively involved in the implementation of the DIR scheme.

As far as possible, the lending institutions should resort to financing particular trade and area etc., so as to acquire efficiency for the successful implementation of the schemes. This would facilitate the reduction in cost and timely recovery.

The lending institutions may appoint special field workers to bring about the necessary rapport between the beneficiaries and the institutions. Measures should be taken to check the tendency to misutilise concessional finance either by the beneficiaries or by the middlemen.

In the absence of adequate income generation, the beneficiaries are left with little reinvestible surplus. Hence, the DIR scheme is of little help to such beneficiaries. Availability of adequate and proper infrastructure and granting of adequate loan amount, therefore, need to be ensured for making the scheme a success.

It is not the lower rate of interest that matters much to the weaker sections. What is urgently required is timeliness and adequacy of credit and simplified procedures of lending. According to a study of the DIR scheme made by the National Institute of Bank Management (NIBM), a higher rate of interest than the present rate is acceptable to the borrowers. It is felt that most of the activities which are financed by the DIR loans yield a return high enough to able to afford a higher than four per cent rate of interest. The banks, however, feel that the present income limits are too small to make the scheme a success and hence the limits are to be raised.

At the grassroots level, preferably for a group of 20 to 30 villages, there is need for creating non-exploitative institutional infrastructure which can provide credit and convert credit into supplies and services.

REFERENCES

1. C.K. Ambastha: 'IRDP Loans: Factors Underlying Growing Overdues', *The Economic Times,* October 8, 1984.
2. Jana Everett and Mira Savara: 'Bank Loans to Lower Class Women in Mumbai: Problems and Prospects', *Economic and Political Weekly,* August 25, 1984, p. M-116 and p. M-117.
3. A.S. Rana: 'How Could Concessional Finance Help the Poor', *Yojana,* May 1-15, 1984, p. 24.
4. M.A. Oommen: 'Differential Interest Rate Scheme: Findings of a Field Survey', *Economic and Political Weekly,* May 24, 1980, p. 22.

5. Natabar Kuntia: 'Differential Rate of Interest Scheme', *Yojana,* July 16, 1980, p. 22.

6. *The Economic Times,* April 30, 1986.

7. *Financial Express* (editorial), December 5, 1978.

8. I. Satya Sundaram: 'A Fresh Look at the DIR Scheme', *Facts for You,* September, 1986.

9. Sudhir K. Jain: 'DIR Scheme: A Review of Achievement of Objectives', *The Economic Times,* July 9, 1984.

10. A.R. Patel: Twelve Years of Differential Rate of Interest Scheme: An Assessment', *The Journal of the Indian Institute of Bankers,* January-March, 1984, p. 34.

Chapter

38 The Lead Bank Scheme

The institutional credit available should be not only adequate, but it should reach all regions, sectors and sections in due proportions. In other words, the services of the banking sector should be shared by all. Special efforts are needed to achieve this objective.

In 1967, the Gadgil Study Group suggested the adoption of area approach to banking development under which commercial banks would be assigned particular districts where they were to act as pace-setters, providing integrated banking facilities. In August 1969, the Reserve Bank of India (RBI) had appointed a Committee of Bankers under the chairmanship of F.K.F. Nariman, which made specific recommendations for setting up lead banks for each of the underdeveloped districts. Accordingly, the lead bank scheme was introduced in December, 1969.

The RBI allotted various districts in the country, other than metropolitan centres and Union Territories of Delhi, Chandigarh and Goa, Daman and Diu, to the public sector banks and three private sector banks. The lead banks would take the lead in surveying the potential for banking development, extending credit facilities after locating viable and potentially viable propositions and mobilising deposits out of rising levels of income.

Under the lead bank scheme, in 1970, the public sector banks and a few other banks were assigned a lead bank role in certain allotted districts. During 1970 to 1972, each lead bank established contacts with other banks and government agencies in the districts and prepared district-wise reports on banking potentiality, containing information about the economy of the districts, population, area, natural resources, administrative set-up, infrastructure, industries and trade. Information was also provided about the banking facilities in the districts, deposits and advances of commercial and co-operative banks, finance provided by other agencies and unbanked and underbanked centres for expanding banking facilities. The task of identification of credit gaps and scope for institutional finance was also undertaken.

During 1971-72, the lead banks constituted district level consultative committees consisting of representatives of local government officers and banks, and convened meetings for the allocation of identified centres for branch expansion and for financing some schemes in the area.

In August 1975, the RBI set up a study group on the lead bank scheme in Gujarat and Maharashtra. It made recommendations for activating DLCC as an effective forum for co-ordination between banks and government agencies, formulation of bankable schemes with the supporting role of various agencies and monitoring.

The concept, methodology and period of the plans were not uniform. So in 1979, the RBI issued guidelines and terminated the old district credit plan by the end of 1979. Since 1980, district credit plans are prepared on a uniform pattern as per the RBI guidelines and are split up into annual action plan and block/branch-wise plans.

In the 1980s, the lead bank scheme was in operation in 398 districts of India excluding the metropolitan centres. Under the lead bank scheme, public sector banks opened 35,192 branches by the end of 4th April, 1981 all over the country and have formulated credit schemes for providing self-employment to unemployed or underemployed persons including rural women-folk. The lead bank scheme constituted a consortium approach to the problem of banking development based on area approach.[1]

Scope and Objectives

Over the years, the lead bank scheme has undergone a distinctive transformation and attained qualitative dimensions. The lead banks were expected to:

(i) Carry out impressionistic surveys of the districts concerned;
(ii) Identify growth centres for opening branches;
(iii) Locate credit gaps;
(iv) Formulate suitable schemes for growth and
(v) Prepare district credit plans to meet the credit requirements of the district in a planned manner in collaboration with other financial institutions at the district level.

One of the important objectives of bank nationalisation was to progressively reduce the disparities among various regions in the availability of institutional credit. Towards the end of 1980s, five states of Andhra Pradesh, Gujarat, Maharashtra, Punjab and Tamil Nadu accounted for 52 per cent of the total agricultural credit supplied.[2] It is also important that the use of bank credit for speculative and other unproductive purposes should be curbed and that the legitimate credit needs of the private industry and trade should be met, keeping of course in view the need for avoiding over-financing.[3]

Following the recommendation of the Western Area Regional Consultative Committee, the RBI has appointed two study groups in August, 1975 for Uttar Pradesh and Madhya Pradesh to suggest guidelines for effective implementation of the lead bank scheme. The reports of these study groups (submitted in January 1976) felt that while branch expansion under the lead bank scheme was impressive, the collaborative effort between various financing and development agencies has not been up to the mark.

Under the district credit plan, the responsibility of the lead bank includes:[4]

(i) Formulation of bankable projects/schemes;

(ii) Implementation of developmental programmes in collaboration with other agencies;

(iii) Monitoring the progress of implementation and

(iv) Evaluation of the progress achieved in relation to targets committed and an assessment of the impact of the credit plan on the district economy. The task of the lead bank is to bring about better co-ordination among the participating financial institutions and between them and the government agencies in the districts.

The lead bank scheme may be divided into two phases: the first phase was the adoption of an area approach under which the various districts in the country were apportioned among all the public and a few of the private sector banks. The second phase may be described as the formulation of the area development programme. The lead banks have to identify the bankable schemes in the districts and cover all economically viable activities. They should seek co-operation from other financing agencies. They should not merely credit demand in the districts but resources mobilisation as well.

The major objectives of the lead bank scheme are:

(i) To specify suitable areas for branch expansion;

(ii) To formulate a phased programme for expanding the branch offices with the object of providing banking facilities to the entire area covered;

(iii) To earmark the potential area for promoting agriculture and small scale industrial schemes inducing local entrepreneurs;

(iv) To assess the major constraints on the development of the district and to induce the appropriate agencies for taking up the follow-up remedial action and

(v) To experiment with financial schemes which can help in mobilising deposits and promoting investment among the local people.

DISTRICT CREDIT PLANS

The third round of district credit plans was formulated in 1982, so that they would be co-terminous with the balance of the Sixth Five Year Plan. In this round of preparation of district credit plans, they covered the period between January 1983 to March 1985. The idea was to switch the district credit plan year to the financial year (April-March) so that necessary co-ordination between the banks and governments could be ensured. The salient features cf the third round of district credit plan are as follows:

(i) Attain by March 1985, a level of 40 per cent of total lending to priority sectors;

(ii) Attain by March 1985, a level of 40 per cent of priority sector advances (i.e., 16 per cent of total advances) for agriculture and allied activities;

(iii) In respect of their total direct advances for agriculture and allied activities, provide, by 1985, to less than 50 per cent to weaker sections (i.e., small and marginal farmers with land holdings of five acres and less and landless labourers and persons engaged in allied activities whose credit limit for such activities in each case does not exeed ₹10,000);

(iv) In respect of advances to small scale industries, attain, by March 1985, a level of 12.5 per cent of such advances to weaker sections (comprising artisans, craftsmen, cottage and village industries and others, small units with credit limits in each case upto ₹ 25,000);

(v) Attain, by March, 1985, a credit deposit ratio of 60 per cent in respect of semi-urban and rural branches;

(vi) Disburse at least one per cent of their total advances as at the end of the previous year under the Differential Interest Rate (DIR) scheme at an interest rate of 4 per cent and ensure that at least 40 per cent of such advances go to SC/ST and further that at least two-thirds of DIR advances are made through rural and semi-urban branches and

(vii) Pay particular attention to the credit needs of SC/ST under the special component plan and tribal plan and make special efforts to prepare bankable schemes for them.

The third round of preparation of district credit plans has shown a vast improvement over the previous rounds of plans in the sense that it has a definite target for achievement with the help of government departments and the on-going anti-poverty programmes.[5] It laid emphasis on a wider dispersal and the IRDP and other anti-poverty programmes have come to occupy prominence. In order to provide for certain environmental changes and thus afford flexibility, the District Credit Plans (DCPs) were divided into the Annual Action Plans (AAPs) and these were sought to be monitored. Quite a few of the state governments designed some special programmes which formed part of the priority sector credit but which did not find a place either in the DCPs or AAPs and pressures were brought on the banks to implement them through the level of state government deposits.[6]

The preparation of the fourth round of DCPs for the three-year period from 1988 to 1990 was undertaken by the lead banks during 1987 as per the RBI guidelines. The National Institute of Bank Management had also conducted short training programmes. As per the time schedule, between May to July 1987, the data regarding actual implementation of DCP of 1985 and 1986 was compiled. The identification of bankable schemes, estimation of credit demand and preparation of the draft district credit plan was circulated to all financing agencies and development departments by October 1987 for their comments.

The revised plan was discussed by the district level review committee and the shares were allotted to the participating banks. By December 1987, the final DCPs were circulated to all the participating banks for working out branch-wise break-up and the implementation of DCPs from 1988. While the DCPs have been prepared for three years, some of the schemes drawn from the plans of various departments have been set up on the basis of the financial years.

For further improvement of the methodology, some blocks have been selected for the formulation and implementation of block level planning. The main features of this approach are:

(i) Grassroot level participation;

(ii) Formulation of village-wise targets for identified activities to arrive at realistic targets for the block, based on needs and potentialities of the area;

(iii) Time schedule for implementing various stages of the schemes;

(iv) Periodical review of physical and financial targets of the schemes to clear bottlenecks, ensure proper linkages etc.

(v) Frequent visits to villages, contacts and discussion with beneficiaries by the bank staff and extension agencies to ensure proper utilisation of funds and smooth implementation of the scheme; and

(vi) Demonstration effect of the schemes implemented in few villages and benefits derived by some persons in the initial stage.

While preparing the fourth round of plans, the banks have taken into account their past experience of financing certain schemes and the need to finance new activities. While formulating new bankable schemes, more emphasis is attached to minor irrigation, dry farming, oilseeds development, wasteland development etc. More emphasis is laid on employment-oriented schemes and those involving local resources to augment the income of the area. Poverty alleviation programmes and certain activities coming under 20-point programme are also to be financed as a part of DCP.

The DCPs formulated in the second phase of the lead bank scheme indicate the volume of credit demand likely to arise under the various bankable schemes in a district or block.

The estimate of credit demand is presented sector-wise, i.e., for crop loans, agricultural term loans and for meeting the working capital and term loan requirements of industries in a district. While estimating the credit demand, the credit needs of tertiary/services sector comprising transportation, retail trade, community services/production schemes for helping the weaker sections are also taken into account. The DCPs are expected to keep under scrutiny the branch expansion policy of commercial banks on the assessment of the strength of the co-operative societies.

The District Consultative Committees (DCCs) were constituted in all the districts of the country. Generally, each DCC has the following composition:

(i) District Collector or Development Commissioner as Chairman;

(ii) Lead Bank Officer of the lead bank of the district as convenor;

(iii) Project Officers or Assistant Development Commissioners of the SFDA, DPAP or IRDP, CAD agency or District Development Agency etc.;

(iv) Deputy Director of Agriculture or the District Agricultural Officer;

(v) Deputy or Joint Director of Industries or General Manager of DIC;

(vi) Executive Officers of the SC/BC Corporation and Women's Welfare Co-operative Society;

(vii) Divisional Co-operative Officer, Deputy Director, Animal Husbandry Programme and

(viii) Representatives of the State Finance Corporation, State Small Scale Industries Corporation. Rural Electrification Corporation or its affiliated co-operative society, executive engineer or superintending engineer of the State Electricity Boards, Chief Executive and Deputy Chief Executive of the District Co-operative Central Bank, Regional Officer of the State Land Development or Land Mortgage Bank, Representatives of all the commercial banks at the controlling level and district level.

For the meetings of DCC in some districts, the BDOs, a few non-officials, a few representatives of the small farmers and even RDOs are invited. The meetings are generally held at the district headquarters, but occasionally they are also held at block headquarters. The DCCs are a useful forum for bankers and administrators to meet and discuss subjects of common interest. Generally these meetings take place once in two or three months. Of course, there are state consultative committees which look into the problems that cannot be solved by the DCCs. Of late, block level consultative committees have also emerged.

Before finalisation, the credit plans are discussed in detail with the government officials at the district level and also with the state level officials. Credit plan documents subsequently prepared incorporate these estimates and circulated among the participating financial institutions and government departments. Thereafter, the credit plan goals were allocated by the DCC among the participating financial institutions, after taking into consideration their organisational and financial resources.[7] The rural planning and credit cell of the Reserve Bank has formulated further guidelines for the preparation of the new district credit plans for the period 1980-82, so as to ensure that all lead banks prepare the new credit plans in a uniform manner, dovetailing them into district development plans.

BLOCK CREDIT PLANS

The major sources of funds for the block plans will be united grants from the state governments, central grants under the IRDP and provision of state sponsored schemes to be implemented at this level and institutional finance. The state-wise targets will be broken down into district and blockwise targets in conformity with the development needs of the area and of the special anti-poverty programmes like the IRDP.

The Working Group on Block Level Planning observed, "If the credit plan is not to remain just a document, then there must be close co-ordination between the banks and the planning machinery to the extent that the banks should be directly involved in preparing the credit plan and be held responsible for the implementation.[8] The credit needs of various schemes to be implemented at the block level either be individuals or government departments should be accepted by the financial institutions. Of course, the projects selected at the block level should have effective linkages with the regional economy.

The Working Group has identified a number of obstacles to the flow of credit to the deserving borrowers. These include: outdated revenue records, uncertainty regarding system of share cropping, oral tenancies, unsatisfactory flow of other inputs, poor extension services, absence of functional experts, absence of crop insurance and ineffective role of the lead bank.

The job of the block credit plan is to allocate resources on a bank-wise and subject-wise basis. But, unless the physical planning is sound, credit planning by itself can do nothing, Moreover, there is a tendency to release funds at the fag end of the year, rendering phasing and sequencing of expenditure and priorities problematic. Effective machinery for plan formulation should emerge at the block level.

Virtually there is no decentralisation in planning. It is only at the implementation stage that some decentralisation has been achieved. In some districts, the Districts Industries Centres (DICs) budgets had become a part of total resources and usually suffered as a result.[9] The DICs and the block plan machinery should jointly identify projects at the block level to be financed by banks. In the absence of this, DICs have been identifying one set of artisans, and the banks are financing another set. For want of various allied facilities, the DICs have also been unable to offer a package of services to the prospective entrepreneurs.

One cannot but notice a lot of duplication of effort at the block level. The lead bank prepares the district plan and the DIC prepares the action plan for industries. The block planning machinery prepares the block plan, though not on scientific lines. The tragedy is that there are no effective linkages among these three plans. At block levels too consultative committees should be constituted for a better co-ordination and understanding among bankers and development agencies.[10]

LEAD BANK SCHEME: SOME PROBLEMS

A number of deficiencies in the working of the lead bank scheme have been brought to light by the two study groups appointed by the RBI. These deficiencies include: inadequate appreciation of the objectives of the scheme by the banks concerned themselves; the unwieldy size of the DCCs, the recurring absence of the District Collectors at the committee meetings in some cases, the failure of the collectors and district officials to keep in mind the viability of the scheme proposed etc.[11]

According to some study groups, the implementation of area development programmes "presents greater difficulties involving as it does, collaborative efforts not only between banks but with various levels and types of government agencies as well." Regarding financing of priority sectors, the groups observed, "These have been through the individual actions of the banks and there are no sizeable schemes of collective action spearheaded by the lead banks." The study groups have also drawn attention to the "feeling, especially among the state governments and local authorities that the lead banks have failed in their responsibility." This is due to their inadequate appreciation of the "scope and content of the Lead Bank Scheme, its limitation and the pre-conditions for its successful operation."

The study groups also deplored the unwieldy size of the district consultative committee and observed: "In some cases, the regular members of the committee included such officials as representatives of the National Seeds Corporation and regulated markets and such non-officials as even journalists. In one district, the DCC consisted of as many as 63 members while there were sub-committees with 25 or more members. While all the members may not attend all the meetings, it is obvious that a large non-homogeneous composition would not serve much purpose beyond perhaps gaining a certain degree of publicity." Very often, the District Collectors do not attend the meetings. The lead bank scheme is thus unable to get the required co-operation from the government departments. No wonder, the DCC meetings are considered as "mere rituals, not to be taken seriously."[12]

A major drawback in the working of the lead bank scheme has been reported to be the lack of co-ordination among the commercial and co-operative banks and other financial institutions operating in the districts as also between the Government officials concerned and the financial institutions. The National Institute of Bank Management (NIBM) arranged training programmes for government and bank officials connected with credit plan implementation. The need for involving the Department of Rural Development of Ministry of Agriculture in the implementation of the lead bank scheme which is essentially a scheme for rural development was appreciated to a large extent.[13]

The slow progress of the lead bank scheme may be attributed to:

(i) The deficiencies in the scheme itself; and

(ii) The built-in shortcomings of the district economy.

The district economy reportedly suffers from:

(i) Inadequacies of the essential inputs;

(ii) Infrastructural inadequacies;

(iii) Inadequate technical and managerial know-how; and

(iv) Weak database.

There is, therefore the need for evolving credit plan for an area smaller than a district. From the implementation point of view (which is more important than more formulation of a credit plan), block level credit planning would be more effective and less costly than their large counterparts.[14]

In the case of many districts, the land records are not upto-date. Therefore, agricultural lending is hampered. Banks are also facing difficulties in getting no due certificates from the co-operative societies. The need of the hour is to have more extension services on the rural side by the bankers and the government. This would facilitate easy implementation of the credit plans in the lead districts by bringing about a better understanding, among the bankers, borrowers and the government agencies.[15]

Due to lack of co-ordination between the lead banks and the government, the banks have faced difficulties in getting no dues certificates while advancing loans.[16]

The lead bank scheme is also greatly handicapped by absence of effective entrepreneurship, which is necessary to promote the level of economic activity to the extent desired. The unprecedented territorial expansion, particularly into the interior parts of the country, coupled with functional diversification and financing of priority and the hitherto neglected sectors caused considerable strain to the concerned bank's manpower resources.[17]

The district credit plans have proved ineffective because:[18]

(i) Of lack of understanding on the part of branch managers and officers of the socio-economic philosophy underlying the concept of district credit plan,

(ii) There is no regular discussion on the progress of implementation of these plans,

(iii) No attempt was made to take advantage of subsidy available from the government,

(iv) Crop loans were neglected,

(v) Branch managers were not familiar with the modalities of financing agricultural schemes,

(vi) There were frequent transfers of managers at some branches,

(vii) Bankable schemes covered under the credit plan were not given due publicity,

(viii) There is interference from local politicians in the working infrastructure of banks,

(ix) DCC meetings are held at the district level instead of at the block level and

(x) The present powers of the commercial banks to sieze movable and immovable assets are said to be inadequate.

Moreover, in preparing the DCPs, the banks fail to take into account the capacity of the state administration to support the proposed programmes. The capacity of the state administration not only varies from one state to another, but also within a state and from one district to another. Therefore, the staffing patter of all the credit institutions and their lending procedures will have to vary for different areas.[19]

A serious drawback of the present credit planning is the absence of proper budgeting and monitoring system in respect of performance of branches of banks *vis-a-vis* credit plan commitments among their branches nor have they fulfilled maintained their commitments annually.[20] Moreover, discussions at the District Consultative meetings mostly centred round the problems of financing rather than of programme implementation.

The general complaint is that the programme data for the individual districts or blocks were never made available and the bankers had to depend to a large extent on their own rough estimates. Naturally, the quality of the credit plans with these data cannot be considered very good.

One significant omission that is noticed generally in the district credit plans is the omission of urban co-operatives from the plan without any credit allocation. This seems ridiculous when one considers that they play a significant role in financing secondary and tertiary sectors, especially rural artisans, village and cottage industries and small scale industries.[21]

The non-availability of inputs has also adversely affected the implementation of district plans. The energisation of wells and also sinking of new wells has been adversely affected by the non-implementation of rural electrification projects. Similarly, loans to dairy farming suffered because supply of animals, the timely availability of veterinary services and arrangements for collection, transportation and purchase of milk were not available.

The district plans are not properly integrated with district development plans. They have not been formulated by personnel having proper training; they have been ineffective as the implementation bodies are already involved and overloaded with other work and finally, they have not generated a sense of participation among other financial institutions working in the district.[22]

The problems facing DCPs are:[23]

(i) The network of rural credit was found to be weak in most of the districts, resulting in severe pressure on the commercial banks;

(ii) There was lack of co-ordination between co-operatives and commercial banks on the one hand and between government agencies and financial institutions on the other. The latter tended to concentrate on government sponsored schemes neglecting others. The question of economic viability was also a point of discord between the government officials and banks;

(iii) The absence of systematic demarcation of area among the banks resulted in concentration of banks in advanced areas and the subsequent neglect of backward areas and

(iv) Extension of credit to the schemes identified under the DCPs often suffered due to inadequate availability of the required inputs like seeds, fertilisers, milch cattle etc. Further, delay in the creation of infrastructural facilities marred the progress in implementation of schemes of DCPs.

A number of factors have contributed to the limited success of DCPs. These include:

(i) In the absence of explicit guidelines, lack of suitably trained personnel and this being the first exercise of its kind attempted by the bank, the formulation of DCPs could not be said to have been done scientifically;

(ii) The lead bank concept entailing active involvement of banks in the socio-economic development being quite a new ideology, failed to evoke the necessary response from the bank personnel at different levels, particularly for service in the smaller villages;

(iii) In the absence of explicit guidelines, allocations of growth centres identified for branch expansion, the bank had to volunteer for those centres which were not accepted by other banks and

(iv) Inadequate co-ordination among the various agencies was another serious bottleneck hampering the pace of implementation of DCPs.

MEASURES TO IMPROVE CREDIT PLANS

The lead bank scheme, though theoretically sound, has been facing a number of problems. Agencies connected with the lead bank scheme have to take various measures to make it cost effective. The study groups appointed by the Reserve Bank of India have suggested that in the preparation of district credit plans during the second phase of the lead bank scheme, "the emphasis should be not so much on methodology excellence in the academic sense as on expeditious preparations of technologically feasible and economically viable schemes and their collective implementation by all financial institutions." The credit plan "should cover only activities for which bankable schemes can be evolved and to areas which are clearly outside the purview of direct expansion by banks."

Deploring the lack of realism in drawing the credit plans, the study groups observed that the targets should be modest. The schemes should be based as far as possible, on the existing infrastructural facilities available throughout the district. The schemes should include details, which would assist in the process of actual extension of credit to individual borrowers. The study groups also felt that the credit authorities should assist the lead banks in identifying areas offering scope for specific schemes.[24]

The DCC has to monitor the progress of the scheme. The study groups observed that collective supervision is important and that a feeling of domination from either the lead bank or the government would have adverse effects on the psychology of the participating banks. With effect from June 1976, the RBI introduced half-yearly progress reports to be submitted by the lead banks in respect of each district allotted to them under the scheme. The Government of India (Department of Revenue and Banking) has also submitted its progress reports. There is, however, some duplication of effort in these reports which should be avoided.

In order to enable the DCC to function more effectively, they must be given wide powers so as to ensure involvement of the agencies concerned in plan implementation in the districts. There must be proper co-ordination among the activities of the rural banks and lead banks. The rural banks benefit a lot from the preparation of the credit plan by the lead bank. If the government machinery helps in the recovery of loans, banks will be willing to lend more money. The joint inspection of the schemes by bankers and officials and a scrutiny of the applications closely, have paid dividends both to the banks and to the beneficiary.[25] The success of the lead bank scheme also depends on the support extended by government agencies in providing infrastructural facilities.

The district planning authority should co-operate with the credit institutions in supervising loan utilisations and in the recovery of loans.[26] The lead banks should prepare annual action plans in December each year, indicating sectoral scheme-wise and institutional group-wise break-up of the total credit outlays.[27] It has been emphasised that the lead banks should also develop their own systems of carrying out evaluation studies of the implementation of the credit plans of their lead districts periodically.

The district credit plans should be integrated with the employment-oriented district plans with a view to generating sizeable employment opportunities. Since the credit plan is an integral part of the district development plan, selected employment-oriented lending schemes have to be suggested in the district credit plans.[28] Our five year plans are formulated more in financial than in real terms, causing less growth and more inflation. The objectives of growth with stability can be achieved if realistic and well target-oriented credit-cum-development plans can be implemented at the grassroots level.[29]

Preparation of DCPs/AAPs is a development-oriented job and the staff both in banks and government departments, should possess the required imagination and techniques of credit planning as to make proper assumptions for credit demand by various sectors and to arrive at a realistic assessment of the magnitude of lending in various sectors.[30] The pre-investment and post-investment benefits should be monitored on an on-going basis jointly by the banks and the sponsoring agencies and the schemes that are not well received by the beneficiaries should be abandoned. Only those schemes which were location-specific should be devised.[31]

There is the most urgent need for reducing the burden of collection and compilation of statistics in various innumerable formats. This prevents the operational staff from paying undivided attention to the development, supervision and follow-up aspects of these schemes.[32]

It is also desirable to assess the physical assets created and the impact of the schemes on the beneficiaries, their role in the economy of the target area and whether a balance economic growth of the area is achieved.[33]

Preparation of credit plans without economic plans at the block level amounts to putting the cart before the horse. It is also necessary to bring about co-ordination among government departments.[34]

The Agricultural Credit Department of the RBI should ensure active participation of co-operatives in credit plan implementation. It is gathered from some co-operative banks that they have not received any communication from their apex bodies advising them about their role in the lead bank scheme. There is need for selecting honest people and motivating them to take up lucrative ventures and gainful vocations.[35] Thus, the lead bank scheme assumes special significance in the context of the implementation of anti-poverty programmes at the micro level.

References

1. *A.K. Mukhopadhyay: 'Rural Credit in India', in Rural Development in India: Some Facets, National Institute of Rural Development, 1979.*
2. *Sixth Five Year Plan 1980-85, p. 109.*
3. *A. Raman: 'Credit planning and Formulation of Credit Policy', in S.L.N. Simha and A. Raman (Ed. 1974): Credit Planning and Policy, Vora & Co. Publishers Ltd., Mumbai.*
4. *Bank of India (1979): Evaluation of District Credit Plan: A Study of Ujjain District, Madhya Pradesh, p. 2.*
5. *S. Balkrishna: 'Lead Bank Scheme: Problems and Prospects', The Journal of the Indian Institute of Bankers, July-September 1984, pp. 146-147.*
6. *B. Yerram Raju: 'Plan Rural Credit Better Way', Yojana, January 1-15, 1986.*
7. *D.J. Kanuinde: 'Methodology for Estimation of Credit Demand Under District Credit Plans', SBI Monthly Review, August 1981, p. 338.*
8. *Report of the Working Group on Block Level Planning, p. 31.*
9. M.N. Upadhayay: 'District Industries Centres: Some Conceptual and Operational Aspects', Economic and Political Weekly, May 31, 1980, p.M-57.
10. B. Satyavati: 'Lead Banks in A.P.: An Evaluation', Financial Express, September 4, 1978.
11. The Hindu, February 29, 1976.
12. Ibid.
13. Aniruddha: 'Lead Bank: The Problem of Co-ordination', *Financial Express,* August 7, 1975.
14. Issac Taler: 'Whither District Credit Plan?', *The Economic Times,* July 19, 1975.
15. B. Ramachandra Rao: 'Lead Bank Workshops on Agriculture', *Financial Express,* September 25, 1978.
16. K. Seshaiah (1985): *The Lead Bank Scheme: An Empirical Study*, Rainbow Publications, Coimbatore.
17. Navin Chandra Joshi: 'Challenges Before Lead Banks', *Financial Express,* June 12, 1975.
18. *Evaluation of District Credit Plan, op. cit.,* pp. 60-65.

19. *Commerce* (editorial), June 6, 1981, p. 1100.

20. A.C. Minocha: 'Credit Planning in a Micro Region: A Case Study of Bhopal Districts Plan', Indian Economic Association Annual Conference, Pune, December, 1980.

21. S. Balkrishna: *op. cit.*, p. 149.

22. Ghanshyam Purbey: 'An Appraisal of District Credit Plans', Indian Economic Association, Annual Conference, Pune, December, 1980.

23. Chitranjan: 'Lead Bank Scheme: A Micro Study', *Financial Express,* September 13, 1982.

24. *The Hindu,* February 29, 1976.

25. Special Report on Banks and Self-Emloyment, *The Hindu,* January 19, 1982.

26. D.J. Kanvinde: .'Districts Credit Planning: Some Problems', *SB1 Monthly Review,* September 1971, p. 318.

27. Reserve Bank of India: *Report on Currency and Finance 1978-79,* p. 121.

28. A.R. Patel: 'Rural Employment: Banks Can Do A Lot', *Kurukshetra,* October 1,1981, p. 35.

29. Bani Mujumdar: "The Lead Bank Scheme and Economic Development', *Financial Express,* May 1, 1982.

30. B.K. Ghose: 'The Lead Bank Scheme: Some Reflections', *The Journal of Indian Institute of Bankers,* April-June 1983, p. 96.

31. *The Hindu,* August 30,1984.

32. A.R. Patel: 'Role of Standing Committee Under Lead Bank Scheme', *Financial Express,* May 15, 1982.

33. J.J. Udeshi: 'District Credit Plans — Fourth Round', *The Economics Times,* September 1, 1988.

34. I. Satya Sundaram: 'Lead Bank Scheme: Problems and Prospects' in I. Satya Sundaram (ed. 1989): *Rural Poverty and Area Planning,* B.R. Publishing Corporation, New Delhi, p. 313.

35. S.K. Achar: 'Lead Banks' Role in Integrated Rural Development', *The Hindu,* December 12, 1987.

Chapter

39 Service Area Approach

The commercial banks are facing a number of problems as they have been assigned the responsibility to meet the credit needs of hitherto neglected sections, sectors and areas. It was thought that a schematic and intensive area approach was on the decline and scattered lending had become common. Social banking can be strengthened only by paying special attention to banking at the grassroots level.

Banks have started adopting the Service Area Approach (SAA) scheme with effect from April 1, 1989. The principal aim of SAA was to ensure that every village in the country, however remote, would have access to banking facilities.

The SAA was the outcome of a high level seminar organised by the Reserve Bank of India on January 9 and 10, 1988. It was felt that the target approach which was needed in the initial stages to push banks into priority sectors had outlived its utility. Under the SAA scheme, the service area of every rural or semi-urban branch has to typically comprise of 15 to 25 villages — proximity to the branch and of villages being the main criteria in allotting contiguity villages to a bank branch.

The area approach is expected to facilitate intensive deployment of credit for development purposes, keeping in view the local needs and problems. The SAA also solves problems associated with the identification of genuine borrowers and supervision of the end-use of credit. It improves the level of co-ordination between banks and other financial and development institutions.

The SAA approach contains five important features:[1]

(i) Identification and allocation of service area for each bank branch;

(ii) Survey of villages in the service area for assessing the potential for lending activities and identification of beneficiaries for assistance;

(iii) Preparation of credit plan on an annual basis for the service area by each branch;

(iv) Co-ordination between credit institutions on the one hand and field level development agencies on the other on an on-going basis for the effective implementation of the credit plans and

(v) System of continuous monitoring of progress in the implementation of the plans.

The SAA would enable the branch manager to understand better the service area. This would subsequently lead to the preparation of branch budgets in a realistic and data-based manner. The ultimate objective of the SAA is meant to improve the quality of lending. The SAA is meant to rationalise rural lending, reduce cost of supervision formulated and adhered to on priority basis both by reducing the number of villages in which the bank branches operate and also by avoiding duplication of efforts in lending in the villages by branches of more than one bank.[2]

The essence of the new approach lies in assigning specific areas to each bank branch. The branch will thus have a development orientation and concentrate on productive lending. The new approach was adopted with a view to ensuring proper utilisation of bank credit to increase production and income levels of the rural poor.

The service area approach consists of a few stages. These include:

(i) Holding meetings on a block-wise basis to decide on the allocation of villages;

(ii) Conducting a survey and preparing a profile of the economic activities of the villages allotted. A need for analysing the infrastructure and linkages available in the area was discussed and those required to be developed to support bank credit;

(iii) Drawing up of annual credit plans by the branch manager for deploying credit in each of the villages in the service area in a phased manner and

(iv) Setting up of a Block Level Bankers' Committee (BLBG) with the lead bank officer as the chairman, and the block development officer and other technical officers as its members. The BLBC has to co-ordinate and monitor the work of all bank branches within a block.

Table: 1
Allocation of Villages Under Service Area Approach

	No. of Branches	*No. of Village Allocated*	*Average Per Branch*
Public Sector Banks	26,016	3,66,382	14
Private Sector Banks	2,489	15,242	6
Regional Rural Banks	13,653	2,36,592	17
TOTAL	42,158	6,18,216	14

The SAA has several advantages. The branch manager can concentrate on the development of the area through productive lending. Multi-agency approach has also resulted in the duplication of efforts which could be avoided, in the new approach. It is now possible to eliminate scattered lending over wide areas in order to ensure planned lending. The accountability on the part of the branch manager in implementing the plan can be assured.[3]

MAJOR PROBLEMS

Though the service area approach is well conceived, it is however likely to create some practical problems. For instance, agricultural development branches of the State Bank of India (SBI), though located in urban areas, are capable of penetrating into the rural and semi-urban areas. Under the new approach, the branches will be barred from lending in rural areas though they are better qualified and equipped than the small branches.

Another problem relates to the pressure on branch managers who are to decide whom to lend to in their particular area and whom to leave out. It is difficult to contain these pressures from different groups within the village.

How to mobilise adequate manpower to man the rural branches with new responsibilities entrusted to the branch managers is another problem. Given the officers' increasing reluctance to posting in rural areas, manning the rural and semi-urban branches in a way that can do justice to the service area concept in letter and spirit is going to be a tremendous task.[4]

Too many responsibilities have been placed on the branch managers. Whether they would visit all the villages under their jurisdiction, devote adequate time and have patience to collect the detailed information called for is the real issue. It may be difficult, with poor infrastructure, for the lead bank office to assist each branch manager of the district in surveying villages. The quality of surveys too is likely to suffer because of the existing poor information sources.

Another serious problem facing the SAA is the general reluctance on the part of the staff to serve the rural areas. Even when they serve rural branches, their residences are generally in nearby urban centres. The bank staff under these circumstances could not devote the attention to local problems expected of them.

It is feared that the SAA may eliminate competition amongst banks. The commercial banks no doubt can compete with co-operatives but this competition is not of much help because of the weak position of co-operatives.[5] With the introduction of SAA, some of the rural branches have become non-viable in the light of restricted potential in the operational area.[6]

STRENGTHENING SERVICE AREA APPROACH (SAA)

Though the service area approach has been well conceived, the following measures should be undertaken to make it effective:[7]

(i) Development and planning skills at the operational level should be given priority to evolve pragmatic credit plans for the service area of each branch;

(ii) There should be frequent interaction with the prospective customers. This is necessary to ensure adequate and timely credit for viable economic activities and also ensure recycling of funds;

(iii) The trends in profitability as a result of formulation of credit plans at the branch level should be closely examined. This is necessary in view of the inevitable rise in operational costs;

(iv) Suitable organisational and monitoring system at the branch level to implement the service area approach more effectively should be developed and

(v) The relationship between the political set-up, grassroot level administration and the banking system should be sufficiently strengthened.

While preparing the credit plans for the service area of each branch, due emphasis should be given to the present district credit plans/annual action plans prepared under the lead bank scheme. It is the branch managers who have to carefully study the viability of each development programme in a service area.

The Reserve Bank of India has observed that:[8]

> It is important that the branch managers exercise their own judgment in the light of village-wise surveys conducted by them, the demand for credit for productive schemes in their service areas and the information which they might gather from local development agencies such as block authorities and local officials of various development departments such as agriculture, animal husbandry, co-operation and small industry.

At the branch level, certain measures need to be initiated. Meetings may be held on a block-wise basis to decide on the allocation of villages. Both the growth potentialities and constraints at the village level need to be assessed on a priority basis. The branch manager had to draw up an annual credit plan for deploying credit in each of the villages. For co-ordinating and monitoring the work of all branches within a block, a Block Level Bankers' Committee (BLBC) was needed at the earliest.

In order to ensure success of SAA, the staffing at the branch level should be strengthened. Currently, most branches lack technical staff. Branches serving areas having growth potentialities alone are now having sufficient staff. But under SAA, the bank branches have the responsibility of identifying growth potentialities and initiating development schemes in such areas.

The SAA should not aggravate the already grave problem of overdues. A vital problem may arise regarding irregular parties being financed by the service area branches, leaving the overdue loans with the erstwhile branches. Here, each service area branch should help in recovery when they lend to such parties.[9]

Rural lending still suffers from paucity of information. The rural poor should have access to correct information about programmes being implemented for them. The benefits of various programmes are at present appropriated by the relatively better-off sections. Under the SAA, camps should be organised to educate the rural people about various schemes, specially about the purpose of the scheme and its benefit to them. This will eliminate the mischief played by middlemen to cheat the rural poor.[10]

The real issue relates to the identification of economically viable programmes at the local level. It is necessary to have a look at the availability of skills to undertake viable activities. Thus, the plan should not only be village specific, but also beneficiary specific. The lead bank officer should have a host of technical and specialised officers with intimate knowledge of rural development, to assist him for preparation and implementation of credit plans.[11]

The 'Cluster of Villages' approach may be adopted to implement credit plans at the micro level. This approach would have to identify activities which are relevant to each of these villages, study their existing infrastructure needs and identify the number of units which can be viable under each of the activities.[12]

The field visits assume special importance in the context of the Service Area Approach (SAA). At present, the approach is carried out in a perfunctory manner. The field visits should aim at educating the borrowers about the proper use of a loan faculty and providing linkages in production and marketing of the produce.[13]

It may be necessary to see that a borrower gets credit from one branch only as far as possible. This would make the borrower careful in utilising credit and repaying the loan as he is denied of alternative sources of finance. There must also be safeguards against the misuse of power by the branch manager.

How to generate credit demand in the service area is the greatest challenge facing the bank manager. It is necessary to publicise economically viable schemes which are entitled to bank credit. The fear of risk of default in repayment needs to be dispelled by publicising success stories. The most important thing is disbursal of credit within a reasonable time.

The SAA would place additional responsibilities on the branch managers. These can be effectively discharged if only the branch managers get co-operation from voluntary agencies, self-help groups and women's organisations.

It is important that the credit plan should not only be village-specific but also beneficiary-specific under the different activities. The inclusion of non-viable activities to meet quantitative targets should not be resorted to.[14]

In spite of the implementation of SAA, each rural branch should have sufficient business. If necessary, the merger of adjoining branches should be allowed. Also, appropriate atmosphere should be created for toning up the performance of the branch manager.

Studies show there is no integration of service area credit plans (SACPs) with development plans. Credit planning will be turn out to be ineffective unless it is linked backward with a development plan in physical terms and it is not sufficient to have forward linkages through the credit disbursing agencies.[15] The service area approach is well conceived. It needs support from administration.

References

1. Reserve Bank of India, May 1988: *Service Area Approach: Formation of Credit Plan,* p. 2.
2. *State Bank of India Monthly Review,* January 1990, p. 13.
3. T.N. Anand and B.K. Narayanaswamy: 'Service Area Approach to Rural Development', *Agricultural Banker,* July-September 1992, pp. 16-17.
4. Keya Sarkar: Service Area Approach: Onus on Branch Managers', *Business India,* 13-26, June 1988, p. 85.
5. T.N. Anand and B.K. Narayanaswamy: *op. cit.*

6. A.R. Patel: 'Rural Banking, Service Area Policy Shift Needed', *Southern Economist,* August 1, 1995, p. 18.

7. N.A. Shanbhag: 'Challenges and Opportunities', *The Economic Times,* November 1,1989.

8. Reserve Bank of India, May 1988: *op. cit.*

9. B. Ramachandra Rao: 'Service Area Approach: Manpower Planning for Rural Banks', *The Economic Times,* December 1, 1988.

10. Rajendra Singh: 'Service Area Approach: A Rejoinder', *The Economic Times,* March 2, 1989.

11. Natabar Khuntia: 'Service Area Approach: Rural Area Financing', *The Economic Times,* November 1, 1989.

12. Kanhaiya Singha: 'Rural Development: Service Area Approach', *The Economic Times,* January 2, 1989.

13. *Economic and Political Weekly,* September 29, 1990, p. A-128.

14. Jag M. Chona: 'Rural Lending: Focus on Service Area Approach', *The Hindu Survey of Indian Agriculture,* 1991, p. 245.

15. V.R. Prabhakaran Nair: ' Problems of integrating the service area credit plans with development plans', Kurukshetra, November 2009. p.9.

Chapter

40 Regional Rural Banks

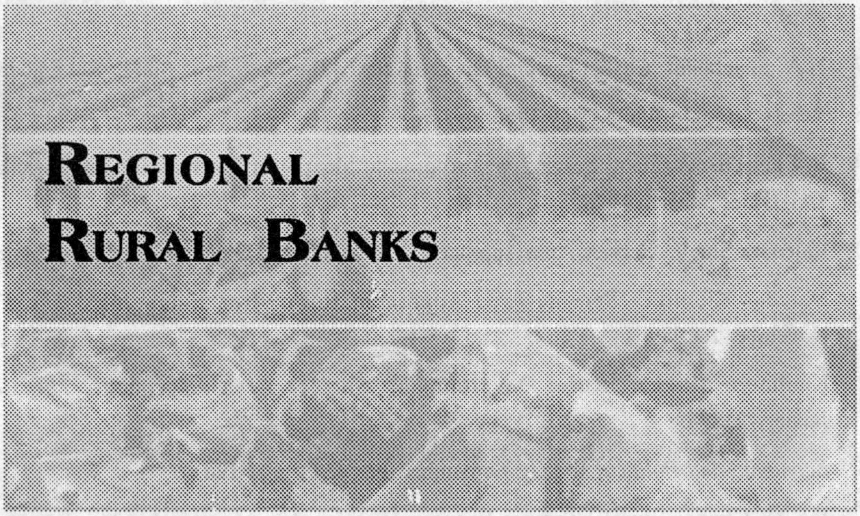

The Regional Rural Banks (RRBs) came into being under the 20-Point Economic Programme launched in 1975. Earlier, the Banking Commission, appointed by the Government to study the structure of banking development in India, mooted the idea of setting up RRBs in its report in 1972. The Government reviewed the recommendations of the Banking Commission, and appointed the Narasimham Study Group on July 1, 1975. It submitted the report in just 30 days and favoured the setting up of RRBs.

The Government of India promulgated the RRBs Ordinance dated 26th September, 1975 which was subsequently replaced by the Regional Rural Banks Act, 1976. On October 2, 1975, five RRBs were established in four states: 2 in Uttar Pradesh, one at Moradabad by the Syndicate Bank and the other at Gorakhpur by the State Bank of India; one in Rajasthan by the United Commercial Bank; one in Bhiwani (Haryana) by the Punjab National Bank and one in Malda (West Bengal) by the United Bank of India.

The RRBs were established with a view to developing the rural economy by providing for the purpose of development of agriculture, trade, commerce, industry and other productive activities in the rural areas, credit and other facilities, particularly to the small and marginal farmers, agricultural labourers, artisans, small entrepreneurs and for matters connected therewith and incidental thereto.

The RRBs are somewhere in between the public sector banks and the co-operative structure. They combine in themselves the characteristics of both these institutions and are expected to play a supporting role in districts where the credit gap is very large and the co-operative structure is weak. In setting up RRBs, certain norms have to be observed. These are:

(i) Areas should be relatively backward or tribal;

(ii) RRBs are to be set up in areas where the co-operative banks are not active;

(iii) There should not be any commercial bank in the area and

(iv) The area should have real potentiality for a development breakthrough with the flow of credit.

While recommending; the setting up of RRBs, the Working Group on Rural Banks appointed by the Government in 1975 opined that each RRB combines in itself the "local feel and familiarity with rural problems which the co-operatives possessed and the degree of business organisation, ability to mobilise deposits, access to central money markets and a modernised outlook which the commercial banks have."

The RRBs are trying to meet the credit requirements of backward areas where coverage by the commercial banks and co-operatives is relatively poor. However, such areas should have growth potentialities and should make rapid progress when once the credit requirements are met. The RRBs appear to be attractive on account of their possibility of combining the relative sophistication of a commercial bank with local bias and low cost structure associated with co-operatives.[1] One of the tasks envisaged from the RRBs is to maintain their cost of operations at a level lower than that of the commercial banks.

SPECIAL POSITION OF RRBs

Each RRB has an authorised capital of ₹ 1 crore and paid-up capital of ₹ 25 lakhs. The share capital is raised by the central government, the state government concerned and the sponsoring bank in the ratio of 50:15:35 respectively. There is no participation of other institutions and individuals in the equity of the RRBs. Each bank has a Board of Directors of 9 members: 4 to be appointed by the central government; 2 by the dominant nationalised banks; one by the state government and 2 by the Government of India.

The strength of RRBs lie in the fact that they combine the good features of both co-operative and commercial banks. No doubt, RRBs are basically scheduled commercial banks, but they differ from the existing commercial banks in several ways:[2]

First, the RRBs area of operation is limited to a particular region;

Second, in granting loans, they concentrate on weaker sections of rural India like the small and marginal farmers, agricultural labourers and rural artisans;

Third, their lending rates are not higher than the prevailing lending rates of co-operative societies in any particular state and

Last, their salary structure is different from that of the commercial banks. It is prescribed by the Central Government, taking into account the salary structure of the employees of the government and local authorities of comparable level and status in that area of operation of the bank. (At present, the staff of RRBs draw salaries on par with those of the commercial banks).

The Banking Commission (1972) has observed that the sponsoring of the RRBs should be aided by the Reserve Bank of India from its National Agricultural Credit (long-term operations) Fund. The RRBs were expected to supplement their deposit resources by loans from their sponsor banks (or, in the case of co-operatives, from the banks at the higher tiers). The Commission also recommended that the liquidity rules applicable to the commercial banks should be relaxed to some extent for the rural banks and that balances maintained with their sponsors should be regarded as liquid assets. It was also provided that for income tax purposes, the RRBs would be treated on par with co-operative societies.

Except the chairman, RRBs can appoint all staff, i.e., branch managers, accountants, field officers, technical officers, field assistants, clerks, cashiers etc. Those within the operational jurisdiction of the respective RRBs and with rural knowledge and orientation are to be selected on the staff, with active secretarial assistance from the sponsoring commercial banks. In fact, as per the RRB Act, 1976, the entire responsibility of staff training, free of cost, lies, with the sponsoring commercial banks for the initial period of five years. Reserve Bank of India has placed RRBs on par with refinance facilities made available to the co-operative banks, i.e., RRBs would be provided refinance at 2 per cent below the bank rate. Like commercial banks, the RRBs also have been made eligible for accommodation against a mere declaration of eligible loans and advances by them.

To achieve viability of the RRBs, the RBI has granted the following concessions:

(i) Statutory Liquidity Ratio (SLR) to be maintained at 25 per cent as against 35 per cent by commercial banks;

(ii) RRBs are allowed to pay half a per cent higher interest to its depositors than the interest rate offered by commercial banks to their depositors;

(iii) Cash reserve requirements of 3 per cent to be maintained with the RBI as against 9.5 per cent by commercial banks;

(iv) They are allowed to charge interest on their direct loans at par with the rate charged by the Primary Agricultural Cooperative Societies (PACS) to its clients;

(v) They are allowed to draw refinance from RBI, and now from NABARD, to the extent of 50 per cent or more depending upon the type of advance of the eligible outstanding loan at concessional rate of interest at 7 per cent per annum;

(vi) Similarly, refinance to the extent of 30 per cent of eligible outstanding loans can be drawn from the sponsoring bank at concessional rate of 8.5 per cent per annum;

(vii) They are entitled to get 9 per cent interest on the balance maintained in the current account by them with the sponsor bank.

(viii) Sponsor bank deputes its own staff to manage the RRB branches till the time thus RRB is able to recruit its own staff;

(ix) All the salary, allowance etc., of such deputed staff are borne by the sponsor bank;

(x) Free remittance is to be allowed in the multiple of ₹ 5,000 between the Head Office of RRB and its different branches through the office of Public Sector Banks;

(xi) Salary, allowance etc. of the chairman of the concerned RRB is also borne by the sponsor bank and

(xii) Sponsor Bank arranges for the training of the RRB staff in its training establishments at its own cost. Further, the sponsor or bank also bears the expenses for training RRB branch managers at the College of Agricultural Banking, RBI, Pune.

FUNCTIONS OF RRBs

A rural bank was described as "a primary banking institution set-up to serve a compact group of villages generally working as a co-operative bank or as a subsidiary of a commercial bank", and its object would be "to provide at one place the special type of credit and banking facilities and related services needed by agriculturists and other rural producers."

The functions of RRBs are:

(i) To mobilise local savings;

(ii) To provide short-term and medium-term credit for agricultural and other purposes on its own and long-term credit as agents of the Land Development Banks;

(iii) To implement programmes of supervised credit tailored to the needs of individual farmers;

(iv) To provide various ancillary banking services to local people;

(v) To set up and maintain godowns;

(vi) To undertake supply of inputs for agriculture and related equipments and in appropriate cases equipment loaning;

(vii) To provide assistance in the marketing of agricultural and other products through marketing organisations and

(viii) To help in the overall development of the villages in its area.[3]

The RRBs are expected to form an integral part of the rural credit structure, along with co-operatives and commercial banks, under the multi-agency approach to rural lending. They are known for their lower cost of operations. Till recently, establishment and operational costs of RRB branches were relatively lower than the rural branches of commercial banks.

RESPONSIBILITY OF SPONSOR BANK

(i) The sponsoring bank has to aid and assist the RRB in all respects. It has to subscribe to the share capital of RRBs;

(ii) Incurring initial expenditure for setting up of RRBs, its head office and providing for stationery and other items of necessity in the initial stage;

(iii) Deputing staff to the branches of RRBs in the initial period of its operations;

(iv) Identifying its own staff for deputing to act as chairman for the initial period of functioning of RRBs;

(v) To arrange for recruitment and training of personnel during the initial functioning of RRBs;

(vi) To suggest nominees of official and non-official for inclusion on the Board of RRBs and

(vii) To lend all the operational/administrative support and guidance in its running successfully.

At present, RRBs are provided refinance facilities on a composite basis. With effect from July, 1984, NABARD has revised its refinance policy whereby Regional Rural Banks, which have completed five years of operation (as on 1st July, 1984), will be provided two separate refinance limits for short-term and medium-term (non-schematic) lendings. Similarly, sanctioning limits of RRBs which have not completed five years has been discontinued from 1986-87. All RRBs, irrespective of their age, are eligible for refinance under Section 21 of the NABARD Act, for short-term credit limits.

As recommended by the Kelkar Committee, the paid-up share capital of each RRB was raised from ₹ 25 lakhs to ₹ 100 lakhs. The formula for refinancing the RRBs was modified so as to reduce the costlier refinance from the sponsor banks. The rate of interest to be charged by the sponsor banks on the refinance provided to the RRBs was reduced from 8.5 per cent to 7 per cent.

Progress of RRBs

At the end of December 1985, the number of branches of RRBs increased to 12,606. The number increased to 13,353 by 31st December, 1987. As of September, 1990, there were 196 RRBs with 14,511 branches covering 380 districts. More than half of these accounting for 53 per cent of total branches, have been sponsored by five major public sector banks.

At the end of December 1985, the deposits of RRBs stood at ₹ 1,285.82 crore. By September 1990, the total deposits mobilised by them stood at ₹ 4,267.52 crore and their outstanding advances totalled upto ₹ 3,355.17 crore. The average deposits and outstanding advances of a RRB were of the order of ₹ 21.77 crore and ₹ 18.14 crore respectively.

By 1995, the 196 RRBs covered 405 districts with a branch network of 14,593 manned by more than 7 lakh employees. The RRB branches alone constitute about 25 per cent of all bank branches in the country and 92.6 per cent of them are in the rural areas (the rest are in semi-urban areas). Indeed, the share of the RRBs in the total number of all rural bank branches is 61.5 per cent. As of March 1992, they gave loans to about 124 lakh small farmers, marginal farmers, agricultural labourers, rural artisans and others with small means of income in the rural areas.

Deposits increased from ₹ 0.20 crore in 1975 to ₹ 1285.82 crore in 1985, and to ₹ 22189.23 crore in 1998.

The average deposits per bank increased from 0.03 in 1975 to ₹ 113.21 crore in 1998. The average deposit per branch was equal to ₹ 1.54 crore in March 1998.

Advances increased from ₹ 0.10 crore in 1995 to ₹ 8718.08 crore in 1997 and to ₹ 9860 crore in 1998.

The advances made per bank increased from ₹ 0.017 crore in 1975 to ₹ 50.31 crore in 1998. The average advance per branch increased more than 115 fold between 1975 and 1998.

The credit deposit ratio was 50 per cent in 1975; 121.79 per cent in 1980, and 70.86 per cent in 1991. It stood at 41.76 per cent in 2002.

In 2002, RRBs advances to agriculture amounted to ₹ 4594 crore (43.46 per cent of the total). Short-term crop loans amounted to ₹ 3812 crore and term loans for agriculture and allied activities ₹ 782 crore.

For the non-agricultural sector, the RRBs advanced in 2002, ₹ 5977 crore (56.54 per cent of the total). Rural artisans, village and cottage industries etc. got ₹ 305 crore, retail trade, self-employed etc. ₹ 1279 crore and others ₹ 4493 crore.

The RRBs as a group made a profit of ₹ 75 crore for the first time during 1997-98 and improved the same further to ₹ 601 crore and to ₹ 608 crore during the years 2000-01 and 2001-02.

The viability based categorisation of RRBs as on 31st March 2002 shows that out of 196 RRBs, 86 have wiped off their accumulated losses and in a way attained a sustainable viability. Also, 89 other RRBs have achieved a turnaround and attained a current viability status. Only 29 RRBs continued to incur losses. The recovery performance of RRBs has shown remarkable improvement from around 40 per cent in 1991-92 to 70 per cent in 2001-02.

By 2004, all the 196 RRBs could cover 511 districts in the country.

The number of branches increased from 14527 in March 1991 to 14,400 in 2004.

The deposits of RRBs increased from ₹ 22,189 crore in March 1998 to ₹ 45,000 crore in 2004.

The outstanding advances increased from ₹ 9861 crore in March 1998 to ₹ 19,000 crore in 2004.

The combined profits of RRBs were ₹ 608 crore but the total accumulated losses amounted to ₹ 2700 crore as on March 31, 2003.

Table: 1
Progress fo Regional Rural Banks

Year	*No. of RRBs*	*No. of districts covered*	*No. of branches*	*Deposit*	*Loans (₹ Crore)*	*Credit deposit ratio*
Dec. 1975	6	12	17	0.20	0.10	50
Dec. 1980	85	144	3279	199	243	122
Dec. 1985	188	333	12,606	1285	1408	109
Dec. 1990	196	380	14,511	NA	3548	NA
Mar. 1995	196	425	14,509	NA	6291	NA
Mar. 1999	196	451	14,425	13,126	11,016	84
Mar. 2005	196	523	14,484	32,688	31,803	97
Mar. 2006	133	525	14,488	36,643	38,520	105

RRBs: RECENT TRENDS

There has been state wide amalgamation of RRBs in many areas. This has reduced their number from 196 to just 102 by end- October 2006. There were significant developments in 2004-05. Aggregate reserves, loans and advances out standing and loans issued increased by 23.26 and 35 per cent respectively while deposits and investments increased by 10 and 2 per cent respectively, over the previous year.

The net profit of RRBs as a group decreased by 2.7 per cent to ₹ 748.11 crore during 2004-05 over the previous year. In all, 166 RRBs showed improvement in their performance, either by way of increase in profits or reduction in losses or by shifting from loss to profit at end-March 2005, as compared to 163 at end- March 2004.

The number of RRBs which had wiped off accumulated losses and attained sustainable viability increased to 111 (from 106), their reserves increased to ₹ 3,807.34 crore and 55 RRBs also attained current viability at end-March 2005. The number of RRBs with accumulated losses declined from 97 (at end March 2003) to 83 (at end March 2005). The accumulated losses of RRBs as a group, however, decreased marginally as on 31st March 2005 from the previous year.

The number of RRBs having recovery of above 80 per cent increased from 59 as at end June 2004 to 88 as at end June 2005. During 2004-2005, 150 RRBs as against 78 during 2003-04 registered a decline in NPAs.

During 2003 to 2005, the number of branches increased from 14,433 to 14,484. Deposits, borrowings, investments and loans and advances increased by 24, 15, 11 and 48 per cent respectively. During 2003 to 2005, the profit earnings of RRBs have increased by 6 per cent and their profit earnings also increased to ₹ 168.83 crores.

The average deposit for RRB was 0.033 Crore, and advances was 0.0166 crore in December 1975. By 1999, there increased to ₹ 66.96.96 crore and ₹ 56.20 crore respectively. By March, 2006, these further increased to ₹ 275.51 crore and ₹ 289.62 crore.

In 2009, the centre decided to inject fresh capital into the weak RRBs with a CRAR (capital risk weighted assets ratio) below 7 per cent. The move is aimed to shore up RRBs capital adequacy so that it can enhance credit flow to poor farmers. The size of the fresh recapitalisation is being working out.

The Government wants fragile RRBs in terms of capital to achieve 7 per cent CRAR by 2010, and 9 per cent by 2012. There were 33 RRBs whose CRAR was below the 7 per cent mark as on March 2008. While there has been some improvement in 2008-09, the finance ministry is yet to release the fresh data relating to the 84 odd RRBs.

MAJOR PROBLEMS OF RRBs

In their actual operation, the RRBs have exhibited a number of weaknesses. At present, the sponsoring commercial bank is not exercising proper control on many crucial points such as location and licence, and the decisions rest with:

(i) The steering committee appointed by the central government;

(ii) The state government concerned and

(iii) The Reserve Bank of India.

The Dantwala Committee suggested that there should be no central control over operational aspects and the steering committee should be wound up.

Reviewing the Report of the Dantwala Committee on RRBs, Bhabatosh Datta has observed that it is irrational to compel a farmer to borrow from a commercial bank at a lower rate of interest than from an RRB or a co-operative society. It is well-known that the borrowers from the commercial banks are likely to be less weak than those borrowing from the special rural institutions.[4]

Besides credit facilities, the RRBs are expected to offer other facilities keeping in view the specific conditions of the areas they are serving. But the performance of RRBs in this respect is quite disappointing. For all practical purposes, they have become an extension version of commercial banking. It is rightly said, "Unless some of these emerging demands on the credit institutions are considered, the RRBs may fast graviate towards being a commercial bank branch, catering particularly to the liberally defined category of weaker sections of the society. The move of the co-operative towards multi-functional and single contact local points and as nerve centres of multi-sided development scores many steps ahead of the uni-purpose monolithic institutions like the RRBs."[5]

The local participation in management is no doubt theoretically sound, but in practice, it is not contributing much for the progress of the bank. It is necessary to examine as to whether state participation in capital ownership has *ipso facto* insured the larger involvement of the state government in the progress of RRBs. The supportive measures offered by the state government at the field level appear to be meagre. Moreover, the interest charged by these banks on loans for agricultural purposes is higher than that levied by commercial banks. The borrowers coming under the scheme of DIR approach the regular commercial banks since the RRBs are apparently not permitted to offer this benefit.

Even the Rural Planning and Credit Cell of the RBI has observed that the RRBs do not have adequate staff required for project preparation to avail of refinance from the Agricultural Refinance and Development Corporation (now NABARD). The Dantwala Committee observed that the RRBs have no plans to make full use of the funds at their disposal. The scheme introduced in 1975 was based on the expectation that only 15 per cent of the loanable funds of the RRBs would come from deposits, while 35 per cent would come as loans from the sponsor banks and 50 per cent as refinance from the Reserve Bank. Few banks have made use of this facility. Not only this, the weightage given to different categories of weaker sections also differed from bank to bank.[6]

The pay scales applicable to clerical and officer staff in RRBs are as per state government pay scales for comparable cadres. This means that the pay scales of the RRB staff varies from state to state. Even though service conditions are laid down in RRB staff regulations, on many issues, the government has advised RRBs to follow the state government guidelines. This once again led to different service conditions in different states.[7]

According to one study, the major problems of RRBs are:[8]

(i) An increasing number of defaulters and preoccupations of the bank officials in recovery work in respect of overdue loans;

(ii) Recovery work of overdue loans together with the normal work of processing new credit proposals and enlisting new beneficiaries hardly allows the bank officials any time for guiding the loanees in adopting improved farming techniques and making a better use of credit and

(iii) A linkage between credit, marketing and other services is practically non-existent and as such the bank is unable to provide a package of economic services like marketing, storage, processing etc., to the beneficiaries.

Another problem with RRBs, spread all over the country, is that effective control over these branches by the Head Office is becoming more and more difficult. Some of the RRBs have grown beyond their optimum size. They have thus become unmanageable. They may have to be restructured.[9] According to one case study, in some cases, the loans given in kind were sold away to meet the contingency needs, and in case of cattle-head, diseases and deaths were reported.[10]

As the credit deposit ratio of many RRBs is high, the RBI and subsequently NABARD evolved a refinance policy to supplement the resources of RRBs. As per the NABARD refinance policy, 30 per cent of the projected lending of RRBs should come from its own sources (deposits), the balance from NABARD (50 per cent) and the rest by the sponsor bank (20 per cent).

The huge overdues of RRBs have rendered many of them ineligible for refinance from NABARD/ sponsor bank and at the same time, due to poor deposit growth, could not go in for fresh lending on their own.[11]

Of the 194 RRBs in 1986,146 have incurred losses to the tune of ₹ 32.46 crore, and of them, 91 have eroded their capital and reserves due to continued losses. By March 1992, the number of loss making RRBs rose to 178 and the accumulated losses to over ₹ 900 crore.

Of the 196 RRBs, only 21 had shown profit in 1991-92, out of these 21 profit making RRBs, one was in Karnataka, seven in Andhra Pradesh, eight in Uttar Pradesh, two in West Bengal and one each in Punjab, Orissa and Bihar. Six such RRBs had profit below ₹ 10 lakhs, while only three, all of them in UP, had made profit exceeding ₹ 1 crore.

The per bank deposit was placed at ₹ 28.26 crore and the per branch deposit at ₹ 38.15 lakh.

The credit deposit ratio of RRBs has been falling ever since 1979 when it peaked at 176 per cent. By September 1993, it has been reduced to 64.7 per cent.

Until 1990, the RRB lending was restricted to weaker sections. Though the restriction was removed, the banks still catered to 125 lakh people in the low income groups with little or no assets.

A majority of 13,429 RRB branches — nearly 92 per cent — are located in interior rural areas. Only 173 are in urban and 941 in semi-urban areas.

At present, interest rates on loans are heavily subsidised at 10-12 per cent, while those on deposits are comparable to rates offered by commercial banks.

However, less than 40 per cent of the RRBs have deposits in excess of ₹ 50 crore and the outstanding deposits of all banks put together account only for ₹ 8,830.58 crore. Ironically, their rate of growth of deposits is a high at 28 per cent, unmatched by any commercial bank.

As on March 31, 1994, of the 196 RRBs, only 23 have showed profits with the remaining 173 or 88.27 per cent of them in the red. The total accumulated losses have gone up to ₹ 1,302.53 crore. According to NABARD, in the fiscal year 1994-95, returns from the 23 profitable RRBs stood at a meagre ₹ 23 crore while for the remaining 173 RRBs/it was ₹ 388 crore.

The mounting losses are due to the fact that the RRBs were compelled to open a large number of branches in rural and semi-urban areas. The RRBs were forced to open branches much beyond their capacity. The 'demand side' alone was taken into account. The 'supply constraints' were ignored. Some branches are managed by the clerical staff. In some cases, the managers belong to clerical cadre.[12]

The overdues as a percentage of loans outstandings, as at the end of March 1992, was 32 per cent (24.7 per cent in December 1984). As at the end of June, 1991, the overdues as a percentage to demand stood at 66 per cent (without taking into account the amounts due under the debt relief scheme).

An analysis of state-wise overdues shows that in some of the agriculturally developed states like Punjab and Haryana, the incidence of overdues is reportedly less. Similarly, in the states where the loans were made for investment purposes like irrigation, tubewells, purchase of tractors and agricultural implements, better recovery was noticed. Generally, recovery was poor in respect of loans sanctioned for major anti-poverty programmes.[13]

The RRBs reportedly lack the initial low cost structure due to certain adverse factors: *(i)* Defective loan policies and procedures; *(ii)* Failure of credit agencies to initiate prompt action for recovery of loans; *(iii)* Lack of active support of the state government for recovery of loans; *(iv)* Inadequate supervision over the end use of credit; *(v)* Political interference in the working of the RRBs and *(vi)* Loan waiver and interest rebate schemes.

The RRB employees very soon began to agitate for salaries on par with those paid by the commercial banks. Subsequently, the 1990 Award of the National Industrial Tribunal put the RRB salary structure on par with that of the commercial banks. Also, the employees' attitude too changed with the spread of trade union activity to RRBs. All these led to mounting wage bill, diminishing productivity and a fall in the level of motivation.[14]

The RRBs have limited income generating opportunities, thanks to the numerous restrictions on their operations. The package of measures announced in December, 1993 has not gone far enough in eliminating these handicaps. Most RRBs are still subject to service area obligations. Again, non-target financing, though raised from 40 to 60 per cent, is permissible only in respect of fresh lending.

Measures to Improve the Performance of RRBs

The Dantwala Committee, which reviewed the performance of RRBs, observed that the superiority of RRB "as an agency of rural credit over the rural branches of commercial banks is derived from its relatively lower cost of operation, its simplicity and low profile, local participation in its management, feel and familiarity of the local staff and close association of the district level agricultural and rural development agencies and personnel." Of course, the cost of operation is going to increase if the differential salary structure is abolished or if the sponsoring banks withdraw their partnership in sharing the establishment cost over a period of time.

The Dantwala Committee, (appointed by the RBI) submitted its Report in 1978. It has placed before the policymakers three options relating to the future programme of RRBs:

(i) To scrap the RRB structure;

(ii) To proceed on a selective basis with the extension programme of establishing RRBs and

(iii) To adopt the RRB pattern for the bulk of rural credit business of commercial banks.

However, the Review Committee felt that considering the conditions under which the RRBs are made to function (they are concentrating on backward areas and weaker sections), their performance is quite satisfactory. They can become economically viable after the completion of the gestation period. The overhead cost of the supervised agricultural credit operations may come down because of large number of accounts to be supervised in a given area.

In judging the performance of RRBs, we have to take note of their problems of feasibility; administrative viability, commercial soundness on the one hand and compulsions of socio-economic realities such as lack of trained personnel, lack of resilience on the part of the existing employees of the sponsoring bank who would initially be deployed in rural areas etc. on the other. [15] In view of these problems, the chairman and branch managers are imparted training at the College of Agricultural Banking (CAB, Pune) and other staff get training at the centres of the respective sponsor banks under the overall supervision of CAB.

The heavy losses are due to poor infrastructural facilities in the areas where the RRBs serve and absence of Farmers' Service Societies and Primary Agricultural Credit Societies etc. through which the RRBs have to advance loans as per the original provisions. As direct lending results in higher distribution, supervision and recovery costs, losses have become enormous. Since the banks are lending exclusively to the rural poor, the number of beneficiaries is more but the total loaned amount remains significantly low which results in low rates of profitability. In order to minimise the operational costs, there must be a pre-conceived model of a viable rural office, more administrative linkage of these branches with selected centres, where expertise and experience are readily available.

The Dantwala Committee has observed, "Indeed, the success of these banks should be judged as much by the efforts at expanding and extending the area of rural credit as by the conventional yardstick of profitability."

Some of the essential conditions of success of RRBs are: active support from the state governments, adequate and effective financing from the sponsor banks, a meaningful relationship with the co-operative system and local participation.[16] The RRBs have to turn to co-operatives to bridge the gap between them and the rural producer. They have to adopt a promotional approach towards co-operatives, rationalise their own methods and operations, actually help in the reorganisation of potentially viable societies so as to make them effective rural intermediaries.[17]

Measures to improve the performance of RRBs should include:[18]

(i) The Primary Co-operative Societies in the area of operation of an RRB should be dissolved and the beneficiaries should be served directly by the bank;

(ii) No commercial bank should be allowed to organise a Farmers' Service Society in the area of operation of the RRB; and

(iii) Any further expansion by a commercial bank in the area of operation of an RRB should be done only with the prior approval of the RRB.

A study on RRBs, undertaken by the Agricultural Finance Corporation, has pointed out that RRBs resort to heavy borrowing from sponsor banks at higher interest rates just to meet their loan obligation under IRDP. It has suggested that sponsor banks should encourage RRBs to participate in an increasing manner in NABARD assisted area-based schemes such as IRDP etc.[19]

The Kelkar Committee (1986) reviewed the working of RRBs. It observed, that "however, to ensure that the large borrowers do not preempt the bulk of loanable funds of the RRBs and the RRBs retain their district mark as the tank of a small man, we suggest that at least 60 per cent of the loan advances by the RRB should be earmarked for the benefit of small farmers, rural artisans and other rural poor."

The Narasimham Committee on Financial System, set up by the Government in 1991, felt that in order to impart viability to their operations, the RRBs should be permitted to engage in all types of banking business, although their focus should continue to lend to the target groups. When this is accepted, the RRBs may be able to function on commercial lines. As a solution to this problem, the Narasimham Committee laid down that "the level of credit to the target group should be maintained as it had obtained during the year 1989-90."

The Committee headed by M.C. Bhandari has, *inter alia,* suggested infusion of a fresh capital of ₹ 25 crore to be shared by the Union Government, the sponsor commercial banks and the state governments in proportion to their earlier share holdings in the RRBs — 50:35:15. That means that the Central Government should release ₹ 12.50 crore, the sponsor banks ₹ 8.75 crore and the state governments together the amount of ₹ 3.75 crore.

The other recommendations include appointment of professionals on RRB boards instead of politicians, investing surplus funds of the RRBs in the Krishi Vikas Patra, the National Saving Schemes, UTI schemes and fixed deposits of financial institutions such as the Industrial Development Bank of India.

The committee set up by NABARD, under the chairmanship of Kishenjit Basu, has suggested, as a step towards restructuring, that a cut-off point should be considered for provisioning norms. While there is to be no provisioning for standard assets, for sub standard assets, 10 per cent provisioning is to be provided and in case of doubtful assets, 100 per cent to which the advance is not covered by the realisable value of the security. The Committee has suggested that the provisioning norms be extended irrespective of whether RRBs have received capitalisation assistance or not.

The Working Group, set up by the RBI in 1995, has recommended that RRBs be allowed to do consortium lending along with the commercial banks in urban areas to improve their balance sheets. The working group has also discussed the possibility of making it mandatory for private sector banks to support loss making RRBs as a pre-condition for opening new branches in major metros.

Many of the weak RRBs have surplus staff. There are three to four staff members working even at a branch where total slips per day is 4 to 10. Such branches should be given freedom to plan in order to achieve more viability and financial muscle. RRBs should give support to branches in implementing the strategies for achieving their respective development action plans.

The content of training should not be limited only to rural banking but cover all subjects of rural development. There should be adequate staff to supervise the credit and other inputs, which are expected to generate increasing income of the rural borrowers and similarly, there must be adequate staff to ensure timely and full recovery.[20]

In 1994, the Government decided to pump in ₹ 275 crore as fresh contribution to the capital of 49 RRBs. However, recapitalisation is not the answer to the present problems of RRBs. In fact, fresh operational losses may wipe out the additional capital.

During 1994-95, 50 of the 196 RRBs were taken up for comprehensive restructuring including the cleansing of their balance sheets and infusion of fresh capital. With effect from January 1, 1994, the proportion of the non-target groups lending has been enhanced to 60 per cent of the fresh lending.

RRBs have since been permitted to extend advances for purchase of consumer durables and loans for various purposes against the security of gold ornaments, National Savings Certificates, Indira Vikas Patras to both target and non-target groups up to 10 per cent of their fresh lending to be accounted for within the overall ceiling of 60 per cent of fresh loans to non-target group lending.

RRBs have also been allowed to issue guarantees on behalf of their customers without any limit on 100 per cent cash margin and up to ₹ 20 lakh on 40 lakh cash margin plus collateral security of more than 50 per cent.

The public sector banks with proven track record and sound fundamentals may come forward to adopt at least one or few weak RRBs and make them viable. Again, only stronger RRBs can help weaker sections cross poverty line. There is, therefore a strong case for the complete deregulation of interest.[21]

RRBs should lay more emphasis on branch level performance and fulfilment of targets in respect of all parameters by branches. Branch managers should be considered the focal point. They should spearhead the process of implementation of Development Action Plan (DAP) targets of their respective branches. With a view to inducing motivation at the branch level, RRBs should introduce a comprehensive performance budgeting exercise with a participation model built into it. The performance budget should be integrated with the DAP.[22]

The viability of RRBs will have to be assessed in terms of increase in business per branch, recovery rate, productivity of staff, cost effectiveness of operations, closer monitoring and socio-economic upliftment and improvement in the standards of living of the clientele.[23]

RRB branches should be given opportunities to participate not only in preparing budgets for outputs like deposits, advances, income and profits, but also in the matter of budgeting for input requirements including staff requirement.[24]

In the light of financial reforms undertaken, the government set up a committee to suggest amendments in the Regional Rural Banks Act, 1976 under the chairmanship of M. V. S. Chalapathy Rao in July 2001. In its report submitted in June 2002, the committee recommemded:

- Change in capital structure and ownership pattern;
- Enlarged role of Sponsor banks;
- Structural consolidation by way of amalgamation on socio-economic zone basis;
- Introduction of capital adequacy norms in a phased manner;
- Additional supervisory authority;
- Computer-based management system; and
- Introduction of asset liability and risk management systems.

An internal group (Chairman:A.V. Sardesai) was set up by the RBI to examine various alternatives available within the existing legal framework for strengthening RRBs and making them viable rural financial institutions. The group submitted its report in June 2005 which has been sent to the government for comments.

The major recommendations of the group include merger/amalgamation of RRBs to improve operational viability, change of sponsor banks to enhance competitiveness, strengthening of balance sheets in respect of merged entities, regulatory and supervisory strengthening, governance and management and scope for improving profitability.

The RRBs have been set up with the specific objective of serving the rural poor. As such, the flaws in their functioning should be removed. The merger of RRBs with their sponsor banks is no solution to the problems associated with rural credit.

REFERENCES

1. S.P. Sinha: 'Agricultural Credit: Development and Prospect', *Commerce* (Annual Number) 1979, p. 111.
2. C.B. Mamoria (1979): *Agricultural Problems of India,* Kitab Mahal, Allahabad, pp. 482-83.
3. J.D. Batra: 'Rural Banks for the Rural Poor', *Kurukshetra,* October 16, 1977, p. 12.
4. *Economic and Political Weekly,* September 9, 1978, p. 1556.
5. Harpal Singh: 'Regional Rural Banks', *Yojana,* December 16, 1979, pp. 14-15.
6. *Economic and Political Weekly,* September 9, 1978, p. 1954.
7. Anil K. Khandwal: Personnel Policies in Regional Rural Banks', *Economic and Political Weekly,* February 22,1986, p. M-30.
8. V. Lakshminarayana: 'Regional Rural Banks: Problems and Prospects', *Financing Agriculture,* April-June 1984, p. 56.
9. *The Economic Times,* October 15, 1984, p. 4.
10. Jagdish Prasad and Sunil Kumar: 'Role of Regional Rural Banks', *Kurukshetra,* May 1985, p. 33.
11. K.S.V. Krishnamadiari: 'RRBs: Sinned Against than Sinners', *The Economic Times,* November 25, 1992.

12. P.N. Joshi: 'Future of Regional Rural Banks: Branch Expansion Stretches Resources', *The Economic Times,* September 15, 1992.
13. T.K. Velayudham and V. Sankaranarayanan: 'Regional Rural Banks and Rural Credit: Some Issues', *Economic and Political Weekly,* September 22, 1990, p. 2159.
14. K. Srinivasa Rao: 'Restructuring RRBs — A Challenge to PSBs, *Financial Express,* August 14, 1994.
15. *Eastern Economist,* January 16, 1976, p. 104.
16. *Economic and Political Weekly,* September 9, 1979, p. 1555.
17. B.N. Choubey: 'Regional Rural Banks and Co-operatives: A Rational Approach to their Lineage', *Indian Co-operative Review,* January 1976, p. 183.
18. B. Yerram Raju (1982): *Commercial Banks and Rural Development: Issues and Trends,* Data News Features, 2nd Floor, Barman Building, Gun Foundry, Hyderabad, p. 55.
19. *The Economic Times,* November 29, 1984.
20. M.G. Shah: 'One Rural Bank for One District', *Commerce,* January 23, 1982, p. 145.
21. J.S. Tomar: 'Regional Rural Banks: Looking Forward', *The Economic Times,* August 17, 1995.
22. K.K. Ammannaya: 'Viability Vital for Success of Regional Rural Banks', *Financial Express,* January 8, 1995.
23. T.K. Velayudham and V. Sankaranarayanan: *op. cit.,* p. 2162.
24. K.K. Ammannaya: 'Regional Rural Banks and Rural Economic Development', *Southern Economist,* April 1 and 15, 1996.

Chapter

41 National Bank for Agriculture and Rural Development

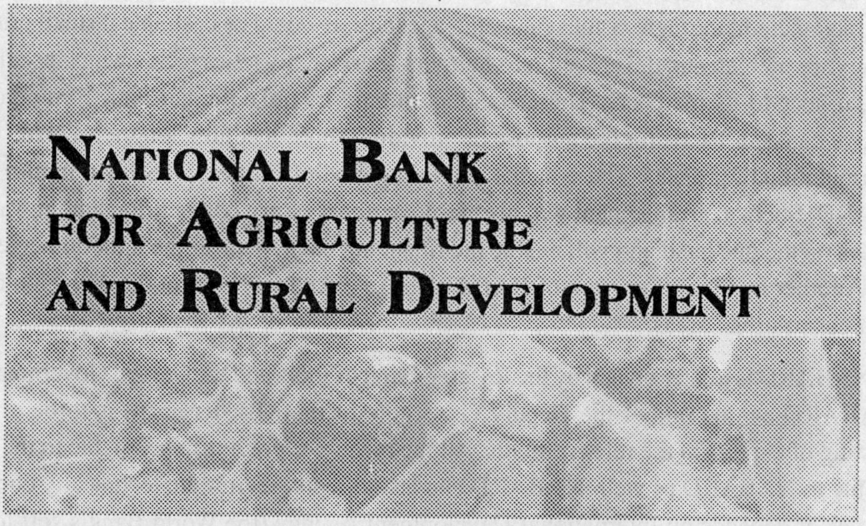

In the rural sector, institutional credit is not only inadequate, but it is unevenly distributed in favour of the affluent sections. This is mainly due to lack of co-ordination amongst various credit agencies. Very often, the loans advanced to the rural rich are given to the poor at a higher rate of interest. Thus, mere establishment of a new credit agency is not likely to bridge the institutional credit gap.

In December 1971, the National Commission on Agriculture (in its interim report on credit services for small and marginal farmers and agricultural labourers) expressed the view that it might be ultimately necessary to set up an Agricultural Development Bank of India on the lines of the Industrial Development Bank of India. The Committee to Review Arrangements for Institutional Credit for Agriculture and Rural Development (CRAFICARD) headed by. B.Sivaraman favoured the setting up of an all-India institution, though there is a view that such an institution will only add to the cost of credit and the red-tape associated with its procedure.

The National Bank for Agriculture and Rural Development (NABARD) is an apex institution of national importance for providing short, medium and long-term credit for financing agricultural and allied activities including processing, storage etc. It started functioning from July 12, 1982. NABARD's authorised share capital is ₹ 500 crore and paid-up capital ₹ 100 crore, contributed equally by the Central Government and RBI. NABARD replaced the agriculture credit department of RBI and the Agricultural Refinance and Development Corporation (ARDC).

NABARD has over 25 regional offices in the country and a paid up capital of ₹ 100 crore, contributed by the Government of India and the Reserve Bank of India. This was raised to ₹ 500 crore later, and at present it has increased to ₹ 2000 crore.

One of the problems of multi-agency approach is over-financing. It is therefore suggested that NABARD should introduce the concept of 'one borrower, one financial agency.' It should co-ordinate the supply of credit through various financing agencies. It would be desirable if small primary agricultural societies are merged and developed into Farmers' Service Societies (FSS) which provide besides credit other services to its members. These societies should be linked either with commercial banks or co-operative banks or RRBs for the purpose of providing short, medium, long-term credit and expertise for the formulation of projects. These banks, providing credit facilities to FSS will in turn be refinanced by NABARD. Such an arrangement will also remove unnecessary competition among various rural credit agencies on the one hand and will enable the financing bank to cover the hitherto neglected areas on the other. Another important function of NABARD is to effectively control the diversion of funds from the rural areas to urban areas.

NABARD is jointly owned by the Reserve Bank of India and the Central Government. The chairman of NABARD can be one of the Deputy Governors of the RBI. Its board is to be a nominated board consisting of experts in the relative fields. All the resources previously available to the ARDC would be available to NABARD as well. NABARD can also directly recruit the technically competent staff. For resources, it depends on International Development Agency (the World Bank's soft loan window), the RBI and the Government of India. It can also float bonds. It can receive deposits from the State Co-operative Banks (SCBs) and State Land Development Banks (SLDBs) and also other deposits such as those accruing incidently in its business. NABARD is to decide the limits of credit to be made available to each of the RRBs, commercial banks, state co-operative banks, state land development banks, although certain guidelines are to be framed by the RBI.

There is need for providing economic size loans, speedily and at one window. This is a pre-requisite for containing, if not ending, the new class of credit middlemen and the attendant corruption.[1] Promoting integrated rural development and ensuring rural prosperity by bringing about an administrative change in the existing arrangements at the apex level, particularly for the promotion of production and investment credit were set as the aims of the Bank.[2]

FUNCTIONS OF NABARD

The functions of NABARD as envisaged by the Sivaraman Committee are:

(i) Development policy, planning and operational matters relating to credit for agriculture, allied activities, rural artisans and industries and other rural developmental activities;

(ii) Training, research and consultancy relating to credit for agriculture and rural development;

(iii) Refinance to commercial banks against term lending (medium-term and long-term) and short-term accommodation for special purposes;

(iv) Refinance, short-term, medium-term and long-term to the co-operatives and RRBs, including co-operative marketing and distribution;

(v) Direct lending, singly or through consortium arrangements in special cases;

(vi) Co-ordination and monitoring of all agricultural and rural lending activities with a view to tying them up with extension and planned development activities in the rural sector;

(vii) Inspection of co-operative banks and RRBs and

(viii) Advise NCDC etc. in regard to the co-operative movement in close collaboration with RBI and the Central government.

SCHEMES AND PATTERNS OF NABARD

NABARD has various schemes for extending refinance for the following purposes:[3]

(i) Development of infrastructure facilities like development of land, construction of worksheds, godowns etc.

(ii) Purchase of machinery, equipment, implements, tools etc.

(iii) Working capital requirements restricted to automatic refinance schemes.

There are two types of schemes covered under automatic refinance scheme as under:

(i) Composing loan upto ₹ 50,000 which covers term loan and working capital and

(ii) Integrated loan upto ₹ 7.50 lakh, term loan plus working capital.

NABARD's refinance is extended through State Financial Corporations, Scheduled Commercial Banks and Co-operative Banks. It has branches in all states. The units are to be automatically financed by the banks and the amount so financed is recouped by NABARD. The schemes involving more than ₹ 7,550 lakh are to be individually examined and prior approval of NABARD is necessary. Under such schemes, only term loan and working capital for a turnover upto ₹ 75 lakhs for each scheme is provided and for additional working capital, normal loan either by the KVIC or banks may be provided which is not covered under the re-finance scheme.

In addition to the above, there are a number of promotional schemes for which NABARD extends financial assistance in the form of grant such as:

(i) Training cum production centres;

(ii) Research and Development Programme;

(iii) Entrepreneur Development Programme;

(iv) The project preparations/formulations; and

(v) Exchange of collaborations and expertise.

NABARD has been providing refinance facilities to base level institutions with a view to ensuring proper flow of credit to agriculture and other priority sectors. Refinance is channelled mainly through four agencies, viz., commercial banks, RRBs, SLDBs and SCBs. While SLDBs deal with long-term lendings, the SCBs are concerned with medium and short-term operations.

NABARD operates all over the country through its 16 regional offices located in the capitals of all the major states and three sub-offices.[4]

Though in exceptional circumstances, NABARD can undertake direct lending, it is essentially a refinancing body for the entire rural lending system. It also undertakes monitoring and evaluation studies. It would also bring about uniformity in systems and procedures between different lending institutions, making it easier for the farmer to choose between them. It may help the state governments in identification of the target groups as also lending programmes. Its attention to the credit delivery systems and recycling of funds might improve the ultimate quality of lending, ensuring timely assistance to the farmer.

NABARD is to ensure better co-ordination and linkage between the banks and state governments. NABARD also should help in drastically reforming the system of refinancing currently in vogue through the ARDC. It has to design a system which would enable free flow of information on all the aspects of implementation of schemes from the retail outlets of banks.

NABARD embodies the principles of integration and decentralisation in so far as it brings together the different parts of rural credit hitherto dealt with in different sections of the RBI, i.e., the Agriculture Credit Department which deals with short-term credit and medium-term credit, ARDC which deals with long-term credit and part of the Department of Banking Operations and Development which deals with agricultural credit by the commercial banks. The organisation of one single institution, integrating all these aspects which are now fragmented in different parts of the RBI, would make for a more effective functioning of the policies and programmes of rural credit. Better results are expected as the federal banking institution has worked out strategies for entrusting the specialised function of agricultural credit to NABARD.

NABARD provides short-term credit to SCBs, RRBs and other financial institutions, repayable over a period not exceeding 18 months for agricultural operations or marketing of crops, of inputs, for commercial and trade transactions, production and marketing of products in the small, cottage and village industries sector.

The short-term loans granted to state co-operative banks and RRBs can be converted into medium-term loans for a period not exceeding 7 years under conditions of drought, famine, natural calamities, military operations or enemy action. NABARD also gives medium-term loans for periods not less than 18 months and not exceeding 7 years to state co-operative banks and RRBs for agriculture and rural development. It will give long-term loans and advances by way of refinance to LDBs, RRBs, Scheduled banks, SCBs and other financial institutions.

NABARD is promoting campaigns to spread the repayment ethic. One of NABARD's important programmes is also to reorganise primary co-operatives and make them viable units. The main problem with the primary co-operatives is that they are too small to engage any trained personnel to serve their needs. NABARD also makes attempts to provide trained personnel who can devote their knowledge and skills to the development of the co-operatives over a period of time. Through technical back-up, NABARD would make broad technical guidance available to commercial banks and co-operative banks. Thus, NABARD is one institution responsible for studying and helping rural development in all its aspects where institutional credit can play a part.[5]

The venture capital fund will have a corpus of ₹ 5 crore. The main purpose of the fund is to:[6]

(i) Assist directly by subscribing to the share capital of companies or promotional concerns adopting innovative ideas or new technologies in agricultural and non-farming and agro processing sectors in rural areas;

(ii) Co-financing for venture capital along with other agencies working in the same area and

(iii) Providing guarantee for the borrowing of voluntary and promotional agencies providing linkage and marketing support to tiny units and craftsmen.

Progress of NABARD

The term credit disbursement of NABARD by way of refinance under schematic tendings crossed ₹ 700 crore during the year 1982-83 — an increase of ₹ 103 crore (17 per cent) against ₹ 600 crore in the previous year by the erstwhile ARDC.

The commercial banks, including the RRBs, took a major share of finance with 61 per cent, the SLDBs 33 per cent and the SCBs 6 per cent. An important feature was a marked improvement in the performance of RRBs in the drawal of refinance under schematic lendings in the year 1982-83, so much so, that their drawals aggregated ₹ 61 crore compared with ₹ 38 crore in the previous year from ARDC.

Minor irrigation was the most important single investment for NABARD with refinance around ₹ 244 crore (35 per cent) out of the ₹ 703 crore provided to it in 1982-83. The working of NABARD during 1982-83 resulted in a surplus of ₹ 94 crore.[7] This surplus was appropriated for strengthening the bank's National Rural Credit (Long-Term Operations) Fund with ₹ 47 crore, the National Rural Credit (Stabilisation) Fund with ₹ 8 crore, Research and Development Fund with ₹ 5 crore and Reserve Fund with ₹ 34 crore.

Refinance facilities provided to co-operative banks for seasonal agricultural operations by the NABARD have crossed ₹ 1,500 crore for the year ended December, 1985. This assistance was barely ₹ 6.12 crore during 1975-76 and ₹ 1,233 crore during 1984-85. The seasonal assistance was provided for agricultural operations, production and marketing activities of weavers and other industrial co-operative societies and rural artisans.

NABARD has taken several measures to ensure that the credit need of new and non-defaulting members of Primary Agricultural Credit Societies (PACs), even in the areas of operation of those Central Co-operative Banks (CCBs) which are ineligible for credit limits from NABARD are fully met. SCBs have been advised to meet such credit needs from their own resources. NABARD, to enable SCBs to achieve this objective, has provided additional short-term credit limits for approved purposes on behalf of eligible CCBs so as to release the resources of SCBs for financing ineligible CCBs.[8]

NABARD has achieved a 18.90 per cent growth in its refinancing activities during 1994-95 over the previous year. Total disbursements, estimated tentatively for the year 1994-95 were placed at ₹ 7,769 crore as against ₹ 6,534 crore for 1993-94.

The average yearly growth for the ten-year period (1983 to 1993) stood at 12.4 per cent. There was a 5.93 per cent growth during 1993-94 with total refinancing amounting to ₹ 6,534 crore for the year. The bank has projected a growth of 17.35 per cent, with a refinancing target of ₹ 9,117 crore for 1995-96.

Ground level investment and production credit jumped from ₹ 15,168 crore in 1992-93 to ₹ 17337 crore for 1993-94 and are tentatively placed at ₹ 20,551 crore in 1994-95. Share of co-operative in rural credit increased from ₹ 9,337 crore in 1992-93 to ₹ 0,117 crore in 1993-94 and was estimated to ₹ 12,000 crore in 1994-95.

During 1994-95, a sum of ₹ 3,010 crore was refinanced towards investment credit of which the LDBs headed the list with ₹ 1,206 crore, followed by commercial banks with ₹ 1,092 crore. Regional rural banks secured ₹ 441 crore while the state co-operative banks were refinanced a sum of ₹ 270 crore.

Under production credit, in 1994-95, NABARD sanctioned credit limits to co-operative banks and RRBs aggregating ₹ 4,648 crore as against ₹ 3,964 crore during 1993-94 for financing agricultural operations. For other purposes like financing for the working capital requirements of handloom/powerloom weavers, industrial co-operatives, rural artisans etc. NABARD during 1994-95, sanctioned short-term credit limits aggregating ₹ 755 crore as against ₹ 690 crore in 1993-94.

NABARD also sanctioned long-term loans of ₹ 68.35 crore during the year to various state governments for enabling them to contribute to the share capital of co-operatives. This has helped to increase the borrowing capacities of co-operatives by improving their equity position. A sum of ₹ 161.57 crore was extended for the conversion of short-term loans into medium-term loans on occurrence of natural calamities.

The Co-operative Development Fund (CDF) created during 1992-93 to improve the viability of co-operatives was augmented by another ₹ 20 crore in addition to the initial corpus of ₹ 10 crore. A total assistance of ₹ 7.74 crore has been sanctioned out of this fund to 15 state co-operative banks and five State Land Development Banks for various purposes.

Purpose-wise refinancing was topped by farm mechanisation with ₹ 685 crore, followed by IRDP with ₹ 620 crore and the non-farming sector with ₹ 410 crore. Minor irrigation was refinanced to an extent of ₹ 390 crore and dairy development with ₹ 170 crore. Plantations and horticulture, a major thrust area received refinancing to the tune of ₹ 129 crore while poultry/sheep/goat and the pig farming sector secured ₹ 139 crore. Of this, the poultry sector stood out with ₹ 96 crore refinancing.

Rural Electricity Corporation secured ₹ 117 crore while the fisheries sector was refinanced with ₹ 100.70 crore. In the latter sector, marine culture farming accounted for ₹ 6.24 crore, inland ₹ 38.21 crore and the remaining ₹ 56.25 crore went to brackish water prawn culture.

Among the states, Uttar Pradesh continued to absorb maximum amount of refinance at ₹ 471 crore, forming 15.6 per cent of the total investment credit refinance, followed by Maharashtra with ₹ 364 crore (12 per cent) and Andhra Pradesh with ₹ 361 crore (also 12 per cent).

The thrust of NABARD is on agriculture. The amount disbursed for agricultural purposes for all the regions of the country was ₹ 772.93 crore in 1988. This increased to ₹ 5268.31 crore in 1993, to ₹ 6914.52 crore in 1998, and to ₹ 18,274.81 crore in 2000.

The amount sanctioned by NABARD for all schemes for all regions of the country was ₹ 704.69 crore in 1982-83. This increased to ₹ 6710.93 crore in 1987-88 to ₹ 16046.65 crore in 1992-93 to ₹ 30,210.52 crore in 1997-98 and to ₹ 39,946 crore in the year 2000 as shown in Table 1.

Table: 1

NABARD: Cumulative Amounts Disbursed for all Schemes

(₹ Crore)

Region	*1982-83*	*1987-88*	*1992-93*	*1997-98*	*2000*
Northern	187.19 (26.56)	1449.93 (21.61)	2795.20 (17.42)	3728.65 (12.34)	6080.76 (15.22)
North-East	13.84 (1.96)	204.12 (3.04)	530.20 (3.30)	1113.44 (3.69)	1365.32 (3.42)
Eastern	89.01 (12.63)	865.74 (12.90)	1912.01 (11.92)	3567.81 (11.81)	4633.45 (11.60)
Western	80.41 (11.41)	935.13 (13.93)	2466.19 (15.37)	5076.94 (16.81)	6966.72 (17.44)
Central	151.00 (82.41)	1414.00 (76.76)	3678.00 (78.84)	6858.98 (69.53)	8334.80 (66.33)
Southern	183.24 (26.00)	1842.01 (27.45)	4664.05 (29.07)	9864.70 (32.65)	12565.36 (31.46)
All India	704.69 (100.00)	6710.93 (100.00)	6046.65 (100.00)	30210.52 (100.00)	39946.50 (100.00)

MAJOR PROBLEMS

Several institutional constraints were identified by NABARD which was inhibiting the free flow of rural credit in the country including the problem of mounting overdues. Under agricultural loans, there was a two-fold increase from ₹ 4,654 crore in June 1986 to ₹ 8,896 crore in June 1992. The recovery climate was vitiated due to loan waivers, interest subsidy schemes and political interference.

Apart from inadequate supervision over credit, there was lack of awareness about development through credit and repayment ethic. In terms of viability, the major problem was erosion of networth of banks/co-operatives aggregating to a staggering amount of ₹ 2,000 crore. Many institutions continued to incur losses, primarily due to administered (low) interest rates resulting in inadequate margins.

NEW MEASURES

NABARD decided to raise a volunteer corporation named 'Vikas Volunteer Vahini' for spreading the message of development through institutional credit. It consists of the beneficiaries of such credit operations all over the country. A volunteer, during his spare time on the farm, would meet neighbouring small farmers, rural artisans etc. and would educate them by sharing his experiences and success with them. The area of his operation will involve administration activities one or two districts adjoining his own, within his state or other neighbouring states, where the language spoken is the one known to the volunteer. In order to enable them to discahrge these functions satisfactorily, they will be given appropriate training by NABARD. In order to co-ordinate the activities of Vikas Volunteer Vahini with those of block extension agencies, the NABARD representative will accompany the volunteers to the village and help them. The volunteer units will be also given a short course of training every year before they are sent out to undertake activites in the villages or blocks assigned to them. The units will be supplied with useful literature in regional languages and other visual aids.[9]

The criteria for eligibility of banking institutions to refinance from the NABARD have been made more stringent as per the recommendations of the World Bank. With effect from July 1, 1986, NABARD, refinancing for PLDBs, LDB branches, RRBs and commercial banks would be classified into four categories, according to the recovery percentage achieved during the previous year. This would be applicable for branches in all parts of the country, excluding the north-eastern region.

Those branches which had a recovery percentage of 75 per cent or more, would fall under category one, which would entitle them to unlimited access in terms of refinancing facility. The present recovery percentage for category one branch is 65 per cent. Branches which had a recovery percentage of 60 to 74 would be classified as category two and would be entitled to refinancing facility for the highest amount lent in any of the last five years, or the average recovered in the previous three years, whichever was greater. Branches with a recovery percentage of 36 to 59 would enjoy refinance facility for the amount recovered in the previous fiscal year or the average amount recovered in the past three years, whichever was greater. Branches with a recovery percentage of between 0 to 35 per cent would be relegated to the last category. During the first year in which a bank fell under category four, refinancing would be limited to 75 per cent of the amount calculated for category three and if the branch failed to improve its recovery by at least seven percentage points, refinancing would be further reduced to 50 per cent in the second year and 25 per cent in the third.[10]

NABARD is seeking an amendment into the NABARD Act of 1982 to increase its authorised capital from the current level of ₹ 500 crore to ₹ 2,000 crore.

This has become necessary with the government and the RBI injecting in a sum of Rs. 170 crore into the bank's capital.

The fresh infusion of ₹ 170 crore will take NABARD's capital to ₹ 500 crore from its present level of ₹ 330 crore. With the paid-up capital reaching its ceiling level, as prescribed in the Act, the bank will need an amendment for any fresh capital injection.

NABARD has also outlined a multi-pronged strategy to tide over its resource crunch during the 1995-96 fiscal, which is estimated to be around ₹ 1,067 crore.

Besides calling for an increase in the government's contribution to its capital, the Board has also asked the government for permission to tap the market with an issue of tax free non-SLR bonds to the order of ₹ 300 crore.

NABARD also plans to take up with the RBI the resumption of the latter's contribution to the Long-Term Operations (LTO) fund. The Reserve Bank of India discontinued its contribution of ₹ 400 crore to the LTO fund in 1992-93. In the subsequent years, 1993-94 and 1994-95, the RBI contribution to the fund was a meagre ₹ 1 crore. This was a token contribution which the RBI had to make as per the provisions of the NABARD Act.

NABARD has been asking the government to negotiate a line of credit from the World Bank to meet its resource needs. It is, however, undecided on the amount of the loan.

In its business budget and resource position for 1995-96, NABARD estimated a total resource requirement of ₹ 9,679 crore while the total planned resources at its command will be only ₹ 8,617 crore, leaving a resource gap of ₹ 1,067 crore.[11]

In the context of resource crunch, NABARD will have to gear itself to raise resources from the market in the coming years on an increasing scale.[12] In the coming years, the debt equity ratio may become adverse. NABARD has to therefore expand its operations, strengthen its equity base or resort to low cost borrowings.

Realising the need for a broad technical wing at the micro level, NABARD proposes to constitute district technical groups. While the idea is quite welcome, NABARD has to strengthen its own technical manpower to man the technical groups at the district level. The groups are expected to concentrate on area-based location specific activities. They can also conduct periodical on the spot training programmes to the technical wings of the banks. Also, NABARD has to pay attention to the qualitative dimensions of credit plans submitted by banks for their service area.[13]

At present, banks provide loans only for buying new tractors and NABARD does not support refinance for secondhand tractors. With thrust on farm mechanisation, the demand for second-hand tractors reportedly increased. Therefore, farmers may be given loans for purchasing second-hand workable tractors which are not more than three years old. The rich farmers too want to replace their old tractors by new ones.[14]

NABARD has introduced an exclusive scheme, viz., Assistance to Rural Women in Non-Farm Development (ARWIND). It is a single window scheme to take care of credit and promotional needs of groups of rural women in non-farm development either for one's own activity or group activity. The scheme envisages an umbrella support for NGOs and other promotional agencies. The total number of projects sanctioned and financial commitments made by NABARD by 1999 were 46 and ₹ 14.9 million respectively. Besides, NABARD has also supported several agencies for conducting Rural Entrepreneurship Development Programmes (REDPs), skill training, setting up Artisans' Guilds and Mother Units/Common Service Centres for rural women.

The Government of India announced in the budget of 1995-96 the scheme for setting up of a Rural Infrastructure Development Fund (RIDF) within NABARD for financing of rural infrastructure projects.

RIDF was set up in 1995-96 with an initial amount of ₹ 2000 crore made up contributions to be received from scheduled commercial banks to the extent of shortfall in agriculture lending in the priority sector target of 18 per cent of their total lending to agriculture. Successive Union Budgets share announced enhanced committed contributions. For instance, in the budget for 2000-2001, it was ₹ 4500 crore.

Till March 31st, 2001, total allocations have an aggregate to ₹ 18,000 crore, NABARD has, for the year 2001-02 further allocated ₹ 5000 crore.

The Fund initially supported projects implemented by state governments. From the year 1999-2000, its scope was extended to cover projects implemented by ground level institutions like Panchayat Raj Institutions (PRIs), SHGs and NGOs.

Till March 31st, 2001, loans aggregating ₹ 766.20 crore have been sanctioned to state governments for projects being implemented by PRIs, SHGs and NGOs.

NABARD is supporting promotional institutions and NGOs in the conduct of Rural Entrepreneurship Development Programme (REDP). The success rate of these programmes as measured by the number of trainees undertaking their own projects is high. So far, nearly 9000 rural youth have been covered under 365 REDPs with financial support of ₹ 20 million.

NABARD has decided to include rural housing as an eligible activity for extension of refinance (investment credit) to all eligible banks, state co-operative banks and scheduled primary (urban) co-operative banks. The scheme is being implemented since April 1, 2001.

Refinance will be provided by NABARD against the loans extended by the banks for housing projects in the rural areas only. In context of the scheme, rural area has been defined as the area belonging to a village or any town where the population does not exceed 50,000.

Individuals, co-operative housing societies, public bodies, housing boards, housing development authorities, improvement trusts, local bodies, voluntary agencies, NGOs and housing finance companies registered with National Housing Bank are eligible borrowers for availing of credit for construction of new houses as well as repairs/renovations of existing houses in rural areas.

With a view to ensuring that the benefit of refinance goes to low and middle income groups, ceilings on cost of dwelling units upto ₹ 7.5 lakh (excluding cost of land), quantum of bank loans for individuals for new houses up to ₹ five lakh, repairs and renovations of existing houses up to ₹ 50,000 has been prescribed by NABARD under the scheme.

NABARD's Progress by 2006

On 12th July 2006, NABARD completed 24 years of service to rural India. Major achievements of NABARD are:

The Micro Finance Programme is the largest of its kind in the world. The programme has helped over 329.90 lakh households through 22.38 lakh SHGs comprising mostly of women members.

NABARD has done a commendable job towards women empowerment. ₹ 872 lakh have been sanctioned by way of assistance to women entrepreneurs.

Through the Rural Infrastructure Development Fund, ₹ 51,283 crore have been sanctioned for ₹ 2,44,651 projects covering irrigation, rural roads and bridges, health and education, soil conservation, drinking water schemes etc.

Watershed Development Fund, with cumulative sanctions of ₹ 578.95 crore for 427 projects in 124 districts of 14 states, has created a 'Peoples Movement' in rural India.

Farmers now enjoy financial access and security through 582.50 lakh Kisan Credit Cards that have been issued through a vast rural banking network.

District Rural Industries Project (DRIP) has generated employment for 23.84 lakh persons with 10.95 lakh units in 105 districts.

Natural Resource Management Initiatives have provided replicable models for sustainable development in resource poor and tribal areas.

NABARD has created Special Funds, namely, Tribal Development Fund, Integrated Development of Backward Blocks, Research and Development Fund, Farm Innovations Fund, Micro Finance Development and Equity Fund for sustainable development interventions.

NABARD has provided rural employment through cluster development, rural haats, rural entrepreneurship, rural industrialisation, skills upgradation of handloom weavers.

NABARD should achieve success in ensuring not only flow of more funds into the rural sector, particularly agricultural sector, but also optimum utilisation of available resources in tune with planned priorities.

REFERENCES

1. L.C. Jain: 'Challenge before NABARD', *Indian Express,* July 21, 1982.
2. S.M. Jha: 'The Role of NABARD in Developing Rural Economy', *Khadigramodyog,* May 1983, p. 305.
3. N.N. Laldas: 'NABARD Nurtures KVI Sector', *Khadigramodyog,* July 1992, pp. 553-54.
4. I. Satya Sundaram: 'NABARD — An Evaluation', *Indian Banking Today & Tomorrow,* March 1991, p. 12.
5. *Commerce,* July 31, 1982, pp. 160-161.
6. *Financial Express,* March 12, 1993.
7. *The Economic Times,* December 12, 1983.
8. *The Economic Times,* April 25, 1986.
9. *The Economic Times,* November 5, 1982.
10. *The Economic Times,* May 3, 1986.
11. *The Economic Times,* April 28, 1995.
12. RBI (August 1989): Report of the Agricultural Credit Review Committee. Chairman Prof. A.M. Khusro.
13. Y.R. Devaprakash: Task Before NABARD at Districts', *Financial Express,* April 28, 1990.
14. Pramon S. Bhatnagar: 'Liberalising Rural Lending', *Yojana,* July 16-31, 1988, p. 31.

Chapter

42 Techniques of Lending for Agriculture

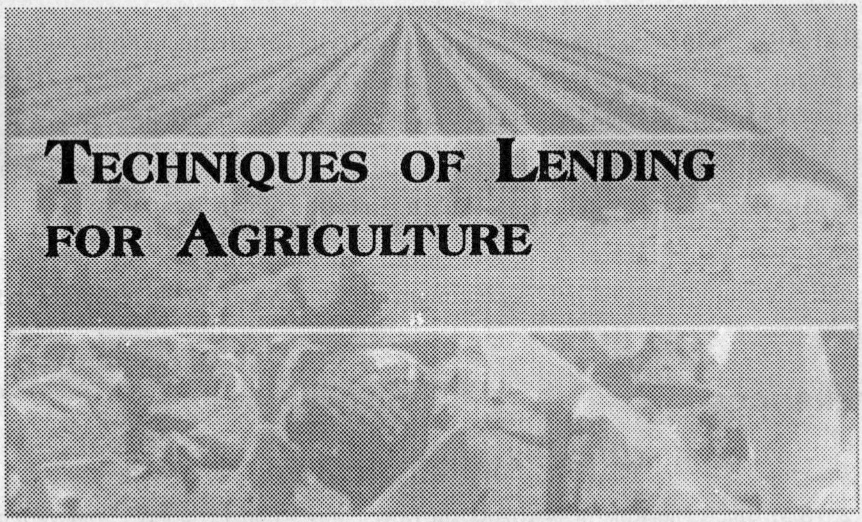

Lending to agriculture, though not risky, is problematic. The problems arise because of the complex nature of agricultural operations, the presence of a large number of uneconomic holdings and the political influence on loans to agriculture. Yet, given the importance of the agricultural sector, lending to agriculture should be streamlined.

Banks should pay attention to certain factors:

(i) The ownership, cultivation and occupational rights of the farmer should be established beyond doubt;

(ii) A mere certificate from the farmer about his encumberances is presently being obtained without insisting on an encumberance certificate and

(iii) A 'no dues' certificate from the co-operative society operating in the area should necessarily be obtained.

Banks are not in a position to realise reasonable returns due to low interest rates on loans, high transaction costs, inadequate marketing support from the government and a poor legal system for recovery. The Narasimham Committee therefore recommended reduction in the targets for the priority sector.

A disturbing trend in agricultural credit is the continuous decline in the recovery to demand ratio. This was 57.4 per cent in 1985-86, 57.5 per cent in 1986-87, 57.0 per cent in 1987-88, 56.0 per cent in 1988-89, 45.0 per cent in 1989-90, 54.09 per cent in 1990-91 and 51.56 per cent in 1991-92. The loan waiver scheme of 1990 has worsened the situation. Recoveries improve only when a special tribunal for recovery of bad debts is set up.

Against a target of ₹ 16,500 crore in 1991-92, total agricultural credit disbursed was around ₹ 11,200 crore — a fall of 11.8 per cent over that in the previous year. Consequently, the target for 1992-93 was scaled down to ₹ 13,000 crore which was met.

However, it is also realised that given the poverty condition in rural India, lending has to be done without waiting for perfect conditions. The CRAFICARD therefore observed, "The creditworthiness of the programme by itself is not sufficient unless growth of income generated by the programme, over time, takes care of the initial non-productive indebtedness and puts the family on its feet."

The commercial banks provide both direct and indirect finance. Under direct finance, we may include development loans, the type of loans eligible for refinance from NABARD, credit provided directly to farmers for financing production and development needs such as purchase of agricultural inputs and machinery also comes under direct finance. Loans granted for development of irrigation potential, reclamation of land development schemes, construction of farm buildings, storage facilities, processing units and subsidiary occupations are other forms of direct finance.

Indirect finance takes the form of credit for financing the distribution of inputs; loans to the electricity boards; loans to farmers through co-operative credit and marketing societies; advances to agro-industries/corporations etc. The commercial banks offer development (term) loans to agriculturists for minor irrigation, sinking of new wells, land improvement, purchase of implements etc. Of course, the interest rates are not uniform for all these activities and also the borrowers are required to offer suitable security.

The RBI, the Government of India and also the state governments have made efforts to simplify the procedures followed for agricultural lending. For instance, the Khanna Committee, appointed by the RBI, made recommendations about adoption of forms, documents, systems etc. by the regional rural banks. Later, the commercial banks too were asked to follow them. The second committee, which worked at the instance of the Government of India, is the Baldev Singh Committee. The Committee made recommendations on the simplification of application forms and lending procedures for loans to agriculture and allied activities by commercial banks. Accordingly, the application forms have been much simplified and security, margin norms etc. have been standardised. But the real problem of the former is the presence of innumerable bank offices and his frequent visit to those offices.[1]

CROP LOAN SCHEME

If the co-operative system has to help the small and marginal farmers, it should take into account the total credit requirements of such farmers. Loans advanced against security of land are not likely to meet the total credit requirements of the rural poor. Therefore, both the Committee of Direction (All India Rural Credit Survey, 1954) and the V.L. Mehta Committee on Co-operative Credit 1960, recommended a purpose-oriented loan policy in the form of crop loan. Under the crop loan scheme, the emphasis has been shifted from the security of the loan to the requirements of credit for the production of a particular crop which was being financed.

ESSENTIAL FEATURES OF CROP LOAN SCHEME

The essential features of the crop loan scheme are:

(i) The primary agricultural credit societies should try to meet in full all short-term credit needs of its members and also the medium-term credit needs as far as possible;

(ii) The creditworthiness of a member should be assessed on the basis of his repaying capacity;

(iii) The society should have a statutory charge on the crop and mortgage security would be justified when the size and period of loan justify it and

(iv) The loan should be advanced only as required and as far as possible in kind.

The crop loan system has brought about a new approach to rural credit. Even the pure tenants have become potential borrowers under the scheme. Moreover, the size of the loan is related to the requirements of business and emphasis on productive purpose. Even if the farmer is not having security, he can get a loan provided he used it productively. Thus, cultivators are given loans with reference to their production requirements in cash and kind. The crop loans are to be repaid out of the sale proceeds of such crops. As such, the sales are generally effected through an agency with which the credit society is linked. Thus, the crop loan system is *'production based'* and *'market-oriented.'*

Though theoretically sound, the crop loan system has not been successful in actual practice. The disbursement of loans in kind is the negligible; mortgage of land is still being insisted upon as security; the agricultural inputs do not reach the farmers in adequate quantities and in time the principle of seasonality in lending and recovery of loans has been neglected; the failure of the crop loan system is also due to ineffective linking of credit with marketing and finally, the procedural delay in application for loans, scrutiny and verification of particulars, delay in sanction and in dispensation of credit has defeated the very purpose of the scheme.

DRAWBACKS OF THE CROP LOAN SYSTEM

The working of the crop loan system suffered from a number of drawbacks. No realistic criterion was evolved to assess the repaying capacity of the borrower. If the requirement of credit is computed as a part of the value of gross output, it fluctuates as and when prices change. It should also be remembered that cultivators have started adopting improved farm practices. Where the cultivator grows a variety of crops during the same agricultural season, it may be necessary to fix the recovery date to coincide with the harvesting period of the most remunerative crop. Recovery of loan has become a problem because there is no effective linking of credit with marketing. Of course, the functioning of the marketing societies needs to be strengthened.

Wilful defaulters should not be financed again until their arrears are cleared. In sanctioning loans to primary societies, the District Co-operative Banks should see that honest borrowers are not denied credit even if the overall performance of the society is poor. It was found that the small farmers faced more difficulties in obtaining crop loan than the medium and large farmers. Crop loans are given only for production purpose. Some consumption loan may be advanced to stop diversion of credit. Provision should also be made to advance loans for investment purposes.[2]

The Government has bailed out farmers through the crop insurance scheme of the General Insurance Corporation (GIC). In the Seventh Plan (1985-90), the premium income collected from the state and central governments was ₹ 120 crore, while the total amount of claims settled by GIC was ₹ 943 crore.

Area Approach to Agricultural Lending

The commercial banks have to follow appropriate lending procedures because credit should not only be adequate, but should also be timely. For instance, in the case of crop loans, applications for loans should be collected and processed well in advance. Of course, while granting term loans, banks should try to get information from reliable and relevant sources regarding, say minor irrigation. Most farmers are illiterate and therefore arrangements must be made for filling up forms either by the bank staff or by those in charge of special schemes. The 'area approach' is adopted to see that the credit requirements of an area are adequately met and viable schemes are identified.

The application forms contain information not only about the borrowers but also about the purposes for which the loans are sought. The bank staff collect information about the borrowers sufficiently in advance, particularly wheri the amounts are large. They also study the economic viability of the schemes to be taken up by the borrowers. The possible increase in income is taken into account for assessing the repaying capacity of the borrowers.

Commercial banks have to formulate agricultural credit schemes within the framework of district credit plans. But, a co-ordinated approach to these schemes is necessary. For instance, schemes for dairy and poultry are to be linked to schemes for financing cattle breeding and calf-rearing, establishment of cattle feed plants, milk collection and chilling centres, milk processing plants, breeding farms for chicks, poultry feed plants and the storage/marketing of poultry products.

The system of providing credit should be streamlined so as to cause least inconvenience to the borrower. As things stand, a number of formalities such as production of evidence regarding ownership/ possession of land, obtainment of no-dues certificate(s), no encumbrance certificate, mortgage of land etc., are required to be completed in many cases before a loan is disbursed. Farmers are thus made to visit the offices of the lending agencies frequently and some amount is incurred for this, besides the loss of wage income.[3]

Group Loaning

The Khusro Committee (ACRC) felt that providing loans to groups of persons or associations of farmers for a common purpose needs to be facilitated and in fact encouraged. Such loans are more secure than individual loans. Those constituting the group exhibit better responsibility including a moral one, to discharge the loan liability.

At a time when the system of group loaning was getting stabilised, it was given up consequently on the recommendation of the Expert Group (Gunvant Desai Committee). This scheme implies lending to a group of individuals for a common purpose to develop an asset individually owned or managed by the members of the group. It was designed:[4]

(i) To induct a sense of collective responsibility among members of a homogeneous group of farmers in the matter of utilisation and repayment of loans and

(ii) To enable a large number of farmers, particularly the small and marginal farmers, to obtain loans at less expense than would have otherwise been possible, if mortgage were to be insisted upon. If the bank groups all the uneconomical farmers, it can provide assets like tubewells. It is thus possible to maximise productivity and prevent eviction of sharecroppers.

However, it is suggested that the size of the group should not be big. Compactness of the group would enable the members to be more cohesive and united. It can also easily and quickly execute bank documents.

PROBLEMS OF GROUP LOANING

Group lending too has given rise to certain problems. If for instance, an irrigation well is financed for the benefit of three or four small/marginal farmers, the problems that might emerge are:

(i) Proportion in which water should be shared and the cost thereof;

(ii) Repayment made individually should be consistent with proper and maximum utilisation of irrigation;

(iii) The well is located in the land of one of the members who may own it later though all have repaid the loan amount and

(iv) Maintenance of the asset may also be a matter of dispute.

It may be, therefore, necessary to have a legal sanction to the effect that the entire group jointly owns the asset and takes up the responsibility of maintaining it. The farmers should be educated on the benefits of group efforts while encouraging formation of groups, and occupational homogeneity should be kept in view. The rural poor are likely to benefit a lot through their individual group effects.[5]

PROJECT APPROACH

A project approach may be necessary for the benefit of the weaker sections like small and marginal farmers. Project methodology consists of:

(i) Identifications;

(ii) Preparation and analysis;

(iii) Appraisal;

(iv) Implementation and

(v) Monitoring and evaluation.

The project should evoke positive response from the target groups. Without active participation of the people for whom it is meant, a project is bound to fall. While designing a project, care should be taken to activate the target groups and motivate them for participation. Second, the technical aspects of project formulation should be carefully studied. Third, the costs and benefits of a project need to be carefully assessed. Last, there must be proper monitoring to see whether the project follows the envisaged course.[6]

CONSORTIUM ADVANCES

In banking parlance, consortium refers to joint financing of an individual, industrial or trading enterprise on certain mutually agreed proportions. Advances to food and procurement agencies are a case in point. The most striking feature of this consortium is that besides being the largest over ₹ 2,500 crore, it consists of over 30 borrowers who are financed jointly by 36 banks for working capital requirement, related to the procurement and distribution of foodgrains in the country. Consortium lending was first examined in depth by an expert group constituted by the RBI in 1974 under the chairmanship of Lakshminarayana.

The consortium approach is likely to limit the risk exposure of a bank in a particular advance. In all consortia, one of the banks is chosen as the lead bank whose role is that of a leader and organiser of various things. Even under consortium approach, borrowers should have the means of effective communication with their bankers and the number of banks they should deal with, should be limited to the circumstances of each case.[7] One advantage of the scheme is that the small co-operative bank with the help of big banks will be able to entertain big credit-proposals and thereby create a good image of themselves in the general public which would result in attracting more business and clientele also.[8]

AGRICULTURAL CREDIT PASS BOOK

The Agricultural Credit Pass Book, provided to every farmer/tenant contains particulars of land owned, cultivated, leased in and leased out, their relative value, continuous record of the various credit limits and the benefits already utilised to him.[9] In Punjab, a new simplified procedure for crop loan purposes known as cheque and pass book was evolved. Under this system, a pass book and a cheque book are issued to each eligible farmer of primary agricultural credit society, indicating his minimum credit limit normally operative for three years, and the member is at liberty to draw the loan both in kind and cash through cheques according to his requirements as and when necessary.[10]

Though the system is sound, it is facing some problems; only 50 per cent of the states have adopted it, it is voluntary in some states and compulsory in others; it is not having legislative backing; and if not updated, it would defeat the very purpose of introducing the scheme. In some states, loans made by the Government alone are recorded and the nature of particulars entered in the books differ from state to state.[11]

CREDIT SUPERVISION

Unsupervised loans are often used for purposes other than those for which they are requested.[12] Supervision in agricultural lendings basically involves developing a proper system under which field staff continuously get information on utilisation from the assets. The crux of the supervision should lie in ensuring that growth is taking place, i.e., the amount lent is generating income to enable the borrower to repay the loan.[13] An information system is to be built up wherein the field staff get information on all matters relevant to their operations.

If the officer can identify a few persons in each village to get a correct picture of the loan utilisation, crop growth and use of assets for income generation, the job is more than done, in the sense that it is precisely what inspection aims at. The officer has to develop an ability to discern and cross check in the case of questionable, dubious and incredible information.[14] Since the field officer cannot stay in an area for a long time, it is absolutely essential for a local person to man banking operations in specified areas. The village head man has to act as co-ordinator or liaison officer between the bankmen and the villagers.[15] The problem of supervision can be partly solved by assigning manageable areas to individual institutions and societies.[16]

Banks would also have to adopt those techniques in respect of agricultural lending which enable them to reduce overdues, exercise better supervision and prevent diversion of credit from productive to unproductive purposes. In short, better lending techniques would mean minimising the misuse of credit.

References

1. C.L. Khemani: 'Systems and Procedures in Agricultural Lending: A Fresh Look', *SBI Monthly Review,* May 1981, p. 213.
2. K.S. Tiwana and A.S. Kahlon: 'Working of Crop Loan System' (in Ludhiana District), *Kurukshetra,* November 1, 1976, p. 8.
3. C.L. Khemani: 'Significance of Encouraging Group Efforts in Rural Lending', *SBI Monthly Review,* June 1981, p. 262.
4. M. Sen Sarma: "The Group Loan Scheme: An Experiment in Farm Finance', *Financing Agriculture,* October 1974, pp. 2-3.
5. C.L. Khemani: 'Significance of Encouraging Group Efforts in Rural Lending', *SBI Monthly Review,* June 1981, p. 265.
6. C.L. Khemani and G.N. Nandi: 'Project Approach in Agricultural Lending and Small Farmers', *SBI Monthly Review,* November 1981.
7. K.V. Rao: 'Banks and Consortium Approach', *Financial Express,* January 14, 1979.
8. S.A. Bedekar: 'Consortium Finance: A Scheme with Promise', *Commerce* (Supplement on Growth of Urban Banks), November 15, 1980, p. 31.
9. *Rural Reconstruction,* October 1971 and January 1972, pp.15-16.
10. H.P. Suneja: 'Agricultural Overdues', *Financial Express,* June 30, 1981.
11. William G. Murray (1959): *Agricultural Finance,* The Iowa State College Press, p. 59.
12. Food and Agricultural Organisation (1955): *Manual of Supervised Credit in Latin America,* p. 4.
13. C.L. Khemani: 'Concept of Supervision in Rural Credit', *SBI Monthly Review,* March 1981, pp. 133-34.
14. *Ibid.*
15. I. Satya Sundaram: 'Monitoring Credit Utilisation', *Capital,* February 16, 1981, p. 5.
16. S.K. Rau: 'Strategies of Rural Development', in *Rural Development in India: Some Facets, op. cit.*

Chapter

43 THE PROBLEM OF OVERDUES

The problem of overdues has been quite challenging to credit institutions in the country. Poor recovery of overdues cripples the capacity of the credit institutions to draw refinance from NABARD. Recycling of funds becomes an impossible task when the overdues reach the dangerous level.

The banking sector is expected to achieve some of the socio-economic objectives of planned development. However, this role can be performed only when banks are financially sound. Because of the phenomenon of mounting overdues, banks are very much enfeebled financially. True, there will be always some 'bad and doubtful debts.' But with greater attention to the priority sector, the problem of overdues has assumed proportions.

INCIDENCE OF OVERDUES

Total overdues of public sector banks stood at ₹ 9,732.31 crore in 1990. Agriculture accounted for ₹ 2,299.91 crore; small scale units and industrial estates ₹ 1,936 crore and medium and large scale units accounted for ₹ 2,613.37 crore.

The Khusro Committee has observed that unless "overdues are contained within an acceptable level, the large scale expansion in the quantum of credit to meet the demand of the agricultural sector, as projected for the last decade of the century, i.e., 1990s, and upto the year 2000 AD cannot be fruitified."

The overdues of agricultural loan advances of all credit agencies at the level of ultimate borrowers increased from about ₹ 42.20 crore in 1985-86 to ₹ 80.25 crore in 1989-90 showing an increase of over 90 per cent during this period.

The proportion of overdues to total demand in respect of agricultural loans of all lending institutions taken together increased from 42.6 per cent of the total demand in 1985-86 to 55 per cent in 1988-89.

The proportion of overdues to demand also remained almost stable between 43 per cent to 44 per cent during the period from 1985-86 to 1988-89, though the demand during the period increased from ₹ 9,894 crore to ₹ 14,268 crore. But the proportion of overdues suddenly shot up from 44 per cent in 1988-89 to 55 per cent in 1989-90 though the demand increased only from ₹ 14,268 crore to ₹ 14,588 crore. This development is due to the existing loan waiver scheme.

The overdues in the agricultural sector have increased at the rate of 14.4 per cent against a rate of 11.7 per cent for issue of loans during 1982-83 to 1991-92. The overdues in the case of RRBs have been growing at a higher rate of 28 per cent. The overdues growth rate is 16 per cent in the case of land development banks and about 15 per cent in the case of commercial banks.

Interestingly enough, only primary agricultural credit co-operatives have a growth rate of 8.8 per cent, which is lower than the average overdues growth rate.

Currently, the recovery rate is quite disappointing at around 50 per cent. In 1987, it was 57.1 per cent which fell to 56.8 per cent in 1988, but rose to 58.1 per cent in 1989. Overdues as a percentage of outstanding advances has been on the rise. It was 14.6 per cent in June, 1985, which rose to 15.7 per cent in June, 1986 and further to 16.8 per cent in June 1987.

The data show that the percentage of recovery of demand in the case of loans given by primary agricultural credit societies increased from 53.48 in 1989-90 to 60.17 in 1991-92 and declined to ₹ 57.15 in 1992-93.

The percentage of overdues in relation to demand was as high as 41 in co-operative credit institutions, 51 in RRBs and 43 in commercial banks.

CAUSES OF OVERDUES

Lending, particularly in the case of rural areas and weaker sections is target-oriented. Banks, in their anxiety to achieve the targets set, are not paying attention to sound norms of lending. It is precisely for this reason that the quality of rural lending has deteriorated. The fact is that lending may be need-based, but not target-based.

The agricultural sector suffers from unsatisfactory repayment and this, largely due to low levels of income generated. In many cases, the incremental incomes actually earned are far below the levels envisaged at the time of sanctioning of schemes to benefit the rural population. This has been attributed to resources not being fully utilised; deficiencies in the formulation of schemes and unrealistic repayment schedules. It needs to be noted that even poor borrowers do not require subsidy if they have viable occupations.

To quote again the Khusro Committee: *"The vitality of the rural financial institutions depends on the vitality of the economy and the activities pursued by the borrowers. Re-organising this inter-linkage, a better co-ordination between development planning and credit planning through a graduation of present 'service area scheme' into a more comprehensive 'development area scheme' is necessary."*

Rural lending is beset with a number of problems. The rural borrowers may not be having the requisite technical know-how and organisational competence. Very often, the loan amount may be inadequate to take up productive schemes. Also, inadequate infrastructure is an important impediment to launching of profitable programmes. Thus, in some cases, the borrowers are willing to repay the loans, but are not able to do so because of some factors beyond their control.

While default may be due to natural calamities and inability of a programme to generate enough income, the tendency to default wilfully is growing stronger and stronger. There are thus defaulters who have the ability to repay, but they do not pay. This is so particularly in the case of co-operative credit institutions which are dominated by the rich and powerful of the rural community. There should be some strict statutory action against such wilful defaulters.

There are many legal hurdles in the recovery process. Very often assets are not available for inspection. The legal procedure is costly and time-consuming. The court fees in some states is as high as 10 per cent of the amount claimed. Lawyers' fees alone claim 10 to 15 per cent of the dues. The Talwar Committee has recommended extension of the Revenue Recovery Act to bank loans.

Important reasons for mounting overdues include:[1]

(i) Deficiencies in credit planning exercise/credit packages/delivery systems;

(ii) Inadequate appreciation of the importance of recycling of funds from the point of ensuring an adequate resources base; to service the ever expanding credit requirements of various target groups;

(iii) Absence of a planned approach as in lending to recovery management through recovery plans and

(iv) Poor performance of credit agencies in bringing about attitudinal changes amongst borrowers as regards repayment ethics/capability to repay.

A study made by the Committee on Agricultural Lending by Commercial Banks (CALCOB) observed that 16 per cent of the overdues is due to internal factors like lack of effective supervision and follow up (12 per cent), defective appraisal (2 per cent) and others like improper selection of borrowers etc. (2 per cent).

The external factors account for 84 per cent of the mounting overdues. The CALCOB study also pointed out that about 53 per cent of overdues can be attributed to borrower's behaviour like wilful default (41 per cent), misutilisation of loans (4 per cent) and others like diversion of funds (8 per cent).

The environment and other factors responsible for 31 per cent of overdues are insufficient incremental income (8 per cent) and others like relief not provided etc. (23 per cent).

The borrowers do not repay the loan overdues due to inadequate repaying capacity. The poor repaying capacity is due to factors like crop failure, increase in domestic expenditure, failure to adopt new cropping systems, delays in disbursal of loan and uneconomic holding with little or no marketable surplus.[2]

Incremental incomes actually earned by borrowers were found to be substantially lower than those envisaged in the schemes. Low and insufficient incremental incomes of borrowers were found to be mainly on account of *(i)* Resources not being fully utilised; *(ii)* Faulty scheme formulations and *(iii)* Unrealistic repayment schedules.[3]

Another important factor is the inability of the banks to initiate timely recovery efforts. The recovery efforts should positively start from the harvestation and marketing of the produce.[4] Also, there is no proper check on the tendency to divert funds to unproductive purposes.[5]

The Government of India has formulated a scheme for providing debt relief to farmers, artisans and weavers. The scheme is called Agricultural and Rural Debt Relief (ARDR) Scheme 1990. It came into force with effect from May 15, 1990. Important features of the scheme are:[6]

(i) The scheme is available to individual farmers, weavers or artisans or landless cultivators who have availed a loan or loans from one or more banks/credit institutions for agricultural and artisan activities and who are non-wilful defaulters;

(ii) Amount of debt relief to a borrower of eligible loan shall not exceed ₹ 10,000;

(iii) The scheme also covers the gold and jewel loans availed for agriculture purposes as defined under Section 2(a) of the scheme, subject to their being otherwise eligible;

(iv) The manager of each bank branch shall determine eligible loan and sanction waiver of the loans as per the guidelines laid down in the scheme;

(v) If the waiver account is sufficient to clear the outstanding principal and interest, such accounts shall be closed and the borrowers be advised in writing about the extent of relief provided and the closure of the account. In case the waiver amount is insufficient, the borrowers should be advised to repay the balance towards principal;

(vi) In cases of borrowers having availed loans from more than one bank, the waiver amount shall be adjusted in proportion to the amount in default to the banks concerned and

(vii) All borrowers whose loan accounts are closed in accordance with the above-mentioned guidelines, are eligible for fresh loans from the bank for ensuring seasonal agricultural operations.

The loan waiver scheme has been criticised on many valid grounds. The scheme has set a bad example on grounds that it may not be a one-time measure. Borrowers otherwise capable of paying also will not pay their dues. The limit of ₹ 10,000 may also be extended. There will be competition amongst the political parties to offer such concessions. The Narasimham Committee on Financial Systems has added an additional element of politicisation of banking apart from the great damage to the concept of credit discipline by encouraging defaulters.

The ARDR scheme was implemented upto March 31, 1991. The Government had released ₹ 5,266 crore to various banks under the scheme upto March, 1995. The Government is at present faced with the job of finding strategies to raise ₹ 2,800 crore to nurse back to health co-operative banks and societies. NABARD thinks that this level of amount is necessary to make these institutions viable by writing off their cumulative losses and bad debt. NABARD has also recommended that this burden be shared on a 50:50 basis by the Centre and the states.

The seven-member agricultural credit review committee, set up in 1986, at the instance of the RBI (Chairman: Prof. A.M. Khusro) submitted its Report in 1989. The Committee condemned the practice of loan melas. The report also notes that as per a sample study, 51 per cent of the applications of 16 branches of a bank were sanctioned on the very day of receipt. Further, 98 per cent of the loans were disbursed on the day of sanction which was the day the loan mela was held. The report has also stated that most of the applications were sponsored by political functionaries.

MEASURES NEEDED TO CURB OVERDUES

It would be better to limit loan waivers to those borrowers reeling under financial crisis due to drought, flood or any other natural calamity including death of the borrowing member and wilful defaulters are to be excluded.[7]

A publicity campaign to educate farmers about the need for repayment of banks' dues should be launched by the Government through newspapers and radio/television network.[8]

No doubt, credit agencies have to study the technical aspects to determine the viability of units. But, it is also equally necessary to impart proper training and education to the beneficiary so as to enable him to use the asset to the fullest extent.[9]

As in the case of State Financial Corporations which provide incentives for prompt repayment to small borrowers, incentives should be allowed by way of concessions in the interest in respect of commercial banks too for prompt repayment.[10]

Providing loans to groups of persons or associations of farmers for a common purpose needs to be encouraged. Such loans are less risky as the group/association assumes the responsibility to repay the loan.

By seeking recourse to litigation, the borrower is at present delaying payments virtually indefinitely. The Tiwari Committee had asked for special legislation to give some teeth to the process of loan recovery.

The special tribunal for recovering bank loans has been successfully challenged in the courts. Hence, further legislation is required to put it back on the rails. The Goswami Committee has made some useful recommendations in order to reduce the time and cost of litigation and make it an attractive option for the banks.[11]

Loan recovery would not be a problem, if the revenue departments worked in liaison with the banks. Only a few states have made honest attempts in this direction. In these states, the bank branches have to make only a single application to the sub-divisional magistrate to recover the dues as arrears of land revenues.[12]

Banks also ought to take cognisance of the economic situation facing the borrowers. The borrowers may lack linkages and supportive services; purchase sub-standard assets when the assets are in short supply; incur unexpected household (consumption) expenditure for which funds are diverted and select schemes which are not appropriate to local conditions. Also, if there is a high concentration of single activity in an area, that would bring down the marketability of the product. The subsidy element for government sponsored schemes is also responsible for scant attention being paid to the viability of these schemes.

It is necessary for us to draw meaningful inferences from the experiences of other countries. For instance, the Comilla system of co-operatives in Bangladesh has yielded extremely good results in respect of repayment of farm loans. The stress is on combining credit with training, production plans, extension, supervision, savings and strict repayment discipline.

Equally interesting and useful is the Korean experience. In Korea, the time of lending and repayment falls at fixed periods. The time is the harvesting season. Loan recovery is done in the two months following harvesting. All the employees of the bank go out to collect their repayment from farmers. Also, farmers are educated about their responsibilities to repay and are assured of fresh loans. A department exclusively for loan recovery has been set up.

NABARD is trying to curb overdues by improving the recovery performance of banks. As a pre-condition to the unrestricted refinance from NABARD, all client banks, except commercial banks, have to become 'viable' by June, 1992 and maintain 80 per cent recoveries each year thereafter in respect of their current demand.

In order to improve the recovery performance of commercial banks, NABARD has evolved the following viability criterion (applicable from the financial year 1992-93):

(i) Branches achieving recovery performance of 80 per cent and above in relation to current demand and 25 per cent recovery under arrears demand would qualify for unrestricted refinance;

(ii) The branches having recovery range of 40 to 80 per cent in relation to current demand and 25 per cent recovery under arrear demand would get restricted refinance; and

(iii) Those branches having recovery below 40 per cent under current demand and less than 25 per cent recovery under arrear demand will not be entitled any refinance facility.

Banks should seriously think of reducing the incidence of overdues not only in their own interests, but in the interests of the sectors and sections they are serving. Without recycling of funds, it is impossible for banks to serve any section/sector for long.

Banks should see that the amount granted is in tune with the borrowers' requirements. The loans should be disbursed in time. The repayment schedule should be based on the convenience of the borrower. If default is due to genuine reasons, the repayment schedule may be modified. There should be no compromise on one issue: The loans taken are put to specific and productive use. This requires co-ordination amongst credit agencies.

Banks have to strengthen pre-sanction scrutiny and post-sanction supervision. There is nothing wrong if the borrowers who are honest are provided with some extra incentives.

What is at stake is the credibility of the banking sector. It is time to realise the simple truth that if the capacity of the banks to recycle funds is crippled as a result of mounting overdues, it would adversely affect the interests of the weaker sections themselves.

REFERENCES

1. A.V. Rajagopalan and M. Balakrishnan: 'Toning Up Recovery Process in Rural Credit', *The Hindu,* December 26, 1991.
2. Balishter: 'Loan Overdues in Agriculture: Suggestions to Break the Impasse', *Yojana,* February 1996, p. 33.
3. Brinda Jagirdar: 'Recovery of Agricultural Loans Under Schematic Lending', *State Bank of India Monthly Review,* July 1988, p. 341.
4. S.P. Sharma: 'Recovery of Agricultural Loans; Need for Innovative Approach', *State Bank of India Monthly Review,* September 1992, p. 445.
5. D.P. Pandey: 'Small Borrowers and Recovery Problems', *Commerce,* March 26, 1983, p. 515.
6. S. Jagannath: 'Agricultural and Rural Debt Relief Scheme 1990', *Agricultural Banker,* October-December 1990, p. 17.
7. T.C. Duhan: 'Waiving Rural Loans; Some Basic Issues', *Agricultural Banker,* October-December 1991, p. 7.
8. S.P. Sharma: *op. cit.,* p. 449.
9. R. Singh: 'Educating Borrowers on Repayment', *Financial Express,* November 13, 1993.
10. V. Prasanna Bhat: 'Recovery of Agricultural Loans', *Agricultural Banker,* January-March 1993, p. 3.
11. J.R. Varma: 'Bad Loans Write Off: Accepting the Inevitable', *The Hindu,* July 6, 1995.
12. J. Panda and M. Altaf Khan: 'Loan Recovery: Courting Problems', *The Economic Times,* January 31, 1991.

Chapter

44 MICROFINANCE IN INDIA

Rural banking in India has made tremendous progress. But, it has also created some problems. The main problem is mounting overdues. The non-performing assets (NPAs) of the banks are rising. The borrowers have to repay the loans taken promptly. This is possible only when the loans are productively utilised. For various reasons, this has not happened. Hence, the group approach to lending has been conceived. Under this scheme, the group, not the individual, is made responsible for repayment. This has many merits. Microfinance is becoming increasingly popular in most developing countries.

BANGLADESH GRAMEEN BANK

The Bangladesh Grameen Bank (BGB) is responsible for popularising the concept of microfinance. The Bank was founded by Prof. Muhammad Yunus, the economist. It was started as a project in Chittagong district in August 1976. It became an independent bank dedicated to poor women of Bangladesh on October 2, 1983. The experience of the Bank made one thing clear: the poor are creditworthy.

The BGB strongly believes in the following principles:[1]

- poverty is not created by the poor, but by the institutions and policies which surround them;
- charity is not an answer to poverty. It serves only to perpetuate poverty and create dependency;
- there is no difference in the ability of a poor person and any other person. The poor people always pay back; and
- lending to women bring greater benefits to the family than lending to men.
- Muhammad Yunus firmly believes that people have to control their fate. The poor are capable of bringing about the desirable change in their lives. Changing the quality of life of the people

below the poverty line is a laudable objective. The poor do not have capital, but they have innate skills.

The BGB has some unique features. A unique feature of the Bank is ownership by borrowers. The target group is the landless poor, particularly the women. Also, all the members have to agree on certain obligations like family planning, growing vegetables, avoidance of dowry and child marriage etc.

The group formation is on gender basis, that is, a group is either for women or men. The BGB has now almost 7 lakh groups and 2.2 crore members throughout Bangladesh.[2]

The interest rate charged by the BGB is high at 16 to 18 per cent. But, borrowers are not worried as they take up economically viable programmes only. As of October 1994, the overdues were 0.74 per cent of the outstanding.

The Bank recognises a group after orientation training and minimum savings. The Bank evolved suitable loan linkages for self chosen income generating activities, very simple procedures and no collaterals. The borrower should not dispose of assets until loan is fully repaid. The first set of two loans are disbursed after a close observation of the group for one or two months.

There is compulsory group saving. The Bank recognises group responsibility for recommending and repaying loans. The members make repayment of loan on weekly basis, failing which the member as well as the group had to face penalty charges.

The BGB has produced many positive results. The increased income and improved living standards of the landless women are clearly visible. They could construct new houses, and improve their health status also.

The factors ensuring the long-term profitability of the BGB are multiple loan products aimed at flexibility, increase in loan outstanding, effective use of staff and assets and of course viable interest rates.[3]

It is said that the BGB has helped non-members also indirectly. As a result of reduced pressure on employment market, the earnings of agricultural labourers have gone up.

The amounts of loans outstanding currently is $250 million, the recovery rate is 99 per cent. The Bank identified what the main barriers for poor people to access money from conventional banks were, and set the course by reversing the principles practised by commercial banks.[4]

The BGB has influenced the social life of the beneficiaries. The members now take interest in sending their children to school, keeping families small, taking joint actions to help the community; rejecting dowry, drinking clean water, growing plants and vegetables; and keeping children and environment clean. Also, their participation in social and political activities is higher than that of non-members.[5]

Grameen Bank II has introduced custom made credit service for its members. Recognising the maturity of the members and the diversification of their needs, the new system introduced loans of different duration suited to the members' needs. Grameen Bank has also introduced a pension fund for the poor which is leading both members and the bank to greater self-reliance.[6]

The BGB tried to understand the reasons for default. One reason is political. The political parties declare waiving of loans upto $95. The other reason is psychological when the payment becomes large, the borrower thinks of ways to avoid repayment.[7]

Provision of appropriate training to field staff is important. The staff have to understand the people and the environment.

SELF-HELP GROUPS

The micro credit is being provided through self-help groups (SHGs). In India, the SHGs have been functioning since 1996. At present, there are over 16 lakh SHGs operating all over the country.

The SHGs are small informal groups aiming at collective action. They are generally formed by the funding agencies and voluntary agencies in the context of micro finance.

The members pool their savings and relend it among themselves on a rotational basis. The SHGs come together for the purpose of solving their common problems through self help and mutual help. The savings are kept with a bank. The common fund is in the name of the SHG. Usually the number of members in one SHG is between 15 and 20. According to NABARD, more than 90 per cent of the SHGs have exclusively women members.

The basic principles of the SHGs are group approach, mutual trust, organisation of small and manageable groups, group cohesiveness, spirit of thrift, demand based lending, collateral free, women friendly loan, peer group pressure in repayment, skill training, capacity building and employment.

There are certain broad principles which govern the functioning of SHGs. These include:

- Savings first, no credit without saving;
- Saving as partial collateral;
- Bank lends to the Group, for on-lending to members;
- Credit decisions for on-lending to member by the group;
- Interest rates and other terms and conditions for loans to members to be decided by the group;
- Joint liability as a substitute for physical collateral;
- Ratio between savings and credit contingent upon creditworthiness of the group, increasing over time with good repayment record; and
- Small loans to begin with.

The SHGs are provided with Revolving Fund of ₹ 25,000 — ₹ 10,000 from the District Rural Development agency and ₹ 15,000 from Bank — after six months of their formation, and upon qualifying the first grading to kick start the loaning activities, second grading is done six months after receiving of Revolving Fund for taking up economic activities.

The revolving fund helps the members draw from it for medical and education expenses or to perform marriages and undertake family obligations. Sometimes, a member may approach it to support her husband's business enterprise.[8]

The SHG selects from among its members a leader called animator. The animator conducts two to three meetings every month. After the group stabilises in management of funds, it gives loan to the members.

Formation of SHG is a viable alternative to achieve the objectives of rural development and to get community participation in all rural development programmes.

The SHGs are able to provide banking services to their members which may not be sophisticated but are cost effective, simple, flexible, accessible to their members and above all without any defaults in repayment of loans.

The SHGs are also facing some problems. Hence, measures should be initiated to strengthen the self-interest and self-motivation on the part of members. Change of leader periodically is necessary. Women should think of occupation mobility to enhance their incomes. The quality of economic activity should be improved.

MICROFINANCE IN INDIA

Banks have accepted microfinance as normal and sustainable banking business operated at market rates of interest.

Micro credit has been defined by the Micro Credit Summit held in 1997 as "programmes that promote credit for self-employment and other financial and business services (including saving and technical assistance) to very poor persons." The delivery is normally through SHG. It is mainly meant to promote self-employment. Microfinance increases the productivity of self-employment in the informal sector of the economy.[9]

Micro finance includes savings, credit, insurance and other financial services for the poor or informal sector communities, whereas micro credit refers to a credit-only approach.[10]

When bank officers are satisfied with the SHG loan performance, members could get five times the funds collected through SHG deposits. Banks normally charge 8.75 per cent to 9 per cent interest for SHG loans upto ₹ 50,000. In fact, the average size of the loans per group is under ₹ 30,000.

The SHG Bank linkage involves having the group save, and then linking it to a bank. Banks are happy with micro credit. Both the leader and the members are responsible for repayment. Banks could drastically reduce supervision and other costs. Some of the risks have been transferred to NGOs. Micro credit has resulted in reduced vulnerability of the poor women to crisis, famine, flood, riots etc.

Based on the study findings, NABARD launched the SHG-Bank linkage programme on pilot basis in February 1992. The RBI based on its working group recommendations in 1994, issued a policy circular to banks to adopt this innovative approach.

Microfinance scheme has made steady progress. NABARD hopes to see a million SHGs serving 20 million households by 2008.

At present, 560 banks, including 48 commercial banks, 196 RRBs and 716 cooperative banks are actively involved in the operation of the programme.

MICROFINANCE: SOME PROBLEMS

The majority of SHGs use loan amount for unproductive purposes i.e. consumption needs and social needs. This led to irregularity in repayment of loan amount.

People like agricultural labourers have to move from their places to other places. More than 60 per cent members of the SHGs become inactive members.

SHG is based on mutual trust. But, actually we find differences among members on the ground of caste, creed, or religion. Some SHGs have therefore become defunct.

Meeting, agenda, minutes, books of accounts are totally new concepts to poor members. The books of accounts are poorly prepared.

It is said that micro loans help most the people above the poverty line. The reason for this is, they can take up risks by investing in new technologies.

As on March 31, 2009, commercial banks had the maximum share of SHG savings with savings of 35,49,509 SHGs (58 per cent) amounting to ₹ 2,772.99 crore (50 per cent); this was followed by RRBs with savings bank accounts of 16,28,588 SHGs (26.6 per cent) and saving amount of ₹ 1,989.75 crore (35.9 per cent) and cooperative banks with saving bank accounts of 9,43,050 SHGS (15.4 per cent) and savings bank account of ₹ 782.88 crore (14.1 percent).

During 2008-09, banks financed 16,09,586 SHGs, including repeat loans to existing SHGs, as against 12,27,770 SHGs during 2007-08 – a growth of 31.1 per cent (number of SHGs had outstanding (cultivative) bank loan of ₹ 22679.85 crore as against 36,25,941 SHGs with outstanding bank loan of ₹ 16,999.90 crore as on March 31,2008.

As on March 31,2009, the average bank loan outstanding per SHG was ₹ 53,689 as against ₹ 46,884 as on March 31,2008. It varied from a high of ₹ 57,037 per SHG in the case of commercial banks to a low of ₹ 31,460 per SHG in the case of cooperative banks.

Table 1
SHG Bank Linkage Programme

Year as on 31st March	*Cumulative No. of SHGS financed*	*Cumulative loan disbursed (in ₹ Crore)*	*Cumulative refinance provided by NABARD (₹ Crore)*
1992-93	255	0.29	0.27
1996-97	8598	11.84	10.65
1999-00	114775	193.00	150.00
2000-01	263825	481.00	395.00
2001-02	46 1478	1026.00	790.00
2002-03	717360	2049.00	1413.00
2003-04	107909 1	3904.00	2118.00
2004-05	16,18,456	6,898.00	3,086.00
2005-06	22,38,565	11,398.00	4,154.00

2006-07*	28,94,505	12,366.49	6,570.39
2007-08	36,25,941	16,999.90	6,849.26
2008-09	42,24,338	22,679.85	12,256.51

Source: NABARD Annual Reports.

Note: *From 2006-07 onwards, data in respect of number . of SHGS financed by banks and bank loans are in clusive of SHGS financed under the Swarnajayanti Gram Swarazgar Yojana and the existing groups receiving repeat loans. Owing to this change, NABARD discontinued compilation of data on cumula-tive basis from 2006-07. Hence, data from 2006-07 onwards are not comparable with the data of the previous years.

The number of SHGs linked to banks reached 10.78 lakh by March 31, 2004, covering an estimated 17 lakh poor families. About 90 per cent of the groups linked with banks are exclusively women groups.

During the period April to December 2004, 1.97 lakh SHGs were provided with bank loan amounting to ₹ 1,134 crore. By the end of July 2005, as many as 16,53,047 SHGs were linked to banks, and the total flow of credit to SHGs was ₹ 7,063 crore. More than 16 million rural households have gained access to bank credit through 60,000 retail credit outlets of the banking sector in rural India.

Microfinance scheme is facing some problems. Measures should therefore be initiated to strengthen it. Projects and programmes should be made economically viable. What is more, we have to increase the credit absorptive capacity of the rural areas. Provision of marketing facilities is also important. Need based training and exposure for the bank personnel is important.

Strict repayment requirements may not be desirable. There should be flexibility in the repayment of individual loans from banks. A well conceived scheme like microfinance needs to be effectively implemented by banks.

REFERENCES

1. Muhummad Yunus: 'Grameen Bank, Micro Credit, and Millennium Development Goals', *Economic and Political Weekly*, September 4, 2004, pp.4077-78.
2. *Mainstream*, August 23, 1997.
3. R. Balakrishnan: 'Are the Poor Creditworthy:Answers from Bangladesh', *The Journal of the Indian Institute of Bankers*, January-March, 1996, p.20.
4. Muhummad Yunus (2004): *op.cit.*, p.4077.
5. *Ibid.*, p.4078.
6. *Ibid.*, p.4079.
7. Md.Nazrul Islam: 'Micro Credit:An Experience of Grameen Bank of Bangladesh', *Southern Economist*, September 15, 2002, p.12.
8. Kausalya Santhanam: 'Advantage Women', *The Hindu*, (Magazine Section), August 1, 2004.
9. Archana Sinha: 'Micro Finance for Women's Empowerment: A Perspective', *Kurukshetra*, April 2004, p.32.
10. *Ibid.*

PART SIX

Rural Delivery System

Chapter

45 AGRICULTURAL MARKETING IN INDIA

The farmers benefit from the new agricultural technology only when there is continuous increase in agricultural productivity and they are able to get a reasonable price for their produce. As the economy develops, marketing assumes importance even in rural areas. The Royal Commission on Agriculture in India (1928) rightly pointed out that —

Until the agriculturist realises that as a seller of produce, he must study the art of sale either as an individual or through a combination of other producers, it is inevitable that he should come off second best in the contest with the highly specialised knowledge and the vastly superior resources of those who purchase his produce.

The rural market for packaging consumer products increased from ₹ 730 crore in 1984 to ₹ 2,080 crore in 1989 and to an estimated ₹ 3,000 crore in 1990. Rural markets were growing at 17 per cent till 1987, increased to 23 per cent in 1988 and boomed to 41 per cent in 1989.

Studies by the National Council of Applied Economic Research reveal that the percentage expenditure on food in the rural areas declined between 1977-78 and 1987-88. A higher proportion of income is being spent on manufactured products and services.

Agricultural marketing involves a number of processes like handling, plucking, washing, cleaning, grading, storage, pre-cooling, preservation, packaging and transportation.

Marketing of agricultural produce tends to be a complex process as agriculture is fundamentally different from manufacturing industries. Agricultural marketing does suffer from special problems: perishable nature of the products, lack of standardisation and storage facilities and price stability.[1] Also, agricultural marketing is dominated by brokers, commission agents and middlemen. There exists a big gap between the farm-gate price and the consumer price.[2]

Since farming in India is largely subsistent farming, marketable surplus, so far as foodgrains are concerned, is low. Marketable surplus is the *theoretical surplus available for sale with the producer, after meeting the requirements of family consumption, payment of wages in land, feed, seed and wastage.* It thus represents arrivals, direct from the producing areas, out of the new crop. It is estimated that marketable surplus is 31 per cent of the total production in the case of rice. The percentage is 45 for wheat, 25 for jowar and 50 for pulses. However, a change in the consumption pattern amongst farmers in favour of non-farm items and the tendency towards greater crop specialisation will increase the size of the marketed surplus.[3]

In the case of foodgrains, the marketable surplus is rather low. The reasons are: First, the productivity per hectare is low; Second, the tendency to hoard more and more by the traders as an insurance against contingencies; Third, higher prices which reduce the inclination to produce more; Fourth, increase in consumption of the agriculturists due to land reforms and better employment opportunities; Fifth, the rural people's desire to consume superior cereals in the place of inferior ones; Sixth, the vast majority of cultivators do not have marketable surplus and finally, farm output responds very little to the movement of prices.

Marketable surplus also plays an important role in determining the pace of development of the economy as a whole, more particularly the prosperity of the farming sector. It is desirable that the marketable surplus should increase along with the increase in production. Otherwise, the tempo of development will be hampered, by reducing supplies available for urban consumption, for industries and for export. Therefore, measures to increase marketable surplus should be initiated. These include: stepping up output, offering price incentives, improving marketing facilities and monetisation of the rural sector.

IMPORTANCE OF MARKETING

The All-India Rural Credit Survey Committee has observed that "Often enough, the cultivator's position is that of having to bargain if he can, with someone, who commands the money, commands the credit, commands the market and commands the transporters."

Marketing enables farmers to dispose off their surpluses at the right time/right place and on right terms. However, in India, in the past, the stress has always been on production levels and marketing did not receive the attention it deserves.

The Eighth Plan document had observed that agricultural marketing assumes special significance in view of the current stress on diversification of the agricultural sector. The plan document observed that unless agricultural marketing is strengthened, it is not possible for the primary producers to realise a fair price.[4]

The National Commission on Agriculture (1976) recommended the following minimum facilities for rural markets in the country:

(i) Availability of physical facilities for grading, weighing and storage;

(ii) An agency to take charge of the cultivator's produce, advance for his immediate needs, process the produce, arrange for further marketing and then make the final payment;

(iii) Availability of an alternative of personal dealing and disposal to the cultivator;

(iv) Means of communication for market information, i.e., post and telegraph office with a provision for telephone;

(v) Provision of shops, selling production inputs and domestic necessities to the producer in the localities where markets are situated and

(vi) Facility of inter-village and intra-village road communication should exist in the market area.

Information technology is the bedrock of modern marketing. In the absence of communication facilities in the villages, farmers do not get the realistic scenario of market prices, the taste, preference, domestic demand, export potential etc.

The size of rural marketing is widening with which the consumption pattern of rural population is also undergoing substantial variations. According to the National Council of Applied Economic Research (NCAER) study, the rural marketing is growing much faster than the urban market. For instance, in 1993-94, villagers bought 53.45 per cent of the total tape recorders, almost a third of the colour television sets, a fourth of the mixers/grinders and a fifth of the refrigerators sold in the country. Of course, products need to be modified to cater specially to the requirements and demands of the rural sector. The corporate sector is now fully aware of the huge purchasing power potential being seen in the rural areas.

The number of regulated markets in the country as on March 31, 1994 was 6809. The Central Government has provided assistance for the creation of infrastructural facilities in the markets and also for setting up of rural godowns. Grading standards have been laid down for 150 agricultural and allied commodities under the Agricultural Produce (Grading and Marketing) Act, 1937.

There are 3124 licensed cold storage with an installed capacity of 8.174 million tonnes as on March 31, 1994. To promote setting up of cold storage under the co-operative sector, the National Co-operative Development Corporation has provided ₹ 74.9 crore for installation of 243 cold storage with an installed capacity of 7.16 lakh tonnes till the end of March 1994.[5]

The special characteristics of agricultural products further enhance the importance of marketing. First, the agricultural products are bulky and therefore require proper storage and transport facilities. Second, most agricultural products are perishable and therefore, suffer from loss in quality. Third, the poor farmers, who are in the majority, sell away their produce immediately after harvest as they urgently require cash. They have a low holding back capacity. Fourth, both the demand for and supply of agricultural products are inelastic. As such, the state has to interfere and initiate in the agricultural price policy in the most cost-effective way. Lastly, the middleman generally determines the grades and standards of agricultural products. In a vast country like India, with such a wide range of products, the tasks to be performed by the marketing system are truly gigantic.

An efficient marketing system acts as an incentive for producers to step up their production. It is the backbone of agricultural development.[7] It ensures a fair price for the marketable surplus. This in turn lead to better capital formation in the agricultural sector. When marketing facilities improve, credit agencies may show greater interest in financing agriculture. In other words, better marketing facilities lead to better credit facilities. Improved marketing facilities also lead to price stability.

An ideal marketing system increases the marketable surplus which directly influences the level of economic development. The small and marginal farmers will be attracted to bring a part of their produce to the market when there is more effective distribution machinery, transport and communication facilities, storage and warehousing facilities and fair marketing practices.

An efficient marketing system should reduce the present dominant role of the middlemen. At present, although the consumer pays a high price, the producer is not benefitted as the middleman's share is considerable. The middlemen are getting more and more profit at the expense of both the producers and the consumers. There is, therefore, a need for reducing the price-spread between the producer and the consumer.

In a situation of scarcity, the middlemen get an opportunity to step up prices to the disadvantage of the consumers. The middlemen also exploit the farmers by keeping the prices of seeds, fertilisers, pesticides and other inputs abnormally high. An efficient marketing system should protect the interests of the consumers and producers.

Government intervention in grain marketing may have an influence on the growth and equity in agricultural sector through.[8]

(i) The level and

(ii) Stability of food prices which in turn will determine the profitability and risk of investment involved.

In India, no producer or manufacturer can ignore the rising rural prosperity as shown in Table 1.

Table: 1
India's Rural Prosperity

Income Group	*1994-95*	*2001-02*	*2006-07**
Above ₹ 1,00,000	1.6	3.8	5.6
₹77,001-1,00,000	2.7	4.7	5.8
₹50,001-77,000	8.3	13.0	22.4
₹25,001-₹50,000	26.0	41.1	36.0
₹25,000-below	61.4	37.4	29.2

* Projections

Source: NCAER

The following facts clearly indicate the growing importance of rural markets in India.

- In 2001-02, LIC sold 55 per cent of its policies in rural India;
- Of the two million BSNL Mobile phone connections, 50 per cent are in rural areas;
- The number of rural super markets (haats) in India is 42,000 that exceed the total number of retail chain stores in the United States (35,000);

- The number of middle and higher income families (having annual income of ₹ 70,000 and above) is 21.7 million and for urban areas it is 24.2 million. No significant difference between these two;
- Electricity consumption by agricultural sector has shown a sharp increase from 17.6 per cent of total consumption in 1980-81 to 29.2 per cent in 1999-2000;
- 24 million Kisan Credit Cards have been issued up to the year 2003. A whopping ₹ 52,000 crore has been sanctioned under KCC Scheme.

PRESENT SYSTEM OF AGRICULTURAL MARKETING

A wide variety of agricultural markets are available in India. In 1980, there were 4,452 regulated markets in the country, comprising of 1,906 principal markets and 2,536 sub-market yards. In addition, there are about 22,000 'haats' or 'shandies' which for a great majority of farmers in India, particularly the small producers, constitute the focal points for disposal of farm produce.[9]

Primary or local markets, also known as *shandies,* are held once or twice a week in the neighbourhood of a group of villages. Each primary market covers an area of 8 to 16 km. radius. Most farmers unload their produce at these markets. It is estimated that these markets account for more than 50 per cent of the total marketed surplus. The village panchayats organise these markets, and prices are mostly determined through bargaining.

Secondary markets, also known as wholesale markets or mandis are permanent in nature in the sense that business in these markets is carried on throughout the year. Each secondary market covers an area of 775 sq. kms. and has a population of 1.32 lakh. The produce is handled in large quantities with the help of a number of middlemen. These markets provide facilities for storage services.

The terminal markets cover a large area, extending over a state or even more. The function of these markets is to carry goods to consumers, final buyers or to places of processing.

Fairs occasionally held are also sources of marketing agricultural produce. These are organised either by local bodies or private agencies.

The Government has set up a series of regulated markets primarily with a view to checking a number of malpractices. In these markets, marketing practices are governed by rules and regulations laid down by the Government.

Co-operative marketing societies have come up with a view to avoiding the middlemen who exploit both the consumers and producers. These societies function on the principle of co-operation and help carry the agricultural produce directly to the consumers.

At present, state trading in foodgrains has become common. The Food Corporation of India (FCI) is maintaining exclusive centres in and around villages. The objective is to procure a good produce at the time of harvest and arrest wide fluctuations in prices.

The methods of sale available at present suffer from a number of defects. Under the open auction system, the agents invite bids for the produce and the highest bidder gets the produce. Under the *dara* system, heaps of different quantities are sold at flat rates without being weighed, grading etc. Under the *Mogum* system, sale is based on the verbal understanding between buyers and sellers. Under private agreement, the seller may invite offers for his produce and may sell to one who will offer the highest price for the produce. In the co-operative and regulated markets, the Government agencies lay down fixed prices for different qualities (and to a great extent the quantities) of agricultural commodities.

The agencies engaged in marketing agricultural produce may be government and quasi-private agencies like the co-operative societies or private agencies. The merchant directly gets the produce from the producer and benefits from the price achieved in his individual capacity. Some merchants visit different villages, collect the produce and take it to the nearest market. The weighmen collect samples of produce from villagers and take them to dealers in towns. The agents are concerned with the assembling and distribution of agricultural produce.

The marketing of agricultural products has been facing a number of problems such as variety of crops, inadequate transport, communication, storage and credit facilities. The price spread (the difference between the price received by the farmer and the price paid by the consumer) is very wide. The marketing system is so defective that as much as 40 per cent of the price paid by the consumer goes to the middlemen.

The inflationary situation has failed to confer much benefits on small and marginal farmers. On the other hand, the benefits have been targeted towards middlemen. The competition which is imperfect, unfair and even monopolistic, is in favour of the middlemen. Naturally, the real income of the farmer is on the decline. Another adverse factor for the farmer is the inadequate marketed surplus of certain items which has declined to a large extent.

DEFECTS OF AGRICULTURAL MARKETING

About 10 per cent of the foodgrains gets wasted due to poor and inadequate storage facilities. Again, foodgrain losses on a percentage basis may be categorised roughly as: field losses to the tune of 25% storage losses between estimated to be 3%.

About 30% of the agricultural produce goes waste for want of post-harvest facilities. Fruit traders are reluctant to invest in high cost storage structures. Of the 260 lakh tonnes of fruits and 501 lakh tonnes of vegetables produced, about 35%, valued at ₹ 3,000 crore, goes waste. Only 1% to 1.5% of the total production of fruits and vegetables is processed.

Cold storage plants are highly capital intensive, and the returns are not attractive. The situation has worsened due to non-availability of uninterrupted power supply. Most of the cold storage capacity is being devoted to potatoes. Around 88% of the plants are in the private sector.[10]

In view of poor transport facilities, farmers are compelled to sell their produce in the local markets or to agents or brokers. Modern transport facilities such as good roads, refrigerated vans for transportation of perishable agricultural commodities from the farmgate to the markets have not been well developed.

A major defect of agricultural marketing in India is the inability of most farmers to postpone the sale of their produce. Since the small and marginal farmers are in debts and therefore urgently require cash, they sell away their produce immediately after harvest when the prices are low and unfavourable to them.

They subsequently face financial crisis and do not get good returns for their produce. In some cases, the crop is mortgaged and the farmer has to sell the produce to the lender only on terms prescribed by him.

The heavy sales in the villages are due to a number of factors. First, the farmer has to honour his debt obligations. Second, due to the unsatisfactory nature of communication with the nearest market, the farmer is tempted to sell away the produce in the village itself. Third, certain perishable goods have to be immediately transported to the market place. If transport facilities are inadequate, the farmer is forced to sell away his produce at a low price in the village itself. Last, most cultivators are hard-pressed for cash and therefore cannot postpone the sale even by a few months.

The farmers who are scattered over a wide area are not properly organised while the buyers, specially in the case of commercial crops, are well organised. There is no organisation to properly guide the small producers and protect their interests. Under these circumstances, the producers of agricultural products as a class are being exploited by a number of middlemen.

Even if the cultivator is capable of postponing his sale to a future date to get remunerative prices, inadequate storage facilities stand in the way. Since rodents eat away a significant part of the produce stored, the farmers are unwilling to keep the stock with them. It is unfortunate that as much as 10% of the total foodgrains output is lost due to poor storage facilities.

Another problem facing the farmers is the inadequate and expensive means of transportation. In spite of the presence of improved bullock carts, the cost of transportation is not within the reach of the small and marginal farmers. But the situation has improved over the years with more faster modes of transport coming in.

The farmers face a number of superfluous middlemen and malpractices. The presence of a long chain of middlemen reduces the profits of the farmers and abnormally increases prices for the consumers. These middlemen function at various stages and indulge in various malpractices like manipulation of scales and weights against sellers; arbitrary deductions and settlement of prices under cover. Moreover, the producers are forced to bear a number of unauthorised charges, particularly in the unorganised markets, and some charges are in kind. These charges are unjust because they are not only high but also not clearly defined and specified.

A serious drawback of agricultural marketing in India is lack of quality-wise grading and standardisation. Much of the produce is marketed in an unsatisfactory condition. In the absence of grading and standardisation, even superior foodgrains are declared inferior and therefore, offered lower prices. It is found that even official agencies resort to this malpractice. The exportation of agricultural products gets greatly hampered in the absence of proper quality-wise grading and standardisation.

The Indian farmers also suffer from lack of market intelligence. The farmers with little contact with the outside world, are not in touch with the existing and emerging trends of the market prices. The information supplied by the middlemen regarding prices in the wholesale market are false and misleading. The farmer is therefore not able to realise reasonable returns for his produce. Even when reliable information is available, prices are not comparable on account of:

(i) The lack of standard grades acceptable to the whole community;

(ii) Variation in the amount of refractions allowed and the terms of standard contracts obtaining in different markets;

(iii) Inaccuracy of information supplied by various agencies concerned;

(iv) Variation in the price quotations given by local and central government and

(v) The considerable variations in weights and measures used in several markets in the absence of standardisation of weights and measures.[11]

Co-operative Marketing

A marketing co-operative can be defined as a group of producers who are basically farmers having come together to sell their marketable surplus at the most remunerative prices for their own benefit. A well knit and efficiently organised co-operative marketing structure would certainly promote the economic standards of the rural masses, the producers and the rural communities as well.[12]

Co-operative marketing aims at strengthening the position of the primary producers by increasing their collective bargaining power. A publication of the Food and Agricultural Organisation of the United Nations observed:

A co-operative, by bargaining for all of its members, can exert more control over the price of their produce and can thus offset monopolistic power in the hands of the buyers, and obtain advantages not attainable if individual members sell independently.

The publication further observed:

> A co-operative can obtain, differentiate sale of produce and it can stimulate demand by advertising and other means that would be uneconomical for the individual members alone. At the minimum, it should be able to increase the bargaining power of the producers and recapture for them part of the value of the product that was being diverted into monopolistic profits.

It is desirable to develop agricultural marketing on co-operative lines. "A marketing society is a co-operative association of cultivators formed primarily for the purpose of helping the members to market their produce more profitably than is possible through private trade." Marketing co-operatives would enable the farmers to have easy access to credit so that distress sales can be avoided. They will do away with many malpractices associated with unregulated markets. The price spread will be reduced and therefore, the consumers too will be benefitted from marketing co-operatives. These co-operatives also help ensure price stability. Hence, production, marketing and processing functions can be linked through co-operative marketing. Co-operative marketing permits a more rational utilisation of physical infrastructure, such as machines, storing facilities and means of transportation. This may contribute to reducing marketing costs especially for small cultivators.[13]

The co-operative movement in India is the largest one in the whole world. We have over 3 lakh co-operative societies of different types with a membership of over 11.2 crore. The movement covers 97 per cent of villages and 50 per cent of the rural population. The movement has a working capital of ₹ 17,000 crore.[14]

For strengthening the co-operative marketing movement, the Report of the All-India Rural Credit Survey Committee has suggested state participation in the share capital marketing societies at all levels, linking of credit with marketing, establishment of a chain of warehouses and godowns and the management of co-operatives by well-trained and efficient personnel. The National Co-operative Development and Warehousing Board was set up in 1956. It was replaced in 1963 by the National Co-operative Development Corporation (NCDC) which plans and promotes programmes for the production, processing, marketing, storage, warehousing and import of agricultural produce through co-operative societies with financial assistance from the Government. As a result of measures taken by NCDC, the value of agricultural produce marketed by co-operatives in India has gone up from ₹ 160 crore in 1962-63 to ₹ 1,189 crore in 1976-77.[15]

The NCDC has been quite successful strengthening the co-operative movement. Thanks to the efforts made by the NCDC, a well-knit co-operative structure has emerged in the agricultural sector, undertaking various activities relating to agricultural marketing. By 1974-75, 3,127 primary marketing societies, covering almost all important secondary markets in the country, have emerged. Primary marketing societies have both individual growers and village primaries as their members. At the end of 1974-75, 92% of the 154 lakh village societies had been affiliated to marketing primaries.

Primary societies have been federated into 25 state level marketing federations of a general type, 7 state federations of tribal co-operatives and one inter-state federation at the national level — National Agricultural Co-operative Marketing Federation. The Federation also permits its membership to primary marketing societies having an annual turnover of ₹ 20 lakh in advanced states and ₹ 10 lakh in the comparatively underdeveloped states. There are also three organised national federations, one each for co-operative spinning mills, co-operative sugar factories and a dairy co-operative.

One of the important recommendations of the All-India Rural Credit Survey Committee was that village primaries should be integrated with marketing societies which would go towards recovering loans due from grower-members from the sale of their produce in these markets. Under the integrated scheme of rural credit, finance is given to agriculturists on conditions that the produce would be sold only through the marketing society, so that recovery of loans being advanced would not be a problem, and further, the farmers would be ensured to get clue price for their produce. Though village societies are organically linked with primary marketing societies, their functional linkage has yet to be developed. To avoid the financial discrepancies reported to be done by the middlemen, what remains to be done is that the marketing societies be permitted to offer production credits to grower members. In the absence of this policy, the credit societies are facing the problem of over-dues.

SUGGESTIONS FOR IMPROVING CO-OPERATIVE MARKETING SYSTEM

Though co-operative marketing system is the ideal one in protecting the interests of both producers and consumers, it has been suffering from a number of weaknesses.

First, the primary co-operative societies at the tehsil level are weak and exhibit uneven performance. Most of them are not taking up marketing and some of them do marketing, but not to the required extent. Most of the societies have failed to effectively cover all the villages in terms of membership of growers and the collection of agricultural produce. Thus, the base of the co-operative marketing system lacks a strong existing base. Measures should be initiated to see that the dormant societies take up marketing business and handle business to the required extent.

Second, the linkage between primaries at the tehsil level and the state and between the State Marketing Federations and the National Agricultural Marketing Federation should be strengthened. Moreover, organisation of societies should be on democratic lines.

Third, sometimes, the co-operatives at various levels work at cross purposes which is due to lack of an integrated plan of business and operations. Co-operatives at higher levels should realise that their objective is to protect the interests of producers and consumers and not secure individually profits for the state or national federations. Co-operatives should not resort to unhealthy competition against each other. Moreover, they should also give up non-co-operative practices like collecting commission charges without performing their individually set aside marketing functions. This is also necessary to win the confidence of the farmers in the rural sector.

Fourth, the marketing co-operatives should undertake a long range programme to market principal agricultural goods. It would be better if the co-operative marketing system handles at least 25% of the agricultural produce. It is also desirable to link co-operative marketing institutions with consumer co-operatives to reduce the price spread.

Lastly, the status of the societies should be improved by enrolling more individuals as members and by collecting additional share capital from the primary agricultural societies. The produce should be marked only after proper grading and processing.

MEASURES TO IMPROVE AGRICULTURAL MARKETING

It is necessary to initiate and implement with immediate effect certain measures to improve agricultural marketing facilities so that the interests of both the producers and consumers are protected. The industrial sector too can secure steady and reliable supplies of raw materials of uniform quality only when the marketing facilities are improved. The following measures are necessary for improving and organising agricultural marketing.

First, the malpractices associated with unregulated markets can be removed by setting up regulated markets. The Government can also exercise proper control over the markets through local bodies or state legislation. In a regulated market, transactions are usually governed by various rules and regulations. Market charges are clearly defined and specified; correct weighment is ensured; arrangements are made to settle disputes and reliable and up-to-date market news are made available. Facilities like sheds for the sale of produce are provided. Marketing committees, having representatives of growers, traders and the Government are responsible for regulating the markets and arresting malpractices. Most wholesale assembling markets in the country now function as successful regulated markets.

Second, storage facilities are essential to avoid loss of crop and enable the farmers to postpone sale to a more favourable time. They enable farmers to regulate the supply of commodities according to the needs. In recent years, storage facilities in the public sector have vastly improved. The central and state warehousing corporations, the Food Corporation of India and the co-operatives are taking special interest in the provision of improved and adequate storage facilities.

The Central Warehousing Corporation was set up in 1982. Its functions go as follows:

- Acquire and build godowns and warehouses at suitable places;
- Arrange facilities for the transport of agricultural produce and inputs;
- Subscribe to the share capital of State Warehousing Corporations and
- Acts as an agent of the Government for the purpose of purchase, sale, storage and immediate distribution of agricultural produce.

Two important institutions are functioning in the co-operative sector. These are: National Co-operative Development Corporation (NCDE) set up in 1963 and the National Co-operative Agricultural Marketing Federation (NAFED) set up in 1958. As a result of the measures initiated so far, the public agencies have been able to provide accommodation to store 14 million tonnes. This is supplemented with cover, plinth storage and rented storage.

Besides, there is the need for improving storage facilities on the following lines:

(i) Encouraging the construction of storage facilities in the private sector through suitable incentives;

(ii) Encouraging multi-purpose co-operative societies at the primary level to expand their storage capacity respectively;

(iii) Arranging storage facilities for inputs and

(iv) Encouraging scientific farm level storage.

Third, the introduction of standard weights and measures safeguards the interests of the consumers by avoiding false or under-weight prices for the produce. The farmers' knowledge of weights and measures should be developed. The metric system of weights and measures has been introduced throughout the country because it is simple, easier to learn and remember. The Standard Weights and Measures Act was brought into force in 1958. Under this Act, the Government weights and measures alone should be used for price transactions. Standard grades of produce should be maintained so that the consumer can purchase items even without personal inspection.

Fourth, in a situation of frequent changes in prices, market information must be useful and timely for the farmers. The buyers too must be aware of price trends. There is no proper co-ordination as between different markets. Therefore, we find price variations even in markets which are not far from each other. Under these circumstances, one market may face over supply, another market may experience shortages of the essential commodities. An efficient market ensures proper flow of produce to each market and protects the interests of both the producers and the consumers by maintaining equality between supply and demand.

Fifth, compatability between improved marketing facilities and better transport facilities would also ensure financial benefits/good returns to farmers. Easy and cheap means of transportation should be developed as would the farmers prefer to market their produce at a favourable time and improve their bargaining power. Rural roads should be developed as they are the connecting links between the rural and the urban marketing centres. The Minimum Needs Programme of the Sixth Plan has given high priority to rural roads. The aim was to link by 1988 every village with a population of 1,000 or more by road. Efforts are also underway to improve the designs of bullock carts which are considered to be the primary of transportation in rural India.

Sixth, one of the important objectives of improved marketing facilities is to ensure proper price for the produce to the farmer. This is being done with the introduction of state trading in foodgrains. The Food Corporation of India has taken the responsibility of purchase, storage, movement, transport, distribution and sale of foodgrains in order to avoid wide fluctuations in their prices.

The Sixth Plan has also aimed to initiate the following measures to improve the existing infrastructure in the marketing system:[16]

(i) Further expansion of the regulated market system in terms of more markets and commodities to be brought within the scope of regulations;

(ii) Strengthening and streamlining the arrangements for enforcement/and inspections to ensure a regulated system of open auctions, trading practices and margins of intermediaries (commission agents) and

(iii) Development of rural markets and 'shandies' and establishment of rural markets in areas where such facility is not available within a reasonable distance.

Research in the field of agricultural marketing has so far been confined mainly to commodity survey reports, which are simple and well suited to the subsistence stage of agriculture. But, institutional, area and functional approaches are likely to be more helpful now in identifying our specific problems and in suggesting solutions.[17] In view of the multiplicity of organisation, there appears to be a strong need for having a co-ordinating agency which can take an overall view of the marketing problems facing the country.[18]

The Government has also accepted as a policy the development of primary markets as multi-purpose growth centres and as effective instruments to give a boost to rural development. Value adding activities like grading, packaging and simple processing should also be introduced at the primary market level. In view of the current stress on liberalisation, developed primary markets could establish a direct link with departmental stores/super bazaars in the urban areas for selling farm-fresh produce.[19]

The multi-marketing channels need cost-effective restructuring to protect the interests of growers and consumers. The growers should develop linkages directly with the retailers/wholesalers, processors and exporters. Farmers' associations/co-operatives can play a vital role in this respect.

The Shankarlal Guru Committee on agricultural marketing submitted its interim report on June 19, 1992 and the final report in the last week of November, 1992. The major recommendations of the Committee include:

(i) Preparing a perspective plan to regulate at least half of the total number of unregulated markets under the respective laws during the Eighth Plan period;

(ii) Setting up of a separate national bank to assist agricultural marketing with its branches in the regulated markets spread all over the country to operate in close collaboration with the marketing committees;

(iii) The states are to ensure regular elections and to constitute State Agricultural Marketing Boards and Market Committees with majority representations to the farmers. The chairman of these committees should be agriculturists and

(iv) Public agencies are to purchase produce directly from farmers and not any intermediaries.

A national level organisation called the National Council of State Marketing Boards (NCOSAMB) was set up in February 1988 as a registered society. The Council was set up as an apex body to provide a common platform to the member boards (State Agricultural Marketing Boards), to discuss problems relating to agricultural marketing, other allied subjects and also to share the experiences of the members. It also formulated guidelines for uniform codes and laws for balanced development of food and agricultural marketing system as a whole. It is expected to undertake studies, surveys, research and projects etc.[20]

A number of rural godowns have been set up under the programme for the National Grid on Rural Godowns and also under schemes for storage in the co-operative and warehousing sector.

It is possible to build rural godowns using locally available materials like bricks, timber, tiles and bamboo. If the rural women are actively involved in the adoption of modern techniques of storage, much of the grain loss after harvest can be prevented.[21]

The Guru Committee (Chairman: Shankar Lal Guru) on Training and Research in Agricultural Marketing, constituted in February, 1994, submitted its report on 27th January, 1995.

The Committee recommended setting up of training colleges for agricultural marketing by state marketing boards. It stressed on the need for starting full-fledged faculties on agricultural marketing by agriculture universities. With emphasis on starting marketing research, the Committee has pleaded for an all-India cadre service in the agricultural sector. Under the cadre, farmers should be exposed to the functioning of various marketing institutions including regulated markets through short-term courses.

Other recommendations of the Committee are (*Kurukshetra,* February, 1995):

(i) There should be close co-ordination between the Directorate of Marketing and Inspection (DMI) and the National Institute of Agricultural Marketing (NIAM) in imparting training to various categories of marketing personnel;

(ii) The state level Agricultural Marketing Cell in NIAM should be developed into a centre for training institution development;

(iii) A new Training Innovations Group should be set up within NIAM, having members from outside faculties;

(iv) The training programmes should also include training of farmers and traders. Agriculture universities and management institutes should be associated with the refresher courses for marketing personnel;

(v) The Ministry of Rural Development, Government of India, may provide grants-in-aid to states to set up adequate training centres with modern facilities. The National Council for State Marketing Boards (COSAMB) should co-ordinate the programmes of the state and central institutions and

(vi) The Agricultural Marketing Boards in the states and Union Territories may be designed as co-ordinating agencies for research work and the application thereof.

There is an urgent need for creation of cadre of well trained and capable managers who can attend to the operation and supervision of the markets. Training facilities are available now at the Directorate of Marketing and Inspection, Faridabad and the National Institute of Agricultural Marketing, Jaipur. In the states, Karnataka has established its own training college at Mysore.

The training programmes should be in tune with the nature of rural markets. They should motivate the producer-sellers in fully availing themselves of the facilities at the rural markets.

Agricultural development programmes should give up priority to improving agricultural marketing arrangements not only to minimise wastage but to enable the farming community to realise reasonable returns from their investments.

REFERENCES

1. A.A. Ansari: 'Co-operative Marketing in India: Progress and Problems', *Khadigramodyog*, November 1994, p. 87.
2. B. Bhushan: 'Agricultural Marketing in India: Structural Weaknesses and Agenda for Reforms', *Kurukshetra*, November 1994, p. 10.
3. Ziabun Y. Jasdanwala: 'Efficient Agricultural Marketing', *Economic and Political Weekly*, December 31, 1977, p. A-133.
4. Planning Commission, Government of India, *Eighth Five Year Plan 1992-97*, Vol. II, p. 11.
5. Ministry of Finance, Government of India, *Economic Survey 1994-95*.
6. Report of the Working Group on Agricultural Marketing and Role of Regulated Markets, Central Advisory Committee, 1979, p. 2.
7. *Sixth Five Year Plan 1980-85*, p. 112.
8. Uma Lele: 'Marketing and Pricing of Foodgrains', in C.H. Shah (Ed. 1979): *Agricultural Development of India: Policy and Problems*, Orient Longman, p. 153.
9. *Sixth Five Year Plan 1980-85*, p. 112.
10. I. Satya Sundaram: 'Vegetables: Case for Co-ordinated Approach', *Financial Express*, September 18, 1993, p. 7.
11. C.B. Memoria (1979): *Agricultural Problems in India*, Kitab Mahal, Allahabad, pp. 766-767.
12. S.K. Verma: 'Rural Development Through Co-operative Marketing', *Kurukshetra*, November 1994, p. 15.

13. U. Aiyasami and H.G. Bohle: 'Market Access as Constraint on Marginal and Small Farmers', *Economic and Political Weekly*, March 28, 1981, p. A-35.

14. M.B. Patil: 'The Co-operative Way to Managing Change', *Kurukshetra*, March 1, 1982.

15. N.N. Sachitanand: 'Co-operative Marketing, Processing: Strength and Weaknesses', *The Hindu*, June 15, 1978.

16. *Sixth Five Year Plan 1980-85*, p. 112.

17. B.S. Saxena and R.A. Khanorkar: 'Role of Agricultural Marketing', *Commerce* (Annual Number), 1979, p. 121.

18. S.C. Verma: 'Recent Trends in Agricultural Marketing', *Kurukshetra*, June 16, 1981, p. 7.

19. R.N. Bansal: 'Development of Rural Markets as Nucleus Growth Centres', *Kurukshetra*, November 1994, p. 8.

20. R. Subramanyam: 'COSAMB: The National Link in Farm Marketing', *Kurukshetra*, November 1994, pp. 25-26.

21. I. Satya Sundaram: 'Plugging the Grain Drain', *Financial Express*, July 6, 1991.

Chapter

46 Rural Development Administration and Panchayati Raj Institutions

The rural poor can derive due benefits from welfare schemes only when they get administrative support. The local level institutions have to ultimately take up the task of rural reconstruction as they can appreciate better local needs and ensure local participation in the formulation of development plans.[1] It is precisely for this reason that the Panchayati Raj Institutions (PRIs) emerged at various levels. This also puts in place the importance of administration for rural development.

The organisational framework of anti-poverty programmes requires careful planning, taking into account the socio-economic features of each area. If greater decentralisation is to be achieved so that the programmes are made responsive to local problems, the needs and potentials, district and block level implementing agencies will have to be given much greater flexibility.[2]

The Government has towards this end, initiated certain measures to strengthen the PRIs. Some of the important features of the Constitutional (Seventy-Third Amendment) Act, 1992 are:

(i) The Gram Sabha will be a body comprising of all the adult members registered as voters in the panchayat area.

(ii) There shall be three-tier system of panchayat at village, intermediate and district levels. Smaller states with population below 20 lakh will have the option to have intermediate level panchayat.

(iii) Seats in panchayats at all the three levels shall be filled by direct election. In addition, chairpersons of village panchayats can be made members of the panchayats at intermediate level and chairpersons at this level can be members of the panchayat at the district level. MPs,

MLAs and MLCs could also be members of panchayats at the intermediate or the district level.

(iv) In all the panchayats, seats would be reserved for SCs and STs in proportion to their population and one-third of the total number of seats will be reserved for women. One-third of the seats reserved for SCs, STs will also be reserved for women.

(v) Every panchayat shall have a uniform five-year term and elections to constitute new bodies shall be completed before the expiry of the term. In the event of dissolution, elections will be compulsorily held within six months. The reconstituted panchayat will serve for the remaining term period of five years.

(vi) It will not be possible to dissolve the existing panchayats by amendment of any act before the expiry of its duration.

(vii) A person who is disqualified under any law for elections to the Legislature of the state or under any law of the state, will not be entitled to become the member of panchayats.

(viii) Specific responsibilities will be entrusted to the panchayats to prepare plans for economic development and social justice in respect of matters listed in XI Schedule. For the implementation of development schemes, the main responsibility will be entrusted to the Panchayat and

(ix) The panchayat will receive adequate funds for carrying out their functions. Grants from the state government will constitute an important source of funding but state governments are also expected to assign the revenue of certain taxes to the panchayat. In some cases, panchayat will also be permitted to collect and retain the revenues raised by them.

I. THE PANCHAYATI RAJ (PR) SYATEM

The Balwant Rai Mehta Committee which was appointed in January, 1957, has suggested a three-tier system of decentralisation. At the village level — village panchayats, at the block level-panchayat samitis and at the district level — Zilla Parishads were suggested. However, no rigid institutional pattern was laid down for the panchayati raj, but the fundamental principles governing the set-up are:

(i) A three-tier structure of local self-governing bodies from the villages structure of local self-governing bodies, from the village to the district, the bodies being organically linked up;

(ii) Genuine transfer of power and responsibility to them;

(iii) Adequate resources should be transferred to these bodies to discharge the responsibilities devolving on them and

(iv) The system should facilitate further devolution and dispersal of power and responsibility in the future.

The village panchayats are the elected bodies of the people. All adults from gram sabhas participate in the elections. The village panchayats send their elected representatives to panchayati samities (at the block level) which act as a link between the village panchayats and the zilla parishads. The samiti elects its president and vice-president. The zilla parishads (at the district level) are constituted by the presidents of the panchayat samitis along with the MPs and MLAs in the district. Of course, the collector and the technical departments of the government offer guidance and assistance to the block panchayat samities. These samities are autonomous. Thus, the panchayat raj is associated with people's representatives at all levels.

FUNCTIONS OF THE PR SYSTEM

While some of the functions of the panchayats are obligatory; others are discretionary, but these differ from state to state. The obligatory functions include: opening and maintenance of burial grounds, maintenance and improvement of public streets; proper drainage, electricity supply, lighting and medical relief; construction and maintenance of public toilets, registration of births and deaths, organisation of melas and fairs, provision of primary education, water supply etc.

The discretionary functions include: plantation of trees, improving the breed of cattle, promotion and improvement of cottage industries, relief against famine; construction of new bridges, dharmashalas and culverts, wells and ponds, provision of medical facilities, reading rooms; control and management of village forests, supervision and control of co-operatives etc.

The panchayats collect taxes, cesses, fees and other dues for the government, regulate harmful trade practices and organise recreational and social functions. Another priority area for the panchayats is working on land reforms. Some of the village panchayats have also been entrusted with judicial powers. These relate to the trial of civil suits for money due on contracts, recovery of movable property or its value. Their powers of punishment are limited to the imposition of moderate fines, and they employ simple and summary procedure for the disposal of cases.

SOURCES OF INCOME FOR PANCHAYATS

The main sources of income for village panchayats are:

(i) Taxes like house tax, profession tax, vehicle tax, octroi, piligrim tax, animal tax, entertainment tax etc. Some taxes are obligatory, others are optional;

(ii) Different types of fees which include fees for services, licence fees, registration fees, fines and penalties etc.;

(iii) Communal income includes income from fisheries, fairs and markets, gross sales, panchayat forests etc. and

(iv) The miscellaneous sources of income include interest and deposits, government assistance, stamp duty, sale of old articles, newspapers, rent and product of land, loans and advances and district board contract work.

The panchayats usually suffer from the want of funds. The Balwant Rai Mehta team had suggested that in all states, panchayats should have the power to levy special tax based on land revenue, house tax or on some other basis of executing specific development projects. It felt that there is an urgent need to convert idle labour into useful public assets.

The Asoka Mehta Committee also observed that the panchayats at all levels should mobilise substantial resources of their own and should not unduly depend on budgetary devolution. It declared: "for discharging the developmental responsibilities entrusted to PRI, the state governments should make available the commensurate funds from its total budget on a continuing basis. The non-plan expenditure pertaining to the decentralised times will be administered by the Zilla Parishad. The financial devolution must correspond to the functional decentralisation."

MERITS OF PR SYSTEM

The PRIs are responsible for the emergence of new leadership which is better than the previous one. They have also contributed significantly to social welfare and increased agricultural production in the rural sector. They have been successful in encouraging the intelligence, self-reliance, initiative and social sense amongst the rural people. The success of anti-poverty programmes depends on the capacity of the rural people to acquire these qualities.

They have provided an opportunity for the people to study the problems facing the village economy. By providing equal opportunities to all, they have strengthened the foundations of democracy at the micro level. If they fail to function well, it is because of the lack of active involvement of the rural people in developmental programmes.

The Asoka Mehta Committee has well summed up the benefits emerged from the PR system. It declared: "Politically speaking, it has become a process of democratic seed-drilling in the Indian soil, making an average citizen more conscious of his rights than before. Administratively speaking, the system has bridged the widening gulf between the bureaucratic elite and the people. Socio-culturally speaking, it has generated a new leadership which was not merely relatively young in age but also modernistic and pro-social change in outlook. Finally, looked at from the developmental angle, the PRI system has successfully helped rural people to cultivate a development psyche."[3]

The PR system has three main advantages:[4]

(i) The people will have a better understanding of what the government proposes to do. In other words, this system is an instrument of self-education;

(ii) The participation of the people both in decision-making and implementation of development programmes helps to choose programmes which serve the felt needs of the people, improve the cost benefit analysis and bring about a radical social change, and

(iii) Involvement of the people in the programmes of economic and social activity increases the likelihood of proper maintenance of such activities.

A purely bureaucratic approach to rural development fails to deliver the goods. Hence, the relationship between administration and the duly elected democratic bodies at the local level should be cordial.

The case for decentralising the planning process rests on the simple truth: the local problems are best understood by the local people themselves. Hence, democracy and devolution of powers should go together.

The PR system, by enlarging the scope of decentralisation, not only ensures the democratic character of the government, but also improves the effectiveness of planned development. Too much power with the bureaucracy no doubt curbs the initiative of the rural people. Decentralisation helps control the power of bureaucracy. It alone can ensure people's participation in the development process.

Despite limitations, the PRIs will help lower castes to move up in governing their own affairs in villages. In a country like India, the shift of power to the rural poor and weaker sections of society has been slow. If the weak use their votes and are encouraged to take wise decisions, they can occupy the driver's seat. The fragmentation and division among themselves must be ironed out.[5]

Thus, the PRIs are local level agencies (to be more specific, democratic institutions) having unique responsibilities to promote and strengthen development consciousness amongst people; ensure people's participation in the planning process; contribute to the success of anti-poverty programmes and bring the marginalised communities into the main stream of progress. Above all, they have the rare opportunity to train the future leaders of the country on the right lines.

Weaknesses of PR System

The panchayat set-up has also created some problems. It has failed to produce benefits expected of it. The major deficiencies of rural development administration in India are:[6]

(i) Development programmes in India have often been marked by a fragmented and compartmentalised approach in formulation on the one hand, and a top-down, inflexible, oneway system of implementation on the other;

(ii) Lack of emphasis on primary tasks, and inadequate appreciation of the linkages between various schemes/ activities and the primary task or core activity;

(iii) A higher salience of power and status orientation, authoritarianism, unresponsiveness, formalism and rigidity;

(iv) Inadequate operational planning, resulting in duplication, wastage, compliance with formal instructions and relative indifference to results and performance and

(v) Defective supervision and reporting, often negative, perfunctory and inquisitorial.

The following are the major weaknesses of the PR system. First, the panchayats are not able to arrive at a consensus due to emerging factions among the villagers. Consequently, there is considerable delay in taking decisions, and the decisions are very often coloured by the factional interests of the members. The elected village panchayats may be free from party politics, but they are not free from village politics.[7]

Second, all is not well with the leadership at this level. Persons who lack a sense of responsibility, integrity and dedication have become leaders. It is but natural that they have failed to inspire the villagers. Political power has been concentrated in the hands of those having money, power and prestige. The role of such leadership in serving the rural poor is bound to be limited.

Third, the development work undertaken by panchayats is sufficiently hampered by political interference. There is also inadequate and vague communication from the higher authorities. Sometimes, the political consequences have to be assessed by the officials before they take an administrative decision.[8] No wonder, qualified and competent persons are generally unwilling to work in these institutions. The posts are treated more as a means of prestige, patronage and power than of service to the community. In practice, the system has turned to be a power mechanism.

Fourth, the attitude of the bureaucracy towards the poor is rather hostile. The officers look upon the elected representatives with contempt and resentment; suffer from superiority complex due to higher education, urban background, higher position, status, power and authority, suffer from general contempt for illiterate and semi-illiterate villagers; and afraid to face the popular leadership for fear of loss of power, prestige and privileges.[9]

Fifth, the benefits of developmental programmes have not been equitably distributed amongst different sections of the rural community. They have been largely appropriated by the high caste and financially well-off sections. Instead of preparing the ground for social equality, the PRIs have allegedly institutionalised injustice, favouritism and factionalism.[10] Benefits such as subsidies extended by the Government are mostly enjoyed by the rural rich. Hierarchy and exploitation are so deep-rooted in rural India, that they are accepted and are running rampant without questioning.[11]

Sixth, a major objective in recommending them is to transfer adequate powers and responsibilities to them. However, in actual practice, this has not been achieved to the desired extent. The government departments are still dominant and the collector is made responsible for every function of the government in the district. Thus, they are converted into mere agents of the state government, without due powers and responsibilities. One of the major causes for the ineffective implementation of land reform measures is the non-involvement of the landless labourers, the insecure tenants and the share-croppers in the process.[12]

Seventh, the financial resources at the disposal of the panchayats are too inadequate to take up developmental works on a significant scale. Naturally, they are showing less interest in development and more interest in petty administrative matters such as posting and transfer, grant of licences or contracts. Some panchayats have also showed an initiative to make use of the matching grants. Yet, panchayat samitis and zilla parishads heavily depend on grants and assigned revenues indicating thereby that the popular representation in these bodies has not led to any appreciable effort to use the available powers of taxation. There is a great potential for receipts for remunerative enterprises which can be developed by a dynamic and imaginative leadership at the official and non-official levels.[13]

Last, the developmental work taken up is not properly planned. The people have had a very limited share in the preparation and execution of the plans even at the village level and therefore they lack any social purpose.[14] The administrative structure is so inappropriate that the whole system revolves around detailed targets set from above and is be-devilled by shortages.[15] The entire structure suffered from party politics, absence of constructive leadership, apathy of bureaucracy and lack of co-operation of rural people.[16]

In a democracy, political will is needed for the success of any programme. A critical factor for the success of PRIs is political will. Yet, this factor is missing. It has been rightly pointed out.[17]

> Evidence suggests that there were deliberate plans by political leaders, in collusion with the bureaucracy and local vested interests, to emasculate and eventually discard panchayati raj.

The lack of political will is understandable. Leaders of the ruling political party may find a danger to their authority and influence in the PRIs. Also, some elections were lost by the ruling political party in areas in which they are strong. The politicians also feared that strengthening them would mean creation of more competing centres of influence and power.[18]

Strengthening the PR System

The Asoka Mehta Committee observed that there is confusion even with regard to the concept of panchayati raj. Some treat it just as an administrative agency; others as an extension of democracy at the grassroot level and still others as a charter of the local rural government.[19] However, there is need for improving the PR infrastructure and not the total abolition of the system.

The Committee has favoured open participation of political parties in panchayati raj affairs as this may 'ultimately convert their mutual competition into constructive co-operation for rural development.' The Committee also felt that funds earmarked for the weaker sections must be subjected to social audit by a district level agency as well as by a committee of legislatures in which scheduled castes and scheduled tribes and MLAs have a majority of representation. It also observed that unless the state governments devolve planned and non-planned funds commensurate with the decentralisation of functions, the scheme of decentralised democratic management would suffer a drawback.

Autonomy to lower formations is essential to improve their effectiveness. There is need to identify the area where such modifications in line authority are required.[20] There is also need for setting up public vigilance committees to see that the schemes meant for the rural poor are effectively implemented. Proper evaluation of the programmes can be entrusted to these committees.

Decentralisation would be effective only when the states are serious about it. Without political will, the PRIs will not be able to discharge their functions successfully.

Some of the pre-conditions for the success of PRIs are:[21]

(i) State governments should set up special organisations devoted to rural planning to train them in the techniques of economic planning;

(ii) Steps should be taken to ensure the administrative neutrality of panchayati raj officers with regard to the policy decisions at the panchayati level;

(iii) The concept of 'partyless democracy' is relevant in the context of the panchayati raj and

(iv) There is need for a separate District Development Officer to look after development and administration of PRIs along with administrative and technical personnel and financial resources.

They should enjoy financial autonomy. Provision of adequate funds is not enough. This brings into focus the need to remove state approaches and supervision over the decisions of these institutions, involving financial commitments relating to budget, taxation, expenditure, contracts, staff appointments, disposal of assets etc., of course, panchayats alone are responsible for their decisions and failures.[22]

They must levy and collect their own taxes and manage their resources. However, most revenue sources under the control of local governments would be of inelastic nature. As such, they find it a challenging task to meet the growing expenditure commitments. Through a judicious allocation of tax sharing and a general and selective grants-in-aid, the state financial commission has to ensure vertical fiscal equity.[23]

The PRIs should be the main mechanism to provide democratic governance at the grassroot level. Strengthening them will go a long way in revamping the rural delivery system. Their success largely depends on the proper mandate, self-governance and financial autonomy which are three areas of priority indicating the power of the PR system.

II. RURAL DEVELOPMENT ADMINISTRATION

A good administrative set up can bring the public and the government closer and ensure maximum participation and co-operation of the masses in the formulation and implementation of target plans initiated to help the rural sector.[24] On the other hand, a bad administration leads to corruption and inefficiency, arrests the spirit of enthusiasm and idealism and results in the wastage of resources.[25]

If returns from huge investments made in the rural sector are not impressive, it is mainly because of faculty planning and inefficient implementation. A rigid bureaucratic administration is not appropriate to tackle the complex problems facing rural India.

The rural people have to develop the capacity to elicit the services of the development administration.[26] The schemes have to be popularised so as to make them more of people's programmes than official programmes.[27]

No doubt new institutions like the District Rural Development Agency (DRDA) and the District Industries Centre (DIC) have emerged, but they suffer from inadequate facilities and are not fully prepared to take up tasks entrusted to them. For instance, the trained personnel available with the DRDA is inadequate, and the frequent transfers of the staff have undermined the efficiency of this institution.

Most project directors are on the verge of retirement and therefore their interest in programmes continue to be at a low ebb. They do not as a rule belong to any specialist cadre. Moreover, the DRDAs have neither the formal authority for co-ordination at the district level nor have they been given direct control over the block agencies.

The PRIs should have greater role in the implementation of anti-poverty programmes. Notwithstanding their limitations, they should be made responsible for the implementation of these programmes. Also, unless the various rural development programmes are brought under one agency, it is difficult to achieve the objectives set with the implementation of the anti-poverty schemes.

The administration also should acquire some additional features such as flexibility, innovativeness and people-oriented stance to undertake the new responsibilities.

There must be co-ordination at both the preparation and implementation stages. Hence, it is rightly said:[29]

> The problem is not only of structural and organisational changes in the attitudes of public servants and the people's representatives and the promotion of decentralised, real self-governing popular institutions.

The block level administration will have to be so structured that the desired degree of horizontal co-ordination is achieved. It should be strengthened by bringing together the various technical officers under the administrative control of the Block Development Officer (BDO). At present, the block level personnel continue to remain under the control of their respective 'line' departments and with the result, the inter-sectoral linkage becomes tenuous.

A single development authority should take up the responsibility of formulating appropriate programmes at the micro level. Again, a single development authority should be made responsible and accountable for the successful implementation of such programmes. A beneficiary should come under only one single programme/scheme and is given adequate assistance to cross the poverty line permanently.

The proposed decentralisation principle is basically sound. But the district/block plan must be in accordance with the national priorities. There is a tendency to ignore this. Another problem relates to the lack of expertise at the district/block level in the art of planning.

In 1987, the Central Government appointed an expert group on 'Systems development for the centrally sponsored schemes' to suggest ways of removing the bottlenecks afflicting these schemes. The group submitted its report in 1988. Its very first recommendation was that "before any new centrally-sponsored scheme is introduced, detailed discussions should be held with the state governments and their views should be given due weight in the guidelines framed for the implementation of the scheme." But, a year later, the JRY was launched without observing this norm.

The development administration in India has become unwieldy. It is highly centralised as most of the programme schemes were designed, implemented and monitored at the central and state levels. Another serious problem relates to limited accountability.

Studies have shown that development administration continued to favour the rich and the powerful. This made the rural population emerge as passive recipients. The administration suffers from deficiency in staff having expertise and specialisation. The system also lacks the much-needed participation culture and therefore neglects effective communication, joint consultation, democratisation and decentralisation. Hence, it continues to suffer from favouritism, nepotism, corruption etc. In short, the present development administration has failed to ensure participation of people and their organisation in the development process.

Any scheme of priorities evolved at the centralised levels is bound to ignore the diverse situations prevailing in rural areas. The multi-disciplinary anti-poverty programmes launched in the country required a more cohesive team to function in a unified manner from a common platform.[29]

The administration should be in constant touch with outsiders, experts, and people's organisations. If necessary, the required changes should be brought about in the structure of administration to achieve this end.

Decentralisation of the administration structure also requires horizontal co-ordination at various levels. An attempt should be made to reduce the number of departments by streamlining the administration on two lines: (i) Avoid splitting of jobs over many departments and (ii) Scrap programmes/schemes when there is overlapping of functions.[30]

The Government has created certain agencies like the DRDA and the DIC to strengthen development administration at the district level. But they can function effectively only when they establish rapport with the elected bodies like the Panchayati Raj Institutions. "Their interaction and interdependence are expected to strengthen development activities as they supplement and complement each other."

The DRDAs are corporate bodies registered under the Societies Registration Act. In most cases, the District Collector is the chairman of the DRDA.

The governing body includes district level officials of different developmental departments, representatives of financial institutions including the Lead Bank, MPs and MLAs of the district, representatives of Scheduled Castes/Scheduled Tribes.

The staff of the DRDA usually consists of a project director, assistant project officers for Agriculture, Animal Husbandry, Rural Industries, Co-operation, Credit Planning Officer and Economist-cum-statistician. Below the district level, the block is the basic unit for IRDP. However, at the block level, the extension staff is depleted. For augmenting the staff, the Ministry of Rural Development has offered to provide 50% of the financial aid needed.

The block plans are prepared by the DRDAs, without proper involvement of block functionaries. Even people's representatives are bypassed. This is responsible for the wrong identification of beneficiaries. Also, wrong decisions are taken by the functionaries. The bureaucrats hardly take any decision due to lack of confidence or their anxiety to play safe.[31]

The DICs were set up to provide assistance to rural artisans, village industries and small industries at pre-investment, investment and post-investment stages of production under one umbrella. The collaboration and co-ordination between the DRDA and DIC is different from state to state.

An important issue in rural development administration is accountability. If rural development, administration is to be accountable only to the superior command at the district and state levels, as is the case at present, administration cannot be responsive to the needs and aspirations of the local people. As such, rural development administration ought to be made accountable to the local population. This alone would ensure that rural projects and investments serve the actual needs and priorities of the rural population. The arrangement would also diminish existing disparities rather than accentuate them or draw as much as possible from local resources. So, there is need for de-emphasising the system of hierarchical and centralised control.[32]

Another important ingredient of rural development administration is giving due importance to technical personnel. Technical, managerial and administrative manpower is available with our large network of technical, social and educational institutions outside the bureaucracy. It is necessary to use this available manpower for successfully implementing rural projects and programmes.[33]

It is necessary to bring the whole rural development programmes under one integrated authority which would call for bringing together all the elements of the programmes right from input supply to marketing of the finished products including planning and extension advice.

REFERENCES

1. Planning Commission, Government of India, *Sixth Five-Year Plan 1980-85*, p. 175.
2. *Ibid.*, p. 92.
3. Report of the Committee on Panchayati Raj Institutions, 1978, Ministry of Agriculture and Irrigation, Government of India, New Delhi, p. 8.
4. Misra, Baidyanath: 'Powers, Functions and Finances of Panchayats', *Kurukshetra*, April, 1996.
5. K.D. Gangrade: 'Power to the Powerless — Dawn of Participatory Democracy', *Kurukshetra*, April, 1995.
6. Shiviah: 'Rural Development Administration', in *Rural Development in India: Some Facets*, National Institute of Rural Development, Hyderabad.
7. George Rosen (1966): *Democracy and Economic Change in India*, Vora & Co., Mumbai, p. 93.
8. G. Ram Reddy: 'Some Aspects of Decision-Making in Panchayati Raj', *Economic and Political Weekly*, October 10, 1970, p. 1704.
9. V.R. Gaikwad (1969): *Panchayati Raj and Bureaucracy*, National Institute of Community Development, Hyderabad, pp. 64-65.
10. C.B. Mamoria (1969): *Agricultural Problems of India*, Kitab Mahal, Allahabad, p. 911.
11. M.N. Srinivas: 'Changing Attitudes in India Today', *Yojana*, October 1,1961.
12. Bikaram Sarkar: 'Defects in Land Reform Administration', Mainstream, February 14, 1981, p. 22.
13. K.V. Narayana Rao: 'Resources of Panchayati Raj Institutions', in *Rural Development in India: Some Facets, op. cit.*
14. Gyan Chand: 'Social Purpose in Planning', in *Problems in the Third Plan: A Critical Miscellany*, Ministry of Information and Broadcasting, Government of India, 1961, p. 80.
15. Guy Hunter (1970): *The Administration of Agricultural Development*, Oxford & IBH, New Delhi, pp. 31-32.
16. B. Sarveswara Rao *et al.*: A Study of 4 Blocks in East Godavari District of Andhra Predesh', in Guy Hunter and Anthony Bottrall (Ed. 1974): *Serving the Small Farmer: Policy Choices in Indian Agricultural Development*, The Overseas Institute, p. 35.
17. George Mathew 1995, *Panchayati Raj: From Legislation to Movement*, Concept Publishing Company, New Delhi, p. 111.
18. *Ibid.*, p. 112.

19. Report of the Committee on Panchayati Raj Institutions, 1978. *op. cit.*, p. 7.

20. T.N. Chaturvedi: 'Why and How to Improve Delivery Systems', *Kurukshetra*, January 1, 1980, p. 11.

21. A. Vijayakumar, 'Management of Panchayati Raj Institutions — A New Thrust Needed', *Southern Economist*, July 15, 1996.

22. George Mathew: 'Transfer of Power to the Local Bodies', *Kurukshetra*, April, 1996, p. 34.

23. Rebindra Kumar Choudhary: 'Financing of Panchayati Raj Institutions', *Kurukshetra*, April 1996.

24. Mansoor Ali (1979): *Missing Links in Indian Planning*, Light and Life Publishers, New Delhi, p. 289.

25. Jagdish Bhagawati 197: *The Economics of Underdeveloped Countries*, Weidenfeld and Nicolson, London, pp. 85-86.

26. K. Seshadri, 1976: *Political Linkages and Rural Development*, National Publishing House, New Delhi, pp. 115-116.

27. *Ibid.*, p. 171.

28. Bhuwan Lai Shah: 'Role of Block Personnel in IRD Programmes', *Kurukshetra*, July 16, 1981, p. 29.

29. R.K. Derhgawen: 'DRDA: Innovation and Administration', *Kurukshetra*, August, 1992.

30. Indira Hirway: 'Seven Pronged Strategy to Make Administration Responsive', *Kurukshetra*, October 1991, p. 55.

31. Hoshiar Singh and Mohinder Singh: 'Role of Bureaucracy in Rural Development', *Kurukshetra*, February 1993, p. 16.

32. L.C. Jain: 'Put People at the Centre for Better Results', *Kurukshetra*, October 1991, p. 8.

33. *Ibid.*, p. 8.

Chapter

47 People's Participation in Rural Development

In any development scheme, people matter because it is for their welfare that such programmes are implemented. Yet, very often people may be passive as they wrongly think that development is the job of the government. Schemes can be successful only when people take an active part in them. Unless people have a stake in their own development, it is unlikely to be sustainable.[1]

The participation of beneficiaries can be understood in terms of participation in (i) decision making; (ii) implementation of development programmes; (iii) monitoring and evaluation of the programme and (iv) sharing the benefits of development.

Importance of People's Participation

Popular participation enriches the planning process by checking the reliability of data, ensuring commitment of the people to targeted projects for the rural sector; rationalising proposals by the agencies concerned; reducing unreasonable pressure through informal channels and finally basing the proposals on the judgement of the people affected by the programmes.[2] People's involvement ensures strict supervision at the cutting edge of level of the administration.[3]

The local communities are in a better position to develop integrated programmes which alone can avoid duplication, minimise delay and ensure easy accountability. As a result of participation, the rural people will be in a better position to assess their own rights and responsibilities. Also, as a result of participation, the talent pool becomes larger.[4]

The way to a successful approach to development lies in enabling the poor to become conscious of the factors leading their critical financial status.[5]

Local people know their problems better and how and where a facility should be located. They are the best judges of their own interest. The government's responsibility is to create an environment that permits the local people to seek their best interests freely.

Popular participation is to be commended as it places obligation on people. The participation relates to decision-making, participation in benefits of growth and implementation of strategies in the work of development. Participation would also enable people to implement meaningful and productive programmes instead of going in for 'softer' projects. Also, as a result of the people's participation, the beneficiaries can get the maximum from the administrative agencies.

According to the Working Group on District Planning, public participation is needed at the local level for the following reasons: (i) To take note of the needs of the population; (ii) To mobilize local resources for plan implementation, including people's labour, (iii) To decrease the level of conflict during the planning and implementation stages; (iv) To increase the speed of implementation by securing the co-operation of the people; (v) To increase the legitimacy of authority; and (vi) To reduce popular resistence to decision.

In the implementation of many anti-poverty programmes, assets have been provided without knowing the capacities/conditions of the beneficiaries. In one case, the beneficiaries belonging to the low caste obtained superior breed of buffaloes. But, they failed to derive any benefit from them as they could not provide them the required dry and green fodder. Some of them are therefore forced to sell them to higher caste big farmers. Likewise, though loans and subsidies are provided to dig open bore wells, electricity is not provided for the pumps. Such costly mistakes could have been avoided, if only people's participation in rural development has been ensured. In the absence of this, even the data collected provided to be unreliable. People's participation is required not only in the construction of assets but also in their proper maintenance.

People's participation is specially important when the government is aiming at providing the basic needs. Participation will also strengthen the claim for material basic goods. For the local people, the basic needs are more important than anything else. As such, they show positive interest in the provision of basic needs.

It has been rightly observed by Rajani Kothari, "participation is not some process of involving everyone and reducing all to a common denominator, rather it consists of evolving institutional structure from which diverse individuals get a sense of dignity and self-respect as beings that are able to determine their own destinies."

The Balwant Rai Mehta Committee observed, "rural development and rural welfare are possible only with local initiative and local direction. In the ultimate analysis, it must be an instrument of expression of the local people's will taking in view the local development."[6]

The main objectives of people's participation can be (i) better planning and implementation of rural development programmes; (ii) mobilisation of additional resources required for rural development programmes and (iii) empowering the people, particularly the poor to play an effective role in rural development.[7]

There should be an in-built mechanism to involve people in the conceptualisation, planning, implementation, monitoring and management of resources (funds). This would go towards increasing the efficacy and acceptance of the programme on the one hand and reducing the operational and administrative cost on the other.[8]

The constitution of the local level institutions like the panchayati raj institutions is based on one simple truth: that is, people not only know what is good for themselves, but also have the power to go about getting it done themselves.[9]

People's participation needs to be ensured in the area of monitoring which is particularly essential to see that benefits flow to the intending beneficiaries. Each programme may have its own constraints or problems at the implementation stage. These can be better understood as a result of participation in the monitoring mechanism.[10]

In the rural sphere, the Participative Rural Appraisal (PRA) technique is recommended for better understanding of rural problems. The PRA is based on certain simple truths: (i) There is a lot of information available with the local people; about local resources and local problems; (ii) If local people are involved in planning any scheme meant for them, they can come up with useful ideas and contribute to the success of the planning process, and (iii) This would also ensure proper use of the facilities made available to them.[11]

The PRA technique help us understand the rural poor and appreciate their perceptions, their needs and aspirations and also involve them in a participatory manner in planning and decision-making for the betterment of their quality of life.[12]

It is rightly said, "The people, for whom all the schemes are chalked out, had not been consulted either for diagnosis of the problem or for the prognosis of the schemes."[13] The officials ought to learn a lot from the experience of the rural poor and this calls for effective interact with them.

In order to implement programmes relevant to rural conditions, a new methodology called PRA is suggested. The PRA is defined as "*a semi-structured process of learning from, with and by rural people about rural conditions.*"

The basic principles governing the PRA are: (i) Learning the rural problems through the methods suitable to them without following tight jacketed programmes; (ii) Offsetting the preconceived notions leading to various kinds of biases about rural development and while collecting the information, the investigator need not hurry, he/she could be calm with the mass, so that much insight could be gained; (iii) Learning with the rural people about their problems, needs and priorities; (iv) Get clarification and justification for their; needs, problems and priorities; and (v) Introspection regarding the work done.[14]

The PRA approach has some merits. It promotes a community forum to study local problems and find out solutions for them. It also serves as catalyst for local and external elements to introduce positive change.[15] In short, people's participation in the planning process enables the government to have a better understanding of local problems.

PEOPLE'S PARTICIPATION: SOME PROBLEMS

Though people's participation in rural development is necessary; there are several problems associated with such participation. We have to first decide at what stage in the planning process is it desirable to ensure the much talked about participation. It is also necessary to understand the value one has to give to the opinions of the villagers. If they put forward a list of demands based on narrow local perspectives, the ultimate gains may not be impressive. Even the collection of data for the people may suffer from personal or group bias.

Under the present set up, the participation of the rural poor in the development process can only be a gradual process. The process can be speeded up only when the poor become conscious of their rights and privileges and subsequently build up strength to achieve justice for themselves in the sharing of benefits of development.[16]

The major obstacles to popular participation are: absence of a strong commitment on the part of the government; unhelpful attitude of the civil servants; monopoly of local organisations by the local elites; divisions among the rural poor themselves and a lax communication media.[17]

Ensuring people's participation has become a difficult task for various reasons; non-involvement of the community and local leadership, lack of awareness among the rural poor about various rural development programmes; village factionalism and rural power structure; apathy of the bureaucracy; lack of incentives for change-agents and inadequate use of the mass media.[18]

The rural society in India is a heterogenous one. The rural population, to a great extent, differs in economic and social status. Generally, the richer sections show an attitude of indifference to programmes meant for the economically poorer sections.

The implementation of anti-poverty programmes may also create a climate of tension, given the rural power structure. The organisation of the beneficiaries has the capacity to work out strategies to ease such tensions.

MEASURES TO STRENGTHEN PEOPLE'S PARTICIPATION

Researchers have also noticed certain pre-conditions for the success of any programme aiming at people's involvement. Of course, a democratic system is essential to ensure a proper place for the people's representatives. The extent of participation depends on the institutional arrangements, the content of programmes and the spectrum of beneficiary groups to which they appeal.

People's participation is to be ensured through generation of awareness and the promotion of motivation. As the rural community is not homogenous, it would be necessary to ensure the much needed participation of the weaker sections in the planning process.

Participation would be meaningful if only the poor have access to correct and reliable information. Institutions need to be set up at the local level through which the poor can express their views pertaining to ongoing programmes, and these views should receive due attention at higher levels.

There is also the danger that participation may be abused. Also, participation may come in the way of taking quick decisions on imminent issues. Yet, without popular participation in the planning process, it would be impossible to change the direction of development in favour of the population which would also end all kinds of exploitation. However, it needs to be remembered that the task of educating and mobilising the people in this direction could be more effectively accomplished when it is institutionalised. The concept of decentralised planning would be nebulous until and unless people's active participation is ensured in the planning process at the grassroot level.

The planner should educate the beneficiaries on the benefits that flow from various programmes and the sacrifices involved. Participation should start at the stage of deciding what to do and how to do it. For proper participation, leaders should preferably emerge from within the rural population. It is also observed that in an egalitarian society, leaders are in a better position to secure people's co-operation.

Beneficiaries should be involved in the review of programmes underway. Their direct feedback will be particularly valuable.[19]

The following measures may be taken to mobilise people to join the mainstream of development:[20]

(i) Measures should be taken to understand the group dynamics and the heterogenous character of society. It is necessary to understand how a community views a particular problem;

(ii) Special attention must be given to identify the resources of the people and to educate them to understand their needs and problems;

(iii) It would be better if individual and household development plans were drawn up and people motivated to take active part in their own development;

(iv) People must realise that the ultimate responsibility of supporting the programme lies with them only and for which they have to work consistently and collectively towards the mobilisation of resources and

(v) Monitoring should be an in-built feature of the programme in order to avoid any undesirable incidents. Attempts should be made to stabilise various interest groups and people's organisations.

Popular participation should be ensured through voluntary organisations which are closer to the local people. Of course, the nature of institutional structure, the prevailing value system and the relationship between the elite group and the citizens do influence the nature and extent of people's participation in development.[21]

Thus, participation is valuable and indispensable from more than one point of view. People themselves are the assets and the largest beneficiaries of such participation. Ultimately, economic development is based on individual and group initiatives.

REFERENCES

1. Parameswaran Iyer: 'Community Participation and Rural Development', *The Economic Times*, September 14, 1995.

2. Y. Venugopal Reddy (1979): 'Multi-Level Planning in India', Vikas Publishing House, New Delhi, p. 124.

3. R.C.Arora (1979: Integrated Rural Development, S.Chand & Co., New Delhi, pp. 350-351.
4. Oroon Kumar Ghosh: 'Planning India's Future', Minerva Associates (Publications), Kolkata, p. 62.
5. Gracious Thomas: 'How Far People Participate in Rural Development, *Kurukshetra*, January, 1992, p. 10.
6. Report of the Team for the Study of Community Projects and National Extension Service Vol. I, Government of India, New Delhi, 1957, pp. 6-8.
7. D.S. Dhillon and B.S. Hansra: People's Participation in Rural Development Programmes', *Kurukshetra*, January, 1995, p. 7.
8. P.K. Bajpai: 'People's Participation in Development, *Mainstream*, July 1,1995, p. 11.
9. B.K. Chandrasekhar and Anand Inbanathan: 'People's Participation in Rural Development,' *The Hindu*, September 10, 1991.
10. Kamta Prasad: 'People's Participation in Rural Development', *Yojana*, August 15,1990, p. 17.
11. M.S.S. Varadan: 'An Exercise that Works Wonders', *The Hindu*, August 29,1993.
12. Neela Mukherjee: 'Participatory Rural Appraisal', *Yojana*, February 16-28,1991.
13. G. Palanithurai: 'Participatory Rural Appraisal and Rural Development, *Southern Economist*, August 15,1992, p. 9.
14. *Ibid.*, p. 10.
15. R.K. Samanta: 'Participatory Rural Appraisal for Purposive Development; *Kurukshetra*, August 1992, p. 32.
16. S.N. Mishra and Kushal Sharma: 'Ensuring People's Participation in RD Programmes', *Kurukshetra*, January, 1985, p. 7.
17. Food and Agricultural Organisation (no year): Review and Analysis of Agrarian Reform and Rural Development in the Developing Countries since the mid-1960s, pp. 84-85.
18. D.S. Dhillon and B.S. Hansra: *op. cit.*, p. 8.
19. M.J.K. Thavaraj: 'Decentralised Planning & People's Participation', *Mainstream*, April 14, 1984, pp. 18-20.
20. P.K. Bajpai: *op. cit.*, pp. 14-15.
21. H.R. Chaturvedi and S.K. Mitra (1982): 'Citizen Participation in Rural Development', Oxford & IBH Publishing Co., New Delhi, p.8.

Chapter

48 Rural Development: Role of Voluntary Agencies

In a vast field like rural development, governmental efforts are certainly inadequate to solve the crucial problems of poverty and unemployment. Rural development is a complex process as it involves continuous reorientation of ongoing development efforts. Even the funds available at the disposal of the government are limited. Also, the bureaucracy suffers from serious limitations and therefore it alone cannot take up the gigantic task of rural reconstruction through various programmes.

The voluntary agencies concentrate less on objectives and more on results. Adopting a broader view, the voluntary agencies can easily move from being on the periphery of the rural economy to becoming active players in the development of the rural areas.[1] Of course, their credibility would be high only when they are accountable in this capacity.

Importance and Changing Role

There are always some missing links in the long chain of rural reconstruction. The voluntary agencies are expected to provide these missing links. Considering the magnitude of rural poverty and unemployment, the government is keen on associating voluntary agencies with its anti-poverty drive.

A new approach to rural development has to be evolved as the existing programmes have reportedly met with limited success. The voluntary agencies, which are in touch with grassroot realities, are expected to help the government in evolving a new strategy to tackle mass poverty and the consequent growing levels of unemployment. Also, development does not mean a mere increase in production output. It ought to include improvement in the quality of human life. The voluntary agencies do enjoy an edge over others in improving the living economic conditions in the targeted rural areas.

One cannot but notice the changing role of voluntary agencies. In the past, these agencies used to undertake relief work whenever there were natural calamities like earthquakes and floods threatening diseases and subsequent outbreaks of life. Gradually, they had taken up welfare and development schemes.

The changing role of voluntary agencies is also understandable. Voluntary action has emerged from social consciousness generated by organised interest groups of people who are committed to the people-centred approach. Local initiative and leadership have received a boost.[2] The action is targeted to benefit individuals on the whole.

The voluntary agencies have given a new boost to rural development. Working with the rural poor is no longer considered *infra dig*. The voluntary agencies have conducted experiments and also provided new leadership at the grassroot level. They are not handicapped by rules and regulations.

Voluntary action has become a major global phenomenon today. There are local level organisations and also international agencies. Most of the voluntary agencies in India are inspired by Gandhian teachings or the Church.

The activities of voluntary agencies can be broadly divided into four categories:

(i) Simple charity, supplementing welfarism of the state;

(ii) Encouraging people's participation and implementing programmes launched by the Government for larger benefit of the rural community at large or the village;

(iii) Involving people in programme planning, raising resources, implementing activities and sharing fruits of development and

(iv) Conscience instilling and organising people thus enabling them to demand and undertake planning and implementation of development programmes beneficial to them.

The development of the local leadership has received new impetus because of the emphasis on the role of the 'change agent' who was expected to act as catalyst in the mobilisation of local manpower and resources and for bringing about development and social change in the rural population.

At present, the voluntary agencies are active in a number of spheres. Some voluntary agencies may not take up development works, but they try to improve the delivery system by placing checks on corruption and inefficiency.

Some voluntary agencies have concentrated on rural technology with the belief that the available technology should come to the rescue of small farmers and artisans. They are interested in areas like improvement in the designs of bullock carts.

A new class of professionals have entered the field of voluntarism which has been appreciated as a significant development. As a result of this, the voluntary agencies are in a position to evolve a low cost delivery system.

Voluntary agencies generally adopt a holistic approach to rural development by planning and organising activities in such a way as to cover all aspects of rural life. However, of late, voluntary agencies started specialising in certain services.

The Bharatiya Agro-Industries Foundation (Urlikanchan, Pune) concentrates on the promotion of hybrid milch animals, fodder development and social forestry.

The Bhartiya Grameena Mahila Sangh organises its training activities for rural women in self-reliance and leadership. The Harijan Sevak Sangh concentrates on constructive work among the Harijans in rural areas.

The Sarvodaya Shramadan Movement (Founder: A.T. Ariyaratne) of Sri Lanka is a unique movement in the share of community development. The movement from its very beginning has been guided by Gandhian ideals. The movement has laid stress on educating people to achieve self-fulfilment and better living standards etc.

The movement is having sixty village centres which co-ordinate development plans in their areas and provide training programmes. The apex body, located outside Colombo, has been taking major decisions concerning policies, priorities and initiating new development programmes. The movement had set up a 'revolving fund' for providing low interest loans for small scale development projects.

The Bhoomi Sena (Land Army) movement in Maharashtra emerged in response to the oppression of the Adivasis (aborigines) by the local elite. The Bhoomi Sena helped the adivasis in securing land forcibly taken away by the landlords. The army has also expanded its activities over a period to such areas like credit, digging wells and trading in grass. The Bhoomi Sena launched campaigns against alcohol and bonded labourers, unnecessary and unproductive expenditure on cultural rituals and social practices. The Land Army has also laid special emphasis on cost effective organisation of the rural sector.

The Social Work Research Centre (SWRC) at Tilonia in Rajasthan has emerged as a reputed voluntary organisation. The organisation is led by young professionally trained experts in various spheres. The emphasis has been on an integrated approach to ensure rural development and a strong linkage between action and research. The SWRC proved beyond doubt that formal educational qualifications are not necessary for serving the financially deprived rural sector.

The SWRC is a non-profit organisation. The professionals are paid nominal remuneration. The staff lead a modest life. The Centre, believes that the ycung professionals should be committed towards rural development a challenge. The work should not be influenced by ideological considerations. There should be flexibility and freedom enough for a change in thinking, in strategies, in emphasis and in shifting responsibility.

The ultimate goal of SWRC has been to call for the effective participation by villagers to initiate projects and take advantage of government programmes that would enable them to bring about change.

The Dasholi Gram Swarajya Mandal (DGSM), founded in 1964 by the creative workers of the district Chamoli in the Central Himalayan range of Uttar Pradesh, aims at conservation of forest wealth, the provision of employment opportunities for the local youth and propagation of the village, industry. The aim has been to encourage forest-based industries. The DGSM launched a scheme to educate the rural people about the evils of alcoholism and strived to preserve the art and culture of the region. The Mandal also worked for the upliftment of women and weaker sections in the region.

Thus, the voluntary agencies are rendering a wide variety of services to the rural population. Their role has completely changed over a period of time. They have started concentrating on both development and change. It is therefore necessary to create a favourable climate for the healthy growth of voluntary agencies.

SUPERIORITY OF VOLUNTARY AGENCIES

The voluntary agencies do enjoy an edge over government departments in many important spheres as they adopt a practical outlook and are guided by a spirit of sacrifice. The voluntary agencies try to see that the communities become as independent as possible. The voluntary agencies are capable of creating the right social climate in support of the state laws.

Voluntary action is said to be essential in areas where awareness and conscious participation of the people is critical for success. Voluntary agencies being small and independent of bureaucratic constraints, can afford to experiment with ideas, technologies, organisation and anything else.[3]

The strength of voluntary organisations lies in their capacity to understand the local needs, problems and resources; their capacity to involve local people and secure their co-operation and participation; and their desire to experiment with new programmes, strategies and approaches for rural development without incurring large expenditures.[4]

The government has been implementing a number of anti-poverty programmes which have failed due to irregularities in the identification of beneficiaries and assets; lack of co-ordination among the activities and agencies; a large incidence of leakages etc. The voluntary agencies can help in removing these deficiencies.

The voluntary agencies adopt a flexible and pragmatic approach which is considered an advantage because of diverse conditions prevailing in the rural areas. Concrete issues are discussed and decided with high degree of participation and commitment. The stress is more on action-based forums than on representative bodies. The voluntary agencies are not only task-oriented but service-oriented, as pointed by Nitish De.[5]

However, the voluntary agencies are specialising in their chosen fields. This is desirable because they can render better service through specialisation. After all, the limited resources available should produce optimum results.

The voluntary agencies have been successful in organising the weaker sections of the people, improving the rural delivery system and countering exploitation of all kinds. Above all, they have given a new boost to local initiatives and efforts.

Some voluntary agencies have made successful innovations in the field of application of science and technology and in the use of local resources. They can thus help exploit the underutilised rural resources.

In a sphere like adult education, voluntary agencies do have an edge over government departments. The adult education programme requires a special quality of service-personnel. People are not generally motivated towards programmes which do not yield immediate rewards or material gains. Educating, the rural adults is no easy task, as they have a low level of motivation. The learning task should be made meaningful by relating it to the day-to-day activities of the adult learners. Post-literacy and follow-up work including the organisation of library services, production and dissemination of literature for neo-literates, creation of organisation of neo-literates etc. are very important. Voluntary agencies which are very close to the local environment are the most appropriate ones to take up responsibility for conducting adult literacy classes.

One of the major causes for failure in the implementation of land reform measures is the non-involvement of the landless agricultural labourers, insecure tenants and the share croppers.[6]

The voluntary agencies can also contribute significantly in the successful implementation of land ceiling laws. The land reform measures failed because of lack of political will. The voluntary agencies can help the informal tenants in getting their tenancies regularised in the village records. They can also identify the benami transfers of surplus lands. Some former land owners, in collusion with local revenue machinery, continue to enjoy land availability. Voluntary agencies command respect among the poor, if only they are able to strengthen the delivery system.

In the sphere of land reforms, the voluntary agencies can — (i) organise the beneficiaries so that they will be made aware of their rights and (ii) bring pressure on the implementing machinery so that the implementation of ceiling laws will be expedited.

The voluntary agencies can ensure people's participation in the development process. They can ensure a mechanism of social control over the developmental bureaucracy. The voluntary agencies can seek, more easily than a government department, people's co-operation. People's participation can be ensured only by genuine grassroot organisations and these alone can keep a watch on the delivery system.[7]

The voluntary agencies are best suited to take up sensitive issues. Organisation of the rural poor is one such issue. Only one per cent of the agricultural labourers is covered by the trade union activity. This implies making them conscious of their deteriorating conditions, their handicaps and their strength.

The organisation of the rural poor is required to secure their full participation in the execution of government plans for integrated rural development. Political parties and mass organisations should see that the benefits of the plan schemes reach those for whom they are intended.

Organising this sector is a complex and difficult task as it is to a large extent divided on caste and other lines. They lack even the mental awareness and eagerness to stand up against injustices done against them. Also, the rural rich try to arrest the emergence of unions. Hence, there may be conflicts whenever attempts are made to unionise the rural poor.

The voluntary agencies must keep in view the various difficulties in attempting to organise the poor. They must seek the co-operation of the government departments and political parties in taking up sensitive issues.

The voluntary agencies can also be helpful in the sphere of monitoring and evaluation of plans targeted to benefit the rural sector. Most programmes at present are not subject to proper evaluation. As a result of this, corrective measures cannot be initiated in time. The voluntary agencies can objectively evaluate the anti-poverty programmes. The voluntary agencies should be involved in concurrent evaluation (ongoing evaluation) and also post-mortem evaluation (evaluation after the completion of a project).

LIMITATIONS OF VOLUNTARISM

True, the voluntary agencies can do significant service in a number of spheres. Yet, in actual operation, they are facing a number of problems. The main problem relates to leadership. Some people who rendered voluntary services earlier have become politicians. Moreover, the success of a voluntary agency largely depends on a charismatic leader and with his exit, the organisation shows either signs of growth or decay. Moreover, the interlocking of leadership results in inadequate and ineffective supervision.

The activities of voluntary agencies are fragmented and spread over a variety of fields. In the case of India, about 60 per cent of the organisations are concentrated in Eastern and Western regions. The central funds too flowed more into areas already developed. Moreover, most voluntary agencies are having their headquarters in urban areas. This is not a healthy trend as a major job opportunity has to be developed in rural areas.

In the case of most voluntary agencies, dedication, rapport with the local people and commitment are on the decline. Most of the organisations still adopt the traditional approach —trying to motivate people and introducing an element of professionalism.

Unfortunately, most voluntary agencies are unwilling to establish even a working relationship with the government departments. This would subsequently deprive the voluntary agencies of their independence, autonomy and identity, leading to unnecessary harassment.

Some feel that voluntary agencies are basically front organisations for political activity. Suspicion, competitiveness, the ambitions of leaders, the loaves and fishes offered by international funding agencies divides voluntary agencies even within one ideological frame.[8] Most agencies also fail to understand the social and economic structures of the community they wish to serve. This alienates them from the community itself. The problem worsens because of unfavourable power structure. Moreover, the number of voluntary agencies which are actively involved in rural development with headquarters in rural areas is very limited.[9]

The specific problems of voluntary agencies include: lack of proper planning and the absence of clearly laid down policies, lack of proper appreciation and recognition, identification with a particular group and a high turnover of the workers.

The major problems facing the voluntary agencies have been summarised as follows:[10]

(i) Inadequacy and lack of certainty of the inflow of funds;
(ii) Ambivalent relations with the government and official agencies;
(iii) Scarcity of competent and committed persons to serve the voluntary agencies;
(iv) Inadequate and only symbolic participation of the beneficiaries in the management of voluntary agencies and their negative inclination towards self-help, the desire to benefit from programmes sponsored by the voluntary agencies and
(v) Antagonism and occasional conflicts with the local political interests.

The rural development bureaucracy does not generally appreciate autonomous institutions like voluntary agencies. The bureaucracy tends to have this attitude to exercise control over these agencies directly or indirectly, to render these agencies unable to extend services to the extent they desire. The situation worsens when local politicians too interfere in the work of the voluntary agencies.

Lack of professionalism is a major problem facing the voluntary agencies. This creates problems in the preparation of project reports. While some agencies have developed professionalism, others do not try to acquire professional help. Hence, they are not in a position to properly assess the development potential of the local and regional resources.[11]

The voluntary agencies do face problems in the mobilisation of funds. There are some voluntary agencies which unduly depend on external institutions and funds. Most voluntary agencies are unable to mobilise resources locally. Also, it is not desirable for the voluntary agencies to spend their limited resources on too many programmes and areas.

The co-operation extended by the people to voluntary agencies is not upto the mark. People generally want benefits only without any sacrifice on their own part. The rural sector by and large feels that the voluntary agencies emerged out of the initiative of the village elite. Even assets like community halls constructed by voluntary agencies are inadequately managed by the villagers.

Concerted efforts should be made to minimise the problems being faced by voluntary agencies. So long as these agencies render service to the community, they deserve the co-operation from the government departments and the people at large.

Strengthening Voluntary Agencies

The voluntary agencies can achieve their goals if only they have clear priorities. It has been rightly pointed out:[12] "Voluntary action should first and foremost mobilise popular support and action for the success of the government plans and efforts through educational and motivational programmes and concrete schemes of employment and production."

The voluntary agencies must concentrate on income generating projects not only in the interests of the beneficiaries, but even for strengthening their own resource base.

It needs to be noted that voluntary agencies by themselves cannot complete the task of rural reconstruction. They must therefore seek the co-operation of the government departments and the local people. In fact, people's active participation in the planning process is necessary for the success of any development and welfare scheme.

Voluntary action cannot be a substitute for the government's role in the rural sphere. These two should be viewed as partners in progress. The relationship between voluntary agencies and government departments should be one of partnership, mutual faith, trust and confidence and utilising the strong points of the other partners in the process.[13]

The voluntary agencies sometimes work in competition with government department. This would only lead to duplication of the infrastructure, leading to wastage of resources. It would be better if the voluntary agencies concentrated on tasks which generally do not receive due attention of the government departments.

There is some rapport between government departments and voluntary agencies. This is seen in the following three areas:[14]

(i) Involving voluntary agencies in select activities like training of service functionaries such as school teachers, auxiliary nurses, mid-wives, community health workers etc.;

(ii) Providing voluntary agencies some annual recurring grants to cover part of their maintenance expenses and

(iii) Nominating them to committees which review programmes at the local level.

Some voluntary agencies may be entrusted with the task of preparation of block plans with support from the government departments. In fact, several state governments have been using the services of reputed voluntary agencies. The state itself is going to be benefited from various experiments being carried out by the voluntary agencies.

The voluntary agencies should help the government departments in successfully implementing anti-poverty programmes. They can help in the proper identification of beneficiaries and also leakages. It would be better if the evaluation work is entrusted to the voluntary agencies.

The government departments can help voluntary agencies in a number of ways. The voluntary agencies may be associated with the preparation of development plans. The government should extend administrative support and encouragement to the voluntary agencies. This includes a great level of interest by the government in the regulation of funds from both national and international agencies and accountability. Voluntary agencies also need technical help which can be provided by the government.

It also needs to be noted that there should be rapport among the voluntary agencies themselves. There is need for co-ordinating the activities of various agencies engaged in rural reconstruction. Interchange of information and experience between organisations engaged in constructive work in different states and across the country would need immediate attention.

Of course, the voluntary agencies should not depend on the government at every stage. They should be free to function on their own and should even be assisted and encouraged to do so.

REFERENCES

1. Narendar Pani: 'NGOs and Liberalisation', *The Economic Times*, January 10,1995.
2. I. Satya Sundaram (1986): *Voluntary Agencies and Rural Development*, B.R. Publishing Corporation, New Delhi, p. 56.
3. Rabindra Kumar Sirtha: 'Rural Development: A Perspective', *Kurukshetra*, August 1984, p. 29.
4. K.K. Mukherjee: "Voluntary Orgaisations in Rural Development', *Voluntary Action*, July-August 1979, Section II, p. 3.
5. *Yojana*, November 1984, p. 11.
6. Bikram Sarkar: 'Defects in Land Reform Administration', *Mainstream*, February 14,1981, p. 22.
7. S.P. Vishnoi: 'Rural Development Policies: An Overview', *Kurukshetra*, March 1984, p. 6.

8. B.G. Verghese: 'Voluntary Action: A New Mission for the New Missionaries', in R.P. Misra and K.V. Sundaram (Ed. 1979): *Rural Area Development: Perspectives and Approaches*, Sterling Publishers Pvt. Ltd., New Delhi, p. 236.
9. Vinod Kumar: 'Limitations of Voluntary Effort in Rural Development', *Kurukshetra*, September 1993, p. 17.
10. R. Ananda Rao: Integrated Rural pevelopment and the Role of Voluntary Agencies, (A Case Study of Bhagvatula Charitable Trust, Visakhapatnam DT), Ph.D. thesis submitted to Andhra University in 1981.
11. Planning Commission, Government of India, 1978, Report of the Working Group on Block Level Planning, p. 10.
12. S. Santigo: 'A Testament of Faith in Self Help', *Yojana*, March 1, 1975, p. 31.
13. D. Paul Chowdhry (1978): *New Partnership in Rural Development*, M.N. Publishers, New Delhi, p. 102.
14. Manu N. Kulkarni: 'Community Participation in Development: Myths and Realities', *Mainstream*, July 23,1983, p. 26.

Chapter

49 Public Distribution System in the Rural Context

The Public Distribution System (PDS) had emerged to ensure the availability of essential goods for the vulnerable sections at reasonable prices. India's PDS is a big one, with 4 lakh fair price shops, covering nearly 56 crore people. The food subsidy is of the order of ₹ 6,000 crore.

The PDS was launched to supply essential commodities such as rice, wheat, imported edible oils, sugar and kerosene below market prices. It is an anti-inflationary measure, having significant bearing on stabilising prices and in improving the nutritional standards of the rural sector. The PDS has been playing an invaluable role in our food security. There is nothing wrong if the PDS is viewed as an anti-poverty measure.[1]

Nearly 75% of the consumers live in the rural areas. More than half of the national income is generated from the rural sector. The rural market is a big one for items like food and agricultural inputs. The rural market in India has grown steadily over a period.

Yet the availability and quality of goods in the rural areas are inadequate as a result of which the rural population has become the most exploited one in terms of urban-rural consumer exploitation.[2]

A recent study of the PDS, conducted by the National Council of Applied Economic Research (NCAER), has shown that 36% of the rural households use PDS on a regular basis.

The level of demand from the rural sector has significantly changed in recent years. A number of items have entered the rural market. These include cosmetics, toilet soaps, washing soaps, books, household utensils, torches and batteries, sewing machines, electrical goods, bicycles and other consumer durables.

The number of fair price shops increased from 3.02 lakh in 1984 to 3.61 lakh in 1990. By February, 1992, the number rose to 3,97,429. These cover a total number of 13.92 crore ration cardholders or about 56 crore people. The rural-urban ratio of the fair price shops is roughly 75:25.

Most state governments are prepared to issue new ration cards. In fact, around 64 lakh cards were issued during 1995-96. More than 15,000 fair price shops were set up. However, because of low purchasing power of the rural poor, the off-take is at a low level. Out of 27 states, as many as 11 showed a significant gap between allocation and off-takes. Studies have shown that the PDS accounts for merely 17.5% of the rice consumption and 11.8% of the wheat consumption by the rural population.

The revamped PDS was launched in January, 1992. The government earmarked 1,700 blocks in the most backward regions of the country as 'identified areas'; fixed a target of 11,225 new fair price shops to be opened, set up vigilance committees to prevent leakages and started a campaign to weed out bogus ration cards.

The 1,700 new blocks include 143 blocks covered under Deserted Development Programme, 596 under the Drought Prone Area Programme, 1,048 under the Integrated Tribal Development project and 55 designated Hill Areas.

The other salient features of the revamped scheme include: opening of additional 11,000 fair price shops, creation of an additional 3.30 lakh tonnes storage capacity and issue of over 2.4 million ration cards. Additional items like tea, salt, soap, clothes and other items will be added to the PDS network to ensure financial viability of the fair price shops.

The RPDS has been extended to another 671 blocks from August 15, 1995, raising the total number of blocks under RPDS to 2,446. About 164 million people have reportedly benefited by the revamped system.

There are about 1,00,000 fair price shops in the consumers' co-operative sector which are engaged in the distribution of select essential consumer goods. The consumer co-operatives also operate mobile shops for making available essential consumer goods in the areas where there are no retail outlets for the distribution of essential consumer goods.

The sales turnover of the consumer co-operatives during the year 1994-95 stood at about ₹ 7,500 crore. The consumer co-operatives now cover about two per cent of the total distributive trade in India. The long-term objective of the co-operatives has been to raise this percentage to 20.

The financial position of most of the consumer co-operatives in India is not sound. They borrow funds and have to bear the interest burden. This subsequently tends to have an adverse effect on the economic viability of the commercial operations.

The tribal population as per the 1981 census formed 7.76% of the total population. In 1981, the tribal population was placed at 58 million; out of this, 42 million were said to be below the poverty line.

The Government supplies foodgrains at special subsidised rates (50 paise below the PDS price) to the people living in Integrated Tribal Development Projects (ITDP) areas. In 1990, 1.88 million tonnes were supplied to the people in such areas.

The scheme has gained significance in its coverage in as much as it covers ITDP areas in 19 States/UTs besides covering the entire population in 6 tribal majority states. The total amount of rice and wheat supplied annually under the scheme has been estimated at 1.75 million tonnes.

The central foodgrains stocks stood at 15.1 million tonnes (10.3 million tonnes of wheat and 4.8 million tonnes of rice) in October 2005 as against the buffer stock norm of 16.2 million tonnes (11 million tonnes of wheat and 5.2 million tonnes of rice).

The food subsidy has been rising. It increased from ₹ 2450 crore in 1990-91 to ₹ 5377 crore in 1995-96, to ₹ 9434 crore in 1999-2000. The revised estimate for 2004-05 is ₹ 25,000 crore.

The PDS issue price for wheat was ₹ 402 per quintal in 1995-96, and it was ₹ 537 for rice.

By 2002-03 July, the wheat price rose to ₹ 415 for people below the poverty line and to ₹ 610 for people above the poverty line. In respect of rice, the respective figures are ₹ 565 and ₹ 830.

The Decentralised Procurement Scheme (DCP) has evoked good response from the State governments. The State of Karnataka and Kerala have joined this scheme in 2004-05 thereby increasing the number of states undertaking this scheme to 11 (including West Bengal, Uttar Pradesh, Madhya Pradesh, Chattisgarh, Uttaranchal, Gujarat, Orissa, Tamil Nadu and Union Territory of Andaman and Nicobar Islands. There was record procurement of 93.6 lakh tonnes of paddy/rice by DCP states in kharif in 2004-05 which were 16.0 lakh tonnes more than the previous record of 77.6 lakh tonnes in kharif in 2003-04.

RURAL PDS: SOME PROBLEMS

However, there is a criticism that the present PDS mostly caters to the needs of the urban people, but fails to meet the needs of the rural population. This is true to some extent because of the low purchasing power of the rural population and the seasonal nature of rural employment.[3]

The regional concentration of the PDS is another problem. For instance, Delhi which accounts for one per cent of the national population, consumed, in 1980, 6% of the national off-take. States like Rajasthan, Madhya Pradesh and Bihar which suffer from high incidence of poverty are not well served by the PDS.

Apart from the inter-regional disparities in the distribution of foodgrains, there is also the problem of the PDS failing to cover casual labourers on daily wages, migrant workers and those without proper residential addresses.

Despite impressive procurement by the Food Corporation of India (FCI), there has been a sharp decline in the off-take in the PDS mainly due to the reduced gap between the prices at ration shops and the open market.

The fall in the purchasing power with the rural poor because of the rising cost of living might have also contributed to the poor off-take. Economist Kirit Parikh has estimated that less than one-fifth of the PDS supplies reach the rural population. Of the rest, about half leaks out to the open market and the rest goes to the non-poor. Leakages are high because of bogus ration cards and non-drawal or rations by the non-poor.[4]

The tribals are not organised enough to fight for their rights. The Government is aware of the special difficulties being experienced in serving the tribals. From the recent newspaper reports, we understand that items like kerosene meant for the tribal people are directed to the open market where prices are three to four times the prices charged by fair price shops. There is need for strengthening the vigilance and monitoring machinery to make the PDS benefit the rural sector for whom it was started.

MEASURES TO STRENGTHEN RURAL PDS

The Centre has urged the states to add a few more items, especially goods like match-boxes, tea, salt, soaps and pulses to the list of commodities supplied through the fair price shops. However, only a few states have initiated measures in this direction. This is so because enlarging the PDS would place additional burden on the states.

The Centre is said to be extending financial assistance to state governments to strengthen the proposed door step PDS delivery system in remote areas. The amount will be used to purchase mobile vans for such areas where due to geographical reasons, static fair price shops are not viable. Expansion of the scheme would not only prevent leakages and delay in delivery, but also ensure steady supply of items in remote areas where the majority of the people live below the poverty line.[5]

Under the present PDS, foodgrains are centrally procured and distributed. This involves huge expenditure on procurement, transportation, storage and re-transportation. The cost of PDS can be reduced by having a village-oriented localised procurement and distribution system. The village panchayat has to take up the responsibility of estimating the food-grain requirement for the entire population of the village.[6]

The PDS has been reoriented to meet the specific needs of the tribal people. More fair price shops are being opened and more ration cards are being issued in tribal dominated blocks. The goods are being taken as near to the people as possible. Purchase of mobile vans for distribution of essential commodities at the doorsteps of tribal population is part of the revamped PDS.[7] Of course, there has been some change in the food habits of tribals.[8] The PDS should take this into account.

Arrangements have been made for the construction of godowns in North-eastern states, Jammu & Kashmir, Himachal Pradesh, Andaman & Nicobar Islands.

As most tribal people are illiterate, the radio and the television should be used for educating them about the facilities available under the PDS. As the tribals still follow the barter system, it is essential to provide more items like soap, tea, kerosene and cloth to the tribals through the PDS.

The PDS should be linked with employment guarantee programmes. The move is certainly having advantages like self-targeting, direct benefits to the poor in terms of employment, indirect benefits to the rural sector through agricultural labour markets, risk benefits and creation of assets.

The PDS should also pay special attention to the needs of the rural population, unorganised housing colonies, slums, jhuggijhopri complexes and camps of construction workers.[9] Food entitlement cards having short-term validity are more appropriate for these groups.

The rural consumers need to be educated to stimulate their awareness and emerge financially strong through schemes started by the Government. The mass media can play a very important role in sending the right message to the rural consumers. Television and radio are particularly useful to consumers who are illiterate. The voluntary agencies can play a useful role in educating the rural consumers. There is need for popular participation and mass movement against unethical exploitation.[10]

Mobile consumer forums should be set up to provide justice to rural consumers at their doorsteps. The rural consumers should be encouraged to report their grievances to the appropriate authorities for their immediate redressal.[11] The PDS, if properly implemented, will be of great help to the rural population.

REFERENCES

1. I. Satya Sundaram: 'Public Distribution System: An Evaluation', *Indian Consumer Co-operator*, October-December, 1995, p. 31.
2. Suresh Misra: 'Imperative of Protecting Rural Consumer', *Kurukshetra*, May 1992, p. 26.
3. Sayulu: 'Rural Public Distribution System: Need for a New Approach', *Kurukshetra*, February 1995, p. 43.
4. *The Economic Times* (editorial), February 21, 1995.
5. *The Financial Express*, April 19, 1992.
6. K. Sayulu: *op. cit.*, p. 43.
7. S.C. Bhatt: 'Is Revamped PDS Benefiting the People', *Kurukshetra*, May 1992, p. 6.
8. Jai Prakash Jha:'Food Distribution in Tribal Area', *Yojana*, May 15, 1992, p. 23.
9. Surinder Sud: 'Operating Revamped PDS Effectively', *Kurukshetra*, May 1992, p. 11.
10. Suresh Misra: *op. cit.*, p. 27.
11. G. Narasimha Murthy and P. Indrasena Reddy: 'Rural Consumer Protection in India', *Khadigramodyog*, May 1995, p. 421.

Chapter

50 BASIC NEEDS OF RURAL INDIA

The basic needs of rural India still remain unmet. Rural areas still suffer from poor housing; health, education, water supply and transport facilities. This chapter examines the progress so far achieved in these spheres, problems these sectors are facing, and also the measures needed to improve the situation.

It is indeed paradoxical that though rural India is having abundance of manpower, this could not be effectively utilised to provide basic services to our villages. The country is now having more than 40 million tonnes of foodgrain surpluses. However, these are not being used to improve the rural infrastructure. Earlier, the food-for-work programme was implemented to generate employment and improve infrastructure in rural areas. There is need for reviving this programme.

As a result of economic reforms undertaken, the flow of funds into the social sectors is likely to slow down. The relative allocations to the sub-sectors of the social sector are found to have been disturbed, even showing declining trends.[1]

Plan and non-plan expenditure of the Central government on various social sector services increased from a level of ₹ 9,608 crore in 1992-93 to ₹ 36,270 crore in 2000-01 (BE); an increase of about four times in eight years. As a ratio to total expenditure, the combined plan and non-plan expenditure of the Centre rose from 8.1 per cent in 1992-93 to 10.7 per cent in 2000-01. Expressed as a ratio to GDP at current market prices, the expenditure on social services of Central government increased from 1.28 per cent in 1992-93 to 1.66 per cent in 2000-01 (BE). Thus, in spite of the severe budgetary pressures faced by the Central government, it has attempted to enhance outlays for the social sectors.[2]

RURAL HOUSING

Housing and shelter have been a basic and fundamental pre-requisite for human existence. Housing facilities ensure decent human existence. Housing is also a labour-intensive activity. Rural housing assumed importance because a section of the rural population appreciated doing business from home, thus making it their work-place.

In India, the problem of housing is both quantitative and qualitative.

PRESENT POSITION

According to the 1991 census, the overall shortage of housing in India was of the order of about 185 lakh dwelling units — the rural areas account for 140 lakh units.

According to the National Building Organisation (NBO), the total housing shortage would be around 200 lakh units in the country by the year 2000 AD. Rural housing shortage would be around 130 lakh units. Also, it was estimated that in the Eighth Plan (1992-97), about 122 lakh units require substantial upgradation to make them habitable.[3]

Table: 1
Housing Shortage in India

(in million units)

Year	*Rural*	*Urban*	*Total*
1991	14.67	8.23	22.90
1992	14.53	8.01	22.54
1993	14.37	7.97	22.34
1994	14.21	7.91	22.12
1995	14.04	7.82	21.86
1996	13.85	7.71	21.56
1997	13.66	7.57	21.23
1998	13.45	7.36	20.81
1999	13.23	7.18	20.41
2000	13.00	6.93	19.93
2001	12.76	6.64	19.40

Source: National Building Organisation

In the rural areas, 91 per cent of the houses do riot have toilets; 93 per cent are without bathrooms, 45 per cent are using a part of the living room as a kitchen and the rest are cooking in the open. The National Sample Survey on housing conditions further revealed that only about five per cent of the rural households have access to tap water supply. Over-crowding and congestion are some of the other disturbing factors in the country's housing scenario.

The average unit cost of house is estimated at ₹ 20,900 and therefore construction of 7.36 million new houses would cost ₹ 15,382 crore. In addition, upgrading of 10.3 million houses at an average unit cost of ₹ 10,000 would amount to ₹ 10,300 crore. Thus, the total funds required to alleviate the housing shortage would be estimated at ₹ 25,700 crore. Of course, a part of this is met by the beneficiaries themselves.[4]

The housing problem continues to be severe because of the rapid growth of population, worsening poverty and high cost of materials and labour. The finances available and the number of houses built is nowhere near solving the rural housing problem. It is also clear that the number of houses have increased, but the conditions have not improved.[5]

The new housing policy (1994) Envisaged a major shift in the government's role from builder to facilitator of housing activities. The policy aimed at providing the poor access to appropriate building materials and technology, besides involving voluntary agencies in house construction activities.

The 1998 National Housing and Habitat Policy, announced on July 30, 1998, aimed at constructing two million dwelling units every year, with focus on the poor. It called for a progressive shift from a subsidy-based housing scheme to cost-sharing, or cost-recovery-cum-subsidy scheme for rural housing.

According to the 2001 census, the housing shortage is placed at 31.1 million dwelling units. The shortage for rural areas is 14.8 million units. The estimated housing shortage does not include the anticipated need arising due to growth of population during the decade 2001-2011.

Under Bharat Nirman Programme, 60 lakh houses are likely to be constructed in the four year period beginning 2005 for below poverty line households.

MEASURES NEEDED

Housing shortage is a multi-dimensional problems and as such, it requires a multi-dimensional approach. The Government holds responsibility to take up different housing schemes, keeping in view their basic requirements and their affordability.[6]

Efforts should be made to utilise to the maximum extent the local materials and low cost technology developed by various institutions. More and more houses in rural India are going to be constructed with biomass materials, depending less and less on burnt bricks. A variety of industrial and agricultural wastes are available and technologies for using them need to be given due publicity.

Too much importance should not be given to cost reduction. With over-emphasis on low cost, there has been a proliferation of structures which are inadequate. It would be much better to construct less number of houses, with pucca roofs, so that the expenditure on upgradation can be avoided year after year.[7]

The financial assistance for housing can be routed through the gram panchayat, and it should ensure proper utilisation of funds. Also, the activities of various agencies should be well coordinated to overcome the problems of overlapping and duplication.[8]

House, as far as possible, should be built in clusters so that common facilities can be provided for the clusters.

RURAL HEALTH

In most developing countries, access to health facilities has not been ensured for the poor for various reasons. As per the World Health Organisation (WHO) statistics, 80 per cent of diseases in the developing countries are related to unsafe water supply and inadequate sanitation, causing high child mortality, low life expectancy and poor quality of life.

PRESENT POSITION

The existing health system has several lacunae. The current outlay for the health sector which is around 3.5 per cent of the GDP, needs to be enhanced to at least 5 per cent. Also, the current situation of almost 80 per cent of the funds available are being spent on salaries and only a meagre balance is available for medicines, and equipment and other necessary supplies is rather deplorable.

During the period 1983 to 1997, the crude birth rate dropped from 33.7 to 27.2; crude death rate from 11.9 to 8.9 and infant mortality rate from 105 to 71.

Life expectancy at birth rose from 55.6 years in 1985-86 to 62.8 years in 1996 in respect of men and from 56.4 to 64.2 in respect of women. Total fertility rate has declined from 4.5 in 1983 to 3.0 in 2001. India is going to achieve polio zero incidence. The incidence of leprosy has been brought down from 57 to 5 per thousand.

India requires 1,34,108 sub-centres (SCs), 22,349 primary health centres (PHCs) and 5,587 community health centres (CHCs). Against this as on June 30, 1998, the country had 1,36,318 SCs, 22,991 PHCs, and 2712 CHCs. At the national level, there is shortage of CHCs only. But, state-wise figures show that out of the 32 States and Union Territories, 13 have shortfall in respect of SCs, 14 have shortfall in respect of PHCs and 22 have shortfall in respect of CHCs.[9]

Nearly 50 per cent of the urban population has no sanitation facilities. Health services in rural areas are so poor that many people prefer to go to private practitioners. Also, studies show that the services are grossly under-utilised due to lack of availability of appropriate institutions, staff, medicine, equipments, transport etc.[10]

The PHCs are normally expected to provide services around six to seven hours a day, but the availability of doctors during these hours varied greatly. The duration of availability of atleast one doctor at PHC in a day was around three hours. There were no fixed timings, and hence, the patients were never sure when the doctor would be available at the PHC.[11]

The total financial requirement for rural primary health infrastructure and manpower to deliver health and family welfare services to the population during the Ninth Plan (1997-2000) is placed at ₹ 18,052.08 crore.[12]

The National Rural Health Mission (NRHM) was launched on April 12, 2005 for a period of 7 years (2005-2012). With a sectorwise approach to family welfare, the programme attempts a decentralised process by inviting each state/UT to prepare its own programme implementation plan based upon a situational analysis of ground realities and requirements.

The Mission would be implemented throughout the country with special focus on 18 states with weak health infrastructure. It wants to mainstream the Indian system of medicines to facilitate comprehensive healthcare. It aims at capacity building, besides increasing the fund allocation to health sector.

One has to welcome NRHM because according to NSSO Report, 2005 three out of every thousand rural households do not get enough to eat.

The National Rural Health Mission (NRHM) was launched in 2005 to provide accessible, affordable and accountable quality health services to rural areas with emphasis on poor persons and remote areas.

There has been a steady increase in healthcare infrastructure available over the plan period. However, there is still a shortage of 20, 486 SCs, 4,477 PHCs and 2,337 CHCs as per the 2001 population norm. Further, almost 29 per cent of the existing health infrastructure is in rented buildings, poor upkeep and maintenance and high absenteeism of manpower in rural areas are the main problems in the health delivery system in the public sector (Economic Survey 2009-10. p.286).

MEASURES NEEDED

The non-availability of government functionaries at their places of duty is a major problem. Two years of rural service should be made mandatory for any medical graduate before he can seek admission for post-graduation. A short-term orientation should also be made mandatory for other PHC staff before they resume duty.[13]

The order to avoid duplication of efforts, all health, population and women and children related welfare programmes at the rural level should be converged.[14]

Village health committees are being organised to help in the planning and implementation of health programmes and the village health guides scheme is increasingly being supervised by such committees.[15]

The village panchayats (or local women bodies) should start and manage village health facilities — commensurate with their resources.[16]

Also, we have vast number of untrained medical practitioners in the countryside. Their services need to be utilised in a rational manner.[17]

Development of mobile clinics is a step in the right direction. Already, some of the medical colleges have adopted certain nearby villages and have been catering to their health and medical needs through mobile clinics.

What rural India requires is low cost health services. Some voluntary agencies like the Bhagavathula Charitable Trust (BCT) at Yellmanchili in Andhara Pradesh have evolved low cost health delivery strategies. For instance, the BCT hires the services of doctors retired from government service. They are paid a nominal honorarium. The patients have to pay the cost of medicines only. Medicines are supplied free of charge to the very poor only.[18]

Experiences indicate that a large proportion of illnesses in the rural areas can be attended by the paramedicals and that they are known to handle such cases of minor ailments effectively.[19]

RURAL EDUCATION

Education is an important conduct by which a person can think of development as an individual and a member of society. Yet, our progress on literacy and education fronts is not upto the mark.

PRESENT POSITION

According to a UNDP report, there were 45 million children out of primary schools in 1995 in India. The figure is however 55 million as per an NCAER survey. Add to this the children in the 11-14 age group as well as those who enrol but drop out before reaching class V and the non-school going child population comes close to 150 million.

In 1967-68, functional literacy programme was started. Non-formal education programme for the age group of 15-25 was introduced in 1975, and the National Adult Education Programme began in 1978 which later became the basis for launching of a massive literacy programme during 1988 in the form of the National Literacy Mission.

Table: 2
Progress of Literacy

(Percentage)

Year	*Male*	*Female*	*Total*	*Rural*	*Urban*
1951	27	9	18	NA	NA
1961	40	15	28	13	24
1971	46	22	34	28	34
1981	57	30	41	34	65
1991	64	39	52	45	73
2001	76	54	65	NA	NA

NA: Not Available.

At the time of independence, the rate of illiteracy was only about 14 per cent, which rose to 52.11 per cent in 1991. According to the 2001 population census, the literacy rate rose to 65 per cent. This means that one-third of all Indians still do not possess even the basic proficiency in literacy. Of course, for the first time, there has been absolute decline in the number of illiterates from 364 million in 1991 to 332 million in 2001. India accounts for one-third of the world's unlettered and 22 per cent of 'out of school' children.

The situation is worse in respect of females. The ratio of female literates to male literates is 4:7. The literacy rate amongst them is only 39.4 per cent as compared to 63.9 per cent amongst males. Females form 62 per cent of total illiterates.

Most educational schemes suffer from inadequate staff. Even adult education programmes have suffered considerably due to transfers and postings of key functionaries at critical junctures of the implementation of the programmes.[20]

The outlay for elementary education proposed under the Eighth Plan (1992-97) is ₹ 8,936 crore — ₹ 2880 crore by the Centre and ₹ 6,056 crore by the states. Although this is more than three times the outlay on elementary education during the Seventh Plan, it is only one-sixth of the required amount for attaining universal elementary education. In 1995, it was estimated that 4.95 lakh new schools were needed by 2000 AD.

Sarva Shiksha Abhiyan (SSA) is being implemented in partnership with the states to address the needs of children in the age group of 6-14 years. The achievements of the SSA till September end 2009 are:

Opening of 2,88,155 new schools, construction of 2,40,888 school buildings, construction of 10,26,831 additional classrooms, 1,84,652 drinking water facilities, construction of 2,86,862 toilets, supply of free textbook to 9.05 crore children, appointment of 10.11 lakh teachers and in-service training for 21.79 lakh teachers.

MEASURES NEEDED

Elementary schooling should become a fundamental right. In the Mohini Jain case, the Supreme Court declared the Right to Education to be a fundamental right, covered by the Right to Life as enshrined in Article 21.

The important ingredients of a universal adult literacy programme should be:[21]

(i) light learning load (without arithmetic);

(ii) less learning time (not more than two months);

(iii) a playful teaching method.

Literacy and primary education are supplementary and complementary to each other. Emphasis on literacy therefore has to be preceded/accompanied and followed by emphasis on the universalisation of primary education.[22]

Our approach to universal primary education should be an integrated one — the questions of literacy, non-formal education and school education should be treated as different aspects of the same universal functional education.[23]

Two major initiatives taken during the Eighth Plan (1992-97) are: the District Primary Education Programme (DPEP) and the Nutrition Support to Primary Education (Midday Meal) programme. These are meant to ensure equity, access, retention and quality at the primary stage.

Improving the teaching quality and teachers' educational qualification and providing good school facilities will be extremely useful in motivating and preparing children to go to schools.[24]

The question of retention is yet another problem. Many who achieve basic minimum essential skills relapse into illiteracy in course of time if follow up programmes are not launched effectively. In fact, the level of literacy is as important or even more important than the content of literacy.[25]

Multiplicity of agencies working in the field of adult literacy should be avoided so that accountability becomes easy.[26]

Also, a healthy combination of approaches, flexible enough to suit the needs of the adults and the volunteers may be adopted instead of a single monolithic strategy.[27]

Decentralisation, coupled with strong accountability systems, with each school linked to the local community could be the answer to our failure on literacy front.[28]

Integrating different schemes of universalisation of primary education with related services such as early childhood care, education, health and nutrition programmes etc. is also needed.[29]

RURAL WATER SUPPLY

Water-borne and other allied diseases are responsible for large incidences of mortality and morbidity in the community. These can be brought under control by providing protected water.

Most villages in India are without adequate facilities for drinking water. True, several rural water supply schemes have been taken up under the programmes for community development, local development works and welfare of backward classes. Towards the end of 1954, the Central Government introduced the National Water Supply and Sanitation Programme (NWSSP).

The village water supply programme (VWSP) was introduced during the Third Plan (1961-66) period. It was intended primarily to deal with rural water supply at the village level. While executing the programme, emphasis was laid on providing water to areas which suffered from water scarcity and salinity and where water-borne diseases were endemic.

The Minimum Needs Programme was introduced in the Fifth Plan. At the beginning of the Sixth Plan (1980-85), 2.31 lakh villages were identified as 'problem villages.' Also, the programme was brought under the revised 20-Point Economic Programme in 1982-83.

In the Seventh Plan (1985-90), low cost methods were preferred. It was realised that the maintenance of the assets created for wafer supply was neglected due to lack of funds and equipment. Therefore, 10 per cent of the plan fund under the minimum needs programme was ear-marked for maintenance of water supply system in rural areas. The help of voluntary agencies was also sought.

In the Eighth Plan (1992-97), the stress was on community management of services, backed up by measures to strengthen local institutions in implementing and sustaining water and sanitation programmes. Importance was also given to sound financial practices, achieved through better management of existing assets and extensive use of appropriate technology.[30]

PRESENT POSITION

At present, about 18 per cent of the rural population and 15 per cent of the urban population has no access to safe drinking water. A survey conducted in 1985 revealed that 1.62 lakh problem villages still remained uncovered for safe drinking water sources. As on April 1,1997, there were 61,724 habitations without safe sources of drinking water (called not covered habitation), 3.78 lakh habitations which were partially covered and 1.51 lakh habitations which had quality problems like excess fluoride, salinity, iron and arsenic etc. In order to cover this backlog in rural drinking water supply, it has been estimated that approximately ₹ 40,000 crore will be required including the funds required for operations and maintenance and funds to tackle quality problems.[31]

Budget 2005-06 allocated ₹ 4,750 crore to increase access to clean potable water. According to the available data, upto 2005, an amount of ₹ 45,000 crore has been spent in a period of 30 years on rural water supply. More than 3.70 million handpumps and 1.7 lakh piped water schemes have been installed in the rural areas.

According to 2001 census figures, almost 77.9 per cent households in India has access to safe drinking water. It includes nearly 90 per cent of the urban households and about 73 per cent rural households.

The rural water supply schemes suffered from many drawbacks:[32]

(i) Personnel at all levels not sufficiently trained;

(ii) Systems were recommended without taking into account the cultural and social realities;

(iii) Technology chosen was often difficult to operate and

(iv) In the absence of workable plane, thousands of handpumps and water supply systems remained unrepaired.

Table: 3
Tenth Plan Outlay (Central) for Rural Drinking Water

(₹ crore)

Year	*Outlay*	*Actual*
2002-03	2110.00	2100.70
2003-04	2585.00	2564.90
2004-05	2900.00	2930.79@
2005-06	4050.00*	4098.03@
2006-07	5200.00	-

*At RE State amount increased to ₹ 4060 crore.

@The increase in actuals is on account of utilisation of unutilised NE funds of Sanitation for Rural Water Supply.

MEASURES NEEDED

The programmes of drinking water supply require:[33]

(i) A more decentralised manner with the involvement of the people and local institutions at all stages — planning, project formulation, execution, operation and maintenance, monitoring and evaluation;

(ii) Technical support from the district planning machinery and

(iii) Appropriate linkage between soil conservation and land/water management and drinking water supply in order to provide sustained supply.

Now, panchayats are given more powers and responsibilities. There is a change in approach. Water supply and sanitation programmes are now conceived with a blend of physical and community-related activities.[34]

RURAL ROADS

Rural transport assumes special significance because the country has 6 lakh villages. These villages cannot hope to develop unless they are connected with towns and cities through better transport systems. In fact, mobility is a sign of modernisation and development. Rural transport would facilitate the introduction of modern inputs such as fertilisers and improved seeds.

Studies show that connecting the habitations to a neighbouring market or to the main road leading to market helps the agricultural producer and those engaged in services and trade to raise their incomes. Lower transport costs increase farmer's access to markets. Banks' costs of doing business also came down.[35]

Construction of rural roads also implies road maintenance. Roads are to be kept in good condition to help efficient and quick movement of goods and passengers.[36]

PRESENT POSITION

The country has to go a long way in providing and improving rural roads. By 1991-92, only one-third of the villages were well connected. Only in small states, the performance is good. Only a few states like Kerala, Punjab and Goa can talk of 100 per cent rural connectivity.

The Road Development Plan for India (1981-2001) envisages total rural connectivity by 2001. In order to connect all the villages with population above 500 in the country has required roads which should be 21,89,000 km, according to an estimate.

Official reports say that 1,12,190 villages out of 1,29,852 villages with a population of 1000 and above in the country are estimated to have been connected by March 1995.

In the Ninth Plan (1997-2002), the target is to ensure that 85 per cent of the village population (not 85 per cent of the villages) are connected by all weather roads. As much as 75 per cent of the villages with population of 500 to 1000 should be covered on a priority basis.

All rural areas should be provided with approach/link roads to centres of business within a particular time frame. The seasonal or untarred roads be converted into tarred or all-season roads.

Construction of rural roads for connectivity has been one of the components of Minimum Needs Programme since the Fifth Five Year Plan (1974-79). The programme continued in the sixth and seventh five-year plans. Rural roads also received importance under schemes like the Rural Landless Employment Guarantee Programme (RLEGP), and National Rural Employment Programme (NREP).

On 15th August 2000, the Government announced a centrally sponsored scheme called the Pradhan Mantri Gram Sadak Yojana (PMGSY). The objective of the programme is to provide road connectivity through good all weather roads to all rural habitations with a population of more than 500 persons by the year 2007.

The Government has to mobilise ₹ 48,000 crore for the rural roads component of the Bharat Nirman Programme. The budget 2006-07 allocated ₹ 4853.06 crore for PMGSY. By 2009, the length of roads to be laid is 1,46,185 km. This would benefit 66,802 villages.

Currently, the funds for rural roads comes partly from the cess on diesel and from external funding.

The Eleventh Five-Year plan has projected an investment requirement of ₹ 41,347 crore (at 2006-07 prices) for rural roads. During the first three years of the Eleventh Plan, the flow of expenditure under Prime Minister's Gameen Sadak Yojna (PMGSY) seems to be on course formetting the plan target. In addition to the PMGSY there are roads built by PWDs and Panchayati Raj institutions in rural areas.

Table: 4

Progress Under the PMGSY

Year	*Length of road work completed (km)*	*Expenditure (₹ Crore)*
2005-06	22,891	4,100.4
2006-07	30,710	7,304.3
2007-08	41,231	10,618.7
2008-09	52,405	15,162.0
Apl-Dec.2009	36,273	12,993.1

Source: Economic Survey 2009-10. p.254.

MEASURES NEEDED

Roads connecting villages could be of earthwork in order to minimise costs, with suitable lasting admixture to permit their all-season use. Roads connecting the primary market centres and towns could be semi-pucca built from locally available wastes of brick kilns or *kankar or murram.*

The Central Road Research Institute (CRRI) has developed a few cost effective technologies which meet the immediate needs of rural India. The CRRI has also developed low cost cross drainage technology involving the use of bitumen drums etc.

To be effective, rural transportation should have the following features:[37]

(i) *Accessibility:* must involve less time to walk between the area and the system;

(ii) *Economica:* save the costs involved in the movement;

(iii) *Efficient*: move the things as speedily as possible;

(iv) *Effective:* save the things moved from damage, leakage etc.

(v) *Durable and Reliable:* must be available round the year and in all seasons; and

(vi) *Adequacy:* must be adequate enough to move things and people.

Thus, achieving full accessibility in a time-bound manner is an important means to ensure rural prosperity. The rural schemes should give importance to rural transport, but funds misuse should be curbed.

CONCLUSION

Funds shortage is no doubt a problem for successfully implementing rural service schemes. However, there is also need for better utilisation of the available funds. Also, the schemes require co-operation from local people, voluntary agencies and self-help groups.

REFERENCES

1. V.R. Panchamukhi: 'Social Impact of Economic Reforms in India: A Critical Appraisal', *Economic and Political Weekly,* march 4, 2000.p. 847.
2. Ministry of Finance, Government of India: Economic Survey 1999-2000, p. 189.
3. Krishna Singh: 'Shelter for All: A Roof Over Your Head', *Kurukshetra,* May-June 1996, p. 43.
4. Planning Commission, Government of India: *Ninth Five Year Plan* 1997-2002, Vol. II, p. 98.
5. Hare Krishna Singh: 'Rural Housing and Indira Awas Yojana: *Kurukshetra,* March 1999, p. 23.
6. P.N. Ansari: 'Hosuing Situation: The Malaise and Some Suggestions', *Yojana,* March 1999, p. 23.
7. Ruddar Dutt: 'National Housing Policy Fails to Assure Shelter for Economically Weaker Sections', *Southern Economist,* October 1, 1998, p. 10.
8. Mohinder Singh: 'Housing for Rural Poor: Problem, Policies and Perspectives', *Kurulcshetra,* July 1999, p. 34.
9. B.S. Padmanabhan: 'Health Care: Cheallenges Ahead', *Yojana,* February 2000, p. 18.
10. P. Durga Prasad: The Nemesis of Health Care System in India: Challenges for the 21st Century', *Fifty Years of Rural Development in India: Retrospect and Prospect,* Vol. II, p. 747.
11. S. Srinivasan: 'Rural Health: Policies, Strategies and Programmes: A Critical Appraisal' in *Ibid*., p. 770.
12. Ninth Five Year Plan 1997-2002, *op. cit.,* Vol. II, p. 93.
13. Alok Mukhopadhyay: 'Revamping Primary Health Care', *Yogana,* August 1998. p. 70.
14. *Ibid*., p. 70.
15. A.A. Siddiqui: 'Health Policy in India', *Mainstream,* December 11, 1999, p. 28.
16. Shyam Ashtekar: 'A Lost Perspective', *The Hindu,* (Magazine Section), January 3, 1999, p. v.
17. *Ibid.*
18. I. Satya Sundaram (1986): *Voluntary, Agencies and Rural Development,* B.R. Publishing Corporation, New Delhi, p. 264.
19. G. Giridhar: 'Access to Social and Health Services for the Rural Poor', paper presented at CIRDAP - IRD Workshop on CPFP. April 3-7, 1995. National Institute of Rural Development. Hyderabad.
20. J.S. Rajput: 'Policy Perspectives in Elementary Education', *Mainstream,* January 21, 1995, p. 30.
21. G.P. Jain: 'The Easy Way to Adult Literacy', *Indian Express,* September 8, 1995.

22. K. Jaya Kumar: 'Literacy: Not a National Priority, Yet', *The Hindu,*December 2, 1997.

23. Hasan Abdullah: 'Universal Primary Education — A Forgotten Objective', *The Hindu,* September 23, 1997.

24. Daljit Singh Bedi and Satyanarayana Patnaik: 'Universalisation of Primary Education: A Myth or Reality', *Kurukshetra,* September 1997. p. 11.

25. Lakshmichar Mishra: 'Total Literacy Campaign: Still an Unwritten Chapter in Indian History', *Mainstream,* September 5, 1992. p. 13.

26. K.V. Ramana: 'Total Literacy Campaign: Some Imperatives', *The Hindu,* November 17, 1992. p. 17.

27. *Ibid*.

28. Vimala Ramachandran: 'Whitber Literacy Programmes?', *The Hindu,* October 13, 1996 (Magazine Section), p. viii.

29. H.D. Dwarakanath: 'Strategies to Improve Primary Education in Rural India', *Kurukshetra,* January 2000. p. 8.

30. Md. Zulfequar Ahmad Khan: 'Rural Water Supply During Plan Periods: An Overview', *Kurukshetra,* March 1996, p. 33.

31. Ninth Five Year Plan 1997-2002, *op. cit.,* p. 97, Vol. II.

32. Dinesh Ghand: 'Rural Water Supply and Sanitation Sector in India: Changing Face', *Kurukshetra,* January 1999, p. 3.

33. Md. Zulfequar Ahmad Khan: *op. cit.,* p. 34.

34. Dinesh Chand: *op. cit.,* p. 4.

35. S.C. Lahiry: 'Rural Road — A Key Component for Rural Development', *Kurukshetra,* October-November 1996. p. 97.

36. J. Bhagyalakshmi: 'Rural Roads: Vital Link to Prosperity', *Yojana,* January 1998. p. 67.

37. R.L. Hyderabad: 'Rural Transportation: Problems and Management,' *Kurukshetra,* October-November 1996. p. 101.

Chapter

51 Communication for Rural Development

Communication plays a very important role in the field of rural development. Given the high rate of illiteracy, the rural people need to be educated about both development and welfare issues. The Government is offering a number of incentives like subsidies. The rural poor should know about governmental schemes meant for them.

The rural people should obtain maximum benefits from the schemes meant for them. Otherwise, they will not take any interest in these schemes. And without people's active participation, rural schemes fail to deliver the goods.

Rural communication must concentrate on 'education' rather than 'publicity.' After all, communication is something more than the mechanical transfer, or even exchange of information. The function of mass communication is to bring about social transformation, and to mobilise human resources to strengthen national effort.[1]

The term "development communication" was first coined by UNESCO. At a symposium at the University of Philippines, development communication was described as the art and science of human communication applied to achieve both growth and social justice by fully utilising human potential.

Importance of Communication

Rural communication is important because economic growth does not depend on economic factors alone. It is related to non-economic factors too like people's attitude to work.

Today, development involves not merely an increase in physical output, but a fair distribution of the benefits of growth. These benefits should be enjoyed by all sections and by all regions. Communication plays a very important role in achieving this objective.[2]

Studies show that mass media is able to bring about a welcome change in the occupational structure in the villages. Earlier, people used to follow caste-based occupations. With access to TV, and also improvement in transport facilities, most people are preferring non-caste occupations.[3]

Communication is the essential element for social change. It can help to inform, motivate, educate and entertain the respective clients. It also helps in imparting training to people, organising community and farm related processes and coordinating various activities.[4] Communication is a catalytic agent that motivates people to take right decision at the right time.[5]

Decentralisation and democratisation of information is very essential in nation-building particularly so in the case of developing countries.[6]

The TV has become a critical agent of change and development. It is an effective means in communicating messages concerning social issues like family planning, personal hygiene, primary healthcare, literacy and basic education. However, there is need for evolving optimum media mix and commercial strategies for rural markets.[7]

The size of the rural market is growing. There is also a change in the consumption pattern with rise in rural income. The rural people are now acquiring more and more consumer durables. There is also increasing use of items like shampoos and soft drinks. The rural consumers are showing interest in branded goods advertised on TV. They should be educated on the merits and demerits of modern products.

Mechanisms of Communication

Mass media includes not only print, radio, television and cinema, but also books, magazines, pamphlets and direct mail literature and posters. Mass media were earlier used for informative, educative and entertaining purposes. At present, they are being increasingly used for development purposes. For effective rural communication, the Government may use posters, pamphlets, exhibitions, wall newspapers, hoardings, wall paintings and booklets.

Wall paintings and posters are better than other means: they stay for a long time. The message is conveyed by the picture alone. However, the design selected must be appropriate to local conditions.[8]

Exhibitions, melas etc. do act as effective means in spreading useful information in the rural areas. In the field of agriculture, kisan melas have proved to be a very popular source of information.

The inexpensive transistor is playing a major role in bringing about change in rural areas. The radio's role in spreading technology particularly relating to agriculture, has been well recognised.

Some Problems

Evolving an effective communication system for rural development is no easy task. There are social, psychological and physical constraints. Even in the sphere of knowledge, those with higher socio-economic status gain more than those with lower socio-economic status. Thus, the gap between the haves and havenots increases.[9] The communication gap between the two groups — the group that has planned the change and the group that is intended to be changed — is large. The job of mass media is to bridge this gap.[10]

There should be two-way communication. Very often, many agricultural development projects have been launched on the basis of findings at research stations. But, no attention was paid to know whether the small farmers have financial backing to carry them through.[11]

Most rural schemes became ineffective because of the indifferent attitude of rural people. People's active participation in the development process is absent. A constant contact is needed between those who administer development and those who are to participate in the process.

TV can be used for both motivation and instructions. Special programmes are being telecast for the farming community. Through TV, it is possible to demonstrate the utility of new technologies. However, according to one study, some farmers expressed the view that the TV programmes are more helpful to large scale farming only.[12]

While mass media contributes to rural development and change, it is necessary to review the impact of media periodically. The medium we use should be situation-specific.

MEASURES NEEDED

People generally resist change. Hence, the media strategies have to first create general awareness amongst the people about what is happening in their surroundings. Then, to motivate them to 'accept' and 'achieve' something significant.[13] The rural press should serve as the information centre about various schemes, plans and projects.[14]

All development programmes must become credible in the sense that the target audience are given an opportunity to meet and discuss their needs with opinion leaders, programme planners and communicators.[15]

In the case of the radio, news and views of a problem solving nature could be broadcast. The staff have to undergo an orientation to the philosophy of development. The producer of the programme should himself be informed before he or she can inform others.[16]

Films are screened in villages occasionally. Though a library of films exists, they are generally outdated or not locally planned. A film language, less dependent on commentary, should be evolved to suit rural viewers and ideas should be explained in simple terms.[17]

The technology selected should be appropriate to local conditions. It is necessary to choose the correct medium for the situation. Of course, radio broadcasting is appropriate for most situations.

Of course, even where one particular medium is obviously best for the job, a greater impact can be achieved by using several media to reinforce one another in an orchestrated way.

Research shows that the message would be very effective if the media are combined with interpersonal, face to face contact with a trained instructor or group leader, preferably drawn from the same social group or area as the audience.[18]

The media should be selected in accordance with the personality of the sender, the nature of messages and the background of the receiver.[19]

In view of the variety of media available, priority should be given to coordination. The lack of coordination is seen among communication agencies as well as between them and development agencies. Also, each means of communication has a unique potential and limitation in terms of reach, expense and ability. We should therefore opt for an optimum mix of existing media.[20]

There is no doubt that communication is an effective tool to bring about the desired rural development. But, it should be handled carefully. The communication revolution can speed up the process of modernisation of the rural economy.

REFERENCES

1. R.K. Chatterjee: *'Mass Communication'*, National Book Trust, New Delhi, 1979.
2. I.Satya Sundaram: 'Communication Support for Rural Development', *Financial Express*, October 9, 1990.
3. P. Kuppuswamy: *'Communication and Development in India'*, Sterling Publishers Private Ltd., New Delhi, 1976.
4. Chandan Kr Deka, Shantanu Kumar and Uma Sah: 'Communication for Rural Development: Concept, Process and Barriers', *Kurukshetra*, March 2003, p.28.
5. Janaki Chundi and Alka Srivastava: 'Role of Media in Rural Areas', *Kurukshetra*, July 2000, p.3.
6. J.Bhagyalakshmi: 'Towards Participatory Rural Communication', *Yojana*, January 2002, p.59.
7. Rajendra K.Aneja: 'Evolving Optimum Media Mix and Communication Strategies for Rural Markets', *Economic and Political Weekly*, May 30, 1992, p.M-75.
8. Malini: 'Communication for Rural Development', in *Rural Development in India:Some Facets*, National Institute of Rural Development, Hyderabad, 1979.
9. Bella Mody: 'Role of Participatory Local Media in Rural Transformation', in R.P.Misra and K.V. Sundaram (Ed.1979), *Rural Area Development:Perspectives and Approaches*, Sterling Publishers, New Delhi, p.156.
10. I.P.Tiwari: 'Communication for Rural Development', *Southern Economist*, August 15, 1978, p.13.
11. R.K. Samanta and R. Chittiraichelvan:'Development Communication — Key to Eradicate Rural Poverty', *Khadigramodyog*, March 2002, p.185.
12. A.Vijayarangan: 'Television for Speedier Rural Development', *Kurukshetra*, September 1992, p.14.
13. Uma Joshi: 'Media Catalyst in Rural Resurgence', *Social Welfare*, June 2005, p.35.
14. H.D. Dwarakanath: 'Mass Media: Crucial Role in Promoting Rural Development', *Kurukshetra*, April 2002, p.10.
15. Uma Tripathi and J.S.Murthy: 'Call for a New Communication Strategy for Rural Development', *Kurukshetra*, January-February 1996, p.55.

16. S.Bashiruddin: 'Radio Programming' (Paper presented at the conference on communication support for rural development held by the Administrative Staff College of India, Hyderabad from 27th to 30th December, 1978, See *Seminar*, March 1979, p.21).
17. Nalini Vittal: 'Communication for Rural Development', in *Rural Development in India:Some Facets,* National Institute of Rural Development, Hyderabad.
18. R.K.Samanta and R.Chithraichelvan (2002): *op.cit.*, p.185.
19. A.Vijayarangan:'Mass Media and Rural Development', *Khadigramodyog*, 1991, p.108.
20. Nalini Vittal: *op.cit.*

PART SEVEN

Rural Development: Experiences of Select Countries

Chapter

52 Rural Development in China

The Chinese rural development experiences offer useful lessons to Third World countries. The Chinese economy experienced ups and downs till 1978 when reforms were undertaken. About 900 million out of the 1200 million Chinese population still live in rural areas.

Chinese Economy

According to official figures, the GDP increased by an average 9.9 per cent per annum between 1979 and 1996, while independent studies place it at 7.9 per cent.

There was a sharp decline in poverty in the first seven years of reform when agriculture and rural industry were in the forefront. In 1978, some 270 million people or 28 per cent of the total population lived below the poverty line. By 1985, that number fell to 97 million, less than 10 per cent of the population. In 1996-97, the number further declined to 70 million.[1]

During the period 1953 to 1976, per capita real income stagnated. However, net rural per capita income increased from 134 yuan in 1978 to 1578 yuan in 1995 — a twelve fold increase from low levels, and rural consumption has similarly risen.

Since the late 1970s, economic growth centred itself in the countryside where rates of industrialisation and exports have outstripped those of the cities.[2]

China's rapid growth and job creation together with direct and indirect subsidies have greatly helped the chronic rural poor.[3]

The *yigong daizhen* (YD) programme is a public works programme linked to work relief. This is an important poverty alleviation programme. The YD programme provided aid in the form of payments in kind to participating households. In the years 1985-91, these programmes contributed to the construction of 1,31,000 kms of roads, 7900 bridges and 2400 kms of inland river channels. Water supply conditions improved for 20 million people and 13 million annually.[4]

Of course, the YD programme has special features. The programme has been organised spatially to target localities such as countries or villages rather than individuals. Payment is exclusively in kind in the form of 'industrial coupons' redeemable at government stores.

The Chinese experiments in the field of rural development offer useful lessons. The country has provided unique opportunities for its people. These include a sense of dignity, the spirit of self-reliance and the opportunity of participation and decision-making. It has been able to bring about.[5]

A fundamental change in values and objectives of development, with greater emphasis on collective rather than individual rewards and on social rather than purely materialistic or technological objectives.

The Chinese experiments in poverty and unemployment reduction in rural areas deserve close study.

Chinese Communes

An important feature of the Great Leap Forward (1958-60) was the formation of the 'communes.' The new set up aimed at freeing China from a family centred society into a community centred society. Private plots, houses and part of one's livestock have come under commune ownership. The rationale of the new set up was decentralisation of power and administration. Each commune has to aim at self-reliance with its own local resources and manpower. The communes started yielding good results.

The Chinese commune has played a very important role in the economic, social and political life of rural China since 1958. Of course, there is variation among communes in terms of income levels and social services provided.

The commune is a composite unit of the local government that encompasses the whole range of economic, social, administrative and political functions for the rural community. Its primary aim is to organise and mobilise the rural population, to develop their land and other resources in order to meet their essential needs. The commune is expected to reduce social inequalities. The concept of commune is based on the principle of self-reliance.

The main function of the commune is to supervise and implement the political and administrative policies of the Government and to strengthen the ideological and political basis of the rural society.

The commune's functions also include providing military training, control of the movement of population and the collection of government taxes. In other words, the commune is responsible for implementing government policy at the local level. It provides leadership, guidance and assistance for agricultural and rural development. It takes up the task of diversification of the rural economy and provision of certain social services.

The people's commune, production brigade and production team were the primary organisations in the countryside. The communes were turned into a revolutionary committee of the production brigade during the cultural revolution.

The average commune was to include 5000 households and was meant to become a self-sufficient unit, combining political, social, economic and cultural functions. The organisation communes emerged in 1961 with stress on food production.[6] The communes provided a viable institutional framework for rural development in China.

The production team enjoys autonomy in making investment decisions. The production team has to meet the quotas fixed by the state which also fixes prices. The production brigade coordinates the annual production plans of the teams. The commune coordinates, supervises and guides the activities of the production teams and production brigades. It undertakes larger projects.

In 1975, there were as many as 50,000 communes. Of course, these communes are linked to the central government through countries and provinces.

The communes have done a good job in the area of rural reconstruction.[7]

First, the communes have productively utilised the surplus labour force available in the rural areas. Of course, the task became easier because of collectivisation.

Second, the commune has been successful in diversifying the agricultural sector and also the entire rural economy by giving importance to small and agro-based industries and also production of farm inputs including machinery.

Third, the communes have also contributed to improvement in the knowledge and skills of the rural population which is essential for agricultural development. The system of rural education and training in China is geared to educating and training the rural population for work within the commune.

Fourth, the communes should ensure equitable distribution of incomes and the benefits of larger production. Besides income from the collective, each member gets some income from private plots which are used mainly for poultry, pigs and for fruits and vegetables. A large portion of the collective land is used for producing foodgrains whose prices are kept low as a matter of policy.

Fifth, the system of communes provides a very effective mechanism of local planning which assumes importance in a vast country like China. Planning in China laid special stress on maximum exploitation of local resources for meeting local needs.

Last, the communes enabled planners to link local level planning to planning at higher levels. True, there is inherent conflict between central planning and local initiative. But the planners in China have succeeded in minimising this conflict.

As a result of rural reforms undertaken, the people's communes were abandoned, and the country introduced "household contact responsibility system, which later on formed a solid base for China's modernisation of sustained economic growth. Under this system, the household which took on lease a particular plot of land had the freedom to choose the crop pattern, but it was bound to give the collective (the state sector) the contracted output from the produce. The surplus production as well as products it made by way of sideline production such as poultry, and piggery was its own and it was free to sell or consume it. This reform increased agricultural production and rural living standards.[8]

The commune system has played a very important role in the rural reconstruction of China. It also offered useful lessons in the field of rural development.

RURAL HEALTH IN CHINA

China's rural health policy is based on four principles: priority for the problems of the masses; use of local and available health resources, priority for prevention and finally mass mobilisation.

China has adopted innovative methods in many spheres. Take the case of rural health. The Chinese recognised the need for low cost curative medicines. Instead of spending huge amounts on buildings and other physical facilities, the Chinese gave importance to what came to be called the programme of barefoot doctors whose total number by 1975 was over one and half a million. About two-thirds of the total budget on medicine is spent in rural areas. Every commune has a hospital with twenty to fifty beds or at least a clinic.

The barefoot doctors are essentially trained peasants or educated youth who can take care of minor ailments through a combination of traditional and modern medicines.

China's 10 lakh 'barefoot doctors' have learned to give first aid, supervise immunisation and conduct public health campaigns for the 8 lakh villages.

The Cultural Revolution laid stress on rural health. Accordingly, commune members with only primary education were selected to receive three months of training. Of course, the skills have been periodically augmented by refresher courses, and they finally become 'barefoot doctors.'

The 'barefoot doctors' (now replaced by better trained rural doctors) at the village health stations constitute the wide base of the health care pyramid of China.

However, as a result of reforms, more and more doctors prefer to do private practice and earn. As a result of this, medical services are becoming costly.[9]

Even today, 85 per cent of Chinese villages have a village health station within a 15 minute walking distance. There are several well equipped village health stations even in the far South hills of Yunnan.

During the period 1952 to 1992, the number of doctors per 1000 persons increased from 0.7 to 1.5 and hospital beds for 1000 population from 0.3 to 3.3.

Infant mortality rate is below 20 per 1000 live births, maternity mortality rate about one in 1000 births, birth rate 17 and death rate 6.5 per 1000. Life expectancy is 70 years plus.

In China, every country has a professional school conducting a two-year course for training rural doctors. After this course, they go through a year long internship at country hospitals, and a national test in the same period. After scoring 60 per cent in the test, they get a green card to practise medicine.

In 1991, medical expenditure throughout China amounted to 60 billion yuan ($ 11 billion accounting for 3.9 per cent of the country's GNP, urban citizens used more than one-third of the total). China's highly subsidised health scheme, of course, created some problems.

In China, health facilities are owned by the local administration — the state — but people pay for most services. Even preventive services are charged for China believes in community financing of health care. The state share of health expenditure remains at around 15 per cent.

Because of economic reforms, the health care ceased to be a collective responsibility. The class of barefoot doctors disappeared, and hospitals in urban areas progressively started becoming commercialised.

CHINESE AGRICULTURE

China moved from a small peasant economy to collective agriculture. This transformation consisted of four stages: *(i)* mutual aid teams; *(ii)* elementary cooperatives; *(iii)* advanced cooperatives and people's communes. China could cross all these states in a short period of six years (1952-1958). This period also witnessed China's First Five Year Plan (1953-07).

The formation of mutual aid teams was the first step towards collectivisation. Some peasants have lands, but not implements. Others had implements and animals but not enough land. To overcome this constraint, six, eight or ten households were grouped into mutual aid teams. While retaining individual ownership, the peasants can pool in their labour, animals and farm implements. Some teams were seasonal, others were permanent. The value of a man's labour or the work done by a member's draught animal was determined through an agreed local standard. Of course, the capacity of these teams is limited.

The elementary cooperatives emerged in 1953. About 70 per cent of the total income was distributed on the basis of work done by each member; the rest was distributed as dividends or rent for land or other means of production contributed by various members. Management of the cooperative was the responsibility of a committee elected each year by all the members.

The advanced cooperatives were a step ahead of elementary cooperatives. Under the new system, the entire income of the cooperative was distributed among members on the basis of the work done for the cooperative, and not on the basis of the land or implements contributed by members. Each advanced cooperative was equal in size to 10 to 20 elementary cooperatives. Thus, advanced cooperatives have enough capital at their disposal.

The relative success of advanced cooperatives resulted in the emergence of the people's communes. It was felt that there was need for a unit of rural development sufficient enough to carry business beyond agriculture. The amalgamation of advanced cooperatives and Hsiangs (lowest administrative units) into people's communes was very rapid and the process was almost complete by the end of September 1958.

Private plots were given to farmers to enable them to produce pigs, poultry and vegetable. Each plot should not exceed 5 per cent of the total land under collective management.

During the period 1979-84, restructuring was confined to rural areas and the agricultural sector where family production and contract responsibility system were introduced. This involved:[10]

(i) Separation of ownership of land from its management by contracting out land (by the state) to farming families with ownership remaining with the collective;

(ii) Abolition of the people's commune system, allowing peasants in some regions to raise their preferred crops and

(iii) Upward revision of the purchasing price of agricultural products.

China has only 8 per cent of the world's cultivable land, but 20 per cent of the world's population. Yet, the country has been able to meet the food and other basic requirements of its growing population.

Despite the vast size of the country, only about 10 per cent of China's geographical area is under cultivation. The net sown area is about 100 million hectares. Cropping intensity is about 150 per cent and approximately 46 per cent of cultivated land is under irrigation. Foodgrain production reached a level of 500 million tonnes.

In China, the cereal productivity was 4161 kg per hectare — much higher than India's 1648 kg per hectare. The Chinese farmers have been making use of all the conceivable sources of organic manures for crop production. Thus, soil health is maintained at the optimum levels.

Arable area declined in China from nearly 108 million hectares in 1952 to less than 95 million hectares in 2000. During the period 1983-86 alone, 2.27 million hectares were lost. This is attributed to industrial, commercial and residential construction, infrastructure building and quite possibly a decline in wasteland reclamation.[11]

Area sown to foodgrains had declined from 120.6 million hectares in 1980 to 110 million hectares in 1994. However, the average annual rate of growth of foodgrains output during the period 1981 to 1990 was 3.4 per cent, well ahead of the population growth rate of 1.2 per cent annually. The Chinese agriculture is subject to natural calamities.

Agricultural productivity in China is high because of certain favourable factors. These include:[12]

(i) Higher use of fertilisers;

(ii) Integrated use of chemical and organic manures;

(iii) Higher use of organic manure;

(iv) Efficient use of inputs including water and

(v) Effective extension system which reduced the gap between knowledge and practice.

State's agricultural subsidies peaked in the year 1978-84, reaching 20 per cent of state revenue in the final three years of the period. By 1944, state investment in agriculture and land improvement had dropped to just 2.6 per cent of all state capital construction investment together with overall decline in investment in agriculture.[13]

Mechanisation of agriculture in China has some special features:[14]

First, the Chinese began to mechanise agriculture *after* achieving a significant diversification of the rural economy. This means a sizeable proportion of the rural population had already been absorbed in non-agricultural activities. Hence, farm mechanisation had no adverse effect on the employment situation.

Second, the mechanisation of agriculture has been financed by the communes and brigades largely from their own savings. The prices of agricultural machinery were relatively low. The distribution of agricultural machinery is subject to the quota system.

Last, the whole range of agricultural machinery is manufactured within China. This has eliminated import of agricultural machinery.

Since 1975, the emphasis has been shifted from selective mechanisation to full scale mechanisation.

Table: 1
Foodgrain Production in China

(in million tonnes)

Year	*Production*
1949	108
1952	154
1957	185
1960	150
1965	200
1970	240
1974	275
1978	305
1984	407
1990	446
1991	435
1993	456
1994	445
1995	467
1998	495
2000	500
2006	498
2007	502

China is a major producer, importer and consumer of fertilisers in the world. During 1990-91, the country accounted for 13 per cent of world's fertiliser production, 16.6 per cent of world imports and 19.7 per cent of the world's fertiliser consumption. Fertiliser use has played an extremely important role in achieving record grain production in 1984.

There has been a sharp rise in fertiliser consumption from around 240 kg/ha in 1981 to over 700 kg/ha in 1990. The total of chemical fertiliser plus organic manures now stand at 2300 kg/ha.

Because of economic reforms, major distortions emerged in the agricultural sector. These include:

(i) The share of public investment in agriculture in the total public investment declined. It was only 3 per cent in the 1980s.

(ii) The community owned means of production accumulated until 1978 were gradually transformed to private hands.

Table: 2
Grain Yield in China

(tonnes/ha)

Year	*Yield*
Pre Reform	
1965	1.64
1970	2.01
1980	2.75
Reform	
1985	3.48
1990	3.94
1991	3.88
1993	4.13
1994	4.06
1995	4.24
2000	4.39

* Estimate

(iii) Peasants who could not acquire these assets fell back on labour-intensive cultivation, leading to decline in mechanised farming;

(iv) There has been deterioration in rural infrastructure and

(v) The cropping pattern changed in favour of cash crops because of price incentives offered.

All these developments led to a sharp drain of wealth from agriculture to the industry.

The second agricultural revolution generated enormous surpluses which were invested in the rural industry. This provided better employment opportunities to millions of workers who were earlier underemployed on the land. In just 17 years — between 1978 and 1995 — the share of agriculture in the labour force dropped from 70 to 50 per cent.

As a result of the second generation economic reforms initiated in 1993, the collective farms were virtually dismantled by leasing out land for private cultivation. Although households were not allowed to own land, they were granted 15 years leases that were freely tradeable. In 1975, these leases were extended to 30 years. The households have to deliver a fixed quota of output to the state at below market prices. Of course, this quota is small, less than five per cent of the output.

The current trends are towards higher value added items, with stress on livestock, aquaculture, processing of foodgrains and forestry. Indeed, China started importing foodgrains.

Agricultural decollectivisation led to an immediate and dramatic improvement in productivity and rural standard of living. Between 1978 and 1984, agricultural value added grew on an average, five times faster that it had during the previous decades. Per capita consumption in rural areas more than doubled.[15] At present, Chinese agriculture is well placed in spite of problems.

CHINESE RURAL INDUSTRIALISATION

Small and medium enterprises have played a significant role in the growth of national economy in China. The Chinese did realise that 'bigger is not always the better.' The small units are seen as more flexible devices to meet changing market demands as also more effective in utilising the vast resources and surplus labour of the countryside.[16]

The communes have played an important role in setting up small industrial units in rural areas.

They set up a large number of small industrial units based on local raw materials or tools producing machinery and other inputs for agriculture. They developed these industries according to their own needs and priorities and trained their workers.

The Chinese pattern of industrialisation is based on forward and backward linkages. Based on the extent and nature of linkages with the local economy, the rural industries in China adopt different techniques for ensuring maximum utilisation of local resources for maximum benefit to the population.

The Chinese experience shows that rural industrialisation should go hand in hand with the development of rural infrastructure. Local initiative, innovation and self-reliance should be developed.

During the period 1978 to 1988, about 2,25,000 privately owned units were set up, leading to creation of 3.6 million jobs. During this period, the number of household units has increased from 1,40,000 to 12.2 millions. More than 50 per cent of them are in the service sector including trade. In the rural areas, a significant role is assigned to the private sector in areas like small scale manufacturing, transport, services and repairs and restaurants.

The economic reforms in China aimed at setting up a large number of rural industries so that the pressure of labour force on land will be eased and most peasants are given the opportunity to become individual entrepreneurs in commerce, transport services and industry. They may also become wage labourers in the new enterprises coming up. The ultimate objective is to shift about 40 per cent of the rural labour force from land to other rural based non-farm activities.

Provision of farm employment and increasing incomes have been important components of the reforms. Earlier, labour movement of the farm was restricted by rural and urban institutions. When many of these barriers were removed, there is an explosion of off-farm work.

Rural industry in China grew substantially employing about 25 per cent of the rural labour force. Nearly 140 million out of a total of 450 million rural labour force now work in non-farm jobs. Townships and Village Enterprises (TVEs) expanded rapidly during the reforms etc. and contributed 40 per cent to the total industrial output. However, of late, rural non-agricultural employment has begun to decline and besides profitability of the TVES is found to be falling.

However, improved incentives for managers of the rural industry and the rise of private rural firms made the sector one of the most dynamic elements of Chinese economy.[17]

The Government has taken a number of supportive measures to encourage small units. These include allocation of foreign exchange and loans to key industries for importing technology and equipment, a special 'spark' programme to diffuse appropriate technology, tax exemption for some time of the products made in the sector and encouraging transfer of scientists and technologists to such enterprises.[18]

So far as rural industrialisation is concerned, China has been following a pragmatic policy, and this has produced good results.

Conclusion

It should be admitted that the rural development in China has combined growth with more egalitarian income distribution. That is why the rural poor in China are much better-off than their counterparts in other less developed countries.[19]

One thing should be said to the credit of China. It has successfully implemented the basic needs strategy. This was made possible "by the production pattern which does not supply luxury goods, by an ownership pattern which does not give large incomes to anyone, and by an ideological movement which frowns on wasteful consumption."[20]

China has been successful in diversifying its rural economy. This has led to provision of essential infrastructure and social services to the rural poor.

Chinese Rural Economy: Recent Trends

China, by 2005, emerged as the world's third largest food donor. It donated 5,77,000 tonnes of food in 2005, mainly to its neighboring countries. China had to feed 1.3 billion mouths, and a land mass largely unsuited to agriculture.

Chinese agriculture has been steadily growing at around 5 per cent in recent years. The yields are high. according to the FAO, between 2003 and 2005, the average yield of rice was 6233 kg/ha. For wheat, it was 4,155 kg/ha. In respect of rape and mustard, it was 1,778 kg/ha.

In 2004, China produced 186 million tones of rice against India's 124 million tonnes. India had 42 million ha. Under paddy cultivation while China had only 24 million ha. Other crops such as wheat and groundnut reveal similar trends, with China well in the lead. China's foodgrain production was 498 million tonnes in 2006, and 502 million tonnes in 2007.

In the case of horticulture, China is marching ahead of India. For instance, in 1980, India's output of fruits and vegetables was 55 million tonnes, and China's output was 60 million tonnes. But by 2003, India's output was 135 million tonnes, that of China increased to 450 million tonnes.

Another advantage for China it the country has a more diversified composition of its agricultural Sector, with animal husbandry and fisheries contributing close to 45 per cent of the total in 2005. This percentage was only 35 for India.

Good performance of Chinese agriculture is attributed to technological improvements accruing from research and development, investment in rural infrastructure, and an increasingly liberalized agricultural policy. The country had over 1000 R & D centres.

According to one source, China invested RMB 151.3 billion (almost $ 20 billion) in the building and reconstruction of 3,25,000 kilometres of rural roads in 2006 alone.

In recent years, China had shown interest in village elections with a view to bring about fundamental changes in the political culture. Direct elections to village councils have gradually been made mandatory across China. In China, for centuries, peasants suffered in the hands of ruthless rulers at the centre.

Since 1998, election to village councils, which comprise between three and seven members, have been institutionalized and are now carried out every three years. The councils take up issues like allocation and use of communal land, the running of village enterprises, and the implementation of family directions.

REFERENCES

1. Sujit Dutta: 'China — Two Decades of Refors', *The Hindu*, December 31, 1998.
2. 'Rural to Urban Migration in.the People's Republic of China', *China Quarterly,*September, 1994, pp. 669-98.
3. Mark Selden: 'Poverty Alleviation, Inequality and Welfare in Rural China', *Economic and Political Weekly,* November 1999, p. 3184.
4. *Ibid*. p. 3185.
5. Sartaj Aziz (1978): *Rural Development: Learning from China,* The Macmillan Press Ltd., London, p. xix.
6. R.P. Misra (Ed. 1985): *Rural Development: Capitalist and Socialist Paths,* Vol. 5, p. 13.
7. Sartaj Aziz (1974): *op. cit.,* pp. 52-61.
8. M.V. Rappai: 'China Turns Back to the Villages', *The Hindu,* November 7, 1998.
9. Robert Weil: 'China at the Brink: Class Contradictions of Market Socialism', *Monthly Review,* December 1994 and January 1995.
10. Dalip S. Swamy: 'Economic Liberalisation in China', *Mainstream,* August 19, 1995, p. 7.
11. Utsa Patnaik and Shriram Natrajan: 'Output and Employment in Rural China: Some Post-Reform problems', *Economic and Political Weekly,* September 16, 2000, p. 3421.
12. B.C. Biswas and T.K. Chanda: 'A Comparative Analysis of Agriculture and Fertiliser Scenario in India and China', *Yojana,* July15, 1992, p. 17.
13. Mark Selden: *op. cit.,* p. 3187.
14. Sartaj Aziz (1974): *op. cit*., pp. 41-42.
15. K.N. Ahmed: 'Economic Liberalisation in China and Russia: Contrasting Experience', *Mainstream,* October 9, 1999, p. 6.
16. Ram K. Vepa: 'Rural Enterprises in China', *The Economic Times,* April 15, 1989.
17. Albert Nyberg and Scott Rozelle (1999): *Accelerating China's Rural Transformation,* The World Bank, Washington, D.C., p. 4.
18. Ram K. Vepa: *op. cit.*
19. Sartaj Aziz (1974): *op. cit.,* p. 58.
20. *Ibid.*, p. 93.

Chapter

53 RURAL DEVELOPMENT IN PAKISTAN

Pakistan, though endowed with rich natural resources, could not solve problems of poverty and unemployment because the economy has not been well managed. The Government itself admitted that in1998-99, there were atleast 36 million people (6 million households) below the poverty line. In 1997, Pakistan's population was 133 million. The geographical area of Pakistan is 796000 sq. kms.

Immediately after the Partition of India and the formation of Pakistan, the economic policy concentrated on the rehabilitation of refugees.

It is said that Pakistan, which is a viable state in economic terms a has become unviable because of economic mismanagement.[1] The situation worsened because of repeated coups and subsequent change of regimes from democracy to military rule.

THE ECONOMY

In 1997, the human poverty index for Pakistan was 42, while it was 44 for Bangladesh and 36 for India. In the mid-1990s, 31.8 million people of Pakistan were below the poverty line. In 1998, the poverty ratio was placed at 46. Adult illiteracy was 59 per cent in 1997.

During 1947-58, when the present Bangladesh was part of Pakistan, Pakistan's GDP grew at an average rate of 3.1 per cent per annum, though the saving ratio was low, and foreign inflows were almost insignificant.

The decade of the 1960s, experienced an impressive growth rate of 6.8. During this period, there was a rise in foreign investment and domestic savings. The Ayub regime followed liberal policies. But, the economy still suffered from income inequalities, regional disparities in development and concentration of economic power.

Separation of East Pakistan (now Bangladesh) in 1971 resulted in a setback to the economy of Pakistan. In the 1970s, the average growth rate was only 3.9 per cent. The situation would have been worse but for liberal policy of manpower exports to the Middle East.

However, during the period 1960 to 1995, the average rate of growth of the economy was 5 per cent. Of course, per capita income was still low. Even now, 45 million people are below the poverty line.

Today, Pakistan's economy is in the doldrums. Its involvement in wars in the past, fighting war against communism, expansionary policy and mismanagement of resources are responsible for this. The country's capacity to generate sustainable growth, reduce poverty and achieve equitable income distribution is crippled.[2]

Pakistan's domestic savings to the GDP ratio remained at a very low level. It increased from 2 per cent in 1949-50 to the highest 16.6 per cent in 1987-88, but has since stagnated around 12 per cent. The investment ratio has been much higher by one-third because the country unduly depends on foreign resources. Even the favourable external factors could not be properly harnessed to ensure self sustained growth.[3]

The total debt of Pakistan constituted 82 per cent of the GDP in 1995 and this ratio is on the rise. Of this, 50 per cent is foreign debt.

Table: 1
Pakistan: Trends in GDP Growth Rates

Decades	*Growth Rate*
1950s	3.1
1960s	6.8
1970s	4.8
1980s	6.5
1990-97	4.6

AGRICULTURE IN PAKISTAN

Foodgrain production in Pakistan is not showing any appreciable growth. It was 16.50 million tonnes in 1980-81 which rose to 17.98 million tonnes in 1982-83, but fell to 16.37 million tonnes.

Table: 2
Trends in Agricultural Growth Rates

Decades	*Growth Rates*
1950s	1.6
1960s	5.1
1970s	2.4
1980s	5.4
1990-97	3.8

Table: 3
Pakistan: Yield of Major Crops in 1995

(kg/hs)

Crop	*Yield*
Wheat	2081
Rice	2179
Barley	994
Maize	1428
Millet	444
Sorghum	575
Cereals	1928

Source: FAO, QBS, Vol. 9, No. 1 /2 -1996.

Table: 4
Pakistan: Compound Growth Rates of Yields of Principal Crops 1980-98

(per cent)

Crop	*Growth Rate of Yields*
Wheat	1.60
Rice	–0.09
Barley	2.07
Maize	0.74
Pearl Millet	–1.76
Sorghum	0.17

Source: FAO Production Year Book, 1980-95.

New agricultural technology allowed large landowners to resume land previously rented out for self cultivation. Tenant farmers were hence evicted. They had to either operate smaller holdings or join the ranks of the landless labourers. In spite of higher agricultural growth in the 1980s, the conditions of those evicted did probably deteriorate. Increased mechanisation led to a decrease in demand for labour which may have been one of the key reasons for the increase in poverty despite high growth rates in output.[4]

It may be noted that Pakistan inherited superior irrigation networks at the time of partition and it's land allocation among foodgrains is more towards rice and wheat — the crops of the Green Revolution.

Sustained development of irrigation over the period 1950 to 1990, has brought about an impressive growth of the agricultural sector at the annual rate of about 5 per cent against the population growth rate of 3 per cent.

In recent years, the scope for developing new irrigation sources has greatly diminished. Hence, there has been a slowdown in the rate of expansion in the irrigated area (1.4 per cent per annum). No wonder, the rate of growth of Pakistani agriculture too decelerated to 2.4 per cent per annum during the eighties.

Under the growth-oriented strategy of the 1960s, physical infrastructure and industry enjoyed priority. Agricultural prices were kept low. Studies show that the agricultural output was below potential because of government price intervention, both direct and indirect especially in the 1970s.[5] It was further stated that the price policy had a negative effect on foreign trade and on the balance of payments.[6]

The improvement in land productivity in Pakistan peaked during the 1960s, the era of the Green Revolution, and since then it stagnated without any acceleration of growth rates.[7]

The compound growth rate or rice yields in Pakistan has been negative during 1980-95. Rice is an important foreign exchange earner for Pakistan, and the negative growth rates during the last 15 years show that little R & D efforts have gone into increasing the productivity of this crop.[8]

A few factors have contributed to the poor performance of agriculture in Pakistan.[9]

First, though Pakistan possesses productive and irrigated soil, and good quality underground water, the feudal structure is still mere. The old Zamindari system of the British period is still continuing.

Two, absence of effective land reforms has resulted in under utilisation and at times waste of biological inputs such as water, fertilisers and seeds. In fact, per hectare fertiliser nutrient consumption in Pakistan was 82 kg as against 68 kg in India during 1993-94. In the same year, irrigated area in Pakistan was 65 per cent as against 27 per cent in India.

Last, the poor performance of agriculture is also due to political uncertainty and military dominance in the decision-making process.

Agriculture growth in Pakistan led to some environmental degradation. In 1988, about 22 per cent of the canal command area suffered from waterlogging conditions. Likewise, 23 per cent of the area was afflicted with the problem of salt accumulation in the crop-root zone. In the saline zones, soil, salinity alone has robbed Pakistan of one-fourth of its potential farm production. The total production loss was put at 6 per cent.[10]

Future efforts should be directed to increasing further the yields of cereals, promoting double cropping, speeding up the diversification of the rural economy in favour of animal husbandry, milk production, fruits and vegetables and encouraging small scale industries.[11]

RURAL INDUSTRIALISATION

Rural industrialisation in Pakistan had faced many problems, mainly arising from partition. Share of small scale industrial production in GDP in 1960 was only 4.4 per cent. The adverse factors include: the breach of traditional links of the cottage industry as a result of cessation of supply of raw materials from India after the partition, and predominance of market methods of regulating the economy.[12]

In the initial stages of development, a much smaller role was assigned to the public sector in the economy. Of course, the economic policy of the military regime led to the strengthening of the government's role in economic development.

The industrial policy announced on 20 the February 1959 enhanced the role of the public sector in the economic sphere. During the period 1959-60 to 1964-65, the share of public sector in investments in the industry grew from 16 to 19 per cent, and only subsequently it started declining.

The gap between the rates of growth of large scale and small scale production decreased from 7.7 per cent in the 1950s to 4.4 per cent in the 1960s. This is attributed to:[13]

(i) links between small units and modernisation of agriculture;

(ii) increase in the inflow of foreign aid for the advantage of small scale entrepreneurs;

(iii) the rise in indirect taxation placed the small enterprises in a more profitable position;

(iv) the emphasis on industrialisation in East Pakistan (now Bangladesh) also provided boost to small and medium entrepreneurs.

But, in contrast to India, small entrepreneurs in Pakistan were not able to achieve either reservation of production for small scale enterprises or an appreciable increase of their share in bank credit.[14]

Thus, rural industrialisation in Pakistan has yet to pick up. It certainly requires pragmatic policies.

CONCLUSION

The rate of growth of the Pakistan economy was lower in the 1990s than in the 1980s. Agriculture could not make satisfactory progress under an unfavourable power structure. In the coming years, the country has to concentrate on better utilisation of available resources.

REFERENCES

1. Ghulam Kibria (1999): *A Shattered Dream,* Oxford University Press, Pakistan.
2. Sanjay Kumar (Book Review): *Economic and Political Weekly,* July 17, 1999. p. 1994.
3. Deena Khatkate (Book Review): *Economic and Political Weekly,* May15, 1999. p. 1183.
4. S. Akbar Zaidi: 'Is Poverty Now a Permanent Phenomenon in Pakistan?' *Economic and Political Weekly,* October 9, 1999, p. 2944.
5. *Indian Journal of Agricultural Economics* (Book Review), January-March 1994. p. 155.
6. *Ibid.*, p. 155.
7. Takashi Kurosaki: 'Agriculture in India and Pakistan 1900-95: Productivity and Crop Mix', *Economic and Political Weekly,* December 25, 1999. p. A-162.
8. I.J. Singh: 'Agricultural Situation in India and Pakistan', *Economic and Political Weekly,* June 28, 1997, p. A-90.
9. *Ibid.*, p.A-90.
10. *Indian Journal of Agricultural Economics* (Book Review), January-March 1994. p. 134.
11. Gilbert Etienne (1985): *Rural Development in Asia; Meeting with Peasants,* Sage Publications, New Delhi, p. 171.
12. A.E. Granovsky (1993): *Economic Development in South Asia,* Agricole Publishing Academy, New Delhi. p. 138.
13. *Ibid.*, p. 153.
14. *Ibid.*, p. 158.

Chapter

54 Rural Development in Bangladesh

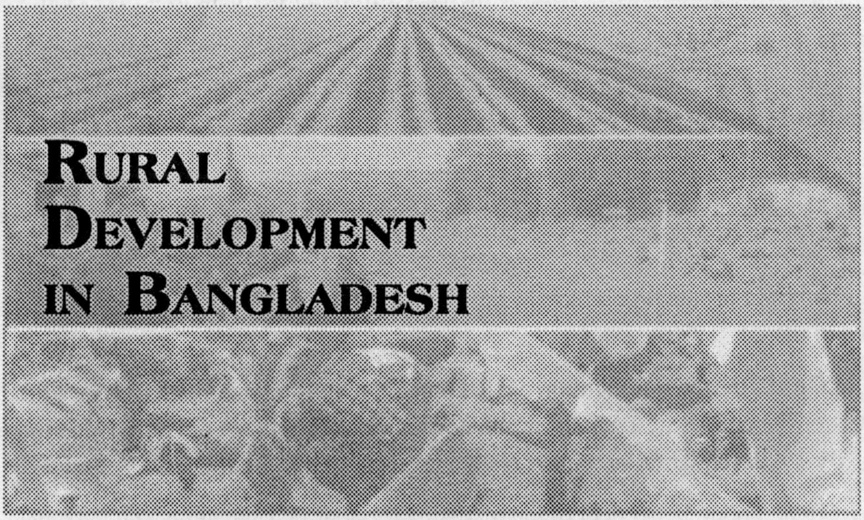

Bangladesh, formerly East Pakistan, came into existence in 1971. It is one of the poorest countries of the world. In 1978-79, the per capita GNP of Bangladesh was less than $100. But the country is rich in resources. The resources are underutilised or unutilised.

The population of the country was 115 million in 1997. The rural population was about 80 per cent of the total. Population may go up to 130 million by 2000 AD. The geographical area of Bangladesh is 144,000 sq. km.

In 1996, 53 per cent of the country's population was below the poverty line. Adult illiteracy rate in 1997 was 61 per cent.

The country also suffers from extreme income inequalities.[1] Gini coefficient for consumption or income distribution show that inequality has increased in Bangladesh. Inequality in the rural areas increased from 25.5 per cent in 1991-92 to 28.8 per cent in 1995-96.

Agriculture in Bangladesh

Bangladesh has still a predominantly agricultural economy. In 1951, 83.2 per cent of the total labour worked in the agricultural sector. By 1974, this declined to 77.4 per cent. Agriculture now accounts for 35 per cent of the GDP.

The net cropped area is 7.7 million hectares. Bangladesh is an intensively cultivated country. In respect of foodgrains, it comes closet to self-sufficiency. The existing irrigation potential covers about 45 per cent of the net cropped area.

During the period 1980 to 2000, the farm size has dropped from 1.5 ha. to 0.9 ha. and the proportion of the landless households increased from 35 per cent to 45 per cent.[2]

The agricultural sector still absorbs 60 per cent of the overall employment. As such, agricultural growth rates are crucial to the economy. Measures need to be initiated towards substantial transformation within this sector.

Bangladesh has a low land-man ratio. In fact, between 1960 to 1980, it is estimated to have declined by one-quarter. Hence, the country is unable to keep up the food-production balance in recent years.

Foodgrain production which in the late 1950s averaged 8 million tonnes increased to 13 million tonnes in the late 1970s.

In the 1970s, the introduction of IR-20 was a major breakthrough in paddy production technology. In parts of the country, especially in the north and west, wheat cultivation also increased rapidly since 1975. By 1990, foodgrain output reached a level of 19 million tonnes.

In 1997, about 38 per cent of the total area is under rice and almost all the wheat cultivated is under HYVs. The Green Revolution is mainly confined to rice and wheat.[3]

Between the early 1960s, and mid-1980s, the area irrigated by modern means increased from only 5 per cent of the cultivated area (about 0.9 million acres) to about 16 per cent of the cropped area (more than 5 million acres).

The use of chemical fertilisers increased from almost nothing to 100 kg per net cropped hectare.

Over the same period (early 1960s and mid-1980s), the area under the high yielding varieties (HYV) developed at the International Rice Research Institute (IRRI), Manila, and Bangladesh Rice Research Institute (BRRI) reached over 20 per cent of the total area under foodgrains.

However, regarding rice, there has been a decline in its imports. Hence, the country has been moving in a sustained way towards rice self-sufficiency. Till 1989-90, imports for rice however has declined by 1.7 per cent per annum.

Imports have played an important role in boosting the total availability for wheat and all foodgrains.

One of the most important impacts of the green revolution in Bangladesh has been a marked increase in cropping intensity each year. The accelerated use of the more crucial ingredients of the HYV package, namely, fertilisers and irrigation might have produced a stabilising impact on the relative viability of production.[4]

Bangladesh is a food deficit country. The shortage per annum on an average is from 1.6 million tonnes to 2.2 million tonnes. The country imports foodgrains from Thailand, India and other rice-producing countries.

Expansion of irrigated land in Bangladesh is slow, far below what is even technically possible. Irrigated area increased from 2.6 million acres in 1969-70 to 3 million acres in 1976-77. Irrigated area forms less than ten per cent of the total cropped area.

The area under HYV increased gradually at a slow rate upto 1975-76, and from the next year, started declining both in absolute terms and as a percentage of the total area under rice cultivation. Farm meachanisation is taking place but it is slow.

Table: 1
Bangladesh: Foodgrain Situation

Year	*Population (million)*	*Net Production (000 tonnes)*	*Imports ('000 tonnes)*	*Per capita availability (grams)*
1973-74	76.4	10911	1666	186.3
1974-75	78.0	10374	2558	187.4
1975-76	79.9	11764	1445	181.9
1976-77	81.8	11005	795	158.1
1977-78	83.7	13268	1635	178.1
1978-79	85.6	13274	1181	185.9
1979-80	87.7	13481	2871	211.2
1980-81	89.9	14855	1078	182.9
1981-82	91.6	14484	1245	191.0
1982-83	93.6	15181	1870	200.8
1983-84	95.7	15560	2134	203.3
1984-85	101.7	15899	1034	178.1
1986-87	104.1	16327	1035	184.4
1987-88	106.6	19669	2967	232.7
1988-89	109.1	16647	2177	195.7
1989-90	111.7	18871	1658	200.1

The use of chemical fertilisers has gone up substantially over the period of two decades from about 108000 tonnes in 1965-66 to 784000 tonnes in 1979-80. But the per hectare use of fertilisers is still low in comparison to the agriculturally prosperous countries of Asia.

So far as the agricultural sector is concerned, four key areas are often highlighted. These are:[5]

(i) Strengthening private sector trade by permanently abolishing restrictions on that trade;

(ii) Making the price stabilisation mechanism more efficient by relying on international trade (both public and private) in place of public storage;

(iii) Targeting food insecurity and moving integrated subsidies that are now captured at least partly by the affluent and

(iv) Making public food operations those commercial activities which can be left to the private sector.

Land ownership is quite skewed in Bangladesh. In 1977, 44.88 per cent of total households owned holdings between 1-2 acres, accounting for 25.17 per cent of the total land area. Those owning 14 acres and above holdings formed 0.92 per cent of the households, but account for 12.91 per cent of the total land area.

Almost all farms of Bangladesh are fragmented. According to the 1960 Census, only 10 per cent of farms and 4 per cent of farmlands were unfragmented. Population growth and laws of inheritance are responsible for this. Highly fragmented holdings are mainly responsible for low agricultural productivity.

The First Five Year Plan of Bangladesh (1973-78) observed that "Radical land reform measures will have to be implemented because the distribution and tenure systems are the fundamental factors determining rural employment and income distribution in a predominantly agricultural society."

The two-year plan (1979-80) also recognised that a land reform policy "will necessarily relate to reduction in the ceiling of landholding per family, elimination of absentee ownership and security of tenure."

The progress of land reforms has been slow. The power structure comes in the way. Because of the delay, many intermediate tenure holders showed land under their own cultivation, and ultimately claimed ownership. The 1972 Presidential Order also fixed the ceiling at 33.5 acres. The rural oligarchy is only marginally affected.

Land rights are often violated by the powerful rural class. It is the government which must act decisively.

Farm products are cheaper in India than in Bangladesh due to larger subsidy component. This component is very marginal in Bangladesh. Thus, the cheap food product dominates the Bangladesh market.[6]

Poor water management has been an impediment to agricultural development. Of course, there is the disturbing excess water problem during the monsoons. Water pricing and cost recovery should receive attention.

There is the need to shift the workforce from agriculture to non-agricultural occupations. The real wages in the agricultural sector have been fluctuating.

Bangladesh suffers from adverse land-man ratio. Increasing cropping intensity is the only means to raise productivity and production. Irrigation expansion can significantly increase cropping intensity. Diversification of agriculture can also help to increase cropping intensity.

RURAL INDUSTRIALISATION

In Bangladesh, the small scale industry contributed more than 85 per cent of the manufacturing sector's share of value added in 1949-50. But this declined to less than 40 per cent in 1969-70.

About 55 per cent of small scale and cottage industrial establishment were located in rural areas in the late 1940s. This moved to 65 per cent by the turn of the 1960s.

Table: 2
Bangladesh: Trends in Real Wages (1970 = 100)

Fiscal Years	*General*	*Agriculture*
1983	88	82
1984	90	70
1985	86	70
1986	95	80
1987	102	86
1988	106	89

1989	107	89
1990	110	94
1991	107	91
1992	107	93
1993	113	99
1994	114	101
1995	111	98
1996	114	97

Source: World Bank (1999): 'Bangladesh: From Counting the Poor to making the poor count.'

The textile manufacturing industry consisting largely of handlooms has always been the largest sector in the rural industry, but its share of the total has been declining over the last 20 years (from 29.5 per cent in 1949 to 27.5 per cent in 1969). In the same period, the food processing industry has increased its share from 20 per cent to 26 per cent. Despite increase in number, the small and cottage industries declined in terms of percentage contribution to GDP.

The Second Five-Year Plan (1980-85) of Bangladesh stressed the need for proper dispersal of industries and observed:

(i) A conscious effort will be made and necessary incentives will be provided for the location of industrial units in new and less developed areas;

(ii) Rural and cottage industries will be promoted as a part of the rural development programme by maximum use of the local natural resources, agricultural produce and human skills and

(iii) An important instrument to encourage rural and small scale industries will be to provide growth centres in rural areas with infrastructure facilities.

Rural industrialisation in Bangladesh has yet to pick up. Programmes in this direction have not been successful because of an unfavourable environment.

BANGLADESH GRAMEEN BANK

In the sphere of rural credit, two things are important: improving the recovery rate and reducing the transactions cost of borrowers.

The Bangladesh Grameen Bank (BGB) was started as a research project at Jabra village by Mohammed Yunus, the then Head of the Department of Economics, Chittagong University in 1976. The BGB officially came into existence in 1983 as a specialised institution for financing the rural poor.

As at the end of 1992, its paid up capital was Tk 149 million with the share of its borrowers and Government of Bangladesh including financial institutions being 88:12.

The essence of the BGB is social development through credit. All the members have to agree on certain obligations which include areas like family planning, growing of vegetables throughout the year, planting of seedlings, education of children, avoidance of dowry and child marriages, ensuring personal and social hygiene and health etc. Members have to put these principles into practice.

By 1995, the Grameen Bank had over 1.2 million borrowers (94 per cent of them women), living in more than 32 villages. The bank's monthly disbursal is over 20 million, the average loan size is 75, and it still has a recovery rate of over 98 per cent.

An important feature of the financing of BGB relates to compulsory savings of a very small amount through different schemes on a weekly basis, utilising such savings for financing consumption expenditure or for emergency needs. This type of saving helps the borrower not only to tide over the situation but also provide an opportunity to the bank to remain in constant touch with the borrowers.

The Bank's activities are under the general direction of the board of governors, consisting of 9 borrower-shareholders and a managing director who is the Chief Executive. Activities are organised and implemented in four administrative tiers, viz., branch office, area office, zonal office and head office.[7]

The clientele of the BGB consist of the landless and the assetless. The family is deemed to be landless if it owned upto half an acre of land and assetless if the value of assets does not exceed Tk 10,000. The loan proposals are entertained by the bank only on a group basis. The intended borrowers have to form themselves into groups. Each group should have at least five members.

The BGB itself identifies borrowers from the group. At the first stage, loans to only two members are issued, and on a satisfactory repayment performance, the remaining members would be covered in batches of two borrowers each, subject to satisfactory repayment performance.

The loans may be general loan, joint loan, housing loan and technology loan.

General loans are the loans given for various economic activities which provide self-employment and help to generate income. There are more than 500 activities for which the bank provides such loans. Of course, priority is shown to milch cow, paddy basking, calf rearing, rice/paddy trade and bullocks. No unit cost of the activity was fixed by the bank.

Joint loans are those loans given to a group of borrowers, and not to individuals for the purposes which required larger investment. These included leasing of land, banana gardens, rice mills etc.

Housing loans are issued for construction of *pacca* houses. Such loans are generally given after assessing the performance of the borrower in respect of other loans both with regard to utilisation and recovery.

Technology loans are those which are issued for investment purposes of such as rice mills, deep tube wells etc. Members are eligible to borrow for any other purpose including consumption loans from the group fund on the basis of the recommendations of the group chairman and centre chief.

The borrower should commit himself in the application that assets would not be disposed of until loan is fully repaid. No security or surety was insisted upon. The loan is generally disbursed within 15 days from the date of application.

In spite of an impressive performance, the BGB suffers from a few weaknesses such as high cost of supervision, absence of financing for investment purposes and lack of proper training facilities for upgrading skills of borrowers.[8]

The bank no doubt charges a high interest rate of 16 to 18 per cent. But the viability of the bank largely depends on the availability of concessional funds from the international agencies.

Countries like, Malaysia, Philippines and Indonesia and even developed countries in Europe are replicating the Grameen Bank credit programme on an experimental basis.

The Comilla Model

The Comilla experiment reasoned that all development tasks in the villages must involve the villagers and could not be imposed upon them from the top.

However, the Comilla model was not without shortcomings. It was not always possible to prevent the control of cooperatives felling into the hands of richer landed elites. Besides, landlessness was much larger in reality than envisioned and the cooperative efforts often failed to create employment for the rural poor.[9]

The experiments conducted in the 1960s at the Comilla Academy of Rural Development ultimately resulted in what is internationally known as the Comilla Model of rural development. The current integrated rural development programme is a derivative of the Comilla Model.

The Comilla Cooperative system wanted to organise small and medium farmers within the existing agrarian structure in order to protect them from the large farmers and moneylenders and to enable them adopt the new agricultural technology.[10]

The model envisaged construction of physical infrastructure, development of irrigation facilities and organisation of groups to make optimum use of such facilities, development of rural institutions for mobilisation of savings and delivery of agricultural inputs, provision of training on improved agricultural practices and a system for its dissemination.[11]

The Comilla model had the following four components:

(i) *The KSS-TCCA Cooperative System:* This is a two tier system to organise village-based peasant cooperatives called 'KSS' (Krishak Samabay Samity or Peasants' Cooperative Association) and to federate them into the Thana Central Cooperative Association (TCCA) at the *thana,* now *upazila* level.

The functions of the cooperatives were to raise savings deposits at weekly meetings of members, to ensure the management of irrigation equipment on a group basis, and to supply institutional credit and other supplementary inputs to overcome the limitations associated with small fragmented holdings, the use of bigger inputs by smaller farmers, and the problem of agricultural credit.

The TCCA was designed as the support and servicing apex organisation to provide credit and other inputs and to provide overall coordination, supervision, training and support services to the KSS.

(ii) *The Thana Training and Development Centre* (TTDC)*:* The idea of the Centre was to coordinate all the specialist government departments concerned with rural administration at the thana level, and to make these services available to the village people. It was intended to be a transmission centre for the diffusion of agricultural technology and modern agricultural practices by training chairmen, managers and model farmers for the KSS at the Centre.

(iii) *Thana Irrigation Plan* (TIP)*:* The plan was designed to organise peasants into groups to control irrigation equipment like low-lift pumps, deep tubewells and shallow tubewells, to provide maintenance services from thana workshops, to train equipment operators and managers of irrigation groups, and to construct field and distribution channels. The groups were eventually to be transformed into cooperatives and federated with TCCA.

(iv) *Rural Works Programme (RWP):* This was designed to construct rural physical infrastructure, like roads, flood protection, embankments, irrigation and drainage canals etc. and to provide employment opportunities to the rural poor during slack seasons. The initial emphasis was on infrastructures that would directly promote agricultural growth.

The Comilla Model, though faced with some problems, offers some useful lessons.

RURAL DEVELOPMENT PROGRAMMES

In the mid-1970s, the 'area development' programme was initiated on an experimental basis to develop a project model for rural development. An attempt was made to develop irrigation and physical infrastructure and to strengthen the TCCA/KSS system in the project areas.

The second project, known as the Serajgonj Integrated Rural Development Project (SIRDP) was launched in July 1977 in four *thanas.* The project laid stress on irrigation and infrastructure development, flood control, and the development of social service facilities such as health, family planning and community education.

The third project, the Noakhali Integrated Rural Development Project (NIRDP) was implemented in July 1978 in three *thanas.* The stress was on health and education.

The fourth project, South-West Rural Development Project (SWRDP) covered 44 *upazilas* in two districts with activities relating to infrastructure development, irrigated agriculture, fisheries development, cooperatives and employment programmes for the poor. It was completed in June 1988.

The programmes however experienced time over runs mainly because of difficulties in coordination among various implementing agencies at the field level. Attempts to develop agriculture, with the present structure of ownership of land, did not help the rural poor. The excessive number of components of the projects created problems of coordination and management and made benefits intractable.[12]

A new strategy for rural development was formulated during the Third Five-Year Plan (1985-90). This strategy gave importance to agriculture and infrastructure. According to this strategy, rural development projects will have one or a combination of the following three major components:

(i) Development of physical infrastructure including roads;

(ii) Irrigated agriculture, minor drainage and flood control works and

(iii) Production and employment programmes for the rural poor (landless and those having up to 0.5 acre of land).

The production and employment programmes for the rural poor have been conceived as an integrated package of five components: *(i)* institution-building; *(ii)* training; *(iii)* credit *(iv)* supply of other inputs, and *(v)* marketing.

In 1982, 460 out of the 495 thanas of the country were upgraded and labelled as *upazilas.* The rationale behind this reorganisation of administrative units was to prevent the bypassing of the local rural communities in the national planning process.

The *upazilas* and the unions under them are expected to draw up their respective development plans and this would ensure a greater realisation of a bottom-up approach and enhance participatory development in the rural areas.

The Comilla Experiment has been transformed into an Integrated Rural Development Programme (IRDP).

Of course, a different approach was adopted by launching the *Shwanirbhar* movement. *Shwanirbhar* means self-reliance and the fundamental goal of this approach was to eliminate dependency and promote the use of unutilised and underutilised local resources through collective efforts. However, the majority of the benefits derived from the *Shwanirbhar* movement were enjoyed by the large landowners.[13]

The Second Five Year Plan (1980-85) aimed at strengthening the IRDP and organise the Bangladesh Rural Development Board (BRDP) to oversee and manage area development projects.

CONCLUSION

Rural development in Bangladesh cannot be merely centred on raising agricultural productivity, but must concern itself with the development of a strategy which can halt or slow down the pace of progressive pauperisation of the rural population.

REFERENCES

1. S. Mahendra Dev: 'Economic Liberalisation and Employment in South Asia', *Economic and Political Weekly,* January 15, 2000, p. 136.
2. Kazi Md. Fazlul Haq and A.K. Wodeyar: 'An Integrated Approach to Development and Plan', *Southern Economist,* February 1, 2000, p. 13.
3. Firdousi Naher: 'Green Revolution in Bangladesh: Production Stability and Food Self-sufficiency', *Economic and Political Weekly,* June 28, 1997, p. A-84.
4. *Ibid.*, p. A-88.
5. Rashid Faruques (Ed.1998): Bangladesh Agriculture in the 21st Century (seminar papers), The University Press, Dhaka.
6. *Economic and Political Weekly,* July 31, 1999, p. 2148.
7. J.S. Tomar: 'Grameen: The Bank of the Poor', *The Economic Times,* July 15, 1995.
8. C.L. Dadhic: 'Bangladesh Grameen Bank: The Pros and Cons', *The Economic Times,* January 12, 1995.
9. H. Ramachandran and J.P. De Campos Guimaraes Ed. 1991): *Integrated Rural Development in Asia: Learning from Recent Experiences,* Concept Publishing Company, New Delhi, p. 43.
10. R.P. Misra (Ed. 1985), Vol. IV, *op. cit.*, p. 273.
11. H. Ramachandran and J.P. De Campos Guimaraes: *op. cit.*, p. 33.
12. *Ibid.*, p. 35.
13. *Ibid.*, p. 44.

Chapter

55 Rural Development in Sri Lanka

Sri Lanka (then Ceylon) achieved independence in 1948. The achievement of its independence was peaceful. Sri Lanka inherited from the British a prosperous export sector organised along commercial lines, high education levels and stable macro economy.

The Economy

Independent Sri Lanka made quite an impressive progress in certain areas of the economy. Adult illiteracy rate (age 15 and above) was only 9 per cent in 1997.

Sri Lanka has a geographical area of 66,000 sq.kms, and a population of 18 million as reported in 1993.

At the time of independence, Sri Lanka had four important characteristics:[1]

(i) high level of involvement into the international division of labour of colonial type;

(ii) extremely conservative character of local bourgeoisie tied to the colonial structure;

(iii) relatively high quality of life based on the sphere of social services and government subsidisation of consumption and

(iv) comparatively high level of political conscience of the working strata.

Annual rate of growth of GDP grew from 3.3 per cent in 1975-77 to 6.8 per cent in 1978-80 and thereupon started steadily decreasing to 5.2 per cent 1981-83 and 4.4 per cent in 1984-86, closely approaching the historical average rate of growth of 4.3 per cent in the years 1957 to 1983.[2]

Sri Lanka achieved an average growth rate of 5 per cent during the period (1977 to 1997) of liberalisation. This growth contributed to diversification of the production structure.[3]

Sri Lanka's per capita gross national product was only 96 in 1960. This rose to only 700 by 1995. Other Asian countries like South Korea (9700), Malaysia (3890), Thailand (2740) and Indonesia (980) marched ahead of Sri Lanka. Particularly during the period 1971 to 1977, the country achieved only a very low rate of growth.

By mid-1977, the maintenance of welfare programmes had become a serious burden. The productive sectors suffered from shortage of much-needed imported inputs. This resulted in under-utilisation of production potential and stagnation of growth.

In spite of its high Human Development Index, Sri Lanka remained a low income country with substantial poverty. In 1990-91, for instance, 22.4 per cent of the country's 17 million population lived below the poverty line.[4] Of course, by 1997, it came down to 19 per cent.

Sri Lanka is well placed in terms of social welfare indicators. In the mid 1990s, the population growth was 1.4 per cent; infant mortality (per thousand live births) was 16, life expectancy at birth was 72 years, and the illiteracy rate was only 10 per cent of population (15 years and above).

During the period 1960 to 1977, nearly 10 per cent of GNP was spent on social welfare programmes. Of course, there are limitations of the direct approach to problems of social equity.

There is another problem: the economy unduly depends on one source — the tea industry. If this industry is wiped out, one-third of the national income would disappear. Of course, from the mid 1970s till 1992, the plantations were mismanaged. In 1992, the value added to the GDP by the tea sector was 3 per cent, while tea exports accounted for 27 per cent of the total exports excluding garments and petroleum products. Since the nationalisation of the estates in 1973, nearly 77 per cent of the production is controlled by state owned corporations.

Tourism is also an important industry, with more than 4 lakh tourist arrivals each year. The ethnic conflict is adversely affecting tourism industry.

AGRICULTURE IN SRI LANKA

Agriculture's share in GDP declined from 29.1 per cent in 1977 to 23.6 per cent in 1987, and to 18 per cent in 1997.

The contribution of agriculture to exports declined from 79.3 per cent in 1977 to 42.4 per cent in 1987, and to 22.8 per cent in 1997.

The essence of policy of reorientation at the second stage of development consisted in shifting emphasis from bringing new land under cultivation to increasing the yield in the traditional rice cultivating areas of the wet zone. The expanding use of tractors is noticeable. But tractorisation has not been followed by other changes like enhanced use of fertilisers and multiple cropping.

The law on land reforms of 1972 envisaged the nationalisation of non-corporate plantations above the size of 12.5 ha, the law of 1975 spread the same ceiling to the joint stock companies. While the influence of land reforms on the rice sector was insignificant, despite the low ceiling of land, only 3.3 per cent of land under the rice was taken over, and the government acquired 63 per cent land under tea, 32 per cent under rubber and 10 per cent under coconut trees.[5]

Poverty Alleviation Programmes

'Samrudhi' is Sri Lanka's poverty alleviation rehabilitation and reconstruction programme. The expenditure on this increased from ₹ 8 billion in 1997 to ₹ 11 billion (BE) in 2001.

However, the targeting of the programme is wide off the mark. The government claims that only 16 per cent of the population is below the poverty line. But, 50 per cent of the population receives cash allowances under the 'Samrudhi' programme. There is therefore the need for rationalising and better targeting the programme.

The district based Integrated Rural Development Programme (IRDP) was initiated in Sri Lanka in 1979 as a public sector investment strategy. Its main objective was to improve the living conditions of the rural population in those districts that do not benefit directly from large, high priority projects. The IRDP is viewed as a supplementary programme designed to accelerate rural development. All the IRD projects rely on foreign funding, bilateral or multilateral.

The IRDP has become popular in Sri Lanka because of its multi-sectoral approach, the integration of activities in time and the flexibility built into the design. The IRDP creates opportunities for local talent. Popular participation is ensured. There has been improved coordination among existing government agencies.

The implementation of IRDP in Sri Lanka offers some useful lessons: These are:[6]

(i) The planning exercise should be entirely in the hands of local planners;

(ii) Multi-sectoral investment packages should be designed on the basis of an indepth analysis of the nature, causes and inter-relations of development issues in the area;

(iii) The planning effort should be a continuous process where understanding is increased over time, vague perceptions are cleared and conclusions revised in the light of new knowledge and of changing conditions.

(iv) A strong effort should be made to institutionalise the local capacity for planning;

(v) Activities selected should contribute to solve a particular problem or problems. Integration implies functional relationships between various activities and purposes; the coordination of activities in time, in space and also in relation to the beneficiaries and

(vi) A coherent policy on IRDP which is consistent with other national policies should be adopted.

However, IRDP too faced some problems. The objectives are often criticised for being vague and unrealistic, and at times contradictory. There are management and organisational problems. The implementation capacity and efficiency are at a low level. The sustainability of activities has been questioned. Also the programme is unduly depending on foreign finance.

CONCLUSION

Sri Lanka is rich in natural resources. But growth has been retarded because of some domestic problems like ethnic conflicts.

REFERENCES

1. A.E. Granovsky (1993): *op. cit.*, p. 229.
2. *Ibid*., p. 252.
3. Saman Kelegam: 'Development in Independent Sri Lanka: What Went Wrong', *Economic and Political Weekly,* April 22, 2000, p. 1485.
4. World Bank (1995): Sri *Lanka: Poverty Assessment.*
5. A.E. Granovsky (1993): *op. cit.,* p. 247.
6. H. Ramachandran and J.P. De Campos Guimaraes: *op. cit.,* pp. 114-115.

Chapter

56 Rural Development in the Philippines

The Philippines is a densely populated country. With a land area of 3 lakh sq. kms, the country has a population of 75 million. The population growth is 2.7 per cent per annum. In 1997, 32 per cent of the population was below the poverty line. Of course, adult illiteracy rate was only 5 per cent in 1997.

The Economy

The national income has grown at 4.5 per cent per year since 1950, but the population growth was high at 2.8 per cent per annum. Even now, it is growing at 2.2 per cent per year, putting pressure on food security and generation of employment for the growing labour force.

About 40 per cent of the population lives in rural areas. Agriculture accounts for 22 per cent of the gross domestic product. About 45 per cent of the labour-force works in the agricultural sector.[1]

The problems facing the economy, particularly the agricultural sector are high population growth, widespread landlessness and lack of diversification of agriculture with the predominance of rice.[2]

Table: 1
The Philippines: GDP Growth Rates

(in per cent)

Year	*Growth Rate*
1992	0.3
1993	2.1
1994	4.4
1995	4.8
1996	5.5

AGRICULTURE IN THE PHILIPPINES

The Green Revolution in the Philippines in respect of rice began in 1966 with the introduction of the miracle rice variety IR 8 by the International Rice Research Institute based in the Philippines.

By 1970, the new varieties were adopted in 50 per cent of the rice areas, and now this percentage stands at 90. As a result of this, the rice yields increased from 1.32 tonnes/ha in 1966 to 3.1 tonnes/ha in 1999. The rice production during this period increased from 4.1 million tonnes to 11.9 million tonnes. Of course, population too increased from 33 million to 75 million during this period.

The land ownership is highly concentrated in the hands of the class called 'Latefundia' — the big landlords.

The Marcos government enacted land reforms in 1972 by imposing ceilings on land holdings at 7 ha to improve the economic conditions of tenants.

The reforms stipulated that share-tenants who worked from a landholding of more than 7 ha could purchase the land they tilled. Those with holdings upto 7 ha. would become leaseholders.

Certificates of land transfers were issued to tenants and emancipation patents were to be granted to new owners when they completed compensation payments to the formal landowners. The plantation crops were left outside the purview of the land reforms.

RURAL DEVELOPMENT PROGRAMMES

The Community Development Programme, which was started in the 1950s under President Ramon Magsaysay, was the first systematic nation-wide effort to integrate all rural development activities at the barrio (village) level. The programme receives massive support from the US government. The programme aimed at strengthening the newly-organised Barrio Councils — the institutional channel for horizontal and vertical communication.

The programme was hampered by the generally low level of productive technology, particularly in agriculture, around which community development programmes were organised.

An attempt was made towards decentralisation and regional development through the creation of the Regional Development Council (RDC) which was composed of the governors and the mayors of the provinces and cities of the region and the regional directors of the national government agencies. The RDC received technical assistance from the regional office of The National Economic Development Authority (NEDA).

Rural development dominated the policy agenda of the RDC and became the overriding goal of the five-year comprehensive regional development plans and the Regional Development Investment Programmes (RDIPs).

Emphasis was placed on spatial integration which would hopefully improve the functional linkages between the region's population centres and their hinterlands and the promotion of employment in farm and non-farm sectors. The Provincial Development Investment Programme (PDIP) provided the substantive inputs into the RDIP.

In the beginning of 1970s, the Philippines adopted Integrated Area Development (IAD) which laid stress on spatial integration and geographical boundaries as determinants of the scale, components and management requirements of IRD projects. This resulted in massive public investments in well-defined geographic areas that were classified as depressed or lagging.[3]

A double objective underlay IAD projects to accelerate economic growth in depressed areas in order to correct regional disparities and to shift benefits in favour of the marginalised poor, thereby achieving social equity. However, the IAD projects heavily depend on foreign assistance.

The complementary objectives of the IAD projects are:

(i) increase the productivity of land and water resources;

(ii) improve the quality of labour through manpower development;

(iii) generate employment opportunities in both farm and non-farm sectors;

(iv) improve social services and

(v) provide for local participation in development.

A unique feature of IAD projects is the simultaneous operation of sector-specific management structures corresponding to the components of the IAD package. The IAD Project Office coordinates all the multi-sectoral components of the IAD package.

The first five years of operation of IAD projects in the Philippines (1975-1979) were a critical period of testing, planning and management methodologies.

It is said that the IAD projects suffered from problems like over-emphasis on infrastructure, limited development capability build-up, failure to conduct immediate baseline studies and the failure to define effective mechanisms for people's participation.[4]

The major drawbacks in IAD planning are attributed to five factors:[5]

(i) over-emphasis on infrastructure;

(ii) difficulty of the special project mode to lead eventually to full integration of activities into the regular functions of the co-operating government line agencies after the project phase-out;

(iii) absence of an explicit provision for building the administrative/institutional capability of the cooperating line agencies and local authorities to sustain post-project operation;

(iv) failure to conduct reliable base-line studies before the start of the project and

(v) failure to define effective and workable mechanisms or participation of target beneficiaries.

In 1978, a permanent institution, the National Council on Integrated Area Development (NACIAD) was created which took over the functions of Cabinet Coordinating Committee for Integrated Rural Development Projects (CCC-RDP). The NACIAD enjoyed support at the highest policy level.

The IRDP approach of the Philippines has six innovative features: *(i)* defined geographical unit; *(ii)* multi-sectoral operation; *(iii)* spatial integration; *(iv)* political commitment; and grass roots participation; *(v)* political commitment and *(vi)* administrative organisational integration.[6]

AGRARIAN REFORM AFTER 1987

After 1987, Philippines gave priority to statutory guarantee of agrarian reforms. In 1988, it passed the comprehensive Agrarian Reform law (CARL). Based on this, the comprehensive agrarian reform programme (CARP) was implemented. The programme was initially for ten years,1988-98, but later extended up to 2008. It has not been so far abolished.

CARP aim at compulsory acquisition and distribution of all agrarian lands without exception. The tiller is the owner of land. There is comprehensive support service to the beneficiaries. Services of non-governmental organisaitions are being used. Of course, the CARP has been financed by the government. By 2008, the programme could achieve 50 per cent of its objectives. Apart from funds shortage, there is strong resistance from landowners. There is need for rationalising land use planning nationwide.

CONCLUSION

The Philippines rural economy is well placed. The country has implemented some programmes to strengthen the agricultural sector.

It has also implemented some rural development programmes which produced good results. Attempts have also been made towards decentralisation of the planning process.

REFERENCES

1. Mahabub Hossain, Fe Gascon and Esther B. Marciano: Income Distribution and Poverty in Rural Philippines: Insight from Repeat Village Study', *Economic and Political Weekly,* December 30, 2000, p. 4650.
2. *Economic and Political Weekly,* July 21, 2001, p. 2763.
3. H. Ramachandran and J.P. De Campos Guimaraes (Ed. 1991): *op. cit.*, p. 135.
4. *Ibid.*, pp. 149-50.
5. *Ibid.*, p. 177.
6. *Ibid.*, p. 171.

Chapter

57 Rural Development in Tanzania

The African country Tanzania, a former German and British colony, became independent in 1961. Initially, the Tanzanian Government concentrated on construction of highly capitalised 'village settlements' in many parts of the country. The experiment was not successful as it proved expensive in terms of capital required and benefitted only a small segment of the population.

Tanzania has been making efforts towards non-violent transition to an egalitarian and self-reliant social economic system. The primary stress has been on organising the ural population to help themselves, first by building rural settlements to live together, then by providing essential social services for everyone and then gradually moving to collective farming and technical progress in agriculture.[1]

Julius Nyerere was Africa's foremost statesman. He became the country's President in 1962, a position which he continued to hold till 1985 when he voluntarily retired from office. He passed away on October 14, 1999.

In 1967, Nyerere proclaimed the famous Arusha Declaration on socialism and self-reliance as Tanzania's twin goals and set the stage for sweeping nationalisation and a momentous attempt to group scattered peasant families in 'ujamaa' cooperative villages. The Scheme produced major benefits in education and health care.[2]

Population in Tanzania is very unevenly distributed depending mainly upon the fertility of the soil, permanence of water supply and certainty of rainfall. Population is concentrated in the highland and coastal border areas with sparse distribution in the central plateau.

APPROACH TO RURAL DEVELOPMENT

People's participation in the formulation and implementation of social, economic and political decisions at both local and national levels is considered central to the country's ideology.

Decentralisation is given due importance by the administration. The District Management Team reviews the villages' plan proposals and prepares the district development programme proposals. These are then reviewed and scrutinised by the District Development Council and approved by the Party District Management Team reviews the villages' plan proposals and prepares the district development programme proposals. These are then reviewed and scrutinised by the District Development Council and approved by the Party District Executive Committee before they are coordinated with other district plans, and considered on a regional basis. The various regional plan proposals are submitted to the Prime Minister's Office to determine their appropriateness.

It has been observed by Mwalimu Nyrere in connection with the need for organising resources:

"The purpose of society is man; but in order to serve man, there must be a social organisation of economic activities which is conducive to the greater production of things useful for the material and spiritual welfare of man. This means that it may well be a function of society to organise and sustain efficient economic organisation and production techniques even when these are in themselves unpleasant or restrictive."

Tanzania's rural development strategy is based on the concept of Ujamaa (cooperative) villages announced in the Arusha Declaration of 1967. The essence of the strategy is cultivation of land collectively with modern techniques of production and to share the proceeds according to the work contributed. The society should be built on the principles of cooperation, mutual respect and responsibility. All members of the society should have equal rights and opportunities.

The establishment of an Ujamaa village consists of three stages:

(i) under 'villagisation', people are persuaded by the local and TANU (Tanganyika African National Union) officials to move from their houses to form a single village and live together as a community. They jointly enjoy common facilities like schools and medical care which are normally built by the members themselves with government help;

(ii) the people were persuaded to develop a small community plot which will be jointly cultivated and the proceeds jointly shared and

(iii) the people were also persuaded to pool their land together, all the members working jointly according to the commonly accepted division of work.

The Ujamaa village has been created in order to:

(i) effectively utilise the potential for increased agricultural and non-agricultural production;

(ii) efficiently utilise public utilities such as drinking water, dispensaries, schools and other supportive services;

(iii) ensure optimum utilisation of labour power;

(iv) check exploitative tendencies among classes and

(v) enhance peasant participation in decision-making implementation.

The villages are self-governing entities — each with a Village Assembly, which oversees amongst others collective farming, transportation and marketing of village agricultural produce.

The *villagisation* policy, aims at improving basic services, increasing agricultural production and broadening rural economic activity. A distinctive characteristic of the country's socialist development strategy is emphasis on the mobilisation and organisation of the population for development.

Agriculture in Tanzania

About 10 per cent of the country's area is considered suitable for cultivation. Studies show that irrigation and flood control could increase the cultivable area by about 20 per cent. Over 90 per cent of Tanzania's population lives in rural areas and depends on agriculture for its income and livelihood. Cotton, coffee, tobacco, tea, wheat and cashewnuts are mainly meant for export.

In the pre-Arusha period, the Government followed the 'transformation' and 'improvement' approaches to agricultural development. Public investment was concentrated on a handful of highly mechanised settlement schemes. Due importance was given to the provision of basic extension services to small holder cash crop producers. This took the form of soil conservation campaign, afforestation, family reserve plots and credit facilities. This, however, strengthened capitalist tendencies as traditional livestock and food crop production was neglected.

In the post-Arusha period, efforts have been made to reverse these trends. One difficulty is the presence of isolated homesteads spreads over a vast country. This did not facilitate the development of an improved and more efficient agricultural and non-agricultural rural production system. This was the rationale for regrouping the widely scattered peasants into the organised village community.

Maize is the major staple food for Tanzania. There have been significant improvements in paddy and wheat production. Overall, the performance of the agricultural sector has been characterised by a sluggish growth.

Until the mid-1960s, the majority of the rural peasantry was excluded from the institutional market for credit. The small farmers had to rely on moneylenders, selling their produce in advance or seeking seasonal employment in the estates. Of course, this situation changed with the establishment of ujamaa villages. To step up institutional credit in the rural areas, the Government set up the Tanzania Rural Development Bank (TRDS) in 1972.

Measures initiated to step up agricultural productivity include creation of price incentives, production cost subsidisation (government subsidises fertilisers directly), improvement in crop husbandry, improved infrastructure and technological adaptation and infrastructure.

Rural Industry

Tanzania inherited a rudimentary industrial structure. The country has been following import substitution industrialisation. The private sector was given importance in the industrialisation of the country. Foreign aid was encouraged. As a result of all these, Tanzania lost a significant part of its potential capital formation.

The Long-term Industrial Strategy (1975-95) of Tanzania considered the following industries as basic:[3]

(i) Those producing essential consumer goods or wage goods;

(ii) Those producing intermediate goods that are inputs into construction, agriculture and manufacturing;

(iii) Those dealing with pre-export processing of traditional raw-material export and

(iv) Those producing capital goods which are domestically adapted to local technology.

The Plan envisages that all the above-mentioned industries will be supported by small scale, decentralised and labour-intensive industrial units.

The small scale units in Tanzania are expected to spread industrial skills to the countryside, thus bridging the rural-urban gap as well as curbing rural-urban drift.[4] The emphasis is on utilisation of local raw-materials.

Too much dependence on foreign aid and multinational corporation (MNCs) has created some problems. The capital intensive technologies worsen the unemployment situation. The other problem is widening inequalities between those employed in this sector and those working in the increasingly marginalised sector. The markets for the informal sector would be reduced. There may be enhanced demand for imported inputs and consumer goods.

CONCLUSION

In spite of the importance given to rural development, the performance of the agricultural sector has not been satisfactory. This is attributed to weak technological and infrastructural base, an inefficient input supply and output marketing systems, and also occasional natural calamities like drought and floods. All these led to widening of urban-rural disparities and inter-regional income differentials.

The Tanzanian approach to rural development is based on principles of self-help, leadership, motivation and voluntary association, sharing equitably whatever resources are available and gradually increasing material and non-material facilities, rather than a rapid growth of agricultural production for its own sake.

REFERENCES

1. Sartaj Aziz (1974): *op. cit.*, p. 171.
2. K. Mathews: 'Remembering Julius K. Nyerere', *Mainstream,* October 14, 2000, p. 11.
3. R.P. Misra (Ed. 1985), Vol. V, *op. cit.*, pp. 127-128.
4. *Ibid.*, Vol. V, p. 142.

Select Bibliography

Acharya, B.T. (1991): *Rural Industrialisation: A Catalyst in Action,* Himalaya Publishing House, Mumbai.

Aggarwal, R.K. (1991): *Evaluation of the Working of Regional Rural Banks,* Mittal Publications, New Delhi.

Ali, Mansoor (1979): Missing *Links in Indian Planning,* Light and Life Publishers, New Delhi.

Arora, R.C. (1979): *Integrated Rural Development,* S. Chand & Sons, New Delhi.

Arora, Ramesh K. (1979): *People's Participation in Development,* The HCM State Institute of Public Administration, Jaipur.

Arumugum, P. (1991): *Lead Bank System and Service Area Approach in India,* UDH Publishing House, Delhi.

Aziz, Sartaj (1978): *Rural Development: Learning from China,* The Macmillan Press Ltd., London.

Basu, C.R. (1990): Commercial *Banking in Planned Economy of India,* Mittal Publications, New Delhi.

Behari, Bepin (1976): *Rural Industrialisation in India,* Vikas Publishing House, New Delhi.

Bhadouria, P.B.S. and Dua, S.C. (1986): *Rural Development Strategy and Perspective,* Anmol Publications, New Delhi.

Bhaduri, Amit (Ed. 1982): *Studies in Rural Participation,* Oxford & IBH Publishing Co., New Delhi.

Bhagawati, Jagdish (1972): *The Economics of Underdeveloped Countries,* Weidenfeld and Nicolson, London.

Bhatia, B.S. et al., (Ed. 1990): *Management of Rural Development,* Deep and Deep Publishers, New Delhi.

Bhattacharya, Sib Nath (1983): *Rural Development in India and Other Developing Countries,* Metropolitan Book Co. Pvt. Ltd., Kolkata.

Brahmananda, P.R., Narayana, B.K., and Kalappa A. (Ed. 1987): *Dimensions of Rural Development,* Himalaya Publishing House, Mumbai.

Brara, J.S. (1983): *The Political Economy of Rural Development: Strategies for Poverty Alleviation,* Allied Publishers, New Delhi.

Centre on IRD for Asia and the Pacific, Comilla, Bangladesh (March 1984): *People's Participation in Rural Development: An Overview of South and South East Asian Experiences.*

Chambers, Robert (1984): *Rural Development: Putting the Past First,* Orient Longman Ltd. Chennai.

Chand, Phul (Ed. 1977): *Unemployment Prpblem in India,* National Publishing House, Delhi.

Chaturvedi, H.R. and Misra S.K. (1982): *Citizen Participation in Rural Development,* Oxford and IBH Publishing Co.

Chaturvedi, T.N. (Ed. 1986): *Rural Development: Some Themes and Dimensions,* Indian Institute of Public Administration, New Delhi.

Chaudhuri, Buddhadeb (1991): *Tribal Development in India,* Inter-India Publications, New Delhi.

Chawdhari, T.P.S. (Ed. 1967): *Selected Readings on Community Development,* National Institute of Community Development, Hyderabad.

Choudhry, S.N. (1987): *Dynamics of Rural Power Structure,* Amar Prakashan, Delhi-35.

Chowdhry, Paul D. (1978): *New Partnership in Rural Development,* M.N. Publishers, New Delhi.

Dak, T.M. (Ed. 1989): *Rural Industrialisation: Challenges and Perspectives,* Northern Book Centre, New Delhi.

Danda, Ajit K. (Ed. 1984): *Studies on Rural Development: Experiences and Issues,* Inter-India Publications, Delhi.-

Danda, Ajit K. (Ed. 1991): *Tribal Economy in India,* Inter-India Publications, New Delhi.

Dantwala, M.L., Ranjit, Gupta and C.D. Souza Keith (1986): *Asian Seminar on Rural Development: The Indian Experience,* Oxford & IBH Publishing Co., New Delhi.

Dasgupta, Biplab (1982): *Rural Development: The CADC Experience,* West Bengal Comprehensive Area Development Corporation, Kolkata.

Deb, K. (1986): *Rural Development in India Since Independence,* Sterling Publishers, New Delhi.

Deb, Kalipada (1988): *Indian Banking Since Independence,* Ashish Publishing House, New Delhi.

Desai, A.R. (1961): *Rural India in Transition,* Popular Book Depot, Mumbai.

Desai, O.K. (1983): *Management in Rural Development,* Oxford & IBH Publishing Co., New Delhi.

Desai, S.S.M. (1986): *Fundamentals of Rural Economics,* Himalaya Publishing House, Mumbai.

Desai, Vasant (1988): *Rural Development (Five Volumes),* Himalaya Publishing House, Mumbai.

Desai, Vasant (1990): *Panchayati Raj,* Himalaya Publishing House, Mumbai.

Dewan, Ritu: *Political Economy of Agrarian Reforms in India,* Himalaya Publishing House, Mumbai.

Dholkia, Ravindra H. and Sudarshan lyengar (1988): *Planning for Rural Development: Issues and Case Studies,* Himalaya Publishing House, Mumbai.

Dube, S.C. (1983): *Development Perspectives for the 1980s,* Abhinav Publications, Hauz Khas, New Delhi -16.

Dubhashi, P.R. (1970): *Rural Development Administration in India,* Popular Prakashan, Mumbai.

Etienne, Gilbert (1985): *Rural Development in Asia: Meeting with Peasants,* Sage Publications, New Delhi.

Food and Agricultural Organisation, Rome (1967): *Agriculture and Industrialisation.*

Food and Agricultural Organisation, Rome (1970): *Marketing: A Dynamic Force in Agricultural Development.*

Food and Agricultural Organisation, Rome (1977): Joint Report on the Expert Consultations, Policies and Institutions for Integrated Rural Development, Colombo and Nairobi Sessions.

Food and Agricultural Organisation, Rome (1979): Report of World Conference on *Agrarian Reform and Rural Development.*

Food and Agricultural Organisation, Rome (1980): *Monitoring Systems for Agricultural and Rural Development Projects.*

Franda, Marcus (1979): *Small is Politics: Organisational Alternatives in India's Rural Development,* Wiley Eastern Limited, New Delhi.

Gaikwad, V.R. (1969): *Panchayati Raj and Bureaucracy,* National Institute of Community Development, Hyderabad.

Gandhi, P. Jegadish (1989): *Indian Economic Issues,* Vol. I, Pointer Publishers, Jaipur.

Gangulee, N.N. (1984): *Problems of Rural India,* Mittal Publications, Delhi — 35.

Gaur, Archana (1985): *Integrated Rural Area Development,* B.R. Publishing Corporation, New Delhi.

Gehlawat, J.K. and Kant (1988): *Strategies for Rural Development,* Arnold Publishers India, New Delhi.

Ghate, Prabhu (1984): *Direct Attacks on Rural Poverty,* Concept Publishing Company, New Delhi.

Govindaiah, T. (1989): *Irrigation Development in India,* Chugh Publications, Allahabad.

Gupta, Ranjit (Ed. 1976): *Planning for Tribal Development,* Ankur Publishing House, New Delhi.

Harbison, Frederick H. (1973): *Human Resources as the Wealth of Nations,* Oxford University Press, London.

Hirschman, Albert O. (1960): *The Strategy of Economic Development,* Yale University Press, New Haven, USA.

Hirway and Abraham (1990): *Organising Rural Workers,* Oxford & IBH Publishing Co. New Delhi, Hoda, Mansur (Ed. 1974): *Problems of Unemployment in India,* India Development Group and Allied Publishers, Mumbai.

Indian Institute of Public Administration, New Delhi (1979): *Management of Agriculture* (Collection of Papers).

International Labour Organisation, Geneva (1961): *Employment Objectives in Economic Development.*

Jain, C.M. and T. Cangan (Ed. 1994): *Forty Years of Rural Development in India,* Print Well, Jaipur.

Jain, L.C. *et al.* (1985): *Grass Without Roots: Rural Development Under Government Auspices,* Sage Publications, New Delhi.

Jain, Pramod Lata (1991): *Co-operative Credit in Rural India,* Mittal Publications, New Delhi.

Jain, S. (1985): *Rural Development Institutions and Strategies,* Rewat Publications, Jaipur.

Jha, L.K. (1994): *India's Forest Policies: Analysis and Appraisal,* Ashish Publishing House, New Delhi.

Jha, S.C. (1971): *A Critical Analysis of Indian Land Reform Studies,* Indian Institute of Asian Studies, Mumbai.

Joshi, P.C. (1976): *Land Reforms in India,* Allied Publishers, Mumbai.

Joshi, P.C. (1990): *Organising Unorganised Labour,* Oxford & IBH Publishing Co., New Delhi.

Kashyap, Chamanlal (1989): *Management and Planning of Rural Development,* Ashish Publishing House, New Delhi.

Khusro, A.M. (1973): *The Economics of Land Reform and Farm Size in India,* Macmillan, Mumbai.

Kohls, Richard L. and Downey, W. David (Ed. 1972): *Agricultural Marketing,* The Macmillan Co., New York.

Krishan, Ram (1966): *Grassroots of Agricultural and Community Development Programme in India,* Allied Publishers, Mumbai.

Krishna Swamy, S.Y. (1980): *Ruralism: A New Socio-Economic Philosophy,* IBH Prakashana, Bangalore.

Kulkarni, V.M. (1969): *Voluntary Action in a Developing Society,* Indian Institute of Public Administration, New Delhi.

Kumar, M. Ashok (1989): *Rural Industrialisation in India: A Strategy for Rural Development,* Mittal Publications, New Delhi.

Kumar, M. Ashok (1990): *Rural Development in India,* Inter-India Publications, New Delhi.

Lakshminarayana, H.D. (1976): *India's Villages at Cross Roads,* National Publishing House, New Delhi.

Lamba, S.K. and J.S. Tomar (1986): *Impact of Land Reforms on Rural Development,* Agricole Publishing Academy, New Delhi.

Lebergott, Stanley (Ed. 1964): *Men Without Work: The Economics of Unemployment,* Prentice Hall Inc. Englewood Cliffs, NJ.

Lewis, John P. (1970): *Quiet Crisis in India,* Asia Publishing House, Mumbai.

Mahajan, R.K. (1991): *Integrated Rural Development Programme,* Concept Publishing Company, New Delhi.

Maheswari, S.R. (1985): *Rural Development in India: A Public Policy Approach,* Sage Publications, Delhi.

Majumdar, D.N. (Ed. 1960): *Rural Profiles,* The Ethnographic and Folk Culture Society, Lucknow.

Mandal, G.C. (1992): *Rural Development: Retrospect and Prospect,* Concept Publishing Company, New Delhi.

Mandal, R.B. (Ed. 1979): *Readings in Land Reforms,* Research Publishers, Monghyr, India.

Marriott, Mc Kim (1963): *Village India,* The University of Chicago Press.

Martin, Anne (1965): *Economics of Agriculture,* Routledge and Kegan Paul, London.

Massachusetts Institute of Technology (1969): *The Role of Popular Participation in Development,* MIT, Report No. 17.

Mathew, George (1994): *Panchayati Raj: From Legislation to Movement,* Concept Publishing Company, New Delhi.

Mathew, George (1994): *Status of Panchayati Raj in the States of India,* Concept Publishing Company, New Delhi.

Mathivaanan, Samuel C. (1991): *Voluntary Agencies and Social Change,* Manas Publications, Delhi-52.

Mathur, Kuldeep (1972): *Bureaucratic Response to Development,* National Publishing House, New Delhi.

Mehta, Balwantray G. (1957) (Chairman): *Report of the Team for the Study of Community Projects and National Extension Service,* Government of India, New Delhi.

Mehta, N.C. and Panandikar V.A. Pai (1974): *Rural Banking,* National Institute of Bank Management, Mumbai.

Mehta, Shiv R. (1984): *Rural Development Policies and Programmes,* Sage Publications, New Delhi.

Mellor, John W. *et al.*, (Ed. 1968): *Developing Rural India,* Cornel University Press, New York.

Mellor, John W. (1969): *The Economics of Agricultural Development,* Vora & Co. Mumbai.

Ministry of Agriculture and Irrigation (1976): Government of India, New Delhi, *Report of the National Commission on Agriculture.*

Ministry of Rural Reconstruction, Government of India, New Delhi (1980): *Manual on Integrated Rural Development.*

Ministry of Rural Reconstruction, Government of India (1982): *Strategy for Full Employment in Rural Areas,* Proceedings of a Conference.

Ministry of Agriculture, Department of Rural Development, Government of India (December 1985): Report of the Committee to *Review the Existing Administrative Arrangements for Rural Development and Poverty Alleviation programmes,* (Chairman: G.V.K. Rao).

Misra, R.P., K.V. Sundaram and V.L.S. Prakasa Rao (1976): *Regional Development Planning in India,* Vikas Publishing House, New Delhi.

Misra, R.P. and K.V. Sundaram (Ed. 1979): *Rural Area Development:* Perspectives and Approaches, Sterling Publishers, New Delhi.

Misra, R.P. (1986): *Rural Industrialisation in the Third World Countries,* Sterling Publishers, New Delhi.

Mishra, S.N. (1984): *Rural Development Planning: Design and Method,* Satvahan Publications, New Delhi.

Mishra, S.N. (1989): *New Horizons in Rural Development Administration,* Mittal Publications, Delhi.

Mountjory, Alan B. (1969): *Industrialisation and Underdeveloped Countries,* Hut Chinson University Library, London.

Mukherjee, Amitava (1995): *Participatory Rural Appraisal,* Vikas Publishing House, New Delhi.

Mukerji, B. (1967): *Community Development in India,* Orient Longman, Kolkata.

Murthy, N.L. and K.V. Narayana (Ed. 1989): *Rural Economy of India,* Mittal Publications, Delhi-35.

Myrdal, Gunnar (1968): *Asian Drama,* Vol. I, II and III. Penguin Books Ltd., London.

Naidu, L.K. (Ed. 1986): *Bank Finance for Rural Development,* Ashish Publishing House, New Delhi.

Naidu, L.K. (Ed. 1988): *Bank Finance for Rural Artisans,* Ashish Publishing House, New Delhi.

Nanjundappa, D.M. (1976): *Development with Social Justice,* Oxford & IBH Publishing Co., New Delhi.

Narula, R.K. and Gopalakrishnan, V. (1982): *Agriculture and Rural Advances by Commercial Banks,* UDH Publishers, Delhi.

National Institute of Rural Development, Hyderabad (1979): *Rural Development in India: Some Facets.*

Neale Walter (1990): *Developing Rural India: Policies, Politics and Progress,* Allied Publishers, New Delhi.

Nurkse, Ragnar (1974): *Problems of Capital Formation in Underdeveloped Countries,* Oxford University Press, Delhi.

Oakley, Peter and David Marsden (1984): *Approaches to Participation in Rural Development,* ILO, Geneva.

Pachauri, S.K. (1985): *Dynamics of Rural Development in Tribal Areas,* Concept Publishing Company, New Delhi.

Pandey, S.M (Ed. 1976): *Rural Labour in India: Problems and Policy Perspectives,* Sri Ram Centre for Industrial Relations, New Delhi.

Parthasarathy, G. (1971): *Agricultural Development and Small Farmers: A Study of Andhra Pradesh,* Vikas Publishing House, New Delhi.

Patel, M.I. (Ed. 1972): *Agro Economic Problems of Tribal India,* Progress Publishers, Bhopal.

Planning Commission, Government of India: *First Five Year Plan to Eighth Five Year Plan Documents.*

Planning Commission, Government of India (1978): *Report of the Working Group on Block Level Planning.*

Planning Commission, Government of India (1978): *Voluntary Participation in Rural Development* (Report of the Voluntary Participation Group headed by B. Sivaraman).

Planning Commission, Government of India (May 1985): *Evaluation Report on Integrated Rural Development Programme.*

Prasad, K.N. (1991): *India's Rural Problems,* Concept Publishing Company, New Delhi.

Punit, A.E. (1978): *Social Systems in Rural India,* Sterling Publishers, New Delhi.

Rajapurohit, A.R. (Ed. 1984): *Land Reforms in India,* Ashish Publishing House, New Delhi.

Ramani, V.C. (1989): *Tribal Economy: Problems and Prospects,* Chugh Publications, Allahabad.

Rao, R.V. (1978): *Rural Industrialisation in India,* Concept Publishing Company, New Delhi.

Ray, Amal and Vanita Venkatasubbiah (1984): *Studies in Rural Development and Administration,* The World Press Pvt. Ltd., Kolkata.

Rayappa, P. Hanumantha and Deepak Grover (1980): *Employment Planning for the Rural Poor: The Case of Scheduled Castes and Scheduled Tribes,* Sterling Publishers, New Delhi.

Rayudu, C.S. (1991): *Rural Credit in India,* Mittal Publications, New Delhi.

Reddy, C.R. (1993): *Overdues Management in Co-operative Banks,* Himalaya Publishign House, Mumbai.

Reddy, K. Venkata (1989): *Rural Development in India (Poverty and Development),* Himalaya Publishing House, Mumbai.

Reserve Bank of India: *Multi-Agency Approach in Agricultural Finance* (Report of the Working Group).

Reserve Bank of India (1954-57): *All India Rural Credit Survey,* Vols. I, II & III (Report of the Committee of Direction).

Reserve Bank of India (1970): *Studies in Agricultural Credit.*

Reserve Bank of India (1978): *Functioning of Public Sector Banks,* Report of the Committee.

Saran, Parmatma (1978): *Rural Leadership in the Context of India's Modernisation,* Vikas Publishing House, New Delhi.

Sarkar, Bikram (1989): *Land Reforms in India,* Ashish Publishing House, New Delhi.

Sarma, P.K. (1991): *Forest Resources and their Utilisation in India.*

Sarma, V.K. (1985): *Water Resources Planning and Management,* Himalaya Publishing House, Mumbai.

Schultz, Theodore W. (1964): *Transforming Traditional Agriculture,* Lyall Book Depot, Ludhiana.

Sen, Bandhudas (1974): *The Green Revolution in India: A Perspective,* Wiley Eastern Pvt. Ltd., Delhi.

Sen, Sudhir (1975): *Reaping the Green Revolution,* Tata McGraw, New Delhi.

Seshadri, K. (1976): *Political Linkages and Rural Development,* National Publishing House, New Delhi.

Seshaiah, K. (1986): *The Lead Bank Scheme: An Empirical Evaluation,* Rainbow Publications, Coimbatore.

Setty, E.D. (1991): *Rural Development: Problems and Prospects,* Inter-India Publications, New Delhi.

Shah, D.R. (Ed. 1989): *Alternatives in Rural Development,* Sterling Publishers, New Delhi.

Shah, Ghanshyam and Chaturvedi, H.R. (1985): *Gandhian Approach to Rural Development: The Valod Experiment,* Ajanta Publications (India), Jawahar Nagar, Delhi.

Shah, S.M. (1977): *Rural Development Planning and Reforms,* Abhinav Publications, New Delhi.

Sharma S.K. and Malhotra S.L. (1977): *Integrated Rural Development: Approach, Strategy and Perspectives.* Abhinav Publications, New Delhi.

Shiviah, M., K.V. Narayana Rao, L.S.N. Murty and G. Mallikarjuniah (1976): *Panchayati Raj – an Analytical Surveys,* National Institute of Rural Development, Hyderabad.

Shiviah, M., M.L. Santhanam., N.Y. Naidu and A.C. Jena (1985): *Improving Delivery System for Rural Development,* National Institute of Rural Development, Hyderabad.

Shrimal, Mohan Lal (1985): *Land Reforms: Promise and Performances,* Metropolitan Book Co. Pvt. Ltd. New Delhi.

Singh, Jasbir (1974): *The Green Revolution in India: How Green It Is,* Vishal Publications, Kurukshetra.

Singh, Katar (1986): *Rural Development: Principles, Policies and Management,* Sage Publications, New Delhi.

Singh, Keder (1974): *Rural Democratisation: X-Rayed,* Vimal Prakashan, Ghaziabad, U.P.

Singh, Mohinder (1992): *Rural Development in India: Current Perspectives,* Intellectual Publishing House, Delhi.

Singh, Ram Yogya (Ed. 1988): *Planning in Integrated Rural Environment,* Deep and Deep Publications, New Delhi.

Sinha, Ajit Kumar (1988): *Rural Industry and Rural Industrialisation,* Pointer Publishers, Jaipur.

Srinivas, M.N. (Ed. 1977): *India's Villages,* Asia Publishing House, Mumbai.

Srinivasa Murthy, A.V. (1991): *Irrigation Planning in India,* Himalaya Publishing House, Mumbai.

Srivastava, A.K. (1986): *Integrated Rural Development Programme in India: Policy and Administration,* Deep & Deep Publications, Delhi.

Subrahmanya, S. and I. Satya Sundaram (Ed. 1987): *Growth of Agriculture and Rural Development in India,* Deep & Deep Publications, New Delhi.

Sundaram, I. Satya (1984): *Anti-Poverty Rural Development in India,* D.K. Publications, New Delhi.

Sundaram, I. Satya (1986): *Voluntary Agencies and Rural Development,* B.R. Publishing Corporation, New Delhi.

Sundaram, I. Satya (Ed. 1989): *Rural Poverty and Area Planning,* B.R. Publishing Corporation, New Delhi.

Suresh, K.A. and Molly Joseph (1990): *Co-operatives and Rural Development in India,* Ashishs Publishing House.

Swarnkar, G.P. (1988): *Women Participation in Rural Development,* Chugh Publications, Allahabad.

Taylor Carl C. *et al.,* (1967): *India's Roots of Democracy: A Sociological Analysis of Rural India's Experiences in Planned Development Since Independence,* Orient Longman, New Delhi.

Thakur, Devendra (1986): Rural *Development and Planning in India,* Deep & Deep Publications, New Delhi.

Thakur, Shrinivas Y. (1985): *Rural Industrialisation in India,* Sterling Publishers, New Delhi.

Thimaiah, G. (Ed. 1979): *Studies in Rural Development,* Chugh Publications, Allahabad.

Thimmaiah, G. and Abdul, Aziz (1984): *The Political Economy of Land Reforms,* Ashish Publishing House, New Delhi.

Thingalaya, N.K. (Ed. 1986): *Rural India – Real India,* Himalaya Publishing House, Mumbai.

Tiwari, R.K. (1990): *Rural Employment Programmes in India, The Implementation Process,* Indian Institute of Public Administration, New Delhi.

Venugopal Reddy, Y. and K. Kosalram (1988): *Multi-Level Planning in India,* Booklinks Corporation, Hyderabad.

Verma, S.V. and S.K. Sharma (Ed. 1984): *Development Administration,* Indian Institute of Public Administration, New Delhi.

Whitby, M.C. *et al.,* (1974): *Rural Resource Development,* Mathue & Co. Ltd. London.

World Bank (1975): *The Assault on World Poverty,* Baltimore, Johns Hopkins University Press.